BIRDS
of
TEXAS

Keith A. Arnold
Gregory Kennedy

with contributions from
Krista Kagume, Chris Fisher & Andy Bezener

LONE
PINE

Lone Pine Publishing International

The Distributor: Lone Pine Publishing
1808 B Street NW, Suite 140
Auburn, WA, USA 98001

Website: www.lonepinepublishing.com

Library and Archives Canada Cataloguing in Publication

Arnold, Keith A
    Birds of Texas / Keith A. Arnold, Gregory Kennedy.

Includes bibliographical references and indexes.
ISBN-13: 978-976-8200-18-1
ISBN-10: 976-8200-18-9

    1. Birds--Texas--Identification. I. Kennedy, Gregory, 1956- II. Title.

QL684.T4A75 2007   598.09764   C2007-900272-2

Illustrations: Gary Ross, Ted Nordhagen, Ewa Pluciennik, Diane Hollingdale
Cover Illustration: Great Horned Owl by Gary Ross
Digital Image Scans: Elite Lithographers Co., ColorSpace Photo-Graphics Inc.

Natural Regions of Texas map: source information provided by and used with permission of Texas Parks and Wildlife.

PC: 15

CONTENTS

ACKNOWLEDGMENTS

The Texas birding community has made numerous contributions to our knowledge of the Texas avifauna during my four decades of studying Texas birds: the advances made in our knowledge in that time have been incredible. To the many persons who have contributed, I am extremely grateful. My wife, Beverly, has been very understanding of my passion for birds, accepting the many times I have been in the field while she remained home with our children. She has also learned to love our Texas birds as much as I and has been patient while I spent countless hours at the computer, working on this book.—*Keith A. Arnold*

Thanks go to our editors Gary Whyte, Wendy Pirk and Sheila Quinlan as well as our design and production staff Volker Bodegom, Patricia Begley, Willa Kung, Trina Koscielnuk, Gerry Dotto, Heather Markham and Elliott Engley for their enthusiasm and expertise in creating this book. Thanks are also extended to the growing family of ornithologists and dedicated birders who have offered their inspiration and expertise to help build Lone Pine's expanding library of field guides. Additional thanks go to John Acorn, Chris Fisher, Andy Bezener and Eloise Pulos for their contributions to previous books in this series. Furthermore, thank you to Gary Ross, Ted Nordhagen and Ewa Pluciennik, whose skilled illustrations have brought each page to life.

Black-bellied Whistling-Duck
size 21 in • p. 41

Fulvous Whistling-Duck
size 20 in • p. 42

Greater White-fronted Goose
size 30 in • p. 43

Snow Goose
size 31 in • p. 44

Ross's Goose
size 24 in • p. 45

Cackling Goose
size 30 in • p. 46

Canada Goose
size 35 in • p. 47

Tundra Swan
size 54 in • p. 48

Wood Duck
size 17 in • p. 49

Gadwall
size 20 in • p. 50

American Wigeon
size 20 in • p. 51

Mallard
size 24 in • p. 52

Mottled Duck
size 21 in • p. 53

Blue-winged Teal
size 15 in • p. 54

Cinnamon Teal
size 16 in • p. 55

Northern Shoveler
size 19 in • p. 56

Northern Pintail
size 23 in • p. 57

Green-winged Teal
size 14 in • p. 58

Canvasback
size 20 in • p. 59

Redhead
size 20 in • p. 60

Ring-necked Duck
size 16 in • p. 61

Greater Scaup
size 17 in • p. 62

Lesser Scaup
size 16 in • p. 63

Bufflehead
size 14 in • p. 64

Common Goldeneye
size 18 in • p. 65

Hooded Merganser
size 17 in • p. 66

WATERFOWL

Common Merganser
size 25 in • p. 67

Red-breasted Merganser
size 23 in • p. 68

Ruddy Duck
size 15 in • p. 69

GROUSE & ALLIES

Plain Chachalaca
size 22 in • p. 70

Ring-necked Pheasant
size 33 in • p. 71

Greater Prairie-Chicken
size 17 in • p. 72

Wild Turkey
size 39 in • p. 73

Scaled Quail
size 11 in • p. 74

Gambel's Quail
size 11 in • p. 75

Northern Bobwhite
size 10 in • p. 76

DIVING BIRDS

Common Loon
size 32 in • p. 77

Least Grebe
size 9 in • p. 78

Pied-billed Grebe
size 13 in • p. 79

Horned Grebe
size 13 in • p. 80

Eared Grebe
size 13 in • p. 81

Masked Booby
size 30 in • p. 82

Northern Gannet
size 36 in • p. 83

American White Pelican
size 65 in • p. 84

Brown Pelican
size 48 in • p. 85

Neotropic Cormorant
size 26 in • p. 86

Double-crested Cormorant
size 29 in • p. 87

Anhinga
size 33 in • p. 88

Magnificent Frigatebird
size 39 in • p. 89

HERONLIKE BIRDS

American Bittern
size 25 in • p. 90

Least Bittern
size 12 in • p. 91

Great Blue Heron
size 51 in • p. 92

Great Egret
size 39 in • p. 93

Snowy Egret
size 24 in • p. 94

Little Blue Heron
size 24 in • p. 95

Tricolored Heron
size 26 in • p. 96

Reddish Egret
size 30 in • p. 97

Cattle Egret
size 20 in • p. 98

Green Heron
size 18 in • p. 99

Black-crowned Night-Heron
size 24 in • p. 100

Yellow-crowned Night-Heron
size 24 in • p. 101

White Ibis
size 22 in • p. 102

Glossy Ibis
size 23 in • p. 103

White-faced Ibis
size 24 in • p. 104

Roseate Spoonbill
size 32 in • p. 105

Wood Stork
size 38 in • p. 106

Black Vulture
size 25 in • p. 107

Turkey Vulture
size 28 in • p. 108

BIRDS OF PREY

Osprey
size 23 in • p. 109

Swallow-tailed Kite
size 23 in • p. 110

White-tailed Kite
size 16 in • p. 111

Mississippi Kite
size 14 in • p. 112

Bald Eagle
size 37 in • p. 113

Northern Harrier
size 20 in • p. 114

Sharp-shinned Hawk
size 11 in • p. 115

Cooper's Hawk
size 16 in • p. 116

BIRDS OF PREY

Harris's Hawk
size 21 in • p. 117

Red-shouldered Hawk
size 19 in • p. 118

Broad-winged Hawk
size 16 in • p. 119

Swainson's Hawk
size 20 in • p. 120

White-tailed Hawk
size 22 in • p. 121

Zone-tailed Hawk
size 20 in • p. 122

Red-tailed Hawk
size 20 in • p. 123

Ferruginous Hawk
size 24 in • p. 124

Rough-legged Hawk
size 21 in • p. 125

Golden Eagle
size 35 in • p. 126

Crested Caracara
size 23 in • p. 127

American Kestrel
size 8 in • p. 128

Merlin
size 11 in • p. 129

Aplomado Falcon
size 16 in • p. 130

Peregrine Falcon
size 16 in • p. 131

Prairie Falcon
size 16 in • p. 132

RAILS, COOTS & CRANES

Clapper Rail
size 14 in • p. 133

King Rail
size 15 in • p. 134

Virginia Rail
size 10 in • p. 135

Sora
size 9 in • p. 136

Purple Gallinule
size 13 in • p. 137

Common Moorhen
size 13 in • p. 138

American Coot
size 14 in • p. 139

Sandhill Crane
size 45 in • p. 140

Whooping Crane
size 56 in • p. 141

Black-bellied Plover
size 12 in • p. 142

American Golden-Plover
size 10 in • p. 143

Snowy Plover
size 6 in • p. 144

Wilson's Plover
size 8 in • p. 145

Semipalmated Plover
size 7 in • p. 146

Piping Plover
size 7 in • p. 147

Killdeer
size 10 in • p. 148

Mountain Plover
size 9 in • p. 149

American Oystercatcher
size 18 in • p. 150

Black-necked Stilt
size 14 in • p. 151

American Avocet
size 17 in • p. 152

Spotted Sandpiper
size 7 in • p. 153

Solitary Sandpiper
size 8 in • p. 154

Greater Yellowlegs
size 14 in • p. 155

Willet
size 15 in • p. 156

Lesser Yellowlegs
size 10 in • p. 157

Upland Sandpiper
size 11 in • p. 158

Long-billed Curlew
size 23 in • p. 159

Marbled Godwit
size 18 in • p. 160

Ruddy Turnstone
size 9 in • p. 161

Red Knot
size 10 in • p. 162

Sanderling
size 8 in • p. 163

Semipalmated Sandpiper
size 6 in • p. 164

Western Sandpiper
size 6 in • p. 165

Least Sandpiper
size 6 in • p. 166

SHOREBIRDS

White-rumped Sandpiper
size 7 in • p. 167

Baird's Sandpiper
size 7 in • p. 168

Pectoral Sandpiper
size 8 in • p. 169

Dunlin
size 8 in • p. 170

Stilt Sandpiper
size 8 in • p. 171

Buff-breasted Sandpiper
size 8 in • p. 172

Short-billed Dowitcher
size 11 in • p. 173

Long-billed Dowitcher
size 12 in • p. 174

Wilson's Snipe
size 11 in • p. 175

American Woodcock
size 11 in • p. 176

Wilson's Phalarope
size 9 in • p. 177

GULLS & ALLIES

Laughing Gull
size 16 in • p. 178

Franklin's Gull
size 14 in • p. 179

Bonaparte's Gull
size 13 in • p. 180

Ring-billed Gull
size 19 in • p. 181

California Gull
size 19 in • p. 182

Herring Gull
size 24 in • p. 183

Lesser Black-backed Gull
size 20 in • p. 184

Glaucous Gull
size 27 in • p. 185

Least Tern
size 9 in • p. 186

Gull-billed Tern
size 14 in • p. 187

Caspian Tern
size 21 in • p. 188

Black Tern
size 9 in • p. 189

Common Tern
size 14 in • p. 190

Forster's Tern
size 15 in • p. 191

Royal Tern
size 20 in • p. 192

Sandwich Tern
size 15 in • p. 193

Black Skimmer
size 18 in • p. 194

Rock Pigeon
size 12 in • p. 195

Eurasian Collared-Dove
size 11 in • p. 196

White-winged Dove
size 12 in • p. 197

Mourning Dove
size 12 in • p. 198

Inca Dove
size 7 in • p. 199

Common Ground-Dove
size 7 in • p. 200

White-tipped Dove
size 11 in • p. 201

Monk Parakeet
size 11 in • p. 202

Yellow-billed Cuckoo
size 12 in • p. 203

Black-billed Cuckoo
size 12 in • p. 204

Greater Roadrunner
size 23 in • p. 205

Groove-billed Ani
size 13 in • p. 206

Barn Owl
size 15 in • p. 207

Western Screech-Owl
size 9 in • p. 208

Eastern Screech-Owl
size 8 in • p. 209

Great Horned Owl
size 22 in • p. 210

Ferruginous Pygmy-Owl
size 6 in • p. 211

Elf Owl
size 5 in • p. 212

Burrowing Owl
size 8 in • p. 213

Barred Owl
size 20 in • p. 214

Long-eared Owl
size 14 in • p. 215

Short-eared Owl
size 15 in • p. 216

NIGHTJARS, SWIFTS & HUMMINGBIRDS

Lesser Nighthawk
size 8 in • p. 217

Common Nighthawk
size 9 in • p. 218

Common Pauraque
size 11 in • p. 219

Common Poorwill
size 8 in • p. 220

Chuck-will's-widow
size 12 in • p. 221

Whip-poor-will
size 9 in • p. 222

Chimney Swift
size 5 in • p. 223

White-throated Swift
size 6 in • p. 224

Buff-bellied Hummingbird
size 4 in • p. 225

Ruby-throated Hummingbird
size 4 in • p. 226

Black-chinned Hummingbird
size 3 in • p. 227

Broad-tailed Hummingbird
size 4 in • p. 228

Rufous Hummingbird
size 3 in • p. 229

Ringed Kingfisher
size 16 in • p. 230

Belted Kingfisher
size 12 in • p. 231

Green Kingfisher
size 8 in • p. 232

WOODPECKERS

Red-headed Woodpecker
size 9 in • p. 233

Acorn Woodpecker
size 9 in • p. 234

Golden-fronted Woodpecker
size 9 in • p. 235

Red-bellied Woodpecker
size 10 in • p. 236

Yellow-bellied Sapsucker
size 8 in • p. 237

Ladder-backed Woodpecker
size 7 in • p. 238

Downy Woodpecker
size 6 in • p. 239

Hairy Woodpecker
size 9 in • p. 240

Red-Cockaded Woodpecker
size 8 in • p. 241

Northern Flicker
size 13 in • p. 242

Pileated Woodpecker
size 17 in • p. 243

Olive-sided Flycatcher
size 7 in • p. 245

Western Wood-Pewee
size 6 in • p. 246

Eastern Wood-Pewee
size 6 in • p. 247

Yellow-bellied Flycatcher
size 5 in • p. 248

Acadian Flycatcher
size 6 in • p. 249

Alder Flycatcher
size 6 in • p. 250

Willow Flycatcher
size 6 in • p. 251

Least Flycatcher
size 5 in • p. 252

Hammond's Flycatcher
size 5 in • p. 253

Gray Flycatcher
size 5 in • p. 254

Dusky Flycatcher
size 5 in • p. 255

Cordilleran Flycatcher
size 5 in • p. 256

Black Phoebe
size 6 in • p. 257

Eastern Phoebe
size 7 in • p. 258

Say's Phoebe
size 7 in • p. 259

Vermilion Flycatcher
size 6 in • p. 260

Ash-throated Flycatcher
size 7 in • p. 261

Great Crested Flycatcher
size 8 in • p. 262

Brown-crested Flycatcher
size 8 in • p. 263

Great Kiskadee
size 9 in • p. 264

Couch's Kingbird
size 8 in • p. 265

Cassin's Kingbird
size 8 in • p. 266

Western Kingbird
size 8 in • p. 267

Eastern Kingbird
size 8 in • p. 268

Scissor-tailed Flycatcher
size 13 in • p. 269

SHRIKES & VIREOS

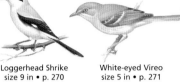

Loggerhead Shrike
size 9 in • p. 270

White-eyed Vireo
size 5 in • p. 271

Bell's Vireo
size 5 in • p. 272

Black-capped Vireo
size 4 in • p. 273

Gray Vireo
size 5 in • p. 274

Yellow-throated Vireo
size 5 in • p. 275

Blue-headed Vireo
size 5 in • p. 276

Hutton's Vireo
size 5 in • p. 277

Warbling Vireo
size 5 in • p. 278

Red-eyed Vireo
size 6 in • p. 279

JAYS & CROWS

Blue Jay
size 12 in • p. 280

Green Jay
size 10 in • p. 281

Western Scrub-Jay
size 11 in • p. 282

American Crow
size 19 in • p. 283

Fish Crow
size 15 in • p. 284

Chihuahuan Raven
size 19 in • p. 285

Common Raven
size 24 in • p. 286

LARKS & SWALLOWS

Horned Lark
size 7 in • p. 287

Purple Martin
size 8 in • p. 288

Tree Swallow
size 5 in • p. 289

Violet-green Swallow
size 5 in • p. 290

Northern Rough-winged Swallow
size 5 in • p. 291

Bank Swallow
size 5 in • p. 292

Cliff Swallow
size 5 in • p. 293

Cave Swallow
size 5 in • p. 294

Barn Swallow
size 7 in • p. 295

Carolina Chickadee
size 4 in • p. 296

Tufted Titmouse
size 6 in • p. 297

Black-crested Titmouse
size 6 in • p. 298

Verdin
size 6 in • p. 299

Bushtit
size 6 in • p. 300

Red-breasted Nuthatch
size 6 in • p. 301

White-breasted Nuthatch
size 6 in • p. 302

Brown-headed Nuthatch
size 4 in • p. 303

Brown Creeper
size 5 in • p. 304

Cactus Wren
size 8 in • p. 305

Rock Wren
size 6 in • p. 306

Canyon Wren
size 5 in • p. 307

Carolina Wren
size 5 in • p. 308

Bewick's Wren
size 5 in • p. 309

House Wren
size 5 in • p. 310

Winter Wren
size 4 in • p. 311

Sedge Wren
size 4 in • p. 312

Marsh Wren
size 5 in • p. 313

KINGLETS, GNATCATCHERS & THRUSHES

Golden-crowned Kinglet
size 4 in • p. 314

Ruby-crowned Kinglet
size 4 in • p. 315

Blue-gray Gnatcatcher
size 4 in • p. 316

Black-tailed Gnatcatcher
size 4 in • p. 317

Eastern Bluebird
size 7 in • p. 318

Western Bluebird
size 7 in • p. 319

Mountain Bluebird
size 7 in • p. 320

Townsend's Solitaire
size 8 in • p. 321

Veery
size 7 in • p. 322

Gray-cheeked Thrush
size 7 in • p. 323

Swainson's Thrush
size 7 in • p. 324

Hermit Thrush
size 7 in • p. 325

Wood Thrush
size 8 in • p. 326

American Robin
size 10 in • p. 327

MIMICS, STARLINGS & WAXINGS

Gray Catbird
size 9 in • p. 328

Northern Mockingbird
size 10 in • p. 329

Sage Thrasher
size 8 in • p. 330

Brown Thrasher
size 11 in • p. 331

Long-billed Thrasher
size 9 in • p. 332

Curve-billed Thrasher
size 9 in • p. 333

European Starling
size 8 in • p. 334

American Pipit
size 6 in • p. 335

Sprague's Pipit
size 6 in • p. 336

Cedar Waxwing
size 7 in • p. 337

Phainopepla
size 7 in • p. 338

Blue-winged Warbler
size 5 in • p. 339

Golden-winged Warbler
size 5 in • p. 340

Tennessee Warbler
size 5 in • p. 341

Orange-crowned Warbler
size 5 in • p. 342

Nashville Warbler
size 5 in • p. 343

Northern Parula
size 4 in • p. 344

Yellow Warbler
size 5 in • p. 345

Chestnut-sided Warbler
size 5 in • p. 346

Magnolia Warbler
size 5 in • p. 347

Yellow-rumped Warbler
size 5 in • p. 348

Golden-cheeked Warbler
size 5 in • p. 349

Black-throated Green Warbler
size 5 in • p. 350

Townsend's Warbler
size 5 in • p.351

Blackburnian Warbler
size 5 in • p. 352

Yellow-throated Warbler
size 5 in • p. 353

Pine Warbler
size 5 in • p. 354

Prairie Warbler
size 5 in • p. 355

Bay-breasted Warbler
size 5 in • p. 356

Black-and-white Warbler
size 5 in • p. 357

American Redstart
size 5 in • p. 358

Prothonotary Warbler
size 5 in • p. 359

Worm-eating Warbler
size 5 in • p. 360

Swainson's Warbler
size 5 in • p. 361

Ovenbird
size 6 in • p. 362

Northern Waterthrush
size 5 in • p. 363

Louisiana Waterthrush
size 6 in • p. 364

Kentucky Warbler
size 5 in • p. 365

Mourning Warbler
size 5 in • p. 366

MacGillivray's Warbler
size 5 in • p. 367

Common Yellowthroat
size 5 in • p. 368

Hooded Warbler
size 5 in • p. 369

Wilson's Warbler
size 5 in • p. 370

Canada Warbler
size 5 in • p. 371

Yellow-breasted Chat
size 7 in • p. 372

Hepatic Tanager
size 8 in • p. 373

Summer Tanager
size 7 in • p. 374

Scarlet Tanager
size 7 in • p. 375

Western Tanager
size 7 in • p. 376

Olive Sparrow
size 6 in • p. 377

Green-tailed Towhee
size 7 in • p. 378

Spotted Towhee
size 8 in • p. 379

Eastern Towhee
size 8 in • p. 380

Canyon Towhee
size 8 in • p. 381

Cassin's Sparrow
size 6 in • p. 382

Bachman's Sparrow
size 6 in • p. 383

Rufous-crowned Sparrow
size 6 in • p. 384

American Tree Sparrow
size 6 in • p. 385

Chipping Sparrow
size 5 in • p. 386

Clay-colored Sparrow
size 5 in • p. 387

Brewer's Sparrow
size 5 in • p. 388

Field Sparrow
size 5 in • p. 389

Vesper Sparrow
size 6 in • p. 390

Lark Sparrow
size 6 in • p. 391

Black-throated Sparrow
size 5 in • p. 392

Lark Bunting
size 7 in • p. 393

Savannah Sparrow
size 5 in • p. 394

Grasshopper Sparrow
size 5 in • p. 395

Henslow's Sparrow
size 5 in • p. 396

Le Conte's Sparrow
size 5 in • p. 397

Nelson's Sharp-tailed Sparrow
size 5 in • p. 398

Seaside Sparrow
size 6 in • p. 399

Fox Sparrow
size 7 in • p.400

Song Sparrow
size 6 in • p. 401

Lincoln's Sparrow
size 5 in • p. 402

Swamp Sparrow
size 5 in • p. 403

White-throated Sparrow
size 7 in • p. 404

Harris's Sparrow
size 7 in • p. 405

White-crowned Sparrow
size 7 in • p. 406

Dark-eyed Junco
size 6 in • p. 407

McCown's Longspur
size 6 in • p. 408

Lapland Longspur
size 6 in • p. 409

Chestnut-collared Longspur
size 6 in • p. 410

Northern Cardinal
size 8 in • p. 411

Pyrrhuloxia
size 8 in • p. 412

Rose-breasted Grosbeak
size 8 in • p. 413

Black-headed Grosbeak
size 7 in • p. 414

Blue Grosbeak
size 6 in • p. 415

Lazuli Bunting
size 5 in • p. 416

Indigo Bunting
size 5 in • p. 417

Painted Bunting
size 5 in • p. 418

Dickcissel
size 6 in • p. 419

BLACKBIRDS & ALLIES

Bobolink
size 7 in • p. 420

Red-winged Blackbird
size 8 in • p. 421

Eastern Meadowlark
size 9 in • p. 422

Western Meadowlark
size 9 in • p. 423

Yellow-headed Blackbird
size 9 in • p. 424

Rusty Blackbird
size 9 in • p. 425

Brewer's Blackbird
size 9 in • p. 426

Common Grackle
size 12 in • p. 427

Boat-tailed Grackle
size 15 in • p. 428

Great-tailed Grackle
size 17 in • p. 429

Bronzed Cowbird
size 8 in • p. 430

Brown-headed Cowbird
size 7 in • p. 431

Orchard Oriole
size 7 in • p. 432

Bullock's Oriole
size 7 in • p. 433

Audubon's Oriole
size 8 in • p. 434

Baltimore Oriole
size 8 in • p. 435

Scott's Oriole
size 9 in • p. 436

FINCHLIKE BIRDS

Purple Finch
size 6 in • p. 437

House Finch
size 6 in • p. 438

Pine Siskin
size 5 in • p. 439

Lesser Goldfinch
size 4 in • p. 440

American Goldfinch
size 5 in • p. 441

House Sparrow
size 6 in • p. 442

INTRODUCTION

BIRDING IN TEXAS

In recent decades, birding has evolved from an eccentric pursuit practiced by a few dedicated individuals to a continent-wide activity that boasts millions of professional and amateur participants. There are many good reasons why birding has become so popular. Many people find it simple and relaxing, while others enjoy the outdoor exercise that it affords. Some see it as a rewarding learning experience, an opportunity to socialize with like-minded people and a way to monitor the health of the local environment. Still others watch birds to reconnect with nature. A visit to any of our region's premier birding locations, such as High Island, Sabine Woods, Davis Mountains State Park or Big Bend National Park, would doubtless uncover still more reasons why people watch birds.

We are truly blessed by the geographical and biological diversity of Texas. In addition to supporting a wide range of breeding birds and year-round residents, our state hosts a large number of spring and fall migrants that move through our area on the way to their breeding and wintering grounds. In all, 629 bird species have been seen and recorded in Texas. Out of these, about 475 species make regular appearances in the state or in its offshore waters.

Christmas bird counts, breeding bird surveys, nest box programs, migration monitoring and birding lectures and workshops all provide a chance for novice, intermediate and expert birdwatchers to interact and share their enthusiasm for the wonder of birds. So, whatever your level, there is ample opportunity for you to get involved!

BEGINNING TO LEARN THE BIRDS

The Challenge of Birding

Birding (also known as birdwatching) can be extremely challenging, and getting started is often the most difficult part. Learning to recognize all the birds in Texas is a long process. But fear not! The species pictured in this guide will help you get started. Although any standard North American field guide will help you identify local birds, such guides can be daunting because they cover the entire continent and present an overwhelming number of species. By focusing specifically on the bird life of Texas, we hope to make the introduction to the world of birding a little less intimidating.

Do not expect to become an expert overnight. To be able to identify any bird at a glance, you will have to spend more than a few hours in the field with binoculars and this guide. It could conceivably take a lifetime of careful study to master the art of birding. After all, only a small number of birders and ornithologists in our state can identify all of our species with confidence. Nevertheless, almost everyone finds the continual learning process of birding to be enjoyable, if not downright thrilling.

Summer Tanager

Classification: The Order of Things

To an ornithologist (a biologist who studies birds), the species is the fundamental unit of classification because the members of a single species look most alike and they naturally interbreed with one another. Each species has a scientific name, usually derived from Latin or Greek, that designates genus and species, which is always underlined or italicized, and a single accredited common name so that the different vernacular names of a species do not cause confusion. A bird has been properly identified only when it has been identified "to species," and most ornithologists use the accredited common name. For example, "American Coot" is an accredited common name, even though some people call this bird a "Mudhen." *Fulica americana* is the American Coot's species name. (*Fulica* is the genus, or generic name, and *americana* is the species, or specific name).

To help make sense of the hundreds of bird species in our region, scientifically oriented birdwatchers lump species into recognizable groups. The most commonly used groupings, in order of increasing scope, are genus, family and order. The American Coot and Common Moorhen are different species that do not share a genus (their generic names are different), but they are both members of the family Rallidae (the rail family). The rail, limpkin and crane families are in turn grouped within the order Gruiformes, which comprises the marsh birds.

Ornithologists have arranged all of the orders to make a standard sequence. It begins with the ducks and their relatives (order Anseriformes), which are thought by many to be the most primitive of modern birds. The sequence ends with those species thought to have been most strongly modified by evolutionary change and most departed from the ancestral form. We have organized this book according to this standard sequence.

At first, the evolutionary sequence might not make much sense. Birders, however, know that all books of this sort begin with waterfowl, followed by grouselike birds, diving birds, birds of prey, and other birds that look more and more like songbirds (formally known as "passerines"). Still, many readers will tell us that we should have arranged this book alphabetically. Although alphabetical organization may seem logical, it assumes that you already know all of the up-to-date, accredited names of the birds. In practice, the tried-and-true method of grouping birds according to similarities and differences provides the best format for learning.

Great-tailed Grackle

TECHNIQUES OF BIRDING

Being in the right place at the right time to see birds in action involves both skill and luck. The more you know about a bird—its range, preferred habitat, food preferences and hours and seasons of activity—the better your chances will be of seeing it. It is much easier to find a Barred Owl in the woodlands than elsewhere, especially at night in spring, when adults are calling for mates. Short-eared Owls, however, are most often seen flying over fields and marshes during the day in winter.

Mississippi Kite

Generally, spring and fall are the busiest birding times. Temperatures are moderate then, and a great number of birds are on the move, often heavily populating small patches of habitat before moving on. Male songbirds are easy to identify on spring mornings as they belt out their courtship songs. Throughout much of the year, diurnal birds are most visible in the early morning hours when they are foraging, but during winter they are often more active in the day when milder temperatures prevail. Timing is crucial because summer foliage often conceals birds and cold weather drives many species south of our region for winter. Birding also involves a great deal of luck.

Binoculars

The small size, fine details and wary behavior of many birds make binoculars an essential piece of equipment for birding. Binoculars can cost anywhere from $50 to $1500, and at times it may seem that there are as many kinds of binoculars as there are species of birds. Most beginners pay less than $200 for their first pair. Compact binoculars are a popular choice because they are small and lightweight, but they are not necessarily cheap—some of the most expensive binoculars can be compact.

Rufous Hummingbird

Binoculars come in two basic types: porro-prism (in which there is a distinct, angular bend in the body of the binoculars) and roof-prism (in which the body is straight). Good porro-prism binoculars are less expensive than good roof-prism binoculars: a first-rate pair of "porros" costs $300 to $400; good roof-prism binoculars, which are often waterproof and fog-resistant (nitrogen-filled), can cost $800 or more. Expensive binoculars usually have better optics and generally stand up better to abuse.

Seaside Sparrow

The optical power of binoculars is described with a two-number code. For example, a compact pair of binoculars might be "8✕21," while a larger pair might be "7✕40." In each case, the first number states the magnification, and the second number indicates the diameter, in millimeters, of the front lenses. Eight-power binoculars are the easiest to use for finding birds; 10-power binoculars give a shakier but more magnified view. Larger lenses gather more light, so a 40 mm or 50 mm lens will perform much better at dusk than a 20 mm or 30 mm lens of the same magnification. For a beginner, eight-power, porro-prism binoculars with front lenses at least 35 mm in diameter (thus 8✕35 or 8✕40) are suitable. Some binoculars have a wider field of view than others, even if the two-number code is identical. We recommend the wider field of view because many beginners have trouble finding birds in compact, narrow-view binoculars.

Look at many types of binoculars before making a purchase. Talk to other birders about their binoculars and ask to try them. Go to a store that specializes in birding—the sales people there will know from personal experience which models perform best in the field.

When birding, lift the binoculars up to your eyes without taking your eyes off the bird. This way you will not lose the bird in the magnified view. You can also note an obvious landmark near the bird (a bright flower or a dead branch, for example) and then use it as a reference point to find the bird with the binoculars.

Spotting Scopes and Cameras

The spotting scope (a small telescope with a sturdy tripod) is designed to help you view birds that are beyond the range of binoculars. Most spotting scopes are capable of magnification by a factor of 20 or more. Some scopes will even allow you to take photographs through them.

If you intend to photograph birds, you should buy a 35 mm single-lens reflex (SLR) camera with a telephoto lens measuring at least 300 mm (or a high-resolution digital SLR camera with an equivalent lens). A solid tripod for the camera is essential. Good quality equipment will help you take photos that are not marred by poor optics or shaky hands. Talk to knowledgeable camera sales staff, and be prepared to spend a lot of money.

Once you have a good camera, you must develop an equally good technique. Most successful bird photographs are taken by quiet, patient photographers—few birds stick around to have themselves photographed by noisy, stampeding admirers.

Birding by Ear

Recognizing birds by their songs and calls can greatly enhance your birding experience. When experienced birders conduct breeding bird surveys in summer, they rely more on their ears than their eyes because listening is far more efficient. There are numerous tapes and CDs that can help you learn bird songs, and a portable player with headphones can let you quickly compare a live bird with a recording.

The old-fashioned way to remember bird songs is to make up words for them. We have given you some of the classic renderings in the species accounts that follow, such as *"peter peter peter"* for the Tufted Titmouse or *"who cooks for you? who cooks for you-all?"* for the Barred Owl. For other species, one has to make up descriptive terms for the bird sounds: for example, some describe the call of the White-breasted Nuthatch as "a tin horn." Some of these approximations work better than others; birds often add or delete syllables from their calls, and very few pronounce consonants in a recognizable fashion. Be aware that songs usually vary from place to place as well. The words and recordings that have helped you identify birds successfully in one area might not work as well elsewhere.

WATCHING BIRD BEHAVIOR

Once you can confidently identify birds and remember their common names, you can begin to appreciate their behavior. Studying birds involves keeping notes and records. The timing of bird migrations is an easy thing to record, as are details of feeding, courtship and nesting behavior if you are willing to be patient. Flocking birds can also provide fascinating opportunities to observe and note social interactions, especially when individual birds can be recognized. Such observations have contributed greatly to our knowledge of birds. However, casual note-taking should not be equated with more standardized, scientific methods of study: your notes can never be too detailed.

Burrowing Owl

Birding, for most people, is a peaceful, nondestructive recreational activity. One of the best ways to watch bird behavior is to look for a spot rich with avian life, then sit back and relax. If you become part of the scenery, the birds, at first startled by your approach, will soon resume their activities and allow you into their world.

BIRDING BY HABITAT

Texas can be separated into nine biophysical regions or "bioregions": Pineywoods, Coastal Plains, Post Oak Savannah, Blackland Prairies, South Texas Brush Country, Edwards Plateau, Rolling Plains, High Plains and Trans Pecos. Each bioregion is composed of a number of different habitats. Each habitat is a community of plants and animals supported by the infrastructure of water and soil and regulated by the constraints of topography, climate and elevation.

Simply put, a bird's habitat is the place in which it normally lives. Some birds prefer the open water, some are found in cattail marshes, others like mature coniferous forest and still others prefer abandoned agricultural fields overgrown with tall grass and shrubs. Knowledge of a bird's habitat increases the chance of identifying the bird correctly. If you are birding in wetlands, you will not be identifying tanagers or towhees; if you are wandering among the leafy trees of a deciduous forest, do not expect to meet Brown Pelicans or Reddish Egrets.

Habitats are like neighborhoods; if you associate friends with the suburb in which they live, you can just as easily learn to associate specific birds with their preferred habitats. Only in migration, especially during inclement weather, do some birds leave their usual habitat.

BIRD LISTING

Many birders list the species they have seen during excursions or at home. It is up to you to decide what kind of list—systematic or casual—you will keep, and you may choose not to make lists at all. However, lists may prove rewarding in unexpected ways. For example, after you visit a new area, your list becomes a souvenir of your experiences there. By reviewing the list, you can recall memories and details that you might otherwise have forgotten. Keeping regular, accurate lists of birds in your neighborhood can also be useful for local researchers. It can be interesting to compare the arrival dates and last sightings of hummingbirds and other seasonal visitors, or to note the first sighting of a new visitor to your area. Try to record accurate numbers for each species, and keep in mind that estimates are better than no numbers at all.

Although there are programs available for listing birds on computers, many naturalists simply keep records in field notebooks. Waterproof books and waterproof pens work well on rainy days, though many birders prefer to use a pocket recorder in the field and then transcribe their observations into a dry notebook at home. Find a notebook you like and personalize it with field sketches, observations, poetry or whatever you wish.

Pyrrhuloxia

BIRDING ACTIVITIES

Birding Groups

We recommend that you join in on such activities as Christmas bird counts, birding festivals and the meetings of your local birding or natural history club. Meeting other people with the same interests can make birding even more pleasurable, and there is always something to be learned when birders of all levels gather. If you are interested in bird conservation and environmental issues, natural history groups and conscientious birding stores can keep you informed about the situation in your area and what you can do to help. Bird hotlines provide current information on the sightings of rarities, which are often easier to find again than you might think.

Organizations

A number of Audubon chapters exist in Texas, especially in metropolitan areas such as Dallas, Fort Worth, San Antonio and Houston. Telephone hotlines exist for a number of these areas, as well as rare bird alerts.

Bird Conservation

Texas abounds with bird life. There are still large areas of wilderness including parks, wildlife refuges and public lands. Nevertheless, agriculture, forestry and development for housing threaten viable bird habitat throughout the region. It is hoped that more people will learn to appreciate nature through birding, and that those people will do their best to protect the natural areas that remain. Many bird enthusiasts support groups such as the Texas Nature Conservancy, the Houston Audubon Society and the Texas Ornithological Society, which help birds by providing sanctuaries or promoting conservation of the natural world.

Landscaping your own property to provide native plant cover and natural foods for birds is an immediate and personal way to ensure the conservation of bird habitat. The cumulative effects of such urban "nature-scaping" can be significant. If your yard is to become a bird sanctuary, you may want to keep the neighborhood cats out—cats kill millions of birds each year. Check with the local Humane Society for methods of protecting both your feline friends and wild birds. Ultimately, for protection of birds, cats are best kept indoors. The Texas Parks and Wildlife Department will help in establishing backyard sanctuaries.

Bird Feeding

Many people set up backyard bird feeders or plant native berry- or seed-producing plants in their garden to attract birds to

*Eastern
Meadowlark*

their yard. The kinds of food available will determine which birds visit your yard. Staff at birding stores can suggest which foods will attract specific birds. Hummingbird feeders are popular in summer to attract our numerous hummingbirds; in some parts of Texas, these feeders can be maintained year-round and attract several species of hummingbirds. Hummingbird feeders are filled with a simple sugar solution made from one part sugar and three to four parts water.

Black Tern

Contrary to popular opinion, birds do not become dependent on feeders, nor do they subsequently forget to forage naturally. Winter is when birds appreciate feeders the most, but it is also difficult to find food in spring before flowers bloom, seeds develop and insects hatch. Birdbaths will also entice birds to your yard at any time of year, and heated birdbaths are particularly appreciated in the colder months. Avoid birdbaths that have exposed metal parts because wet birds can accidentally freeze to them in winter. There are many good books about feeding birds and landscaping your yard to provide natural foods and nest sites.

Nest Boxes

Another popular way to attract birds is to set out nest boxes, especially for Eastern Bluebirds, Tufted and Black-crested Titmice, Carolina Chickadees and Purple Martins. Not all birds will use nest boxes; only species that normally use cavities in trees are comfortable in such confined spaces. Larger nest boxes can attract kestrels, owls and cavity-nesting ducks.

Cleaning Feeders and Nest Boxes

Nest boxes and feeding stations must be kept clean to prevent birds from becoming ill or spreading disease. Old nesting material may harbor a number of parasites, as well as their eggs. Once the birds have left for the season, remove the old nesting material and wash and scrub the nest box with detergent or a 10 percent bleach solution (one part bleach to nine parts water). You can also scald the nest box with boiling water. Rinse it well and let it dry thoroughly before you remount it. For some birds such as screech-owls, do not place nesting materials in their boxes and they will not need cleaning.

Feeding stations should be cleaned monthly. Feeders can become moldy and any seed, fruit or suet that is moldy or spoiled must be removed. Unclean bird feeders can also be contaminated with salmonellosis and possibly other avian diseases. Clean and disinfect feeding stations with a 10 percent bleach solution, scrubbing thoroughly. Rinse the feeder well and allow it to dry completely before refilling it. Discarded seed and feces on the ground under the feeding station should also be removed. We advise that you wear rubber gloves and a mask when cleaning nest boxes or feeders.

West Nile Virus

Since the West Nile Virus first surfaced in North America in 1999, it has caused fear and misunderstanding—some people have become afraid of contracting the disease from birds, and health departments in some communities have advised residents to eliminate feeding stations and birdbaths. To date, the disease affects 138 species of birds. Corvids (crows, jays and ravens) and raptors have been the most obvious victims because of their size, though the disease also affects some smaller species. The virus is transmitted to birds and to humans (as well as some other mammals) by mosquitoes that have bitten infected birds, but not all mosquito species can carry the disease. Humans cannot contract the disease from casual contact with infected birds, and birds do not get the disease from other birds. According to the Centers for Disease Control and Prevention (CDC), only about 20 percent of people who are bitten and become infected will develop any symptoms at all, and less than one percent will become severely ill.

Because mosquitoes breed in standing water, birdbaths have the potential to become mosquito breeding grounds. Birdbaths should be emptied and the water changed at least weekly. Drippers, circulating pumps, fountains or waterfalls that keep water moving will prevent mosquitoes from laying their eggs in the water. There are also bird-friendly products available to treat water in birdbaths. You can contact your local nature store or garden center or do some research on-line for more information on these products.

TOP BIRDING SITES IN TEXAS

There are hundreds, if not thousands, of good birding areas throughout Texas. The following areas have been selected to represent a broad range of bird communities and habitats, with an emphasis on accessibility.

High Plains, including the Panhandle
1. Lake Meredith NRA
2. Gene Howe WMA
3. Buffalo Lake NWR
4. Palo Duro Canyon SP
5. Caprock Canyons SP
6. Muleshoe NWR
7. Buffalo Springs Lake, Lubbock
8. Lake Six, Lubbock
9. Big Spring SP
10. Lake Colorado City SP

Rolling Plains
11. Lake Arrowhead SP
12. Abilene SP
13. Possum Kingdom SP
14. Lake Brownwood SP

Oak & Prairies, Blackland Prairies
15. Hagerman NWR
16. Lewisville Lake Park
17. Village Creek Wastewater Treatment Plant
18. Fort Worth Nature Center
19. White Rock Lake, Dallas
20. Cedar Hill SP
21. Lake Tawakoni SP
22. Dinosaur Valley SP
23. Fairfield Lake SP
24. Waco Lake
25. Granger Lake
26. Bastrop SP
27. Lake Somerville SP

Pineywoods
28. Wright Patman Lake
29. Daingerfield SP
30. Lake O' the Pines
31. Caddo Lake SP
32. Tyler SP
33. Martin Dies, Jr. SP

34. Lake Livingston SP
35. Huntsville SP
36. W.G. Jones SF
37. Big Thicket National Preserve

Trans Pecos
38. Franklin Mountains SP
39. Hueco Tanks State Historic Site
40. Guadalupe Mountains NP
41. Red Bluff Reservoir
42. Davis Mountains SP
43. Balmorhea Lake
44. Big Bend Ranch SP
45. Big Bend NP
46. Black Gap WMA
47. Seminole Canyon SP

Edwards Plateau
48. San Angelo SP
49. Meridian SP
50. Inks Lake SP
51. Enchanted Rock SNA
52. Pedernales Falls SP
53. Guadalupe River SP
54. Balcones Canyonlands NWR
55. Wild Basin Wilderness Preserve, Austin
56. Hornsby Bend Wastewater Plant, Austin
57. Garner SP
58. Lost Maples SNA

South Texas Brush Country, including the lower Rio Grande valley
59. Friedrich Wilderness Park, San Antonio
60. Mitchell Lake, San Antonio
61. Braunig and Calaveras Lakes, San Antonio
62. Chaparral WMA
63. Goliad SP
64. Choke Canyon SP
65. Laredo Nature Preserve
66. Lake Corpus Christi SP
67. Falcon Dam and Falcon SP
68. Anzalduas County Park
69. Bentsen-Rio Grande Valley SP
70. Santa Ana NWR
71. Frontera Audubon Sanctuary, Weslaco
72. Estero Llano Grande SP
73. Sabal Palm Audubon Sanctuary
74. South Padre Island Convention Center
75. Boca Chica, mouth of the Rio Grande
76. Laguna Atascosa NWR

Coastal Plain
77. Sabine Woods
78. Sea Rim SP
79. Anahuac NWR
80. High Island
81. Bolivar Flats Shorebird Sanctuary
82. East Beach & East Jetties, Galveston Island
83. Galveston Island SP
84. San Luis Pass, Galveston Island
85. Quintana Nature Preserve
86. Sheldon Lake SP
87. Baytown Nature Center
88. Jesse H. Jones Park, Spring Creek
89. Edith Moore Nature Sanctuary, Houston
90. Bear Creek Pioneer Park, Houston
91. Brazoria NWR
92. San Bernard NWR
93. Brazos Bend SP
94. Magic Ridge, Calhoun County
95. Aransas NWR
96. Goose Island SP
97. Port Aransas
98. Blucher Park, Corpus Christi
99. Hazel Bazemore County Park, Corpus Christi
100. Padre Island National Seashore

NP =	National Park
NRA =	National Recreation Area
NWR =	National Wildlife Refuge
SF =	State Forest
SNA =	State Natural Area
SP =	State Park
SRA =	State Recreation Area
WMA =	Wildlife Managment Area

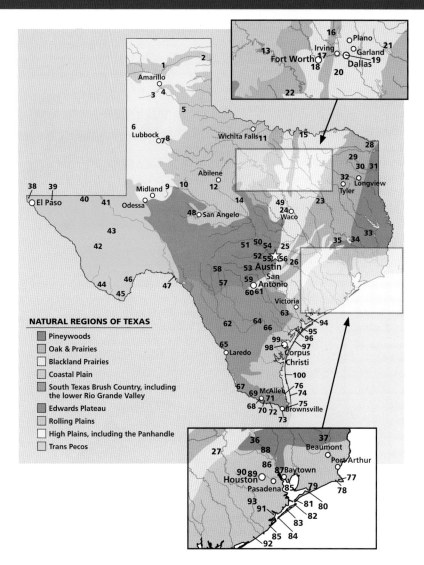

NATURAL REGIONS OF TEXAS

- Pineywoods
- Oak & Prairies
- Blackland Prairies
- Coastal Plain
- South Texas Brush Country, including the lower Rio Grande Valley
- Edwards Plateau
- Rolling Plains
- High Plains, including the Panhandle
- Trans Pecos

TOP 20 BIRDING LOCATIONS

These sites have been selected for one or more of the following reasons: the presence of unique species of avifauna; the presence of particular ecosystems; or proximity to urban populations.

Aransas National Wildlife Refuge

Located on the Coastal Plain in Aransas County, this 115,000-acre refuge hosts the wintering flock of the Whooping Crane, now some 237 individuals. At one time, this endangered species number but 15 birds. The refuge also serves many other water birds, including large numbers of waterfowl. Several neotropical species also occur on the refuge.

Attwater Prairie Chicken National Wildlife Refuge

An 8000-acre tract in Colorado County on the Coastal Plain, this refuge was established to help preserve the endangered Attwater's Prairie-Chicken. Unfortunately, only two populations remain in Texas and both must be supplemented by captive-reared birds to sustain these populations. The refuge has developed water resources that attract large numbers of wintering geese and Bald Eagles. Other nesting birds include Fulvous and Black-bellied whistling-ducks, White-tailed Hawks, Crested Caracaras, Common Moorhens, Black-necked Stilts and Dickcissels.

Greater Prairie-Chicken

Balcones Canyonlands National Wildlife Refuge

One of the newer members of our national refuge system, it was established for the express purpose of protecting two endangered species of birds, the Black-capped Vireo and the Golden-cheeked Warbler. Management plans on the refuge are designed to protect and increase habitats for these two species, but many other land birds of the Edwards Plateau occur on the refuge. This tract of land, destined to reach 30,000 acres, takes in property in Burnet, Travis and Williamson counties.

Bentsen-Rio Grande Valley State Park

In Hidalgo County in the Lower Rio Grande Valley is a 760-acre tract of subtropical brushland that also serves as the headquarters of the World Birding Center. The park holds a number of tropical bird species, including Tropical Parulas, Clay-colored Robins, Hook-billed Kites, Great Kiskadees and many other "Mexican specialties" found nowhere else in the United States but Texas. The park checklist includes 370 species of birds.

Great Kiskadee

Big Bend National Park

Established in 1933, this park of more than 800,000 acres in Brewster County of the Trans-Pecos region includes the Chisos Mountains, a northern extension of the Mexican Sierra Oriental. The park shares a large number of lowland birds with adjacent parts of the Trans-Pecos, and even some montane species with the Davis and Guadalupe Mountains, but it is known for the only breeding population of the Colima Warbler in the United States. Other species that attract birders to this park include the Flammulated Owl, Blue-throated Hummingbird, Lucifer Hummingbird, Mexican Jay and Painted Redstart.

Bolivar Flats Shorebird Sanctuary

The original tract consisted of 550 acres owned by the State of Texas but leased to the Houston Audubon Society, and about 500 acres of mudflats on the Bolivar Peninsula of Galveston County. The Society has since added about 600 acres to preserve an area very important on the Texas coast for migrating and wintering shorebirds, waterfowl and other water birds. The sight of thousands of American White Pelicans or American Avocets is spectacular. Brown Pelicans abound in the area, and Least Terns nest at the Sanctuary.

American White Pelican

Davis Mountains State Park

Located in Reeves County of the Trans-Pecos, the park takes in slightly more than 2700 acres of the somewhat isolated Davis Mountains. The park is situated about halfway between Guadalupe Mountains NP and Big Bend NP. These mountains give a birder the best opportunity to observe the Montezuma Quail. Lucifer Hummingbirds also nest in these mountains, as do a number of other western and Mexican species such as the Acorn Woodpecker, White-breasted Nuthatch and Black-headed Grosbeak. In winter, all three species of bluebirds, Mountain Chickadees and Townsend's Solitaires may appear in the park.

Guadalupe National Park

The 86,425 acres of this park include the four highest peaks in Texas, with the highest, Guadalupe Peak, at 8749 feet. Located in Culberson County and adjacent parts of New Mexico, these are often looked upon as the southern-most limits of the Rocky Mountains. Breeding birds here include the endangered Spotted Owl and the Northern Saw-whet Owl (rarely), the Band-tailed Pigeon, the White-throated Swift, the Blue-throated Hummingbird, the Magnificent Hummingbird, the Violet-green Swallow and the Juniper Titmouse.

Violet-green Swallow

Hagerman National Wildlife Refuge

Located in Grayson County on the shores of Lake Texoma, this 11,000-acre refuge with 3000 acres of marshland and open water attracts large numbers of migrating and wintering waterfowl. Five species of geese, including large numbers of Ross's Geese, and 21 species of ducks, occur regularly on the refuge. On rare occasions, Tundra Swans appear for brief periods. With the large area of marshland, the refuge also attracts many species of shorebirds. The 8000 upland acres attract a large variety of land birds.

Hazel Bazemore County Park

Groove-billed Ani

A small tract on the west side of Corpus Christi, this Coastal Plain location has a number of South Texas species, such as the White-tipped Dove, Groove-billed Ani, Long-billed Thrasher and Olive Sparrow, that reach their northern limits on the central Coastal Plain. The park is also well known for migrant land birds in spring but is best known for migrating raptors. A well-organized program for counting migrating raptors over this park produces up to a half-million birds of prey, including hundreds of thousands of Broad-winged Hawks. Seventeen species are regularly encountered in these migrations.

High Island

An area, rather than a park, refuge or wildlife management area, this is one of the most well-known and important migrant "traps" on the upper Texas coast. Located in Galveston County, the "island" consists of oak mots and other highlands surrounded by marshes. Under certain weather conditions, migrating birds pile up in large numbers either coming off the Gulf of Mexico in spring or before heading out over the Gulf in fall. Birders anticipate a "fall-out" when hundreds of birds literally drop out of the sky when weather conditions force them to seek the nearest land after completing a flight across the Gulf. The Houston Audubon Society has four sanctuaries at High Island: Smith Oaks, Boy Scout Woods, Eubanks Woods and S.E. Gast Red Bay. The Texas Ornithological Society added to the sanctuary system at High Island with the Crawford Sanctuary and the Connie Herring Hooks Sanctuary.

Hornsby Bend Wastewater Treatment Plant

Located in southeast Austin, Travis County, this treatment plant also has an environmental learning center associated with it. The settling ponds hold an assortment of waterfowl during winter, and the drying beds attract large numbers of shorebirds in migration. Recently, Ringed Kingfishers and Green Kingfishers have become regular around the area.

Green Kingfisher

Lake O' the Pines

Located in Harrison County of the Pineywoods region, this lake of over 18,000 surface acres is one of the better locations for the "specialties" of the region: Red-cockaded Woodpeckers, Brown-headed Nuthatches, Pine Warblers and Bachman's Sparrows. Several species of warblers breed in areas around the lake. Although one park exits near the dam, the adjacent roads provide access to other parts of the lake and to the habitats used by these specialty land birds. The lake itself attracts a large number of waterfowl and other water birds.

Lake Tawakoni

The lake is situated on the Sabine River at the junction of Rains, Hunt and Van Zandt counties. Although a state park exists in Hunt County, several other access points allow birders to view much more of the lake. While the lake hosts large numbers of wintering waterfowl, it has gained a reputation for some of the rarer water birds such as Pacific and Red-throated loons, Western and Red-necked grebes, all three species of scoters (rare inland), jaegers and Black-headed, Sabine's and Little gulls. Land birds such as Sprague's Pipits, Sedge Wrens, LeConte's Sparrows and Smith's Longspurs appear here regularly.

Sedge Wren

Mitchell Lake

San Antonio has several lakes with associated property. Mitchell Lake is a former wastewater treatment plant. Its 600 acres attract a large number of water birds. Least Grebes nest here, and both species of cormorants appear regularly. The local checklist includes 40 species of shorebirds and 18 species of gulls and terns—a number of rare species appear on this list. An extensive list of land birds have also been recorded from this facility: Cave Swallows overwinter in the area, and a few South Texas species reach their limits here.

Muleshoe National Wildlife Refuge

The oldest national wildlife refuge in Texas, Muleshoe NWR is located in Bailey County of the High Plains. Most of the refuge's 5809 acres consist of short-grass rangeland, but the lakes on the refuge, when full, have 600 acres to attract waterfowl and large numbers of Sandhill Cranes: usually 10,000 to 25,000 cranes. Snowy Plovers, American Avocets and Horned Larks are among the nesting birds on the refuge.

Sandhill Crane

Santa Ana National Wildlife Refuge

This 2088-acre parcel of subtropical thornscrub sits in eastern Hidalgo County of the Lower Rio Grande Valley. The nearly 400 species of birds includes a large contingent of neotropical species such as Plain Chachalacas, Hook-billed Kites, Gray Hawks, Pauraques, Buff-bellied Hummingbirds, all three species of kingfishers, Couch's and Tropical kingbirds and Northern Bearded-Tyrannulets. The refuge also contains marshlands and small bodies of water known as "resacas," which attract a number of water birds such as Masked Ducks and Least Grebes.

Village Creek Wastewater Treatment Plant

Located in Tarrant County in the city of Arlington, this wastewater treatment plant provides a wide variety of birdlife for birders of the western parts of the Metroplex. Black-bellied Whistling-Ducks, Common Moorhens and Black-necked Stilts all nest on the property. In migration, one might expect Cinnamon Teals, Glossy Ibises and Buff-bellied Sandpipers; in winter, look for LeConte's Sparrows, Harris's Sparrows and Rusty Blackbirds.

Black-bellied Whistling-Duck

White Rock Lake

Located in the city of Dallas, this relatively small lake and its surroundings offer a variety of birding opportunities. The lake attracts migrating and wintering waterfowl and gulls, including some rare species such as the Little Gull and Mew Gull. The Dallas Arboretum and Botanical Garden adjacent to the lake offers excellent birding for migrants in spring. Ponds on the old fish hatchery have nesting Wood Ducks and Yellow-crowned and Black-crowned night-herons. A small colony of Monk Parakeets also nests here.

W.G. Jones State Forest

Located in Montgomery County not far north of Houston, this 1700-acre tract offers perhaps the best opportunity to view Red-cockaded Woodpeckers. The Texas Forest Service manages the area for this species. Also present are Brown-headed Nuthatches and Pine Warblers and, occasionally, Bachman's Sparrows.

Red-cockaded Woodpecker

ABOUT THE SPECIES ACCOUNTS

This book gives detailed accounts of 401 species of birds that are listed as regular by the *Texas Ornithological Society*; these species can be expected on an annual basis. Eighty-four less common or occasional species are briefly mentioned in an illustrated appendix. The order of the birds and their common and scientific names follow the American Ornithologists' Union's *Check-list of North American Birds* (7th edition, July 1998) and *The Forty-third Supplement 2003*. Common birds are included in these accounts, as well as exciting rarities.

As well as discussing the identifying features of a bird, each species account attempts to bring a bird to life by describing its various character traits. Personifying a bird helps us to relate to it on a personal level. However, the characterizations presented in this book are based on the human experience and most likely fall short of truly defining the way birds perceive the world. The characterizations should not be mistaken for scientific propositions. Nonetheless, we hope that a lively, engaging text will communicate our scientific knowledge as smoothly and effectively as possible.

One of the challenges of birding is that many species look different in spring and summer than they do in fall and winter. Many birds have breeding and nonbreeding plumages, and immature birds often look different from their parents. This book does not try to describe or illustrate all the different plumages of a species; instead, it focuses on the forms that are most likely to be seen in our area.

Common Pauraque

ID: It is difficult to describe the features of a bird without being able to visualize it, so this section is best used in combination with the illustrations. Where appropriate, the description is subdivided to highlight the differences between male and female birds, breeding and nonbreeding birds and immature and adult birds. The descriptions use as few technical terms as possible and favor easily understood language. Birds may not have "jaw lines," "eyebrows" or "chins," but these and other scientifically inaccurate terms are easily understood by all readers. Some of the most common features of birds are pointed out in the glossary illustration.

Size: The size measurement, the average length of the bird's body from bill to tail, is an approximate measurement of the bird as it is seen in nature. The size of larger birds is often given as a range, because there is variation among individuals. In addition, wingspan (from wing tip to wing tip when fully spread) is given for all birds in the book. Please note that birds with long tails often have large measurements that do not necessarily reflect body size.

Status: A general comment, such as "common," "uncommon" or "rare" is usually sufficient to describe the relative abundance of a species. Wherever possible, we have also indicated status at different times of the year. Situations are bound to vary somewhat since migratory pulses, seasonal changes and centers of activity tend to concentrate or disperse birds.

Habitat: The habitats we have listed describe where each species is most commonly found. In most cases it is a generalized description, but if a bird is restricted to a specific habitat, the habitat is described precisely. Because of the freedom flight gives them, birds can turn up in almost any type of habitat. However, they will usually be found in environments that provide the specific food, water, cover and, in some cases, nesting habitat that they need to survive.

Tricolored Heron

Nesting: The reproductive strategies used by different bird species vary. In each species account, nest location and structure, clutch size, incubation period and parental duties are discussed. Remember that birding ethics discourage the disturbance of active bird nests. If you disturb a nest, you may drive off the parents during a critical period or expose defenseless young to predators. The nesting behavior of birds that do not nest in our region is not described.

Feeding: Birds spend a great deal of time foraging for food. If you know what a bird eats and where the food is found, you will have a good chance of finding the bird you are looking for. Birds are frequently encountered while they are foraging; we hope that our description of their feeding styles and diets provides valuable identifying characteristics, as well as interesting dietary facts.

Voice: You will hear many birds, particularly songbirds, which may remain hidden from view. Memorable paraphrases of distinctive sounds will aid you in identifying a species. These paraphrases only loosely resemble the call, song or sound produced by the bird. Should one of our paraphrases not work for you, feel free to make up your own—the creative exercise will reinforce your memory of the bird's vocalizations.

Hammond's Flycatcher

Similar Species: Easily confused species are discussed briefly. If you concentrate on the most relevant field marks, the subtle differences between species can be reduced to easily identifiable traits. You might find it useful to consult this section when finalizing your identification; knowing the most relevant field marks will speed up the identification process. Even experienced birders can mistake one species for another.

Best Sites: If you are looking for a particular bird, you will have more luck in some locations than in others, even within the range shown on the range map. There are many excellent sites in Texas; unfortunately, we cannot list them all. We have listed places that, besides providing a good chance of seeing a species, are easily accessible. As a result, many nature centers, state game areas, national lakeshores and state and national parks are mentioned.

Range Maps: The range map for each species represents the overall range of the species in an average year. Most birds will confine their annual movements to this range, although each year some birds wander beyond their traditional boundaries. These maps do not show differences in abundance within the range—areas of a range with good habitat will support a denser population than areas with poorer habitat. These maps also cannot show small pockets within the range where the species may actually be absent, or how the range may change from year to year.

Unlike most other field guides, we have attempted to show areas of the region where birds may appear in migration while en route to nesting or winter habitat. Many of these migratory routes are "best guesses," which will no doubt be refined as new discoveries are made. The representations of these routes do not distinguish high-use migration corridors from areas that are seldom used.

Range Map Symbols

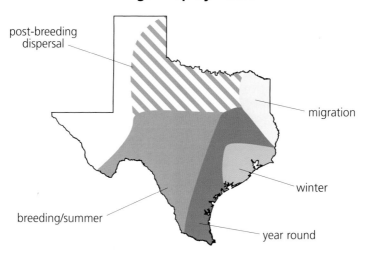

post-breeding dispersal

migration

breeding/summer

winter

year round

NONPASSERINES

Nonpasserine birds represent 18 of the 19 orders of birds found in Texas, about 53% of the species in our region. They are grouped together and called "nonpasserines" because, with few exceptions, they are easily distinguished from the "passerines," or "perching birds," which make up the 19th order. Being from 18 different orders, however, means that nonpasserines vary considerably in their appearance and habits—they include everything from the 4-foot-tall Great Blue Heron to the 3-inch-long Rufous Hummingbird.

Generally speaking, nonpasserines do not "sing." Instead, their vocalizations are referred to as "calls." There are also other morphological differences. For example, the muscles and tendons in the legs of passerines are adapted to grip a perch, and the toes of passerines are never webbed. Many nonpasserines are large, so they are among our most notable birds. Waterfowl, raptors, gulls, shorebirds and woodpeckers are easily identified by most people. Some of the smaller nonpasserines, such as doves, swifts and hummingbirds, are frequently thought of as passerines by novice birders, and can cause those beginners some identification problems. With a little practice, however, they will become recognizable as nonpasserines. By learning to separate the nonpasserines from the passerines at a glance, birders effectively reduce by half the number of possible species for an unidentified bird.

Waterfowl

Grouse & Allies

Diving Birds

Heronlike Birds

Birds of Prey

Rails, Coots & Cranes

Shorebirds

Gulls & Terns

Doves, Parrots & Cuckoos

Owls

Nightjars, Swifts & Hummingbirds

Woodpeckers

BLACK-BELLIED WHISTLING-DUCK

Dendrocygna autumnalis

Sporting a red bill, pink legs and distinctive body plumage, the Black-bellied Whistling-Duck is a popular pondside attraction. North-central Texas and Arizona mark the northernmost limit of this subtropical duck's range, but populations continue to spread northward, aided by agricultural expansion, human-made water holes and nest boxes. • Particularly active at night, whistling-ducks can be located by their constant in-flight chattering. They retreat to treed areas when disturbed. The genus name *Dendrocygna* ("tree swan") reflects their preference for nesting and perching in trees. • Unlike most ducks, whistling-ducks mate for life, with the male aiding in incubation and in rearing the young. Female Black-bellied Whistling-Ducks are known for "dump nesting" (placing their eggs into other nest cavities). Nests have been found with as many as 101 eggs, though not all eggs will hatch, and some parasitized nests are never incubated.

ID: long, pink legs; long neck; brown upperparts; black underparts with brown breast; gray head; white eye ring; red bill; pink feet. *In flight:* bold white wing stripe.

Size: *L* 21 in; *W* 30 in.
Status: increasing in numbers; locally common permanent resident in much of its range of the Coastal Plain and southern Texas to the southeastern Edwards Plateau and the north-central region; retreats from the northern portions during winter.

Habitat: freshwater marshes, lakes and ponds; flooded agricultural fields.
Nesting: on the ground in a nest woven of soft vegetation or in a tree cavity or nest box with little or no added material; pair incubates 12–16 white eggs for 25–30 days.
Feeding: on the ground or in water; grazes on grass seeds, waste grain and aquatic vegetation; also eats insects.
Voice: nasal, wheezing whistle of 4–5 syllables, like squeezing a rubber ducky.
Similar Species: *Fulvous Whistling-Duck* (p. 42): rich tawny underparts and head; orange bands on dark back; dark gray bill and legs; white tail band.
Best Sites: Laguna Atascosa NWR; Brazos Bend SP; Mitchell L. (San Antonio).

41

FULVOUS WHISTLING-DUCK

Dendrocygna bicolor

Occurring mainly in subtropical and tropical climates, the distinctive Fulvous Whistling-Duck has a worldwide distribution, and migratory populations also breed in temperate regions, including the Coastal Plain of Texas. • Fulvous Whistling-Ducks expanded their range northward into the rice fields of the Gulf Coast in the 1950s. Today, most birds arrive in early spring as planting begins and depart in August or late September. After breeding, small roving flocks occasionally travel hundreds of miles northward, straying as far as southern Canada. • The Fulvous Whistling-Duck looks like a cross between a domestic duck and a domestic goose, often displaying impressively straight posture. • Unlike most waterfowl, whistling-ducks tend to feed at night in groups, preferring damp or shallowly flooded fields with an abundance of seeds or grain.

ID: long neck; long, dark gray legs; rich tawny underparts and head; brown back with orange bands; bold white stripes on flanks; black rump; black tail with broad white band; blackish wings; white undertail coverts; dark gray bill and feet.
Size: *L* 18–21 in; *W* 26 in.
Status: uncommon to locally common summer resident on the Coastal Plain; rarely winters within this area.
Habitat: freshwater marshes, ponds or lakes; flooded agricultural fields.

Nesting: in a rice field or cattail marsh; unlined ground nest of woven grass, sedges or cattails may feature a canopy; pair incubates 12–14 whitish eggs for 24–26 days (parasitized nest may contain up to 60 eggs).
Feeding: mostly at night; prefers damp fields for foraging habitat; forages in water by gleaning from the surface, tipping or occasionally diving; eats mainly plant material, including aquatic vegetation, grain and seeds.
Voice: gives loud, rising whistle in flight.
Similar Species: *Black-bellied Whistling-Duck* (p. 41): brown upperparts; black underparts with brown breast; gray face; red bill; bold white wing stripe visible in flight.
Best Sites: Coastal Plain, especially in rice fields.

GREATER WHITE-FRONTED GOOSE

Anser albifrons

Greater White-fronted Geese breed on the Arctic tundra and winter in the southern U.S. and Mexico. They commonly migrate through central Texas and overwinter along the Coastal Plain or in agricultural areas. Groups can be seen foraging in coastal marshes for aquatic plants or feeding on waste grain in ploughed fields. • Watch for Greater White-fronted Geese among flocks of Canada or Snow Geese. The slightly smaller Greater White-fronts are best distinguished by their bright orange feet, which shine like beacons as the birds stand on marshes or fields, and by the laughing notes they utter in flight. • The Greater White-fronted Goose has an almost circumpolar Arctic distribution. It is the only North American representative of the five species of gray geese found in Eurasia. Like most geese, the Greater White-front is a long-lived bird that mates for life, with both parents caring for the young.

ID: brown overall; black-speckled belly; pinkish bill; white around bill and on forehead; white hindquarters; black band on upper tail; orange feet. *Immature:* unspeckled, pale belly; little or no white on face.
Size: *L* 27–33 in; *W* 4½–5 ft.
Status: common winter resident on the upper and central Coastal Plain and uncommon elsewhere.

Habitat: croplands, fields, open areas and shallow marshes.
Nesting: does not nest in Texas.
Feeding: dabbles in water and gleans the ground for grass shoots, sprouting and waste grain and occasionally aquatic invertebrates.
Voice: high-pitched "laugh."
Similar Species: *Canada Goose* (p. 47): white "chin strap"; black neck; unspeckled, pale belly. *Snow Goose* (p. 44): blue morph has white head and upper neck and all-dark breast and belly.
Best Sites: McFaddin NWR; San Bernard NWR; Attwater's Prairie Chicken NWR.

43

SNOW GOOSE

Chen caerulescens

Snow Geese breed in the High Arctic from Alaska to Greenland, and they overwinter in the southern U.S. and Mexico. In recent years, their populations have increased dramatically in North America, taking advantage of human-induced changes to the landscape and to the food supply. Oscillating, wavy lines of Snow Geese begin to appear over eastern Texas in early October and remain in suitable coastal and agricultural areas until mid-March. • Snow Geese grub for their food, often targeting the underground parts of plants. Their strong, serrated bills are well designed for pulling up the root stalks of marsh plants and for gripping slippery grasses.

"Blue Morph"

There is concern that their large numbers may be degrading the sensitive tundra environment used for nesting. • Snow Geese occur in two color morphs: white and blue. Until 1983, each morph was considered a separate species—the "Snow Goose" and "Blue Goose," respectively. In Texas, the white morph occurs statewide, and the blue morph is found mainly along the Gulf Coast.

"White Morph"

ID: white overall; black wing tips; pink feet and bill; dark "grinning patch" on bill; plumage is occasionally stained rusty red. *Blue morph:* dark bluish gray body below upper neck. *Immature:* gray or dusty white plumage; dark bill and feet.
Size: *L* 28–33 in; *W* 4½–5 ft.
Status: abundant winter resident on the Coastal Plain, sometimes moving inland later in winter; uncommon to locally common in western Texas.

Habitat: shallow fresh or salt marshes, lakes, agricultural fields and suburban areas.
Nesting: does not nest in Texas.
Feeding: grazes on aquatic vegetation, grasses, sedges and roots; also takes grain in agricultural fields.
Voice: loud, nasal, constant *houk-houk* in flight.
Similar Species: *Domestic (Graylag) Goose:* larger; white wing tips; usually in city parks or farm and ranch ponds. *Ross's Goose* (p. 45): smaller; shorter neck; no black "grinning patch." *Tundra Swan* (p. 48): larger; white wing tips.
Best Sites: Coastal Plain.

ROSS'S GOOSE

Chen rossii

Ross's Geese look so similar to Snow Geese that inexperienced birders can easily get the two confused, and these small geese are often overlooked, particularly when a few individuals are mixed within large flocks of migrating Snow Geese. • Most of the world's Ross's Geese nest along the remote Arctic coastline of northeastern Canada. • This bird was named after Bernard Rogan Ross, a former chief factor of the Hudson's Bay Company and correspondent of the Smithsonian Institute. The species occurs regularly and in increasing numbers along with Snow Geese. Although Ross's Goose occurs widely scattered in the eastern two-thirds of the state, the largest numbers are encountered in the Coastal Plain.

ID: white overall, occasionally stained rusty by water-borne iron; black wing tips; dark pink feet and bill; no "grinning patch" on bill; small, bluish or greenish "warts" on base of bill. *Blue morph* (very rare): white head; bluish gray body plumage. *Immature:* gray plumage; dark bill and feet.

Size: *L* 23 in; *W* 3¾ ft.

Status: uncommon to common migrant in most of the state, absent from the South Plains south to the Rio Grande; common winter resident on the Coastal Plain and the northern half of the High Plains, uncommon to locally common in extreme western Trans-Pecos and a few inland locations in the eastern half of the state.

Habitat: grasslands, rice and other grain fields and pastures.

Nesting: does not nest in Texas.

Feeding: grazes on waste grain and new sprouts; also eats aquatic vegetation, grasses, sedges and roots.

Voice: similar to the Snow Goose, but higher pitched.

Similar Species: *Snow Goose* (p. 44): larger; longer neck; dark "grinning patch" on bill. *Tundra* (p. 48), *Trumpeter* and *Mute swans:* much larger; white wing tips. *American White Pelican* (p. 84): much larger bill and body.

Best Sites: Coastal Plain.

CACKLING GOOSE

Branta hutchinsii

The Canada Goose was split into two species in 2004. The smaller, Arctic-breeding subspecies has been renamed the Cackling Goose, whereas the larger subspecies that breeds mainly in the central states and Canada is still known as the Canada Goose. Birders face an interesting challenge as they search through various homogeneous and mixed flocks seeking to distinguish the various subspecies. • Two subspecies of Cackling Goose occur in Texas. Our smallest, palest form, the "Richardson's Goose" *(B.h. hutchinsii)* is distinguished by its stocky build, square-shaped head and short bill. It migrates through eastern and central Texas in late October and overwinters in the southern plains and along the Gulf Coast. "Taverner's Goose" *(B.h. taverneri)* is a rare migrant and winter visitor throughout Texas. Both subspecies often travel with flocks of Canada Geese but generally split up into flocks of their own type on the wintering grounds.

ID: generally dark brown; stubby, black bill; rounded, white "chin strap"; relatively long, black neck; white rump and undertail coverts; short, black tail; black legs and feet.

Size: *L* 25–35 in; *W* 3–4 ft.

Status: common migrant east of the Pecos R.; common winter resident along the Coastal Plain and on the High Plains.

Habitat: along water bodies and marshes; croplands and parks.

Nesting: does not nest in Texas.

Feeding: grazes on new sprouts, aquatic vegetation, grass, roots, berries and seeds (particularly grains); tips up for aquatic roots and tubers.

Voice: cackling call similar to the Canada Goose's *ah-honk,* but higher pitched.

Similar Species: *Canada Goose* (p. 47): larger; generally lighter in color. *Greater White-fronted Goose* (p. 43): brown neck and head; no white "chin strap"; orange legs; white around base of bill; dark-speckled belly. *Brant* (p. 443): no white "chin strap"; white "necklace"; black upper breast. *Snow Goose* (p. 44): blue morph has white head and upper neck.

Best Sites: Buffalo Lake NWR; Hagerman NWR; Anahuac NWR; Brazoria NWR.

CANADA GOOSE

Branta canadensis

Thousands of Canada Geese descend on Texas each winter to enjoy the abundant food supply found in agricultural fields and coastal marshes. Few people realize that at one time Canada Geese were hunted almost to extinction. Populations have since been reestablished and, in recent decades, these large, bold geese have inundated urban waterfronts, picnic sites, golf courses and city parks. Today, many people even consider them pests. • Canada Geese mate for life and are devoted parents. Unlike with most birds, a family stays together for nearly a year, which increases the survival rate of the young. Rescuers who care for injured geese report that these birds readily adopt their human caregivers. However, wild geese can be aggressive, especially when defending young or competing for food. Hissing sounds and low, outstretched necks are signs that you should give these birds some space.

ID: brown body, paler below; black bill; white "chin strap"; long, black neck; white undertail coverts; short, black tail; black legs and feet.

Size: *L* 21–48 in; *W* 3½–5 ft.

Status: common winter resident, especially in the Panhandle; rarely breeds in the Panhandle.

Habitat: ponds and lakes, farmland, residential areas and city parks; originally wintered in salt and brackish marshes and bays.

Nesting: on an island or shoreline; usually on the ground but may use a heron rookery; female builds a nest of plant materials lined with down; female incubates 3–8 white eggs for 25–28 days while the male stands guard.

Feeding: grazes on new sprouts, aquatic vegetation, grass and roots; tips up for aquatic roots and tubers.

Voice: loud, familiar *ah-honk*.

Similar Species: *Cackling Goose* (p. 46): smaller; generally darker in color. *Greater White-fronted Goose* (p. 43): brown neck and head; no white "chin strap"; orange legs; white around base of bill; dark-speckled belly. *Brant* (p. 443): no white "chin strap"; white "necklace"; black upper breast. *Snow Goose* (p. 44): blue morph has white head and upper neck.

Best Sites: Buffalo Lake NWR; Hagerman NWR; McFaddin NWR.

TUNDRA SWAN

Cygnus columbianus

Tundra Swans breed in the Arctic and winter along the Atlantic and Pacific coasts. They turn up in winter on inland lakes throughout Texas and annually in the Panhandle. • The magnificent Tundra Swan is a long-lived species that mates for life. The young remain with their parents for the first winter, and the family flies back to the breeding grounds together. Young birds can be distinguished by their light gray plumage. • The eastern North America population of Tundra Swans is estimated at over 100,000 birds, with numbers growing steadily. These birds traditionally fed on aquatic plants, but in recent years they have taken a liking to more widely available waste grain. As flocks of Tundra Swans migrate through the interior U.S., they often stop in agricultural fields to refuel on corn, soybeans or wheat shoots. • In the early 19th century, members of the Lewis and Clark expedition found this bird near the Columbia River, thus the term *columbianus* in its scientific name.

ID: white plumage; large, black bill; black feet; often shows yellow lores; holds neck straight up; neck and head show rounded, slightly curving profile. *Immature:* light grayish plumage; gray bill.
Size: *L* 4–5 ft; *W* 6–7 ft.
Status: irregular and rare winter visitor.
Habitat: shallow areas of lakes, rivers and wetlands.

Nesting: does not nest in Texas.
Feeding: tips up, dabbles and surface gleans for aquatic vegetation and aquatic invertebrates; grazes for tubers, roots and waste grain.
Voice: migrating flocks constantly repeat high-pitched, quivering *oo-oo-whoo*.
Similar Species: adult is distinctive. *Snow Goose* (p. 44) and *Ross's Goose* (p. 45): smaller; shorter neck; pinkish bill; black wing tips. *American White Pelican* (p. 84) large, orange bill with distinct pouch; black wing tips.
Best Sites: unpredictable.

WOOD DUCK

Aix sponsa

The male Wood Duck is one of North America's most colorful water birds; books, magazines, postcards and calendars routinely celebrate his beauty. The female, although much subtler in plumage, shares the drake's crest and sports large, teardrop-shaped white eye patches. • Pairs or small flocks of Wood Ducks are often seen around dawn or dusk, flying to or from night-roosting areas. These forest birds nest in tree cavities up to a mile from the nearest water body. Newly hatched ducklings may have to jump 20 feet or more out of their nest to follow their mother to the nearest body of water. The little bundles of down bounce well, seldom sustaining injury when they hit the ground. • Wood Ducks can be attracted by nest boxes placed above or near swamps, tree-lined ponds or marshes.

ID: *Male:* extremely colorful; multi-colored head with long, slicked-back, greenish crest edged with white; red eyes; white throat extends into neck ring and facial "spur"; mostly reddish bill; rusty breast with small white spots; black and white shoulder slashes; golden sides. *Female:* mostly grayish brown upper-parts; brown face with teardrop-shaped, white eye patch; mottled, white-streaked, brown breast.

Size: *L* 15–20 in; *W* 30 in.

Status: fairly common permanent resident in eastern Texas and south into the Lower Rio Grande Valley; summer resident in eastern Texas and west to the eastern Panhandle and Edwards Plateau and south to the Rio Grande.

Habitat: swamps, ponds, marshes and lake-shores with wooded edges.

Nesting: usually near water; in a hollow or tree cavity, as high as 30 ft up, or in an artificial nest box; cavity is lined with down; female incubates 9–14 white to buff eggs for 25–35 days.

Feeding: gleans the water's surface and tips up for aquatic vegetation, especially duckweed, aquatic sedges and grasses; picks nuts from the ground.

Voice: *Male:* ascending whistle. *Female:* slurred, squeaky note.

Similar Species: *Hooded Merganser* (p. 66): slim, black bill; black and white breast; male has black head with white crest patch.

Best Sites: Lake O' the Pines (Marion Co.); Huntsville SP; Lake Sheldon SP; Brazos Bend SP.

GADWALL

Anas strepera

Generally nondescript, Gadwalls are gray or brown ducks with white bellies. Although male Gadwalls lack the striking plumage of most other male ducks, they have a dignified appearance and a subtle beauty. Once you learn their field marks—a black rump and white wing patches—Gadwalls are surprisingly easy to identify. • Ducks in the genus *Anas*, the dabbling ducks, are most often observed tipping up their hindquarters and submerging their heads to feed, but Gadwalls dive more often than others of this group. These ducks feed equally during the day and night, a strategy that reduces the risk of predation, because the birds avoid spending long periods of time sleeping or feeding. • Since the 1950s, this duck has expanded its range throughout North America. The majority of Gadwalls winter along the Gulf Coast and in Mexico, although increasing numbers over-winter on inland lakes across the country.

ID: *Male:* dark above with grayish brown head; dark eyes and bill; yellow legs; black breast patch; gray flanks; black upper- and undertail coverts and tail. *Female:* mottled brown overall; blackish bill with orange sides. *In flight:* white speculum.

Size: *L* 18–22 in; *W* 33 in.

Status: abundant migrant and winter resident statewide; rarely nests in the Panhandle.

Habitat: freshwater lakes or ponds; less common in brackish or saline ponds or estuaries.

Nesting: well-concealed in tall vegetation, in a grassy, down-lined hollow, sometimes far from water; female incubates 8–12 creamy to very light green eggs for 24–27 days.

Feeding: dabbles for aquatic plants; also grazes on grass and waste grain.

Voice: quacks.

Similar Species: gray plumage and black hindquarters of male are unique; female resembles females of several other ducks but look for blackish bill with orange sides and white speculum.

Best Sites: Muleshoe NWR; L. Tawakoni; Hornsby Bend (Austin); Mitchell L. (San Antonio); Warren L. (Harris Co.).

AMERICAN WIGEON

Anas americana

The American Wigeon breeds throughout Alaska and Canada, and it winters along both coasts, in the West Indies and south to Central America. In Texas, this duck is common on brackish or freshwater habitats and sometimes grazes in agricultural fields. • Although wigeons frequently dabble for food, they favor the succulent stems and leaves of pond-bottom plants. These plants grow far too deep for dabbling ducks, so wigeons often pirate from accomplished divers such as American Coots, Canvasbacks, Redheads and scaup. In contrast to other ducks, the wigeons are good walkers and are commonly observed grazing on shore. • The American Wigeon nests farther north than any other dabbling duck with the exception of the Northern Pintail. Pair bonds are strong and last well into incubation. • The male's bright white crown and forehead have earned this bird the nickname "Baldpate."

ID: rufous brown overall; rounded head; pale bluish gray bill with black tip. *Male:* rusty breast and sides; gray head; white forehead and crown; wide, iridescent, green cheek patches; white belly; black undertail coverts. *Female:* grayish head; brown underparts; dusky undertail coverts. *In flight:* large white upperwing patches.

Size: *L* 18–22½ in; *W* 32 in.

Status: common migrant and winter resident statewide.

Habitat: shallow wetlands, lakes, ponds and estuaries.

Nesting: does not nest in Texas.

Feeding: dabbles and tips up for the leaves and stems of pondweeds and other aquatic plants; also grazes on land; may eat some invertebrates.

Voice: *Male:* nasal, frequently repeated whistle. *Female:* soft, seldom-heard quack.

Similar Species: male's head pattern is distinctive. *Gadwall* (p. 50): white speculum rather than large white patch on upperwing; male has wholly grayish brown head; female has orange-sided bill. *Eurasian Wigeon:* gray "wing pits"; male has rufous head, without green eye swipe, with cream forehead and rosy breast; female usually has browner head.

Best Sites: White Rock L. (Dallas); L. Tawakoni; Mitchell L. (San Antonio); Brazoria NWR.

MALLARD

Anas platyrhynchos

Mallards can be seen almost any day of the year, often in flocks and always near open water. These confident ducks have even been known to take up residence in local swimming pools. • Wild Mallards will freely hybridize with domestic ducks, which were originally derived from Mallards in Europe. The resulting offspring, often seen in city parks, are a confusing blend of both parents. • After breeding, male ducks lose their elaborate plumage, helping them stay camouflaged during their flightless period. In early fall, they molt back into breeding colors. • A brooding female's body heat increases the growth rate of nearby grasses, which she then manipulates to further conceal her nest.

ID: orange feet. *Male:* glossy, green head; yellow bill; chestnut brown breast; white "necklace"; gray body plumage; black central tail feathers curl upward. *Female:* mottled brown overall; black-mottled, orange bill. *In flight:* white-bordered, dark blue speculum.

Size: *L* 20–27½ in; *W* 35 in.

Status: common migrant and winter resident in northern Texas and less common in the south; replacing the "Mexican Duck" in the Trans-Pecos region through interbreeding.

Habitat: lakes, wetlands, rivers, city parks, agricultural areas and sewage lagoons.

Nesting: in tall vegetation or under a bush, often near water; lines nest of grass and other plant material with down; female incubates 7–10 light green to white eggs for 26–30 days.

Feeding: dabbles in shallows for plant seeds; also eats insects, aquatic invertebrates, larval amphibians and fish eggs.

Voice: *Male:* deep, quiet quacks. *Female:* loud quacks; very vocal.

Similar Species: *Mottled Duck* (p. 53): resembles female Mallard, but with wholly yellow or yellowish orange bill, unstreaked throat and more narrowly bordered speculum. *Mallard x Mottled Duck hybrids:* increasingly common; variable plumage. *Northern Shoveler* (p. 56): much larger bill; drake has white breast. *American Black Duck:* very rare; darker than female Mallard; wholly olive or greenish yellow bill; unbordered, purple speculum.

Best Sites: Muleshoe NWR; Six Lakes (Lubbock), Granger L. (Williamson Co.).

MOTTLED DUCK

Anas fulvigula

The Mottled Duck's resemblance to a female or nonbreeding male Mallard has led some experts to argue that it is a nonmigratory race of the Mallard rather than a separate species. One clue to identification is the bluish green speculum, which has only a very narrow white border, if any. • The warm, productive waters of the Gulf Coast provide all the nutrients and structure this duck needs to successfully raise young and to survive year-round. However, pesticide use and the drainage and degradation of coastal wetlands, as well as hybridization with domestic Mallards, are ongoing problems for the Mottled Duck. Protection efforts include public education programs aimed at discouraging the release of domestic ducks and the creation of coastal sanctuaries, including Anahuac, Attwater's Prairie-Chicken and Brazoria national wildlife refuges. • Local names for this bird include "Black Mallard" and "Summer Mallard."

ID: stocky body; green speculum bordered with black; wholly yellow or yellow-orange bill; unstreaked, buffy throat; brown tail.

Size: *L* 20–22 in; *W* 30 in.

Status: locally common resident on the Coastal Plain; increasing summer resident in the northeastern and north-central parts of Texas.

Habitat: primarily freshwater marshes, ponds, lakes, or flooded agricultural fields; also in brackish estuaries.

Nesting: on dry ground usually close to water; shallow bowl of grass, rushes, reeds or aquatic vegetation concealed by surrounding vegetation; female incubates 8–12 whitish to buffy olive eggs for 24–28 days.

Feeding: dabbles for aquatic vegetation and invertebrates; also grazes on land.

Voice: loud, Mallardlike *quack*.

Similar Species: *Mallard* (p. 52): paler; white tail; blue speculum bordered with white; male has contrasting rusty breast in eclipse plumage; female has black mottling on orange bill. *American Black Duck:* accidental in Texas; darker overall, with more contrasting white underwings; streaked throat; purple speculum.

Best Sites: Anahuac NWR; J.D. Murphree WMA; Brazos Bend SP, Brazoria NWR.

BLUE-WINGED TEAL

Anas discors

Renowned for its aviation skills, the speedy Blue-winged Teal can be identified by its small size, sharp twists and precisely executed turns. • Despite a similar name, the Green-winged Teal is not this bird's closest relative. The Blue-winged Teal is more closely related to the Northern Shoveler and the Cinnamon Teal, which have similar bills, forewings and speculums. • The Blue-winged Teal is a dabbling duck; it feeds by tipping up its tail and dunking its head underwater, and it has small feet situated near its body center. Other ducks, such as scaup, scoters and Buffleheads, dive underwater to feed, propelled by large feet set farther back on their bodies. • Blue-winged Teals migrate farther than most ducks, summering as far north as the Canadian tundra and wintering mainly in Central and South America. Some birds overwinter in Texas, remaining here until late April or May.

ID: blackish bill; yellow legs. *Male:* bluish gray head; bold white crescent on face; black-spotted, rusty breast and sides. *Female:* mottled brown overall; fairly bold dark eye line; white throat. *In flight:* bold pale blue patch on leading edge of upperwing.
Size: *L* 14–16 in; *W* 23 in.
Status: common migrant statewide; common winter resident in the Coastal Plain and in southern Texas; rare and irregular to uncommon breeder in much of Texas, especially in the High Plains.
Habitat: ponds, lakes, shallow marshes and estuaries; frequents areas with short, dense emergent vegetation.

Nesting: in grass close to water; nest is built with grass and down; female incubates 8–13 whitish eggs for 23–27 days.
Feeding: gleans the water's surface for sedge and grass seeds, pondweeds, duckweeds and aquatic invertebrates.
Voice: *Male:* soft *keck-keck-keck. Female:* soft quacks.
Similar Species: *Cinnamon Teal* (p. 55): female resembles female Blue-winged Teal but is richer brown, with larger, more spatulate bill. *Green-winged Teal* (p. 58): smaller; female has smaller bill and black and green speculum and has no blue forewing patch. *Northern Shoveler* (p. 56): much larger bill with paler base; male has green head and unspotted underparts.
Best Sites: Hornsby Bend (Austin); Mitchell L. (San Antonio); Village Creek Treatment Plant (Arlington); Warren L. (Harris Co.), Brazos Bend SP.

CINNAMON TEAL

Anas cyanoptera

Surely, if the Stetson is the "hat of the West," the Cinnamon Teal is the "duck of the West." The principal distribution of both the hat and the bird define that great reach of arid country where the presence of water is dramatic and important. The Cinnamon Teal breeds in the Canadian Prairies and the Great Plains but visits southern Texas in winter, as far inland as El Paso. • You will instantly recognize the intense reddish brown plumage of the male Cinnamon Teal, accented by his ruby red eyes. The drab female and eclipse plumages, however, closely resemble that of the female Blue-winged Teal and are hard to differentiate in the field. • Female ducks of most species are abandoned by their mates during nesting, but female Cinnamon Teals may be accompanied by their partners throughout the nesting cycle.

ID: large bill. *Male:* intense cinnamon red head, neck and underparts; red eyes. *Female:* mottled warm brown overall; dark eyes. *In flight:* conspicuous pale blue forewing patch; green speculum.
Size: *L* 15–17 in; *W* 20–22 in.
Status: common migrant in the western half of Texas and less common and irregular in the eastern half; locally uncommon winter resident along the coast; rarely nests in the High Plains.
Habitat: freshwater ponds, marshes, sloughs and flooded swales with emergent or submergent aquatic vegetation.
Nesting: in tall vegetation, occasionally far from water; nest of grass and down is placed in a concealed hollow; female incubates 7–12 white to buffy eggs for 21–25 days; ducklings fly after 7 weeks.
Feeding: gleans the water's surface for grass and sedge seeds, pondweeds, duckweeds and aquatic invertebrates.
Voice: not often heard; male utters a whistled *peep;* female gives a rough *karr, karr, karr.*
Similar Species: *Blue-winged Teal* (p. 54): male has white crescent in front of eye; female is difficult to distinguish. *Ruddy Duck* (p. 69): male has white cheek, blue bill and stiff, upward-angled tail. *Green-winged Teal* (p. 58): small bill; no forewing patch.
Best Sites: Buffalo Lake NWR; O.C. Fisher Reservoir (San Angelo), Balmorhea L. (Reeves Co.); Fort Hancock (Hudspeth Co.).

NORTHERN SHOVELER

Anas clypeata

Using its extra-large, spoonlike bill, the Northern Shoveler strains small invertebrates from the water and from the bottoms of ponds. This strangely handsome duck eats much smaller organisms than do most other water-fowl, and its intestines are elongated to prolong the digestion of these hard-bodied invertebrates. The shoveler's specialized feeding strategy means that it is rarely seen tipping up; it is more likely to be found in the shallows of ponds and marshes, where the mucky bottom is easiest to reach. • The word *clypeata*, Latin for "furnished with a shield," possibly refers to the chestnut patches on the flanks of the male. This species was once placed in its own genus, *Spatula*, the meaning of which needs no explanation.

ID: large, spatulate bill; blue forewing patch; green speculum. *Male:* green head; yellow eyes; white breast; chestnut brown flanks. *Female:* mottled brown overall; orange-tinged bill.
Size: *L* 18–20 in; *W* 30 in.
Status: common migrant and winter resident statewide; occasional breeder in the Panhandle and rarely in other parts of the state.
Habitat: ponds, lakes, shallow marshes and estuaries.
Nesting: in a shallow hollow on dry ground, usually within 150 ft of water; female builds a nest of dry grass and down

and incubates 10–12 pale buff olive eggs for 21–28 days.
Feeding: dabbles in shallow and often muddy water; strains out plant and animal matter, especially aquatic crustaceans, insect larvae and seeds; also takes small fish.
Voice: generally quiet in Texas, although courtship begins on the wintering grounds; occasional raspy chuckle or quack.
Similar Species: spatulate bill is distinctive in all plumages. *Mallard* (p. 52): blue speculum bordered by white; no pale blue forewing patch; male has chestnut brown breast and white flanks. *Blue-winged Teal* (p. 54) and *Cinnamon Teal* (p. 55): smaller overall; much smaller bill; male has white crescent on face and black-spotted breast and sides.
Best Sites: Hagerman NWR; L. Tawakoni; Mitchell L. (San Antonio); San Bernard NWR.

NORTHERN PINTAIL

Anas acuta

The elegant Northern Pintail's trademark is the male's long, tapering tail, which makes up one-quarter of his body length. The elongated tail feathers are easily seen in flight and point skyward when this duck dabbles in shallow wetlands, intertidal habitats or estuaries. • Although Northern Pintails were once among the most numerous ducks in North America, populations have declined steadily in recent decades. Drought, wetland drainage and loss of grassland habitat are serious threats for many waterfowl species, but Northern Pintail populations have suffered more than most. These ducks are especially susceptible to lead poisoning, often mistaking the lead shot left behind by hunters for seeds. One ingested pellet contains enough lead to poison a bird. Fortunately for waterfowl, lead shot has been banned in many states.

ID: long, slender neck; glossy, dark bill. *Male:* grayish above and below; white of neck extends onto hind-neck as narrow wedge; brown head; long, tapering, black tail feathers. *Female:* mottled light brown overall; plain, paler head. *In flight:* slender body; brownish speculum with white trailing edge.
Size: *L* 21–25 in; *W* 34 in.
Status: common migrant and winter resident statewide; local and uncommon breeder in the High Plains.
Habitat: estuaries, impoundments, marshes, lakes and ponds.

Nesting: in a small depression in vegetation, usually near water; nest of grass, leaves and moss is lined with the female's down; female incubates 6–9 creamy to greenish eggs for up to 24 days.
Feeding: dabbles in shallows for the seeds of grasses and sedges; also eats aquatic invertebrates.
Voice: generally silent in Texas. *Male:* soft, whistling call. *Female:* rough quack.
Similar Species: male is distinctive. *Mottled Duck* (p. 53), *Mallard* (p. 52) and *Gadwall* (p. 50): females are chunkier, usually have dark or 2-tone bills and do not have tapering tails or long, slender necks. *Blue-winged Teal* (p. 54): female is smaller, with green speculum and blue forewing patch.
Best Sites: Hagerman NWR; Hornsby Bend (Austin); Brazos Bend SP; Sea Rim SP; Anahuac NWR.

GREEN-WINGED TEAL

Anas crecca

Our smallest dabbling duck, the Green-winged Teal is one of the speediest and most maneuverable of waterfowl. When disturbed, it flies up from the water's surface, circles overhead in tight, fast-flying flocks, then returns to the water after the threat has passed. A predator's only chance of catching a healthy teal is to snatch it from the water. • Although most birds molt their flight feathers gradually, many ducks lose all their flight feathers at once, rendering them flightless for a few weeks. During this vulnerable time, these ducks hide in thick vegetation or roost on open water, where they can scan for predators. Male Green-winged Teals often undertake a partial migration before molting into their duller postbreeding colors; this "eclipse plumage" is similar to the female's plumage. • The name "teal" possibly originated from the medieval English word *tele* or the old Dutch word *teling*, which both mean "small."

ID: small, dark bill; green and black speculum. *Male:* chestnut head with green cheek stripe outlined in white; gray flanks with white vertical shoulder slash; creamy breast spotted with black; pale gray sides; yellow undertail coverts; black tail. *Female:* mottled brown overall; dark eyeline.

Size: *L* 12–16 in; *W* 23 in.

Status: uncommon migrant and winter resident statewide, although more abundant on the upper Coastal Plain.

Habitat: marshes, ponds and shallow lakes.
Nesting: does not nest in Texas.
Feeding: dabbles in shallows for seeds of sedges, grasses and other aquatic plants; also eats mollusks and aquatic invertebrates.
Voice: *Male:* crisp whistle. *Female:* soft quack.
Similar Species: male is unmistakable. *Blue-winged Teal* (p. 54): female has larger bill, blue forewing patch and heavily spotted undertail coverts.
Best Sites: Anahuac NWR; Lake Sheldon SP; Attwater's Prairie-Chicken NWR; San Bernard NWR.

CANVASBACK

Aythya valisineria

The Canvasback's back and unique profile are unmistakable field marks. The male has a bright, clean back that appears to be wrapped in white canvas. In profile, both the male and the female cast a noble image—the long bill meets the forecrown with no apparent break in angle, allowing them to be distinguished at long range. • Canvasbacks are diving ducks that are typically found on large areas of open water. Because these birds prefer large lakes and bays and the deepest areas of wetlands, birders often need binoculars to admire the male's wild, red eyes and mahogany head. • Canvasbacks may be found throughout Texas during migration, and many birds converge along the Gulf Coast in winter. However, the draining of wetlands on their breeding grounds in the Great Plains and the Canadian Prairies poses a serious threat, and their populations are declining. • In the scientific name, *valisineria* refers (with altered spelling) to one of the Canvasback's favorite foods, eel grass or wild celery (*Vallisneria americana*).

ID: head slopes upward from bill to forehead. *Male:* pale body; chestnut head; red eyes; black breast and hind-quarters. *Female:* pale body; light brown head and neck; dark eyes.
Size: *L* 19–22 in; *W* 29 in.
Status: uncommon and local migrant and winter resident statewide.
Habitat: bays and estuaries; salt marshes; occasionally visits inland marshes and lakes.
Nesting: does not nest in Texas.

Feeding: dives 10–15 ft underwater to feed on seeds, roots, tubers and other plant material; occasionally eats aquatic invertebrates.
Voice: generally quiet in winter. *Male:* occasional coos and "growls" during courtship. *Female:* low, soft, "purring" quack or *kuck;* also "growls."
Similar Species: *Redhead* (p. 60): rounded rather than sloped forehead; male has gray back and bluish bill with black tip.
Best Sites: Hornsby Bend (Austin); Mitchell L. (San Antonio); Aransas NWR; Laguna Atascosa NWR.

REDHEAD

Aythya americana

October brings great numbers of Redheads that descend on the coastal bays of the lower Texas coast. Half of the Redheads in the world overwinter on coastal waters between Rockport, Corpus Christi and Languna Atascosa National Wildlife Refuge. Watch for flocks surfing just offshore with scaup. • The Redhead and the Canvasback have very similar plumages and habitat preferences. The best way to distinguish the two species is by head shape. The Redhead has a round head that meets the bill at an angle, whereas its close cousin has a sloping head that seems to merge with the bill. In males, the most obvious difference between them is the color of their back—white in the Canvasback and gray in the Redhead. • The Redhead is a diving duck, but it will occasionally feed on the surface of a wetland like a dabbler. Seagrass and shoal grass form a large part of its winter diet.

ID: rounded head; black-tipped, bluish gray bill. *Male:* red head; yellow eyes; black breast and hindquarters; gray back and sides. *Female:* dark brown overall; lighter chin and cheek patches.
Size: *L* 18–22 in; *W* 29 in.
Status: common migrant throughout Texas; common to abundant winter resident on the central and lower coasts and locally uncommon elsewhere; rare summer resident in the Panhandle.
Habitat: bays and estuaries; salt marshes; occasionally visits inland marshes or lakes.

Nesting: does not nest in Texas.
Feeding: dives to depths of 10 ft; primarily eats aquatic vegetation, especially ditch-grass, sedges and water lilies; occasionally eats aquatic invertebrates.
Voice: generally quiet in Texas. *Male:* catlike meow in courtship. *Female:* rolling *kurr-kurr-kurr; squak* when alarmed.
Similar Species: *Canvasback* (p. 59): clean white back; bill slopes onto forehead. *Ring-necked Duck* (p. 61): female has more prominent white eye ring, white ring on bill and peaked head; restricted to fresh water. *Lesser Scaup* (p. 63) and *Greater Scaup* (p. 62): males have dark heads and whiter sides; females have white at bases of bills.
Best Sites: Aransas NWR, Laguna Atascosa NWR and points in between.

RING-NECKED DUCK

Aythya collaris

The Ring-necked Duck's distinctive tricolored bill, angular head and black back are field marks that immediately strike an observer. Many birders wonder why this bird was not named "Ring-billed Duck." However, the name originated with an ornithologist looking at an indistinct cinnamon "collar" on a museum specimen, not a birder looking at a live duck through binoculars. • In Texas, Ring-necked Ducks overwinter south of the Panhandle but are most common on wooded marshes along the coast. Like scaup, Redheads and Canvasbacks, Ring-necked Ducks are diving ducks, but they prefer to feed in shallower shoreline waters, frequently tipping up for food. They ride high on the water and tend to carry their tails clear of the water's surface. Ring-necks are generalized feeders, capitalizing on the scarce resources found in their subarctic and boreal nesting grounds.

ID: distinctive tricolored (bluish gray, white and black) bill; distinctive peaked crown. *Male:* black upperparts; dark purple head; yellow eyes; black breast and hindquarters ; gray sides; white shoulder slash. *Female:* brown overall, with paler head and whitish face; white eye ring extends behind eye as narrow line.
Size: *L* 14–18 in; *W* 25 in.
Status: uncommon to locally common statewide migrant and winter resident.
Habitat: ponds vegetated with lily pads and other surface vegetation, swamps, marshes and lakes.
Nesting: does not nest in Texas.

Feeding: dives for aquatic vegetation, including seeds and tubers of smartweed, water lilies and other plants; rarely eats aquatic invertebrates and mollusks.
Voice: generally silent in Texas. *Male:* low-pitched, hissing whistle. *Female:* growling *churr*.
Similar Species: *Greater Scaup* (p. 62) and *Lesser Scaup* (p. 63): little habitat overlap (rare on fresh water, but Lessers may be found on large, deep lakes, where Ring-necks are unlikely); gray back and all-white sides; rounder crowns; bluish bill with black tip; female has white face patch.
Best Sites: Village Creek Wastewater Treatment Plant (Arlington); L. Tawakoni; Hornsby Bend (Austin); Mitchell L. (San Antonio); Warren L. (Harris Co.).

GREATER SCAUP

Aythya marila

Scaup are uncommon migrants throughout Texas and locally uncommon winter residents, found along the Gulf Coast or on large reservoirs. The specific identity—Greater or Lesser—of many scaup cannot be accurately determined in the field. The primary field mark to distinguish the two scaup species is that the white wing stripe of the secondary flight feathers extends onto the primaries on Greater Scaup, whereas it is dull gray on the primaries of Lesser Scaup. It can be seen when the birds are in flight or when stretching their wings while resting on the water. Some field guides state that an additional field mark is the male's head color: green for Greater Scaup and purple for Lesser. However, scaup head color is the result of iridescence, not pigment, and males of one species can show iridescence supposedly diagnostic of the other species, so this characteristic is not entirely reliable.

ID: rounded head; yellow eyes. *Male:* iridescent head usually appears greenish; bluish bill with black tip; pale back; white sides; black breast; dark hindquarters. *Female:* brown overall; well-defined white patch on face. *In flight:* white wing stripe extends onto primary feathers.
Size: *L* 16–19 in; *W* 28 in.
Status: rare to uncommon migrant statewide; uncommon to locally common winter resident on the Coastal Plain and in the eastern third of the state.
Habitat: large lakes, reservoirs, ocean, bays and estuaries; less common in coastal impoundments.
Nesting: does not nest in Texas.

Feeding: dives for crustaceans and other aquatic invertebrates and the seeds of glasswort and other aquatic plants.
Voice: generally silent in Texas.
Similar Species: *Lesser Scaup* (p. 63): shorter white wing stripe; slightly smaller bill. *Ring-necked Duck* (p. 61): black back; peaked crown; white shoulder slash; bluish gray, white and black bill; virtually no habitat overlap (limited to freshwater marshes and ponds). *Redhead* (p. 60): female has dark eyes and lacks well-defined white face; male has red head and darker back and sides.
Best Sites: Laguna Madre region.

LESSER SCAUP

Aythya affinis

The tricolor appearance of the male Lesser Scaup makes this widespread diving duck easy to recognize and remember. In nonbreeding plumage, he has a black head and chest, a brown midsection and a dark tail, but in breeding plumage he shows a white midsection. • Large groups of Lesser Scaup are found along the Gulf Coast from mid-October to early May. They are more abundant than Greater Scaup, which are found mainly on the Atlantic Coast and Pacific Coast. • A member of the *Aythya* genus of diving ducks, the Lesser Scaup leaps up neatly before diving underwater, where it propels itself with powerful strokes of its feet. • In the scientific name, *affinis* is Latin for "adjacent" or "allied"—a reference to this scaup's close association to other diving ducks. "Scaup" might refer to a preferred winter food of this duck—shellfish beds are called "scalps" in Scotland—or it might be a phonetic imitation of one of its calls. • Both the Lesser Scaup and the Greater Scaup are known by the nickname "Bluebill."

ID: yellow eyes. *Male:* head usually appears purplish; bluish bill with black tip; grayish back; white sides; black breast and hindquarters. *Female:* dark brown overall; dark eyes; well-defined white patch at base of bill.

Size: *L* 15–18 in; *W* 25 in.

Status: common migrant and winter resident east of the Pecos R., locally uncommon in the Trans-Pecos region.

Habitat: coastal areas; rarely inland on large lakes.

Nesting: does not nest in Texas.

Feeding: dives for seeds, plant fibers and mollusks, crustaceans and other aquatic invertebrates.

Voice: generally silent in Texas; deep *scaup* alarm call.

Similar Species: *Ring-necked Duck* (p.61): male has white shoulder slash and black back; white-ringed bill. *Redhead* (p. 60): female has less white at base of bill; male has red head and darker sides. *Greater Scaup* (p. 62): rounded head; slightly larger bill; longer white wing stripes.

Best Sites: White Rock L. (Dallas); L. Tawakoni; Mitchell L. (San Antonio); Warren L. (Harris Co.).

BUFFLEHEAD

Bucephala albeola

A simple, bold pattern makes Buffleheads easy to notice as they bob among piers and wharves in saltwater bays. The males are strikingly dressed in black and white, their most characteristic feature a great white patch on the rear of the head. The females are somber but appealing, their sooty heads ornamented with a pretty white cheek spot. • Tiny Buffleheads are right at home in coastal bays and estuaries amid their larger relatives. During their winter stay in Texas, Buffleheads ride the waves, diving for mollusks, mostly snails. If you are lucky, you may even see a whole flock dive at the same time. • Both the common and scientific names refer to this bird's large head: "Bufflehead" is short for "buffalo-head," and *Bucephala* means "ox-headed" in Greek. The word *albeola* is Latin for "white," a reference to the male's plumage.

ID: rounded appearance; short, gray bill; short neck. *Male:* white wedge on back of head, which is otherwise iridescent, dark green or purple, usually appearing black; dark back; white neck and underparts. *Female:* dark brown head; oval, white ear patch; light brown sides. *In flight:* white speculum.

Size: *L* 13–15 in; *W* 21 in.

Status: common migrant and winter resident statewide.

Habitat: ocean, bays and estuaries; also on large inland lakes.

Nesting: does not nest in Texas.

Feeding: dives for aquatic crustaceans, insects and other invertebrates; also eats seeds of glasswort and other aquatic plants.

Voice: generally quiet in Texas. *Male:* growling call. *Female:* harsh quack.

Similar Species: *Hooded Merganser* (p. 66): larger; longer, slender bill; yellow eyes; brown flanks; white crest outlined in black; female has shaggy crest on all-dark head. *Common Goldeneye* (p. 65): larger; yellow eyes; male has all-greenish head with round white facial patch; female has yellow-tipped bill.

Best Sites: White Rock L. (Dallas); Hornsby Bend (Austin); Warren L. (Harris Co.); Mitchell L. (San Antonio).

COMMON GOLDENEYE

Bucephala clangula

A crisp white patch contrasted against a dark head easily identifies the Common Goldeneye. • Common Goldeneyes spend their entire lives in North America, dividing their time between breeding grounds in the boreal forests of Canada and Alaska and winter territory in marine bays and estuaries along the Atlantic Ocean and Pacific Ocean. They grace the upper and central coasts of Texas in winter and are occasionally found inland on larger lakes or rivers. State parks and wetlands have become increasingly important for Common Goldeneyes, because much of their winter habitat has been altered or lost. • Fish, crustaceans and mollusks make up a major portion of the Common Goldeneye's winter diet, but in summer this diving duck eats large amounts of aquatic invertebrates and tubers, and the female is often found nesting beside fishless lakes.

ID: steep forehead with peaked crown; black wings with large white patches; dark bill; golden eyes. *Male:* iridescent, dark green head; round, white cheek patch; dark back; white sides and belly. *Female:* chocolate brown head; lighter breast and belly; grayish brown body plumage; yellow tip on bill in spring and summer.
Size: *L* 16–20 in; *W* 26 in.
Status: uncommon migrant and winter resident in most parts of Texas; locally more common on the upper and central coast regions.

Habitat: ocean, bays and estuaries; rare on large inland lakes.
Nesting: does not nest in Texas.
Feeding: dives for crustaceans, mollusks and aquatic insect larvae; may also eat tubers, leeches, frogs and small fish.
Voice: generally silent in Texas. *Male:* nasal *peent* and hoarse *kraaagh* courtship calls. *Female:* harsh croak.
Similar Species: *Hooded Merganser* (p. 66): white crest outlined in black. *Bufflehead* (p. 64): male is smaller, with white wedge on back of head.
Best Sites: Hornsby Bend (Austin); Mitchell L. (San Antonio); Balmorhea L. (Reeves Co.); White Rock L. (Dallas).

HOODED MERGANSER

Lophodytes cucullatus

Extremely attractive and exceptionally shy, the Hooded Merganser is one of the most sought-after ducks from a birder's perspective, and most of the attention is directed toward the handsome male. The male Hooded Merganser's crest is usually held flat but is raised in moments of arousal or agitation. The male flaunts his full range of colors and athletic abilities in elaborate late-winter courtship displays and chases. • All mergansers have thin bills with small, toothlike serrations to help the birds keep a firm grasp on slippery prey. The smallest of the mergansers, Hoodies have a more diverse diet than their larger relatives. They add crustaceans, insects and even acorns to the usual diet of fish. • Female Hooded Mergansers have been known to share the incubation of eggs with female Wood Ducks and goldeneyes.

ID: slim body; crested head; thin, pointed, dark bill. *Male:* black head and back; bold white crest outlined in black; white breast with 2 black slashes; rusty sides. *Female:* dusky brown body; shaggy, reddish brown crest. *In flight:* small white wing patches.

Size: *L* 16–18 in; *W* 24 in.

Status: uncommon to locally common migrant and winter resident in most of Texas; uncommon local summer breeder in the Pineywoods region and increasingly breeding in the northeast.

Habitat: bays, estuaries, lakes, ponds and marshes.

Nesting: usually in a nest box placed for Wood Ducks; female incubates 5–12 white eggs for 31 days.

Feeding: diverse diet; dives for small fish, crustaceans, aquatic insects and the seeds and roots of aquatic plants.

Voice: usually silent in winter; low grunts and croaks. *Male:* froglike *crrrrooo* during courtship display.

Similar Species: *Bufflehead* (p. 64): breeding male has entirely white underparts and no black outline on white crest. *Red-breasted Merganser* (p. 68) and *Common Merganser* (p. 67): females have much longer, orange bills and gray backs. *Other diving ducks* (pp. 59–69): females do not have crests.

Best Sites: Village Creek Treatment Plant (Arlington); Hagerman NWR; Hornsby Bend (Austin); Mitchell L. (San Antonio).

COMMON MERGANSER

Mergus merganser

Lumbering like a jumbo jet, the Common Merganser must run along the surface of the water, beating its heavy wings, to gain sufficient lift to take off. Once up and away, this large duck flies low over the water, making broad, sweeping turns to follow the meandering shorelines of rivers and lakes. • Common Mergansers are highly social and often gather in large groups during migration. In winter, any source of open water with a fish-filled shoal will support good numbers of these skilled divers. In some years, they can be common on large lakes and rivers of the Panhandle and Trans-Pecos in the western half of the state. • As the name suggests, the Common Merganser is the most abundant merganser in North America. "Merganser" is derived from the Latin for "diving goose." This species is also found in Europe and Asia, where its English name is "Goosander."

ID: large, elongated body; long, red bill. *Male:* glossy, green head without crest; brilliant orange to blood red bill and feet; white body plumage; black spinal stripe; large white patch on upper forewing. *Female:* rusty head; clean white neck and throat; gray body. *In flight:* shallow wing-beats; body is compressed and arrowlike; white speculum.

Size: *L* 22–27 in; *W* 34 in.

Status: uncommon to locally common migrant and winter resident in the western third of Texas and rare east to the north-central region.

Habitat: large, often fast-flowing rivers and deep lakes; may also use estuaries and coastal lagoons.

Nesting: does not nest in Texas.

Feeding: dives underwater (up to 30 ft) for small fish, usually trout, carp, suckers, perch and catfish; may also eat shrimp, sala-manders and mussels.

Voice: generally silent in winter. *Male:* utters a harsh *uig-a*, like a guitar twang. *Female:* harsh *karr karr.*

Similar Species: *Red-breasted Merganser* (p. 68): shaggy crest; male has spotted, red breast; female has pale brownish throat. *Mallard* (p. 52): male has chestnut breast. *Common Goldeneye* (p. 65): male has white cheek patch. *Common Loon* (p. 77): breeding bird has black bill and white-spotted back.

Best Sites: Lake Meredith NRA (Panhandle); Buffalo Lake NWR; McNary Reservoir (El Paso Co.).

RED-BREASTED MERGANSER

Mergus serrator

Glossy, slicked-back crests and wild, red eyes give Red-breasted Mergansers the disheveled, wave-bashed look of adrenalized windsurfers. At home in salt water, they winter in estuarine shallows, shipping channels and sections of relatively protected open ocean along the entire stretch of coast. A few birds appear well inland during migration periods, typically in late fall and early winter, favoring larger reservoirs. Red-breasted Mergansers associate only loosely with other waterfowl but are commonly found sprinkled individually among grebes and loons or in loose flocks of their own kind. • Red-breasted Mergansers appear to feed over featureless sandy bottoms, and groups sometimes fish cooperatively, funneling fishes for easier capture. Sizable concentrations assemble on bays, at harbor entrances and in ocean coves wherever small schooling fishes are abundant.

breeding

breeding

ID: large, elongated body; red eyes; thin, serrated, orange bill; shaggy, slicked-back head crest. *Breeding Male:* green head; white collar, light rust breast spotted with black. *Female and nonbreeding male:* grayish brown overall; reddish head; white chin, foreneck and breast.

Size: *L* 19–26 in; *W* 30 in.

Status: common migrant and winter resident in coastal regions and less common on inland reservoirs in the eastern half of the state.

Habitat: coastal waters and estuaries; also on large inland lakes.

Nesting: only 1 nesting record; does not usually nest in Texas.

Feeding: dives underwater for small fish; also eats aquatic invertebrates and crustaceans.

Voice: generally silent in Texas. *Male:* catlike *yeow* during courtship and feeding. *Female:* harsh *kho-kha.*

Similar Species: *Common Merganser* (p. 67): male has clean white breast and blood red bill and no head crest; female's rusty foreneck contrasts with white chin and breast.

Best Sites: along coasts; large inland water bodies.

RUDDY DUCK

Oxyura jamaicensis

The Ruddy Duck is a small bay duck that winters in large flocks along the Gulf Coast or on large interior lakes. It has a flattened and somewhat elongated head, short neck and short tail, which is often held upraised at an angle. The male has a gleaming white cheek patch that contrast with its black crown and grayish brown body. The female is similar, but her cheek is marked with a wide, dark line across it. • On rare occasions, the Ruddy Duck has bred in Texas. In his resplendent breeding plumage, the male has a bright rusty body and vivid azure bill. Sacs in his neck are inflated with air as part of his courtship display, which also involves tilting his head backward and emitting a series of notes. Despite her small size, the female Ruddy Duck lays the largest eggs of any waterfowl, and she commonly lays up to 10 eggs at a time.

breeding ♂

♀

♀

breeding

breeding ♂

ID: large bill and head; short neck; long, stiff tail feathers (often held upward). *Breeding male:* white cheek; chestnut red body; blue bill; black tail and crown. *Female:* brown overall; dark cheek stripe across whitish face; darker crown and back. *Nonbreeding male:* similar to female, but with all-white cheek.
Size: *L* 15–16 in; *W* 18½ in.
Status: common migrant and winter resident throughout most of the state; less common in winter in the Panhandle; rarely breeds in the extreme western Trans-Pecos and the South Plains.
Habitat: bays, estuaries and the ocean; also uses large inland lakes.

Nesting: in cattails, bulrushes or other emergent vegetation; female suspends a woven platform nest over water; female incubates 5–10 rough, whitish eggs for 23–26 days.
Feeding: dives for aquatic vegetation and lesser amounts of crustaceans and insects.
Voice: generally silent in Texas. *Male: chuck-chuck-chuck-chur-r-r-r* during courtship display.
Similar Species: *Cinnamon Teal* (p. 55): brown or red cheeks; dark bill. *Masked Duck:* rare and irregular visitor; nonbreeding bird has tawny face with 2 stripes and black bill tip. *Other diving ducks* (pp. 59–68): females do not have long, stiff tails and dark facial stripes.
Best Sites: Village Creek Wastewater Treatment Plant (Arlington); Hagerman NWR; Hornsby Bend (Austin); Mitchell L. (San Antonio); Laguna Atascosa NWR.

PLAIN CHACHALACA

Ortalis vetula

The Plain Chachalaca is the only member of the chickenlike Cracidae family to venture out of the tropics and into the U.S. This tree-dwelling bird has expanded northward from Mexico into the riparian woodlands and scrub of the South Texas Brush Country. • These secretive birds are not common, but groups are easy to locate once they begin to call. They are very social and especially noisy during the breeding season. To attract a mate, a lone male begins with his low-pitched call, and soon a female will chime in with her higher, screechy reply. • The Plain Chachalaca resembles a cross between a turkey and a roadrunner. Surprisingly, this mix makes for a very agile tree inhabitant. The long, broad tail aids in balancing on precariously small branches, and the short wings do not get in the way of a Chachalaca flying through dense brush. • This bird's onomatopoetic common name imitates its call. The word *vetula* is Latin for "little old woman," which jokingly refers to the bird's constant calling.

breeding

ID: grayish brown upperparts; buffy underparts; long, scaly legs with long talons; dark gray-blue face; long, dark brown tail with white tip. *Breeding:* red patch of skin on throat.

Size: *L* 22 in; *W* 24–28 in.

Status: uncommon to locally common and restricted to the brushlands of the Lower Rio Grande Valley, downriver from the Falcon Reservoir.

Habitat: riparian woodlands and woody thickets near water.

Nesting: close to water; in a tree, up to 15 ft above the ground; sometimes built on top of another species' old nest; loose bed of sticks, vines and twigs is lined with Spanish moss and has a small depression in the center; female incubates 2–3 white eggs for 25 days.

Feeding: takes food while perched in a tree or on the ground; eats berries, seeds, green vegetation and flower buds; sometimes takes insects and other invertebrates.

Voice: flocks of up to 20 birds may call together, creating a constant, rough *cha-cha-lac-a;* males have a lower tone than females; during courtship, males call first.

Similar Species: *Greater Roadrunner* (p. 205): head crest; streaky, brown and whitish plumage.

Best Sites: Bentsen-Rio Grande Valley SP; Anzalduas CP (Hidalgo Co.); Santa Ana NWR; Falcon SP.

RING-NECKED PHEASANT

Phasianus colchicus

Mainly intended as quarry for hunters, the spectacular Ring-necked Pheasant was introduced to North America from Asia in the mid-1800s. Today, this well-known, colorful gamebird continues to thrive through the stocking of hatchery-raised young and private releases. First introduced to Texas in the 1930s, the Ring-necked Pheasant is now found throughout the Panhandle and northern South Plains. One small population also persists near Anahuac. Despite widespread introduction programs, Ring-necked Pheasant populations tend to remain small and concentrate locally because of diverse climatic conditions and intense hunting pressure. • Male pheasants are heard much more often than they are seen. Their distinctive, loud *krahh-krawk!* can be heard echoing near farmyards and brushy suburban parks. • This gamebirds' flight muscles are not well developed for flight. As a result, it does not fly long distances, but it will explode in bursts of flight to travel over small areas or to quickly escape a predator.

ID: long, barred tail; unfeathered legs. *Male:* green head; white collar; bronze underparts; naked, red face patch. *Female:* mottled brown overall; light underparts.

Size: *Male: L* 30–36 in; *W* 31 in. *Female:* 20–24 in; *W* 31 in.

Status: common permanent resident in the Panhandle, northern South Plains and in Chambers Co.

Habitat: agricultural lands, brushy and weedy fields, stubble fields, croplands and shrubby, overgrown hillsides at low elevations.

Nesting: on the ground, among grass or sparse vegetation or next to a log or other natural debris; in a slight depression lined with grass and leaves; female incubates 10–12 olive brown eggs for up to 25 days.

Feeding: *Summer:* gleans the ground and vegetation for weed seeds and terrestrial insects. *Winter:* eats mostly buds, seeds and waste grain.

Voice: hoarse *ka-ka-ka, ka-ka* when flushed or running. *Male:* loud, raspy, roosterlike *krahh-krawk!* promptly followed by a muffled whirring of wings.

Similar Species: male is distinctive. *Greater Roadrunner* (p. 205): raised head crest; longer bill; red patch of bare skin surrounds eye; unbarred, dark tail.

Best Sites: Lake Meredith RA; Muleshoe NWR; Buffalo Lake NWR.

GREATER PRAIRIE-CHICKEN

Tympanuchus cupido

When seen dancing on their leks, male Greater Prairie-Chickens are a crowd-pleaser, especially to the females that gather around to decide which contender has best intimidated the other males and shown his dancing prowess. The dancing includes the stomping of feathered feet and occasional jumps and turns. The large, colorful air sacs on the males' necks emit the low booming sound that underlies the drama of whoops and cackles at the lek—some sounds can be heard up to a mile away. • Greater Prairie-Chicken *(T.c. pinnatus)* populations are now fragmented and local, having become scattered around the central and northern states since the coming of large-scale agriculture. Of the two other races of this species, the "Heath Hen" *(T.c. cupido)* lived along the Atlantic Coast and became extinct in 1932. The Attwater's race *(T.c. attwateri)*, now found only on the Coastal Plain of Texas, may soon follow the path of the "Heath Hen."

"Attwater's Prairie-Chicken"

ID: large, chickenlike body; striped, black and tan plumage; feathered legs; black terminal tail band; pinnae black at back. *Male:* large, yellow air sacs on sides of neck; thick, orange eye combs.

Size: *L* 17–18 in; *W* 28 in.

Status: decreasing within current habitat; near extinction, with populations supplemented by birds from breeding programs.

Habitat: tallgrass prairie.

Nesting: on the ground, under grass cover; female scratches out a nest and lines it with feathers and grass; female incubates 7–10 buff eggs, with dark brown speckles, for 23–25 days.

Feeding: snatches food from the ground or low vegetation. *Breeding:* buds, grasshoppers and fruits. *Winter:* historically fed on acorns in nearby oak savannah but now eats mostly waste grain such as oats and wheat.

Voice: *Male:* low-frequency booming *whhooo-doo-dooohh* on the lek. *Female:* low *kuk, kwerr* and *brirrb* calls.

Similar Species: *Lesser Prairie-Chicken* (p. 444); restricted to northern Texas; smaller; less streaking on underparts; darker orange or red air sacs; higher voice.

Best Sites: Attwater's Prairie-Chicken NWR; Texas Nature Conservancy Preserve (Galveston Co.).

WILD TURKEY

Meleagris gallopavo

The Wild Turkey was once very common throughout most of eastern North America, but habitat loss and overhunting took a toll on this bird during the 20th century. Several restoration programs sponsored by the Texas Parks and Wildlife Department have restored the species to much of its original range in our state. • Although turkeys forage on the ground and travel mostly by foot, they can fly strongly for short distances. Surprising as it may seem, turkeys avoid predation by bobcats and other terrestrial predators by roosting in trees at night! • This charismatic bird is the only native North American animal that has been widely domesticated. The wild ancestors of most other domestic animals came from Europe. • If Congress had taken Benjamin Franklin's advice in 1782, our national emblem would be the Wild Turkey instead of the majestic Bald Eagle.

ID: unfeathered head; iridescent, glossy, dark body plumage; barred, copper-colored tail. *Male:* long, central breast tassel; colorful head and body.

Female: smaller; bluish gray head; less iridescent body.
Size: *Male: L* 3–3½ ft; *W* 5½ ft. *Female: L* 3 ft; *W* 4 ft.
Status: uncommon to common resident in the eastern woodlands, southern Coastal Plain, much of the Edwards Plateau and north to the eastern half of the Panhandle.
Habitat: open deciduous or mixed woodlands or cypress swamps adjacent to pastures and other open fields.

Nesting: in a woodland or at a field edge; in a depression on the ground under thick cover; nest is lined with grass and leaves; female incubates 10–12 brown-speckled, pale buff eggs for up to 28 days.
Feeding: in open woodlands or fields near protective cover; forages on the ground for acorns, seeds and fruits; also eats insects, especially beetles and grasshoppers; may take small amphibians.
Voice: wide array of sounds; courting male gobbles loudly; loud *pert* alarm call; clucking gathering call; loud *keouk-keouk-keouk* contact call.
Similar Species: none.
Best Sites: Gene Howe WMA; Buffalo Lake NWR; Garner SP; Welder Wildlife Refuge (San Patricio Co.).

SCALED QUAIL

Callipepla squamata

These quirky little birds can be found hiding underneath farm equipment or mesquite bushes in their arid scrubland habitat. Groups known as "coveys" form in winter and then break into breeding pairs in March or April. The timing and occurrence of breeding depend on the amount of summer precipitation; if conditions allow, females lay more than one clutch. • Black edges on the feathers of its neck and underparts gives this bird a "scaly" appearance. Male Scaled Quails show off their plumage atop fence posts, calling to claim their breeding territories. Their showy plumage has earned them the name "Cottontop." The females have less "cotton" on their heads and do not have the buffy throat patches of the males. • Scaled Quail populations are decreasing because of habitat loss. Overgrazing removes the greenery, and fire suppression allows shrubbery to encroach, forming habitat more suitable for the adaptable Gambel's Quail.

ID: stocky body; pale gray and brown plumage overall; horizontal white stripes along sides; 1 white wing bar; gray-tipped tail; gray "scales" around neck and down front; white head tuft. *Male:* larger head tuft; buffy throat patch. *Female:* gray throat.
Size: *L* 10–12 in; *W* 14 in.
Status: uncommon to locally common resident in the western half of Texas; populations fluctuate greatly with droughts.

Habitat: arid scrub and grasslands; may be found in coveys around log piles or farm equipment; usually close to water.
Nesting: on the ground; makes a small depression under thick vegetation; female incubates 12–14 creamy, brown-speckled eggs for 22–23 days.
Feeding: eats seeds, insects and vegetation.
Voice: throaty *chip-Chuk!* when separated; various clicks and trills. *Male:* loud *sheesh!*
Similar Species: *Gambel's Quail* (p. 75): female has chestnut sides, buffy chest and thin, black plume on head.
Best Sites: Muleshoe NWR; Palo Duro Canyon SP; Big Spring SP.

GAMBEL'S QUAIL

Callipepla gambelii

A half-curled forehead plume adds a dash of style to the head-bobbing gait of the plump, robin-sized Gambel's Quail. • During summer, to survive the dry climate, avoid the hot sun and elude predators, these quails feed only during early morning and late evening. At night, coveys of up to 40 birds roost within thickets or dense shrubbery, emerging in the morning to visit nearby streams or water holes. They also derive water from their food. • Courting males perch atop shrubs or rocks, throw their heads back and utter boisterous *chi-ca-go-go* calls. Within 10 days of hatching, young Gambel's Quails can fly short distances on undersized, partially developed wings. • This bird is named after American naturalist William Gambel; *callipepla* comes from *kalli* and *peplos*, Greek for "beautiful robe."

ID: gray breast and upperparts; white-streaked, chestnut sides; teardrop-shaped, black plume. *Male:* black face and forehead bordered by white; rusty crown; buffy belly with black inner patch. *Female:* brownish head; all-buff belly; smaller plume.

Size: *L* 11 in; *W* 15 in.

Status: common resident in the extreme west Trans-Pecos and uncommon along the Rio Grande to the Big Bend region.

Habitat: frequents honey mesquite thickets; desert scrublands, canyons and brushy open country, especially near water sources.

Nesting: on the ground (or may use an existing nest in a low shrub); shallow depression, sheltered by a shrub or grass, is lined with vegetation; female incubates 10–12 white or buff eggs for about 21 days; pair tends the young.

Feeding: forages (usually within coveys) on or near the ground for seeds, leaves, buds and tender shoots; also eats cacti, fruit and occasional insects; may visit suburban yards or gardens for seeds and grains.

Voice: calls include a loud 4-note *chi-ca-go-go,* a sorrowful *qua-al* and various cackling, crowing, grunting and clucking noises.

Similar Species: *Scaled Quail* (p. 74): white head crest; "scaly" neck and underparts. *Montezuma Quail* (p. 444): male has rounded, brown crest, black and white facial pattern and white-dotted, dark upperparts; female is brownish overall. *Northern Bobwhite* (p. 76): brown and chestnut overall; no forehead plume.

Best Sites: Franklin Mountains SP; Hueco Tanks SP.

NORTHERN BOBWHITE

Colinus virginianus

During spring, the characteristic whistled *bob-white* call of our most common quail rings out through the farmlands and forests of eastern Texas. The male's well-known call is often the only evidence of the Northern Bobwhite's presence among the dense, tangled vegetation of its rural woodland home. • Throughout fall and winter, Northern Bobwhites typically travel in large family groups called "coveys," collectively seeking out sources of food and huddling together during cool nights. When they huddle, all members of the covey face outward, enabling the group to detect danger from any direction. With the arrival of summer, breeding pairs break away from their coveys to perform elaborate courtship rituals in preparation for another nesting season. • Bobwhites benefit from habitat disturbance, using the early successional habitats created by fire, agriculture and forestry.

ID: mottled brown, buff and black underparts; short tail; slightly peaked, brown crown; bold black and brown horizontal stripe from bill back past eye; chestnut flanks marked with black and white stripes. *Male:* white throat; broad, white eyebrow. *Female:* buffy throat and eyebrow.

Size: *L* 10 in; *W* 13 in.

Status: uncommon to common resident east of the Pecos R.; populations fluctuate with rainfall.

Habitat: open woodlands and woodland edges, grassy or brushy fields and prairies.

Nesting: on the ground; shallow depression, often concealed by surrounding vegetation or a woven partial dome, is lined with grass and leaves; pair incubates 12–16 white to pale buff eggs for 22–24 days.

Feeding: eats seeds, fruit, leaves and acorns; also takes insects and other invertebrates.

Voice: gives whistled *hoy-hee* year-round. *Male:* whistled, rising *bob-white* or *oh-bob-white* in spring and summer.

Similar Species: *Scaled Quail* (p. 74): white-tipped crest; dark-edged, grayish breast and belly feathers give "scaly" look. *Montezuma Quail* (p. 444): male has rounded, brown crest, black and white facial pattern and black and brown mottling on back and wings; female is brownish overall and has distinctive head pattern. *Lesser Prairie-Chicken* (p. 444) and *Greater Prairie-Chicken* (p. 72): larger; heavily barred breast.

Best Sites: state parks in the eastern two-thirds of Texas.

COMMON LOON

Gavia immer

Anything but ordinary, the Common Loon's haunting call and elegant black and white breeding plumage are famous throughout the northern boreal forests. • Loons overwintering in Texas are generally silent and wear their dull brown alternate plumage, but these skilled diving birds are still fascinating to watch. Look for Common Loons on coastal waters north of Corpus Christi and inland on large lakes or reservoirs. • Unlike most birds, loons have nearly solid bones that reduce buoyancy and make diving easier. Their legs are placed well back on their bodies for better underwater propulsion. On land, however, this placement makes walking difficult, and with their heavy bodies and small wing size, loons require a lengthy sprint over water to achieve takeoff. • Common Loons also occur in the Old World, where their English name is "Great Northern Diver."

nonbreeding

nonbreeding

ID: thick, stout bill. *Breeding:* green-black head; red eye. *Nonbreeding:* brown back, nape and back of head; white "indentation" where necks meets body; white underparts. *In flight:* hunchbacked appearance; legs trail behind tail.
Size: *L* 28–35 in; *W* 4–5 ft.
Status: uncommon migrant statewide; uncommon to locally common winter resident along the coast and on many inland bodies of water.
Habitat: coastal waters, such as offshore, estuaries and bays; large inland lakes.
Nesting: does not nest in Texas.

Feeding: pursues small fish underwater to depths of 180 ft; occasionally eats amphibians and large aquatic invertebrates.
Voice: generally silent in winter; quavering tremolo alarm call; long, wailing *where aaare you?* contact call; breeding notes are soft, short hoots. *Male:* territorial call is an undulating, complex yodel.
Similar Species: *Cormorants* (pp. 86–87): all-black plumages; hooked bill tips; tilt head slightly upward when swimming. *Red-throated Loon:* rare; smaller; slender bill; sharply defined white face and white-spotted back in nonbreeding plumage. *Pacific Loon* (p. 444): rare; thin, brown "chin strap" on nonbreeding adults.
Best Sites: L. Tawakoni; Offat's Bayou (Galveston); Galveston Island SP; Texas City dike.

77

LEAST GREBE

Tachybaptus dominicus

Grebes are sleek diving birds with long necks, individually lobed toes and tiny, nearly invisible tail feathers. They anchor their floating nests to aquatic vegetation and are known for carrying their newly hatched, striped young on their backs. The young can stay aboard even when the parents dive underwater. • The Least Grebe is highly nomadic and frequents water bodies ranging from trenches and large ponds in summer to coastal areas in winter. • In Texas, nesting may take place year-round and is accompanied by the tinny duets of mated pairs. Least Grebes tend to hide in the reeds, so the couple's trumpeting may be the only clue to their whereabouts. • *Tachybaptus* means "quick dip" in Greek, but this grebe is more likely to fly than dive to escape danger.

breeding

ID: grayish body; dark crown; bright yellow eye; slender bill; short neck; white tail coverts fluffed high; white outer flight feathers. *Breeding:* face and bill blacken.

Size: *L* 9–10 in; *W* 11 in.

Status: uncommon resident in southern Texas, north to Calhoun Co. and Del Rio; occasional and irregular visitor year-round up the Rio Grande to Big Bend and north to Travis Co.

Habitat: ditches, sloughs and ponds; requires surrounding vegetation for nest material.

Nesting: on water; semifloating nest is anchored to aquatic vegetation and consists of wet, decomposing vegetation; male and female incubate 4–6 pale eggs for 21 days; up to 4 broods per year.

Feeding: snatches insects from the air and water; occasionally takes crustaceans, tadpoles and small fish.

Voice: rattling, high-pitched, descending whine.

Similar Species: *Eared Grebe* (p. 81): nonbreeding bird has whitish neck and chin, dark tip on light bill and dark orange eye. *Pied-billed Grebe* (p. 79): much larger; "chicken bill."

Best Sites: Bentsen-Rio Grande Valley SP; Santa Ana NWR; Brazos Bend SP; Mitchell L. (San Antonio).

PIED-BILLED GREBE

Podilymbus podiceps

With relatively solid bones and the ability to partially deflate its air sac, the Pied-billed Grebe can float low in the water or sink below the water's surface like a tiny submarine, with only its nostrils and eyes showing above the surface. This bird tends to stick to the shallow waters of quiet freshwater ponds and rivers but is occasionally found in saltwater bays during winter. Dark plumage, a chickenlike bill and individually webbed toes distinguish the Pied-billed Grebe from other waterfowl. • These grebes build their floating nests among sparse vegetation, so that they can see their numerous predators—including Great Blue Herons, small turtles and water snakes—approaching from far away. When frightened by an intruder, they cover their eggs and slide underwater, leaving a nest that resembles a mat of debris. • In the scientific name, *podiceps*, meaning "rump foot," is a reference to how far back on its body this bird's feet are located.

breeding

ID: stocky body; short, laterally compressed "chicken bill"; very short tail. *Breeding:* all-brown body; black ring on pale bill; black throat; white undertail coverts; pale belly; pale eye ring. *Nonbreeding:* yellow eye ring; unringed, yellow bill; white chin and throat; brownish crown.

Size: *L* 12–15 in; *W* 16 in.

Status: common migrant and winter resident statewide; locally uncommon summer resident east of the Pecos R.

Habitat: ponds, marshes, impoundments and backwaters; flooded agricultural lands. *Winter:* may use saltwater bays.

Nesting: in a sheltered bay, pond or marsh; among sparse emergent vegetation; floating platform nest is made of wet and decaying plants; pair incubates 4–5 white to buff eggs for about 23 days; pair raises the young.

Feeding: dives for aquatic invertebrates, small fish and amphibians; occasionally eats aquatic plants.

Voice: loud, whooping call begins quickly, then slows: *kuk-kuk-kuk cow cow cowp cowp cowp.*

Similar Species: *Horned Grebe* (p. 80) and *Eared Grebe* (p. 81): short, thin bill; red eyes; black and white nonbreeding plumage. *Least Grebe* (p. 78): smaller; thin bill; yellowish eyes. *American Coot* (p. 139): wholly black body; white of bill extends onto forehead.

Best Sites: Village Creek Wastewater Treatment Plant (Arlington); Mitchell L. (San Antonio); Hornsby Bend (Austin); Brazos Bend SP.

HORNED GREBE

Podiceps auritus

This compact little grebe rides high in the water, has a rounded head outline and slightly puffed cheeks and holds its neck somewhat curved or thrust forward when swimming. • The Horned Grebe flies more readily than most grebes, with a strong, direct, loonlike flight that reveals a large white patch at the rear of the inner wing. • Grebes catch their food in long dives that may last up to three minutes, and they can travel as far as 400 feet while underwater. The birds start their dives with a pronounced upward and forward leap, and they propel themselves underwater solely with their feet. • This bird's common name and the word *auritus* (eared) both refer to the golden feather tufts, or "horns" that this species acquires in its breeding plumage. In winter, look for this grebe along the upper coast and at large inland reservoirs in Texas.

nonbreeding

ID: red eyes; flat crown; white underparts. *Breeding:* rufous neck and flanks; black head; golden "ear" tufts; dark back. *Nonbreeding:* no "ear" tufts; dark upperparts; white cheek and foreneck. *In flight:* wings beat constantly; hunchbacked appearance; legs trail behind tail.
Size: *L* 12–15 in; *W* 18 in.
Status: rare to uncommon migrant across the state; uncommon winter resident on the Coastal Plain and at scattered inland locations.

Habitat: coastal areas; wetlands and large lakes.
Nesting: does not nest in Texas.
Feeding: dives shallowly and gleans the water's surface for aquatic insects, crustaceans, mollusks and small fish.
Voice: silent in migration and winter.
Similar Species: *Pied-billed Grebe* (p. 79): mostly brown body; short, thick neck; thick bill. *Eared Grebe* (p. 81): rare; head mostly black, with white crescent behind eye; dark foreneck. *Red-necked Grebe:* larger; dark eyes; no "ear" tufts; white cheek and red neck in breeding plumage.
Best Sites: Hornsby Bend (Austin); Mitchell L. (San Antonio); Texas City dike.

EARED GREBE

Podiceps nigricollis

For nine to ten months of every year—longer than for any other flying bird—the Eared Grebe is flightless. During these cyclical grounded periods, the Eared Grebe's internal organs and pectoral muscles shrink or swell, depending on whether or not the bird needs to migrate (only a few individuals stay to breed). • Like other grebes, the Eared Grebe eats feathers. The feathers often pack the digestive tract, and it is thought that they protect the stomach lining and intestines from sharp fish bones or parasites, or perhaps they slow the passage of food, allowing more time for complete digestion. • The Eared Grebe inhabits parts of Europe, Asia, Central Africa and South America, making it the most abundant grebe not only in North America but also in the world. • In the scientific name, *nigricollis* means "black neck," a characteristic of this bird's breeding plumage.

nonbreeding

ID: red eyes. *Breeding:* black neck, cheek, forehead and back; red flanks; fanned-out, golden "ear" tufts; white underparts; thin, dark bill; slightly raised crown. *Nonbreeding:* dark cheek and upperparts; white underparts; dusky upper foreneck and flanks. *In flight:* wings beat constantly; hunchbacked appearance; legs trail behind tail.
Size: *L* 11½–14 in; *W* 16 in.
Status: common migrant and winter resident statewide; locally uncommon summer resident in scattered locations east of the Pecos R. but rarely nests in Texas.

Habitat: coastal waters near shore; freshwater wetlands, larger lakes and sewage disposal ponds.
Nesting: singly or in loose colonies; floating platform nest is anchored to pondweeds; pair incubates 4–5 white eggs (often stained by rotting vegetation) for 20–23 days.
Feeding: makes shallow dives and gleans the water's surface for aquatic insects, crustaceans, mollusks and small fish.
Voice: usually quiet outside the breeding season.
Similar Species: *Pied-billed Grebe* (p. 79): thicker, stubbier bill; mostly brown body. *Least Grebe* (p. 78): smaller; slender bill; yellow eyes; grayish plumage. *Horned Grebe* (p. 80): rufous neck in breeding plumage; white cheek in nonbreeding plumage.
Best Sites: *Winter:* most bodies of water.

MASKED BOOBY

Sula dactylatra

Boobies are tropical seabirds that feed by plunge-diving into the sea, often from heights of 30 or more feet. Most often found offshore, especially around oil rigs, they are never seen from the Texas mainland except after tropical storms, when they may be driven to shore. Four species occur in North America, but only the Masked Booby occurs regularly in our area. The other boobies are found only as accidental or rare visitors to our offshore waters. • The Masked Booby is the largest of the boobies, with a wingspan of 5 feet or more. Unlike the Brown Booby and the Red-footed Booby, which commonly roost in trees or on buoys or channel markers, the Masked Booby roosts on land or on the water. Breeding colonies are located on tropical islands throughout the world. In the U.S., the Masked Booby breeds only in the Hawaiian Islands and at Hospital Key, Florida.

ID: mostly white, with black mask, flight feathers and tail; long, yellowish bill. *Immature:* dark brown back, wings and head.

Size: *L* 27–33 in. *W* 5 ft.

Status: uncommon migrant along the coast; usually appears along the coast as a summer or winter visitor but may occur at any time of the year.

Habitat: *Nonbreeding:* open ocean.

Nesting: does not breed in Texas.

Feeding: tucks back wings and dives head-first into the ocean to feed on fish and squid.

Voice: *Male:* hoarse whistles. *Female:* deep honks.

Similar Species: *Northern Gannet* (p. 83): larger; white tail; black in wings restricted to primaries; yellow on head and neck; entirely dark juvenile plumage. *Red-footed Booby:* white morph is accidental; smaller; bluish bill; red feet.

Best Sites: offshore; often seen from Quintana and Freeport jetties.

NORTHERN GANNET

Morus bassanus

Northern Gannets are the only pelagic birds that you are likely to spot from shore in Texas. From fall through spring, small to occasionally large numbers of gannets can be seen feeding just offshore. They fly along slowly, scanning the surface of the water from heights of 50 feet or more. When a school of fish is sighted, these birds suddenly fold back their wings and plunge headfirst into the ocean. To cushion the brain from diving impacts, Northern Gannets have evolved a reinforced skull. • Each summer, these gentle-looking birds return to their large sea-cliff nesting colonies in eastern Canada and the Old World. They do not breed until age five, and they often mate for life, reestablishing pair bonds each year at their nest sites with elaborate face-to-face nest-duty exchange sequences that involve wing raising, tail spreading, bowing, sky-pointing and preening.

1st-year juvenile

ID: white overall; black wing tips; buffy wash on nape; thick, tapered bill; long, narrow wings; pointed tail. *Immature:* various stages of mottled gray, black and white.
Size: *L* 3 ft; *W* 6 ft.
Status: uncommon migrant and winter visitor along the coast; occasionally appears in large flocks.

Habitat: open ocean; often seen from shore.
Nesting: does not nest in Texas.
Feeding: dives for fish or squid; also forages by submerging its head while floating on the water's surface.
Voice: generally silent at sea.
Similar Species: *Masked Booby* (p. 82): smaller; black mask; black tail; more white on underwings; immature has white collar and dark brown back, wings and head.
Best Sites: offshore; often seen from Quintana and Freeport jetties.

AMERICAN WHITE PELICAN

Pelecanus erythrorhynchos

With its impressive wingspan, the American White Pelicans is a majestic wetland presence. • Unlike most birds, American White Pelicans feed cooperatively—a group of foraging pelicans paddles with their feet to herd fish together, then dip their bills to scoop up the prey. • The porous, bucketlike bill is dramatically adapted for feeding. As a pelican lifts its bill from the water, the fish are held within its flexible pouch while the water drains out. The bill can hold over 3 gallons of water and fish, which is about two to three times the stomach capacity. • Astoundingly, an isolated group of white pelicans nests in the Laguna Madre in Texas, 1400 miles from the nearest colony, which is in Utah. • A black pigment, melanin, makes this bird's flight feathers stronger and more resistant to wear.

nonbreeding

nonbreeding

ID: very large, stocky body; white overall; long, orange bill; orange throat pouch; naked orange skin patch around eye; short tail. *Breeding:* small, keeled plate on upper mandible; pale yellow crest on back of head. *Nonbreeding* and *immature:* brown-tinged plumage. *In flight:* black wing tip and trailing edge.
Size: *L* 4½–6 ft; *W* 9 ft.
Status: common migrant over eastern Texas and less common in the west; common winter resident along the coast and on many inland reservoirs; rare breeder, with 1 breeding colony at Laguna Madre (Nueces Co).

Habitat: estuaries, bays and freshwater lakes; also uses flooded agricultural fields. *In migration:* may be seen over any habitat.
Nesting: colonial; on bare, low-lying islands; nest scrape may be lined with pebbles and debris; pair incubates 2 dull white eggs for about 33 days.
Feeding: groups cooperatively "herd" fish into shallows, then scoop up prey with bills.
Voice: generally quiet; rare piglike grunts.
Similar Species: no other large white bird has a long bill and pouch. *Brown Pelican* (p. 85): smaller and less stocky; darker overall. *Wood Stork* (p. 106) and *Whooping Crane* (p. 141): fly with necks extended and long legs trailing beyond tail.
Best Sites: Bolivar Flats Shorebird Sanctuary (Galveston Co.); Oso Bay (Nueces Co.); most large inland reservoirs.

BROWN PELICAN

Pelecanus occidentalis

Brown Pelicans are among the most conspicuous waterbirds, perching on beaches, rocks and pilings or coursing the troughs in single file. • Unlike the American White Pelican, the Brown Pelican is primarily a coastal species and is seldom encountered away from marine or intertidal habitats. • Among the world's six species of pelicans, the Brown Pelican has a unique foraging method: it flies slowly over the water at a height of up to 60 feet, then folds back its wings, pulls back its head and dives head-first into the water. All other pelicans scoop up prey while swimming in shallow water.

• In the 1950s and 1960s, reproductive problems caused by DDT resulted in the near disappearance of the Brown Pelican in Texas, California and much of the Southeast. When the Texas coastline was surveyed in 1969, only 116 Brown Pelicans were found. Since the banning of this highly persistent pesticide, populations have recovered throughout the South.

breeding

ID: grayish brown body; very large bill. *Breeding:* yellow head; white stripe down side of neck; dark brown hind-neck; red pouch. *Nonbreeding:* white neck; head washed with yellow; pale yellowish pouch.

Size: *L* 4 ft; *W* 7 ft.

Status: increasingly common resident on the upper and central coasts; occasionally appears at inland reservoirs.

Habitat: bays, estuaries and shores; rare on large inland lakes.

Nesting: on the ground or in mangroves; nest may be a scrape or an elaborate platform woven from sticks and lined with vegetation; pair incubates 2–3 bright chalky white eggs under foot webs for 29–32 days; pair cares for the young.

Feeding: forages almost exclusively for fish, which are caught by diving headfirst into the water from heights of up to 60 ft; fish are held in the flexible pouch until water is drained.

Voice: generally silent away from colonies.

Similar Species: *American White Pelican* (p. 84): all-white body; orange bill and pouch; extensive black in wings.

Best Sites: anywhere from the Louisiana border to Corpus Christi.

NEOTROPIC CORMORANT

Phalacrocorax brasilianus

With an air of confidence, the Neotropic Cormorant perches on narrow branches, signs or even slender wires. This versatile species inhabits both freshwater and saltwater environments from southern Texas to the tip of South America. A versatile, year-round resident, the Neotropic Cormorant flies only short distances between wintering and breeding grounds. • Neotropic Cormorants nest in colonies along the Gulf Coast, often in association with larger Double-crested Cormorants. Most eggs are laid in spring, although nesting can occur from February to mid-November. • As solitary hunters, mostly of fish, cormorants dive underwater and propel themselves with their large, webbed, black feet. Occasionally the birds cooperate, funneling fish to the surface by beating their wings on the water. • This species was formerly known as "Olivaceous Cormorant" and is also referred to as "Mexican Cormorant" or "Brazilian Cormorant."

breeding

ID: slender, black body; glossy feathers; thick, hooked bill; yellow throat patch ends in point behind mouth. *Breeding:* white outline on throat patch; white plume on back of head.

Size: *L* 23–29 in; *W* 3¼ ft.

Status: uncommon to locally common resident on the coast; rare resident and breeder on a number of inland reservoirs.

Habitat: varied habitat includes freshwater and saltwater environments with protected surroundings; reservoirs.

Nesting: in a live or dead tree or bush (or on bare ground); platform stick nest is lined with grass or seaweed; pair incubates 3–4 light blue eggs for 25–30 days.

Feeding: dives underwater for small fish; also takes frogs and shrimp.

Voice: guttural warning grunts to surrounding individuals in breeding areas.

Similar Species: *Double-crested Cormorant* (p. 87): larger; thicker body and bill; orange throat patch reaches above eye and is rounded on cheek; no white outline on throat patch or white plume in breeding plumage. *Common Loon* (p. 77): grayish brown back; light underparts; holds straight bill level while swimming. *Anhinga* (p. 88): black body; wings streaked with silver and white; thinner, longer neck, usually held outstretched; fanlike tail; red eyes; female has buffy head and neck; restricted to fresh water.

Best Sites: High Island Rookery (Galveston Co.); Anahuac NWR; Brazoria NWR; Brazos Bend SP; Fort Hancock Reservoir (Hudspeth Co.).

DOUBLE-CRESTED CORMORANT

Phalacrocorax auritus

Double-crested Cormorants are commonly seen in large V-shaped or single-file flocks flying between foraging and roosting areas. After foraging, they often perch on channel markers or piers with their wings partially spread to dry their feathers. • Most water birds have waterproof feathers, but Double-crested Cormorant feathers allow water in, making this bird less buoyant, which aids diving. • Japanese fishermen once used other species of cormorants to catch fish. A ring was placed around the bird's throat to prevent it from swallowing the fish, and a leash was attached to the ring to reel the cormorant in when it caught a fish. In recent years, the Double-crested Cormorant has been a problem for fish farms in Texas.

1st-year juvenile

breeding

Nesting: colonial; in a shrub or tree, usually on an island or in swamp; nest is built of sticks; pair incubates 3–4 bluish white eggs for 25–29 days; feeds young by regurgitation.
Feeding: long underwater dives for fish, to depths of 30 ft or more; surfaces to swallow prey.
Voice: generally quiet away from breeding colonies.
Similar Species: *Neotropic Cormorant* (p. 86): smaller, more slender body; thinner bill; breeding bird has white head plumes and white outline on throat patch. *Common Loon* (p. 77): grayish brown back; light underparts; holds straight bill level while swimming. *Anhinga* (p. 88): black body; wings streaked with silver and white; thinner, longer neck, usually held outstretched; fanlike tail; red eyes; female has buffy head and neck; restricted to fresh water.
Best Sites: anywhere along the coast; large inland water bodies.

ID: all-black body; long, crooked neck; thin bill, hooked at tip; blue eyes. *Breeding:* throat pouch becomes intense orange-yellow; fine, black plumes trail from eyebrows. *Immature:* brown upperparts; buff throat and breast; yellowish throat patch.
Size: *L* 26–32 in; *W* 4½ ft.
Status: common to abundant migrant statewide; common winter resident along the coast and on inland reservoirs; breeding reported from scattered inland locations.
Habitat: open fresh water or salt water; avoids small ponds. *Roosting* and *nesting:* trees or shrubs.

87

ANHINGA

Anhinga anhinga

The Anhinga, which ranges from the southeastern U.S. to northern South America and the West Indies, is the sole New World member of the Darters (Anhingidae), a family related to cormorants but restricted to fresh water. • The Anhinga's ability to control its buoyancy makes it a stealthy hunter and an ominous presence in freshwater ponds and canals. With dense bones and easily waterlogged feathers, it swims almost completely submerged, holding its curved neck just above the water, often appearing snakelike. One quick lunge and a stab of the Anhinga's long bill captures its prey. Serrations on the top of the bill keep the prey secure until the Anhinga flips it in the air and swallows it headfirst. • Following a swim, the Anhinga *breeding* dries out its feathers and warms up by perching on a protruding snag and unfolding its silver-decorated wings. • The name "Anhinga," from the Tupi language of the Amazon, means "evil spirit of the woods."

♂

ID: black body; wings streaked with silver and white; long, curved neck; fanlike tail; red eyes. *Breeding:* bluish green orbital ring. *Female* and *immature:* buffy head and neck.

Size: *L* 2½–3 ft; *W* 4 ft.

Status: uncommon to common migrant in the eastern half of the state; uncommon summer resident on the Coastal Plain and in the eastern third of the state; rare to uncommon winter resident on the Coastal Plain and in the Lower Rio Grande Valley.

Habitat: sheltered, slow-moving or still fresh water.

Nesting: in a colony with cormorants and herons; in a tree above or near calm water; female uses sticks brought by male or may use an abandoned egret or heron nest; pair incubates 2–5 whitish eggs for 25–29 days.

Feeding: swims submerged or perches motionless, then stabs prey; feeds primarily on fish; may also take frogs and snakes.

Voice: descending metallic clicks while perched.

Similar Species: *Double-crested Cormorant* (p. 87) and *Neotropic Cormorant* (p. 86): thicker, black bodies; heavy, hooked bills; blue eyes; yellow or orange throat patches; dive for prey; often feed in salt water.

Best Sites: Caddo Lake SP; High Island Heronry; Brazos Bend SP; Richland Chambers WMA.

MAGNIFICENT FRIGATEBIRD

Fregata magnificens

The Magnificent Frigatebird often employs kleptoparasitism as a feeding strategy. A gull, tern, shorebird or other bird carrying food is harassed in mid flight until it drops or regurgitates its meal. Once food is dropped, the frigatebird swoops down to snatch the falling item before it hits the water or ground. This agile aerial acrobat can even snatch food directly from the bill of another bird during a spectacular aerial dogfight. • During courtship, groups of males put on a unique performance for onlooking females. The males inflate their throat sacs like large, red balloons and simultaneously raise their bills, vibrate their wings and shake their heads, uttering hoarse, cackling calls. The only known Magnificent Frigatebird breeding colonies in the U.S. occur in the Florida Keys and the Dry Tortugas. Other breeding sites are found in the Caribbean and Central and South America. • Relative to its body weight, the Magnificent Frigatebird has the largest wing surface area of any bird alive. With great wings and a deeply forked tail, this bird is virtually unsurpassed at soaring and aerial maneuvers.

ID: long, deeply forked tail; long, narrow wings; long, hooked bill. *Male:* glossy, black plumage with inflatable red throat patch. *Female:* blackish brown plumage with white breast. *Immature:* variable amount of white on head and breast.
Size: *L* 3–3½ ft; *W* 7–8 ft.
Status: uncommon summer visitor along the coast and rare in winter.

Habitat: *Roosting:* among mangroves on coastal islands. *Foraging:* along coastal waters or offshore.
Nesting: does not nest in Texas.
Feeding: swoops down to snatch prey off the water's surface or steals prey from other birds; eats mostly fish but occasionally takes jellyfish, crustaceans or even small birds.
Voice: silent except at nesting colonies, where it utters hoarse, cackling notes.
Similar Species: none. *Swallow-tailed Kite* (p. 110): might be mistaken for juvenile Magnificent Frigatebird if short bill is overlooked.
Best Sites: Bolivar ferry crossing; offshore.

AMERICAN BITTERN

Botaurus lentiginosus

The American Bittern is a large, elusive wading bird that breeds over much of southern Canada and the northern U.S., and it winters in the southern U.S. and along the Pacific Coast to British Columbia. At the approach of an intruder, an American Bittern's first reaction is to freeze with its bill pointed skyward—its vertically streaked, brown plumage blends in with the surrounding reeds. Intruders usually pass by without noticing the bird. The American Bittern prefers to hunt at dawn or dusk, when its camouflage is most effective. • The American Bittern's distinctive call is rarely heard in Texas. Seldom seen in our state because of its retiring habits and usually inaccessible wetland habitats, the American Bittern is a locally uncommon migrant and uncommon winter resident on the Coastal Plain. There are several reports of breeding from eastern Texas.

ID: brown upperparts; buff streaking on neck and breast; straight, stout bill; yellow legs and feet; black "mustache" streak. *In flight:* pointed wings; distinctive blackish flight feathers.
Size: *L* 23–27 in; *W* 3½ ft.
Status: rare to common migrant statewide; uncommon winter resident along the coast and local inland; occasional summer resident; rare breeder in the eastern third of the state.
Habitat: shallow freshwater wetlands.
Nesting: in a cattail or bulrush marsh; above the waterline in dense vegetation;

nest platform of grass, sedges and dead reeds often has separate entrance and exit paths; female incubates 4–5 buffy brown to olive buff eggs for about 28 days.
Feeding: patient stand-and-wait predator; strikes at small fish, crayfish, frogs and snakes.
Voice: generally silent in Texas; gives a deep, slow, resonant, "pumping" *pomp-er-lunk* around dawn or dusk.
Similar Species: *Night-Herons* (pp. 100–01): juveniles have dark brown upperparts flecked with white; no "mustache" streaks; often in saline habitats.
Best Sites: Anahuac NWR; San Bernard NWR; Brazoria NWR; Brazos Bend SP.

LEAST BITTERN

Ixobrychus exilis

One of North America's most reclusive marsh birds, the Least Bittern is the smallest of the herons. It moves about dense marshland habitat with ease, its slender body passing freely and unnoticed through the cattails. An expert climber, the Least Bittern clings to vertical stems to climb over the water and access deeper feeding areas. • A good number of Least Bitterns breed in the marshes of eastern Texas, and they can be fairly common in some areas during summer. However, they are rarely seen because of their secretive behavior and solitary lifestyle. When an intruder approaches, the bittern freezes with its bill pointed skyward—its vertically streaked, brown plumage blends perfectly with the surrounding marsh.

nonbreeding

♂

Habitat: freshwater marshes with cattails and other dense emergent vegetation.

Nesting: on top of bent marsh vegetation, usually well concealed within dense vegetation; mostly the male constructs a platform of dry plant stalks; pair incubates 4–5 pale green or blue eggs for 17–20 days; pair feeds the young by regurgitation.

ID: rich buff flanks and sides; buff-streaked foreneck; white underparts; mostly pale bill; yellowish legs; short tail. *Male:* black crown and back. *Female* and *immature:* chestnut brown head and back; immature has darker streaking on breast and back. *In flight:* large, buffy shoulder patches; dark flight feathers.

Size: *L* 11–14½ in; *W* 17 in.

Status: uncommon migrant statewide; uncommon to locally common summer resident east of the Pecos R. and rare in the Big Bend region and El Paso Co.; rare winter resident along the coast and occasionally inland.

Feeding: stabs prey with bill; eats mostly small fish; also takes large insects, tadpoles, frogs and crayfish.

Voice: *Male:* rapid 3-syllable cooing; staccato *kuk-kuk-kuk-kuk-kuk* call.

Similar Species: *American Bittern* (p. 90): much larger; boldly brown-streaked underparts; black streak from bill to shoulder. *Night-Herons* (pp. 100–01): immatures have dark brown upperparts with white flecking. *Green Heron* (p. 99): longer neck; entirely dark wings; frequents the ground in open areas.

Best Sites: Sea Rim SP; Anahuac NWR; Lake Sheldon SP; Brazos Bend SP.

91

GREAT BLUE HERON

Ardea herodias

The sight of a majestic Great Blue Heron is always memorable, whether you are observing its stealthy, often motionless hunting strategy or tracking its graceful wingbeats. • Unlike cranes, which fly with their necks outstretched, herons fly with their long necks tucked toward their bodies. • To avoid terrestrial predators such as raccoons, rookeries (heron colonies) are usually located on isolated islands or in wooded swamps. Rookeries are also sensitive to human disturbance, so be careful to observe them from a distance. • Great Blue Herons use their bills to spear fish or frogs, then swallow their catch whole. Anglers occasionally catch a fish with distinctive triangular scars—evidence that it survived a heron attack. • Although Great Blue Herons are most common along the coast, they use a wide variety of habitats throughout their extensive range. They may turn up at virtually any water body that supports fish, from small riparian creeks to large reservoirs.

breeding

breeding

ID: bluish gray overall; long, curving neck; long, dark legs; bluish gray back and wing coverts; straight, yellow bill; chestnut brown thighs. *Breeding:* richer colors; plumes streak from crown and throat. *White morph:* white overall; buffier legs. *In flight:* neck folds back over shoulders; legs trail behind body; slow, steady wingbeats.
Size: *L* 4–4½ ft; *W* 6 ft.
Status: uncommon to common resident; may withdraw from northern areas in winter.
Habitat: forages along the edges of various types of wetlands, from saline to freshwater; also stalks fields or yards.
Nesting: colonial; in a tree, snag, tall bush or marsh vegetation; stick and twig platform can be up to 4 ft in diameter; pair incubates 3–5 pale bluish green eggs for 25–29 days.

Feeding: patient stand-and-wait predator; spears fish, snakes, amphibians, even rodents, then swallows prey whole.
Voice: deep *frahnk-frahnk-frahnk* when startled.
Similar Species: *Sandhill Crane* (p. 140): unfeathered, red crown; flies with neck outstretched. *Little Blue Heron* (p. 95): much smaller; dark overall; dark bill. *Tricolored Heron* (p. 96): smaller; darker upperparts; white underparts. *Great Egret* (p. 93): smaller; white overall; black legs.
Best Sites: any state or national park, wildlife refuge or management area with water bodies; reservoirs; coastal regions.

GREAT EGRET

Ardea alba

Widely used to decorate hats in the early 20th century, the plumes of the Great Egret and Snowy Egret once sold for up to $32 per ounce—more than gold at that time. As a result, egret populations began to disappear. Some of the first conservation legislation in North America was enacted to outlaw the hunting of the Great Egret. In 1903, Teddy Roosevelt established the nation's first national wildlife refuge at Pelican Island, Florida, where it became illegal to hunt egrets for the feather trade. The Great Egret is also the symbol for the National Audubon Society, one of our country's oldest conservation organizations. • Egrets are named after the silky breeding plumes—aigrettes—that most species produce during courtship. The aigrettes of a Great Egret can grow up to 4½ feet long! • Found mainly along the coast, Great Egrets are common permanent residents in Texas but often occur at inland water bodies. Long legs and long necks allow them to forage in deeper water than other egrets.

nonbreeding

breeding

ID: all-white plumage; black legs; yellow bill. *Breeding:* white plumes trail from throat and rump; green skin patch between eyes and base of bill. *In flight:* neck folds back over shoulders; legs extend backward.
Size: *L* 3–3½ ft; *W* 4 ft.
Status: uncommon to common resident in the eastern third of the state south to the Lower Rio Grande Valley and west through the Edwards Plateau, and in extreme western Trans-Pecos; common summer resident in the north-central region; rare to uncommon post-breeding disperser in all parts of the state.
Habitat: edges of marshes, lakes and ponds; flooded agricultural fields.

Nesting: colonial; in a tree or tall shrub; pair builds a platform of sticks and incubates 3–5 pale bluish green eggs for 23–26 days.
Feeding: patient stand-and-wait predator; occasionally stalks slowly; feeds primarily on fish and aquatic invertebrates.
Voice: generally silent away from colonies; deep, low *kroow* or *kraaa*.
Similar Species: *Great Blue Heron* (p. 92): white morph is larger, with yellow bill and dull yellow legs. *Snowy Egret* (p. 94): much smaller; black bill; yellow feet. *Little Blue Heron* (p. 95): immature is much smaller, with yellowish olive legs and bluish gray bill.
Best Sites: any state or national park, wildlife refuge or management area with water bodies; reservoirs; coastal regions.

SNOWY EGRET

Egretta thula

Looking as if it stepped in a can of yellow paint, the Snowy Egret flaunts bright yellow feet, a black bill and legs and spotless white plumage. Come breeding season, this egret's facial skin turns reddish, its feet deepen to orange, and long plumes extend from its neck and back. These delicate breeding plumes were in high demand in the 1900s, and the Snowy Egret was nearly hunted to extinction. Once public outrage made the feather trade illegal, egrets made a strong comeback. • Herons and egrets, particularly Snowy Egrets, use a variety of feeding techniques. By poking their feet through the mire of a wetland, these birds spook aquatic life out of hiding places and then use their bills for stabbing their prey. They are also known for extending their wings over open water to create shade, which provides better visibility and may attract fish seeking shelter from the sun. Some paleontologists have even suggested that this usage was one of the original functions of bird wings.

nonbreeding

breeding

ID: white plumage; black bill and legs; bright yellow feet; yellow lores. *Breeding:* long plumes on throat and rump; reddish lores.

Size: *L* 22–26 in; *W* 3½ ft.

Status: uncommon migrant statewide; uncommon to common summer resident in the eastern half of the state and uncommon in El Paso Co. and Hudspeth Co.; rare to uncommon postbreeding wanderer statewide; rare to uncommon in winter in coastal areas and inland areas.

Habitat: edges of marshes, rivers, lakes and ponds; flooded agricultural fields.

Nesting: colonial; in a tree or tall shrub; pair builds a platform of sticks and incubates 3–5 pale bluish green eggs for 23–26 days.

Feeding: stand-and-wait predator; also actively chases after fish in shallows.

Voice: generally silent away from colonies; very rasping or nasal *hraa,* higher in tone than the Great Egret.

Similar Species: *Great Egret* (p. 93): much larger; yellow bill; black feet. *Cattle Egret* (p. 98): yellow-orange legs and bill; inhabits pastures and backyards. *Little Blue Heron* (p. 95): immature has yellowish olive legs and bluish gray bill.

Best Sites: High Island Heronry; Sea Rim SP; Mitchell L. (San Antonio); Brazos Bend SP; Aransas NWR.

LITTLE BLUE HERON

Egretta caerulea

immature

With their dark plumage and less attractive aigrettes, Little Blue Herons were not as sought after by the plume hunters as the white-feathered egrets, but they suffered nonetheless at the rookeries. Because many wading birds breed in mixed colonies, the persecution of one species harmed them all. • Little Blue Herons are common in eastern Texas and along the Gulf Coast in summer, wandering westward after breeding. Although the dark adult plumage is quite distinctive, immature Little Blues are white for the first year. The birds gradually molt, with blue patches of feathers appearing during the second year, giving rise to the name "Calico Heron." • The Little Blue Heron often seems tentative and stiff while hunting, jabbing awkwardly at prey.

breeding

ID: slate blue overall. *Breeding:* shaggy, maroon-colored head and neck; black legs and feet. *Nonbreeding:* smooth, purple head and neck; dull green legs and feet. *Immature:* white overall, with dusky-tipped primaries; yellowish olive legs; bluish gray bill; becomes spotted with slate blue when molting to adult plumage.
Size: *L* 24 in; *W* 3½ ft.
Status: common summer resident in eastern Texas on the Coastal Plain; uncommon post-breeding wanderer statewide; uncommon winter resident in coastal areas in the south-eastern third to the Lower Rio Grande Valley.
Habitat: edges of marshes, ponds, lakes and ponds; flooded agricultural fields.
Nesting: nests in a shrub or tree above water; male brings sticks and female builds a bulky platform nest; pair incubates 3–5 pale greenish blue eggs for 22–24 days.
Feeding: patient stand-and-wait predator; also wades slowly to stalk prey; primarily eats fish, amphibians and aquatic invertebrates.
Voice: generally silent away from colonies; hoarse *squacks* and squeals, higher in tone than the Snowy Egret.
Similar Species: *Snowy Egret* (p. 94): black bill; yellow lores; black legs; bright yellow feet. *Cattle Egret* (p. 98): stocky, yellow bill; yellow legs and feet; immature has black feet; inhabits pastures and backyards.
Best Sites: Caddo Lake SP; L. Tawakoni; Sea Rim SP; Brazos Bend SP.

TRICOLORED HERON

Egretta tricolor

nonbreeding

Blue, white and brown are the three plumage colors for which the Tricolored Heron was named. This heron is easily identified by its extremely long, thin neck and bill and by its unique plumage, which is dark above and white below. • Although it is most partial to coastal habitats such as estuaries, the Tricolored Heron is found in many types of wetlands, including inland ones. When foraging, it is one of the most active wading birds, often pursuing fish in shallow water or "canopy feeding," in which the wings are arched above the body to attract prey to the shadows. However, this heron's preferred habitat of brackish marshes and mangrove swamps are increasingly threatened by coastal development. • This bird was formerly named "Louisiana Heron" by ornithologist Alexander Wilson, because the first specimen was collected by Lewis and Clark within the vast tract of land obtained in the Louisiana Purchase.

breeding

ID: long, slender bill, neck and legs; purplish to grayish blue plumage; white underparts and foreneck; pale rump. *Breeding:* long plumes appear on head and back.

Size: *L* 26 in; *W* 3 ft.

Status: common summer resident in coastal regions and locally at scattered areas inland; postbreeding wanderer to all parts of the state south of the Panhandle.

Habitat: edges of marshes, mangrove swamps, estuaries, lakes and ponds; flooded agricultural fields.

Nesting: colonial; in a tree or shrub; male brings sticks and vegetation for female to build a bulky platform; pair incubates 3–4 greenish blue eggs for 21–25 days.

Feeding: stand and wait predator; also stalks or stirs bottom sediments to catch primarily small fish.

Voice: generally silent away from colonies; nasal groaning more reminiscent of an ibis than other herons or egrets.

Similar Species: *Reddish Egret* (p. 97): shaggy, reddish head and neck; dark underparts; pinkish bill with black tip in breeding plumage. *Little Blue Heron* (p. 95): all-dark plumage; breeding bird has shaggy pinkish neck.

Best Sites: Sea Rim SP; Anahuac NWR; Sheldon Lake SP; Port Aransas.

REDDISH EGRET

Egretta rufescens

Our rarest and most range-restricted wading bird, the Reddish Egret is fairly common in suitable areas. When foraging among the saltwater habitats of the southern coast, this large wader of coastal habitats is most entertaining. It typically feeds by lurching through shallow water in a weaving half-run while stabbing its bill in all directions, attempting to catch a fish off guard. At other times, it rakes the murky waters with its spindly feet to expose bottom-dwelling prey. Occasionally, the Reddish Egret takes a more calculated approach to feeding by standing motionless with outstretched wings. The shade produced provides better visibility by reducing the sun's glare and may also attract fish seeking shelter from the sun. • Reddish Egrets occur in two color morphs, red—which is by far more common throughout Texas—and white. On occasion, a red-morph egret is seen with scattered white feathers in the wings.

breeding

dark morph

ID: bluish gray overall; rusty neck and head; bluish legs; pale eyes. *Breeding:* shaggy neck plumes; pinkish bill with black tip. *Nonbreeding:* dark bill. *Juvenile:* gray with cinnamon head, neck and inner wing; dark bill. *White morph:* all-dark legs and feet; pinkish bill with black tip in breeding plumage.
Size: *L* 27–32 in; *W* 3½–4 ft.
Status: uncommon to common resident along the coast; occurs rarely inland south of the Panhandle as a postbreeding wanderer.
Habitat: coastal lagoons, tidal flats, estuaries and mangrove swamps.

Nesting: colonial; often in mangroves; pair builds a platform nest of sticks or grass; pair incubates 3–4 pale bluish green eggs for about 26 days; pair feeds the young.
Feeding: various foraging methods, some quite active; feeds mainly on small fish.
Voice: generally silent away from colonies; low-pitched groans resembling those of the Tricolored Heron.
Similar Species: *Tricolored Heron* (p. 96) and *Great Blue Heron* (p. 92): necks not shaggy or rusty; bills not pink with dark tip. *Snowy Egret* (p. 94): white overall, with black legs and yellow feet. *Little Blue Heron* (p. 95): smaller; all-dark plumage; immature is white with yellowish olive legs and bluish gray bill
Best Sites: Sea Rim SP; Bolivar Flats Shorebird Sanctuary (Galveston Co.); Brazoria NWR; Aransas NWR; Laguna Atascosa NWR.

CATTLE EGRET

Bubulcus ibis

Over the last century the Cattle Egret dispersed from Africa to inhabit every continent except Antarctica. After a tropical storm deposited a group of Cattle Egrets in Brazil, the species spread north through the Caribbean to Florida. It showed up in Texas in 1955 and rapidly spread across the U.S. • *Bubulcus* means "belonging to or concerning cattle" and reflects the bird's habit of following grazing animals. Other egrets feed in swamps, but the Cattle Egret's diet consists mostly of terrestrial invertebrates found around ungulates. When foraging, the Cattle Egret sometimes uses a "leapfrog" feeding strategy in which birds leap over one another, stirring up insects for the birds that follow. This egret is mistakenly reputed to remove ticks from grazing animals, but the majority of its prey is taken from the ground.

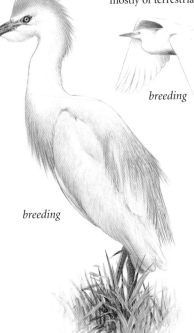

breeding

breeding

ID: relatively short legs and neck; white plumage. *Breeding:* long plumes on throat and lower back; buff orange throat, rump and crown; orange-red legs, feet and bill. *Nonbreeding:* yellow-orange bill; yellowish or dark legs *Immature:* dark bill, legs and feet.
Size: *L* 19–21 in; *W* 3 ft.
Status: common to abundant summer resident along the coast and inland east of the Balcones Escarpment and locally uncommon in the west; uncommon away from the colonies after breeding; uncommon winter resident along the coast and more abundant in the Lower Rio Grande Valley.

Habitat: primarily fields and pastures; also backyards.
Nesting: colonial; in a tree or tall shrub; male supplies sticks for female to build a platform; pair incubates 3–4 pale blue eggs for 21–26 days.
Feeding: picks grasshoppers and other invertebrates from fields; often associated with livestock; also stalks anole lizards in yards.
Voice: short quacks in breeding colony and low, nasal *brek* elsewhere.
Similar Species: *Great Egret* (p. 93): much larger; black legs and feet. *Snowy Egret* (p. 94): yellow feet; black legs. *Little Blue Heron* (p. 95): immature has yellowish olive legs and bluish gray bill.
Best Sites: *Breeding* and *in migration:* pastures with cattle.

GREEN HERON

Butorides virescens

Sentinel of mangroves and marshes, the Green Heron can show up at just about any watering hole in Texas, from a drainage ditch to a large lake. This crow-sized heron often perches just above the water's surface along wooded streams, waiting to stab frogs and small fish with its daggerlike bill. One of the few North American birds known to use tools, it has also been observed dropping feathers, leaves or other small debris into the water to attract fish within range. • Unlike most herons, the Green Heron nests singly rather than communally, but it can sometimes be found in loose colonies. Although some of this heron's habitat has been lost to wetland drainage or channelization, the digging of farm ponds and reservoirs has created habitat in other areas. • The word *virescens*, Latin for "growing or becoming green," refers to this bird's transition from a streaky brown juvenile to a greenish adult.

nonbreeding

nonbreeding

ID: stocky body; greenish black crown; chestnut face and neck; white foreneck and belly; bluish gray back and wings shaded with iridescent green; relatively short, yellow-green legs; bill dark above and greenish below; short tail. *Breeding male:* bright orange legs. *Immature:* heavy streaking along neck and underparts; dark brown upperparts.
Size: *L* 15–22 in; *W* 26 in.
Status: common summer resident in the eastern two-thirds of Texas and uncommon in El Paso Co. and Hudspeth Co.; rare winter resident along the coast and in the Lower Rio Grande Valley.
Habitat: marshes, lakes and canals; mangroves.

Nesting: nests singly or in small, loose groups; male begins and female completes a stick platform in a tree or shrub, usually near water; pair incubates 3–5 pale blue-green to green eggs for 19–21 days; feeds young by regurgitation.
Feeding: slowly stalks or stands and waits; stabs prey with bill; eats mostly small fish.
Voice: generally silent; loud *skow* alarm call.
Similar Species: *Night-herons* (pp. 100–01): juveniles much larger, with brownish plumage and white-streaked or spotted upperparts. *Least Bittern* (p. 91): buffy yellow shoulder patches, sides and flanks.
Best Sites: any state park, wildlife management area or national wildlife refuge along the coast; eastern wooded areas with water.

BLACK-CROWNED NIGHT-HERON

Nycticorax nycticorax

When dusk's long shadows shroud the marshes and the cricket frog's clicking fills the air, Black-crowned Night-Herons arrive to hunt in the marshy waters. Crouching motionless, they use their large, light-sensitive eyes to spot prey lurking in the shallows. They remain alongside water until morning, when they flap off to treetop roosts. Not entirely nocturnal, they may also forage during daylight hours, especially when nesting. • Young night-herons, both this species and its Yellow-crowned cousin, are commonly seen around large cattail marshes in fall. Both species are medium-sized herons with streaked juvenile plumage reminiscent of an American Bittern. The Black-crowned Night-Heron is the stockier species, with a short, thick neck, short legs and a hunched posture. • *Nycticorax*, meaning "night raven," refers to this night-heron's loud call: a single *quock!* that is often heard as the bird flies to and from roosting or feeding areas.

immature

breeding

ID: stocky body; black cap and back; white cheek, foreneck and underparts; gray neck and wings; dull yellow legs; stout, black bill; large, red eyes. *Breeding:* 2 white plumes trail down from crown. *Juvenile:* lightly streaked underparts; brown upperparts with white flecking; yellowish bill. *In flight:* only tips of feet project beyond tail.

Size: *L* 23–26 in; *W* 3½ ft.

Status: common coastal resident; uncommon to locally common summer resident in nearly all inland areas; uncommon local winter resident inland.

Habitat: various wetlands, although most common in fresh water.

Nesting: colonial; in a tree or shrub; male gathers nest material and female builds a platform of twigs lined with finer materials; pair incubates 3–4 pale green eggs for 21–26 days.

Feeding: often at dusk; patient stand-and-wait predator; stabs for fish, crustaceans, amphibians and other aquatic prey.

Voice: deep, guttural *quock!*

Similar Species: *Yellow-crowned Night-Heron* (p. 101): rare inland; juvenile resembles juvenile Black-crowned but back is mostly brown with smaller white spots; wholly black bill; legs extend farther beyond tail in flight. *American Bittern* (p. 90): similar to juvenile Black-crowned Night-Heron but larger; black "mustache"; rarely seen in open; never in flocks.

Best Sites: Sea Rim SP; Galveston Island SP; Sheldon Lake SP; Goose Island SP.

YELLOW-CROWNED NIGHT-HERON

Nyctanassa violacea

Although night-herons are named for their habit of hunting from dusk until dawn, the Yellow-crowned Night-Heron also hunts during daylight hours. Its movements are slow and nearly imperceptible until it strikes—then, with a sudden lunge, it captures its prey. • Unlike the Black-crowned, which relies primarily on fish, the Yellow-crowned specializes in catching crustaceans. This solitary hunter is often seen standing quietly along a beach or among mangrove roots as it waits for a ghost crab or fiddler crab to pass by. When a crab is captured, its legs are removed, and then the body is swallowed whole. • To catch up on sleep and replenish energy reserves, Yellow-crowned Night Herons roost safely in the treetops.

breeding

immature

ID: black head; white cheeks and crown, yellowish forehead; stout, black bill with pale base to lower mandible; slate gray neck and body; yellow legs. *Breeding:* long, white head plumes extend down back of neck. *Juvenile:* brown plumage with white spotting; all-black bill; green legs. *In flight:* legs extend well beyond tail.
Size: *L* 24 in; *W* 3½ ft.
Status: uncommon to locally common summer resident from east Texas west to about Val Verde Co. and north to Lubbock; locally common winter resident in the lower coastal region and occasionally appears inland.
Habitat: beaches, mudflats and mangroves; less commonly inland at swamps and springs.

Nesting: singly or in colonies, occasionally with other wading birds; in a shrub or tree; builds a platform above the ground or water; pair incubates 2–4 pale bluish green eggs for 21–25 days; pair raises the young.
Feeding: stands and waits or engages in slow, methodical walking or wading; eats primarily crabs, crayfish and fish.
Voice: high, short *woc* call.
Similar Species: *Black-crowned Night-Heron* (p. 100): feet barely project beyond tail in flight; juvenile is similar to juvenile Yellow-crowned, but back and wing coverts have larger white spots and bill is mostly yellow. *American Bittern* (p. 90): similar to juvenile Yellow-crowned Night-Heron, but with black streak from bill to shoulder and lighter tan overall.
Best Sites: Sea Rim SP; Anahuac NWR; High Island sanctuaries; Brazos Bend SP; Goose Island SP.

WHITE IBIS

Eudocimus albus

Often found with herons or shorebirds, White Ibises congregate on the coastline from April to November, rhythmically probing the mud for crabs or crayfish. These highly nomadic birds commute between nesting and feeding areas in long, cohesive lines or V-patterns. • Once one of North America's most plentiful wading birds, the White Ibis has declined from historic levels. Whereas ancient Egyptians worshipped ibises and Asian masters immortalized them in art, in the West they have been slaughtered as a game species or as vermin. However, ibises do not threaten commercial crayfish farms, because they also take a variety of other shellfish, insects and small vertebrates. • Breeding is heavily dependent on the rainy season of May and June, when freshwater pools form, a necessity for feeding salt-sensitive young. At this time, "bachelor parties" of hopeful males are commonly seen preening, soaring in circles or performing graceful acrobatics. A pair forms when a female accepts a male's stick offering. Nesting ibises are sensitive to disturbance, so do not enter colonies during the breeding season.

ID: white body; black wing tips; red face and legs; long, down-curved, red bill. *Juvenile:* brown upperparts with white rump; orange face and bill; dull orange legs; streaked neck and breast; white belly; gradual transition to adult plumage.
Size: *L* 22 in; *W* 3 ft.

Status: common coastal resident; breeder inland in eastern Texas; postbreeding wanderer statewide; very rare winter visitor throughout much of the breeding range.
Habitat: estuaries, mangroves and swamps; flooded agricultural fields and roadsides.
Nesting: colonial; in mangroves, thickets or forested swamps; nests from ground level up to 15 ft; nest is a platform of sticks, cordgrass or reeds; pair incubates 2–4 brown-splotched, buff or bluish eggs for 21–22 days; pair cares for the young.

Feeding: probes for fish, crustaceans or worms; looks for insects in fields.
Voice: mostly silent; muffled *hunk-hunk-hunk* alarm or flight call.
Similar Species: *Glossy Ibis* (p. 103): all-dark plumage; thinner bill. *Long-billed Curlew* (p. 159): mottled, brown plumage; finer bill; restricted to saline habitats; never in flocks.
Best Sites: Hornsby Bend (Austin); Bear Creek Pioneer Park (Houston); Sea Rim SP; Anahuac NWR; Galveston Island SP.

GLOSSY IBIS

Plegadis falcinellus

Originally restricted to the Old World, the Glossy Ibis is thought to have colonized North America in the early 1800s. Rare until the 1930s, this largish wading bird is still expanding its range on the continent. Like the Cattle Egret several decades later, the Glossy Ibis probably used the trade winds to fly westward from Africa and colonize the West Indies and then the Southeast. In eastern Texas, the Glossy Ibis is a local and increasing permanent resident. • Glossy Ibises reach their abundance in the Coastal Plain, where small flocks forage among rice plantings or in freshwater marshes. • This species and the White-faced Ibis present one of the more difficult field identification problems—they are virtually indistinguishable in the nonbreeding plumage.

breeding

breeding

ID: dark plumage; thin, downcurved, yellowish to brownish bill; dark facial skin bordered by 2 bluish stripes. *Breeding:* chestnut head, neck and sides; green and purple iridescence on upperparts. *Nonbreeding:* white streaks on grayish brown head and neck. *In flight:* fully extended neck; hunchbacked appearance; flocks fly in lines or V-formations.
Size: *L* 22–25 in; *W* 3 ft.
Status: rare to locally uncommon resident in the upper and central coastal regions, increasing in numbers inland in the state's eastern half and found upriver to El Paso.

Habitat: primarily freshwater marshes, swamps and lakes; flooded agricultural fields; less commonly in estuaries.
Nesting: in a mixed colony; over water, in a shrub or tree; builds a bulky platform of sticks; pair incubates 3–4 pale blue or green eggs for about 21 days.
Feeding: probes bill into mud or sand; eats crayfish, fish, reptiles, amphibians and insects.
Voice: generally silent away from colonies; series of nasal moans or quacks.
Similar Species: *White Ibis* (p. 102): juvenile has brown upperparts, white rump, white belly and orange bill. *White-faced Ibis* (p. 104): red eyes (dark on juvenile); breeding bird has reddish face with white border and redder legs.
Best Sites: in appropriate habitat from Jefferson Co. to Calhoun Co.

WHITE-FACED IBIS

Plegadis chihi

The White-faced Ibis inhabits large wetlands of interior western North America. It is perhaps most at home in the expansive reedbeds and muddy shallows of wildlife refuges and in flooded croplands. With long legs, slender toes and a downcurved bill, this bird is well adapted to life in the marsh. It forages in wet or pooled meadows and reed-fringed muddy shorelines, picking food from the saturated soil. • Disappearing wetlands and heavy pesticide use in rice fields have taken their toll on White-faced Ibises, and populations are declining. Ibises require high-quality marshes for nesting and, like most other colonial birds of similar habitat, they abandon disrupted or altered breeding sites. • Ibises fly rapidly, readily traversing the miles that may separate secluded nesting colonies and outlying feeding locations. White-faced Ibises tend to stick to traditional migration flyways, so they may be common in some regions but scarcely known a few miles away.

breeding

breeding

ID: slender; long, downcurved bill; dark red eyes. *Breeding:* dark chestnut overall, with iridescent, greenish lower back and wing coverts; narrow strip of white feathers borders naked red facial patch; rich red legs. *Nonbreeding:* grayish legs; brownish overall with less distinct greenish gloss. *In flight:* outstretched neck and long, downcurved bill visible at long range.
Size: *L* 19–26 in; *W* 3 ft.
Status: common coastal resident and local breeder in eastern Texas; migrant postbreeding wanderer statewide.
Habitat: marshes, lake edges, mudflats, rice fields, wet pastures and irrigation ditches.
Nesting: colonial; in bulrushes or other emergent vegetation; deep cup nest of coarse materials is lined with fine plant matter; pair incubates 3–4 bluish green eggs for about 22 days.

Feeding: probes and gleans soil and shallow water for aquatic invertebrates, amphibians and other small vertebrates.
Voice: generally quiet; occasionally gives a series of low, ducklike quacks.
Similar Species: *Glossy Ibis* (p. 103): dark eyes; dark face with pale blue lines; darker legs. *White Ibis* (p. 102): immature has brown body with white abdomen. *Herons* and *egrets* (pp. 90–101): bill not thick-based or downcurved.
Best Sites: Sea Rim SP; Anahuac NWR; Galveston Island SP; Aransas NWR; Laguna Atascosa NWR.

ROSEATE SPOONBILL

Platalea ajaja

One of the crown jewels of the Texas coast, the Roseate Spoonbill is a large, flamboyant wading bird. It sports a shocking pink body, scarlet shoulders, orange tail and featherless, greenish head. Of the world's six species of spoonbills, the Roseate is unique in having colored plumage—all other spoonbills are white. Another peculiarity is its unfeathered head in adult plumage. • The Roseate Spoonbill engages in an odd and unexplained behavior called "sky-gazing," in which a bird momentarily cranes its neck and points its bill skyward when another spoonbill passes overhead. • These exotic-looking birds were hunted almost to extinction in the 1800s, when plume hunters marketed the rosy wings as fashionable fans. Fewer than 200 spoonbills remained in Texas in 1920! Fortunately, enough of the birds survived among the thick mangroves of Texas and the Gulf Coast for populations to rebuild. • Spoonbills forage by sweeping their uniquely-shaped bills back and forth in shallow water.

ID: pink plumage; long, spoon-shaped bill; white neck and back; unfeathered, greenish head; red shoulders; orange tail. *Juvenile:* mostly white; pale pink wings; white-feathered head.
Size: *L* 32 in; *W* 4–4½ ft.
Status: locally common resident in the coastal regions, with reduced numbers in winter; rare to uncommon postbreeding wanderer to most areas east of the Pecos R.
Habitat: estuaries and bays; mangrove swamps, coastal islands; flooded agricultural fields.

Nesting: colonial; usually above ground or water in a mangrove, shrub or low tree; male brings sticks and vegetation for female to construct a bulky platform nest; pair incubates 2–3 whitish eggs for 23–24 days; pair raises the young.
Feeding: sweeps bill back and forth in shallow water to capture fish, crustaceans, mollusks and other aquatic animals.
Voice: generally silent.
Similar Species: *Wood Stork* (p. 106): white overall; dark flight feathers; sickle-shaped bill. *Greater Flamingo:* accidental in Texas; pink overall; extremely long neck and legs; unique bill shape and foraging posture.
Best Sites: Sea Rim SP; Galveston Island SP; Brazoria NWR; Aransas NWR; Padre Island National Seashore.

WOOD STORK

Mycteria americana

A striking inhabitant of cypress swamps, the Wood Stork is the only stork regularly found in North America. It is protected nationwide as an endangered species. Because this huge wading bird has specific habitat needs, it is considered an indicator species. Monitoring one or more indicator species allows scientists to judge the overall state of an ecosystem without untangling its intricate details. In other words, a change in the size or the health of the Wood Stork population could indicate a change in the environment. • The Wood Stork was once a breeding species in Texas, but all of the current birds appear as postbreeding dispersers, mainly juveniles, probably from eastern Mexico.

ID: slightly down-curved, large, dark bill; white plumage with black flight feathers and tail; unfeathered, blackish head and neck. *Juvenile:* yellow bill; feathered head and neck. *In flight:* often soars in flocks.

Size: *L* 3–3½ ft; *W* 5–5½ ft.

Status: endangered (USFWS); uncommon to locally common postbreeding wanderer from Mexico to the coastal regions and inland reservoirs of central and east Texas, and less common in the northern areas.

Habitat: freshwater ponds and marshes, cypress swamps, ponds and mangroves; flooded agricultural fields.

Nesting: does not nest in Texas.

Feeding: sweeps partly open bill back and forth in shallow water while wading, shutting it quickly upon contact with prey; also forages for fish, reptiles, amphibians and crustaceans.

Voice: generally silent.

Similar Species: *American White Pelican* (p. 84): large, yellow bill evident in flight but legs inconspicuous. *Whooping Crane* (p. 141): much rarer; larger; white-feathered head with red crown; white secondary feathers and tail; often forages in uplands. *Great Egret* (p. 93): all white plumage; straight bill.

Best Sites: unpredictable; may appear for extended periods in shallow coastal waters or on inland reservoirs, ponds and river flats.

BLACK VULTURE

Coragyps atratus

Until recently, American vultures were thought to be related to hawks and other raptors, but recent examination of the genetic structure, anatomical features and behaviors of vultures shows that they are more closely related to storks. The two species of vultures found in North America are common to abundant permanent residents virtually throughout Texas. The Black Vulture is arguably the less abundant species. • Both of our vultures are large, black soaring birds that feed primarily on carrion, which usually consists of road-killed armadillos and other animals. Unlike the Turkey Vulture, the Black Vulture does not have a well-developed sense of smell. Instead, the Black Vulture relies on its eyesight to spot prey, sometimes resorting to following Turkey Vultures to a meal. • Despite the abundance and wide range of Black Vultures and Turkey Vultures in Texas, few birders have been fortunate to find a nest here. Although communal and conspicuous otherwise, vultures become secretive when nesting, hiding their nests in dense undergrowth, uprooted trees or shallow caves.

ID: black body with silvery primary feathers; short, broad tail; unfeathered, grayish head.
Size: *L* 25 in; *W* 4½ ft.
Status: common resident eastward from the Pecos R. and uncommon in the Panhandle and the Big Bend region; fewer birds remain in winter in the northern parts of the range.
Habitat: *Foraging:* over open country. *Roosting* and *nesting:* forested areas.
Nesting: on the ground, often under saw palmettos; no nest is built; pair incubates 1–3 pale grayish eggs with brown markings for 28–32 days.
Feeding: mostly carrion; also eats discarded human food.
Voice: generally silent.
Similar Species: *Turkey Vulture* (p. 108): red head; dark wing linings and light flight feathers; longer, narrower wings and tail; usually holds wings in shallow "V."
Best Sites: over open country, especially pastures and rangelands; best seen coming from winter roosts.

TURKEY VULTURE

Cathartes aura

Turkey Vultures are intelligent, playful and social birds. Groups live and roost together in large trees. Some roost sites are over a century old and have been used by the same vulture family for several generations. • Turkey Vultures are unmatched at using updrafts and thermals—they can tease lift from the slightest pocket of rising air and patrol the skies when other soaring birds are grounded. Pilots have reported vultures soaring at 20,000 feet. • A vulture's bill and feet are much less powerful than those of eagles, hawks or falcons, which kill live prey. It may appear grotesque, but the featherless, red head allows the bird to stay relatively clean while feeding on messy carcasses. • Turkey Vultures are renowned for their highly developed sense of smell. U.S. engineers once located gas pipelines leaks by adding a substance with a carrion-like scent and then watching where Turkey Vultures gathered.

ID: black body with paler flight feathers; featherless, red head; longish, slender tail. *Juvenile:* gray head. *In flight:* head appears small; dark wing linings and light flight feathers; holds wings in shallow "V"; rocks from side to side when soaring.
Size: *L* 26–32 in; *W* 5½–6 ft.
Status: common resident statewide; less common in the northern areas and virtually absent from the Panhandle and much of the Trans-Pecos in winter.
Habitat: *Foraging:* over open country. *Roosting* and *nesting:* forested areas.

Nesting: on the ground, often under saw palmettos; no nest is built; pair incubates 2 white eggs blotched with reddish brown for 38–41 days; feeds young by regurgitation.
Feeding: solely carrion, often road-killed mammals, especially nine-banded armadillos.
Voice: generally silent; occasional hisses or grunts if threatened.
Similar Species: *Black Vulture* (p 107): shorter, rounded wings with bold silver tips; short, rounded tail; gray head. *Golden Eagle* (p. 126) and *Bald Eagle* (p. 113): less contrast between wing linings and flight feathers; hold wings flat in flight; do not rock when soaring; heads more visible in flight.
Best Sites: over open country such as pastures and rangelands; best seen coming from winter roosts.

OSPREY

Pandion haliaetus

One of the most widely distributed birds, the Osprey occurs on all continents except for Antarctica. It feeds nearly exclusively on fish and is often called "Fish Hawk." • The large, powerful Osprey is almost always found near water. This bird often hovers in the air while hunting for fish, its dark eye line blocking the sun's glare off the water. Once a fish is spotted, the Osprey folds its wings and hurls itself downward in a dramatic headfirst dive toward the target. An instant before striking the water, it flips upright and thrusts its feet forward, often striking the water with a tremendous splash. The Osprey has specialized feet for gripping slippery prey—two toes point forward, two point backward, and all four are covered with spines.

ID: dark brown upperparts; white underparts; dark eye line; yellow eyes; light crown; fine, dark "necklace" (may be absent on male). *In flight:* long wings held in shallow "M"; dark "wrist" patches; banded, brown and white tail.
Size: *L* 22–25 in; *W* 4 ½–6 ft.
Status: rare to uncommon migrant statewide; rare summer resident and winter resident along the coast and up the Rio Grande to Falcon Reservoir and inland on the reservoirs of east Texas; rarely nests in Texas, in Nacogdoches Co.

Habitat: lakes and slowly flowing rivers and streams.
Nesting: on a treetop, usually near water; may also use a specially made platform, utility pole or tower up to 100 ft high; massive stick nest is reused over many years; pair incubates 2–4 yellowish, blotched eggs for about 38 days; pair feeds the young, but the male hunts more.
Feeding: dramatic, feet-first dives into the water; fish, averaging 2 lbs, make up almost all of the diet.
Voice: series of melodious ascending whistles: *chewk-chewk-chewk;* also an often-heard *kip-kip-kip.*
Similar Species: *Bald Eagle* (p. 113): immature is larger, always has some black on body, holds its wings flatter and has larger bill with yellow base and yellow legs.
Best Sites: along the coast and on inland reservoirs, especially in winter.

SWALLOW-TAILED KITE
Elanoides forficatus

A subfamily of hawks with very long, narrow wings and tails, kites can soar or glide for great distances with little effort. Three kite species regularly occur in Texas. • Powerful, swept-back wings and a long, forked tail give the Swallow-tailed Kite incredible maneuverability. This raptor's acrobatics and elegant, black and white plumage make it the favorite of many Texas birders. • The Swallow-tailed Kite migrates early, often passing through between March and May and departing for South American wintering grounds in late summer. Because of wetland drainage and habitat loss, this kite, once found as far north as the Great Lakes, now has a breeding range confined to the Deep South. In 1989, after a 75-year absence from Texas, several birds returned to nest in the densely forested swamps north of Hampshire; the species has since become established throughout much of southeast Texas.

Nesting: in a tall tree (often a pine or cypress); builds a platform of sticks lined with lichens and moss; pair incubates 3–4 brown-blotched, white eggs for 28–31 days.
Feeding: forages aerially, plucking large insects (especially dragonflies) and small vertebrates (tree frogs, small snakes, nestling birds) out of the air or off foliage; often eats prey in flight.
Voice: generally silent except around nest or roost; shrill *klee-klee-klee* call.
Similar Species: bold black and white plumage and long swallow tail generally unmistakable. *Magnificent Frigatebird* (p. 89): juvenile is larger, has long bill, always has some black on underparts and favors island mangroves and coastal and offshore waters.
Best Sites: *Breeding:* Liberty Co. between Liberty and Dayton. *In migration:* Smith Point (Chambers Co.); Hazel Bazemore CP (Corpus Christi).

ID: white body; black back and wings; long, deeply forked, black tail. *In flight:* long, slender wings; white underwing linings with black flight feathers.

Size: *L* 23 in; *W* 4 ft.
Status: rare migrant east of the Pecos R. and south of the Panhandle; rare local nester in extreme southeastern Texas.
Habitat: open woodlands, cypress swamps and riparian forests. *Foraging:* over most habitats.

WHITE-TAILED KITE

Elanus leucurus

The White-tailed Kite, formerly known as "Black-shouldered Kite," forages for small mammals, such as cotton rats, shrews and small rabbits. It exhibits swings in abundance, with natural cycles fluctuating along with the rodent populations. In the 20th century, persecution nearly extirpated this kite from the U.S. It has recently made a strong comeback, perhaps partially as a result of the introduction of the house mouse, a readily available food source. • The White-tailed Kite is an uncommon to common resident in the eastern third of Texas. During winter, White-tailed Kites occasionally gather in southern Texas at communal roosts that can contain over 100 kites. In 1986, after an 80-year absence, White-tailed Kites returned to Texas to breed.

ID: gray back and wings with black shoulders; white head with gray crown and nape; red eyes; white underparts; gray tail with white outer feathers. *Juvenile:* "scaly" brown back, nape and crown; brown breast streaking. *In flight:* white underwings with black "wrist" marks; white tail; buoyant flapping; hovers with body held at steep angle.
Size: *L* 15–17 in; *W* 3–3½ ft.
Status: uncommon to locally common resident in the Coastal Plain and South Texas Brush Country; summer resident north through the southern half of central and east Texas.

Habitat: pastures with scattered trees; wet prairie.
Nesting: in a shrub or tree; pair build a bulky stick platform lined with grass; female incubates 3–4 brown-blotched, creamy white eggs for 26–32 days.
Feeding: flies slowly over grassland, often hovering; drops to ground feet first to capture prey, primarily small mammals.
Voice: generally silent away from nest; shrill *keep-keep-keep* call.
Similar Species: *Mississippi Kite* (p. 112): gray shoulders and underparts; black tail; favors woodlands and riparian areas. *Northern Harrier* (p. 114): conspicuous white rump; gray or brown shoulders; does not hover.
Best Sites: Sabine Woods Bird Sanctuary (Jefferson Co.); Brazoria NWR; Laguna Atascoa NWR; Santa Ana NWR.

MISSISSIPPI KITE

Ictinia mississippiensis

The Mississippi Kite catches flying insects on the wing or hawks them out of the air and often eats them in flight. Occasional acrobatic aerial pursuits end in the capture of larger prey, including bats, swallows and swifts. • This sociable woodland inhabitant relies on the protection of tall trees for nesting and nighttime roosting but requires adjacent open areas for hunting. • In fall, large flocks of Mississippi Kites funnel through Texas and Mexico en route to wintering grounds in southern South America. They typically arrive back in Texas to breed in May. Traditionally restricted to the southern states, these raptors seem to be expanding their breeding range, with sightings as far north as New England.

ID: dark gray back, wings and underparts; pale head; dark gray; black tail. *Male:* paler head and nape. *Juvenile:* dark brownish upperparts; underparts heavily marked with rufous; banded tail. *In flight:* gray below, with darker tail and wing tips; long wings and tail.
Size: *L* 14 in; *W* 3 ft.
Status: common breeding resident of the Panhandle and Rolling Plains from April to September and rare to locally uncommon in the Trans-Pecos, the Pineywoods and parts of the upper coast region; uncommon to common migrant statewide.
Habitat: deciduous or mixed woodlands; riparian areas.

Nesting: in a tall tree; pair constructs a flimsy stick platform lined with leaves; pair incubates 2 bluish white eggs for 30–32 days.
Feeding: plucks insects out of the air or small invertebrates from foliage.
Voice: generally silent; *kee-kew, kew-kew* alarm call; fledgling gives an emphatic *three-beers* call.
Similar Species: *White-tailed Kite* (p.111): black shoulders; white underparts and tail; black "wrist" patches on underwings; favors pastures with scattered trees or wet prairie. *Swallow-tailed Kite* (p. 110): black and white plumage; long, deeply forked tail. *Peregrine Falcon* (p. 131): dark "helmet;" finely barred undersides. *Northern Harrier* (p. 114): male is rare in summer, has white rump, does not hover and favors open habitats.
Best Sites: Buffalo Lake NWR; Abilene SP; Lake Mineral Wells SP; Brazos Bend SP. *In migration:* Hazel Bazemore CP (Corpus Christi).

BALD EAGLE

Haliaeetus leucocephalus

immature

The Bald Eagle, a symbol of freedom, longevity and strength, became the emblem of the U.S. in 1872. • Two subspecies of Bald Eagles occur in Texas. A wintering population (*H.l. alascanus*) is found throughout the northern two-thirds of the state, and a breeding population (subspecies *H.l. leucocephalus*), estimated at 140 pairs, inhabits the eastern third of the state. Nesting activities begin in December, and most eggs hatch in February. By April, the young fledge, and most leave the state. • Beginning in the late 1940s, populations of eagles and other fish-eating species suffered dramatic declines that were linked to DDT poisoning. The banning of DDT has allowed eagle populations to recover in Texas from a low of about 15 pair in the 1970s. • Bald Eagles molt into their adult plumage in their fourth year, only then acquiring the characteristic white head and tail.

ID: white head and tail; dark brown body; yellow bill and feet. *Juvenile:* variable amounts of white mottling on upperparts, underwings and undertail; mostly dark bill; acquires adult plumage in 4th year. *In flight:* huge, dark bird that soars on broad, flat wings.
Size: *L* 30–43 in; *W* 5½–8 ft.
Status: threatened species (USFWS); locally uncommon resident on the Coastal Plain and eastern third of the state; uncommon to locally common migrant and winter resident east of the Pecos R. and north of the Lower Rio Grande Valley.

Habitat: *Foraging:* over large water bodies. *Nesting:* close to water.
Nesting: in a large live pine or cypress; massive nest is used for several years; pair incubates 1–3 white eggs for 34–36 days.
Feeding: eats primarily fish and waterbirds; frequently pirates fish from Ospreys.
Voice: thin, weak squeal or gull-like cackle.
Similar Species: adult is distinctive. *Golden Eagle* (p. 126): dark overall, except for golden nape; immature has prominent white patches on wings and base of tail.
Best Sites: *Winter:* Lake Meredith (Hutchinson Co.); Fairfield Lake SP; Brazos Bend SP; Lake Buchanan (Llano Co.); Lake Texoma SP.

NORTHERN HARRIER

Circus cyaneus

With its prominent white rump and distinctive slightly upturned wings, the Northern Harrier may be the easiest raptor to identify in flight. Unlike other midsized birds, this raptor often flies close to the ground, cruising low over fields, meadows and marshes, relying on sudden surprise attacks to capture prey. Owl-like parabolic facial discs allow the Northern Harrier to hunt by sound when prey is hidden in the vegetation. • Along with the loss of wetland habitat, the North American population of harriers has declined in recent years. However, these raptors are common winter residents in Texas and very rarely breed in the Panhandle or along the coast. • The Northern Harrier was once known as "Marsh Hawk" in North America, and it is still called "Hen Harrier" in Britain. Britain's Royal Air Force was so impressed by this bird's maneuverability that it named its Harrier aircraft after this bird.

ID: *Male:* gray upperparts; white underparts with faint rusty streaking; black tail bands. *Female:* dark brown upperparts; buff underparts streaked with dark brown. *Juvenile:* rich brown upperparts; head and upper breast streaked with brown. *In flight:* long wings and tail; black wing tips; conspicuous white rump; flies low over marshes.

Size: *L* 16–24 in; *W* 3½–4 ft.

Status: common migrant and uncommon to locally common winter resident statewide; has bred locally statewide, more regularly in the Panhandle.

Habitat: open habitats, such as fields, pastures and marshes.

Nesting: on the ground; usually in tall vegetation or on a raised mound; shallow depression is lined with grass, sticks and cattails; female incubates 4–6 bluish white eggs for 30–32 days.

Feeding: flies low, often skimming the top of vegetation; eats rats, small rabbits, snakes and birds such as the Red-winged Blackbird.

Voice: generally silent; high-pitched *ke-ke-ke-ke-ke-ke* near the nest.

Similar Species: *Red-tailed Hawk* (p. 123): brown rump; shorter, wider tail.

Best Sites: may occur on any open pasture, grassland or marsh.

SHARP-SHINNED HAWK

Accipiter striatus

Accipiters are small to medium-sized woodland hawks that prey mostly on birds. They have short, rounded wings and long, rudderlike tails to help maneuver quickly to chase and capture their feathered quarry. After a successful hunt, the Sharp-shinned Hawk often perches on a favorite "plucking post," grasping its meal in its razor-sharp talons. • The Sharp-shinned Hawk breeds over much of North America and winters across the continental U.S., the West Indies and Central America. It is an uncommon migrant and winter resident in Texas and often stakes out backyards with bird feeders to prey on the doves and other birds that frequent the feeders. • Raptors are an example of reverse sexual dimorphism, in which the females are larger than the males.

immature

ID: blue-gray upperparts; pale face with dark crown and nape; red eyes; white underparts heavily barred with orange. *Juvenile:* brown upperparts; yellow eyes; white underparts heavily streaked with brown. *In flight:* short, rounded wings; long, square-tipped tail; flap-and-glide flight.
Size: *Male: L* 10–12 in; *W* 20–24 in. *Female: L* 12–14 in; *W* 24–28 in.
Status: uncommon to common migrant and winter resident statewide; breeds at scattered locations.
Habitat: forages over any wooded or semi-wooded habitats, even suburban yards.
Nesting: builds a stick nest in a live tree or may remodel an abandoned crow nest; female incubates 4–5 brown-blotched, bluish white eggs for 30–35 days; male feeds the female during incubation.
Feeding: chases or dives at small to medium-sized landbirds.
Voice: silent except around nest; gives an intense *kik-kik-kik-kik.*
Similar Species: *Cooper's Hawk* (p. 116): larger; more rounded tail tip has broader terminal band; crown is darker than nape and back. *American Kestrel* (p. 128): long, pointed wings; 2 dark facial stripes; typically seen in open country. *Merlin* (p. 129): pointed wings; rapid wingbeats; 1 dark facial stripe; brown streaking on buff underparts; dark eyes.
Best Sites: *Winter:* any park with sufficient open woodlands, often in exurban and suburban areas. *Migration:* Smith Point (Chambers Co.), Hazel Bazemore CP (Corpus Christi).

COOPER'S HAWK

Accipiter cooperii

Larger and heavier than the Sharp-shinned Hawk, the Cooper's Hawk glides silently along swamps and flood plains, using surprise and speed to snatch its prey from midair. The female can seize and decapitate birds as large as a chicken, which has earned this bird the name "Chicken Hawk." • This medium-sized raptor is now protected by law in some states, and it is increasing in numbers and slowly recolonizing former habitats in the region. • Distinguishing the Cooper's Hawk from the Sharp-shinned Hawk is challenging. In flight, the Cooper's has a shallower, stiffer-winged flight, whereas the Sharpie has deeper wingbeats with more bending in the wings. The Cooper's tail often looks more rounded. As well, the Cooper's Hawk can be seen perching on fence posts, poles and tree branches, whereas the Sharp-shin perches almost exclusively on tree branches.

immature

rare to uncommon summer resident in much of Texas except the High Plains, far west Trans-Pecos and the north-central and southeastern areas.

Habitat: *Foraging:* over any wooded or semiwooded habitats, even suburban yards.

Nesting: in a fork of a tree; nest consists of sticks and twigs; may reuse an abandoned squirrel nest; female incubates 4–5 bluish white eggs for 30–36 days.

Feeding: chases or dives at medium-sized landbirds, often following the target bird into vegetation.

Voice: silent except around nest; fast *cac-cac-cac-cac.*

Similar Species: *Sharp-shinned Hawk* (p. 115): rare during summer; smaller; square tail tip; dark nape. *American Kestrel* (p. 128): long, pointed wings; 2 black facial stripes; typically seen in open country, often perched on powerlines. *Merlin* (p. 129): 1 dark facial stripe; brown streaking on buff underparts; dark eyes; pointed wings; rapid wingbeats.

Best Sites: *Winter:* in any park with sufficient open woodlands; may occur in exurban and suburban areas year-round. *Migration:* Smith Point (Chambers Co.), Hazel Bazemore CP (Corpus Christi).

ID: long, straight, heavily barred, rounded tail; dark barring on pale undertail and underwings; squarish head; blue-gray back; red horizontal barring on underparts; red eyes; white terminal tail band. *Immature:* brown overall; dark eyes; vertical brown streaks on breast and belly. *In flight:* short, rounded wings; flap-and-glide flier.

Size: *Male: L* 15–17 in; *W* 27–32 in. *Female: L* 17–19 in; *W* 32–37 in.

Status: uncommon migrant and rare to locally uncommon winter resident statewide;

HARRIS'S HAWK

Parabuteo unicinctus

Harris's Hawks are highly sophisticated, social, cooperative feeders that use different hunting strategies for specific prey. Before each hunt, up to five birds assemble for a hunting "ceremony," sitting motionless on the same perch before commencing the hunt. Depending on the type of prey, the birds may all converge at the same time, or one may flush the animal while the others ambush from other directions. Birds switch off as lead chaser until the exhausted prey is caught. The order of feeding indicates the hierarchy of the social unit, which consists of two to seven hawks. • Nest building begins five weeks before breeding. Only the dominant pair in a social unit breeds; the subordinate "helper" hawks that help defend the nest and feed the young may be immatures up to three years old or lone adults. • The Harris's Hawk is threatened by urban expansion and illegal capture for falconry. • This medium-sized raptor is named after Edward Harris, a friend and benefactor of John James Audubon. *Unicinctus* is Latin for "once girdled," referring to the large black band around the hawk's tail.

ID: dark brown body; chestnut shoulders and thighs; white rump and undertail; tail has thick black band and white tip; yellow legs and beak. *Juvenile:* vertically streaked, white and brown belly. *In flight:* broad wings.
Size: *L*: 17–24 in; *W* 3½ ft.

Status: common resident in the South Texas Brush Country, less common northward through the Trans-Pecos, the southern Edwards Plateau and the South Plains and a vagrant north and east of these areas.
Habitat: desert savanna with saguaro and dead trees appropriately spaced for perch-and-fly hunting; proximity to water is very important.
Nesting: on a saguaro or stable perch; large platform of eucalyptus, ironwood, mesquite or soapberry is lined with cactus pieces and leaves; mostly the female incubates 3–4 white

or bluish-white eggs for 31–36 days; may breed year-round if the spring clutch fails.
Feeding: groups hunt cooperatively using various techniques; eats rabbits, small birds and mammals.
Voice: single long, harsh note; defensive *kah-kah-kah-kah*.
Similar Species: *Red-tailed Hawk* (p. 123) and *Swainson's Hawk* (p. 120): no white rump or rufous shoulder patch.
Best Sites: L.E. Ramey CP (Kingsville); Mitchell L. (San Antonio); Chaparral WMA; Choke Canyon SP; Laguna Atascosa NWR.

RED-SHOULDERED HAWK

Buteo lineatus

Preferring wetter habitats than the closely related Broad-winged Hawk and Red-tailed Hawk, the Red-shouldered Hawk nests in mature trees, usually around river bottoms and in lowland tracts of woods alongside creeks. As spring approaches, this normally quiet hawk forms pair bonds and utters loud, shrieking *key-ah* calls. Be forewarned that Blue Jays and Brown Jays have mastered an impressive impersonation of the Red-shouldered Hawk's calls. • During summer, the dense cover of this medium-sized raptor's forested breeding habitat allows few viewing opportunities. However, during migration, the Red-shouldered Hawk can be found hunting from exposed perches such as telephone poles and fence posts, sometimes up to one-half mile from the nearest stand of trees, and it is often seen perched on powerlines. • If left undisturbed, Red-shouldered Hawks remain faithful to productive nesting sites, returning yearly. After the parents die, one of the young carries on the family nesting tradition.

ID: bold black and white barring on back and wings; rusty or pale grayish head; whitish underparts with bold orange or buffy barring; prominent rusty shoulder patch; banded tail with wider black bars. *Juvenile:* brown upperparts; wide, teardrop-shaped brown streaks on white underparts; shoulder may have faint rusty patch. *In flight:* light and dark barring on underside of flight feathers and tail; white crescent at base of primaries.
Size: *L* 19 in; *W* 3½ ft.
Status: common resident in eastern and central Texas and less common in the Panhandle, the South Plains and the western Edwards Plateau.

Habitat: virtually any wooded or semi-wooded habitat that contains oaks or cypress.
Nesting: in any of various trees; pair builds a bulky nest of sticks and twigs or reuses an old nest; female incubates 2–4 darkly blotched, bluish white eggs for about 33 days.
Feeding: drops down on prey from a perch; eats various animal prey, ranging from insects to snakes, frogs, small mammals and rarely birds.
Voice: *key-ah,* often uttered as a series.
Similar Species: *Broad-winged Hawk* (p. 119): entirely brown wings; wide tail bands.
Best Sites: Tyler SP; Lake Livingston SP; Bear Creek Pioneer Park (Houston); Armand Bayou Nature Center (Harris Co.).

BROAD-WINGED HAWK

Buteo platypterus

Generally shy and secretive, Broad-winged Hawks are best seen during fall migration, when kettles of these buteos funnel through Texas to wintering grounds in Central and South America. In the last weeks of September, tens of thousands of Broad-tailed Hawks can be seen daily at some "hawkwatch" sites. They take advantage of thermals to rise upward and soar, sometimes gliding for hours without flapping. • This medium-sized raptor shuns the open fields and forest clearings favored by other buteos, such as the Red-tailed Hawk, to seclude itself in dense, often wet forests. Its short, broad wings and highly flexible tail help it maneuver in the heavy growth. • Most hunting is done from a high perch with a good view. If flushed from its perch, the Broad-winged Hawk returns and resumes its vigilant search. • Of all raptors, the Broad-winged Hawk is the one most likely to be seen clutching a snake.

dark morph

light morph; juvenile

ID: brown upperparts; broad black and white tail bands; white underparts with heavy rusty barring; broad wings with pointed tips. *Juvenile:* white underparts with teardrop-shaped, dark brown streaking; buff and dark brown tail bands. *In flight:* pale underwings outlined with dark brown.
Size: *L* 14–19 in; *W* 32–39 in.
Status: common to abundant migrant in eastern Texas and rare to uncommon in the west; rare to uncommon summer resident in the east, west to the Balcones Escarpment and to the north-central region.
Habitat: dense mixed and deciduous forests and woodlots. *In migration:* escarpments and shorelines; also uses riparian and deciduous forests and woodland edges.

Nesting: usually in a deciduous tree, often near water, in a crotch 20–40 ft above the ground; builds new bulky stick nest; mostly the female incubates 2–4 brown-spotted, whitish eggs for 28–31 days; pair raises the young.
Feeding: swoops from a perch for small mammals, amphibians, insects and young birds; often hunts from roadside telephone poles in northern areas.
Voice: high-pitched, whistled *peeeo-wee-ee;* generally silent during migration.
Similar Species: *Red-shouldered Hawk* (p. 118): barred upperparts; rusty shoulders; white crescent at base of primaries; juvenile has heavily brown-streaked underparts.
Best Sites: *In migration:* Smith Point (Chambers Co.); Hazel Bazemore CP (Corpus Christi). *Breeding:* Daingerfield SP; Martin Dies, Jr. SP; Huntsville SP.

SWAINSON'S HAWK

Buteo swainsoni

Although the Red-tailed Hawk dominates the skies over much of Texas, the Swainson's Hawk takes center stage where open country far exceeds forests, especially in grassy expanses where ground squirrels are abundant. The Swainson's Hawk breeds largely in western North America; in Texas, this midsized soaring hawk is most common west of Dallas and San Antonio. • The Swainson's Hawk undertakes the longest migration of any Texan raptor: in winter, it travels as far south as the southern tip of South America. Pesticide use on this bird's South American wintering grounds has dealt the population a blow—reminding us that the conservation of migratory species urgently requires international cooperation.

light morph

ID: very small bill. *Light morph:* dark "bib"; white belly; finely barred tail. *Dark morph:* brown overall. *In flight:* long, narrow wings; white wing linings and "bib" contrast with dark flight feathers (light morph) or all-dark below (dark morph); holds wings in conspicuous "V"; fan-shaped tail.
Size: *Male: L* 19–20 in; *W* 4¼ ft.
Female: L 20–22 in; *W* 4¼ ft.
Status: common summer resident in western Texas and expanding eastward, especially in the Coastal Plain; uncommon to abundant migrant statewide, except for the Pineywoods region of east Texas; rare and irregular winter vagrant in coastal areas.
Habitat: grasslands, open fields, oak savanna, croplands, pastures and scattered tree groves in open country. *In migration:* may use mountain ridges or appear at coastal "hawkwatch" sites.

Nesting: often in a solitary tree in an open field; builds a large stick nest or uses an abandoned raptor, crow, raven or magpie nest; repeatedly reuses the same nest; female incubates 2–3 white eggs, lightly speckled or blotched, for about 28–35 days.
Feeding: dives to the ground for voles, mice and ground squirrels; also eats snakes, small birds and large insects, such as grasshoppers and crickets; hawk concentrations may attend outbreaks in crops.
Voice: generally silent; high, weak *keeeaar*.
Similar Species: *Red-tailed Hawk* (p. 123): bulkier overall; larger bill; orange tail; lacks dark chest band; holds wings nearly flat while soaring. *Red-shouldered Hawk* (p. 118): rusty shoulders; underwing linings and barred underparts are reddish in adults; white crescent at base of primaries.
Best Sites: *Breeding:* Lake Meredith NRA; Buffalo Lake NWR; San Angelo SP. *Migration:* Hazel Bazemore CP.

WHITE-TAILED HAWK

Buteo albicaudatus

The White-tailed Hawk is a stately presence in southern Texas skies, meditatively soaring above the coastal grasslands. This thick-bodied, midsized raptor declined in numbers from the 1950s to the 1970s as a result of both habitat loss to expanding agriculture and DDT thinning their eggshells. Brush thinning and the ban on DDT has slowed the decline, but the hawk is still troubled by the overgrazing of grassland. • The White-tailed Hawk has learned that the edges of a brush fire make lucrative hunting grounds, and small mammals that escape their fiery demise may run straight into the talons of a waiting hawk. This hawk is also known to catch large insects in flight. • Giving the illusion of thinner wings, the White-tailed Hawk has four notched wing tips (or "fingers") instead of five, a feature it shares with the Broad-winged Hawk and the Swainson's Hawk.

ID: gray upperparts, including face; all-white underparts; black wings extend beyond tail at rest; gray bill; yellow legs; chestnut shoulder patch. *Immature:* dark barring on lower belly and legs; darker head and back; thinner wings; longer tail. *In flight:* black band on white, fanlike tail.
Size: *L* 21–23 in; *W* 3½–4 ft.
Status: uncommon resident in the Coastal Plains, although less common on the upper coast; rare winter and spring visitor to the Balcones Escarpment and into the Trans-Pecos.
Habitat: savanna, Coastal Plain and semi-arid brush; common around ranches, unless heavily grazed.
Nesting: in a low tree or cactus; stick nest is lined with grass; mostly the female incubates 2–3 white eggs for 29–32 days.

Feeding: hunts from perches in shrubs and trees, diving after prey; eats small mammals, such as rabbits; also takes reptiles, amphibians and small birds.
Voice: high pitched *keee ke-HAA ke-HAA ke-HAA.*
Similar Species: *Swainson's Hawk* (p. 120): dark brown upperparts; white, rufous or brown underparts, often with white face and rufous or brown "bib". *Broad-winged Hawk* (p. 119): dark brown overall; brown undertail coverts; 1 white tail band in flight. *Other hawks* (pp. 114–25): show 5 (not 4) notched primaries in flight.
Best Sites: Attwater's Prairie Chicken NWR; Brazos Bend SP; Aransas NWR; Laguna Atascosa NWR.

121

ZONE-TAILED HAWK

Buteo albonotatus

Lazily soaring and tilting among warm thermal updrafts, the Zone-tailed Hawk holds its wings in a V-shape. This hawk's flight pattern, slightly translucent flight feathers and dark underwing linings are reminiscent of a Turkey Vulture, and these two raptors are often found soaring together. To distinguish the two, watch for the Zone-tailed Hawk's feathered, blackish head, thinly barred flight feathers and black and white tail barring. Feeding strategies can also lend a clue to identity. The Zone-tailed Hawk swoops down to prey on small animals, whereas the vulture scavenges for its prey. This hawk is most often found in canyons and riparian woodlands.

Status: uncommon summer resident in the Trans-Pecos Mts. and rare eastward through the western part of the Edwards Plateau; rare winter visitor from the Rio Grande to the southeastern edge of the Edwards Plateau.
Habitat: open country habitats, including chaparral, desert scrub and grassland, desert mountains, canyons and streamside woodlands.
Nesting: in a tall tree (often a cottonwood or pine) near a cliff or stream and high above the ground; builds a bulky stick platform; both adults incubate 1–3 spotted, pale bluish white eggs for about 35 days.
Feeding: makes swooping attacks from a high perch or from the air for seasonally available small mammals, reptiles, amphibians and birds; may eat carrion.
Voice: alarm call is a long, screaming whistle.
Similar Species: *Turkey Vulture* (p. 108) and *Black Vulture* (p. 107): no barring on wings and tail. *Common Black-Hawk* (p. 446): rare; shorter, broader wings and tail; 1 wide white tail band. *Golden Eagle* (p. 126): much larger; unbarred flight feathers and tail (immature has white at base of tail).
Best Sites: Guadalupe Mountains NP; Davis Mountains SP; Big Bend NP; Black Gap WMA.

ID: dark gray to slate black overall; alternating black and grayish white tail bands; bright yellow legs; black-tipped, yellow bill. *Immature:* more tail bands but with less contrast; white-flecked breast. *In flight:* pale underwing flight feathers with fine dark barring; wings held in "V"; often tilts side-to-side.
Size: *L* 18½–21½ in; *W* 4–4½ ft.

RED-TAILED HAWK

Buteo jamaicensis

"Harlan's Hawk"

North America's most common hawk, the Red-tailed Hawk often uses rising air currents, known as thermals and updrafts, to soar. This hawk is so adept at teasing lift out of air currents that it can fly almost 2 miles during migration without flapping once. On cool days without much lift, this bird saves energy by scanning the fields from a high perch. • During their spring courtship, excited Red-tailed Hawks dive at each other, sometimes locking talons and tumbling through the air together before breaking off to avoid crashing to the ground. • The Red-tailed Hawk's impressive piercing call is often misleadingly paired with the image of an eagle in TV commercials and movies. • This hawk's tail obtains its brick red coloration only upon maturity.

dark morph

and the Lower Rio Grande Valley; common migrant and winter resident statewide.

Habitat: open country with scattered trees.

Nesting: in open pinewoods or at a woodland edge; often in a pine; bulky stick nest is usually augmented each year; pair incubates 2–4 brown-blotched, whitish eggs for 28–35 days; male brings food to the female and nestlings.

Feeding: scans the ground from a tall perch and then captures prey after a short flight; eats mostly rodents.

Voice: powerful, descending scream given year-round.

Similar Species: *Red-shouldered Hawk* (p. 118): reddish shoulders and underparts. *Swainson's Hawk* (p. 120): all-dark back; more pointed wing tips; dark flight feathers and pale (or all-dark) wing linings in flight; holds wings in shallow "V." *Rough-legged Hawk* (p. 125): dark "wrist" patches on underwings; white undertail with broad, dark terminal band.

Best Sites: *Breeding:* in rural or exurban areas with open fields and pastures that have large trees for nesting. *Winter:* roadsides in open country.

ID: mottled, brown wings and back; brown head; white throat; white or pale buff underparts with brown belly band; orange tail (is white, mottled with dark spots, on Harlan's subspecies). *Juvenile:* brown tail with dark bands. *In flight:* white or buffy underwing linings; dark leading edge on pale underwings with faint barring.

Size: *Male: L* 18–23 in; *W* 3½–4½ ft. *Female: L* 20–25 in; *W* 4–5 ft.

Status: common resident in most of Texas but absent from the western High Plains

FERRUGINOUS HAWK

Buteo regalis

Coursing the contours of rolling, grassy hills, circling high above the landscape, or sitting alertly in a barren field, the Ferruginous Hawk favors open country. This large grassland hawk spends much of its time perched low in a tree or on a fencepost, watching for unsuspecting rodents. Hunting from the air, this powerful bird strikes unexpectedly, often swooping at its prey from great heights. • Once considered pests, Ferruginous Hawks were previously shot and poisoned, but, because their diet comprises mostly rabbits, ground squirrels and gophers, they can actually be of service to ranchers and farmers. However, conversion of pristine grasslands and rodent control campaigns have reduced and localized Ferruginous Hawks. • These birds breed primarily on the Great Plains and in the northern Great Basin. Some pairs use nesting platforms that have been built to replace logged trees.

dark morph

light morph

ID: pale flight feathers. *Light morph:* rusty red upperparts; white underparts; dark rusty "leggings"; pale head; rust-tipped, pale tail. *Dark morph:* rare; dark underparts; white tail. *Immature:* white "leggings." *In flight:* pale, rust-marked (light morph) or dark (dark morph) wing linings; holds wings in shallow "V" while soaring.
Size: *L* 22–27 in; *W* 4¾ ft.
Status: rare summer resident in the western Panhandle; locally common winter resident in the western third of Texas, rare to locally uncommon from north-central regions to the Coastal Plain and generally absent from the Pineywoods region.

Habitat: grasslands, open pastures and brushlands with scattered trees.
Nesting: does not nest in Texas.
Feeding: spots prey while soaring or hunts from a low perch or from the ground; eats primarily small rodents; also takes snakes and small birds.
Voice: generally silent; loud, squealing *kaaarr* alarm call, usually dropping at the end.
Similar Species: *Red-tailed Hawk* (p. 123): smaller; darker underparts; dark abdominal belt; orange (adult) or brown (juvenile) tail; raspier call. *Swainson's Hawk* (p. 120): dark flight feathers contrast with light wing linings (dark forms are all dark underneath). *Rough-legged Hawk* (p. 125): dark "wrist" patches; dark-streaked breast; dark brown belly band or dark-streaked belly.
Best Sites: Rita Blanca National Grasslands; Muleshoe NWR; Buffalo Lake NWR.

ROUGH-LEGGED HAWK

Buteo lagopus

Each fall, arctic-nesting Rough-legged Hawks drift south in search of warmer habitat in southern meadows and sage-brush. The irregular annual abundance of these large, bulky hawks in northern Texas results from the interplay of annual reproductive success, small mammal abundance and fluctuations of early winter weather. In years when the number of small mammals on the tundra is high, Rough-legs may produce up to seven young; in lean years, a pair may raise but a single chick.
• Foraging Rough-legged Hawks can easily be identified at great distances, because few other large hawks routinely hover over prey.
• The word *lagopus*, meaning "hare's (or rabbit's) foot," refers to this bird's distinctive feathered feet—an insulating adaptation for survival in cold climates.

*immature,
light morph*

♀

light morph

ID: legs and feet feathered to toes. *Light morph:* white tail with wide, dark subterminal band; wide, dark belly band; darkly streaked breast and head; dark upperparts. *Dark morph:* dark wing linings, head, body and underparts; light flight feathers and undertail; dark subterminal tail band. *Juvenile:* lighter streaking on breast; bold belly band; white at base of upperwing flight feathers. *In flight:* light underwings with dark "wrist" patches; long wings; frequently hovers.
Size: *L* 19–24 in; *W* 4–4¾ ft.
Status: rare to uncommon winter resident in northern Texas and much less common in the southern half.
Habitat: open grasslands, savanna, sage-brush flats, coastal plains, agricultural fields, meadows, pastures and open river valleys.

Nesting: does not breed in Texas.
Feeding: hunts from a perch or from the ground; eats mostly small rodents; occasionally captures birds, amphibians, reptiles and large insects.
Voice: seldom heard in Texas; alarm call is a catlike *kee-eer,* usually dropping at the end.
Similar Species: *Red-tailed Hawk (Harlan's subspecies)* (p. 123): similar to Rough-legged dark morph; white streaks on dark breast; grayish tail lacks dark band. *Other Buteos* (pp. 118–24): no dark "wrist" patches or dark subterminal band on otherwise light tail; rarely hover. *Northern Harrier* (p. 114): slimmer; long tail; facial disc; cruises slowly.
Best Sites: Balmorhea L.; Lake Meredith NRA; Buffalo Lake NWR; Buffalo Springs L. (Lubbock); Benbrook L. (Tarrant Co.).

GOLDEN EAGLE

Aquila chrysaetos

For many centuries, the Golden Eagle has embodied the wonder and wildness of the North American landscape. However, this noble bird became the victim of a lengthy persecution from the late 1800s. It was perceived as a threat to livestock, and bounties were offered, encouraging its shooting and poisoning. Today, the Golden Eagle is protected under the Migratory Bird Act. • The Golden Eagle is more closely related to the *Buteo* hawks than it is to the Bald Eagle. Unlike the Bald Eagle, the Golden Eagle is an active, impressive predator, taking prey as large as foxes, cranes and geese. It can soar high above mountain passes for hours, sometimes stooping at great speeds—150 to 200 miles per hour—for prey or for fun. • This large, western bird of mountainous areas is an unforgettable treat for birders in western Texas. Its migration route along the Rocky Mountains was discovered in 1992.

immature

ID: brown overall; golden tint to neck and head; brown eyes; dark bill; brown tail has grayish white bands; yellow feet; fully feathered legs. *Juvenile:* white tail base; white patch at base of underwing primaries. *In flight:* relatively short neck; long tail; long, large, rectangular wings.
Size: *L* 30–40 in; *W* 6½–7½ ft.
Status: rare to uncommon resident in the Panhandle and much of the Trans-Pecos; very rare to uncommon winter resident statewide, although more common in the western half.
Habitat: semi-open woodlands and fields.

Nesting: usually in a tree in open habitats; builds a huge stick nest, reused for many years; pair incubates 1–2 white eggs for 43–45 days; pair feeds the young.
Feeding: swoops on prey from a soaring flight; eats hares, grouse, rodents, foxes and occasionally young ungulates; often eats carrion.
Voice: generally quiet in winter; thin, weak squeal or gull-like cackle: *kleek-kik-kik-kik* or *kah-kah-kah*.
Similar Species: *Bald Eagle* (p. 113): immature has longer neck, shorter tail and less distinct white underparts in flight. *Turkey Vulture* (p. 108): naked, red head; pale flight feathers; dark wing linings. *Rough-legged Hawk* (p. 125): dark morph has pale flight feathers and white tail base.
Best Sites: Guadalupe Mountains NP; Davis Mountains SP; Big Bend NP; Lake Meredith NRA; Muleshoe NWR.

CRESTED CARACARA

Caracara cheriway

Although the Crested Caracara has the featherless, yellow legs of a chicken, the profile and stature of a hawk and some of the feeding habits of vultures, this large, carrion-eating raptor it is taxonomically classified as a relative of the falcons. Often seen patrolling in pairs over highways during early morning hours in search of fresh roadkill, this odd raptor's weak grasp and naked face are more suited to scavenging than hunting. The Crested Caracara often resorts to piracy—chasing larger vultures away from carrion or harassing larger birds in flight until they disgorge their meal. • Celebrated south of the border as Mexico's national bird, the Crested Caracara is struggling to survive in America. More and more of its natural habitats, the southern grasslands of Texas and the semi-open fields of the Southwest, are plowed, paved or irrigated for agricultural and urban uses. • The caracara's unusual name is derived from a native South American word for its guttural, cackling call.

ID: long, yellow legs; black body; white head; black crest and crown; unfeathered, reddish facial skin; barred, black and white neck. *Juvenile:* brown body; streaked, brown and white neck. *In flight:* white wing tips; white tail with wide, black subterminal band.

Size: *L* 23 in; *W* 4 ft.

Status: uncommon to locally common resident from the South Texas Brush Country north along the southern half of the Edwards Plateau to north-central Texas, and rare to locally uncommon on the upper coastal plain and in the Trans-Pecos.

Habitat: prairies, pastures and other upland grasslands.

Nesting: typically at the top of a cabbage palm; builds a bulky stick nest that may be used over successive years; pair incubates 2–3 heavily blotched, whitish eggs for about 28 days.

Feeding: terrestrial forager; primarily eats carrion along roadsides; also walks through pastures and flips over "cow patties" in search of insects and other invertebrates; may also take small vertebrates.

Voice: seldom-heard harsh, cackling call.

Similar Species: none; plumage and terrestrial habits unique.

Best Sites: Attwater's Prairie Chicken NWR; Brazos Bend SP; Brazoria NWR; Aransas NWR; Laguna Atascosa NWR.

127

AMERICAN KESTREL

Falco sparverius

Common and widespread, the colorful American Kestrel was formerly known as "Sparrow Hawk." Not shy of human activity, it is adaptable to habitat change. This robin-sized falcon has benefited from the grassy rights-of-way created by interstate highways, which provide habitat for prey such as grasshoppers. Watch for it along rural roadways, perched on poles and telephone wires or hovering over agricultural fields, foraging for insects and small mammals. While perched, it often repeatedly lifts its tail. • The American Kestrel is small enough to nest in tree cavities, which help protect defenseless young kestrels from predators. • Studies have shown that the Eurasian Kestrel can detect ultraviolet reflections from rodent urine on the ground. Whether the American Kestrel shares this ability is unclear. • The American Kestrel was the first falcon to be bred by artificial insemination and has aided in studying the effects of pesticides on birds of prey.

ID:
rufous
back barred
with black;
gray crown; white
face with 2 black
stripes; buffy nape
with black patch;
whitish underparts; rufous tail. *Male:* blue wings; underparts spotted with black; bold black subterminal band on tail. *Female:* rufous wings; underparts streaked with rufous; banded rufous and black tail. *In flight:* frequently hovers.
Size: *L* 7½–8 in; *W* 20–24 in.
Status: common migrant and winter resident statewide; uncommon summer resident statewide except on the Edwards Plateau and the Coastal Plain and in the Lower Rio Grande Valley.

Habitat: virtually any open or semiwooded habitat.
Nesting: in a tree cavity (may use a nest box); mostly the female incubates 4–6 finely speckled, white to pale brown eggs for 29–30 days; pair raises the young.
Feeding: swoops from a perch or hovers overhead; eats primarily insects and small vertebrates.
Voice: shrill *killy-killy-killy.*
Similar Species: *Merlin* (p. 129): larger; gray or brown back, wings and tail; single facial stripe; does not hover. *Sharp-shinned Hawk* (p. 115): blue-gray upperparts; no facial stripes; does not hover; flap-and-glide flight.
Best Sites: *Winter:* usually seen along roadsides in open country. *In migration:* Smith Point (Chambers Co.); Hazel Bazemore CP.

MERLIN

Falco columbarius

The Merlin is one of the smallest of the six-regularly-occurring falcons seen in Texas. It breeds in Alaska, most of Canada and parts of the northwestern continental U.S. and winters along the U.S. Pacific, Atlantic and Gulf coasts, in the Great Plains and West Indies and south to northern South America. It is also found in the Old World. • In Texas, the Merlin is generally rare to uncommon statewide during winter and migration. During winter, it tends to occur along the coast to take advantage of the large flocks of shorebirds that winter along our shores. The Merlin is a solitary species, even when migrating. • Merlins feed nearly exclusively on birds, which can be as large as doves and are captured from steep dives or after short chases from a perch. Unlike American Kestrels, Merlins seldom perch on powerlines. Instead, they usually hunt from a snag or other conspicuous perch. • Three different populations of the Merlin, with differing plumage coloration, inhabit North American. Two of them, the dark gray taiga population *(F.c. columbarius)* and the somewhat paler-plumaged prairie population *(F.c. richardsonii),* occur in Texas.

"Taiga Merlin"

ID: dark crown and nape; narrow, pale eyebrow; pale face with single dark "sideburn;" white throat; white underparts heavily streaked with brown; black tail with white bands. *Male:* gray back and wings. *Female:* brown back and wings. *In flight:* very rapid, shallow wingbeats.
Size: *L* 10–12 in; *W* 23–26 in.
Status: rare to uncommon migrant statewide; rare winter resident on the Coastal Plain and very rare inland.

Habitat: virtually any open habitat, usually near water.
Nesting: does not breed in Texas.
Feeding: flies from a perch to drop on prey or overtakes prey in flight; eats primarily birds.
Voice: generally silent in Texas.
Similar Species: *American Kestrel* (p. 128): smaller and more colorful; 2 facial stripes; often hovers. *Other falcons* (pp. 130–32): significantly larger.
Best Sites: *Winter:* Bear Creek Pioneer Park. *Migration:* Smith Point (Chambers Co.); Hazel Bazemore CP (Corpus Christi).

129

APLOMADO FALCON

Falco femoralis

Coastal Plain, high-elevation grasslands and savannas from southern Texas to Peru form the habitat of the striking, long-tailed Aplomado Falcon. • Thinning of egg shells by pesticide contamination and loss of native grassland habitat led to the decline of the northern subspecies *(F.f. septentrionalis)* of this medium-sized falcon. In 1989, the Peregrine Fund, Inc. and the U.S. Fish and Wildlife Service began a captive breeding program to reintroduce this colorful falcon back into its original American range. For the population to remain stable, cross-border conservation efforts, including riparian management and responsible pesticide use, must continue. • A pair of Aplomado Falcons may hunt cooperatively to flush out prey. The female usually flies closer to the ground, attempting to scare prey upward toward the male. These falcons may also feed by walking along the ground to search for insects or perching to scan for prey. They are most active at dusk and dawn.

ID: bluish gray above; black cap, eye line and "mustache"; white eyebrow and "bib"; cinnamon lower belly with dark belly band; long legs. *Juvenile:* white "bib" is streaked with black. *In flight:* long, dark tail with thin, white stripes; striped wing edges; dark inner wings.
Size: *L:* 16 in. *W:* 35 in.
Status: endangered (USFWS); rare to locally uncommon resident established from introduced birds on the Coastal Plain from the Rio Grande to about Calhoun Co., with recent sightings as far north as Galveston I., and in Reeves Co. in the Trans-Pecos.
Habitat: prefers open prairie or savanna, especially open areas near the coast.
Nesting: in a low tree; in an abandoned raptor stick nest; will use a nest platform; pair incubates 2–3 white or pinkish white eggs for 31–32 days; pair tends the young.
Feeding: hunts in flight, from a perch or on the ground; varied diet includes birds, insects, small mammals and reptiles.
Voice: *kik-kik-kik-kik-kik-kik-kik!* warning and alarm call. *Female:* long, sharp wails to demand food when brooding.
Similar Species: *Peregrine Falcon* (p. 131): heavier; shorter tail; darker helmet with no eyebrow. *Prairie Falcon* (p. 132): heavier body; paler, brown plumage; white patch behind eye; diagnostic dark "wing pits" in flight.
Best Sites: Laguna Atascosa NWR.

PEREGRINE FALCON

Falco peregrinus

No bird elicits more admiration than a hunting Peregrine Falcon in full flight, and nothing causes more panic in a tightly packed flock of ducks or shorebirds. This large, powerful raptor matches every twist and turn the flock makes, until a weaker or less-experienced bird falls behind. Diving at speeds of up to 220 miles per hour, the Peregrine clenches its feet and then strikes its prey with a lethal blow that often sends both falcon and prey tumbling. • The Peregrine Falcon's awesome speed and hunting skills were little defense against the pesticide DDT. The chemical caused contaminated birds to lay eggs with thin shells, which broke when the adults incubated the eggs. This bird was completely eradicated east of the Mississippi River by 1964. DDT was banned in North America in 1972, and, in 1975, the Eastern Peregrine Recovery Program was created and has successfully reintroduced the Peregrine Falcon in the eastern U.S. • Peregrines nest on every continent except Antarctica.

ID: blue-gray back and wings; prominent black helmet; white face with bold black "sideburn"; pale underparts with fine black barring; black-banded, blue-gray tail. *Juvenile:* brown replaces blue-gray; pale crown; narrower but distinct "sideburn"; brown-streaked breast. *In flight:* wide, pointed wings; often soars.
Size: *Male: L* 15–17 in; *W* 3–3½ ft.
Female: L 17–19 in; *W* 3½–4 ft.
Status: uncommon migrant statewide, although more common along the coast; rare summer resident in Culberson Co. and Brewster Co. where it is a rare and local breeder; rare winter resident in the lower Rio Grande valley and the lower Coastal Plain.
Habitat: various open habitats, including coastal areas.
Nesting: usually on a rocky cliff; may use a sky-scraper ledge; site is often reused and littered with prey remains; pair incubates 3–5 white eggs with reddish specks for 32–34 days.
Feeding: high-speed, diving stoops; strikes prey, such as ducks, shorebirds and gulls, with clenched feet in midair.
Voice: generally silent except at the nest; loud, harsh, continuous *cack-cack-cack-cack-cack*.
Similar Species: *Merlin* (p. 129): smaller; no prominent dark helmet; heavily streaked breast and belly. *American Kestrel* (p. 128): smaller; 2 facial stripes; more colorful; often hovers. *Prairie Falcon* (p. 132): sandier brown upperparts; diagnostic dark "wing pits"; no dark helmet.
Best Sites: *Summer:* Guadalupe Mountains NP; Big Bend NP. *Migration:* Smith Point (Chambers Co.); Hazel Bazemore CP.

PRAIRIE FALCON

Falco mexicanus

Rocketing overhead like a super-charged fighter jet, the Prairie Falcon seems to appear out of nowhere. • During spring and summer, Prairie Falcons often concentrate their hunting efforts over ground squirrel colonies, readily swooping over expanses of windswept grass to pick off naive youngsters. As summer fades to fall, large flocks of migrating songbirds often capture the attention of these pallid "ghosts of the plains." • Freshly fledged, inexperienced falcons risk serious injury or death when pushing the limits in early hunting forays. Swooping falcons can easily misjudge their flight speed or their ability to pull out of a dive. • The Prairie Falcon is a medium-sized falcon that commonly soars for long periods on updrafts or along ridgelines.

ID: brown upperparts; pale face with narrow, dark brown "mustache"; white underparts with brown spotting. *In flight:* diagnostic dark "wing pits"; pointed wings; long, narrow, banded tail; quick wingbeats; direct flight.
Size: *Male: L* 14–15 in; *W* 3–3¼ ft. *Female: L* 17–18 in; *W* 3½ ft.
Status: uncommon migrant and rare winter resident in the western half of the state north of the Lower Rio Grande Valley; rare summer resident in the western Panhandle and Trans-Pecos Mountains
Habitat: *Summer:* mountains of the central Trans-Pecos and canyons of the Panhandle. *Winter* and *in migration:* treeless country, such as open fields, pastures, grasslands and sagebrush flats.

Nesting: on a cliff ledge, in a crevice or on a rocky promontory; rarely in an abandoned nest of another raptor or crow; nest is usually unlined; mainly female incubates 3–5 whitish eggs, spotted with brown, for 29–30 days; male brings food to the female and young.
Feeding: high-speed strike-and-kill by diving swoops, low flights or chases on the wing; eats ground squirrels, small birds, other small vertebrates and large insects; females consume more mammalian prey than do males.
Voice: generally silent; rapid, shrill *kik-kik-kik-kik* alarm call near nest.
Similar Species: dark "wing pits" are diagnostic. *Peregrine Falcon* (p. 131): distinctive dark helmet. *Merlin* (p. 129): much smaller. *American Kestrel* (p. 128): smaller; much more colorful; 2 bold facial stripes; often hovers.
Best Sites: Muleshoe NWR; Hueco Tanks SP; Davis Mountains; Big Bend NP.

132

CLAPPER RAIL

Rallus longirostris

With a characteristic tail flick, the Clapper Rail wades through tidal marshes and mangroves in search of prey. A thin profile and long, spreading toes allow quick, efficient movement. The Clapper Rail is more often heard than seen, especially at sunrise and sunset, when it vehemently issues loud *kek* calls. • For years, Clapper Rail habitat throughout North America has been under siege by humans hoping to convert marshland into airports, malls and landfills. A common resident of brackish marshes here in Texas, this rail has been extirpated from much of the U.S. • Clapper Rails can lay up to a dozen eggs over several days. Within hours of the first young hatching, one adult often moves to a nearby auxiliary nest to brood the vulnerable new hatchlings in safety while the other stays to incubate any remaining eggs. • Four recognized subspecies, with differing brightness of coloration, inhabit Texas.

ID: long, slightly down-curved bill; pale-edged, generally darker back feathers; grayish brown to cinnamon breast; barred flanks of gray to brown and white; grayish face.
Size: *L* 14 in; *W* 19 in.
Status: common resident in coastal saltwater marshes.
Habitat: tidal saltwater marshes of pickleweed and cordgrass. *Foraging:* often along marshy tidal channels at low tide.
Nesting: in dense cover above or near water; pair builds a cup nest of vegetation, usually with a domed canopy and an entrance ramp; pair incubates 7–11 brown-blotched, olive brown eggs for 20–23 days; pair raises the young.

Feeding: hunts while walking in shallow water or among dense marsh vegetation; probes, snatches or gleans aquatic insects, crustaceans and small fish from the water, ground or vegetation; may also eat seeds, amphibians, worms and other small items.
Voice: loud, harsh *kek* note series, accelerating at first, then slowing; single bird often causes an entire marsh to erupt with widely scattered "chime-ins" from other unseen rails.
Similar Species: *King Rail* (p. 134): rufous brown overall; cinnamon shoulders and underparts; strongly barred flanks. *Virginia Rail* (p. 135): much smaller; gray face. *Least Bittern* (p. 91): streaked neck and back; inhabits shallow freshwater wetlands.
Best Sites: Sea Rim SP; Anahuac NWR; Galveston Island SP; Brazoria NWR; Aransas NWR; Laguna Atascosa NWR.

KING RAIL

Rallus elegans

North America's largest rail, the King Rail is only roughly the size of a farmyard chicken. Unlike some of the more secretive rails, it is often seen wading through shallow water along the edge of a freshwater marsh, stalking its prey within full view of eager onlookers. Crayfish, crabs, small fish, spiders, beetles, snails, frogs and a whole host of aquatic insects keep this formidable hunter occupied and well fed. • King Rail nests, which are commonly built above shallow water, often include a protective dome of woven vegetation and a well-engineered entrance ramp. Despite these deluxe features, young rails and their attending parents desert the nest mere hours after the eggs hatch.

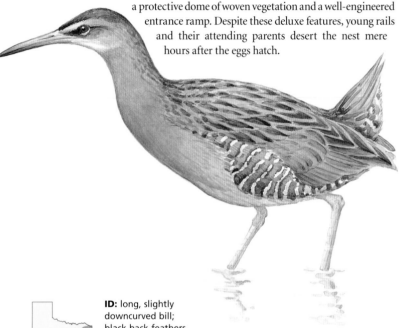

ID: long, slightly downcurved bill; black back feathers with buffy or tawny edges; cinnamon shoulders and underparts; strongly barred, black and white flanks; grayish brown cheeks. *Immature:* lighter, washed-out colors.
Size: *L* 15 in; *W* 20 in.
Status: common resident in freshwater marshes on the Coastal Plain, less common and local in the eastern third of the state and at isolated places in the western third; rare to uncommon migrant statewide.
Habitat: freshwater marshes, shrubby swamps, marshy riparian shorelines and flooded fields with shrubby margins.
Nesting: among clumps of grass or sedge just above the water or ground; male builds most of the platform nest with a canopy and entrance ramp using marsh vegetation; pair

incubates 6–12 lightly spotted, pale buff eggs for 21–23 days; pair cares for the young.
Feeding: catches small fish and amphibians in shallow water, often in or near dense plant cover; also eats aquatic insects, crustaceans and occasionally seeds.
Voice: chattering call is 10 or more evenly spaced *kek* or *bup* notes.
Similar Species: *Virginia Rail* (p. 135): much smaller; brown back feathers; gray face; red bill. *Clapper Rail* (p. 133): mottled, gray-brown and black back feathers; grayish brown to cinnamon breast; gray to brown and white barring on flanks. *Least Bittern* (p. 91): solid black back feathers without pale edging; buff-orange face and wing patches; thicker bill.
Best Sites: Sea Rim SP; Anahuac NWR; Galveston Island SP; Brazoria NWR; Aransas NWR.

VIRGINIA RAIL

Rallus limicola

The best way to meet a Virginia Rail is to sit alongside a wetland marsh in winter, clap your hands three or four times to imitate this bird's *ki-dick* calls and wait patiently. If you are lucky, a Virginia Rail will reveal itself for a brief instant, but usually you will only hear the bird. • When pursued by an intruder or predator, rails almost always attempt to scurry away through dense, concealing vegetation rather than risk exposure in a getaway flight. Modified feather tips and flexible vertebrae allow these very narrow birds to squeeze through the confines of their marshy homes. • The Virginia Rail and the Sora often inhabit the same marshes. The secret of their successful coexistence is in their microhabitat preferences and distinct diets. The Virginia Rail typically favors dry shorelines of marshes and eats invertebrates, whereas the Sora prefers waterfront property and eats plants and seeds.

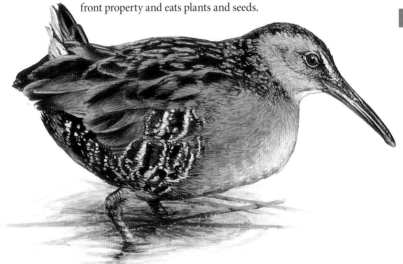

ID: long, down-curved, reddish bill; gray face; rusty breast; barred flanks; chestnut brown wing patch; very short tail. *Immature:* much darker overall; pale bill.

Size: *L* 9–11 in; *W* 13 in.

Status: uncommon migrant statewide; rare to locally uncommon summer resident on the High Plains and western half of the Edwards Plateau and rare on the central and upper Coastal Plain; rare to uncommon winter resident on the Coastal Plain and in northeast Texas; breeds in the far west Trans-Pecos and in the South Plains.

Habitat: wetlands, especially cattail and bulrush marshes.

Nesting: usually suspended just over the water, concealed in emergent vegetation; constructs a loose basket nest of coarse grass, cattail stems or sedges; pair incubates 5–13 spotted, pale buff eggs for about 20 days; pair cares for the young.

Feeding: probes into soft substrates and gleans vegetation for invertebrates, such as beetles, snails, spiders, earthworms, insect larvae and nymphs; also eats some pondweeds and seeds.

Voice: often-repeated, telegraph-like *ki-dick, ki-dick* call; also "oinks" and croaks.

Similar Species: *King Rail* (p. 134): much larger; paler bill; less gray in face; immature is mostly pale gray. *Sora* (p. 136): short, yellow bill; black face and throat. *Yellow Rail* (p. 446): smaller; short, pale yellowish bill; striped, black and tawny back.

Best Sites: Sea Rim SP; Galveston Island SP; Mustang Island SP; Goose Island SP.

135

SORA

Porzana carolina

Soras have small bodies and large feet with long, spreading toes. Even without webbed feet, these unusual creatures swim quite well over short distances. • Although the Sora is the most common and widespread rail species in North America, it is seldom seen. This secretive bird prefers to remain hidden in dense marshland, only occasionally venturing into the shallows to search for aquatic insects and mollusks. • Try throwing a small stone into the water or clapping your hands to locate the Sora, which may respond with an alarmed *keek* call. In addition to alarm notes, the Sora has two main calls: a clear, whistled, easy-to-imitate *coo-wee* and a strange, descending whinny that is most often heard at dawn or dusk on the breeding grounds. • Although it appears to be a weak and reluctant flier, the Sora migrates hundreds of miles each year between breeding grounds in Canada and the central U.S. to wintering wetlands in Central and South America. In Texas, it is seen mostly during migration. • The species name *carolina* means "of Carolina"; this bird is also known as "Carolina Rail."

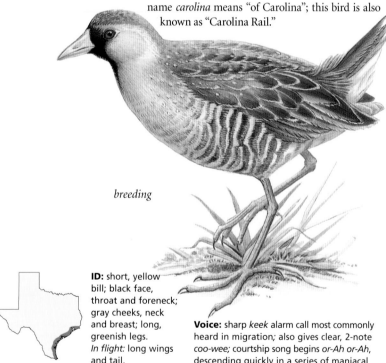

breeding

ID: short, yellow bill; black face, throat and foreneck; gray cheeks, neck and breast; long, greenish legs. *In flight:* long wings and tail.

Size: *L* 8–10 in; *W* 14 in.

Status: locally common migrant statewide; locally rare summer resident; common winter resident in the coastal marshlands and rare to uncommon inland.

Habitat: wetlands with abundant emergent cattails, bulrushes, sedges and grasses.

Nesting: does not nest in Texas.

Feeding: gleans and probes for seeds, plants, aquatic insects and mollusks.

Voice: sharp *keek* alarm call most commonly heard in migration; also gives clear, 2-note *coo-wee;* courtship song begins *or-Ah or-Ah,* descending quickly in a series of maniacal *weee-weee-weee* notes.

Similar Species: *Virginia Rail* (p. 135) and *King Rail* (p. 134): larger; long, downcurved bill; redder upperwing; cinnamon or rusty breast. *Yellow Rail* (p.446): streaked, tawny upperparts; white throat; white trailing patches on wings visible in flight.

Best Sites: Sea Rim SP; Galveston Island SP; Brazoria NWR; Aransas NWR; Laguna Atascosa NWR.

PURPLE GALLINULE

Porphyrio martinica

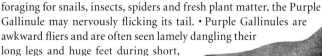

I f a group of children were given a box of paints and let loose on a bird, the color-ful result would likely resemble the Purple Gallinule. This unique bird is one of the treasures of the southeastern swamps and a "must-see" for visitors to Texas. Watch for the Purple Gallinule swimming through the shallows, bobbing its head with great zeal. • This bird's large feet and long toes distribute the bird's weight, allowing it to walk on top of floating lily pads and mats of vegetation. While foraging for snails, insects, spiders and fresh plant matter, the Purple Gallinule may nervously flicking its tail. • Purple Gallinules are awkward fliers and are often seen lamely dangling their long legs and huge feet during short, reluctant flights.

breeding

ID: all-white under-tail coverts; glossy, purplish blue head and underparts; greenish upperparts; light blue forehead shield; red bill with yellow tip; yellow legs and feet. *Immature:* tawny brown overall, with greenish tinge in wings; darkish bill and crown.

Size: *L* 12–14 in; *W* 22 in.

Status: rare to uncommon migrant in eastern Texas and very rare in the west; rare summer resident in the east and very rare in the west; rare winter resident in the coastal marshlands.

Habitat: freshwater swamps, lagoons, marshes and ponds with floating vegetation and dense cover.

Nesting: over water in dense, standing marsh vegetation; pair builds a platform of cattails, sedges and grasses; extra nests may be built; pair incubates 5–10 finely spotted, creamy buff eggs for 22–25 days; pair cares for the young.

Feeding: gleans food from vegetation or water by walking or swimming; omnivorous diet includes seeds, fruits, leaves, insects, spiders, worms, small fish and snails.

Voice: noisy henlike clucking sounds; gives cackling *kek kek kek* call in flight.

Similar Species: *Common Moorhen* (p. 138): gray-black body with brown back; red forehead shield. *American Coot* (p. 139): gray-black body; white forehead shield

Best Sites: Sea Rim SP; Galveston Island SP; Brazos Bend SP; Brazoria NWR; Padre Island National Seashore.

COMMON MOORHEN

Gallinula chloropus

T his curious-looking creature, appears to have been assembled from bits and pieces left over from other birds: it has a chicken's bill, a duck's body and the long legs and large feet of a small heron. As it strolls around a wetland, its head bobs back and forth in synchrony with its legs, producing a comical, chugging stride. Unlike most other members of the rail family, the Common Moorhen is quite comfortable feeding in open areas. • For moorhens, the responsibilities of parenthood do not end when their eggs have hatched—parents feed and shelter their young until they can feed themselves and flying on their own. • Although the Common Moorhen resembles its close relative, the American Coot, its delicate manner and elusive tendencies easily distinguish it from the loud and gregarious coot. • Until recently, this bird was known as "Common Gallinule."

breeding

ID: reddish forehead shield; red bill with yellow tip; gray-black body; brownish upperparts; white-streaked flanks; long, greenish yellow legs. *Breeding:* brighter bill and forehead shield. *Immature:* paler plumage; duller legs and bill; white throat.
Size: *L* 12–15 in; *W* 21 in.
Status: uncommon resident from east-central Texas to the coast; common to abundant summer resident in the Lower Rio Grande Valley and the extreme west Trans-Pecos and rare to uncommon elsewhere.
Habitat: freshwater marshes, ponds, lakes and sewage lagoons.
Nesting: in shallow water or along a shoreline; pair builds a platform nest or a wide,

shallow cup of bulrushes, cattails and reeds, often with a ramp to the water; pair incubates 8–14 buff-colored, spotted or blotched eggs for 19–22 days.
Feeding: eats mostly aquatic vegetation, berries, fruits, tadpoles, insects, snails, worms and spiders; may take carrion and eggs.
Voice: various sounds, including chickenlike clucks, screams, squeaks and a loud *cup*. *Male:* harsh *ticket-ticket-ticket* when courting.
Similar Species: *American Coot* (p. 139): mostly white bill and forehead shield; all-gray flanks. *Purple Gallinule* (p. 137): glossy, purplish blue head and underparts; greenish upperparts; light blue forehead shield; all-white undertail coverts; yellow legs.
Best Sites: Village Creek Wastewater Treatment Plant (Arlington); Brazos Bend SP; Brazoria NWR; Mustang Island SP; Mitchell L. (San Antonio).

AMERICAN COOT

Fulica americana

Truly an all-terrain bird in its quest for food, the American Coot dives and dabbles like a duck, grazes confidently on land and swims about skillfully with its lobed feet. A strong swimmer, it uses both its lobed toes and wings to paddle quickly through the water. • Young American Coots often hitch a ride on their parents' backs, even staying aboard for underwater dives. Coots can completely submerge to avoid predators, although the young often fall victim to pike or other fish. • Coots gather amicably in large winter groups of possibly thousands of birds. Pendulous head movements while swimming make them easy to spot. They are also the only birds in Texas with white bills, which stand out against their dark bodies. Occasional pairs stay on to breed, especially in central Texas, but most birds nest farther north. • The American Coot is colloquially known as "Mud Hen," "Pond Crow" or "White-bill." Many people mistakenly believe it to be a species of duck.

ID: gray-black overall; white, chickenlike bill with dark ring near tip; white forehead shield with reddish spot; long, greenish yellow legs; lobed toes; red eyes. *Immature:* lighter body color; darker bill and legs; no forehead shield.
Size: *L* 13–16 in; *W* 24 in.
Status: common to abundant winter resident statewide; uncommon to common summer resident and irregular breeder in many parts of the state.
Habitat: shallow marshes, ponds and wetlands with open water and emergent vegetation; also sewage lagoons.
Nesting: in emergent vegetation; pair builds a floating nest of cattails and grass;

pair incubates 6–11 brown-spotted, buffy white eggs for 21–25 days.
Feeding: gleans the water's surface; sometimes dives, tips up or even grazes on land; eats aquatic vegetation, invertebrates, tadpoles and fish; may steal food from ducks.
Voice: frequent *kuk-kuk-kuk-kuk-kuk* calls in summer, day and night; also grunts.
Similar Species: *Ducks* (pp. 49–69, 443): no white, chickenlike bills; bodies not uniformly black. *Grebes* (pp. 78–81): no white forehead shield; plumage not wholly dark. *Common Moorhen* (p. 138): reddish forehead shield; yellow-tipped bill; white-streaked flanks. *Caribbean Coot:* broader forehead shield may have yellow tinge.
Best Sites: any water body with submerged vegetation and adjacent grassy fields.

SANDHILL CRANE

Grus canadensis

Deep, resonant, rattling calls announce the approach of Sandhill Cranes long before they pass overhead. The coiling of the trachea adds harmonies to the notes, making them louder and able to carry farther. In flight, the snapping upstroke and slower downstroke of the cranes differentiate them from similar long-necked birds. • One of the world's most spectacular wildlife migrations occurs each spring, when half a million Sandhill Cranes converge on the banks of the Platte River in Nebraska. Before continuing their journey northward, tens of thousands of these birds refuel on invertebrates or waste grain. However, as with so many of our rivers, an increasing demand for water is reducing flows along the Platte, posing a serious threat to an essential migratory stopover for millions of birds. • Sandhill Cranes mate for life, reinforcing pair bonds each spring with an elaborate courtship dance. With a lifespan of more than two decades, they are among the longest living birds.

ID: gray plumage, often stained rusty by iron oxides in the water; long neck and legs; naked, red crown; long, straight bill. *In flight:* extends neck and legs; often glides, soars and circles.

Size: *L* 3½–4 ft; *W* 6–7 ft.

Status: uncommon to common migrant in the west and less common in the east, although basically absent in the Pineywoods region; common winter resident on the Coastal Plain, in the Panhandle and in the playa areas of the High Plains.

Habitat: agricultural fields and shorelines.

Nesting: does not nest in Texas.

Feeding: probes and gleans the ground for insects, soft-bodied invertebrates, waste grain, shoots and tubers; frequently eats small vertebrates.

Voice: loud, resonant, rattling *gu-rrroo gu-rrroo gurrroo.*

Similar Species: *Great Blue Heron* (p. 92): no red forehead patch; folds neck back over shoulders in flight. *Whooping Crane* (p. 141): all-white plumage; black-tipped wings.

Best Sites: Muleshoe NWR; Sandhill Crane Sanctuary (Big Spring); Galveston Island SP; Brazoria NWR; Mustang Island SP.

WHOOPING CRANE

Grus americana

The Aransas National Wildlife Refuge houses the world's only wild population of Whooping Cranes, a small group of about 180 overwintering birds that nests exclusively in Canada's Wood Buffalo National Park. These extraordinary cranes wavered on the brink of extinction in the 1940s, when the world population dipped to only 15 birds. One of the most intensive conservation programs in history managed to increase that number to about 400 wild and captive birds by 2005. Increasing the numbers is a challenge, because these cranes do not reach maturity until five years of age and usually lay only one egg per year. These birds also face many dangers during migration. • Most reintroduced Whooping Cranes are found in Florida, where conservation agencies have been experimenting with both migratory and nonmigratory populations since 1993. In 2000, a pair of Florida birds hatched the first two chicks born in the American wild in over six decades. Biologists hope to establish breeding populations in other states, because Texas's Aransas NWR lies next to the busy Intercoastal Waterway, where an oil spill or other disaster could decimate the Whooping Crane population.

ID: mostly white overall; black-tipped wings; bare, red skin on forehead and chin; long, pointed bill; black legs. *In flight:* extends neck and legs.

Size: *L* 4¼–5 ft; *W* 6½–8 ft.

Status: endangered (USFWS); winter resident at Aransas NWR and nearby adjacent marshlands; rare migrant from the eastern Panhandle along a narrow pathway through central Texas to Aransas NWR, but occasionally appears elsewhere.

Habitat: lakes, coastal and freshwater marshes; prefers remote areas.

Nesting: does not nest in Texas.

Feeding: picks food from the water or the ground; eats invertebrates and small vertebrates, including fish, amphibians, reptiles and small mammals; also eats plant material such as roots, acorns and berries.

Voice: gravely *ker-loo ker-lee-loo* rattle like that of the Sandhill Crane.

Similar Species: *Sandhill Crane* (p. 140): gray overall. *Tundra Swan* (p. 48): all-white wings; short legs. *Great Egret* (p. 93): all-white wings and head.

Best Sites: Aransas NWR.

BLACK-BELLIED PLOVER

Pluvialis squatarola

Tight flocks of Black-bellied Plovers are commonly seen along the coast during winter and migration, running along mudflats at low tide. These plovers forage with a robinlike run-and-stop technique, frequently pausing to lift their heads and scan their surroundings. They are usually found in coastal habitats but are equally comfortable foraging inland near freshwater. • Their striking black-bellied breeding plumage, for which they are named, may be seen in Texas in late spring or early fall, but these shorebirds are gray for most of winter. Instead, watch for small flocks flashing their bold white wing stripes as they fly low over the water.

nonbreeding

• The Black-bellied Plover is unique for several reasons. North America's largest plover, it has large eyes, an adaptation that allows it to search for prey at night. Also, whereas most plovers have three toes, the Black-belly has a fourth toe higher on its leg, like a typical sandpiper.

breeding

ID: short, black bill; long, black legs. *Breeding:* black face, breast, belly and flanks; white under-tail coverts; white stripe leads from crown down collar, neck and sides of breast; mottled, black and white back. *Nonbreeding:* mottled, gray brown upperparts; lightly streaked, pale underparts. *In flight:* bold white wing linings with black "wing pits"; whitish rump.
Size: *L* 10½–13 in; *W* 29 in.
Status: uncommon to common migrant east of the Pecos R. and rare in the Trans-Pecos;

common to abundant winter resident and rare summer resident along the coast.
Habitat: coastal mudflats and beaches; plowed fields, sod farms and meadows; edges of lakeshores, reservoirs, marshes and sewage lagoons.
Nesting: does not nest in Texas.
Feeding: run-and-stop foraging technique; eats insects, mollusks and crustaceans.
Voice: rich, plaintive, 3-syllable *pee-oo-ee* whistle, usually given in flight.
Similar Species: *American Golden-Plover* (p. 143): gold-mottled upperparts; black undertail coverts in breeding plumage; gray "wing pits."
Best Sites: any accessible beach along the coast.

AMERICAN GOLDEN-PLOVER

Pluvialis dominica

Only 150 years ago, the American Golden-Plover population was among the largest of any bird population in the world, but, in the late 1800s, market gunners mercilessly culled the great flocks in both spring and fall—a single day's shooting often yielded tens of thousands of birds. Populations have recovered somewhat, but they will likely never return to their former numbers. • Although this bird is boldly marked, the white stripe down its side disrupts the vision of a predator, confusing the hunter as to where the bird's head or tail is. The cryptic coloration of speckles on the top of the body blends well with the golden, mottled earth of its arctic breeding grounds. • The Eskimo Curlew (*Numenius borealis*), now possibly extinct, once migrated with the American Golden-Plover between the Canadian Arctic and South America. If the Eskimo Curlew does still exist, it may be found traveling alongside the American Golden-Plover.

nonbreeding

breeding

ID: straight, black bill; long, black legs. *Breeding:* black face and underparts, including undertail coverts; white "S" stripe from forehead to shoulders; dark upperparts speckled with gold and white. *Nonbreeding:* broad, pale eyebrow; dark streaking on pale neck and underparts; much less gold on upperparts. *In flight:* gray "wing pits."
Size: *L* 10–11 in; *W* 26 in.
Status: common spring migrant and rare fall migrant east of the Pecos R., very rare fall migrant in the Trans-Pecos; occasionally winters along the coast.

Habitat: cultivated fields, meadows and airports; lakeshores and mudflats along the edges of reservoirs, marshes and sewage lagoons; coastal sand flats.
Nesting: does not nest in Texas.
Feeding: run-and-stop foraging technique; snatches insects, mollusks and crustaceans; also takes seeds and berries.
Voice: soft, melodious, whistled *quee, quee-dle* flight call.
Similar Species: *Black-bellied Plover* (p. 142): white undertail coverts; whitish crown; no gold speckling on upperparts; conspicuous, black "wing pits" in flight.
Best Sites: coastal pastures, grasslands and rice fields.

SNOWY PLOVER

Charadrius alexandrinus

A subtle, year-round patron of the Gulf Coast, the Snowy Plover breeds on the drier shorelines of our remaining undisturbed beaches. For most of the year, this plover blends unseen into its surroundings, moving ghostlike over isolated coastal dunes and open sandy beaches. The Snowy Plover used to be more numerous along the Gulf Coast, but human development now restricts this threatened species to a few unspoiled areas. • Snowy Plover nests are notoriously difficult to spot and might easily be crushed under a carelessly placed foot. Also, nesting activities can be easily disrupted by well-intentioned birders or their dogs, which inadvertently keep the parent away from its nest for prolonged periods. Therefore, this bird should be sought out only in the nonbreeding season, when the effects of human disturbances are minimized and the plover population is boosted by the arrival of overwintering birds.

breeding

breeding

ID: *Breeding:* white underparts; light brown upperparts; thin, black bill; variable dark patches on ear, shoulder and forehead; slate gray legs. Non*breeding:* no dark patches.

Size: *L* 6–7 in; *W* 17 in.

Status: rare to uncommon migrant statewide; uncommon summer resident on the Gulf Coast and locally rare from the southern half of the High Plains and Rolling Plains south to the western half of the Edwards Plateau; uncommon winter resident on the Gulf Coast.

Habitat: coastal birds use sandy beaches (especially ones backed by dunes), sand spits and the drier shoreline areas of tidal estuaries, bayshore sandflats and salt evaporation ponds; interior birds use alkaline lake shorelines.

Nesting: on bare ground, usually near a grass clump or piece of driftwood; lines a shallow scrape with pebbles, shells, grass and other debris; pair incubates 3 black-dotted, pale buff eggs for 26–32 days; young leave the nest within hours of hatching; 1–2 broods per year.

Feeding: uses run-and-stop foraging technique to catch tiny crustaceans, mollusks, marine worms and some insects; inland birds consume more insects.

Voice: soft, whistled *ku-wheat* or *chu-wee* flight call; also gives a low *krut.*

Similar Species: *Semipalmated Plover* (p. 146): darker back; complete breast band; black-tipped, orange bill; orange legs. *Killdeer* (p. 148): 2 black breast bands; much larger; darker back; rusty tail.

Best Sites: Sea Rim SP; Bolivar Flats Shorebird Sanctuary (Galveston Co.); Galveston Island SP; Mustang Island SP; Padre Island National Seashore.

WILSON'S PLOVER

Charadrius wilsonia

The Wilson's Plover, with its unusually long, heavy, black bill, affords us the opportunity to easily identify at least one species among the hordes of shore-dwelling species. Whereas most other plovers use their much smaller bills to snatch tiny marine worms and insects, the larger-billed Wilson's Plovers can handle crayfish, fiddler crabs and small shellfish. Further scrutiny of this beachcomber also reveals a broad, dark breast band that is black on the male and brown on the female. • Of the four small plovers that occur in Texas, this species seems least affected by human activities, other than development in the coastal regions. • This plover was named after the father of American ornithology, Alexander Wilson.

breeding

ID: long, thick, black bill; brownish upperparts; grayish pink legs white underparts. *Breeding male:* broad, black band across breast; black band on forehead. *Breeding female:* brown replaces black on breast and head. *Nonbreeding:* resembles breeding female with incomplete breast band.
Size: *L* 7³/4 in; *W* 19 in.
Status: common summer and rare winter resident along the coast.
Habitat: sandy beaches, tidal mudflats, dredge-spoil islands and coastal islands.
Nesting: near a concealing piece of vegetation or debris; female chooses one of several scrapes in dry sand excavated by the male; nest is sparsely lined with grass, pebbles, shell fragments or debris; pair incubates 2–3 heavily marked, creamy buff

eggs for 24–32 days; pair tends precocial young; 1–2 broods per year.
Feeding: forages by sight, running and pausing to snatch prey from ground or low vegetation; crustaceans, insects, worms and small mollusks form most of the diet.
Voice: calls include a shrill *wheat!* alarm whistle and a lower *quit.*
Similar Species: *Semipalmated Plover* (p. 146): small, orange bill with black tip; orange legs; male's dark forehead band connects to eye. *Killdeer* (p. 148): larger; 2 black bands encircle chest; orange rump; black subterminal tail band. *Piping Plover* (p. 147): small, orange bill with black tip; orange legs; pale gray upperparts; narrow breast band. *Snowy Plover* (p. 144): thin bill; broken breast band.
Best Sites: Sea Rim SP; Bolivar Flats Shorebird Sanctuary (Galveston Co.); Galveston Island SP; San Bernard NWR; Padre Island National Seashore.

145

SEMIPALMATED PLOVER

Charadrius semipalmatus

Overwintering along our coast, the Semipalmated Plover spends much of its time searching for worms and crustaceans along the damp mudflats. Because this adaptable plover uses a variety of habitats and exploits a number of food sources, it is one of the few plover species with numbers that are increasing. • Long, slender wings make this bird a fast flier, able to reach speeds of 31 miles per hour. With its powerful wing beats, the Semipalmated Plover can negotiate strong winds with relative ease. It migrates both during the day and at night, although nighttime collisions with lighthouses or towers can prove fatal. • The scientific name *semipalmatus* means "half-webbed" and refers to the slight webbing between the toes of this plover. The webbing is thought to give the bird's feet more surface area when it walks on soft substrates.

breeding

nonbreeding

ID: dark brown back; white breast with 1 dark horizontal band; long, orange legs; stubby, black-tipped, orange bill; white patch above bill; white throat and collar; brown head. *Breeding:* black band across forehead, extending rearward below eye; small, white eyebrow.
Size: *L* 7 in; *W* 19 in.
Status: common migrant in much of the state, uncommon in the Panhandle and South Plains and rare in the Trans-Pecos and the northeast quarter; summer vagrant and common winter resident along the coast.

Habitat: mainly coastal; rarely seen inland; mudflats and sandy beaches.
Nesting: does not nest in Texas.
Feeding: usually on damp shorelines and beaches; run-and-stop foraging technique; eats crustaceans, worms and insects.
Voice: crisp, high-pitched, 2-part, rising *tu-wee* whistle.
Similar Species: *Killdeer* (p. 148): larger; 2 black bands across breast. *Piping Plover* (p. 147): much lighter upperparts; no dark band through eyes; narrower breast band is incomplete in females and most males. *Wilson's Plover* (p. 145): larger; heavy black bill; pink legs.
Best Sites: Sea Rim SP; Bolivar Flats Shorebird Sanctuary (Galveston Co.); Galveston I.; Mustang I.; Padre Island National Seashore.

PIPING PLOVER

Charadrius melodus

The Piping Plover is hardly noticeable when it settles on shorelines and beaches. Its pale, sand-colored plumage is the perfect camouflage against a sandy beach. As well, the dark bands across its forehead and neckline resemble scattered pebbles or strips of washed-up vegetation. However, this plover's cryptic plumage has done little to protect it from the draining of wetlands, increased predation and disturbance by humans. The recreational use of beaches during summer and an increase in human-tolerant predators, such as gulls, raccoons and skunks, has impeded this plover's ability to reproduce successfully. The Piping Plover is threatened in North America, although good numbers sometimes gather in winter on undisturbed coastal beaches in Texas. • On beaches with wave action, these birds often employ a foot-trembling strategy to entice invertebrates to the surface.

breeding

nonbreeding

ID: pale sandy upperparts; white underparts; orange legs. *Breeding:* black-tipped, orange bill; black forehead band; black "neck-lace" (sometimes incomplete, especially on female). *Nonbreeding:* all-black bill; pale sandy fore-head and "necklace."

Size: *L* 7 in; *W* 19 in.

Status: threatened (USFWS); uncommon migrant in the eastern half of the state and vagrant west of the Balcones Escarpment; locally common winter resident on the coast, with some birds remaining as summer stragglers.

Habitat: sandy, undisturbed coastal beaches.

Nesting: does not nest in Texas.

Feeding: run-and-stop foraging technique; eats worms and insects; takes almost all its food from the ground.

Voice: clear, whistled melody: *peep peep peep-lo.*

Similar Species: *Semipalmated Plover* (p. 146): dark band continues from forehead rearward below eye; much darker upperparts. *Killdeer* (p. 148): larger; 2 breast bands; much darker upperparts.

Best Sites: Sea Rim SP; Bolivar Flats Shorebird Sanctuary (Galveston Co.); Galveston I.; Mustang I.; Padre Island National Seashore; Boca Chica (Cameron Co.).

147

KILLDEER

Charadrius vociferus

Often the first shorebird a birder learns to identify, the Killdeer is ubiquitous. Its boisterous calls rarely fail to catch the attention of people passing through its wide variety of nesting environments. The Killdeer's preference for open fields, gravel driveways, beach edges, golf courses and abandoned industrial areas has allowed it to thrive throughout our rural and suburban landscapes. • If you happen to wander too close to a Killdeer nest, the parent will try to lure you away by issuing loud alarm calls and feigning a broken wing. In most instances, a predator will take the bait and be led safely away from the nest, at which point the parent suddenly "recovers" from its "injury" and flies off while sounding its piercing calls. • The word *vociferus* aptly describes this vocal bird, but double-check all calls in spring, when the Killdeer is often imitated by frisky European Starlings.

ID: long, dark yellow legs; white upperparts with 2 black breast bands; brown back; white underparts; brown head; white eyebrow; white face patch above bill; black forehead band; rufous rump; tail projects beyond wing tips at rest.
Size: *L* 9–11 in; *W* 24 in.
Status: common to abundant resident throughout Texas; absent from the Panhandle during winter in some years.

Habitat: open ground, fields, lakeshores, sandy beaches, mudflats, gravel streambeds, wet meadows and grasslands.
Nesting: on open ground; in a shallow depression, usually unlined; pair incubates 4 darkly blotched, pale buff eggs for 24–28 days; occasionally raises 2 broods.
Feeding: run-and-stop foraging technique; eats mostly insects; also takes spiders, snails, earthworms and crayfish.
Voice: loud, distinctive *kill-dee kill-dee kill-deer* and variations, including *deer-deer*.
Similar Species: *Semipalmated Plover* (p. 146): smaller; 1 breast band. *Piping Plover* (p. 147): smaller; lighter upperparts; 1 breast band.
Best Sites: any open field, parking lot or gravelly area statewide.

MOUNTAIN PLOVER
Charadrius montanus

Don't let the name fool you—this plover prefers to inhabit vast, open areas, far from the mountains. The Mountain Plover breeds in the western Great Plains, then migrates to wintering grounds in northern Mexico and the southwestern U.S. It clings to its traditional migratory routes as tightly as any shorebird, and a "lost" individual is only infrequently encountered. This bird of dry grasslands is found locally in the Trans-Pecos and the northwestern Panhandle in summer and in the Coastal Plain north to the southern Blackland Prairies in winter. Many Texan birdwatchers have made pilgrimages to find this rare species. • Like the Upland Sandpiper, the Mountain Plover does little to announce its shorebird heritage—it only rarely approaches shorelines. It is indeed more of a "grass-piper" than a sandpiper.

nonbreeding

ID: thin, dark bill; light underparts; sandy upperparts; white forehead; thin black eye line; light legs. *Breeding:* black forecrown and lore stripe **Size:** *L* 9 in; *W* 23 in.

Status: candidate for threatened species status; rare migrant in western Texas, east into the north-central area and west of the Brazos R.; rare to locally common winter resident on the central Coastal Plain and north to the southern parts of the Blackland Prairie, Edwards Plateau and South Plains regions; rare summer resident in higher grasslands of Trans-Pecos and in the northwest Panhandle; has bred in the Davis Mountains of the Trans-Pecos.

Habitat: sparse, dry prairies, heavily grazed pastures and mudflats.

Nesting: near a dry hummock, cactus plant or cow chips; in a shallow scrape lined with small amounts of grass, cow chips and roots; pair incubates 3 light olive or olive-buff eggs for about 30 days.

Feeding: gleans the ground for insects, especially grasshoppers.

Voice: shrill call note; whistles during spring and summer.

Similar Species: *Upland Sandpiper* (p. 158): longer neck; mottle upperparts; lightly streaked breast, sides and flanks. *Killdeer* (p. 148): 2 breast bands.

Best Sites: *Winter:* fields south of Granger L. (Williamson Co.); western Bexar Co. *Breeding:* Davis Mts. grasslands.

149

AMERICAN OYSTERCATCHER

Haematopus palliatus

One of the few birds with a bill sturdy enough to pry open a mollusk shell, the American Oystercatcher eats a variety of shellfish, including oysters, clams and mussels. When their tastebuds cry out for more, they gladly eat a host of other intertidal invertebrates, including crabs, marine worms, sea urchins and even jellyfish. This large shorebird usually forages silently and alone, but it issues loud whistles as it flies between mudflats and shellfish beds. • During the summer breeding season, watch for mating pairs performing their loud "piping" courtship display. These birds begin breeding at three or four years of age and may mate for life. American Oystercatchers may form a breeding trio consisting of two females and one male. Together, the group tends up to two nests and takes care of the young for the first weeks.

ID: long, orange-red bill; black head and neck; brown back; white wing and rump patches; white underparts.
Size: *L* 18½ in; *W* 32 in.

Status: rare to locally uncommon resident along the coast.
Habitat: coastal marine habitats, including saltwater marshes, sandy beaches and tidal mudflats; will nest on dredge spoil islands.
Nesting: in sand; pair scrapes out a depression and may line it with shells or pebbles; pair incubates 2–4 yellowish to buff eggs, with bold spots, blotches or streaks, for 27 days; precocial young leave nest soon after hatching to be fed and tended by pair.
Feeding: walks in shallow water, on rocks or on mud to scan or probe for intertidal life, including mollusks, crustaceans, marine worms and other invertebrates; shellfish, which form the bulk of the diet, are either hammered open or quickly stabbed through an opening and cut open.
Voice: loud *wheet!* call; often given in series during flight.
Similar Species: none.
Best Sites: Bolivar Flats Shorebird Sanctuary (Galveston Co.); Texas City Dike; Galveston I.; Mustang I.; Padre Island National Seashore.

BLACK-NECKED STILT

Himantopus mexicanus

The Black-necked Stilt strides daintily around coastal and interior wetlands on its long, gangly legs. Whether this bird is wandering along a smelly sewage lagoon or wading along the shorelines of an impoundment, the stilt's dignity adds a sense of subtle glory to the bleak landscape with which it is most often associated. • On hot summer days, adult Black-necked Stilts routinely take turns sheltering their eggs from the warmth of the hot sun. The parents repeatedly wet their belly feathers in order to cool off their eggs and young during incubation. • Proportionately, this bird has the longest legs of any North American bird, making it truly deserving of the name "stilt."

ID: very long, pink legs; dark upperparts; clean white underparts; long, straight, needlelike bill; small, white eyebrow. *Male:* blacker upperparts. *Female:* browner upperparts.

Size: *L* 14–15 in; *W* 29 in.

Status: common summer resident on the coast and locally inland, except for the eastern wooded areas; rare to uncommon migrant statewide except very rare in the eastern wooded areas; uncommon winter resident along the coast and inland to the edge of the Edwards Plateau and in El Paso Co.

Habitat: *Breeding:* along the margins of freshwater, brackish and saltwater marshes and on the marshy shorelines of lakes, ponds and tidal mudflats; also forages in flooded agricultural fields, impoundments and salt-evaporation ponds.

Nesting: in a shallow depression on slightly raised ground near water; nest is lined with shells, pebbles or vegetative debris; pair incubates 4 darkly blotched, buff eggs for about 25 days; pair tends the precocial young.

Feeding: picks prey from the water's surface or from the bottom substrate; eats primarily insects, crustaceans and other aquatic invertebrates; rarely eats seeds of aquatic plants.

Voice: not vocal during migration; loud, sharp *yip-yip-yip-yip* in summer; *kek-kek-kek-kek* in flight.

Similar Species: *American Avocet* (p. 152): upturned bill; no black on head.

Best Sites: Mitchell L. (San Antonio); Anahuac NWR; Brazoria NWR; Padre Island National Seashore; Laguna Atascosa NWR.

AMERICAN AVOCET

Recurvirostra americana

The full breeding plumage of an American Avocet is a sight to remember. The rusty head, needlelike bill and bold black and white body paint an elegant picture against the uniform mudflats. Often by August, the rusty hood has been replaced by the more subdued gray seen most of the year. No other avocet undergoes a yearly color change. • The American Avocet usually walks rapidly or runs about in fairly deep water, swinging its bill from side to side along the muddy bottom. The upcurved bill is also ideal for efficiently skimming aquatic vegetation and invertebrates off the surface of shallow water. • If disturbed while standing in its one-legged resting position, this bird takes off, switches legs in midair and lands on the rested leg. • Avocets remain in Texas year-round but are most abundant in winter and during migration, when thousands may gather along the coast.

breeding

nonbreeding

ID: long, upturned, black bill (longest on male and most upturned on female); long, pale blue legs; black wings with wide, white patches; white underparts.
Breeding: rust-colored head, neck and breast.
Nonbreeding: gray head, breast and neck.
Size: *L* 17–18 in; *W* 31 in.
Status: rare to common migrant statewide; common winter resident on the coast and inland in El Paso Co., the South Plains and southern Edwards Plateau; rare to locally common summer resident in the west and the Edwards Plateau, breeding in many areas.
Habitat: tidal mudflats and brackish coastal marshes; inland on marshy lakeshores or flooded fields.
Nesting: semi-colonial; along a dried mud-flat, exposed shoreline or open area, always near water; in a shallow depression; pair creates a shallow scrape or mound of vegetation lined with debris; pair incubates 4 darkly blotched, pale brownish eggs for 23–25 days.
Feeding: sweeps bill from side to side along the water's surface for aquatic invertabrates and occasional seeds; sometimes swims and tips up like a duck.
Voice: harsh, shrill *plee-eek plee-eek*.
Similar Species: *Black-necked Stilt* (p. 151): straight bill; mostly black head; red legs. *Willet* (p. 156): straight, heavy bill; flashy flight pattern is grayish overall.
Best Sites: McNary Reservoir (El Paso Co.); Mitchell L. (San Antonio); Bolivar Flats Shorebird Sanctuary (Galveston Co.); Brazoria NWR; Laguna Atascosa NWR.

SPOTTED SANDPIPER

Actitis macularius

Even though its breast spots are not noticeable from a distance, the Spotted Sandpiper's stiff-winged, quivering flight pattern and tendency to burst from the shore are easily recognizable. This bird is also known for its continuous "teetering" behavior as it forages. • It wasn't until 1972 that the unexpected truth about the Spotted Sandpiper's breeding activities were realized. The female Spotted Sandpiper defends a territory and mates with more than one male in a single breeding season, leaving the male to tend the nest and eggs. This unusual nesting behavior, known as polyandry, is found in about one percent of all bird species. The Spotted Sandpiper's breeding range extends from the central U.S. to the Arctic. In Texas, it occasionally breeds in the Panhandle. • The word *macularia* is Latin for "spot," referring to the spots on this bird's underparts in breeding plumage.

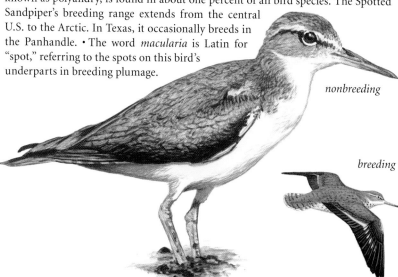

nonbreeding

breeding

ID: teeters almost continuously. *Breeding:* white underparts heavily spotted with black; yellow-orange legs; black-tipped, yellow-orange bill; white eyebrow. *Nonbreeding* and *immature:* pure white breast, belly, foreneck and throat; brown bill; dull yellow legs. *In flight:* flies close to water's surface with very rapid, shallow wingbeats; white upperwing stripe.
Size: *L* 7–8 in; *W* 15 in.
Status: common migrant statewide; uncommon to common winter resident in much of the state, but rare in west Texas and absent from the High Plains and northern Rolling Plains; rare and scattered breeder in the western third of Texas.

Habitat: coastal areas; shorelines, gravel beaches, ponds, marshes, alluvial wetlands, rivers, streams, swamps and sewage lagoons; occasionally visits cultivated fields.
Nesting: usually near water; sheltered by vegetation; shallow scrape is lined with grass; male incubates 4 darkly blotched, creamy buff eggs for 20–24 days.
Feeding: picks and gleans along shorelines for terrestrial and aquatic invertebrates; snatches flying insects from the air.
Voice: sharp, crisp *eat-wheat, eat-wheat, wheat-wheat-wheat-wheat.*
Similar Species: *Solitary Sandpiper* (p. 154): complete eye ring; yellowish bill with dark tip; streaking and barring on breast and sides. *Other sandpipers* (pp. 155–72): black bills and legs; breasts generally unmarked, streaked or barred rather than spotted.
Best Sites: *In migration* and *winter:* almost any body of water, including rivers.

153

SOLITARY SANDPIPER

Tringa solitaria

True to its name, the Solitary Sandpiper is usually seen alone, bobbing its body like a spirited dancer as it forages for insects. Every so often, though, a lucky observer may happen upon a small group of these birds during spring or fall. • A favorite foraging method of the Solitary Sandpiper is to wade in shallow water, slowly advancing and vibrating its leading foot, stirring the bottom to disturb prey. In this way, it captures aquatic insects and their larvae, including water boatmen and small crustaceans. • Solitary Sandpipers closely resemble both yellowlegs species. However, Solitary Sandpipers have a distinctive behavior that distinguishes them from yellowlegs: they slowly bob their hind end as they forage or rest. Their explosive *peet-wheet* call is also different. • Like the Spotted Sandpiper, this bird often frequents the shores of small lakes and ponds.

breeding

nonbreeding

ID: *Breeding:* white eye ring; short, green legs; dark, yellowish bill with black tip; white lores; spotted, gray-brown back; fine white streaks on gray-brown head, neck and breast; dark uppertail with barred, black and white sides. *Nonbreeding:* paler upperparts.
Size: *L* 7½–9 in; *W* 22 in.
Status: rare to uncommon migrant statewide; rare winter resident in coastal regions and inland in the southeastern Edwards Plateau and irregular further inland.
Habitat: freshwater coastal sites; wet meadows, sewage lagoons, muddy ponds, sedge wetlands, beaver ponds and wooded streams.
Nesting: does not nest in Texas.
Feeding: feeds in shallow water on small invertebrates, often disturbing the soft substrate with its feet to dislodge its prey.
Voice: high, thin *peet-wheet* or *wheat wheat wheat.*
Similar Species: *Lesser Yellowlegs* (p. 157): no eye ring; longer, bright yellow legs. *Spotted Sandpiper* (p. 153): incomplete eye ring; spotted breast in breeding plumage; black-tipped, yellow-orange bill. *Other sandpipers* (pp. 155–72): black bills and legs; many have short legs or lack eye rings.
Best Sites: Sea Rim SP; Sheldon Lake SP; Galveston I.; Mustang I.; Laguna Atascosa NWR.

GREATER YELLOWLEGS

Tringa melanoleuca

Seen in small flocks during migration and in winter, the Greater Yellowlegs is the more solitary of the two yellowlegs species. This species often performs a lookout role among mixed flocks of shorebirds. At the first sign of danger, this large sandpiper bobs its head and calls incessantly. If forced to, the Greater Yellowlegs usually retreats into deeper water, becoming airborne only as a last resort. • During migration, many shorebirds, including the Greater Yellowlegs, often stand or hop around beachflats on one leg, a stance that may conserves body heat. • Despite its long bill, the Greater Yellowlegs does not probe for food; instead it picks aquatic insects off the water's surface or swings its bill from side to side through the water to locate prey. This side-sweeping behavior may be a clue that you are looking at a Greater Yellowlegs and not a Lesser, which uses this technique far less often.

nonbreeding

nonbreeding

Habitat: almost all wetlands, including lakeshores, marshes, flooded fields and river shorelines; salt- and freshwater ponds.
Nesting: does not nest in Texas.
Feeding: usually wades in water over its knees; sometimes sweeps its bill from side to side and occasionally snatches prey from the water's surface; eats primarily aquatic invertebrates but also small fish.
Voice: quick, whistled *tew-tew-tew* series, usually 3 notes.
Similar Species: *Lesser Yellowlegs* (p. 157): smaller; straight bill, shorter than width of head; typical call is 2 higher notes: *tew-tew*. *Willet* (p. 156): black and white wings; heavier, straighter bill; dark greenish legs.
Best Sites: Village Creek Wastewater Treatment Plant (Arlington); Mitchell L. (San Antonio); Sea Rim SP; Galveston I.; Mustang I.; Laguna Atascosa NWR.

ID: long, bright yellow legs; slightly upturned, dark bill, noticeably longer than head width. *Breeding:* brown-black back and upperwing; fine, dense, dark streaking on head and neck; dark barring on breast often extends onto belly; subtle, dark eye line; pale lores. *Nonbreeding:* gray overall; fine streaks on breast.
Size: *L* 13–15 in; *W* 28 in.
Status: common migrant statewide; uncommon winter resident in the southern two-thirds of the state and rare and irregular in the northern third; rare summer straggler in coastal regions.

WILLET

Tringa semipalmata

When grounded, the Willet cuts a rather dull figure, but in flight or when displaying, the Willet has a striking black and white appearance and calls attention to itself with a loud, rhythmic *will-will willet, will-will-willet!* If you look closely, you may notice that the white markings across the Willet's wingspan form a rough "W" as it flies away. Other shorebirds may use the bright, bold flashes of the Willet's wings as alerts of imminent danger. • Willets are loud, social, easily identified birds—a nice change when dealing with sandpipers. Willets are abundant residents in the salt marshes or dune grasses along our coastlines. They are also uncommon migrants throughout the state. • There are two distinct subspecies of the Willet, a western one (*C.s. inornatus*) and an eastern one (*C.s. semipalmatus*). The eastern race rarely ventures far from the Atlantic Coast, whereas the western one breeds far inland and winters mostly on the Pacific Coast.

breeding

ID: plump; heavy, straight, black bill; pale throat and belly; dark greenish legs. *Breeding:* dark streaking and barring overall. *Nonbreeding:* grayer upperparts. *In flight:* bold black and white wing pattern.
Size: *L* 14–16 in; *W* 26 in.
Status: common resident along the coast; rare to uncommon migrant statewide.
Habitat: freshwater coastal habitats; wet fields and shorelines of marshes, lakes and ponds.
Nesting: on the ground, well hidden among vegetation in a salt marsh or field; shallow

depression is lined with leaves and dry grass; pair incubates 4 heavily spotted, olive or buff eggs for 24–26 days.
Feeding: feeds by probing muddy areas; also gleans the ground for insects; occasionally eats shoots and seeds.
Voice: loud, rolling *will-will willet, will-will-willet.*
Similar Species: *Hudsonian Godwit* (p. 447) and *Marbled Godwit* (p. 160): larger; much longer, pinkish yellow bills with slightly upturned, dark tips; more muted or cinnamon-toned wing patterns. *Greater Yellowlegs* (p. 155): long, yellow legs; slightly upturned bill; plainer wings, dark above and pale below.
Best Sites: any accessible beach along the coast.

LESSER YELLOWLEGS

Tringa flavipes

With a series of continuous, rapid-fire *tew-tew* calls, the Lesser Yellowlegs streaks across wetlands, lakeshores and beaches. It is relatively common throughout Texas during spring and fall migration. • Many birders find it a challenge to distinguish the Lesser Yellowlegs and the Greater Yellowlegs in the field. With practice, you will notice that the Lesser's bill is finer, straighter and not noticeably longer than the width of its head. The Lesser appears to have longer legs and wings, making it seem slimmer and taller than the Greater, and it is also more commonly seen in flocks. If your sight proves inadequate, open your ears: the Lesser Yellowlegs gives a pair of peeps, whereas the Greater gives three. If you are still puzzled at a bird's identity, simply write "yellowlegs spp." in your field notes and try again next time. • The word *flavipes* is derived from Latin words meaning "yellow foot."

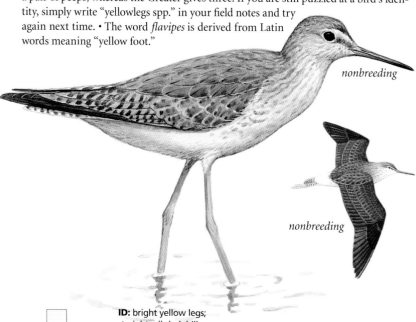

nonbreeding

nonbreeding

ID: bright yellow legs; straight, all-dark bill, shorter than width of head. *Breeeding:* brownish black back and upperwings; dense, dark streaking on head, neck and breast; barred, white belly; subtle dark eye line; pale lores. *Nonbreeding:* fine streaking on back; no barring on belly.
Size: *L* 10–11 in; *W* 24 in.
Status: common migrant statewide; common winter resident in coastal areas and irregular inland; rare summer straggler along the coast.
Habitat: coastal freshwater ponds; shorelines of lakes, rivers, marshes and ponds; sod farms.
Nesting: does not nest in Texas.

Feeding: snatches prey from the water's surface; frequently wades in shallow water; eats primarily aquatic invertebrates but also small fish and tadpoles.
Voice: typically a high-pitched pair of *tew* notes.
Similar Species: *Greater Yellowlegs* (p. 155): larger; slightly upturned bill, noticeably longer than width of head; *tew* call usually given in 3-note series. *Solitary Sandpiper* (p. 154): white eye ring; greenish legs. *Willet* (p. 156): much bulkier; black and white wings; heavier bill; dark greenish legs.
Best Sites: Sea Rim SP; Galveston I.; Brazoria NWR; Mustang I.; Boca Chica.

UPLAND SANDPIPER

Bartramia longicauda

Upland Sandpipers are usually seen in grassy habitats, moving with a ploverlike stop-and-start run. During migration, their soft, distinctive *quip-ip-ip-ip* calls can be heard at night as they fly overhead. • Twice each year, these wide-ranging shorebirds migrate through Texas, usually east of the Pecos River. They fly from their breeding grounds in the Great Plains and Canadian Prairies to overwinter in South America. • During the late 1800s, high market demand for Upland Sandpiper meat led to severe overhunting and catastrophic declines in this species' population over much of North America. Its numbers have since improved, but recent declines in grassland habitats again threaten this sandpiper's welfare. • This species was formerly known as "Upland Plover."

ID: small head; long, streaked neck; large, dark eyes; yellow legs; mottled, brownish upperparts; lightly streaked breast, sides and flanks; white belly and undertail coverts; bill about same length as head.
Size: *L* 11–12½ in; *W* 26 in.
Status: common spring and uncommon fall migrant in the eastern half of Texas; uncommon spring and common fall migrant in the western half; rare summer resident in the northern Panhandle and adjacent parts of the Rolling Plains.

Habitat: sod farms, ungrazed pastures, grassy meadows, abandoned fields, natural grasslands, airports and coastal plains.
Nesting: no recent nesting records for Texas.
Feeding: gleans the ground for insects, especially grasshoppers and beetles.
Voice: soft *quip-ip-ip-ip* nocturnal flight call; airy, whistled *whip-whee-ee you* courtship song; *quip-ip-ip* alarm call.
Similar Species: *Willet* (p. 156): longer, heavier bill; dark greenish legs; bold black and white wings in flight. *Buff-breasted Sandpiper* (p. 172): shorter neck; larger head; daintier bill; no streaking on cheek and foreneck. *Pectoral Sandpiper* (p. 169): streaking on breast ends abruptly; smaller eyes; shorter neck; usually seen in larger numbers.
Best Sites: grassy fields and pastures on the Coastal Plain.

LONG-BILLED CURLEW

Numenius americanus

With a bill more than seven inches long, the Long-billed Curlew—North America's largest sandpiper—is an imposing and remarkable bird. The long, downcurved bill is a dexterous tool ideal for extracting buried mollusks from soft, penetrable mud or picking grasshoppers from dense prairie grasslands. • These Curlews may be seen throughout Texas during migration, and a good many overwinter here. Individual Long-Billed Curlews return to—and defend—the same winter foraging territory each year. These large, long-necked sandpipers prefer quiet, undisturbed coastal beaches and pastures. Breeding records exist for the northwest Panhandle and the coast. • The gun and the plow have caused a decline of this once numerous bird. The future of the Long-billed Curlew is largely tied to adoption of conservative range and grassland management strategies.

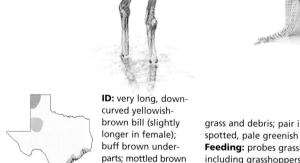

ID: very long, down-curved yellowish-brown bill (slightly longer in female); buff brown under-parts; mottled brown upperparts; unstriped head; long legs. *In flight:* orange-cinnamon underwing linings.
Size: *L* 20–26 in; *W* 3 ft.
Status: common migrant in much of the state but uncommon in the South Plains and rare in the Trans-Pecos and the north-west quarter; summer vagrant and common winter resident along the coast.
Habitat: *Nonbreeding:* coastal grasslands, pastures, tidal mudflats, estuaries, saltwater marshes and tidal channels. *Breeding:* prairies and pastures.
Nesting: usually on dry prairie or pastures; in a slight depression sparsely lined with

grass and debris; pair incubates 4 heavily spotted, pale greenish eggs for 27–30 days.
Feeding: probes grasslands for insects, including grasshoppers and beetles; probes shorelines and coastal mudflats for mollusks, crabs, crayfish, marine worms and insects; may eat nestling birds, eggs and some berries.
Voice: most common call is a loud whistle: *cur-lee cur-lee cur-lee;* also, a melodious, rolling *cuurrleeeuuu.*
Similar Species: *Marbled Godwit* (p. 160): shorter, slightly upturned, yellow-orange bill with dark tip; often found among or near curlews along the coast. *Whimbrel* (p. 447): smaller; much shorter bill; dark and pale striping on head; unmarked, white belly.
Best Sites: Sea Rim SP; Bolivar Flats (Galveston Co.); Galveston I.; Brazoria NWR; Mustang I.; Aransas NWR.

159

MARBLED GODWIT

Limosa fedoa

Even with a long bill, buried prey seems to be just beyond reach of the Marbled Godwit, so this bird is frequently seen with its head submerged beneath the water or with its face pressed into a mudflat. These deep probings apparently pay off for this large, resourceful shorebird, and a godwit looks genuinely pleased with a freshly extracted meal and a face covered in mud. • Unlike Hudsonian Godwits, which undertake long migrations from the Arctic to South America, Marbled Godwits migrate comparatively short distances from breeding grounds in the Great Plains and Canadian Prairies to coastal wintering areas in the southern U.S. and Central America. These birds turn up along our coastlines during winter and may be fairly common in some locations but rare in others. • The genus name *Limosa*, meaning "muddy," refers to this bird's preference for muddy foraging habitats.

breeding

nonbreeding

ID: long, yellow-orange bill with dark, slightly upturned tip; long neck and legs; mottled, buff brown plumage is darkest on upperparts; long, blue-black legs. *Breeding:* heavily barred breast and belly. *Nonbreeding:* buff breast and belly. *In flight:* cinnamon wing linings.
Size: *L* 16–20 in; *W* 30 in.
Status: very rare to rare migrant statewide; common winter resident and rare summer straggler on the coasts.
Habitat: coastal beaches, inlets and mudflats.
Nesting: does not nest in Texas.

Feeding: probes deeply in soft substrates for worms, insect larvae, crustaceans and mollusks; picks insects from grass; may also eat the tubers and seeds of aquatic vegetation.
Voice: usually silent in Texas.
Similar Species: *Hudsonian Godwit* (p. 447): smaller; chestnut red neck and underparts; dark tail; white rump. *Greater Yellowlegs* (p. 155): shorter, all-dark bill; bright yellow legs. *Long-billed Dowitcher* (p. 174) and *Short-billed Dowitcher* (p. 173): smaller; straight, all-dark bills; white rump wedge; yellow-green legs. *Long-billed Curlew* (p. 159): down-curved bill; unstriped head; lighter underparts.
Best Sites: any coastal area with appropriate mudflats.

RUDDY TURNSTONE

Arenaria interpres

nonbreeding

nonbreeding

Small flocks of boldly patterned Ruddy Turnstones run along our coastal shores, mingling and foraging among the shorebirds. Their painted faces and eye-catching black and red backs set them apart from the multitudes of brown and white sandpipers. In Texas, their striking breeding plumage may be seen in spring before these shorebirds depart for their northern breeding grounds. • Ruddy Turnstones are truly long-distance migrants. Individuals that nest along the shores of the Arctic routinely fly to South America or western Europe to avoid frosty winters. Ruddy Turnstones routinely stop to refuel along Texas shorelines during spring and fall migration and many winter along the Gulf Coast. • The name "turnstone" is appropriate for this bird, which uses its bill to flip over pebbles, shells and washed-up vegetation to expose hidden invertebrates. The short, stubby, slightly upturned bill is an ideal utensil for this unusual foraging style. The Ruddy Turnstone eats whatever food is readily available, including berries, the eggs of crabs or other birds and even leftover french fries.

ID: white belly; black "bib" curves up to shoulder; stout, slightly upturned, black bill; orange-red legs. *Breeding:* ruddy upperparts (female is slightly paler); white face; black collar; dark, streaky crown. *Nonbreeding:* brownish upperparts and face.
Size: *L* 9½ in; *W* 21 in.
Status: statewide migrant, common along the coast but rare inland; common winter resident and uncommon summer visitor on the coast.

Habitat: coastal beaches, shores of lakes, reservoirs, marshes and sewage lagoons; also in flooded fields.
Nesting: does not nest in Texas.
Feeding: probes under and flips rocks, weeds and shells for food items; picks, digs and probes soil or mud for invertebrates; also eats berries, seeds, spiders and carrion.
Voice: low, repeated contact notes; also, a sharp *cut-a-cut* alarm call.
Similar Species: *Other sandpipers* (pp. 153–72): plainer plumage and wing markings in flight. *Plovers* (pp. 142–49): bold plumage in significantly different patterns.
Best Sites: on the coastal beaches and rocky dikes.

161

RED KNOT

Calidris canutus

Small flocks of Red Knots appear briefly during migration. These tubby birds are rarely in their colorful red breeding plumage as they pass through Texas, appearing instead in their drab gray and white winter colors. • These birds fly up to 19,000 miles in a single year, some traveling from breeding grounds in the Arctic to wintering grounds at the southern tip of South America. • Migrating Red Knots have traditionally stopped over in Delaware Bay, New Jersey, timing their arrival to the horseshoe crab spawn. For a few weeks each year, they gorge on crab eggs, doubling their body weight to continue their journey north. Recently, horseshoe crab numbers have been decreasing as a result of habitat degradation and the overharvest of crabs or crab eggs for commercial fishing bait. The disappearing food source has meant that many Red Knots are too weak to reach their breeding grounds, and populations are facing serious declines. In an effort to reverse this alarming trend, a portion of Delaware Bay has been protected, and coastal states have placed restrictions or moratoriums on the crab harvest.

nonbreeding

nonbreeding

ID: chunky, round body; dark greenish legs; faint barring on white rump. *Breeding:* brown, black and buff upperparts; rusty face, breast and underparts. *Nonbreeding:* pale gray upperparts; white underparts with some faint streaking on upper breast. *Immature:* buff-washed breast; "scaly" back. *In flight:* white wing stripe.
Size: *L* 10½ in; *W* 23 in.
Status: statewide migrant, uncommon to common on the coast and rare and local inland; rare summer straggler on the upper coast.

Habitat: coastal beaches, lakeshores, marshes and plowed fields.
Nesting: does not nest in Texas.
Feeding: gleans shorelines for insects, crustaceans and mollusks; probes soft substrates, creating lines of small holes.
Voice: melodious, soft *ker ek* in flight.
Similar Species: *Long-billed Dowitcher* (p. 174) and *Short-billed Dowitcher* (p. 173): much longer bills; barred undertail and flanks; white wedge on back. *Buff-breasted Sandpiper* (p. 172): buff underparts; finer, shorter bill. *Curlew Sandpiper:* longer bill; breeding bird has redder rusty color.
Best Sites: Bolivar Flats Shorebird Sanctuary (Galveston Co.); Galveston I.; Brazoria NWR; Padre Island National Seashore; Laguna Atascosa NWR.

162

SANDERLING

Calidris alba

Lively Sanderlings grace sandy shorelines around the world, forever running toward the surf and back. Their well-known habit of chasing waves has a simple purpose: to snatch washed-up aquatic invertebrates before the next wave rolls into shore. To vary their diet, Sanderlings are also expert tweakers of marine worms and other soft-bodied critters just below the surface of wet mudflats. • When engaged in the rapid sprints of their beach-foraging strategy, Sanderlings move so fast on their dark legs that they appear to be gliding across the sand. When resting, Sanderlings often tuck one leg up to preserve body heat. • Sanderlings are among the world's most cosmopolitan creatures. They breed across the Arctic in Alaska, Canada and Asia and spend winters running up and down sandy shorelines in more temperate climates on every continent except Antarctica.

nonbreeding

breeding

ID: straight, sturdy, black bill; black legs. *Breeding:* rusty head and breast with dark spotting or mottling. *Nonbreeding:* white underparts; very pale gray upperparts; black shoulder patch (often concealed).

Size: *L* 7–8½ in; *W* 17 in.

Status: common to abundant migrant along the coast and less common and local inland; common winter resident and summer visitor on the coast.

Habitat: lower wave zone of sandy ocean beaches; also uses rocky shorelines, breakwaters, tidal mudflats and estuaries; occasional on inland freshwater shorelines and mudflats.

Nesting: does not nest in Texas.

Feeding: pecks at sand and mud to obtain prey; winter diet is mainly coastal invertebrates; may eat carrion; summer diet includes mostly insects and some leaves, seeds and algae.

Voice: generally vocal; flocks converse and flush with electric *twik* notes, sometimes continued in an irregular series.

Similar Species: *Least Sandpiper* (p. 166): smaller and browner. *Dunlin* (p. 170): darker back; streaked breast; slightly downcurved bill. *Red Knot* (p. 162): larger; faintly barred, whitish rump; breeding bird has rusty underparts. *Western Sandpiper* (p. 165) and *Semipalmated Sandpiper* (p. 164): smaller; head and upper breast not uniformly copper color in breeding plumage; sandy upperparts in winter.

Best Sites: any exposed coastal beach.

SEMIPALMATED SANDPIPER

Calidris pusilla

Among the swarms of similar-looking *Calidris* sandpipers that migrate through Texas, the small, plain Semipalmated Sandpiper can be difficult to identify. Because of the similarity in their high-pitched calls, the Semipalmated, Least, Western, White-rumped and Baird's sandpipers are known collectively as "peeps." These strikingly similar "miniatures" can make shorebird identification either a complete nightmare or an uplifting challenge. • Semipalmated Sandpipers raise up to four young during the short Arctic summer, then fly almost the entire length of the Americas during migration. To replenish their body fat during the long journey, Semipalmated Sandpipers gather at key coastal stopovers (staging areas) that provide an ample food supply. Birds from the Great Plains travel south through Texas, continuing on over the Gulf to winter in South America. Birds from the Eastern Arctic leave the mainland at New England or southern Canada and then fly over the ocean to South America, an incredible nonstop journey of 2000 miles.

nonbreeding

nonbreeding

ID: short, straight, black bill; white eyebrow; black legs. *Breeding:* mottled upperparts of white, black and brown; slight tinge of rufous on ear patch, crown and scapulars; faint streaks on white upper breast and flanks. *Nonbreeding:* gray-brown upperparts; white underparts with light brown wash on sides of upper breast. *In flight:* black line through white rump and tail.
Size: *L* 5½–7 in; *W* 14 in.
Status: rare to locally common migrant statewide.
Habitat: coastal mudflats and the shores of ponds and lakes.

Nesting: does not nest in Texas.
Feeding: probes soft substrates and gleans for aquatic insects and crustaceans.
Voice: harsh *cherk* flight call; sometimes a longer *chirrup* or a chittering alarm call.
Similar Species: *Least Sandpiper* (p. 166): yellowish legs; darker upperparts. *Western Sandpiper* (p. 165): longer, slightly downcurved bill; bright rufous wash on crown and ear patch in breeding plumage. *Sanderling* (p. 163): paler upperparts in nonbreeding plumage; white stripe on wing. *White-rumped Sandpiper* (p. 167): larger; white rump; folded wings extend beyond tail. *Baird's Sandpiper* (p. 168): larger; longer bill; folded wings extend beyond tail.
Best Sites: exposed mudflats at reservoirs, wastewater treatment plants and the coast.

WESTERN SANDPIPER

Calidris mauri

Western Sandpipers overwinter primarily along the Pacific and Gulf coasts, picking over the mudflats for marine invertebrates. In spring, large flocks of these birds migrate northward to the Copper River Delta in Alaska, where as many as 6.5 million Western Sandpipers converge to breed. • Many identification guides tell you to look for this bird's downcurved bill, and on paper this seems like a sensible plan. In the field, however, as angles and lighting change, the bills of "peeps" can look downcurved one moment, straight the next and anything in between when double-checked. It is a good idea to spend some time getting to know the peeps before trying to identify them. The Western Sandpiper can easily be confused with other peeps, in particular the Semipalmated Sandpiper, which also has black legs.

nonbreeding

nonbreeding

ID: black, slightly downcurved bill; black legs. *Breeding:* rufous crown, ear patch and scapulars; V-shaped streaks on upper breast and flanks; light underparts. *Nonbreeding:* white eyebrow; gray-brown upperparts; white underparts; streaky, light brown wash on upper breast. *In flight:* narrow, white wing stripe; black line through white rump.

Size: *L* 6–7 in; *W* 14 in.

Status: uncommon to common migrant statewide, although less common inland; uncommon to common winter resident and rare and irregular in the Panhandle, north Texas and Trans-Pecos.

Habitat: pond edges, lakeshores and mudflats.

Nesting: does not nest in Texas.

Feeding: gleans and probes mud and shallow water; primarily eats aquatic insects, worms and crustaceans.

Voice: high-pitched *cheep* flight call.

Similar Species: *Semipalmated Sandpiper* (p. 164): shorter, straight bill; less rufous on crown, ear patch and scapulars. *Least Sandpiper* (p. 166): smaller; yellowish legs; darker breast wash in all plumages; lacks rufous patches. *White-rumped Sandpiper* (p. 167): larger; white rump; folded wings extend beyond tail; lacks rufous patches. *Sanderling* (p. 163): nonbreeding plumage shows pale gray upperparts, blackish trailing edge on flight feathers and bold, white upperwing stripe in flight.

Best Sites: exposed mudflats at reservoirs, wastewater treatment plants and the coast.

165

LEAST SANDPIPER

Calidris minutilla

Least Sandpipers are the smallest North American shorebirds, but their size does not deter them from performing migratory feats. Like most other "peeps," many Least Sandpipers migrate from the Arctic to the southern tip of South America and back. • Arctic summers are short, so shorebirds must maximize their breeding efforts. Least Sandpipers lay large eggs relative to those of other sandpipers, and the entire clutch might weigh over half the weight of the female! The young hatch in an advanced state of development, giving them an early start on preparations for fall migration. These tiny shorebirds begin moving south as early as the first week of July, so they are some of the first sandpipers to arrive back in Texas for winter. • Although light-colored legs are a good field mark for this species, bad lighting or mud can confuse matters. Dark mud can make the legs look dark, whereas light-colored mud can make the legs of other species lighter.

breeding

nonbreeding

ID: black bill; yellowish legs; chestnut, white and black mottled back. *Breeding:* buff brown breast, head and nape; light breast streaking; prominent white "V" on back. *Nonbreeding:* more gray brown overall.

Size: *L* 5–6½ in; *W* 13 in.

Status: common to abundant migrant statewide; uncommon to locally common winter resident in most of the state except for the northern part of the High Plains.

Habitat: tidal pools, sewage lagoons, mudflats, lakeshores, ditches and wetland edges.

Nesting: does not nest in Texas.

Feeding: probes or pecks for insects, crustaceans, small mollusks and occasional seeds.

Voice: high-pitched *kreee.*

Similar Species: *Semipalmated Sandpiper* (p. 164): black legs; paler upperparts; rufous tinge on crown, ear patch and scapulars. *Western Sandpiper* (p. 165): slightly larger; black legs; lighter breast wash in all plumages; rufous patches on crown, ear and scapulars in breeding plumage. *Other peeps* (pp. 164–68): larger; dark legs.

Best Sites: exposed mudflats at reservoirs, wastewater treatment plants and the coast.

WHITE-RUMPED SANDPIPER

Calidris fuscicollis

Just as a die-hard shorebird-watcher is about to go into a peep-induced stupor, small, brownish heads emerge from hiding. Back feathers are ruffled, wings are stretched, and, almost without warning, the birds take flight and flash pure white rumps. There is no doubt that the beautiful White-rumped Sandpiper has been identified. • This sandpiper's white rump may serve a similar purpose to the tail of a white-tailed deer, to alert other birds when danger threatens. • When flocks of White-rumps and other sandpipers take to the air, they often defecate in unison. This spontaneous evacuation might assist them by reducing their weight for takeoff. Flocks of White-rumped Sandpipers have also been known to collectively rush at a predator and then suddenly scatter in its face. • Like many sandpipers, White-rumps are accomplished long-distance migrants, often flying for stretches of 60 hours nonstop.

breeding

nonbreeding

ID: black legs; black bill, about as long as head width. *Breeding:* brown-mottled upperparts; dark streaking on breast, sides and flanks. *Nonbreeding:* gray upperparts and breast. *In flight:* white rump; dark tail; indistinct wing bar.
Size: *L* 7–8 in; *W* 17 in.
Status: uncommon to common spring migrant in most of the state, although rare in the Trans-Pecos; rare fall migrant in the eastern half of Texas.

Habitat: coastal tidal pools and mudflats; inland on lakeshores, marshes, sewage lagoons and flooded and cultivated fields.
Nesting: does not nest in Texas.
Feeding: gleans the ground and shorelines for insects, crustaceans and mollusks.
Voice: characteristic squeal-like *tzeet* flight call is higher in pitch than that of any other peep.
Similar Species: *Other peeps* (pp. 164–68): all have dark line through rump. *Baird's Sandpiper* (p. 168): grayish brown rump; breast streaking does not extend onto flanks. *Stilt Sandpiper* (p. 171) and *Curlew Sandpiper:* much longer legs trail beyond tail in flight.
Best Sites: exposed mudflats on reservoirs, wastewater treatment plants and the coast; recently flooded rice fields.

BAIRD'S SANDPIPER

Calidris bairdii

The Baird's Sandpiper is a modest-looking bird with extraordinary migratory habits. Like many shorebirds, this small, long-winged, brown sandpiper remains on its Arctic breeding grounds for a very short time. As soon as newly hatched chicks can fend for themselves, the adult birds abandon their nests and flock together to begin their southward migration to South America in July. Thus, southbound migrants often reach Texas while some birds are still northbound. A few weeks after the parents have departed, the young form a second wave of southbound migrants. • This elegant wader was named after Spencer Fullerton Baird, an early director of the Smithsonian Institution who organized several natural history expeditions across North America.

breeding

breeding

ID: black legs and bill; fine dark streaks on buffy brown breast; white belly. *Breeding:* large, black diamond-like patterns on back and wing coverts. *Nonbreeding:* gray-brown upperparts, head and breast.
Size: *L* 7–7 ½ in; *W* 17 in.
Status: uncommon to common migrant in all areas.
Habitat: upper ocean beach waveslope, drier estuarine and freshwater mudflats, damp alkali flats and margins of sewage ponds.
Nesting: does not nest in Texas.
Feeding: walks slowly along, picking insects and other invertebrates from the water's surface; rarely probes; much less inclined to wade than other sandpipers of similar appearance and habitat.
Voice: soft, reedy, rolling *creeep creeep*, often repeated in flight; usually silent while foraging.
Similar Species: *Pectoral Sandpiper* (p. 169): striped (not "scaly") upperparts; legs usually dull yellowish. *Least Sandpiper* (p. 166): smaller; streakier upperparts; yellowish legs. *Dunlin* (p. 170): longer bill with downcurved tip; distinct upperwing stripe in flight; wades in water. *Western Sandpiper* (p. 165) and *Sanderling* (p. 163): noticeably shorter wings; generally in large, busy flocks in or near water.
Best Sites: exposed mudflats at reservoirs, wastewater treatment plants and the coast.

PECTORAL SANDPIPER

Calidris melanotos

The Pectoral Sandpiper is named for the location of the male's prominent air sacs. When displaying on his Arctic breeding grounds, the male inflates these air sacs, causing his breast feathers to rise. While displaying, the male also emits a hollow hooting sound that has been likened to the sound of a foghorn. • During their epic annual migrations, these widespread travelers have been observed in every state and province in North America. In spring and fall, large flocks of over a thousand Pectoral Sandpipers are conspicuous along our coastlines and in wet, grassy fields throughout Texas. When threatened, the flocks suddenly launch into the air and converge into a single, swirling mass. • Unlike most sandpipers, the Pectoral exhibits obvious sexual dimorphism, with the female being is only two-thirds the size of the male. • Because of its preference for wet meadows and grassy marshes, the Pectoral Sandpiper is sometimes referred to as "Grass Snipe."

ID: brown breast streaks end abruptly at edge of white belly; white under-tail coverts; mottled upperparts; black bill has slightly down-curved tip; may have faintly rusty, dark crown and back; long, yellow legs; folded wings extend beyond tail. *Immature:* less spotting on breast; broader white feather edges on back form 2 distinct white V-shapes.

Size: *L* 9 in; *W* 18 in (female noticeably smaller).

Status: locally common migrant statewide; possible summer straggler statewide.

Habitat: lakeshores, marshes, mudflats and flooded fields or pastures.

Nesting: does not nest in Texas.

Feeding: probes and pecks for small insects; eats mainly flies but also takes beetles and some grasshoppers; may eat small mollusks, crustaceans, berries, seeds, moss, algae and some plant material.

Voice: sharp, short, low *krrick krrick*.

Similar Species: combination of well-defined "bib" of dark streaking and yellow legs is unique among the peeps.

Best Sites: exposed mudflats at reservoirs, wastewater treatment plants and the coast; recently flooded rice fields.

DUNLIN

Calidris alpina

Outside the breeding season, Dunlins form dynamic, synchronized flocks. More exclusive than other shorebird troupes, these tight flocks rarely include other species. Sometimes hundreds of these birds are seen flying wing tip to wing tip. Unlike many shorebirds that make long migrations to South America, Dunlins overwinter in coastal areas of Mexico and the southern Unite States—few ever cross the equator. They gather in flocks that can number in the tens of thousands. • Dunlins are fairly distinctive in their breeding attire: their black bellies and legs make them look as though they have been wading belly-deep in puddles of ink. • This bird was originally called "Dunling," meaning "little dark one," but with the passage of time, the "g" was dropped. It was also known as "Red-backed Sandpiper" because of its rufous back in breeding plumage.

nonbreeding

nonbreeding

ID: slightly down-curved, black bill; black legs. *Breeding:* black belly; gray streaking on white neck and underparts; rufous-marked wings, back and crown. *Nonbreeding:* pale gray underparts; brownish gray upperparts; light brown streaking on breast and nape. *In flight:* white wing stripe.
Size: *L* 7½–9 in; *W* 17 in.
Status: rare to locally common migrant statewide, more so on the coast; common winter resident on the coast, rare at scattered inland locations; occasional summer straggler on the coast.

Habitat: mudflats and the shores of ponds, marshes and lakes.
Nesting: does not nest in Texas.
Feeding: gleans and probes mudflats for aquatic crustaceans, worms, mollusks and insects.
Voice: grating *cheezp* or *treezp* flight call.
Similar Species: black belly in breeding plumage is distinctive. *Western Sandpiper* (p. 165) and *Semipalmated Sandpiper* (p. 164): smaller; nonbreeding plumage is browner overall and mottled; less downcurved bill tip. *Least Sandpiper* (p. 166): smaller; yellowish legs; nonbreeding bird has darker, mottled upperparts. *Sanderling* (p. 163): paler; straight bill; usually seen running in the surf.
Best Sites: exposed mudflats at reservoirs, wastewater treatment plants and the coast; recently flooded rice fields.

STILT SANDPIPER

Calidris himantopus

With the silhouette of a small Lesser Yellowlegs and the foraging behavior of a dowitcher—birds with which it often associates—the Stilt Sandpiper is easily overlooked by most birders. Named for its relatively long legs, this shorebird prefers to feed in shallow water, where it digs like a dowitcher, often dunking its head completely underwater. • When identifying this species, it helps to know that, because of its short bill, the Stilt Sandpiper must hunch its back and lean farther forward than a dowitcher to reach prey. Moving on tall, stiltlike legs, this sandpiper will also wade into breast-deep water in search of a meal. The Stilt Sandpiper eats anything from insects to seeds and occasionally sweeps its bill from side to side to snag freshwater shrimp, insect larvae or tiny minnows. • Unlike many of its *Calidris* relatives, the Stilt Sandpiper never gathers in large flocks.

nonbreeding

nonbreeding

ID: long, greenish legs; long, dark bill droops slightly at tip. *Breeding:* chestnut red ear patch; white eyebrow; striped crown; streaked neck; dark-barred, white-marked, dark upperparts. *Nonbreeding:* fainter eyebrow; dirty white neck and breast; white belly; dark, brownish gray upperparts. *In flight:* white rump; legs trail behind tail; no wing stripe.
Size: *L* 8–9 in; *W* 18 in.
Status: locally common migrant east of the Pecos R. and rare to the west; uncommon winter resident in the Lower Rio Grande Valley and rare on the coast and inland to the southern edge of the Edwards Plateau.

Habitat: shores of lakes, reservoirs, marshes and sandy coastal beaches.
Nesting: does not nest in Texas.
Feeding: probes deeply in shallow water, but will also feed in deeper water; occasionally picks insects from the water's surface or the ground; eats mostly invertebrates but also takes seeds, roots and leaves.
Voice: simple, sharp *querp* or *kirr* in flight; clearer *whu.*
Similar Species: *Greater Yellowlegs* (p. 155) and *Lesser Yellowlegs* (p.157): larger; yellow legs; straight bills; no red ear patches. *Curlew Sandpiper:* more obviously curved bill; black legs; paler gray upperparts in nonbreeding plumage. *Dunlin* (p. 170): shorter, black legs; long, downward curving bill; dark rump; whitish wing bar.
Best Sites: exposed mudflats at reservoirs, wastewater treatment plants and the coast; recently flooded rice fields.

BUFF-BREASTED SANDPIPER

Tryngites subruficollis

Shy in behavior and humble in appearance, the Buff-breasted Sandpiper is an uncommon migrant that is seen mainly in eastern Texas. This sandpiper regularly mingles with flocks of foraging Black-bellied Plovers and American Golden-Plovers in cultivated fields, pastures and grasslands. • The Buff-breasted Sandpiper prefers drier habitats than most other sandpipers. When feeding, this subtly colored bird stands motionless, blending beautifully into a backdrop of cultivated fields, mudflats or managed sod farms. Only when moving prey comes within range does the Buff-breasted Sandpiper become visible, making a short, forward sprint to snatch at a fresh meal. • The Buff-breasted Sandpiper breeds in Alaska and the Canadian Arctic, and it winters in southern South America, generally avoiding the eastern and western edges of the continent, then continues through Central America. • These birds appear dovelike with their somewhat bulbous heads, thin necks and short legs.

ID: buffy, unpatterned face and foreneck; large, dark eyes; very thin, straight, black bill; buff underparts; small spots on crown, nape, breast, sides and flanks; "scaly" look to back and upperwings; yellow legs. *In flight:* pure white underwings; no wing stripe.
Size: *L* 7½–8 in; *W* 18 in.
Status: rare to uncommon migrant in the eastern half of Texas and rare in the western half; more common in fall than in spring.

Habitat: shores of lakes, reservoirs and marshes; sod farms, airports, highway ditches, cultivated fields and flooded fields.
Nesting: does not nest in Texas.
Feeding: gleans the ground and shorelines for insects, spiders and small crustaceans; may eat seeds.
Voice: usually silent; calls include *chup* or *tick* notes; *preet* flight call.
Similar Species: *Upland Sandpiper* (p. 158): bolder streaking on breast; longer neck; smaller head; larger bill; streaking on cheek and foreneck.
Best Sites: wet grassy fields and pastures, especially ones adjacent to bodies of water.

SHORT-BILLED DOWITCHER

Limnodromus griseus

Short-billed Dowitchers tend to be stockier than most shorebirds, and they generally avoid venturing into deep water. While foraging along shorelines, these birds use their bills to "stitch" up and down into the mud with a rhythm like a sewing machine. This drilling motion, which is helpful for long-range field identification, liquefies the mud or sand, allowing the dowitchers to reach their prey. • These plump shorebirds migrate through eastern Texas but are usually seen along our coastal mudflats, marshes and beaches. • The best way to distinguish between Short-billed Dowitchers and the very similar Long-billed Dowitchers is by their flight calls or by listening to them feeding. Long-bills chatter softly while feeding, whereas Short-bills feed silently.

nonbreeding

nonbreeding

ID: chunky body; long, straight, dark bill; white eyebrow; yellowish green legs. *Breeding:* white belly; reddish buff neck and upper breast with dark spots or bars; prominent dark barring on white sides and flanks. *Nonbreeding:* dirty gray upperparts; dirty white underparts. *In flight:* white wedge on rump and lower back; barred, black and white tail.

Size: *L* 11–12 in; *W* 19 in.

Status: common migrant along the coast, less common in the eastern half of the state and rare in the western half; locally common winter coastal resident.

Habitat: coastal mudflats, shores of lakes, reservoirs and marshes.

Nesting: does not nest in Texas.

Feeding: wades in shallow water or mud, probing deeply with a rapid up–down bill motion; eats aquatic invertebrates; may also eat seeds, aquatic plants and grasses.

Voice: generally silent; mellow, repeated *tututu*, *toodulu* or *toodu* flight call.

Similar Species: *Long-billed Dowitcher* (p. 174): breeding bird has black and white barring on reddish flanks, very little white on belly; dark barring on neck and upper breast; high-pitched *keek* alarm call. *Red Knot* (p. 162): much shorter bill; all-gray tail and white wedge on back in flight; unmarked breast in breeding plumage. *Wilson's Snipe* (p. 175): heavily striped head, back, neck and breast; shorter legs. *American Woodcock* (p. 176): unmarked, buff underparts; yellow bill; pale bars on black crown and nape; short legs.

Best Sites: mudflats and shallow waters on the coast; Bolivar Flats (Galveston Co.); Galveston I.; Brazoria NWR; Mustang I.

LONG-BILLED DOWITCHER

Limnodromus scolopaceus

Each winter, mudflats and marshes host small numbers of enthusiastic Long-billed Dowitchers. These chunky, sword-billed shorebirds diligently forage in shallow water and mud for invertebrates. A diet of insects and shellfish provides migrating and overwintering Long-bills with plenty of fuel for flight and essential calcium for bone and egg development. • Compared to other shorebirds of similar size, Dowitchers have short wings and require a series of hops to become airborne during a water takeoff. • Mixed flocks of shorebirds demonstrate a variety of foraging styles: some species probe deeply, while others pick at the water's surface or glean the shorelines. Different feeding strategies and specialized diets probably allow large numbers of shorebird species to coexist without exhausting the food supply.

nonbreeding

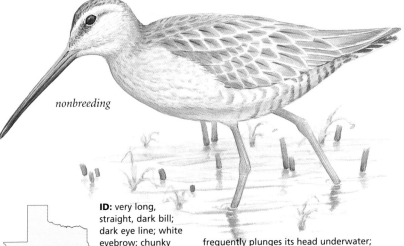

nonbreeding

ID: very long, straight, dark bill; dark eye line; white eyebrow; chunky body; yellowish green legs. *Breeding:* black and white barring on reddish underparts; some white on belly; mottled, dark upperparts. *Nonbreeding:* gray upperparts; dirty white underparts. *In flight:* white wedge on rump and lower back.

Size: *L* 11–12½ in; *W* 19 in.

Status: uncommon to common migrant statewide and abundant on the coast; common winter resident along the coast, uncommon and local in southern Texas west to the Pecos R. and rare in the rest of the state.

Habitat: mudflats, salt marshes, lakeshores and shallow marshes; prefers fresh water.

Nesting: does not nest in Texas.

Feeding: probes in shallow water and mudflats with a repeated up–down bill motion; frequently plunges its head underwater; eats a variety of aquatic invertebrates.

Voice: loud, high-pitched *keek* alarm call, occasionally given in a series.

Similar Species: *Short-billed Dowitcher* (p. 173): white sides, flanks and belly; more spots than bars on reddish sides and flanks; brighter feather edges on upperparts; call is lower-pitched *toodu* or *tututu*. *Red Knot* (p. 162): much shorter bill; all-gray tail and white wedge on back in flight; unmarked breast in breeding plumage. *Wilson's Snipe* (p. 175): heavily striped head, back, neck and breast; shorter legs. *American Woodcock* (p. 176): unmarked, buff underparts; yellow bill; pale bars on black crown and nape; short legs.

Best Sites: exposed mudflats and shallow fresh water at reservoirs, wastewater treatment plants and the coast.

WILSON'S SNIPE

Gallinago delicata

While in Texas, the well-camouflaged Wilson's Snipe is shy and secretive, often remaining concealed in vegetation. Only when an intruder approaches too closely does the snipe flush from cover, performing a series of aerial zigzags—an evasive maneuver designed to confuse predators. Hunters skilled enough to shoot a snipe came to be known as "snipers," a term later adopted by the military. • The snipe's eyes are placed far back on its head, allowing the bird to see both forward and backward. This bird is also equipped with a specialized flexible bill tip that is useful for snatching up underground prey. • Each spring, the eerie, hollow, winnowing sound of courting male Wilson's Snipes is heard above wetlands in the northern U.S. and Canada. The sound is produced when the snipe's specialized outer tail feathers vibrate rapidly through the air during daring, headfirst dives high above the marshland.

ID: long, sturdy, yellowish bill, darker toward tip; relatively short legs; heavily striped head, back, neck and breast; dark eye stripe; dark-barred sides and flanks; unmarked white belly. *In flight:* quick zigzags on takeoff.

Size: *L* 10½–11½ in; *W* 18 in.

Status: common migrant statewide; common winter resident in the eastern two-thirds of Texas and less common and local in the western third.

Habitat: cattail and bulrush marshes, poorly drained floodplains or fields, roadside ditches and muddy lakeshores.

Nesting: does not nest in Texas.

Feeding: probes soft substrates for soft-bodied invertebrates; also eats mollusks, crustaceans, spiders, small amphibians and some seeds.

Voice: nasal *scaip* alarm call; often sings *wheat wheat wheat* from an elevated perch.

Similar Species: *American Woodcock* (p. 176): unmarked, buff underparts; yellowish bill; pale bars on black crown and nape. *Short-billed Dowitcher* (p. 173) and *Long-billed Dowitcher* (p. 174): no heavy striping on head, back, neck and breast; all-dark bill; longer legs; white patch on back in flight; usually in flocks. *Marbled Godwit* (p. 160): much larger; slightly upturned bill; much longer legs.

Best Sites: *Winter:* shallow waters and wet grassy fields.

AMERICAN WOODCOCK

Scolopax minor

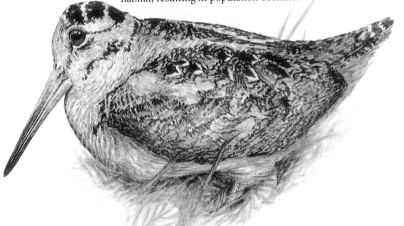

The American Woodcock's behavior usually mirrors its cryptic, inconspicuous attire. Found in moist woodlands and damp thickets, the male American Woodcock is a quiet and reclusive bird for most of the year, until the breeding season reveals his true character. Just before dawn or just after sunset, he struts provocatively in an open woodland clearing while calling out with a series of loud *peeent* notes. He then launches into the air, twittering upward in a circular flight display until, with wings partly folded, he plummets to the ground in the zigzag pattern of a falling leaf, chirping at every turn. • The secretive American Woodcock has endured many changes to its traditional nesting grounds. The clearing of forests and draining of woodland swamps has degraded and eliminated large tracts of woodcock habitat, resulting in population declines.

ID: chunky body; short legs; large head; pale bars on black crown and nape; long, sturdy bill; large, dark eyes; short neck; unmarked, buff underparts. *In flight:* rounded wings.

Size: *L* 11 in; *W* 18 in.

Status: rare to locally uncommon migrant statewide; rare winter resident and very rare nester (between January and April) in eastern Texas, as far west as the eastern Edwards Plateau.

Habitat: moist woodlands and brushy thickets near grassy clearings or abandoned fields.

Nesting: on the ground in woods or in an overgrown field; female digs a scrape and lines it with dead leaves and other debris; female incubates 4 brown-blotched, pinkish buff eggs for 20–22 days; female tends the young.

Feeding: probes in soft, moist soil for earthworms and insect larvae; also takes spiders, snails, millipedes and some plant material, including seeds, sedges and grasses.

Voice: twitters when flushed from cover. *Male:* nasal *peent* and high-pitched, twittering, whistling sounds during courtship.

Similar Species: *Wilson's Snipe* (p. 175): heavily striped upperparts; dark-barred sides and flanks. *Long-billed Dowitcher* (p. 174) and *Short-billed Dowitcher* (p. 173): all-dark bill; longer legs; no pale bars on dark crown and nape; usually seen in flocks.

Best Sites: any eastern Texas park or wildlife management area with open, moist woodlands.

WILSON'S PHALAROPE

Phalaropus tricolor

halaropes are the wind-up toys of the bird world: they spin and whirl about in tight circles, stirring up the water. Then, with needlelike bills, they help themselves to the insects and small crustaceans that funnel toward the surface. • Phalaropes are "polyandrous," meaning that a female mates with several males and often produces a clutch of eggs with each mate. She abandons each mate after egg laying and leaves him to incubate the eggs and tend the young while she seeks out other males. This reversal of gender roles includes a reversal of plumage characteristics—the female is more brightly colored than her male counterpart. • Of the three North American phalarope species, the Wilson's Phalarope is the only one that migrates mainly over land. The more terrestrial Wilson's Phalarope lacks the lobed, or individually webbed, feet of other phalaropes.

nonbreeding

breeding

ID: *Breeding female:* gray cap, chestnut brown neck sides; black eye line that extends down side of neck and onto back; black legs. *Breeding male:* duller overall; dark cap. *Nonbreeding:* gray upperparts; white eyebrow; gray eye line; white underparts; dark yellowish or greenish legs.

Size: *L* 9–9½ in; *W* 17 in.

Status: common to abundant migrant nearly statewide; irregular and locally uncommon summer resident in the Panhandle with some nesting reported; very rare winter coastal resident north to southern edge of the Edwards Plateau and the South Plains.

Habitat: coastal mudflats; lakeshores, flooded fields, marshes and sewage lagoons.

Nesting: on bare ground with overhanging vegetation at the edge of shallow wetlands; hollow is lined with grasses; female lays 3–4 creamy eggs heavily marked with spots or blotches; male incubates the eggs for 20–21 days.

Feeding: whirls in tight circles in water to stir up prey, then picks insects and small crustaceans from the water's surface or just below it; on land, makes short jabs to pick up invertebrates.

Voice: generally silent; grunting *work work* or *wu wu wu*, usually given on the breeding grounds, occasionally heard in Texas.

Similar Species: *Red-necked Phalarope* (p. 447): rufous stripe down side of neck in breeding plumage; dark nape and line behind eye in nonbreeding plumage. *Lesser Yellowlegs* (p. 157): larger; yellow legs; streaked neck; mottled upperparts.

Best Sites: Lake Meredith NRA; Village Creek Wastewater Treatment Plant; Hornsby Bend Wastewater Treatment Plant; Mitchell L. (San Antonio); McNary Reservoir (El Paso Co.).

LAUGHING GULL

Larus atricilla

A broken, white eye ring and a drooping bill give Laughing Gulls in their black-headed breeding plumage a stately appearance. Still, Laughing Gulls are not above begging for handouts and are frequently seen loitering in parking lots, around beaches or following ferries, keeping a sharp eye out for human leftovers. • The Laughing Gull's breeding range includes North America's Atlantic Coast and Gulf Coast. Colonies often nest on small, offshore islands, where they are protected from human disturbance but vulnerable to spring storms that may flood shoreline nests or even submerge entire islands, resulting in the loss of eggs and young. • Laughing Gulls were nearly extirpated from the Atlantic Coast in the late 19th century, when commercial markets demanded eggs and feathers for women's hats. Populations gradually recovered once feather and egg trades were outlawed, and these gulls are once again abundant.

breeding

nonbreeding

ID: dark gray mantle; *Breeding:* black head; broken, white eye ring; red bill and legs. *Nonbreeding:* white head with pale gray streaking on the back; black bill and legs. *Immature:* variable brown to gray and white overall; broad, black subterminal tail band in flight. *In flight:* gray upperwing, black at tip.
Size: *L* 15–17 in; *W* 3 ft.
Status: abundant resident along the coast and up the Rio Grande to Amistad Reservoir; irregular fall and winter visitor inland in the eastern half of the state.
Habitat: primarily coastal in bays and estuaries; also on salt marshes and sandy beaches; occasionally on inland shores, steams or landfills.

Nesting: colonial; on a dry island, sandy coastal beach or salt marsh; on the ground; cup-shaped nest of marsh vegetation may be attached to vegetation to float during storm tides; pair incubates 3 darkly splotched, buff to dark brown eggs for 22–27 days.
Feeding: omnivorous; gleans the ground or water for insects, small mollusks, crustaceans, spiders and small fish; may steal food from other birds; may eat other birds' eggs and nestlings; often scavenges at landfills.
Voice: loud, high-pitched, laughing call: *ha-ha-ha-ha-ha-ha.*
Similar Species: *Franklin's Gull* (p. 179): slightly smaller; shorter, slimmer bill; nonbreeding bird has black at back of head. *Bonaparte's Gull* (p. 180): slimmer, black bill; paler mantle; smaller hood on breeding bird; dark ear patch in nonbreeding plumage; white forewing wedge in flight.
Best Sites: anywhere along the coast.

FRANKLIN'S GULL

Larus pipixcan

Although we refer to the Franklin's Gull as a "sea gull," this bird spends much of its life away from salt water. It nests on inland lakes in the Canadian Prairies and northern Great Plains and is found along coastlines only in winter. Flocks pass through the eastern two-thirds of Texas during spring and fall migration, traveling to and from wintering grounds in Central and South America. A few birds may overwinter along the Texas coast, mixing with resident Laughing Gulls. • The Franklin's Gull is often called "Prairie Dove" because it has a dove-like profile and often follows tractors across agricultural fields, snatching up exposed insects and worms, in much the same way that its cousins follow fishing boats. • The word *pipixcan* is from an Aztec word for "Mexico," where one of the first specimens was collected.

breeding

nonbreeding

ID: gray mantle; white eye ring; black wing tips with white spots; white underparts. *Breeding:* black head; white eye ring; red bill and legs; breast often has a pinkish tinge. *Nonbreeding:* white head; dark patch on back of head; dark bill and legs. *In flight:* mainly white underwing; white stripe and black band at wing tip.
Size: L 14½ in; W 3 ft.
Status: uncommon to common migrant statewide, often in large numbers; irregular and rare winter visitor on the coast and on some inland reservoirs.

Habitat: coastal areas, agricultural fields, marshlands, meadows, lakes, river mouths and landfills.
Nesting: does not nest in Texas.
Feeding: opportunistic; gleans agricultural fields and meadows for insects; catches flying insects in midair.
Voice: mewing, shrill *weeeh-ah weeeh-ah* in migration.
Similar Species: *Laughing Gull* (p. 178): longer bill; all-dark wing tips; nonbreeding bird has gray smudges on head. *Bonaparte's Gull* (p. 180): black bill; white forewing wedge in flight.
Best Sites: at most reservoirs and the coast; often migrates along major rivers.

BONAPARTE'S GULL

Larus philadelphia

With its delicate plumage and behavior, the small Bonaparte's Gull is nothing like its brash relatives. This gull is the smallest to appear in Texas. It avoids landfills, preferring to dine on insects caught in midair or crustaceans plucked from the water's surface. • Bonaparte's Gull raises its soft, scratchy voice in excitement only when it spies a school of fish or an intruder near its nest. • During winter, Bonaparte's Gulls are seen flying about for hours on end, wheeling and flashing their pale wings. Flocks are fairly common along the coast and are occasionally spotted at large inland lakes during migration. • This gull was named after Charles-Lucien Bonaparte, a nephew of French emperor Napoleon Bonaparte and a naturalist who made significant contributions to the study of ornithology in the 1800s.

nonbreeding

breeding

ID: gray mantle; black bill; white underparts. *Breeding:* black head; broken, white eye ring; orange legs. *Nonbreeding:* white head; dark ear patch; paler legs. *In flight:* white forewing wedge; black wing tips.
Size: *L* 11½–14 in; *W* 33 in.
Status: rare to uncommon migrant across Texas; uncommon to common winter resident on the coast and on many inland reservoirs in the eastern two-thirds of the state.

Habitat: coastal areas or inland near large lakes, rivers and marshes.
Nesting: does not nest in Texas.
Feeding: dabbles and tips up for aquatic invertebrates, small fish and tadpoles; gleans the ground for terrestrial invertebrates; also captures insects in the air.
Voice: scratchy, soft *ear ear* while feeding.
Similar Species: *Laughing Gull* (p. 178): longer bill; all dark wing tips; nonbreeding bird has gray smudges on head. *Franklin's Gull* (p. 179): larger; breeding bird has orange bill; nonbreeding bird has black at back of head; white stripe and black band at wing tip in flight.
Best Sites: any beach along the coast; most large inland reservoirs.

RING-BILLED GULL

Larus delawarensis

Few people can claim they have never seen this common and widespread gull. Highly tolerant of humans, the Ring-billed Gull is part of our everyday lives, scavenging our litter and frequenting our parks. This omnivorous gull eats almost anything and swarms parks, beaches, golf courses and fast-food parking lots looking for food handouts, making a pest of itself. However, few species have adjusted to human development as well as the Ring-billed Gull, which is something to appreciate. • During winter, the Ring-bill is our most common gull. It resembles a Herring Gull but is smaller, with subtle differences in the bill and legs. The Ring-bill has a black ring around the tip of its bill, whereas the Herring Gull has a small red dot. Also compare the Ring-billed Gull's yellow legs to the Herring Gull's pink ones.

nonbreeding

nonbreeding

ID: pale gray mantle; black ring around tip of yellow bill; yellow eyes; white underparts; yellow legs. *Breeding:* white nape, cheek and crown. *Nonbreeding:* dusky streaking on nape, cheek and crown. *Immature:* brown wings and breast. *In flight:* black wing tips with white spots.
Size: *L* 18–20 in; *W* 4 ft.
Status: common migrant across Texas; common winter resident along the coast and on inland reservoirs in most of the state; rare summer visitor on the coast and on inland reservoirs.
Habitat: coastal areas; lakes, rivers, landfills, golf courses, fields and parks.
Nesting: does not nest in Texas.

Feeding: gleans the ground for human food waste, spiders, insects, rodents, earthworms, grubs and some waste grain; scavenges for carrion; surface-tips for aquatic invertebrates and fish.
Voice: high-pitched *kakakaka-akakaka;* also, a low, laughing *yook-yook-yook.*
Similar Species: *Lesser Black-backed Gull* (p. 184): rare; larger; much darker mantle; much less white on wing tips; no bill ring. *Herring Gull* (p. 183) and *Glaucous Gull* (p. 185): larger; pinkish legs; red spot near tip of lower mandible; no bill ring. *California Gull* (p. 182): larger; black and red spot near tip of lower mandible instead of ring; dark eyes.
Best Sites: along coastal beaches and on inland reservoirs.

CALIFORNIA GULL

Larus californicus

The California Gull is a western species that appears along our coastline in small numbers during migration and winter, perhaps from populations on the Great Plains or the Pacific coast. Sightings of this gull have increased since 1990, likely because more birdwatchers are visiting landfills or coastal hotspots. • It takes a sharp eye to recognize a California Gull as it roosts among Ring-bills, but if you watch keenly, you may be able to distinguish the larger California Gull's longer bill and slightly narrower wings. Adults also have a black and red dot on their bill. • In 1848 and 1855, Utah's harvests were threatened by swarms of grasshoppers, until large numbers of California Gulls appeared and ate the pests. A monument in Salt Lake City honors this prairie gull, which is now the state bird of Utah, despite its name.

nonbreeding

nonbreeding

ID: gray mantle; yellow bill with black and red spot near tip; yellow-green legs; dark eyes; black wing tips. *Breeding:* white head; white underparts.
Nonbreeding: dark spotting on head and gray streaking on neck. *Immature:* mottled brown overall; pinkish legs; pale bill with black tip.
Size: *L* 21 in; *W* 4½ ft.

Status: rare migrant and winter visitor along the coast and on inland reservoirs.
Habitat: coastal areas; inland at large lakes and landfills.
Nesting: does not nest in Texas.
Feeding: gleans the ground for terrestrial invertebrates; scavenges; surface-tips for aquatic invertebrates.
Voice: generally silent away from breeding colony; high-pitched, nasal *kiarr-kiarr*.
Similar Species: *Ring-billed Gull* (p. 181): slightly smaller; paler eyes; shorter bill with broad, black ring. *Herring Gull* (p. 183): larger; pale eyes; pink legs.
Best Sites: coastal beaches; landfills.

HERRING GULL

Larus argentatus

Although skilled at scrounging beach handouts, Herring Gulls prefer wilderness areas over urban settings. They settle on lakes and large rivers where their Ring-billed relatives are not usually found. • Herring Gulls are proficient hunters that enjoy a variety of foods, allowing them to live in diverse habitats. These large, resourceful gulls have even learned how to drop shellfish on rocks or pavement to break open the shell and expose the tasty meat inside. • Like many gulls, the Herring Gull has a small red spot on the lower mandible that serves as a target for nestlings. When a chick pecks at the lower mandible, the parent regurgitates its meal. • When Herring Gulls arrive on their northern breeding grounds in spring, the landscape may still be covered in snow, but gulls can stand on ice for hours without freezing their feet. The arteries and veins in their legs run close together, so that blood flowing to the extremities warms the cooler blood traveling back to the core.

nonbreeding

nonbreeding

ID: yellow bill; red spot on lower mandible; light eyes; light gray mantle; pink legs. *Breeding:* white head; white underparts. *Nonbreeding:* brown wash on white head and nape. *Immature:* mottled brown overall. *In flight:* black wing tips with white spots.
Size: *L* 23–26 in; *W* 4 ft.
Status: common migrant and winter resident on the coast and uncommon at inland reservoirs; uncommon summer visitor on the coast and at inland reservoirs; 2 recent nesting records from Cameron Co.
Habitat: along the coast; occasionally near large lakes, wetlands, rivers, landfills and urban areas.

Nesting: nests consist of vegetation piled on a hollow in sand; mostly the female incubates 2–3 olive to greenish eggs, with light to heavy speckling or blotches, for 25–33 days.
Feeding: surface-tips for aquatic invertebrates and fish; gleans the ground for insects and worms; scavenges dead fish and human food waste; eats other birds' eggs and young.
Voice: loud, buglelike *kleew-kleew;* alarmed *kak-kak-kak.*
Similar Species: *Ring-billed Gull* (p. 181): smaller; black bill ring; yellow legs. *Glaucous Gull* (p. 185): rare; paler mantle; no black on wings. *Lesser Black-backed Gull* (p. 184): rare; much darker mantle. *California Gull* (p. 182): rare; smaller; dark eyes; yellowish legs; black and red spot on lower mandible.
Best Sites: coastal beaches; landfills; inland reservoirs.

LESSER BLACK-BACKED GULL

Larus fuscus

Equipped with a large wingspan for long-distance flights, the Lesser Black-backed Gull leaves its familiar European and Icelandic surroundings in small numbers each fall to make its way to North America. Most of these birds settle along the U.S. Atlantic Coast during winter. In recent years, Lesser Black-backed sightings have increased in North America, so it is possible that this Eurasian species will soon colonize North America. Birders are advised to keep a close eye on coastal shores and landfills—the most likely locations to find the Lesser Black-backed Gull. • Of the other gulls found in Texas, the Herring Gull is the most similar, but the Lesser Black-backed Gull has darker wings and yellow legs. Occasionally, the Lesser Black-backed Gull crossbreeds with the Herring Gull, so we may see even more puzzling hybrids in the future.

nonbreeding

ID: dark gray mantle; mostly black wing tips; yellow bill with red spot on lower mandible; yellow eyes; yellow legs. *Breeding:* white head and underparts. *Nonbreeding:* brown-streaked head and neck. *Immature:* eyes may be dark or light; black bill, becoming pale with black tip; varying amounts of gray on upperparts and brown flecking over entire body.
Size: *L* 21 in; *W* 4½ ft.

Status: rare winter resident along the coast and very rare at inland landfills.
Habitat: coastal beaches; landfills and open water on large lakes and rivers.
Nesting: does not nest in Texas.
Feeding: eats mostly fish, aquatic invertebrates, small rodents, seeds, carrion and human food waste; scavenges at landfills.
Voice: screechy call is like a lower-pitched version of the Herring Gull's call.
Similar Species: *Herring Gull* (p. 183): paler mantle; pink legs. *Glaucous Gull* (p. 185): much paler mantle; white wing tips; pink legs. *Ring-billed Gull* (p. 181): smaller; paler mantle; dark ring on yellow bill.
Best Sites: coastal beaches; landfills; inland reservoirs.

GLAUCOUS GULL

Larus hyperboreus

Glaucous Gulls are Arctic birds, wintering southward in temperate latitudes only sparingly. They can make a living through scavenging, but they are also powerful predators, taking small mammals and birds on their breeding grounds. • Adults often linger farther north in winter than do immatures, so most of the modest number of Glaucous Gulls seen each year along the Gulf Coast are in subadult plumages. As with many species, first-winter birds outnumber older subadult age classes because fewer birds will survive their second or third winter. • Despite their inexperience, first-winter Glaucous Gulls are notable among other young gulls for their ability to defend food sources. Teetering atop a mound of freshly bulldozed garbage, a gull secures a chosen food item through an intimidating "mantling" using its widespread wings and the well-aimed, no-nonsense jabs of a snapping bill.

nonbreeding

1st winter

ID: large, stout body; very pale gray mantle; pale eyes; pure white wing tips; yellow bill with red spot near tip of lower mandible; *Breeding:* white head and neck. *Nonbreeding:* rare in Texas; variable head and neck streaking. *1st-winter:* pale overall, often whitish; long, heavy, pinkish bill tipped with black; subtle broken white eye arcs on darker individuals; dusky barring on undertail coverts.
Size: *L* 27 in; *W* 5 ft.
Status: rare migrant and winter resident along the coast and very rare inland.

Habitat: chiefly marine and estuarine habitats, including the ocean, river mouths, beaches, industrial waterfronts and garbage dumps.
Nesting: does not nest in Texas.
Feeding: omnivorous; forages in the manner of most other large gulls, snatching almost any edible item, living or dead.
Voice: seldom heard away from the breeding grounds.
Similar Species: *Other large gulls* (pp. 182–84): most are smaller and have at least some black or blackish areas on wing tips.
Best Sites: coastal beaches; landfills; inland reservoirs.

LEAST TERN

Sternula antillarum

The Least Tern sticks close to water, breeding locally along the Gulf Coast before it migrates to Central and South America for winter. However, much of its breeding habitat has been lost to development and disturbance, and only a few colonies persist in our region today. • Terns are known for their elaborate courtship displays, which include distinctive calls, flights and parading. While displaying a fish in its beak, a breeding male will lead several other terns—and these can be both sexes—in a dramatic aerial performance. The ritual reaches a climax when the female tern accepts the male's offering of fish. • Adult Least Terns shelter their eggs from heavy rains by rolling them to drier areas. In hot weather, adults use their bodies to provide shade, or they may wet their undersides, then drip the cool water onto the eggs or chicks.

breeding

ID: gray upperparts; white underparts; orange-yellow legs; white forehead. *Breeding:* black cap and nape; black-tipped, orange-yellow bill. *1st-summer:* black bill, legs and eye line extending into nape; grayish cap; white forehead. *Nonbreeding:* black eye line; dark cap; white forehead; black bill and feet. *In flight:* dashing, rapid wingstrokes; black wedge on upper side of outer primaries.
Size: *L* 9 in; *W* 20 in.
Status: federally endangered (USFWS); common summer resident on the coast and rare at scattered inland localities; rare to uncommon migrant in the eastern two-thirds of Texas and very rare in the western third; very rare winter resident along the coast.

Habitat: coastal beaches; inland on some lakes and rivers.
Nesting: colonial; on undisturbed flat ground or a flat rooftop near water; shallow scrape is often lined with pebbles, grasses or debris; pair incubates 1–3 variably marked, buff to pale olive eggs for 20–22 days.
Feeding: hovers before plunging to or below the water's surface; eats mostly fish, crustaceans and insects; may eat mollusks; also takes insects on the wing and snatches prey from the ground or water's surface.
Voice: loud, high-pitched *chirreek!* and *kip kip kip* calls.
Similar Species: *Other terns* (pp. 187–93): larger; breeding birds have black foreheads and different bill colors.
Best Sites: Sea Rim SP; Bolivar Flats Shorebird Sanctuary (Galveston Co.); Galveston I.; Mustang I.; Padre Island National Seashore.

GULL-BILLED TERN

Gelochelidon nilotica

Unlike most terns, which plunge into the water in pursuit of fish, the large Gull-billed Tern typically flies into the wind, scooping up airborne insects in its path. This tern's characteristic thick, gull-like bill also allows for the occasional meal of nontraditional tern foods, such as lizards, frogs and mice. • In defiance of human alterations to its customary salt-marsh nest sites, the Gull-billed Tern has adapted to nesting on secluded islands and out-of-reach gravel rooftops. • Young Gull-billed Terns leave the nest within days of hatching, taking shelter under nearby vegetation or debris. For the next five weeks, before they learn to fly, they may have a hard time eluding predators and other dangers. The surviving birds stay with their parents for three months or more to learn how to fly and forage.

breeding

ID: pale gray upperparts; white underparts; black legs; thick, black bill. *Breeding:* white head with black cap and nape. *Nonbreeding:* black ear patch; darkish nape patch. *Immature:* similar to nonbreeding adult, but with dark mottling on head and mantle.

Size: *L* 14 in; *W* 34 in.

Status: common resident on the coast, although less so in winter; casual inland to central Texas in summer.

Habitat: open ocean, saltwater marshes, coastal bays, farmlands and open country near the ocean.

Nesting: colonial, sometimes with other gulls or skimmers; in soil, sand or gravel; pair lines a shallow depression with vegetation or debris; pair incubates 2–3 variably marked, creamy to yellowish buff eggs for 22–23 days.

Feeding: eats mostly insects caught on the wing, on the ground or on the water's surface; may also eat crustaceans, mollusks, other invertebrates and small amphibians, reptiles and mammals; rarely plunge-dives.

Voice: raspy *kay-weck* or *zah zah zah* call; immature gives a high, faint *peep peep*.

Similar Species: *Sandwich Tern* (p. 193): black crest at back of head; black wedge near tip of upperwing; long, thin, yellow-tipped bill. *Royal Tern* (p. 192): larger; black crest; orange bill. *Caspian Tern* (p. 188): larger; slight black crest; red-orange bill.

Best Sites: Bolivar Flats Shorebird Sanctuary (Galveston Co.); Galveston I.; Brazoria NWR; Mustang I.; Padre Island National Seashore.

CASPIAN TERN

Hydroprogne caspia

With its size and habits, the mighty Caspian Tern bridges the gulf between the smaller terns and the larger, raucous gulls. It is North America's largest tern, and its wingbeats are slower and more gull-like than those of most other terns—a trait that often leads to its misidentification as a gull. However, this tern's distinctive heavy, red-orange bill and forked tail usually give away its identity. • Caspian Terns are usually seen together with gulls on shoreline sandbars and mudflats during migration or during the breeding season, when they nest in colonies on exposed islands and elevated areas of protected beaches. • This species was first collected from the Caspian Sea, hence its name, and it nests the world over, even Australia.

breeding

ID: light gray mantle; white underparts; heavy, red-orange bill with faintly black tip; black legs; shallowly forked tail. *Breeding:* black cap. *Nonbreeding:* black cap streaked with white. *In flight:* long, frosty, pointed wings; dark gray on underside of outer primaries.
Size: *L* 19–23 in; *W* 4–4½ ft.
Status: common coastal resident; rare to locally uncommon migrant and winter visitor in eastern Texas and in the western Trans-Pecos.
Habitat: coastal areas; wetlands and shorelines of large lakes and rivers.

Nesting: on bare sand, lightly vegetated soil or gravel; shallow scrape is sparsely lined with vegetation, or rocks; pair incubates 1–3 darkly spotted, pale buff eggs for 20–22 days.
Feeding: hovers over water and plunges headfirst after small fish, tadpoles and aquatic invertebrates; also feeds by swimming and gleaning the water's surface.
Voice: low, harsh *ca-arr;* loud *kraa-uh*.
Similar Species: *Common Tern* (p. 190) and *Forster's Tern* (p. 191): much smaller; daintier bills. *Sandwich Tern* (p. 193): smaller; frazzled, black crest at back of head; black wedge on outer primaries of upperwing; yellow tip on long, thin, black bill. *Royal Tern* (p. 192): shaggy, black crest; large, orange bill. *Gull-billed Tern* (p. 187): smaller overall; smaller, black bill; long legs.
Best Sites: coastal beaches; inland reservoirs.

BLACK TERN

Chlidonias niger

Wheeling about in foraging flights, the acrobatic Black Tern picks small minnows from the water's surface or catches flying insects in midair. It passes through Texas during migration, from April to mid-June and from early August to October. • Black Terns nest in the northern U.S. and Canada. They are finicky nesters and refuse to return to sites that show even slight changes in water level or in the density of emergent vegetation. This selectiveness, coupled with the degradation of marshes across North America, has contributed to a significant decline in populations of this bird over recent decades. Commitment to restoring and protecting valuable wetland habitats can eventually help this bird reclaim its once prominent place in North America's bird kingdom.

breeding

nonbreeding

ID: black bill; reddish black legs. *Breeding:* black head and underparts; gray back, tail and wings; white undertail coverts. *Nonbreeding:* white underparts and forehead; molting fall birds may be mottled with brown. *In flight:* long, pointed wings; shallowly forked tail.
Size: *L* 9–10 in; *W* 24 in.
Status: common migrant statewide; very rare winter resident along the coast.

Habitat: shallow freshwater cattail marshes, wetlands, lake edges and sewage ponds with emergent vegetation.
Nesting: does not nest in Texas.
Feeding: snatches insects from the air, tall grass and the water's surface; also eats small fish.
Voice: shrill, metallic *kik-kik-kik-kik-kik* greeting call; typical alarm call is *kreea*.
Similar Species: *Other terns* (pp. 186–93): mostly larger; much paler overall.
Best Sites: Hornsby Bend Wastewater Treatment Plant (Austin); Mitchell L. (San Antonio); Sea Rim SP; Galveston I.; Mustang Island SP.

COMMON TERN

Sterna hirundo

Throughout much of North America, the sleek appearance and graceful flight of the Common Tern are a familiar sight. This tern migrates north to nest in large colonies, mostly in Canada, over summer, passing through the eastern half of Texas each spring and fall. • During the late 19th century, ladies' hats with feathers—or sometimes whole, stuffed terns—were popular fashion items. The hat trade nearly extirpated the Common Tern from the Atlantic Coast. After laws were enacted to protect nesting colonies, this bird's populations quickly recovered, and the Common Tern became a symbol of successful conservation efforts. • Terns are effortless fliers, and they are some of the most impressive long-distance migrants. A Common Tern banded in Great Britain was once recovered in Australia.

nonbreeding

breeding

ID: *Breeding:* black cap; thin, black-tipped, red bill and legs; grayish underparts. *Nonbreeding:* black nape; white forehead; black bill and legs; white underparts. *In flight:* long, pointed wings; dark gray wedge near lighter gray upperwing tip; white rump; shallowly forked, white tail with gray outer edges.

Size: *L* 13–16 in; *W* 30 in.

Status: common migrant along the coast and rare inland; rare winter resident along the coast and casual at inland reservoirs; rare summer resident on the coast; rarely nests on the coastal beaches and islands.

Habitat: open ocean; coastal beaches; inland reservoirs.

Nesting: primarily colonial; usually on a beach or other open area without vegetation; small scrape is sparsely lined with pebbles, vegetation or shells; pair incubates 1–3 variably marked, white to greenish eggs for 20–23 days.

Feeding: hovers over water and plunges headfirst for small fish and aquatic invertebrates.

Voice: most commonly heard at colonies but also in foraging flights; high-pitched, drawn-out *keee-are*.

Similar Species: *Forster's Tern* (p. 191): gray tail with white outer edges; upper primaries have silvery look; black eye band in nonbreeding plumage. *Caspian Tern* (p. 188): much larger overall; much heavier, red-orange bill; dark primary underwing patch.

Best Sites: Bolivar Flats Shorebird Sanctuary (Galveston Co.); Galveston I.; Mustang I.; Padre Island National Seashore.

FORSTER'S TERN

Sterna forsteri

The Forster's Tern so closely resembles the Common Tern that the two often seem indistinguishable. Only when these terns acquire their distinct fall plumages do birders begin to note the Forster's presence. • Most terns are known for their extraordinary ability to catch fish in dramatic headfirst dives, but the Forster's excels at gracefully snatching flying insects in midair. • The Forster's Tern has an exclusively North American breeding distribution, but it bears the name of a man who never visited this continent: German naturalist Johann Reinhold Forster. Forster, who lived and worked in England and who accompanied Captain Cook on his 1772 voyage around the world, examined tern specimens sent from Hudson Bay, Canada. He was the first to recognize this bird as a distinct species. Taxonomist Thomas Nuttall agreed, and in 1832, he named the species "Forster's Tern" in his *Manual of Ornithology*.

nonbreeding

breeding

ID: light gray mantle; pure white underparts. *Breeding:* black cap and nape; thin, orange bill with black tip; orange legs; white rump. *Nonbreeding:* white head with black patch behind eye. *In flight:* forked, gray tail with white outer edges; long, pointed wings.

Size: *L* 14–16 in; *W* 31 in.

Status: uncommon to common migrant in most of Texas; common resident along the coast; locally common winter resident on inland reservoirs.

Habitat: coastal beaches; brackish wetlands; freshwater lakes, rivers and marshes.

Nesting: does not nest in Texas.

Feeding: hovers above the water and plunge-dives for small fish and aquatic invertebrates; catches flying insects and snatches prey from the water's surface.

Voice: short, nasal *keer keer* flight call; also, a grating *tzaap*.

Similar Species: *Common Tern* (p. 190): darker red (or black) bill and legs; mostly white tail; gray wash on underparts; dark wedge near tip of primaries. *Caspian Tern* (p. 188): much larger; much heavier, red-orange bill.

Best Sites: any coastal beach; many inland reservoirs and wastewater treatment plants.

ROYAL TERN

Thalasseus maximus

The regal-looking Royal Tern begins its annual breeding ritual with elegant courtship displays that include spiraling aerial flights, stylish strutting, respectful bowing and offerings of fish. • Female Royal Terns usually lay a single egg amidst a tightly packed colony of a thousand nests or more. Both adults take responsibility for incubation through hot, sun-drenched days, cool coastal nights and brutal summer storms. Most of the eggs in the colony hatch within a period of a few days, instantly turning the beach into a raucous muddle of commotion. Parenting terns herd their semi-precocial young into a massive group ("creche") of fluffy, hungry newborns. Constantly supervised by incoming squadrons of food-carrying adults, the creche remains well protected while the adults hunt. The parents recognize their young by voice. • A loss of nest sites may threaten these birds in the near future.

breeding

ID: long, orange bill; legs usually black but can be orange; white underparts; pale gray mantle. *Breeding:* black cap, frayed at back of head. *Nonbreeding:* retains frayed fringe at back of head. *Immature:* duskier than nonbreeding adult, with dusky tail tip. *In flight:* thick, dark wedge on tip of upperwing; narrow dark edging on outer underwing primaries; deeply forked tail.

Size: *L* 20 in; *W* 3½ ft.

Status: common resident along the coast, although less so in winter; casual inland to central Texas in summer.

Habitat: coastal habitats, including sandy beaches, estuaries, saltwater marshes, islands, bays and lagoons.

Nesting: colonial; usually on sandy ground; shallow depression is sparsely lined with vegetation; pair incubates 1–2 darkly blotched, whitish eggs for 20–25 days.

Feeding: hovers, then plunges into water; may snatch items from the ground or from the water's surface; eats mostly small fish and crabs; may also take squid and other crustaceans.

Voice: high-pitched *kee-er* bleating call and a whistling *turreee.*

Similar Species: *Caspian Tern* (p. 188): thicker bill; no crest or deeply forked tail; black cap streaked with white in nonbreeding plumage; harsh *ka-raa* call. *Common* (p. 190), *Forster's* (p. 191), *Least* (p. 186) and *Sandwich* (p. 193) *terns:* much smaller; daintier bills.

Best Sites: Sea Rim SP; Bolivar Flats (Galveston Co.); Galveston I.; Mustang I.; Padre Island National Seashore.

SANDWICH TERN

Thalasseus sandvicensis

The increasingly scarce and strictly coastal Sandwich Tern frequently keeps company with the Royal Tern, often forming tightly packed mixed nesting colonies on undisturbed sandy beaches, islands and offshore sandbars. However, these vital nesting habitats are in high demand by humans and are slowly being claimed for housing development and recreation. • Watching Sandwich Terns forage and frolic over open water is an exciting spectacle. They dive nearly straight down into deep water, and sometimes one emerges with several fish lined up in its bill. Occasionally these terns dive immediately after Brown Pelicans to capture escaped fish. Both adult and young terns entertain themselves by repeatedly dropping seaweed into the water from high above, then diving down to retrieve it.

breeding

ID: black bill with yellow tip; black legs; deeply forked tail; dark wedge on upper surface of primaries; dark border on lower surface of primaries. *Breeding:* black cap with shaggy crest. *Nonbreeding:* white forehead. *Immature:* shorter crest; less deeply forked tail; mottled upperparts.
Size: *L* 14–16 in; *W* 34 in.
Status: common summer resident and uncommon winter resident along the coast.
Habitat: pelagic; coastal waters, beaches, lagoons, estuaries and islands.
Nesting: colonial; undisturbed beaches or islands; shallow scrape nest in sand may be lined with debris; pair incubates 1–2 variably

marked, yellowish white eggs for 21–25 days; pair feeds the young.
Feeding: hovers, then plunges headfirst into water; eats mostly fish, plus shrimp, squid and marine worms; may take flying insects on the wing.
Voice: calls include a grating *kee-rick* and a quick *gwit gwit*.
Similar Species: *Gull-billed Tern* (p. 187): thicker bill without yellow tip; no frayed head crest; nape is dusky (not black) in nonbreeding plumage. *Royal Tern* (p. 192) and *Caspian Tern* (p. 188): much larger; heavier bills.
Best Sites: Sea Rim SP; Bolivar Flats Shorebird Sanctuary (Galveston Co.); Galveston I.; Mustang I.; Padre Island National Seashore.

BLACK SKIMMER

Rynchops niger

The Black Skimmer is a unique, wonderful bird to observe as it propels through the air on long, swept-back wings. It forages by skimming its lower mandible just below the water's surface, slamming its upper mandible down when it senses contact with a fish. The Black Skimmer is the only bird in North America with a lower mandible that is longer than its upper mandible. • The Black Skimmer's vertical pupils, similar to those of a cat's or rattlesnake's eyes, have evolved to reduce the blinding glare of sun-drenched beaches and reflective ocean water. • The squawking of young skimmers contributes to the loud, chaotic atmosphere of typical breeding colonies. When young wander too far from their nest, they will attempt to lie flat or even burrow underneath the sand to elude predatory gulls and crows.

breeding

ID: black upperparts; white underparts; long, thick, red bill with black tip and protruding lower mandible. *Breeding:* black nape. *Non-breeding:* white nape; duller upperparts. *Immature:* mottled, dull brown upperparts.
Size: *L* 18 in; *W* 3½ ft.
Status: locally common resident along the coast and casual and irregular inland, especially in the eastern half of the state.
Habitat: coastal marine habitats including estuaries, lagoons, sheltered bays and inlets.

Nesting: colonial; on a beach, sandy island, exposed shell bank or, rarely, on a gravel roof; digs a shallow scrape; pair incubates 3–5 darkly blotched, creamy white to buff eggs for 23–25 days; both adults feed the young by regurgitation; family sometimes remains together through winter.
Feeding: flies low over water, with lower mandible skimming just below the water's surface to catch small fish; may eat some crustaceans.
Voice: call is a series of yapping notes.
Similar Species: none.
Best Sites: Bolivar Flats Shorebird Sanctuary (Galveston Co.); Galveston I.; Brazoria NWR; Mustang I.; Padre Island National Seashore.

ROCK PIGEON

Columba livia

Introduced to North America in the early 17th century, Rock Pigeons have settled wherever cities, towns and farms are found. Most birds seem content to nest on buildings or farmhouses, but "wilder" members of this species can occasionally be seen nesting on tall cliffs, usually along lakeshores. • It is believed that Rock Pigeons were domesticated from Eurasian birds as a source of meat in about 4500 BC. Since their domestication, they have been used as message couriers (both Caesar and Napoleon used them), scientific subjects and even as pets. Much of our understanding of bird migration, endocrinology and sensory perception derives from experiments involving Rock Pigeons. • All members of the pigeon family, including doves, feed their young "pigeon milk", a thick, nutritious liquid produced by glands in the bird's crop. A chick insert its bill down the adult's throat to reach the fluid. • No other "wild" bird varies as much in coloration—a result of semi-domestication and extensive inbreeding over time.

ID: highly variable color (iridescent, blue gray, red, white or tan); usually has white rump and orange feet; dark bill with white cere; dark-tipped tail. *In flight:* glides with wings in deep "V."
Size: *L* 12–13 in; *W* 28 in.
Status: abundant year-round resident.
Habitat: urban areas, railroad yards and agricultural areas; high cliffs.
Nesting: on a ledge in a barn or on a cliff, bridge, building or tower; flimsy nest consists of sticks, grass and assorted vegetation; pair incubates 2 white eggs for 16–19 days; pair feeds the young "pigeon milk"; may raise broods year-round.
Feeding: gleans the ground for waste grain, seeds and fruit; occasionally eats insects.
Voice: soft, cooing *coorrr-coorrr-coorrr.*
Similar Species: *Mourning Dove* (p. 198) and *White-winged Dove* (p. 197): smaller; slimmer; pale brown plumage; Mourning Dove has long tail and wings. *Eurasian Collared-Dove* (p. 196): black half-collar with white edges. *Merlin* (p. 129): lighter bodied; longer tail; wings not in "V"; wings do not clap on takeoff.
Best Sites: statewide in urban and rural areas.

EURASIAN COLLARED-DOVE

Streptopelia decaocto

Streptopelia is Greek for "twisted dove," an appropriate name for a species that seems to be effortlessly winding its way around the world. Originally from the Middle East, the Eurasian Collared-Dove expanded through Europe along with the human population in the 20th century. The species spread to the Western Hemisphere when 50 individuals were released in the Bahamas in 1974. From there, some birds made their way to mainland Florida, and, soon afterward, the species spilled over into neighboring states. • In warmer climates, the Eurasian Collared-Dove can breed six times per year. Young will disperse long distances, which helps the population spread. With a love of suburban areas and at ease around humans, there is little doubt that this bird's rapidly expanding range will soon include much of North America.

ID: pale gray overall; white outer tail; gray band across wing coverts; black half-collar with white outline across back of neck.

Size: *L* 12–13 in; *W* 18–20 in.
Status: uncommon to locally common resident statewide.
Habitat: coastal areas; suburbs and farmland; parks with both open ground and tree cover.
Nesting: in a tree or bush or in cavities or crevices in buildings; female builds a platform nest of twigs and sticks; pair incubates 2 white eggs for about 14 days; may raise 3 or more broods per year; initially feeds young on "pigeon milk."
Feeding: frequent at feeders, in backyards and on farmland where it feeds on grain.
Voice: a soft, repeated *coo-COO-coo*.
Similar Species: *Mourning Dove* (p. 198), *Common Ground-Dove* (p. 200) and *White-winged Dove* (p. 197): no black collar. *Rock Pigeon* (p. 195): stockier; white rump; black tail band.
Best Sites: seen in almost any human community, especially around grain elevators.

WHITE-WINGED DOVE

Zenaida asiatica

The glowing light of early morning is sometimes punctuated by the soothing coos of the White-winged Dove. The piercing glance of hot red eyes contained in cooling pools of azure blue skin make this bird captivating to observe at close range, especially when it is feeding among the bright colors of an orange grove. • In the late 1800's, the Lower Rio Grande Valley was home to several million White-winged Doves, but their numbers rapidly declined at the turn of the century following excessive hunting and clearing of their native brushland nesting habitat. Several decades later, this species began to recover, adapting to new nesting territory in citrus groves. White-winged Doves are now common in summer throughout southern Texas and are rapidly expanding their range northward. Although most birds retreat to Central America for winter, increasing numbers are overwintering in our urban centers.

ID: light brownish gray overall; large white crescent at edge of wing; blunt, rounded tail with white corners; bold blue patch around red eye. *In flight:* large white crescent across middle of upperwing.

Size: *L* 11–12 in; *W* 19 in.

Status: common resident in the southern half of the state; locally uncommon into north-central Texas and west to Midland, Lubbock and Amarillo; generally absent from wooded areas of east Texas.

Habitat: variety of semi-open habitats, including farmland, townsites, brushlands, tree groves, riparian woodlands and chaparral.

Nesting: rarely colonial; in a tree or shrub; on a horizontal limb or in a fork; builds a flimsy stick platform; pair alternates incubation of 1–4 (usually 2) white or pale buff eggs for 13–14 days; feeds young "pigeon milk."

Feeding: forages on the ground and occasionally in trees, shrubs and on cactus flowers; eats mostly seeds, plus some berries and fruit.

Voice: variable cooing call: *who-cooks-for-you?*

Similar Species: *Mourning Dove* (p. 198) and *Common Ground-Dove* (p. 200): no white patches on wings; dark spots on upperwings; Common Ground-Dove is smaller. *Rock Pigeon* (p. 195): stockier; white rump; black tail band. *Eurasian Collared-Dove* (p. 196): black half-collar with white edges.

Best Sites: parks and suburban areas in all major metropolitan areas.

MOURNING DOVE

Zenaida macroura

The soft cooing of the Mourning Dove filtering through our broken woodlands and suburban parks and gardens is often mistaken for the muted sounds of a hooting owl. • One of North America's most abundant, widespread native birds, this species is one of the most popular game birds. It has benefited from human-induced changes to the landscape—its numbers and distribution have increased over recent centuries. Encountered in both rural and urban habitats, it avoids heavy forest. • Despite its fragile look, the Mourning Dove is a swift, direct flier. Its wings often whistle as it cuts through the air at high speed. When this bird bursts into flight, its wings clap above and below its body. • The common name reflects the sad, cooing song, and *Zenaida* honors Zenaïde, Princess of Naples and the wife of naturalist Charles-Lucien Bonaparte, nephew of the French emperor.

ID: sleek body; buffy, gray-brown plumage; small head; dark, shiny patch below ear; dark bill; dull red legs; pale rosy underparts; long, tapering, white-trimmed tail; black spots on upperwing.

Size: *L* 11–13 in; *W* 18 in.

Status: common resident statewide; large numbers from more northerly states increase winter populations.

Habitat: open and riparian woodlands, woodlots, forest edges, agricultural and suburban areas and open parks.

Nesting: in a shrub or tree, in a fork, or occasionally on the ground; female builds a fragile, shallow platform nest using twigs supplied by the male; pair incubates 2 white eggs for 14 days; young are fed "pigeon milk."

Feeding: gleans the ground and vegetation for seeds; visits feeders.

Voice: mournful, soft, slow *oh-woe-woe-woe*.

Similar Species: *White-winged Dove* (p. 197): bold blue patch around red eye; dark patch below eye; white patches on wings; shorter tail. *Eurasian Collared-Dove* (p. 196): less common; black half-collar with white edges. *Rock Pigeon* (p. 195): stockier; white rump; shorter tail; iridescent neck. *Yellow-billed Cuckoo* (p. 203) and *Black-billed Cuckoo* (p. 204): curved bill; long tail with white spots and broad, rounded tip; brown upperparts; white underparts.

Best Sites: virtually anywhere with trees.

INCA DOVE

Columbina inca

In the broiling heat of midday, Inca Doves shelter in shade trees or seek out cool, watered lawns. These scaly-looking doves are often found close to human dwellings, where they benefit from reliable sources of water, plenty of shade and ledges for nesting. Their affinity for urban areas has allowed them to expand their range in the face of human development, and they are now found as far north as Amarillo and Tyler. • Inca Doves breed year-round, hatching several broods per year. The male sits on the nest by day, relinquishing his incubation duties to his mate in the evening. Like most doves and pigeons, adult Inca Doves share all of the essential parenting duties, including feeding the young "pigeon milk." • To stave off the cold, Inca Doves huddle together in a pyramid-shaped roost to conserve heat, with up to a dozen individuals piled atop each other three layers high.

ID: gray-brown plumage; barring gives "scaly" appearance to head, breast, upperwings, back, belly and flanks; long tail, black bill; red eye with faint blue eye ring (visible at close range). *In flight:* white-edged tail; rufous primaries.
Size: *L* 7–8 in; *W* 11 in.
Status: common resident in the southern half of Texas; less common and local in the northern half, usually in towns and cities; absent from most of the Panhandle.
Habitat: open to semi-open habitats, including parks and gardens, townsites, farmlands and occasionally riparian areas; close association with human dwellings.

Nesting: on a tree, shrub or artificial surface (building, wire, etc.); female builds a small platform of twigs and vegetation; pair incubates 2 white eggs over 15–16 days; may raise 4–5 broods per year.
Feeding: mainly forages on the ground for seeds; may eat cactus fruit.
Voice: repeated, mournful, 2-syllable call that sounds like "no hope."
Similar Species: *Common Ground-Dove* (p. 200): shorter, slightly white cornered tail; plain gray back, belly and flanks; large dark spots on upperwings; reddish bill with black tip. *Mourning Dove* (p.198): larger; black spots on upperwings; not "scaly." *White-winged Dove* (p. 197): larger; prominent white wing patch; not "scaly."
Best Sites: occurs locally in many towns and cities.

COMMON GROUND-DOVE

Columbina passerina

The Common Ground-Dove may be found trotting briskly through coastal agricultural areas, rhythmically bobbing its head to an unheard beat. This small dove is very tame but, unlike other doves, is not often found in urban environments. True to its name, the Common Ground-Dove favors the ground, preferring to walk along roadsides or grain fields in search of food. • Common Ground-Doves will flock in winter, then pair up (recent studies suggest for life) when the weather allows. To charm the female, the male will prance around with his feathers puffed out, tail up and head bowed while emitting an enticing *coo*. • These doves are marathon "cooers," perching for hours on end, while calling their inquisitive *cooOOO*s. The call is so soothing and soft that Common Ground-Doves often go unnoticed.

ID: "scaly" head and breast; brown upperparts; pink-brown underparts; black spots on side; pink legs; pink bill with black tip; iridescent, blue and gray head.
In flight: rufous primaries and wing linings.
Size: *L* 6–7 in; *W* 10½ in.
Status: uncommon to locally common in south Texas, up the coast to Galveston Bay and north through east Texas, up the Rio Grande to El Paso and inland to the southern half of the Edwards Plateau.
Habitat: quiet areas such as fields, suburbs and woodland edges.

Nesting: in a tree (rarely on the ground); nest is a flat, simple stick platform; pair incubates 2–3 white eggs for about 14 days; 2–4 broods per year.
Feeding: walks along the ground seeking seeds, grains, insects and sometimes berries.
Voice: call is a sequence of *woot woot woot* or *wroo*, repeated 4–5 times.
Similar Species: most other doves or pigeons are larger. *Inca Dove* (p. 199): slender; "scaly" appearance; pale cheek; long tail. *Mourning Dove* (p. 198): long tail and wings. *White-winged Dove* (p. 197): large, white patch across center of upperwing; white-tipped tail; bold blue patch around red eye.
Best Sites: Choke Canyon SP; Park Chalk Bluff (Uvalde Co.); Santa Ana NWR; Bentsen-Rio Grande Valley SP; Anzalduas CP (Hidalgo Co.).

WHITE-TIPPED DOVE

Leptotila verreauxi

Another Texas specialty, the White-tipped Dove is found in the Lower Rio Grande Valley but nowhere else in the U.S. Unlike other doves that frequent open fields and parks, the secretive White-tipped Dove hides among thorn-scrub thickets, where it is more often heard than seen. • White-tipped Doves have a robotic walk, bobbing their heads in time with each step. When startled, they often lift their tails in an exaggerated manner. • A courting male White-tip seems to send out mixed signals. Sometimes he bows deeply and coos, as if to say "I'll do anything for you." At other times he hunches his shoulders, lowers his head and charges the female insistently. • Doves and pigeons drink an incredible amount of water. They are the only group of birds in North America that can drink continuously by sucking water into their throats. Other species must fill their beaks, then tilt their heads back.

ID: pale face; pale grayish tan body with slightly darker upperparts; red eye ring; red legs. *In flight:* reddish brown underwing obvious against pale body; square, white-tipped tail.

Size: *L* 11½ in; *W* 18 in.

Status: common resident in the Lower Rio Grande Valley and less common up the central coast and north through the South Texas Brush Country.

Habitat: thorn scrub thickets; woodlands with dense understories.

Nesting: in dense vines or vegetation; low to the ground; nest varies from a flimsy platform of twigs to a more sturdy bowl structure;

pair incubates 2–3 white or cream-colored eggs for 14 days.

Feeding: on the ground; diet, probably insects and seeds, is not well known.

Voice: low cooing *oo-ooooooooo* call resembles the sound of blowing into a bottle.

Similar Species: *Mourning Dove* (p. 198): slender; tan overall; pale bluish eye ring; black spots on upperwings; long, pointed tail. *White-winged Dove* (p. 197): red iris and blue eye ring; white wing crescent. *Rock Pigeon* (p. 195): considerable color variation; often darker or with darker patches; white cere; white rump visible in flight on most birds.

Best Sites: Hazel Bazemore CP (Nueces Co.); Chaparral WMA; Santa Ana NWR; Bentsen-Rio Grande Valley SP; Lake Corpus Christi SP.

MONK PARAKEET

Myiopsitta monachus

The Monk Parakeet is just one of several nonnative parrots that now breed in Texas. Originally found only in South America, the Monk Parakeet now occurs worldwide. In the late 1960s, a boom in the pet industry resulted in both accidental and intentional releases, allowing this bird to establish in many urban parks. Unlike most parrots, the Monk Parakeet originated in comparatively temperate regions and can survive in cooler climates, especially when bird feeders provide a year-round food source. • Monk Parakeets are considered agricultural pests in their native lands because they feed mainly on fruit and seeds. Despite attempts to eradicate American populations in the 1970s, Monk Parakeets continue to thrive in the U.S. and occur as far north as Illinois. • Monk Parakeets are the only parrots that nest communally. Whereas other parrots nest in cavities, groups of Monk Parakeets weave bulky, condominium-style stick nests that contain separate areas and entrances for each pair.

ID: green upperparts; gray-white underparts and forehead; blue outer wings; pink bill. *Immature:* green patch on forehead. *In flight:* long, pointed, diamond-shaped, green tail.
Size: *L* 11–12 in; *W* 19 in.
Status: locally common in several metropolitan areas.
Habitat: treed parks and backyards; visits feeders in winter.

Nesting: colonial; on a pole or high in a tree; group builds a large, multi-compartment nest of twigs, sticks and grass with an "apartment" for each pair; pair incubates 6–8 white eggs for 25–30 days; may have 2 broods per year.
Feeding: on the ground or at feeders; takes birdseed, grass seeds and weed seeds.
Voice: rough chattering and shrieking.
Similar Species: *Green Parakeet* (p. 449): green overall; pale eye ring; may have some orange neck feathers. *Red-crowned Parrot* (p. 449): larger; red crown; blue nape; square, yellow-tipped tail in flight.
Best Sites: established colonies in Houston, Corpus Christi, Austin, Temple, Dallas and several other towns and cities.

YELLOW-BILLED CUCKOO

Coccyzus americanus

Large tracts of hardwood forest and riparian areas provide valuable habitat for the Yellow-billed Cuckoo, a declining species that has disappeared in parts of America. Like songbirds, it is more vulnerable to predators in the small, fragmented forest patches created by development. The riparian habitat preferred by the cuckoo is also steadily disappearing as waterways are altered or dammed. • Usually, the Yellow-billed Cuckoo skillfully negotiates its tangled home within impenetrable deciduous undergrowth in silence, relying on obscurity for survival. Then, for a short period during nesting, the male cuckoo tempts fate by issuing a barrage of loud, rhythmic courtship calls. The Yellow-billed Cuckoo, also known as "Rain Crow," has a propensity for calling on dark, cloudy days, predicting the coming rainstorms. • Yellow-billed Cuckoos breed in higher densities and lay larger clutches when outbreaks of cicadas or tent caterpillars provide an abundant food supply.

ID: olive brown upperparts; white underparts; down-curved bill with black upper mandible and yellow lower mandible; yellow eye ring; long tail with large white spots on underside; rufous tinge on primaries.

Size: *L* 11–13 in; *W* 18 in.

Status: common migrant and summer resident statewide; casual and irregular winter visitor on the Coastal Plain.

Habitat: semi-open deciduous habitats; dense tangles and thickets at the edges of orchards, urban parks, agricultural fields and roadways; sometimes woodlots.

Nesting: in a deciduous shrub or small tree; on a horizontal branch within 7 ft of the ground; flimsy platform of twigs is lined with roots and grass; pair incubates 3–4 pale bluish green eggs for 9–11 days.

Feeding: gleans deciduous vegetation for insect larvae, especially hairy caterpillars; also eats berries, small fruits, small amphibians and occasionally the eggs of small birds.

Voice: long series of deep, hollow *kuks*, slowing near the end: *kuk-kuk-kuk-kuk kuk kop kow kowlp kowlp*.

Similar Species: *Black-billed Cuckoo* (p. 204): all-black bill; no rufous tinge on primaries; less prominent undertail spots; red eye ring; juvenile has buff eye ring and may have buff wash on throat and undertail coverts. *Mourning Dove* (p. 198): short, straight bill; pointed, triangular tail; buffy gray-brown plumage; black spots on upperwing.

Best Sites: any park with open woods.

BLACK-BILLED CUCKOO

Coccyzus erythropthalmus

Black-billed Cuckoos do not sound anything like their famous European relative, nor do they sound quite like any other birds in Texas. From shrubby thickets, they vocalize in loud bursts repeating deep *ca, coo* and *cow* notes in tangled melodies. Migrating through Texas in spring and fall, these birds quietly hop, flit and skulk through low, dense deciduous vegetation in their ultra-secretive search for sustenance. • The Black-billed Cuckoo is one of few birds that thrives on hairy caterpillars, particularly tent caterpillars, and there is evidence to suggest that cuckoo populations increase when a caterpillar infestation occurs in their area. • This cuckoo is reluctant to fly more than a short distance during nesting, but it migrates to wintering grounds as far away as northwestern South America.

ID: brown upperparts; white underparts; long tail with white-spotted underside; downcurved, dark bill; reddish eye ring. *Juvenile:* buff eye ring; may have buff tinge on throat and undertail coverts.
Size: *L* 12 in; *W* 18 in.
Status: rare to uncommon migrant in the eastern two-thirds of Texas; very rare west to central Trans-Pecos.
Habitat: dense second-growth woodlands, shrubby areas and thickets; tangled riparian areas and abandoned farmlands with low deciduous vegetation and adjacent open areas.

Nesting: nesting has not been confirmed in Texas since the 1880s.
Feeding: gleans leaves, branches and trunks for hairy caterpillars; also eats other insects and berries.
Voice: fast, repeated *cu-cu-cu or cu-cu-cu-cu-cu;* also a series of *ca, cow* and *coo* notes.
Similar Species: *Yellow-billed Cuckoo* (p. 203): yellow bill; rufous tinge to primaries; larger, more prominent undertail spots; no red eye ring. *Mourning Dove* (p. 198): short, straight bill; pointed, triangular tail; buffy, gray-brown plumage; black spots on upperwing.
Best Sites: Sabine Woods Bird Sanctuary (Jefferson Co.); High I. (Galveston Co.); Lafitte Cove Nature Preserve (Galveston); Jesse H. Jones Park (Harris Co.); Edith Moore Sanctuary (Houston).

GREATER ROADRUNNER

Geococcyx californianus

Celebrated in legends and cartoons, the Greater Roadrunner lives up to its reputation as a speedy and spirited bird, commonly dashing along and across highways and gravel roads bisecting its brushy habitat. • This large member of the cuckoo family spends much of its time on its long, spindly legs, chasing insects, lizards and small rodents at speeds of up to 15 miles per hour. The Greater Roadrunner rarely flies, and when it does resort to the air, it passes quickly and directly over short distances. When alarmed or intrigued, it raises its crest and cocks its tail. • Roadrunner courtship is an energetic affair involving high-speed foot chases followed by long, breath-catching pauses. The male typically leads the performance by running away from his mate with both tail and wings held over his body. Then, after a few graceful bows and some affectionate tail wagging, both adults seal their bond by exchanging offerings of sticks or vegetation.

ID: streaky, brown and whitish plumage; long, thick bill with hooked tip; raised crest; blue and red patch of bare skin surrounds eye; thick, "scaly" legs; short, rounded wings; very long tail.

Size: *L* 23 in; *W* 22 in.

Status: uncommon to common resident throughout most of Texas, although less common in the northeast.

Habitat: thorn forest, desert and arid woodlands of pinyon-pine and juniper; agricultural lands and suburbs.

Nesting: usually in a cactus, dense shrub or low tree; cup-shaped stick nest is lined with vegetation and feathers (may include snake-skin and dried cow manure); pair incubates 3–6 white eggs for 20 days; may mate for life and defend breeding territory year-round.

Feeding: varied diet; catches insects, small mammals, lizards, snakes and small birds by running them down; also eats scorpions, snails, fruit and seeds.

Voice: descending, dovelike cooing; loud bill clattering.

Similar Species: *Ring-necked Pheasant* (p. 71): female has no raised head crest or colorful bare skin behind eye and has shorter bill and barred tail; inhabits croplands.

Best Sites: almost any state park west of the Brazos R.

GROOVE-BILLED ANI

Crotophaga sulcirostris

Especially common along the Lower Rio Grande Valley, Groove-billed Anis are summer residents in southern Texas. Some birds overwinter along the Gulf Coast, but most head south to warmer areas. Although anis are weak flyers, post-breeding birds have wandered as far north as southeastern Canada. • Small flocks of Groove-billed Anis congregate in thick vegetation next to open fields or woodlands. These strange birds give away their location with soft, scratchy *ti–jo* calls. • Up to four pairs of Groove-billed Anis will brood in one large, cup-shaped nest. Although nesting communally may provide protection and allow the sharing of incubation duties, it also results in direct competition. Females must protect their eggs from being pushed out of the nest by other group members. • *Crotophaga* is Greek for "bug-eater," referencing the Groove-billed Ani's habit of following cattle to pick off the insects stirred up by the herd. *Sulcirostris* means "furrowed bill" in Latin.

ID: black overall; large, black eyes; scruffy head feathers; large bill with parallel furrows on upper mandible; "scallops" with green or purple iridescence on upper back; long tail.
Size: *L* 13½ in; *W* 17 in.
Status: common summer resident in south Texas north to the Edwards Plateau and upriver to Webb Co.; rare to locally uncommon through the Edwards Plateau to the Llano Estacado; rare to uncommon winter resident in theLower Rio Grande valley and on the Coastal Plain to Galveston County.
Habitat: brushy areas close to open fields or range land; marshes or wooded riversides.

Nesting: communal nest with 1–4 pairs and occasional unpaired "helpers"; low in a tree; all members help build a stick nest lined with vegetation; each female lays 3–4 blue eggs, with up to 16 eggs per nest; all birds take turns incubating during the day; dominant male takes over at night.
Feeding: on the ground or in low bushes; eats large insects and occasionally berries and seeds.
Voice: 5–6 scratchy, sharp, short notes before a repeated, fluttering *ti-jo!*
Similar Species: none; parrotlike bill is diagnostic.
Best Sites: Mitchell L. (San Antonio); Port Aransas; Hazel Bazemore CP (Nueces Co.); Santa Ana NWR; Bentsen-Rio Grande Valley SP.

BARN OWL

Tyto alba

The haunting look of this night hunter has inspired superstitions among many people. However, this owl helps keep farmlands and even city yards free of undesirable rodents. • Like the House Sparrow and the Rock Pigeon, the Barn Owl has found success by associating with urban and agricultural areas. Its nocturnal habit, taste for small rodents and general tolerance of humans has allowed this adaptable bird to prosper on six continents. • Normally these nocturnal birds hunt alone or in pairs, but during winter they may gather at local feeding sites. All owls have night vision 100 times more sensitive than that of humans, and they can locate prey using sound alone.

ID: heart-shaped, white facial disc; dark eyes; pale bill; golden brown upperparts spotted with black and gray; creamy white, black-spotted underparts; white undertail and underwings; long legs.
Size: *L* 12½–18 in; *W* 3¾ ft.
Status: rare to locally common resident statewide; absent from the Trans-Pecos Mts.
Habitat: *Roosting* and *nesting:* cliffs, hollow trees, barns and other unoccupied buildings, mine shafts, caves and bridges. *Foraging:* open areas, including agricultural fields, pastures, marshy meadows and streamsides.
Nesting: in a natural or artificial cavity, often in a sheltered, secluded hollow of a building; may dig a hole in a dirt bank or use an artificial nest box; no actual nest is built; female incubates 3–8 whitish eggs for 29–34 days; male feeds incubating female.
Feeding: eats mostly small mammals, especially rodents; may take snakes, lizards,

birds and large insects; rarely takes frogs and fish.
Voice: calls include harsh, raspy screeches and hisses; also makes metallic clicking sounds.
Similar Species: *Short-eared Owl* (p. 216): yellow eyes set in black sockets; vertical streaks on breast and belly; black "wrist" patches. *Barred Owl* (p. 214): barred chest; streaking on belly; darker facial disc.
Best Sites: open grasslands of the western half of Texas.

WESTERN SCREECH-OWL

Megascops kennicottii

Two screech-owls occur in Texas, with their range overlapping along the Pecos River and on the western half of the Edwards Plateau. The Western Screech-Owl occurs in the arid regions of west Texas, whereas the Eastern Screech-Owl inhabits the rest of the state. • Screech-owls occur in woodlands, parklands, agricultural areas and suburbs. They require little more than a secluded roosting site, a tree hollow for nesting and semi-open ground for hunting. • Despite its small size, the Western Screech-Owl is an adaptable hunter, capturing insects, amphibians, small mammals and birds larger than itself. It hunts nocturnally, then passes the early morning and daylight hours concealed in dense shrubs or a hollow tree. • Western Screech-Owls are most vocal in Texas between March and June, when their distinctive courting whistle percolates through both natural and suburban habitats. Their bouncing-ball whistles are easily imitated and can often draw an owl into flashlight range.

ID: gray overall; yellow eyes; "ear" tufts; dark bill; heavy, dark vertical barring on breast.
Size: *L* 7–11 in; *W* 18–24 in.
Status: uncommon local resident in the Trans-Pecos and the western half of the Edwards Plateau.
Habitat: open or broken lowland oak, conifer or mixed woodlands; riparian woodlands, parklands, suburbs and ranches, especially on dry ridges.
Nesting: in a nest box or natural cavity; no nesting material is added; female incubates 2–5 white eggs for about 26 days; male feeds incubating female; pair feeds the young.

Feeding: hunts at night; swoops from a perch to capture invertebrates, small rodents, amphibians and occasionally songbirds; can capture animals larger than itself.
Voice: distinctive series of soft, accelerating, evenly pitched whistles and notes, with a rhythm like that of a bouncing ball coming to a stop; pairs often appear to "countersing"; variations occur.
Similar Species: *Eastern Screech-Owl* (p. 209): slightly less heavy barring on breast, with more fine crossbars; greenish bill; may be red or brown overall. *Ferruginous Pygmy-Owl* (p. 211): orange-brown overall; streaked crown; no "ear" tufts; black false eye spots on back of head. *Great Horned Owl* (p. 210) and *Long-eared Owl* (p. 215): much larger. *Other owls:* no "ear" tufts.
Best Sites: Hueco Tanks SP; Big Bend NP; Seminole Canyon SP; Big Spring SP; San Angelo SP.

EASTERN SCREECH-OWL

Megascops asio

The diminutive Eastern Screech-Owl is a year-round resident of deciduous woodlands east of the Pecos River. Most screech-owls sleep away the day inside a tree cavity or an artificial nest box but mobbing hordes of chickadees or squawking gangs of Blue Jays can alert you to its presence. Smaller birds that mob an owl during the day often do so after losing a family member during the night. More commonly, you will find this owl by listening for the male's eerie, "horse-whinny" courtship calls and loud, spooky trills on spring nights. These calls are helpful in differentiating between this owl and the Western Screech-Owl. • Unique among Texas' owls, Eastern Screech-Owls are polychromatic: they show red, brown or gray color morphs. The brown birds are more common in Texas. A pocket of gray morphs also occurs in southern Texas, although they are usually more common in the northern U.S.

gray morph

ID: reddish or grayish overall; yellow eyes; short "ear" tufts; dark barring on breast, with fine horizontal lines; pale grayish bill.
Size: *L* 8–9 in; *W* 20–22 in.
Status: common year-round resident in most of Texas; absent from the South Plains and the western half of the Trans-Pecos.
Habitat: mature deciduous forests and open deciduous and riparian woodlands.
Nesting: in a natural cavity or artificial nest box; no lining is added; female incubates 4–5 white eggs for about 26 days; male feeds incubating female.

Feeding: hunts at dusk and at night; takes small mammals, earthworms, fish, birds and insects, including moths, in flight.
Voice: horselike "whinny" that rises and falls.
Similar Species: *Western Screech-Owl* (p. 208): heavy, dark barring on breast, with few horizontal lines; darker bill. *Ferruginous Pygmy-Owl* (p. 211): orange-brown overall; streaked crown; no "ear" tufts; black false eye spots on back of head. *Great Horned Owl* (p. 210) and *Long-eared Owl* (p. 215): much larger. *Other owls:* no "ear" tufts.
Best Sites: any wooded park in the eastern half of the state.

GREAT HORNED OWL

Bubo virginianus

The highly adaptable and superbly camouflaged Great Horned Owl has sharp hearing and powerful vision that allow it to hunt at night as well as by day. It can swoop down from a perch onto almost any small creature that moves. An apparently poor sense of smell might explain why it is the only consistent predator of skunks. • An owl has specially designed feathers on its wings to reduce noise. The leading edge of each flight feather is fringed rather than smooth, which interrupts airflow over the wing and allows the owl to fly noiselessly. • Great Horned Owls often begin their courtship as early as January, when their hooting calls make them quite conspicuous. By February and March, females are already incubating their eggs. By the time other birds to fledge, Great Horned owlets are learning to hunt.

ID: overall plumage varies from light gray to dark brown; heavily mottled, gray, brown and black upperparts; yellow eyes; tall, wide-set "ear" tufts; fine, horizontal barring on breast; black-outlined, rusty orange facial disc; white chin.
Size: *L* 18–25 in; *W* 3–5 ft.
Status: common resident statewide, although less common in east Texas woodlands.
Habitat: fragmented forests, agricultural areas, woodlots, meadows, riparian woodlands, wooded suburban parks and the wooded edges of landfills.
Nesting: in the abandoned stick nest of another bird; may also nest on a cliff; adds little or no material to the nest; mostly the female incubates the 2–3 dull whitish eggs for 28–35 days.
Feeding: mostly nocturnal but also hunts at dusk or by day in winter; usually swoops from a perch; eats small mammals, birds, snakes, amphibians and even fish.
Voice: breeding call is 4–6 deep hoots: *hoo-hoo-hoooo hoo-hoo* or *Who's awake? Me too;* male also gives higher-pitched hoots.
Similar Species: *Eastern Screech-Owl* (p. 209) and *Western Screech-Owl* (p. 208): much smaller; heavy, vertical breast streaks. *Short-eared Owl* (p. 216) and *Barred Owl* (p. 214): no "ear" tufts. *Long-eared Owl* (p. 215): smaller; thinner; vertical breast streaks; "ear" tufts are close together.
Best Sites: any wooded park.

FERRUGINOUS PYGMY-OWL

Glaucidium brasilianum

With a fondness for daytime activities and a small body size, the Ferruginous Pygmy-Owl might be mistaken for a common perching bird. • In general, it seems that the smaller an owl is, the more aggressive it can be. The Ferruginous Pygmy-Owl is no exception, attacking much larger prey, including waterfowl. • Occasionally Ferruginous Pygmy-Owls nest close to a human residence or drink from a backyard birdbath. If you live near a clearing and want to attract one of these tiny owls to your backyard, be sure that water is available and your nest box entrance is between 1⅞ and 2⁵⁄₁₆ inches across. Nest boxes can be set up as early as December, because these owls choose their mates and nest location well before the eggs are laid.

ID: small, round body; brownish orange overall; large head; finely streaked crown; obvious white eyebrows; no "ear" tufts; black false eye spots on back of head; brown streaks on breast; relatively long tail; wags tail when perched. *Female:* larger; more reddish brown overall. *In flight:* orange tail; pale underwing.
Size: *L* 6¾ in; *W* 12 in.
Status: rare to locally common resident in the Lower Rio Grande Valley and adjacent parts of the South Texas brushlands.
Habitat: varies from dry desert scrub to lush forest.
Nesting: at a clearing edge near water; in a natural cavity or next box (sometimes in a tree fork); female incubates 3–4 white eggs for 30 days; pair feeds the hatchlings.
Feeding: hunts during the day or at twilight; diet varies with season and location;

eats insects, reptiles. amphibians, birds and small mammals.
Voice: rapid twitters, hoots and *took* noises, about 3 per second; slightly rising *pwip pwip pwip*; piercing yelps.
Similar Species: *Elf Owl* (p. 212): smaller; brown facial disc; gray back with white flecks; indistinct streaks on breast. *Eastern Screech-Owl* (p. 209) and *Western Screech-Owl* (p. 208): prominent "ear" tufts; heavy barring on breast.
Best Sites: Santa Ana NWR; Bentsen-Rio Grande Valley SP; Anzalduas CP (Hidalgo Co.); Falcon SP.

ELF OWL

Micrathene whitneyi

Male Elf Owls return to southern Texas in early to late spring to find a suitable nesting cavity and fiercely defend their territory, collectively mobbing intruders such as snakes or larger owls. On warm spring nights, yappy, chirping calls can often be heard coming from within a hollow tree—a determined male's attempt to coerce a female into his well-guarded nesting site. • The tiny Elf Owl avoids direct competition with other owls by squeezing into smaller nest cavities and sticking to a diet of mainly insects. This reliance on insects, which become increasingly scarce in cold weather, forces this owl to migrate south for winter. • The Elf Owl is the smallest owl in the world. It weighs about the same as a small candy bar.

ID: very small body; mottled, buff upperparts; yellow eyes; prominent white eyebrows; no "ear" tufts; indistinct buff-brown streaking on white undersides; very short tail.

Size: *L* 5–6 in; *W* 13 in.

Status: uncommon to locally common summer resident from the Lower Rio Grande Valley and from the Big Bend region north to the western half of the Edwards Plateau.

Habitat: deserts with saguaro cactus and mesquite; low-elevation canyons with large sycamores and oaks; riparian zones in mountain canyons.

Nesting: in a saguaro cactus, large tree or utility pole; in an old woodpecker hole; may use same site over many years; female incubates 2–4 white eggs over about 24 days;

male feeds the female and newly hatched young.

Feeding: swoops from a perch to catch insects, spiders and scorpions with its talons; may hover low over prey or snatch prey from low flight; rarely takes small mammals and reptiles.

Voice: variable, loud, rapid chirps and puppy-like barks used to defend territory and attract mate.

Similar Species: *Ferruginous Pygmy-Owl* (p. 211): long, barred tail; distinct streaking on breast; black false eye spots on back of head. *Eastern Screech-Owl* (p. 209) and *Western Screech-Owl* (p. 208): prominent "ear" tufts; heavy barring on breast.

Best Sites: Santa Ana NWR; Bentsen-Rio Grande Valley SP; Anzalduas CP (Hidalgo Co.); Big Bend NP; San Angelo SP.

BURROWING OWL

Athene cunicularia

Easily identified by their long legs and oversized eyes, Burrowing Owls inhabit the prairie and desert, heavily grazed pastures and disturbed areas in extensive grasslands. They nest in underground burrows and are often seen perched atop fence posts or rocks near their burrow entrances. Because Burrowing Owls use abandoned animal burrows for nesting, the extermination of ground squirrels and prairie dogs in the Great Plains has greatly reduced the number of suitable nest sites. Collisions with vehicles, agricultural chemicals and the conversion of native grasslands to cropland are also thought to be challenges facing this endangered bird. • When winter brings an influx of raptors to our state, Burrowing Owls become increasingly nocturnal, spending much of the day underground to avoid predation.

ID: long legs; rounded head; no ear tufts; yellow bill; short wings; white breast spotting; dark barring on belly; brown upperparts flecked with white.

Size: *L* 8–9 in; *W* 20–24 in.

Status: uncommon to common resident in the open country of the western third of Texas; rare and irregular migrant and winter visitor eastward, but absent from the Pineywoods of east Texas.

Habitat: dry, open grasslands, rolling hills and prairies; cleared land, including airports and golf courses.

Nesting: often loosely colonial; in an abandoned animal burrow; uses talons to enlarge burrow up to 7 ft deep; may add grass, sticks or other debris; female incubates 7–10 white eggs for 28–30 days while male brings food.

Feeding: often forages by evening or night; stalks prey, pouncing from a mound or swooping down from flight or from a fence post perch; eats mostly ground insects, such as grasshoppers, beetles and crickets; also eats small rodents, birds, amphibians and reptiles.

Voice: harsh *chuk* or *QUEE! kuk-kuk-kuk-kuk-kuk* call; rasping, rattlesnake-like warning call when inside burrows. *Male:* mournful *coo-coo-roo* in courtship.

Similar Species: *Short-eared Owl* (p. 216): larger; heavy, dark breast streaking; short legs; long wings with dark "wrist" marks; black eye discs.

Best Sites: Rita Blanca National Grassland; Buffalo Lake NWR; Muleshoe NWR; Big Spring SP.

BARRED OWL

Strix varia

Each spring, the sound of courting Barred Owls echoes through our forests: *Who cooks for you? Who cooks for you-all?* The escalating laughs, hoots and gargling howls reinforce the bond between pairs. At the height of courtship and when raising young, a pair of "Old Eight-Hooters" may continue their calls well into daylight hours. • With its relatively weak talons, the Barred Owl often chooses small prey. It is usually most active between midnight and 4 AM, when the forest floor rustles with the movements of rodents, which this owl can locate and follow using sound alone. • Barred Owls once inhabited moist, deciduous woodlands and swamps, but their numbers have declined with the destruction of these habitats. In the absence of suitable tree hollows for nesting, Barred Owls may resort to abandoned stick nests or even ground nests.

ID: mottled, dark gray-brown plumage; horizontal barring around neck and upper breast; vertical streaking on belly; dark eyes; pale bill; no "ear" tufts.

Size: *L* 17–24 in; *W* 3½–4 ft.

Status: uncommon to common resident in eastern Texas, extending along riparian woods into the eastern Panhandle, the southern and northern edges of the Edwards Plateau and down to the central coastal region.

Habitat: mature deciduous and mixedwood forests, especially in dense stands near fresh water.

Nesting: in a natural tree cavity, broken treetop or abandoned stick nest; very little material added; female incubates 2–3 white eggs for 28–33 days while male supplies food.

Feeding: nocturnal; swoops down on prey from a perch; eats mostly mice, cotton rats and squirrels; also takes amphibians, muskrats and small birds.

Voice: most characteristic of the owls; gives loud, hooting, rhythmic, laughing call year-round but mostly in spring: *Who cooks for you? Who cooks for you all?*

Similar Species: *Great Horned Owl* (p. 210): larger; "ear" tufts; horizontal barring on entire breast. *Western Screech-Owl* (p. 208) and *Eastern Screech-Owl* (p. 209): "ear" tufts; light-colored eyes. *Short-eared Owl* (p. 216): yellow eyes; no horizontal barring on upper breast.

Best Sites: any wooded park in eastern Texas.

LONG-EARED OWL

Asio otus

Long-eared Owls either inflate or compress their bodies in response to certain situations. To scare an intruder, this owl expands its air sacs, puffs its feathers and spreads its wings, doubling its size in a threat display. To hide from an intruder or predator, it compresses itself into a long, thin, vertical form to blend into the stumps and branches that surround it. • This nocturnal predator hunts in open areas but returns to dense stands of trees to roost by day. • Despite the common use of "eared" in many owl names, the tufts on top of the Long-eared Owl's head are made only of feathers. An owl's ear openings, in fact, are located on the sides of their head and are often asymmetrical, helping the owl to correctly judge the where a sound originates.

ID: long "ear" tufts are relatively close together; slim body; vertical belly markings; light brown facial disc; mottled brown plumage; yellow-orange eyes; white area around bill.

Size: *L* 13–16 in; *W* 3–4 ft.

Status: rare to uncommon winter resident in most of Texas; absent from the forests of east Texas.

Habitat: dense, mixed forests and tall shrub-lands, usually next to open spaces such as grasslands and meadows; may hunt over extensive semi-open terrain.

Nesting: often in an abandoned crow, magpie or hawk nest; occasionally in natural tree cavities; female incubates 4–5 eggs for 25–30 days.

Feeding: nocturnal; flies low, pouncing on prey from the air; eats mostly voles and mice but occasionally shrews, pocket-gophers, small rabbits, small birds and amphibians.

Voice: low, soft *quoo-quoo* breeding call; *weck-weck-weck* alarm call.

Similar Species: *Western Screech-Owl* (p. 208) and *Eastern Screech-Owl* (p. 209): smaller; "ear" tufts are farther apart; body is less compressed. *Great Horned Owl* (p. 210): much larger; "ear" tufts are farther apart; body is less compressed.

Best Sites: areas with thickets adjacent to open fields, from the central coast to the Edwards Plateau.

SHORT-EARED OWL

Asio flammeus

The Short-eared Owl fills the open-country niche left unoccupied by forest-dwelling owls. It occupies habitats such as wet meadows, marshes, fields and bogs. Often difficult to locate, it remains well hidden during the day as it roosts in grassy meadows, sand dunes and ditches. Usually solitary, the Short-eared Owl may form colonial winter roosts on the ground. • Short-eared Owl populations grow and decline over many years in response to dramatic fluctuations in prey availability. Cold weather and decreases in small mammal populations occasionally force large numbers of these owls, especially immature birds, to become temporary nomads, often sending them to areas well outside their usual breeding range. • You can learn to identify the Short-eared Owl from afar by its characteristic flight. Like a big butterfly, it beats its long wings slowly and deeply as it courses erratically low over meadows and fields. • All owls cough up "pellets" containing the indigestible parts of their prey, such as bones, feathers and fur.

ID: yellow eyes set in black sockets; heavy, vertical streaking on buff belly; straw-colored upperparts; short, inconspicuous "ear" tufts. *In flight:* dark "wrist" crescents; deep wingbeats; long wings.
Size: *L* 13–17 in; *W* 3–4 ft.
Status: rare to locally common migrant and winter resident statewide, less so in the Trans-Pecos.
Habitat: open areas, including grasslands, wet meadows, marshes, fields, airports and forest clearings.

Nesting: does not nest in Texas.
Feeding: forages while flying low over marshes, wet meadows and tall vegetation; pounces on prey from the air; eats mostly voles and other small rodents; also takes insects, small birds and amphibians.
Voice: generally quiet away from the nest; squeals and barks like a small dog.
Similar Species: *Long-eared Owl* (p. 215) and *Great Horned Owl* (p. 210): long "ear" tufts; rarely hunt by day. *Barred Owl* (p. 214): dark eyes; horizontal barring on upper breast; nocturnal hunter.
Best Sites: Anahuac NWR; Bolivar Flats Shorebird Sanctuary (Galvston Co.); Galveston I.; Brazoria NWR; San Bernard NWR.

LESSER NIGHTHAWK

Chordeiles acutipennis

With an erratic flight that is distinctive from that of the Common Nighthawk, the Lesser Nighthawk flies low over open fields at dusk, feeding on flying insects. Shaped like a boomerang with an added head and tail, this nighthawk zigzags across darkening skies, occasionally uttering its trilling call. • Along with their quick, manic flight, nighthawks are marked by very wide mouth gapes that are fringed with feather shafts (vibrissae) to increase the chance of catching insects. • Unlike other nighthawks, the Lesser does not dive during its courtship display. The Lesser Nighthawk also tends to fly quite low to the ground, whereas the Common Nighthawk hunts high above the fields. • Watch for both nighthawks feeding at parking lots or sports fields with bright outdoor lights that attract plenty of insects.

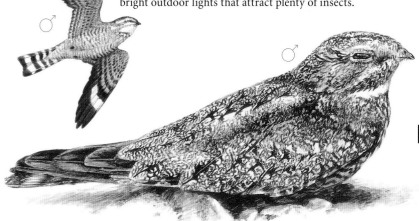

ID: mottled, brown upperparts; buffy underparts with faint dark barring; small bill; white (male) or buffy (female) forecollar. *In flight:* long, pointed wings; white (male) or buffy (female) bar across "wrist" (near wing tip); long, rectangular tail (with broad, white band on male).

Size: *L* 8–9 in; *W* 22 in.

Status: common migrant and summer resident from the Trans-Pecos east through the lower South Plains and Edwards Plateau and south to the Rio Grande and the central Coastal Plain; rare migrant on the upper Coastal Plain.

Habitat: sandy, coastal scrub; areas with sparse brush or scrub vegetation; open, arid fields and deserts.

Nesting: on open, barren ground, sometimes shaded by a small shrub; mostly the female incubates 2 white to pale gray eggs with fine dark dots, for 18–19 days; pair feeds the young by regurgitation.

Feeding: catches insects in flight using its gaping mouth; usually forages at dusk but may also feed during daylight and at night.

Voice: distinctive soft, rapid, tremulous trill.

Similar Species: *Common Nighthawk* (p. 218): slightly larger; darker overall; whitish underparts with prominent dark bars; white bar on primaries is further from wing tip. *Common Poorwill* (p. 220), *Chuck-will's-widow* (p. 221) and *Whip-poor-will* (p. 222): bulkier necks; shorter, rounded tails and wings; white-tipped tail corners; no white wing bar. *Common Pauraque* (p. 219): white-tipped tail corners.

Best Sites: Franklin Mountains SP; Balmorhea L.; Goliad SP; Mitchell L. (San Antonio); Falcon SP.

COMMON NIGHTHAWK

Chordeiles minor

Each May and June, the male Common Nighthawk flies high above suburban areas, forest clearings and lakeshores, gaining elevation in preparation for the climax of his noisy aerial dance. From a great height, he dives swiftly, thrusting his wings forward in a final braking action as he strains to pull out of the steep dive. This quick thrust of the wings produces a deep, hollow *vroom* that attracts female nighthawks. • Like its close relatives, the Common Nighthawk has a gaping mouth surrounded by feather shafts that funnel flying insects into its mouth. A nighthawk can eat over 2600 insects—including mosquitoes, blackflies and flying ants—in one day. • Nighthawks are generally less nocturnal than other nightjars, but they still spend most of the daylight hours resting on a tree limb or on the ground. With their very short legs and small feet, they sit along the length of a tree branch, not across it as do most perched birds.

ID: cryptic, mottled plumage; barred underparts. *Male:* white throat. *Female:* buff throat. *In flight:* bold white "wrist" patch on long, pointed wings; shallowly forked, barred tail; erratic flight.
Size: *L* 8½–10 in; *W* 24 in.
Status: uncommon to common migrant statewide; common summer resident in most of the state except the forests of east Texas.
Habitat: forest openings, burns, bogs, rocky outcroppings, gravel rooftops and sometimes fields with sparse cover or bare patches; also in most cities.
Nesting: on bare ground or a gravel rooftop; no nest is built; female incubates 2 heavily marked, creamy white eggs for about 19 days; pair feeds the young.

Feeding: primarily at dawn and dusk; catches insects in flight, often high in the air, sometimes around streetlights; eats mosquitoes, midges, beetles, moths and other flying insects.
Voice: frequently repeated, nasal *peent peent. Male:* wings make deep, hollow *vroom* during courtship flight.
Similar Species: *Lesser Nighthawk* (p. 217): slightly smaller; paler overall; white "wrist" bar closer to wing tip. *Common Poorwill* (p. 220), *Whip-poor-will* (p. 222) and *Chuck-will's-widow* (p. 221): no white "wrist" patches; shorter, rounder wings; rounded tails. *Common Pauraque* (p. 219): white-tipped tail corners.
Best Sites: any town or city with flat rooftops or gravel parking lots.

COMMON PAURAQUE

Nyctidromus albicollis

A bird of our southern brush country, the Common Pauraque is most vocal and active during clear nights when the moon is full. Its eerie, wailing cries have earned it a place in Central and South American folklore. Locals say that the presence of a Common Pauraque near a dwelling has resulted in virgins becoming pregnant. • Unlike with other nightjars, the eggs are incubated by both sexes. An incubating male always sits with his tail facing the sun, probably to transfer maximum heat. Whereas the Common Pauraque relies on cryptic coloration for protection, the eggs are ironically conspicuous and must be kept under cover to avoid hungry predators. • The Common Pauraque's scientific name comes from *albus*, meaning "white" and *collum* for "neck," in reference to the chevron-shaped mark on the bird's neck.

ID: long tail; black, triangular false eye spots on back of neck; V-shaped white throat patch. *Female:* less white on tail; buffy throat patch. *In flight:* blunt, rounded wing tips; buffy belly and underwing; broad, white bar across primary feathers; white on outer tail feathers.
Size: *L* 11 in; *W* 24 in.
Status: common resident from the Lower Rio Grande Valley to the southern part of the Edwards Plateau and along the coast to Calhoun Co.
Habitat: woodlands and brush during the day; open fields and forest edges at night.
Nesting: scrape nest on the ground or bed of leaves; pair incubates 2 salmon or buffy eggs, with pink, lavender, cinnamon or gray markings, for an estimated 20 days.
Feeding: forages near the ground or makes short flights; eats night-flying insects, mainly beetles.
Voice: several bizarre, wailing cries, such as a hoarse, whistled *who are you* and a *hip-hip hip-hip hip-hip hooray* cry that gets faster as the night goes on.
Similar Species: *Other Nightjars* (p. 217–22): no white "wrist" patch; less white on tail; no false eye spots on back of neck; pointed wings in flight. *Nighthawks* (pp. 217–18): may have buffy to white "necklace"; pointed wings in flight; smaller white "wrist" patches.
Best Sites: Hazel Bazemore CP (Nueces Co.), Choke Canyon SP, Santa Ana NWR, Bentsen-Rio Grande Valley SP, Anzalduas CP (Hidalgo Co.).

COMMON POORWILL

Phalaenoptilus nuttallii

In December, 1946, the scientific community was surprised by the discovery of a Common Poorwill in southern California that appeared to be hibernating through winter in a rock crevice. It was cold to the touch and had no detectable breath or heartbeat. Although poorwills do not enter true hibernation to survive cold periods, they enter into short-term torpor in which their body temperature drops as low as 43° F. Most poorwills migrate to warmer climates for winter but some may survive as year-round residents by entering a state of torpor during cold spells. The 1946 discovery was clearly not the first suggestion of this strange habit in poorwills: in 1804, Meriwether Lewis found a mysterious "goatsucker...to be passing into the dormant state" and, in an earlier era, the Hopi had named this bird *Holchoko*, "the sleeping one."

ID: cryptic, mottled plumage; light to dark brown overall; pale throat; finely barred underparts. *Male:* white tail corners. *Female:* buff tail corners. *In flight:* mothlike or batlike fluttering; rounded wings and tail.

Size: *L* 7½–8½ in; *W* 17 in.

Status: uncommon to common summer resident in the western half of the state and south to the Lower Rio Grande valley; rare in migration into the north-central region.

Habitat: arid, open, grassy environments, pinyon-juniper woodlands, chaparral, brushy slopes, sagebrush flats and open shrublands; occasional in logging clearcuts.

Nesting: on bare ground; no actual nest is built; pair incubates 2 white eggs for 20–21 days; pair feeds the young.

Feeding: at dawn and dusk and on moonlit nights; catches a variety of flying insects on the wing, mostly moths and beetles.

Voice: *poor-will* is frequently heard at dusk and through the night; at close range, a hiccuplike sound can be heard at the end of the phrase.

Similar Species: *Nighthawks* (pp. 217–18): long, pointed wings with white "wrist" patches; longer tails; feed mainly at dawn and dusk and often during daylight hours. *Common Pauraque* (p. 219): white "wrist" bars. *Whip-poor-will* (p. 222): slightly larger; pale gray stripes on upper back. *Chuck-will's-widow* (p. 221): much larger.

Best Sites: South Llano River SP; Choke Canyon SP; Guadalupe Mountains NP; Hueco Tanks SP; Big Bend NP.

CHUCK-WILL'S-WIDOW

Caprimulgus carolinensis

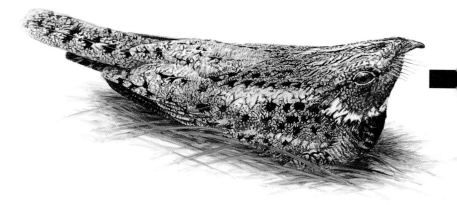

By day, you would be lucky to see this perfectly camouflaged bird roosting on the furrowed bark of a tree limb or sitting among scattered leaves on the forest floor. Even during nesting, the Chuck-will's-widow is virtually undetectable, incubating its eggs and raising its young on the ground. At dusk, however, the Chuck-will's-widow is hard to miss, whistling its own name while patrolling the evening skies for flying insects. • The Chuck-will's widow is our largest nightjar, and it can eat thousands of insects in a day. Tiny, stiff hairs (vibrissae) encircle the Chuck-will's-widow's bill and funnel prey into its large mouth as it flies. This bird's yawning gape allows it to capture flying insects of all sizes. Occasionally, the Chuck-will's-widow will even take a small bird!

ID: mottled, brown and buff body with overall reddish tinge; pale brown to buff throat; whitish "necklace"; dark breast; long, rounded tail. *Male:* white inner edges on outer tail feathers.

Size: *L* 12 in; *W* 26 in.

Status: common migrant in the eastern half of Texas and rare on the High Plains and western part of the Edwards Plateau; common summer resident in the eastern half of the state.

Habitat: riparian woodlands, swamp edges and deciduous and pine woodlands.

Nesting: on bare ground; no nest is built; female incubates 2 heavily blotched, creamy white eggs for about 21 days and raises the young alone.

Feeding: catches large flying insects on the wing or by hawking.

Voice: 3 loud whistling notes often paraphrased as *chuck-will's-widow*.

Similar Species: *Whip-poor-will* (p. 222): smaller; "necklace" contrasts with black throat; grayer coloration overall; male shows much more white in tail feathers; female's dark tail feathers are bordered with buff on outer tips. *Common Pauraque* (p. 219) and *Nighthawks* (pp. 217–18): white patches on wings; white (male) or buff (female) throat. *Common Poorwill* (p. 220): much smaller.

Best Sites: any wooded park or wildlife management area in the eastern half of the state.

WHIP-POOR-WILL

Caprimulgus vociferus

Because of its camouflaged plumage, sleepy daytime habits and secretive behavior, you must literally stumble upon a Whip-poor-will to see it. This elusive bird blends seamlessly into lichen-covered bark or the forest floor. Only occasionally is this bird seen roosting on an exposed tree branch or alongside a quiet road. • Whip-poor-wills apparently time their egg-laying so that hatchlings can be fed during the light of the full moon. Within days of hatching, young Whip-poor-wills can scurry away from their nest in search of protective cover if disturbed. • The Whip-poor-will is a member of the nightjar or "goatsucker" family, so named during the days of Aristotle, when superstition held that these birds would suck milk from the udders of female goats and cause the goats to go blind!

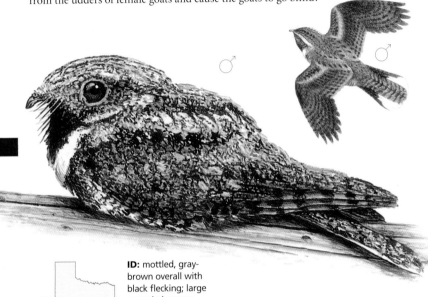

ID: mottled, gray-brown overall with black flecking; large eyes; dark crown stripe; dark throat; reddish tinge on rounded wings; longish, rounded tail. *Male:* white outer tail feathers and "necklace." *Female:* buff "necklace" and outer tail feathers. *Red morph:* mottled, rufous overall; pale gray markings on wings.

Size: *L* 9–10 in; *W* 16–20 in.

Status: common summer resident in the Trans-Pecos Mts.; common migrant in eastern Texas and rare on the western Edwards Plateau and High Plains.

Habitat: open deciduous and pine woodlands; often along forest edges.

Nesting: on the ground in leaf or pine needle litter; no nest is built; female incubates 2 whitish eggs, with brown blotches, for 19–20 days; pair raises the young.

Feeding: catches large night-flying insects in flight; eats mostly moths, beetles and mosquitoes; takes some grasshoppers.

Voice: loud, whistled *whip-poor-will,* with emphasis on the *will.*

Similar Species: *Chuck-will's-widow* (p. 221): larger; pale brown to buff throat; whitish "necklace"; darker breast; more reddish overall; much less white on male's tail; different call. *Nighthawks* (pp. 217–18): shallowly forked, barred tail; white wing patches; white (male) or buff (female) throat; much more conspicuous behavior.

Best Sites: any wooded park in eastern Texas; Davis Mountains SP; Guadalupe NP; Big Bend NP.

CHIMNEY SWIFT

Chaetura pelagica

Swifts are the "frequent fliers" of the bird world—they feed, drink, bathe, collect nesting material and even mate while they fly! Chimney Swifts spend much of their time sailing above urban neighborhoods in search of insects, touching down only to sleep or nest. They can also spotted flying low over grassy fields after it has rained. • Swifts migrate at night in a sleeplike state. They apparently use only half their brains during nocturnal flight, automatically adjusting to changing wind conditions to remain on course. Migrating Chimney Swifts may fly as high as 10,000 feet; above this altitude aircraft are required to carry oxygen. • Chimney Swifts got their name from their second choice for nest sites—brick chimneys. They also nest in abandoned buildings and silos and have adapted to special structures erected for them. • Chimney Swifts have small, weak legs and cannot take flight again if they land on the ground, so they usually cling to vertical surfaces.

ID: slim brown body; long, thin, pointed, crescent-shaped wings; squared tail. *In flight:* rapid wing-beats; boomerang-shaped profile; erratic flight pattern.

Size: *L* 4½–5½ in; *W* 12–13 in.

Status: common migrant east of the Pecos R. and less common in the Trans-Pecos; common summer resident throughout most of Texas except the Lower Rio Grande Valley.

Habitat: *Foraging:* over cities and towns. *Roosting* and *nesting:* chimneys and swift "towers"; may nest in tree cavities in more remote areas.

Nesting: often colonial; inside a chimney or tree cavity or in the attic of an abandoned building; pair uses saliva to attach a half-saucer nest of twigs to a vertical wall; pair incubates 4–5 white eggs for 19–21 days; pair feeds the young.

Feeding: swallows flying insects whole during continuous flight.

Voice: rapid, chattering flight call: *chitter-chitter-chitter;* rapid series of *chip* notes.

Similar Species: *White-throated Swift* (p. 224): found in western Texas; white throat; white flank patches. *Swallows* (pp. 288–95): broader, shorter wings; smoother flight patterns; most have forked or notched tails.

Best Sites: best seen in towns and cities with numerous chimneys.

WHITE-THROATED SWIFT

Aeronautes saxatalis

The White-throated Swift is found in the mountains of western Texas, where it replaces the Chimney Swift of the east. This bird asks little more than persistently fair skies and a vertical or even overhanging rock face in which to nest. Mountain canyons and rocky crags support this swift, as do the concrete buildings and bridges of the urban wilderness. • During its lifetime, the average White-throated Swift is likely to travel more than a million miles—enough to take it around the earth more than forty times! It is also considered the fastest North American swift, timed at up to 200 miles per hour. At this speed, this native Texan would certainly rank among the fastest birds in the world.

ID: sleek body; dark upperparts; white throat tapers to belly; black flanks with white patches. *In flight:* long, tapering wings angle backward; slightly forked tail, often held in point.

Size: *L* 6–7 in; *W* 15 in.

Status: common summer resident in the Trans-Pecos Mtns. and east to Val Verde Co.; rare migrant from the western Panhandle to the western Edwards Plateau; locally uncommon winter resident in the Trans-Pecos and in Palo Duro Canyon of the Panhandle.

Habitat: forages widely over a variety of open habitats. *Breeding:* on cliffs and canyon walls in the mountains; also on tall buildings, freeway overpasses and under bridges.

Nesting: colonial; in a crack or crevice on a cliff face; shallow saucer of twigs and conifer needles is glued together with saliva; pair incubates 4–5 eggs for 18–19 days.

Feeding: on the wing, flying perhaps hundreds of miles each day; feeds almost entirely on flying insects.

Voice: loud, shrill, descending laugh: *skee-jee-ee-ee-ee-ee-ee-ee.*

Similar Species: *Chimney Swift* (p. 223): found in eastern Texas; dark underparts. *Bank Swallow* (p. 292): all-white underparts except for dark collar. *Violet-green Swallow* (p. 290) and *Tree Swallow* (p. 289): all-white underparts. *All Swallows:* broader wings.

Best Sites: Hueco Tanks SP; Davis Mountains SP; Big Bend NP; Seminole Canyon SP.

BUFF-BELLIED HUMMINGBIRD

Amazilia yucantanensis

The Buff-bellied Hummingbird is probably one of the least studied birds to ever cross the U.S. border from Mexico into southern Texas. Found mainly in the Lower Rio Grande Valley, this hummingbird has recently been expanding its range inland and up the coast. Each fall, hundreds of birds gather on the Coastal Sand Plain in preparation for migration. Although most of the population ventures south for winter, some Buff-bellies migrate northeast along the Gulf Coast, delighting birdwatchers in Louisiana and occasionally in Florida. • To attract Buff-bellied Hummingbirds, hang a sugarwater feeder and plant red flowers. For nesting, these birds like sparse, bushy areas with shrubs such as hackberry or willow. The females use spider webs and plant fibers to build their nests and then hang lichen and flower petals on the outside as camouflage. Unlike other hummers, male and female Buff-bellied Hummingbirds look very similar.

Nesting: nest saddles a horizontal branch; cup nest of leaves, lichens and other plant material is woven together with spider silk; nest is lined with soft plant material; usually lays 2 glossy white eggs.

Feeding: frequents feeders and bright flowers (preferably red); occasionally eats insects.

Voice: call consists of 2–4 high, sharp notes, weaker notes when perched; chase call consists of sharp buzzes.

ID: bright green head and chest; green back with rusty tinge; rusty flanks and outer tail feathers; buff belly; white eye ring; downcurved, red and black bill. *Male:* more red on bill.

Size: *L* 4–4½ in; *W* 5¾ in.

Status: uncommon to locally common summer resident from the Lower Rio Grande Valley to the central coast; winter visitor up the Coastal Plain to Galveston Bay and inland to at least Washington Co. and Bexar Co.

Habitat: sparse woodland or thickets; frequents backyards with nectar feeders.

Similar Species: *Ruby-throated* (p. 226), *Black-chinned* (p. 227) and *Broad-tailed* (p. 228) *hummingbirds*: no rufous or orange on bodies or tails; dark tail feathers; males have distinctive throat patches. *Rufous Hummingbird* (p. 229): male has bright reddish orange on flanks and back; female has red-spotted throat and reddish flanks.

Best Sites: Rockport Hummingbird Garden; Corpus Christi Botanical Gardens; Santa Ana NWR; Frontera Audubon Sanctuary (Welaco); Bentsen-Rio Grande Valley SP.

RUBY-THROATED HUMMINGBIRD

Archilochus colubris

Like bees, hummingbirds feed on the sweet, energy-rich nectar of flowers, pollinating the flowers in the process. To attract these delightful birds, plant nectar-producing native plants in your yard or maintain a clean sugarwater feeder in a safe location (do not add red food coloring—it is poisonous to hummingbirds).
• Weighing about as much as a nickel, a hummingbird can briefly achieve speeds of up to 62 miles per hour. It is also among the few birds that can fly vertically and in reverse. In straight-ahead flight, hummingbirds beat their wings up to 80 times per second, and their hearts can beat up to 1200 times per minute! • Each year, Ruby-throated Hummingbirds migrate across the Gulf of Mexico—an incredible, nonstop journey of more than 500 miles. To accomplish this feat, these little birds first double their body mass by fattening up on insects and nectar.

ID: long bill; iridescent, green back; light underparts; dark tail. *Male:* ruby red throat; black chin. *Female and immature:* fine, dark throat streaking.

Size: *L* 3½–4 in; *W* 4½ in.

Status: common summer resident in eastern Texas and south along the central Coastal Plain; common migrant east of the Pecos R. and rare west of it; rare winter resident on the Coastal Plain, casual and irregular inland.

Habitat: open, mixed woodlands, wetlands, orchards, tree-lined meadows, flower gardens and backyards with trees and feeders.

Nesting: on a horizontal tree limb; tiny, deep cup nest of plant down and fibers is bound with spider silk and camouflaged with lichens and leaves; female incubates 2 white eggs for 13–16 days; female feeds the young.

Feeding: probes blooming flowers and sugarwater feeders; also eats small insects and spiders.

Voice: noticeable soft buzzing of the wings; loud *chick* and other high squeaks.

Similar Species: *Black-chinned Hummingbird* (p. 227): longer bill; usually duller green back, but difficult to distinguish; male has dark purple throat patch. *Rufous Hummingbird* (p. 229): male has bright reddish orange on flanks and back; female has red-spotted throat and reddish flanks. *Broad-tailed Hummingbird* (p. 228): rufous in lower part of outer tail feathers; white line from bill through eye and down neck.

Best Sites: any garden with red or orange flowers. *In migration:* concentrates at feeders.

BLACK-CHINNED HUMMINGBIRD

Archilochus alexandri

The Black-chinned Hummingbird is the western counterpart of the Ruby-throated Hummingbird of the East—the females of these two species are virtually indistinguishable in the field. The Black-chinned Hummingbird is most commonly seen in western Texas during summer. This remarkably adaptable hummingbird may be found in many different habitats, from deserts to lush gardens, and at any elevation between sea level and 6000 feet. • Naturalist and hummingbird taxonomist H.G.L. Reichenbach was deeply influenced by Greek mythology. He named several hummingbird genera after Greeks, including *Archilochus,* a notable Greek poet; *alexandri* honors a doctor who collected specimens in Mexico.

to uncommon migrant in the western two-thirds of Texas; rare winter resident along the coast and casual and irregular inland.

Habitat: *Breeding:* in lowland riparian woodlands, orchards and shrub-filled canyons. *In migration* and *postbreeding:* may feed in gardens and meadows in the foothills and mountains.

Nesting: tiny cup nest of plant down and spider webs is saddled atop a branch; female incubates 2 white eggs for up to 16 days.

Feeding: probes flowers for nectar; eats small insects and visits sugarwater feeders.

Voice: soft, high-pitched, warbling courtship songs; buzz and *chip* alarm calls; male's wings buzz in flight.

Similar Species: *Broad-tailed Hummingbird* (p. 228) and *Rufous Hummingbird* (p. 229): females and immatures have rufous or peach color on sides and flanks. *Ruby-throated Hummingbird* (p. 226): male has red gorget.

Best Sites: gardens with red or orange flowers. *In migration* and *winter:* at feeders.

ID: iridescent, green upperparts; long, thin bill; small, white crescent behind eye. *Male:* black throat with iridescent, violet band; white underparts with green "vest." *Female* and *immature:* black eye line; white throat, usually unmarked, but may have faint gray or greenish streaks; white underparts, often with pale grayish sides and buff tinge on flanks.

Size: *L* 3–3½ in; *W* 4¾ in.

Status: common summer resident of the Trans-Pecos, the Edwards Plateau and northern South Texas and rare south to the Lower Rio Grande Valley and west to the South Plains and the southern Panhandle; rare

227

BROAD-TAILED HUMMINGBIRD

Selasphorus platycercus

The Broad-tailed Hummingbirds that breed in high-elevation mountainous regions of the western U.S. overwinter in Mexico. In Texas, they are locally common summer residents of subalpine meadows in the Guadalupe, Chisos and Davis mountains. They migrate through the western third of the state and individuals occasionally overwinter at feeders. • Best known for the metallic trill produced by the male's wings, Broad-tailed Hummingbirds are often heard before they are seen. They breed during the short montane flowering season and can conserve energy during food shortages or cool nights by lowering their respiration rate and body temperature. • Whereas most hummingbirds survive three to five years in the wild, one female Broad-tailed Hummingbird lived a record 12 years.

ID: iridescent, bright green crown and back; long, straight bill. *Male:* rosy red throat; green and buffy wash to underparts; dark tail; wings whistle in flight. *Female:* dark streaking on cheeks and throat; buffy sides; broad, dark tail with rufous base and white tips.

Size: *L* 4 in; *W* 5¼ in.

Status: uncommon summer resident in most of the Trans-Pecos Mts.; uncommon migrant in western Texas east through the Edwards Plateau to the central coast and rare to the east and north; rare winter visitor in the Lower Rio Grande Valley and up the Coastal Plain to Harris Co.

Habitat: subalpine meadows and montane forests, especially cypress-pine-oak or pinyon-juniper-oak woodlands, often near streams; gardens.

Nesting: on a branch, often overhanging a stream; female builds cup nest of plant material lined with or plant down spiders webs and decorated with lichen or bark; female incubates 2 white eggs for 14–17 days; may have 2 broods.

Feeding: eats flower nectar (favors tubular red flowers) and small insects; visits hummingbird feeders.

Voice: high *chip* notes; male's wings produce a unique, metallic trill in flight.

Similar Species: *Ruby-throated Hummingbird* (p. 226): male has deep red throat and black mask, with no rufous in tail, and does not produce wing-trill in flight. *Black-chinned Hummingbird* (p. 227): male has deep blue throat and no rufous in tail. *Rufous Hummingbird* (p. 229): smaller; smaller tail; more rufous than female Broad-tailed Hummingbird.

Best Sites: Guadalupe Mountains NP; Davis Mountains SP; Big Bend NP.

RUFOUS HUMMINGBIRD

Selasphorus rufus

The Rufous Hummingbird is, like the Summer Tanager and the Townsend's Solitaire, the northernmost representative of a family with mostly tropical affiliations. It breeds throughout most of the Pacific Northwest to southern Alaska and overwinters in the southernmost states and Mexico. This species follows an elliptical migration pattern, heading north along the Pacific Coast but returning south through western Texas. • The tiny Rufous Hummingbird is a delicate avian jewel, but its beauty hides a relentless mean streak. Male hummers are aggressively territorial, exhibiting remarkable feistiness near concentrated food sources. • Plants with colorful flowers and sweet, energy-rich nectar attract hummingbirds. As hummingbirds visit flowers for the food, they spread pollen from one flower to another, ensuring the plants' survival.

ID: long, thin, black bill; mostly rufous tail. *Male:* orange-brown back, tail and flanks; iridescent, orange-red throat; green crown; white breast and belly. *Female:* green back; red-spotted throat; rufous sides and flanks contrast with white underparts.

Size: L 3¼–3½ in; W 4½ in.

Status: common migrant in the western third of Texas and rare to uncommon in the rest of the state; rare to locally uncommon winter resident on the Coastal Plain and in the Lower Rio Grande Valley; rare and irregular inland.

Habitat: nearly any habitat with abundant flowers, especially hibiscus and salvia; mixed-wood forests; hummingbird feeders.

Nesting: does not nest in Texas.

Feeding: probes mostly red flowers for nectar while hovering; also eats small insects, sap and sugar water.

Voice: low *chewp chewp* call; also utters a rapid and exuberant confrontation call: *ZEE-chuppity-chup!*

Similar Species: *Broad-tailed Hummingbird* (p. 228): female does not have red spotting on throat and has much less rufous in tail and much paler sides and flanks. *Ruby-throated Hummingbird* (p. 226) and *Black-chinned Hummingbird* (p. 227): no rufous or orange on body and tail.

Best Sites: gardens with red or orange flowers. *Winter:* at feeders.

RINGED KINGFISHER

Ceryle torquatus

The conspicuous Ringed Kingfisher is the largest of the three kingfishers found in North America, and it reaches the northern limit of its range in southern Texas. This colorful waterside resident is usually found perched on a prominent branch or hovering above a pool in search of fish. Its loud, rattling, machine gun–like call is slower and deeper than the Belted Kingfisher's call. • The Ringed Kingfisher is a relative newcomer to the U.S. Common in Central and South America, but considered rare outside of Mexico until the 1960's, this species appears to be slowly expanding its range northward. The Ringed Kingfisher is a locally common resident along the Lower Rio Grande Valley, and it is being reported more frequently along the Nueces, Guadalupe and Colorado rivers and the central Gulf Coast.

ID: blue upperparts; rusty underparts; shaggy, blue-gray crest; large, sturdy bill; white throat and collar; rusty belly; barred tail. *Male:* rusty breast. *Female:* thick, blue breast band bordered in white. *In flight:* female has rusty underwings; male has white underwings.

Size: *L* 16 in; *W* 25 in.

Status: locally common resident in the Lower Rio Grande Valley and upriver to Val Verde Co., inland onto the eastern half of the Edwards Plateau and along the coast to Nueces Co.

Habitat: riparian areas; low-lying streams, lakeshores, dams and lagoons.

Nesting: in an earth or sand bank overlooking water; both adults excavate a burrow and incubate 3–5 glossy white eggs for about 22 days; both adults tend the young.

Feeding: dives headfirst into the water, either from a perch or from hovering flight; eats mostly small fish, aquatic invertebrates and tadpoles.

Voice: loud, deep, rattling *ke ke ke ke ke* call is slower than Belted Kingfisher's.

Similar Species: *Belted Kingfisher* (p. 231): smaller; mainly white underparts.

Best Sites: Laguna Atascosa NWR; Boca Chica; Sabal Palm Audubon Sanctuary; Santa Ana NWR; Bentsen-Rio Grande Valley SP; Falcon SP.

BELTED KINGFISHER

Ceryle alcyon

Never far from water, the boisterous Belted Kingfisher bird utters its distinctive rattling call while perched on a bare branch that extends out over a productive pool. With a precise headfirst dive, this bird can catch fish at depths of up to 2 feet or snag a frog immersed in only a few inches of water. It has even been observed diving into water to elude avian predators. • Belted Kingfishers breed locally in northern Texas. A pair of kingfishers typically takes turns excavating the nest burrow. The birds use their bills to chip away at an exposed sandbank and then kick loose material out of the tunnel with their feet. • In Greek mythology, Alcyon (Halcyone), the daughter of the wind god, grieved so deeply for her drowned husband that the gods transformed them both into kingfishers.

ID: bluish upperparts; shaggy crest; blue-gray breast band; white collar; long, straight bill; short legs; white under-wings; small white patch near eye.
Female: rusty belt (may be incomplete).
Size: *L* 11–14 in; *W* 20 in.
Status: uncommon to locally common summer resident throughout most of Texas, although less common on the upper coast and in the Lower Rio Grande Valley; common winter resident in the northeast and on the upper coast, uncommon in the western third and rare and irregular elsewhere.
Habitat: rivers, large streams, lakes, marshes and beaver ponds, especially near exposed soil banks, gravel pits or bluffs.
Nesting: in a sand or clay bank; pair excavates a cavity at the end of an earth burrow that is often up to 6ft long; pair incubates

6–7 white eggs for 22–24 days; pair feeds the young.
Feeding: dives headfirst into water, either from a perch or from hovering flight; eats mostly small fish, aquatic invertebrates and tadpoles.
Voice: fast, repetitive, cackling rattle, a little like a teacup shaking on a saucer.
Similar Species: *Ringed Kingfisher* (p. 230): larger; huge bill; rufous underparts and wing linings. *Green Kingfisher* (p. 232): much smaller; green upperparts and head. *Blue Jay* (p. 280): more intense blue color; smaller bill and head; different behaviours.
Best Sites: any park with a lake, stream or river and adjacent trees and shrubs.

GREEN KINGFISHER

Chloroceryle americana

The colorful Green Kingfisher, with its disproportionately large head and huge bill, is a gem of the Lower Rio Grande Valley. Appearing slightly top-heavy, the smallest of the kingfishers often bobs its head and tail while perched. Watch for it resting on low branches near clear ponds or small streams, searching for fish in the shallows of waterways and seasonally flooded channels that are not productive enough for larger kingfishers. Although this bird flies low over the water, it does not hover before diving for prey. • At the northern limit of its range, the Green Kingfisher has never been common in Texas. After World War II, damming, pollution and alteration of waterways caused it to disappear near our major cities, but recent conservation efforts have helped slightly. • Fire ants destroy more Green Kingfisher nests than all other predators combined. The ants pester incubating adults until their eggs accidentally crack, providing an easy meal for the ants.

ID: dark green upperparts with white markings; small crest; white collar; green spotting on belly. *Male:* rufous chest band. *In flight:* white outer tail feathers

Size: *L* 7–9 in; *W* 11–13 in.

Status: uncommon resident from the Lower Rio Grande Valley upriver to at least Val Verde Co., onto the southern half of the Edwards Plateau and up the coast to Jackson Co.; rare up the Rio Grande to El Paso and throughout the northern Edwards Plateau.

Habitat: clear streams, seasonally flooded channels (resacas) and ponds surrounded by bushes and trees.

Nesting: in a stream bank; 5–8 ft above the water line, pair digs out a 2–3 ft tunnel; pair incubates 4–6 eggs for 20 days.

Feeding: dives headfirst into the water for small fish; occasionally takes insects in flight; may take lizards and grasshoppers in dry years.

Voice: quick *tik-tikeee-tik* followed by a short rattle; high-pitched *tseep* flight call.

Similar Species: *Belted Kingfisher* (p. 231): larger; shorter bill; blue-gray upperparts; rusty belt on female. *Ringed Kingfisher* (p. 230): much larger; large, heavy bill; mostly blue with rusty underparts.

Best Sites: Lost Maples SP; South Llano River SP; Santa Ana NWR; Bentsen-Rio Grande Valley SP; Falcon SP.

RED-HEADED WOODPECKER

Melanerpes erythrocephalus

Closely related to the western Acorn Woodpecker, the Red-headed Woodpecker is a bird of the East that lives mostly in deciduous woodlands, in urban parks and in fields with open groves of large trees. • Red-headed Woodpeckers were once common throughout their range, but their numbers have declined dramatically over the past century. Introduced European Starlings have largely out-competed Red-headed Woodpeckers for nesting cavities. As well, these woodpeckers are often struck by vehicles when they dart over roadways to catch flying insects. • During the breeding season, the Red-headed Woodpecker will hawk for flying insects and store them, as well as acorns and other nuts, in cracks and bark crevices. It is one of only four woodpecker species that regularly caches food.

juvenile

ID: bright red head, chin, throat and "bib" with black border; black back, wings and tail; white breast, belly, rump, lower back and inner wing patches.

Size: *L* 9–9½ in; *W* 17 in.

Status: rare to locally common resident from eastern Texas through the north-central region to the eastern Panhandle; rare winter visitor in west Texas to the Pecos R.

Habitat: open deciduous (especially oak) woodlands, urban parks, river edges and roadsides with groves of scattered trees.

Nesting: in a dead tree or limb; male excavates a cavity; pair incubates 4–5 white eggs for 12–13 days; pair feeds the young.

Feeding: flycatches for insects; hammers dead and decaying wood for grubs; eats mostly insects, earthworms, spiders, nuts, berries, seeds and fruit; may also eat some young birds and eggs.

Voice: loud series of *kweer* or *kwrring* notes; occasional chattering *kerr-r-ruck;* drums softly in short bursts.

Similar Species: adult is distinctive. *Red-bellied Woodpecker* (p. 236): whitish face and underparts; black-and-white-barred back. *Yellow-bellied Sapsucker* (p. 237) and *Red-naped Sapsucker* (p. 451): white and black markings on head; large white wing patch.

Best Sites: Caddo Lake SP; Huntsville SP; W.G. Jones State Forest; Big Thicket National Preserve; Bear Creek Pioneer Park (Houston).

ACORN WOODPECKER

Melanerpes formicivorus

Well known for their unique communal lifestyle, Acorn Woodpeckers live in family groups of a dozen or more birds, cooperating to protect shared food-storage sites and nesting cavities. Groups include both breeding birds and nonbreeding helpers, usually young from the previous year. Although mating systems vary between populations, up to seven breeding males typically vie for one to three egg-laying females. Competition is especially intense among females that share a joint nest cavity, and females regularly remove and then eat eggs laid by their co-breeders. Nonbreeding group members help to raise the young and protect the group's feeding territory. • Acorn Woodpeckers eat a variety of food, but almost half of their diet consists of acorns that they hoard in hole-studded "granary trees" for later consumption. An oak or sycamore snag may be perforated with up to 50,000 holes.

ID: white patches on face and throat; pale eyes; throat often yellowish; glossy, black upperparts; white underparts streaked with black; white wing patches and rump. *Male:* red crown and nape. *Female:* red on the nape only.
Size: *L* 9 in; *W* 17½ in.
Status: common resident in several mountain passes of the Trans-Pecos and locally common in Kerr Co. and Real Co. of the Edwards Plateau; irregular winter visitor in the rest of the Trans-pecos and the High Plains.
Habitat: closely associated with many species of oak; oak and pine-oak woodlands; also found in riparian woodlands and parks.
Nesting: colonial; group excavates a cavity in a standing dead tree; breeding adults and occasionally nonbreeding helpers incubate 4–6 white eggs for 11 days; young are raised communally.

Feeding: harvests and stores acorns in holes drilled into bark or standing dead-wood; gleans tree bark or foliage for insects (especially ants) or catches them on the wing during short, swooping flights; also eats fruit, seeds and bird eggs; drills small, shallow sap wells.
Voice: raucous *ja-cup, jap-cup, jap-cup* call, often becoming a chorus.
Similar Species: *Red-headed Woodpecker* (p. 233): non-overlapping ranges; all-red head; large white patch on back.
Best Sites: Guadalupe Mountains NP; Big Bend NP; Davis Mountains SP.

GOLDEN-FRONTED WOODPECKER

Melanerpes aurifrons

Conspicuous Golden-fronted Woodpeckers inhabit the mesquite brushlands and dry woodlands of central and southern Texas, drawing attention to themselves with raucous *kaaaaaaak!* calls. Unlike other woodpeckers, they rarely drill into wood, instead catching insects in flight or feeding on fruit and nuts. In summer, Golden-fronted Woodpeckers gorge themselves on the fruit of prickly pear cactus, smudging their faces with purple juice. In winter, they favor pecans and are often found in riparian areas searching out these nuts. • This bird is now a common visitor to urban backyards and parks. If you wish to attract one to your yard, a bird bath and a handful of corn will go a long way toward pleasing this species. • The Golden-fronted Woodpecker is closely related to the Red-bellied Woodpecker of the East, and these two species occasionally hybridize.

ID: black and white horizontal stripes on back; white rump with black tail; buffy head and underparts; yellow nasal patch; orange-yellow nape. *Male:* red crown patch.
Size: *L* 9½ in; *W* 17 in.
Status: common resident from the Panhandle south through the Edwards Plateau to the Rio Grande and the central coast and west through the South Plains and the Trans-Pecos.
Habitat: urban parks and yards; mesquite scrub, pecan groves and dry woodlands.
Nesting: in standing dead wood or a live tree; pair excavates a small hole and lines bottom of cavity with wood chips; pair incubates 4–7 eggs for 12–14 days; pair raises the young.
Feeding: catches insects in flight; also eats fruit and nuts.

Voice: repeated, raspy rattle.
Similar Species: *Red-bellied Woodpecker* (p. 236): darker underparts; white rump with black spots; male has continuous red from crown to nape; female has red nape only. *Northern Flicker* (p. 242): gray crown; brown back with dark barring; black "bib"; dark-spotted underparts. *Yellow-bellied Sapsucker* (p. 237): juvenile has tan facial stripes and a large, white wing patch.
Best Sites: any park in western Texas with open brushland.

RED-BELLIED WOODPECKER

Melanerpes carolinus

No stranger to suburban backyards, the familiar Red-bellied Woodpecker some-times nests in birdhouses. It is found year-round in woodlands throughout the southeastern states, but numbers fluctuate depending on habitat availability and weather conditions. During mild winters, more Red-bellied Woodpeckers frequent the northern parts of their range. • Unlike most woodpeckers, Red-bellies consume large amounts of plant material, seldom excavating wood for insects. When occupying an area together with Red-headed Woodpeckers, Red-bellies nest in the trunk, below the foliage, and the Red-heads nest in dead branches among the foliage. • The Red-bellied Woodpecker's "red belly" is only a small reddish area that is dif-ficult to see in the field. • In the wild, Red-bellied Woodpeckers have a life span of more than 20 years.

Nesting: female selects one of several cavities excavated by the male, an existing cavity or a birdhouse; pair incubates 4–5 white eggs for 12–14 days; pair raises the young.

ID: black-and-white-barred back; red nape; white patches, speckled with black, on rump and central tail feathers; reddish tinge on belly. *Male:* red nape extends to forehead. *Juvenile:* dark gray crown; streaked breast.

Size: *L* 9–10½ in; *W* 16 in.

Status: common to abundant resident in eastern Texas and west through the north-central region to the eastern Panhandle; rare migrant and winter visitor from the western Panhandle south through the South Plains and Edwards Plateau to the Lower Rio Grande Valley.

Habitat: mature deciduous woodlands; occasionally in wooded residential areas.

Feeding: forages in trees, on the ground or occasionally on the wing; eats mostly insects, seeds, nuts and fruit; may also eat tree sap, small amphibians, bird eggs or small fish.

Voice: soft, rolling *churr* call; drums in second-long bursts.

Similar Species: *Golden-fronted Wood-pecker* (p. 235): lighter upperparts; yellow nasal patch; orange-yellow nape; white rump; black central tail feathers; male has red crown patch. *Northern Flicker* (p. 242): yellow under-wings; gray crown; brown back with dark barring; black "bib"; large, dark spots on underparts. *Red-headed Woodpecker* (p. 233): all-red head; unbarred, black back and wings; white patch on trailing edge of wing.

Best Sites: any eastern Texas park with open woods; often in suburban areas.

YELLOW-BELLIED SAPSUCKER

Sphyrapicus varius

Yellow-bellied Sapsuckers visit Texas in winter, occasionally uttering their quiet *keer* call. The drumming of sapsuckers—with its slow, irregular rhythm reminiscent of Morse code—differs from that of other local woodpeckers. The Yellow-bellied Sapsucker's range overlaps with the Red-naped Sapsucker's in the Trans-Pecos, where these similar birds are often found in the same habitat. • Lines of freshly drilled parallel "wells" in tree bark are a sure sign that sapsuckers are nearby. A pair of sapsuckers might drill a number of sites within their forest territory. The wells fill with sweet, sticky sap that attracts insects; the sapsuckers then make their rounds, eating both the trapped bugs and the pooled sap. Sapsuckers do not actually "suck" sap—they lap it up with a tongue that resembles a paintbrush. • Species such as hummingbirds, kinglets, warblers and waxwings also benefit from the wells made by Yellow-bellied Sapsuckers, especially when flying insects, fruit and nectar are rare.

ID: black "bib"; red forecrown; black and white face, back, wings and tail; large, white wing patch; yellow wash on lower breast and belly. *Male:* red chin. *Female:* white chin. *Juvenile:* brownish overall, but with large, clearly defined wing patches.
Size: *L* 7–9 in; *W* 16 in.
Status: uncommon to locally common migrant and winter resident in most of Texas, rare in the western Trans-Pecos.
Habitat: deciduous and mixed forests, especially dry second-growth woodlands.
Nesting: does not nest in Texas.
Feeding: hammers trees for insects; drills "wells" in live trees to collect sap and trap insects; also flycatches for insects.
Voice: nasal, catlike *meow* is given occasionally in winter; territorial and courtship hammering has a quality and rhythm similar to Morse code.

Similar Species: *Red-naped Sapsucker* (p. 451): 2 rows of white marking on back; male has red chin with black border. *Red-headed Woodpecker* (p. 233): juvenile has no white patch on wing. *Downy Woodpecker* (p. 239) and *Hairy Woodpecker* (p. 240): red nape; white back; lack large, white wing patches and red forecrown.
Best Sites: any area with open woods, including suburban areas.

237

LADDER-BACKED WOODPECKER

Picoides scalaris

The Ladder-backed Woodpecker is a common visitor to ranches and rural towns throughout the southwestern U.S., taking over areas that the equally numerous Downy Woodpecker avoids. Formerly called "Cactus Woodpecker," the Ladder-back frequently feeds and nests in cacti. This small, speckled woodpecker is also seen flitting between scrub, dried riverbeds and pine-oak woodlands. • Male and female Ladder-backed Woodpeckers seem to use different foraging techniques and feed on different plant species, possibly as a result of limited food availability in their arid habitats. Some studies have suggested that females prefer to feed near the tops and outer branches of trees or mesquite, whereas males are more likely to feed closer to the trunk or near the ground.

Female: black crown. *Juvenile male:* smaller red crown patch.
Size: *L* 7–7½ in; *W* 13 in.
Status: rare to common resident in the western two-thirds of Texas; rare vagrant further onto the upper coast and Pineywoods.
Habitat: mesquite, desert savanna, scrubland and thorn forests.
Nesting: in a tree, cactus, agave, yucca or utility pole; in a cavity, likely drilled by the male and lined with woodchips; 2–7 creamy white eggs hatch within 13 days.
Feeding: mainly eats insects such as ants and beetles; also eats cactus flowers; may feed on or near the ground or dig under bark.
Voice: quick, descending laugh with raspy ending; quick *chip* contact call; drums quickly.
Similar Species: *Downy Woodpecker* (p. 239): black upper back and nape; white patch on upper back; white underparts; shorter bill; male has red only on back of crown. *Yellow-bellied Sapsucker* (p. 237): large, white wing patch; red forecrown; lacks red nape and clean white back.
Best Sites: any park with open brushland in the western two-thirds of Texas.

ID: black back with thick, white horizontal stripes turning to spots on the wings; white or buffy underparts with black spotting; black tail with striped, white and black outer coverts; white face and throat; black eye line joins with black bill line; faint white "mustache." *Male:* red crown with white dots on forehead.

DOWNY WOODPECKER

Picoides pubescens

A birdfeeder well stocked with peanut butter and peanut hearts may attract a pair of Downy Woodpeckers to your backyard. These approachable little birds tolerate human activities better than most other woodpeckers, and they visit feeders more often than the larger, more aggressive Hairy Woodpeckers. • The Downy Woodpecker's small bill is extremely effective for poking into tiny crevices and extracting invertebrates and wood-boring grubs. • Like other members of the woodpecker family, the Downy has evolved a number of features that help to cushion the repeated shocks of a lifetime of hammering. These characteristics include a strong bill, strong neck muscles, a flexible, reinforced skull and a brain that is tightly packed in its protective cranium. Feathered nostrils filter out the sawdust produced when hammering.

ID: black eye line and crown; short, stubby bill about half as long as head is wide; white belly; black wings with white bars; white back patch; black tail with black-spotted, white outer feathers. *Male:* small red patch on back of head.
Size: *L* 6–7 in; *W* 12 in.
Status: common resident in the eastern half of Texas through the north-central region and the eastern half of the Edwards Plateau to the central Coastal Plain, rare to uncommon in the eastern Panhandle and local elsewhere; rare migrant and winter resident in the western third of Texas.
Habitat: wooded environments, especially deciduous and mixed forests and areas with tall deciduous shrubs.
Nesting: in a dying or decaying trunk or limb; pair excavates a cavity and lines it with wood chips; pair incubates 4–5 white eggs for 11–13 days; pairs feeds the young.
Feeding: forages on trunks and branches, often in saplings and shrubs; chips and probes for insects, from eggs to adults; also eats nuts and seeds; visits suet feeders.
Voice: long, unbroken trill; sharp *pik* or *ki-ki-ki* and whiny *queek queek* calls; more frequent, higher-pitched drumming than the Hairy Woodpecker, usually on small trees and dead branches.
Similar Species: *Hairy Woodpecker* (p. 240): larger; longer bill; unspotted outer tail feathers. *Ladder-backed Woodpecker* (p. 238) barred back and outer tail feathers; black-streaked underparts. *Red-cockaded Woodpecker* (p. 241): rare; white cheek patch; barred back; black-spotted underparts.
Best Sites: any park with open woods.

HAIRY WOODPECKER

Picoides villosus

Glimpsing a Hairy Woodpecker at your feeder is a treat, because this bird tends to visit less frequently than the similar Downy Woodpecker. The Hairy is quite aggressive, thrashing seeds around with its sturdy bill. At close range, the larger size, bigger bill and pure white outer tail feathers of the Hairy distinguish it from the Downy. • The secret to a woodpecker's feeding success is its very long tongue—in some cases more than four times the length of the bill—made possible by twin structures that wrap around the perimeter of the skull and store the tongue much like a measuring tape in its case. Long and maneuverable, the tongue has a tip that is sticky with saliva and finely barbed to help seize reluctant wood-boring insects. • Rather than singing during courtship, woodpeckers drum rhythmically on trees.

to the edge of the Edwards Plateau, in the Trans-Pecos Mts. and in the eastern Panhandle; rare migrant and winter visitor in the rest of the Panhandle, the Rolling Plains and Edwards Plateau.

Habitat: lowland deciduous and mixed forests; burned areas.

Nesting: in a live or decaying tree trunk or limb; pair excavates a cavity and lines it with wood chips; pair incubates 4–5 white eggs for 12–14 days; pair feeds the young.

Feeding: chips, hammers and probes bark for insects, from eggs to adults; also eats nuts, fruit and seeds; visits suet feeders, especially in winter.

Voice: loud, sharp *peek peek* call; long, unbroken trill: *keek-ik-ik-ik-ik-ik;* drums less regularly and at a lower pitch than the Downy Woodpecker, always on tree trunks and large branches.

ID: black cheek and crown; bill length about equals head width; black wings with white spots; white patch on back; pure white belly; black tail with unspotted, white outer feathers.
Male: small, red hindcrown patch.

Size: *L* 8–9½ in; *W* 15 in.

Status: uncommon to locally common resident in the eastern third of Texas south

Similar Species: *Downy Woodpecker* (p. 239): smaller; shorter bill; dark spots on outer tail feathers. *Yellow-bellied Sapsucker* (p. 237): large white wing patch; red forecrown; barred back. *Ladder-backed Woodpecker* (p. 238) smaller; barred back; buff underparts streaked with black; barred outer tail feathers.

Best Sites: Guadalupe Mountains NP; Davis Mountains SP; Big Bend NP; Daingerfield SP; Martin Dies, Jr. SP.

RED-COCKADED WOODPECKER

Picoides borealis

The rare Red-cockaded Woodpecker is a highly social bird with intricate nesting requirements. "Clans" (family groups) include the breeding pair and up to eight helpers. The group drills a cluster of cavities into live trees, often choosing large longleaf pines infected with red heart fungus. The average cavity takes two years to excavate but may be reused for two decades. • Nest cavities are protected by rows of tiny holes or resin wells drilled above and below the entrance. Gum seeping from these wells forms a barrier against climbing predators such as rat snakes. Wildfires are important for suppressing understory vegetation that could otherwise grow above this sap barrier. • Red-cockaded Woodpecker colonies were once more common; the remaining populations are mostly in isolated islands of old-growth pines. Fire suppression and the logging of mature forests continues to threaten this species, but management efforts have led to increased numbers. • This woodpecker's "cockades," red patches of feathers on the head, are often difficult to see in the field.

ID: black and white ladder pattern on back and wings; distinctive white cheeks; black spots on white belly; broad, black "mustache" extends from bill to neck. *Male:* red patch behind eye (may be difficult to see).

Size: L 8½ in; W 14 in.

Status: endangered federally (USFWS); rare to locally uncommon resident in the Pineywoods of east Texas.

Habitat: open pine forest, 80 years old or older, with little understory; most common in fire-resistant longleaf pines.

Nesting: in a live pine; cavity 30–50 ft above the ground is reused; both parents and sometimes helpers incubate 2–5 shiny white eggs for 10–15 days; pair raises the young.

Feeding: flakes off bark on pine trees to expose insects and spiders; sometimes eats seeds and berries.

Voice: most common call is a *sklit* or *szrek*, given every few seconds; grating and clicking rattle call ends with a hoarse snarl.

Similar Species: *Downy Woodpecker* (p. 239) and *Hairy Woodpecker* (p. 240): broad, black eye line; white patch on back.

Best Sites: Alabama Creek WMA; Sam Rayburn Reservoir; Huntsville SP; W.G. Jones SF.

NORTHERN FLICKER

Colaptes auratus

"Red-shafted Flicker"

Unlike most woodpeckers, the Northern Flicker spends a lot of time on the ground. It appears almost robinlike as it hops about. • Two forms inhabit Texas—the "Yellow-shafted Flicker" breeds east of Dallas, Austin and San Antonio and the "Red-shafted Flicker" breeds throughout the western Panhandle and the Trans-Pecos—and they frequently intergrade. • Flickers often bath in dusty depressions. The dust particles absorb excess oils and kill harmful bacteria. For more thorough cleaning, flickers squish ants and preen themselves with the remains: ants contain formic acid, which can kill small parasites. • The Northern Flicker has zygodactyl feet—each foot has two toes facing forward and two toes pointing backward—which allows the bird to move vertically up and down tree trunks. As well, stiff tail feathers help to prop up the bird's body as it scales trees and excavates cavities.

"Yellow-shafted Flicker"

ID: black-barred, brown back and wings; black-spotted, buff to whitish underparts; black "bib"; long bill; brownish to buff face; brown or gray crown. *Male:* black or red "mustache" stripe.

Size: *L* 12½–13 in; *W* 20 in.

Status: rare to locally uncommon resident in the Trans-Pecos Mts., the Panhandle, north and east Texas and the wooded areas of the upper Coastal Plain; common migrant and winter resident statewide.

Habitat: open deciduous, mixed and coniferous woodlands and forest edges; fields and meadows; beaver ponds and other wetlands.

Nesting: in a dead or dying deciduous tree (or nest box); pair excavates a cavity and lines it with wood chips; pair incubates 5–8 white eggs for 11–16 days; pair feeds the young.

Feeding: forages on the ground for ants and other terrestrial insects; probes bark; also eats berries and nuts; occasionally flycatches.

Voice: loud, laughing, rapid *kick-kick-kick-kick-kick-kick; woika-woika-woika* issued during courtship.

Similar Species: *Golden-fronted Wood-pecker* (p. 235): yellow-orange nape; black and white back; all-buffy underparts; male has red crown. *Red-bellied Woodpecker* (p. 236): more red on head; black and white back; unspotted underparts.

Best Sites: Guadalupe Mountains NP; Davis Mountains SP; Big Bend NP. *Winter:* any open woods.

PILEATED WOODPECKER

Dryocopus pileatus

With its flaming red crest, swooping flight and maniacal call, this impressive deep-forest dweller can stop hikers in their tracks. Using its powerful, dagger-shaped bill and stubborn determination, the Pileated Woodpecker chisels out uniquely shaped rectangular cavities in its unending search for grubs and ants. • As a primary cavity nester, the Pileated Woodpecker plays an important role in forest ecosystems. Ducks, small falcons, owls and even flying squirrels frequently nest in its abandoned cavities. • Not surprisingly, a woodpecker's bill becomes shorter with age. In his historic painting of the Pileated Woodpecker, John J. Audubon correctly depicted the bills of the juveniles as slightly longer than those of the adults. • Because they require large home territories, these magnificent birds are usually not frequently encountered. A pair of breeding Pileated Woodpeckers generally needs more than 100 acres of mature forest in which to settle. However, in some parts of its range, these birds actually breed in backyards.

ID: predominantly black; white wing linings; red crest; yellow eyes; stout, dark bill; white stripe from bill to shoulder; white chin. *Male:* red "mustache"; red forehead. *Female:* black "mustache"; gray-brown forehead.

Size: *L* 16–19 in; *W* 29 in.

Status: rare to locally common resident in eastern and central Texas, from the Red R. south and along the riparian woodlands of the upper Coastal Plain.

Habitat: extensive tracts of mature deciduous, mixed or coniferous forests; some occur in riparian woodlands or wood-lots in suburban and agricultural areas.

Nesting: in a dead or dying tree trunk; pair excavates a cavity and lines it with wood chips; pair incubates 3–5 white eggs for 15–18 days; pair feeds the young.

Feeding: often hammers the base of rotting trees, creating fist-sized or larger, rectangular holes; eats carpenter ants, wood-boring beetle larvae, berries and nuts.

Voice: loud, fast, laughing, rolling *woika-woika-woika-woika;* long series of *kuk* notes; loud, resonant drumming.

Similar Species: *Other woodpeckers* (pp. 233–42, 451): much smaller. *Ivory-billed Woodpecker:* extirpated in Texas; larger; black face and throat; large, white wing patch; ivory bill. *American Crow* (p. 283) and *Common Raven* (p. 286): no white or red markings; no crest.

Best Sites: Tyler SP; Lake Tawakoni SP; Huntsville SP; Jesse H. Jones Park (Harris Co.).

PASSERINES

Passerines are also commonly known as songbirds or perching birds. Although these terms are easier to comprehend, they are not as strictly accurate, because some passerines neither sing nor perch, and many nonpasserines do sing and perch. In a general sense, however, these terms represent passerines adequately: they are among the best singers, and they are typically seen perched on a branch or wire.

It is believed that passerines, which all belong to the order Passeriformes, make up the most recent evolutionary group of birds. Theirs is the most numerous of all orders, representing about 47% of the bird species in Texas, and nearly three-fifths of all living birds worldwide.

Passerines are grouped together based on the sum of many morphological and molecular similarities, including such things as the number of tail and flight feathers and reproductive characteristics. All passerines share the same foot shape: three toes face forward and one faces backward, and no passerines have webbed toes. Also, all passerines have a tendon that runs along the back side of the bird's knee and tightens when the bird perches, giving it a firm grip.

Some of our most common and easily identified birds, such as the Carolina Chickadee, American Robin and House Sparrow, are passerines. However, some of the most challenging and frustrating birds to identify, —at least until their distinctive songs and calls are learned—are passerines as well.

Flycatchers

Shrikes & Vireos

Jays & Crows

Larks & Swallows

Chickadees, Nuthatches & Wrens

Kinglets, Bluebirds & Thrushes

Mimics, Starlings & Waxwings

Wood-Warblers & Tanagers

Sparrows, Grosbeaks & Buntings

Blackbirds & Orioles

Finchlike Birds

OLIVE-SIDED FLYCATCHER

Contopus cooperi

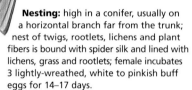

The *Tyrannidae* family (tyrant flycatchers) is one of the largest bird families in the world. Tyrant flycatchers are named for their feisty behavior and are characterized by large heads and broad, flat bills surrounded by stiff bristles that funnel insects toward their mouth in flight. They feed by looping out from exposed perches to snatch flying insects in midair. • The Olive-sided Flycatcher perches with a distinctive, upright, attentive stance. Its large, peaked head and fluffy, white rump patches distinguish it from other flycatchers of the suborder known as suboscines, characterized by their simple calls and drab plumage. • The Olive-sided Flycatcher may be the least noticeable of the tyrant-flycatchers, but its enthusiastic *hic-three-beers!* call makes it a favorite with many birders. In late summer, it changes its tune to a subdued, but persistent *pip-pip, pip.*

Nesting: high in a conifer, usually on a horizontal branch far from the trunk; nest of twigs, rootlets, lichens and plant fibers is bound with spider silk and lined with lichens, grass and rootlets; female incubates 3 lightly-wreathed, white to pinkish buff eggs for 14–17 days.

Feeding: flycatches flying insects; honeybees are important prey in some places.

Voice: snappy *pip-pip, pip* location call. *Male:* lively *hic-three-beers* song in the east, with the 2nd note highest in pitch; loud, liquid *what peeves you* song in the west.

Similar Species: *Eastern Wood-Pewee* (p. 247) and *Western Wood-Pewee* (p. 246): smaller; no white rump tufts; gray breast; 2 faint wing bars. *Eastern Phoebe* (p. 258): no white rump tufts; all-dark bill; often wags tail. *Eastern Kingbird* (p. 268): no white rump tufts; all-dark bill; white-tipped tail.

Best Sites: *Breeding:* Guadalupe Mountains NP. *In migration:* any park with open woods, especially on the Coastal Plain.

ID: dark olive gray "vest"; light throat and belly; olive gray to olive brown upperparts; white tufts on rump sides; dark upper mandible and dull yellowish orange base of lower mandible; inconspicuous eye ring. *In flight:* fairly long, pointed wings and shortish, broad tail; somewhat jerky flight, returning to same or nearby treetop perch.

Size: *L* 7–8 in; *W* 13 in.

Status: rare to uncommon migrant; rare breeder in the Guadalupe Mts. and probably in the Davis Mts.

Habitat: *Breeding:* semi-open mixed and coniferous forests at higher altitudes. *In migration:* any wooded area.

WESTERN WOOD-PEWEE

Contopus sordidulus

Aspiring birders quickly come to recognize the burry, down-slurred call of the Western Wood-Pewee as one of the most common summertime noises in woodlands of western Texas. This bird's generalized habitat, feeding and nesting requirements contribute to its success. Found in forest clearings, edge habitats or riparian areas, the small, drab male sings persistently throughout the summer afternoons. • This wood-pewee occasionally launches into aerobatic, looping ventures in search of flying insects, usually returning to the same perch. • Overall numbers of Western Wood-Pewees appear to be declining. Loss or alteration of riparian habitat through clear-cutting or grazing and the destruction of tropical rain forests on their wintering grounds are likely contributing factors.

ID: dark olive brown upperparts; 2 faint grayish wing bars; pale underparts; blurry dark "vest"; no eye ring; pale throat; slightly peaked hindcrown; mainly dark bill; light undertail coverts; fairly long, notched tail.

Size: *L* 6½ in; *W* 10–11 in.

Status: rare to locally common summer resident in the Trans-Pecos Mts. and on the High Plains and the western edge of the Edwards Plateau; common migrant in the west and from the southern edge of the Edwards Plateau to the Rio Grande.

Habitat: *Breeding:* open deciduous and coniferous forests and woodland edges, orchards, riparian growth, aspen woodlands, juniper and mountain mahogany stands, homesteads and residential woodlots. *In migration:* almost any woodland habitat.

Nesting: on a horizontal limb of a tree far from the trunk; fairly large, deep cup of plant fibers and down is bound to the branch with spider webs and lined with fine materials; female incubates 2–4 creamy white eggs, marked with brown and purple, for 12–13 days; young fledge at 14–18 days.

Feeding: sallies, hovers and gleans for insects; eats some berries.

Voice: plaintive, nasal, whistling *dree-yurr* or *brreeer* and other clearer, whistled phrases; flat, sneezy *dup* contact call.

Similar Species: *Eastern Wood-Pewee* (p. 247): indistinguishable except by vocalization: higher, clearer, whistled song and drier calls. *Olive-sided Flycatcher* (p. 245): larger; white rump tufts; explosive song and calls. *Townsend's Solitaire* (p. 321): larger; gray overall; white eye ring; peach-colored wing patches; pale rump; long, thin black tail with white outer feathers.

Best Sites: Davis Mountains SP; Guadalupe Mountains NP; Big Bend NP.

EASTERN WOOD-PEWEE

Contopus virens

One of our most common woodland flycatchers, the Eastern Wood-Pewee breeds in central and eastern Texas. The male is readily detected by his plaintive, whistled *pee-ah-wee pee-oh* song, which is repeated all day long throughout summer. Some of the keenest suitors even sing late into the evening, long after most birds are silent. • Like other flycatchers, the Eastern Wood-Pewee loops out from exposed perches to snatch flying insects in midair, a technique often referred to as "fly-catching" or "hawking." • Many insects have evolved defense mechanisms to avert potential predators such as the Eastern Wood-Pewee. Some flying insects are camouflaged, whereas others are distasteful or poisonous and flaunt their foul nature with vivid colors. Interestingly, some insects even mimic their poisonous allies, displaying warning colors even though they are perfectly edible.

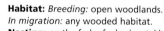

ID: brownish olive upperparts; inconspicuous eye ring; short, yellow-based bill; dingy underparts with partial vest; black wings with 2 white (adult) or buffy (juvenile) wing bars.
Size: *L* 6–6¾ in; *W* 10 in.
Status: rare to locally common summer resident in eastern Texas and west through the north-central region to the eastern edge of the Panhandle and the eastern parts of the Edwards Plateau; rare to locally common migrant statewide.

Habitat: *Breeding:* open woodlands. *In migration:* any wooded habitat.
Nesting: on the fork of a horizontal branch, well away from the trunk; open cup of grass, plant fibers and lichen is bound with spider silk; female incubates 3 darkly blotched, whitish eggs for 12–13 days.
Feeding: flycatches insects from a perch; may also glean foliage for insects, especially while hovering.
Voice: ascending *pee-wee* call; clear, slow, plaintive *pee-a-wee, pee-ooh* song.
Similar Species: *Western Wood-Peewee* (p. 246): almost identical; distinguished only by voice; inhabits mountains of western Texas. *Eastern Phoebe* (p. 258): faint wing bars, if any; all-dark bill; often pumps tail. *Eastern Kingbird* (p. 268) larger; white-tipped tail; brighter white underparts; all-dark bill. *Empidonax flycatchers* (pp. 248–56): smaller; more conspicuous wing bars; eye rings.
Best Sites: any eastern park with open woodlands.

YELLOW-BELLIED FLYCATCHER

Empidonax flaviventris

The Yellow-bellied Flycatcher is one of ten *Empidonax* species found in Texas. The "empids"—small flycatchers that often flip up their tails—are among the most challenging birds to identify. Habitat and vocalizations are key to identifying these species, but many are silent as they pass through Texas, and many individuals cannot be identified to species. Therefore, readers of this book are advised to record "*Empidonax* species" for most individuals seen in Texas. • The Yellow-bellied Flycatcher is the most elusive and secretive of this confusing genus. It hides deep within soggy, mosquito-infested bogs and fens as it migrates through eastern Texas. In spring, it is typically seen from late April to late May as it journeys northward to nesting grounds in the pine forest of the northeastern states and Canada. In fall, this flycatcher passes through eastern Texas between mid-August and mid-October, heading for winter territories in Central and South America.

ID: olive green upperparts; 2 whitish wing bars; yellowish eye ring; white throat; yellow underparts; pale olive breast.
Size: *L* 5–6 in; *W* 8 in.

Status: uncommon to common migrant in the eastern two-thirds of the state; very rare in the western half of the Trans-Pecos.
Habitat: woodlands with a dense shrub understory.
Nesting: does not nest in Texas.
Feeding: flycatches for insects at low to middle levels of the forest; also gleans vegetation for larval and adult invertebrates while hovering.
Voice: generally silent in Texas; calls include a chipper *pe-wheep*, *preee*, *pur-wee* or *killik*.

Male: song is a soft *che-luck* or *che-lek* (2nd syllable is lower pitched).
Similar Species: *Acadian* (p. 249), *Alder* (p. 250), *Willow* (p. 251), *Cordilleran* (p. 256) and *Least* (p. 252) *flycatchers:* no extensive yellow wash from throat to belly; white eye rings; different songs; all but Acadian have browner upperparts. *Dusky Flycatcher* (p. 255): longer bill and tail; white edges on outer tail feathers; male usually has 2-phrased song and clearer whistles. *Gray Flycatcher* (p. 254): paler gray overall; longer, pale-based bill; dips tail persistently.
Best Sites: any wooded migrant "trap" along the coast.

ACADIAN FLYCATCHER

Empidonax virescens

Because it breeds in the state and vocalizes frequently, the Acadian Flycatcher is the *Empidonax* most familiar to Texas birders. The quick, forceful *peet-sa* call is key to identifying this species. Whereas many other flycatchers are silent in Texas, the Acadian Flycatcher can be heard singing on its breeding grounds in the eastern third of the state. • The bird's speedy, aerial courtship chases and the male's hovering flight displays are sights to behold. This flycatcher nests deep within swampy woodlands, cypress swamps and near river edges, habitat where mosquitoes and other insects thrive, providing plenty of food. The nest, which may be up to 20 feet above the ground, can be quite conspicuous because of dangling loose material that gives it a sloppy appearance.

ID: narrow, yellowish eye ring; 2 buff to yellowish wing bars; large bill has dark upper mandible and pinkish yellow lower mandible; white throat; faint olive yellow breast; yellow belly and undertail coverts; olive green upperparts; very long primaries.

Size: *L* 5¾–6 in; *W* 9 in.

Status: common migrant in the eastern half of the state and very rare from the western parts of the Edwards Plateau south to the Lower Rio Grande Valley; common summer resident in the eastern half from Cooke Co. south through the eastern parts of the Edwards Plateau to Matagorda Co.

Habitat: fairly mature deciduous woodlands, riparian woodlands and wooded swamps.

Nesting: low in a deciduous tree, usually near water; on a horizontal branch, 6–13 ft above the ground; female builds a loose cup nest of moss, bark strips, fine twigs and grasses held together with spider silk; female incubates 3 lightly spotted, creamy white eggs for 13–15 days; pair raises the young.

Feeding: forages primarily by hawking or by gleaning foliage while hovering; takes insects and insect larvae; may also eat berries and small fruit.

Voice: call is a softer *peet;* may issue a loud, flickerlike *ti-ti-ti-ti-ti* during breeding season. *Male:* forceful *peet-sa* song.

Similar Species: *Alder Flycatcher* (p. 250): *fee-bee-o* song; narrower, white eye ring is often inconspicuous; browner overall; smaller head relative to body. *Willow Flycatcher* (p. 251): explosive *fitz-bew* song; browner overall; smaller head; very faint eye ring. *Least Flycatcher* (p. 252): clear *che-bek* song; prominent white eye ring; rounded head; shorter wings. *Yellow-bellied Flycatcher* (p. 248): liquid *che-lek* song; yellow wash from throat to belly.

Best Sites: any local or state park in the eastern half of the state.

ALDER FLYCATCHER

Empidonax alnorum

The Alder Flycatcher, which nests in the northeastern states and Canada but migrates through much of eastern Texas, is indistinguishable from other *Empidonax* flycatchers until it opens its small, bicolored beak: with a hearty *fee-bee-o* or *free beer,* its identity is revealed. The nondescript Alder Flycatcher is well named because it is often found in alder and willow shrubs on its breeding grounds. Where their breeding ranges overlap, the Alder Flycatcher frequently competes against the Willow Flycatcher for control over dense, riparian alder and willow thickets. • Once this aggressive bird has been spotted, its feisty behavior can often be observed without distraction as it drives away rivals and pursues flying insects. • Many birds have to learn their songs and calls, but Alder Flycatchers instinctively know the simple phrase of their species. Even if a young bird is isolated from the sounds of other Alder Flycatchers, it can produce a perfectly acceptable *fee-bee-o* when it matures. • The Willow Flycatcher is a close relative of the Alder Flycatcher, and until 1973 these two species were grouped together as a single species known as "Traill's Flycatcher."

ID: olive brown upperparts; 2 dull white to buff wing bars; faint, whitish eye ring; dark upper mandible; orange lower mandible; long tail; white throat; pale olive breast; pale yellowish belly.

Size: *L* 5½–6 in; *W* 8½ in.

Status: uncommon to locally common migrant in the eastern half of the state, including the Lower Rio Grande Valley.

Habitat: thickets, especially bordering lakes or streams.

Nesting: does not nest in Texas.

Feeding: flycatches for beetles, bees, wasps and other flying insects; also eats berries and occasionally seeds.

Voice: generally silent in Texas; *wheep* or *peep* call; snappy *free beer* or *fee-bee-o* song.

Similar Species: *Eastern Wood-Pewee* (p. 247): larger; no eye ring or conspicuous wing bars. *Willow Flycatcher* (p. 251): explosive *fitz-bew* song; mostly found in drier areas. *Least Flycatcher* (p. 252): clear *che-bek* song; bolder white eye ring; greener upperparts; pale grayish white underparts. *Acadian Flycatcher* (p. 249): forceful *peet-sa* song; yellowish eye ring; greener upperparts; yellower underparts. *Yellow-bellied Flycatcher* (p. 248): song is a liquid *che-lek;* yellowish eye ring; greener upperparts; yellower underparts.

Best Sites: migrant "traps" along the coast and inland in parks with appropriate habitat.

WILLOW FLYCATCHER

Empidonax traillii

Willow Flycatchers are named for their breeding habitat—dense willows and thickets that surround swamps and river edges—but they are strictly migrants in Texas. They often perch low to the ground, skulking in the shadows until a tasty insect happens by. Willow Flycatchers may forage on the ground but more commonly capture flying insects in midair or snatch unsuspecting spiders that dangle from silky threads. • The Willow Flycatcher was once grouped together with the closely related Alder Flycatcher, which shares very similar plumage and haunts. The only sure way to identify these two birds in the field is by their calls: Willow Flycatchers give a characteristic, sneezy *fitz-bew* song, whereas Alder Flycatchers sing a distinct *fee-bee-o*. Because both these birds rarely sing as they pass through our state, Texan birders often settle for marking "*Empidonax* sp." on their checklists.

ID: olive brown upperparts; 2 whitish wing bars; little or no eye ring; white throat; yellowish belly; pale olive breast. *In flight:* large-headed; fairly long, rounded wings; broad, straight-sided tail; 2 whitish wing bars.
Size: *L* 5½–6 in; *W* 8–9 in.
Status: rare to uncommon migrant state-wide; rare and local summer resident on the western Edwards Plateau.
Habitat: willows and cottonwoods and adjoining farmlands.
Nesting: does not nest in Texas.
Feeding: flycatches insects; also gleans vegetation for insects, usually while hovering.

Voice: generally silent in Texas; call is a quick, upslurred *whit*; quick, sneezy *fitz-bew* song.
Similar Species: *Eastern Wood-Pewee* (p. 247) and *Western Wood-Pewee* (p. 246): larger and duller; no eye rings or conspicuous wing bars. *Alder Flycatcher* (p. 250): usually darker and more olive gray; smaller bill; different song and call; prefers drier areas. *Least Flycatcher* (p. 252): bolder white eye ring; greener upperparts; pale gray and white underparts; different song and habitat. *Acadian Flycatcher* (p. 249) and *Yellow-bellied Flycatcher* (p. 248): yellowish eye rings; greener upperparts; yellower underparts; different songs and habitat.
Best Sites: shrubby growth alongside rivers and on the edge of old fields.

LEAST FLYCATCHER

Empidonax minimus

A common migrant in the eastern two-thirds of Texas, the Least Flycatcher is less frequently seen further west. It breeds in deciduous and mixed forest across much of Canada and the northern third of the continental U.S., and it winters from Florida and Mexico south through Central America. • The Least Flycatcher may be the only *Empidonax* that can often be identified based on plumage alone. Its bold white eye ring and clear white wing bars stand out at close view. Like other flycatchers, this little bird is olive brown above and pale below, but it does not have the obvious yellow tones of other flycatchers, and its call is a clear, sharp *whit*. • *Empidonax* flycatchers are aptly named: the literal translation, "mosquito king," refers to their insect-hunting prowess.

ID: olive brown upperparts; fairly long, narrow tail; 2 white wing bars; bold white eye ring; mostly dark bill has yellow-orange lower base; white throat; gray breast; grayish white to yellowish belly and undertail coverts.

Size: *L* 4¾–6 in; *W* 7¾ in.

Status: common migrant in most of the state, but rare in the extreme western Trans-Pecos and in the Rolling Plains; rare winter resident along the coast and in the Lower Rio Grande Valley.

Habitat: open deciduous or mixed woodlands; forest openings and edges; often in second-growth woodlands and occasionally near human habitation.

Nesting: does not nest in Texas.

Feeding: flycatches insects; gleans trees and shrubs for insects while hovering; may also eat some fruit and seeds.

Voice: generally silent in Texas. *Male:* constantly repeated, dry *che-bek che-bek* song.

Similar Species: *Eastern Wood-Pewee* (p. 247): larger; no eye ring or conspicuous wing bars. *Alder Flycatcher* (p. 250): *fee-bee-o* song; faint eye ring; prefers wetter areas. *Willow Flycatcher* (p. 251): explosive *fitz-bew* song; no eye ring; yellower underparts. *Acadian Flycatcher* (p. 249) forceful *peet-sa* song; yellowish eye ring; greener upperparts; yellower underparts. *Yellow-bellied Flycatcher* (p. 248): liquid *che-lek* song; yellowish eye ring; greener upperparts; yellower underparts. *Ruby-crowned Kinglet* (p. 315): broken eye ring; much daintier bill; shorter tail.

Best Sites: coastal migrant "traps"; inland parks with open woodland.

HAMMOND'S FLYCATCHER

Empidonax hammondii

The retiring, diminutive Hammond's Flycatcher breeds beneath the shady, dense canopy of mature conifers throughout the Rocky Mountains. During spring and fall, this uncommon migrant seeks out similar habitat west of the Pecos River. As a rare winter resident in the Lower Rio Grande Valley, it inhabits both Franklin Mountains State Park and Memorial Park near El Paso. • The Hammond's Flycatcher is easily confused with the more common Dusky Flycatcher. Fortunately, a few clues help distinguish the two species. The Dusky Flycatcher prefers sun-drenched brushfields and scattered young conifers, but the Hammond's "closets-up" within the inner canopy of firs and pines. Also, the Hammond's has a darker breast and a shorter tail, which is held almost vertically when the bird is perched, whereas the Dusky tends to have a darker tail, usually held at an angle, that contrasts with a lighter-colored rump. • This bird was named for William Hammond, an army surgeon who sent animal specimens from western North America to the Smithsonian Institution for scientific classification.

ID: olive grayish upperparts; 2 white wing bars; distinct light eye ring; gray face; tiny, all-dark bill; light gray throat; thin, dark tail with gray outer edge; hindcrown often slightly peaked.

Size: *L* 5½ in; *W* 8¾ in.

Status: rare to uncommon migrant and very rare winter visitor in the western Panhandle and in the Trans-Pecos; occasional in winter east onto the Edwards Plateau.

Habitat: various habitats ranging from chaparral and riparian woodlands to suburban parks and deciduous forests.

Nesting: does not nest in Texas.

Feeding: flycatches and hover-gleans vegetation for insects, generally well within the mid-canopy.

Voice: generally silent in Texas; soft, but incisive *peep* or *bik* call; easily overlooked, low and spiritless *dissup…wassup* song.

Similar Species: *Dusky Flycatcher* (p. 255): slightly longer bill and tail; white-edged outer tail feathers. *Eastern Wood-Pewee* (p. 247) and *Willow Flycatcher* (p. 251): larger; no eye ring. *Cordilleran Flycatcher* (p. 256): pale yellowish chin; yellower underparts; longer, broader bill with conspicuously pale lower mandible. *Gray Flycatcher* (p. 254): paler gray overall; slightly longer, pale-based bill; dips tail persistently.

Best Sites: Davis Mountains SP; Guadalupe Mountains NP; Big Bend Ranch SP; Big Bend NP.

GRAY FLYCATCHER

Empidonax wrightii

Pine-dotted sagebrush flats and the pinyon pine–juniper woodlands of the Davis Mountains are favorite summer habitats of a small breeding population of Gray Flycatchers. These birds favor a mixture of scattered dry-site conifers and an extensive growth of tall sagebrush or bitterbrush. • Helping to distinguish this *Empidonax* from its nearly identical relatives—the Dusky and the Hammond's— are the Gray's deliberate downward tail-bobbing, slender proportions and tendency to drop to the ground frequently in pursuit of insects, a useful foraging strategy in high country where frosts may occur nightly. • This distinctly western species is named in honor of Charles Wright, a botanist who accompanied the Pacific Railroad surveys during the mid-1800s.

ID: drab grayish upperparts, becoming olive-tinged in fall; whitish underparts; faint eye ring; 2 thin, white wing bars; pale lower mandible with dark tip; long tail with thin, white border.

Size: *L* 5¼–6 in; *W* 8¾ in.

Status: uncommon migrant and rare winter resident in the western half of the Trans-Pecos and the Panhandle; locally uncommon summer resident in the Davis Mts.

Habitat: *Breeding:* above 4000 ft on sagebrush flats and in pine or juniper woodland; avoids dense forest. *In migration:* varied habitats.

Nesting: may form loose colonies; in a vertical sagebrush fork or on a horizontal branch of pinyon pine or juniper; mostly the female builds a deep, cup nest of grass, twigs and bark, lined with feathers; female incubates 3–4 creamy white eggs for about 14 days.

Feeding: takes insects by hawking, hovering or a short flight to the ground.

Voice: loud *whit* call; *chawip seeahl* song (1st note often doubled, 2nd note often omitted), often followed by an aspirated *whea* or liquid *whilp*.

Similar Species: *Dusky Flycatcher* (p. 255): usually darker and plumper overall; restricted pale on lower mandible; more contrast between upperparts and underparts; does not bob tail downward. *Hammond's Flycatcher* (p. 253): darker, more contrasting "vest"; plumper; tiny, all-dark bill; often flicks wings and short, thin tail. *Willow Flycatcher* (p. 251): browner upperparts; entirely pale lower mandible; bolder wing bars. *Cordilleran Flycatcher* (p. 256): white eye ring expands slightly behind eye; dark olive green upperparts; yellowish underparts; entirely pale lower mandible.

Best Sites: Davis Mountains SP.

DUSKY FLYCATCHER

Empidonax oberholseri

Many novice birders might wonder why three virtually identical-looking birds, the Dusky, Hammond's and Gray flycatchers, are not just lumped together as a single species. It's not surprising that even prominent ornithologists of the past considered the Dusky Flycatcher to be a subspecies of the Gray Flycatcher. However, closer inspection of collected specimens, DNA analysis and detailed studies of bird behavior and habitat requirements have revealed that each of these birds indeed deserves a distinct status. • The scientific name *oberholseri* honors Dr. Harry Oberholser, one of the finest 20th-century ornithologists. He worked for the U.S. Fish and Wildlife Service and the Cleveland Natural History Museum.

ID: olive brown upperparts; 2 faint white wing bars; light-colored eye ring; white throat; dark bill with orange at base of lower mandible; long, dark tail trimmed with white.

Size: *L* 5–6 in; *W* 8¼ in.

Status: common migrant in the Trans-Pecos and rare to very rare in the rest of west Texas; rare winter resident in the southern part of the Trans-Pecos; very rare summer resident in the Davis Mts.

Habitat: *Breeding:* montane forest openings and brushy meadows at higher elevations of the Davis Mts. *In migration:* a variety of open woodland habitats, riparian woodlands and brushlands.

Nesting: in a fork of a small shrub; small cup nest consists of weeds, plant fibers, feathers, grass and fur; female incubates 3–4 white or creamy white eggs for 15–16 days.

Feeding: flycatches for aerial insects; also gleans and hover-gleans leaves, limbs and bark for larval and adult insects.

Voice: flat *wit* call-note. *Male:* quick, whistled *PREE-tick-preet* call, rising at the end; repeated *du...DU-hie* summer song.

Similar Species: *Hammond's Flycatcher* (p. 253): bill and tail are slightly shorter; no white edges on outer tail feathers; prefers shady forest habitat. *Eastern Wood-Pewee* (p. 247) and *Willow Flycatcher* (p. 251): no eye ring. *Cordilleran Flycatcher* (p. 256): yellow underparts; longer, broader bill has an all-pale lower mandible. *Gray Flycatcher* (p. 254): paler gray overall; slightly longer bill; dips tail persistently.

Best Sites: Davis Mountains SP; Big Bend Ranch SP; Big Bend NP.

CORDILLERAN FLYCATCHER

Empidonax occidentalis

The Cordilleran Flycatcher and the Pacific-slope Flycatcher were formerly lumped together into one species, the "Western Flycatcher." Although they are now regarded as distinct species, their similar field characteristics remain a troubling issue that perpetuates their uncertain status. Much remains to be learned about the distribution and migration of these new species, especially where their ranges overlap in the interior northwest U.S. • The Cordilleran Flycatcher is found in the western U.S., east of the Rocky Mountains and south to the mountainous regions of Mexico. It is an uncommon summer resident in Texas, found primarily in the montane forests of the Trans-Pecos. • The scientific name *occidentalis* is Latin for "western."

ID: olive green upperparts; 2 white wing bars; yellowish throat; light-colored eye ring; orange lower mandible.
Size: *L* 5½ in; *W* 8 in.
Status: rare migrant in the Trans-Pecos, very rare east on to the Edwards Plateau; uncommon summer resident in Davis, Guadalupe and Chisos mts.
Habitat: coniferous and riparian woodlands or shady deciduous forests, often near seepages and springs, in the mountains.
Nesting: in a cavity in a small tree, bank, bridge or cliff face; cavity is lined with moss, lichens, bark, fur and feathers; female incubates 3–4 creamy white eggs for 15 days.
Feeding: flycatches for insects.
Voice: *Male:* call is a chipper whistle: *swee-deet.*
Similar Species: *Willow Flycatcher* (p. 251) and *Eastern Wood-Pewee* (p. 247): no eye ring. *Least* (p. 252), *Hammond's* (p. 253) and *Dusky* (p. 255) *flycatchers*: no almond-shaped eye ring or completely orange lower mandible; songs are very useful in field identification.
Best Sites: Davis Mountains SP; Guadalupe Mountains NP; Big Bend Ranch SP; Big Bend NP.

BLACK PHOEBE

Sayornis nigricans

Dark and handsome, the Black Phoebe is a locally uncommon to rare resident of shady streamsides and other semi-open, moist habitats at low and middle elevations throughout the Trans-Pecos and southwestern Texas. • An expert flycatcher, this phoebe can capture just about any insect that zips past its perch. The Black Phoebe is most often seen on an exposed low perch, such as a fence post, stump or building eaves. • This bird collects a large proportion of its invertebrate prey by delicate sallies from perch to ground. In eroded streambeds without overhanging tree limbs, it resorts to flycatching from stones as small as streamside cobbles. • During cold weather, Black Phoebes tend to concentrate in protected lowlands and are often seen scattered throughout suburban and urban areas, occurring in greatest numbers about small lakes, ponds, parks and gardens.

ID: mostly black; white belly and undertail coverts; long, thinly white-edged tail. *Immature:* dark brown plumage; retains cinnamon wing bars and rump until late fall.
Size: *L* 6¾ in; *W* 11 in.
Status: rare to uncommon resident in the Trans-Pecos and southern Edwards Plateau, very rare in the western portion of the Lower Rio Grande Valley; rare migrant in the southern Panhandle and High Plains.
Habitat: semi-open habitats near water, including riparian woodlands, steep-walled canyons, cities, farmlands with wet areas.
Nesting: on a cliff, bridge, building or culvert; site may be reused for years; cup-shaped or semi-circular nest built from vegetation, hair and mud is usually placed on a flat surface or vertical face with shelter from above; female incubates 4–5 white eggs for 15–18 days; pair raises the young.
Feeding: flycatches for aerial insects; gleans plant foliage by fluttering or snatching; commonly takes insects from the ground or from the water's surface; regurgitates indigestible parts of prey as pellets.
Voice: penetrating *tsip!* or *tsee* call note. *Male:* exclamatory *f'BEE, f'BEER!* song.
Similar Species: *Eastern Phoebe* (p. 258): paler plumage; round, not peaked, head; pale gray breast; pumps slightly shorter tail slower and lower. Empidonax *flycatchers* (pp. 248–56): smaller; most have wing bars and eye rings. *Eastern Kingbird* (p. 268): larger; white-tipped tail; black upperparts.
Best Sites: Balmorhea SP; Big Bend NP; Davis Mountains SP; Seminole Canyon SP.

EASTERN PHOEBE

Sayornis phoebe

Whether you are poking around a barnyard, a city park or a nature center, you may stumble upon an Eastern Phoebe, a small, drab, tail-wagging flycatcher of open country found year-round in our state. • The Phoebe's characteristic tail pumping, absence of wing bars and solid, dark tail distinguish it from *Empidonax* flycatchers and Eastern Kingbirds. In summer, listen for the Eastern Phoebe's whistled *fee-bee* song, for which it is named. In winter, its frequent *chip* notes set it apart from similar birds. • All three North America Phoebe species are found in Texas, but the Eastern Phoebe is the most widespread. • Once limited to nesting on natural cliffs and fallen riparian trees, this adaptive flycatcher now nests on buildings and bridges, sometimes reusing the same nest site for many years.

ID: grayish brown upperparts; dark head and tail; white throat; short, black bill; dark gray wings, possibly with faint wing bars; white underparts, sometimes with faint yellow wash.

Size: *L* 6¾–7 in; *W* 10¾ in.

Status: uncommon to common summer resident in much of northern and central Texas east of the Pecos R., but absent south of the Edwards Plateau; breeds rarely in the western Panhandle and Trans-Pecos; rare to common migrant statewide, although very rare in the western Trans-Pecos; rare to common winter resident in the eastern two-thirds of Texas and vagrant in the west.

Habitat: *Breeding:* under bridges near water, usually near or in open woodlands. *In migration* and *winter:* open country, such as pastures, fields, or open woodlands.

Nesting: under the ledge of a building, culvert, bridge, cliff or well; cup-shaped

mud nest is lined with moss, grass, fur and feathers; female incubates 4–5 sparsely spotted, white eggs for about 16 days; pair feeds the young.

Feeding: sallies for flying insects or gleans foliage for insects and spiders.

Voice: sharp *chip* call. *Male:* hearty, snappy *fee-bee* song, delivered frequently.

Similar Species: *Black Phoebe* (p. 257): peaked head; dark breast; slightly longer tail; pumps tail faster and higher. *Eastern Wood-Pewee* (p. 247): olive brown above, including head; yellow-orange lower mandible; does not pump tail. *Empidonax flycatchers* (pp. 248–56): smaller; most have wing bars and eye rings. *Eastern Kingbird* (p. 268): larger; white-tipped tail; black upperparts.

Best Sites: city and state parks in central and eastern Texas.

SAY'S PHOEBE

Sayornis saya

Say's Phoebes occupy an expansive summer range that extends from Mexico through western Texas and into Alaska. Partial to dry environments, Say's Phoebes thrive in sun-parched grassy valleys and hot, dry canyons. They are particularly common where abandoned or little-used farm buildings provide sheltered, reusable nest sites and where livestock conveniently stir up insects. Watch for these phoebes hawking insects from a fence post or other low perch. • This bird is the only one whose genus and species names honor the same person, Thomas Say. A versatile naturalist, his primary contributions were in the field of entomology. • The name "phoebe" comes from the call of the closely related Eastern Phoebe.

ID: apricot buff belly and undertail coverts; dark tail; brownish gray breast and upperparts; dark head; no eye ring; very faint wing bars; constantly bobs tail.

Size: *L* 7½ in; *W* 13 in.

Status: rare to common year-round resident in the western third of the state; rare migrant and winter resident from the central coast to the north-central region.

Habitat: canyons, ravines, rimrocks, valleys and gullies dominated by grass and shrubs; may also use agricultural areas and scrublands; grassy coastal bluffs in winter.

Nesting: in a niche on a cliff face or beneath an eave or bridge; bulky, shallow nest consists of grass, moss and fur; female incubates 4–5 white eggs for up to 17 days.

Feeding: flycatches for aerial insects; also gleans buildings, vegetation, streamsides and the ground for insects; sometimes runs short distances in pursuit of prey.

Voice: softly whistled *pee-ur* call; *pitseedar* song.

Similar Species: *Other flycatchers* (p. 245–69, 451–52): bellies not apricot.

Best Sites: Balmorhea SP; Big Bend NP; Davis Mountains SP; Seminole Canyon SP.

VERMILION FLYCATCHER

Pyrocephalus rubinus

The adult male Vermilion Flycatcher is one of the most brilliantly colored birds in Texas. Indeed, the names *Pyrocephalus* ("fire head") and *rubinus* ("ruby-red") describe the stunning plumage of the adult male. • In Texas, Vermilion Flycatchers are found in open areas, such as marshes, pastures, fields and golf courses, invariably close to a pond or lake. These small flycatchers often perch on fences or trees from which they watch for prey. • The Vermilion Flycatcher is a year-round resident from the Desert Southwest through central South America. Some birds migrate to breed in the southern U.S., including Texas.

ID: *Male:* brownish black back and wings; shockingly bright red head and underparts; brownish black ear patch and nape; short, black bill. *First-year male:* red color variably patchy. *Female:* grayish brown upperparts and head; white eyebrow; dark mask; white throat; white breast narrowly streaked with brown; lower belly and under-tail coverts dark pinkish (adult) or yellowish (first-year).

Size: *L* 6 in; *W* 10 in.

Status: uncommon to common summer resident from the Trans-Pecos and the Edwards Plateau south to the Lower Rio Grande Valley and very rare and local to the east and north; rare to uncommon migrant statewide; rare to uncommon winter resident from the Trans-Pecos through the Edwards Plateau and the Coastal Plain.

Habitat: open habitats with scattered trees, and near open water.

Nesting: in the fork of a horizontal branch of a tree or shrub; female constructs a cup-shaped nest of twigs, vegetation, hair, spider webs and lichen; female incubates 2–4 cream-colored, speckled eggs for 12–14 days; pair raises the young; male may tend first brood while female begins a second nest.

Feeding: sallies for insects on or near the ground.

Voice: sharp *pitsk* call. *Male:* soft *pit-a-see pit-a-see* in courtship.

Similar Species: none if seen well. *Say's Phoebe* (p. 259): superficially similar to adult female but larger, with gray throat and unstreaked, gray breast.

Best Sites: Balmorhea SP; Big Bend NP; Garner SP; Seminole Canyon SP.

ASH-THROATED FLYCATCHER

Myiarchus cinerascens

Some of the most familiar summer sounds in the canyons and river valleys of western Texas are the shrill, whistled calls of Ash-throated Flycatchers. Although they spend summer in arid junipers, pines or oaks, Ash-throated Flycatchers require a shaded cavity in which to nest. If a suitable tree cavity cannot be found, a bluebird box, old machinery or an unused mailbox is expropriated by this opportunistic secondary cavity nester.

• The Ash-throated Flycatcher belongs to a large group of subtropical and tropical flycatchers that are characterized by prominent crests and rufous tails. The Ash-throat is a paler version of the Great Crested Flycatcher found in eastern Texas.

with large, old trees. *In migration*: occurs in a wide variety of tree and shrub associations.

Nesting: in a natural or artificial cavity; pair amasses a nest of soft vegetation, hair and feathers; female incubates 4–5 darkly blotched, creamy white eggs for about 15 days; pair feeds the young.

Feeding: rarely catches prey in midair and tends to forage low among trees and shrubs; eats mostly insects; also takes fruit, rarely small lizards and even mice.

Voice: voice vaguely suggests a referee's whistle; distinctive, year-round *prrrt* call; also issues a burry *ka-BREER!* or a harsh, abrupt *ka-brick;* song is a series of similar calls.

Similar Species: *Great Crested Flycatcher* (p. 262): darker; dark gray throat and breast; brighter yellow underparts. *Brown-crested Flycatcher* (p. 263): large bill; slightly brighter yellow underparts; more rufous on tail. *Couch's* (p. 265), *Western* (p. 267) and *Cassin's* (p. 266) *kingbirds:* uncrested; paler gray on heads; yellower below; no wing bars or rufous feathering; black tails thinly edged in white.

Best Sites: Davis Mountains SP; Guadalupe Mountains NP; Hueco Tanks SP; Lost Maples SP.

ID: grayish brown upperparts; gray throat and breast; yellow belly and undertail coverts; stout, dark bill; fluffy crown; 2 whitish wing bars; no eye ring; ample dark brown tail shows some rufous in the webbing.

Size: *L* 7–8 in; *W* 12 in.

Status: uncommon to common summer resident in western Texas; rare migrant east to the Blackland Prairies; very rare winter resident along the Rio Grande and on the Coastal Plain.

Habitat: *Breeding*: taller mixed chaparral, oak groves and woodland, riparian corridors

GREAT CRESTED FLYCATCHER

Myiarchus crinitus

Loud, raucous *wheep!* calls give away the presence of the brightly colored Great Crested Flycatcher. Listen for this large flycatcher along forest edges and in virtually any woodland throughout eastern Texas. This species breeds across the eastern U.S. and extreme southern Canada, and it winters from Florida to northern South America. • Compared to most other flycatchers, the *Myiarchus* flycatchers have unusual nesting habits. Instead of building a traditional cup nest, they lay their eggs in a natural or artificial cavity, which may be a nest box, mailbox or other structure. Most nests incorporate shed snake skins, onion skins or even translucent plastic wrap into the lining. • This large flycatcher sallies from perches to capture prey. It generally remains inside foliage and it rarely perches in the open on power lines.

ID: olive back and slightly crested head; gray face and throat; large bill with yellow lower mandible; dark wings with rufous primaries; bright yellow belly and undertail coverts; rufous tail.

Size: *L* 8–9 in; *W* 13 in.

Status: uncommon migrant and summer resident in the eastern two-thirds of the state from the eastern Panhandle through the Edwards Plateau, and very rare in extreme western Trans-Pecos; common spring migrant in the Lower Rio Grande Valley, and rare in most of the western parts of the state.

Habitat: virtually any wooded habitat.

Nesting: in a tree cavity or nest box; nest is lined with grass, bark strips and feathers; may hang a shed snakeskin or plastic wrap from the entrance hole; female incubates 5 variably marked, white to buff eggs for 13–15 days.

Feeding: usually forages high in foliage; sallies for flying insects; also takes some fruit.

Voice: call is a loud, burry whistled *wheep!;* song consists of clear, rising notes—*quitta, queeto, quitta.*

Similar Species: *Western Kingbird* (p. 267): superficially similar but typically perches on wires in the open; light gray head with black mask; black tail with white outer feathers. *Brown-crested Flycatcher* (p. 263): paler underparts; wholly black lower mandible; clear *whit* call. *Ash-throated Flycatcher* (p. 261): paler underparts with whitish throat; dark tail tip; rough *prrrt* call.

Best Sites: most local parks with open woodlands in eastern Texas.

BROWN-CRESTED FLYCATCHER

Myiarchus tyrannulus

The Brown-crested Flycatcher is the largest of the three *Myiarchus* species seen in Texas. In extreme southern Texas, it replaces the Great Crested Flycatcher of the East and the Ash-throated of the West. Nesting in open woodlands of mesquite, hackberry and ash, the Brown-crested Flycatcher relies on the cavities hammered out by local woodpeckers. Across their breeding range, these flycatchers are found in sharply different habitats: riparian woodlands and arid columnar cactus groves. • Loudly aggressive in defending its home, the Brown-crested Flycatcher will take on larger birds, including ravens and jays. Because it arrives on its breeding grounds relatively late, it must be very aggressive to outcompete the European Starling and other cavity nesters. • *Myiarchus* is Greek for "fly ruler," appropriate for birds that snag insects as large as dragonflies and even take hummingbirds on rare occasions. When not hawking for insects, the Brown-crested Flycatcher hovers above foliage, gleaning the leaves for insects.

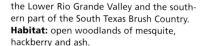

the Lower Rio Grande Valley and the southern part of the South Texas Brush Country.

Habitat: open woodlands of mesquite, hackberry and ash.

Nesting: in a cavity; cup nest consists of bark, fibers, feathers, hair and often snake skin; female incubates 3–5 creamy-white eggs for 14–15 days.

Feeding: hawks or hovers above tree leaves to glean for insects; eats occasional berries and other fruit.

Voice: varied vocalizations, including rolling whistles with strong first notes and a descending *teeerrr*.

ID: brown crest and back; brown face; large bill with hook on upper mandible; long tail with reddish undertail coverts; red-edged primary flight feathers; yellow belly; light gray breast, throat and chin; dark legs.

Size: *L* 8½–9 in; *W* 13 in.

Status: common summer resident in the Lower Rio Grande Valley, becoming rarer north to the southern part of the Edwards Plateau and to the central Coastal Plain, and very rare along the Rio Grande in the Trans-Pecos; very rare winter resident in

Similar Species: *Ash-throated Flycatcher* (p. 261): paler underparts with whitish throat; dark-tipped tail; rough *prrrt* call. *Great Crested Flycatcher* (p. 262): smaller bill; brighter yellow underparts; more rufous on tail; loud *wheep!* call.

Best Sites: Bentson-Rio Grande SP; Falcon SP; Santa Ana NWR; San Ygnacio.

263

GREAT KISKADEE

Pitangus sulphuratus

With its boisterous *kis-ka-dee!* calls, the Great Kiskadee can be heard throughout the day in the swampy woodlands of the Rio Grande Valley. The Great Kiskadee is the only yellow-bellied tropical flycatcher to venture into the U.S. but has many relatives in the Central and South American lowlands. Southern Texas marks the northern extension of this bird's range, which stretches south to Argentina.

• Great Kiskadee pairs bond for life and aggressively defend their territory even outside of the breeding season. They can be seen chasing much larger birds from their territory, but they avoid anything (even a painted stick) that resembles one of their predators, the coral snake, which is banded with red, black and yellow. • The Great Kiskadee is omnivorous and, in addition to insects, consumes frogs, young birds and berries. • *Pitangus* is a derivative of its native Brazilian name, and *sulphuratus* refers to the bright yellow belly.

ID: stocky; boldly striped, black and white head; heavy bill; white throat; yellow underparts; bright rusty tail and wingtips; reddish brown upperparts.

Size: *L* 9–10 in. *W* 16 in.

Status: locally common year-round resident from the Lower Rio Grande Valley to the southern half of the Edwards Plateau and rare in the central Coastal Plain; seems to be expanding northward and up the Coastal Plain; in summer up to Galveston Bay.

Habitat: usually near water; wooded riparian thickets, parks and orchards.

Nesting: in dense branches of a tree; hollow globe 1 ft in diameter, with side entrance, consists of bark, grass and moss; female incubates 2–5 creamy white eggs sparsely marked with dark spots for approximately 2 weeks.

Feeding: omnivorous; dives into water for large aquatic insects, minnows and frogs; takes young birds, lizards, mice, berries and seeds; also takes insects on the wing.

Voice: call is a squealed *weeeee!*; song consists of a whistling, repeated *KIS-ka-DEE-ee*.

Similar Species: head pattern and bright yellow underparts make this bird distinctive.

Best Sites: Bentson-Rio Grande SP; Falcon SP; Laguna Atascosa NWR; Santa Ana NWR.

COUCH'S KINGBIRD

Tyrannus couchii

Lieutenant Darius N. Couch took a leave of absence from his service in the U.S. Army in 1835 to lead a zoological expedition through northeastern Mexico. A new species discovery, the Couch's Kingbird, was the fruit of this expedition. It looks so similar to the Tropical Kingbird that it endured over 100 years as a Tropical Kingbird subspecies. In the 1980s, the Couch's Kingbird was reinstated as a separate species, because it has a different call and does not interbreed with the Tropical Kingbird where their ranges overlap in southern Texas. • Although aggressive, this kingbird may nest cooperatively with other birds, such as Great Kiskadees or other kingbirds. The birds may steal nest material from each other, but partnerships provide added protection from predators and parasitic cowbirds. • Couch's Kingbirds are found in treed urban regions or in shrubby mesquite ranges, usually near water. • Most of the Couch's Kingbirds in Texas migrate south of the border for winter, although a few may remain in the Lower Rio Grande Valley.

ID: gray cap; black bill; white chin; olive gray upperparts; bright yellow underparts.
Size: *L* 8–9 in; *W* 15½ in.
Status: common summer resident from the Lower Rio Grande Valley to the southern edge of the Edwards Plateau, uncommon north and east onto the mid-Edwards Plateau and rare up the Rio Grande to the Big Bend area; uncommon winter resident in the Lower Rio Grande Valley.
Habitat: open areas with surrounding shrubs or tall perches; chaparral; some riparian areas; suburban settings.
Nesting: nests on a horizontal branch; untidy nest of grass, moss and twigs is lined with plant down; 2–4 brown-spotted, buff eggs are incubated for an unknown period.
Feeding: hawks from high perches or gleans leaves for insects; sometimes eats berries or fruit.
Voice: sharp, raspy single notes; panicked, coupled ascending phrase, followed by a lower finishing note: *quick-quick, quick quick, quick quick! Oh there you are!*
Similar Species: *Tropical Kingbird* (p. 452): very rapid *pip-pip-pip-pip* call must be heard to distinguish from Couch's. *Western Kingbird* (p. 267) and *Cassin's Kingbird* (p. 266): different calls; much shorter bills; gray upper breasts; black tails; Western has white outer tail margins; Cassin's is found in Trans-Pecos Mts.
Best Sites: Bentson-Rio Grande SP; Laguna Atascosa NWR; Sabal Palm Grove Audubon Sanctuary; Santa Ana NWR.

CASSIN'S KINGBIRD

Tyrannus vociferans

Although it is by no means commonly seen in the mountains of the Trans-Pecos, the Cassin's Kingbird certainly makes itself known. When this bird decides to claim its territory of grassy ranchland or tree groves, it belts out a loud, tirelessly repeated call. • Assuming you can overlook their noisy nature, a pair of Cassin's Kingbirds nesting in your yard can be a blessing. Experts at catching pesky flying insects, kingbirds can help you to enjoy summer evening barbecues without you having to bathe in insect repellent first. • Bold and fiesty Cassin's Kingbirds work in pairs to defend their nesting territory, attacking larger birds such as hawks, ravens, crows and magpies. • The scientific name *vociferans* was given to this bird in recognition of its loud calls.

ID: dark bluish gray upperparts; whitish chin; black bill; yellow belly and undertail coverts; dark wings without bars; thinly pale-tipped, brown tail.

Size: *L* 8–9 in; *W* 16 in.

Status: uncommon summer resident in the Trans-Pecos, especially at high altitudes; rare to uncommon migrant east to the High Plains and western Edwards Plateau and south to the coast.

Habitat: open woodlands, dry savannas interspersed with small tree groves and shrubby windbreaks adjacent to agricultural fields.

Nesting: well above the ground, on a horizontal branch of a large tree such as an oak, pine or cottonwood; bulky cup of twigs, leaves, feathers, hair and other debris is lined with plant fibers and other soft materials; female incubates 3–4 white eggs, with heavy dark blotches, for about 18 days; pair feeds the young.

Feeding: eats mostly insects caught by hawking or gleaned from the ground or foliage while hovering; also takes some berries and other small fruits.

Voice: common year-round loud *chick-weeer* or *chi-bew* call; also issues an excited *kideedeedee* or *ki-dear ki-dear ki-dear;* loud, rising "dawn song": *burg-burg-burg-BURG.*

Similar Species: *Western Kingbird* (p. 267): lighter head, throat and upper breast; white outer tail feathers; *whit-ker-whit* call. *Tropical Kingbird* (p. 452): much longer bill; olive yellow upper breast; distinctive rapid, twittering *pip-pip-pip-pip* call.

Best Sites: Big Bend NP; Guadalupe Mountains NP; Davis Mountains SP.

WESTERN KINGBIRD

Tyrannus verticalis

Once you have witnessed a kingbird's brave attacks against much larger birds, such as crows and hawks, you'll understand the reason for the regal common name. Like any kingbird, the Western Kingbird does not hesitate to take on perceived threats to its nest and young. Feisty and argumentative for the most part, it may allow Eastern Kingbirds close if food is plentiful. • The tumbling aerial courtship display of this flycatcher is a common sight throughout western Texas. At other times, this kingbird is a more conventional performer and is often seen surveying for prey from fence posts, barbed wire and power lines. Once it spots a flying insect, especially a dragonfly, bee or butterfly, the kingbird quickly pursues its prey for 40 feet or more.

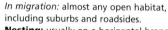

ID: pale gray head and breast; whitish throat; stout, black bill; dark gray mask; concealed orange-red crown patch; yellow belly, sides and under-tail coverts; narrowly white-edged, long, black tail. *In flight:* long wings and tail; bright yellow underparts and wing linings.
Size: *L* 8–9 in; *W* 15–16 in.
Status: common summer resident statewide, except for the eastern wood-lands; rare to common migrant statewide.
Habitat: *Breeding:* open country near ranch houses, towns, isolated groves and cottonwood-lined stream courses.

In migration: almost any open habitat, including suburbs and roadsides.
Nesting: usually on a horizontal branch against or near the trunk of a tree or on a human-built structure; cup nest is lined with hair, cotton and plant down; female incubates 3–4 heavily-mottled, white to pinkish eggs for 18–19 days.
Feeding: darts out from a perch to pounce on insects; also eats some berries.
Voice: alarm and threat calls are a rapid, rising series of shrill, sputtering *widik* and *pik* notes or twittering *kit* repetitions. *Male:* high-pitched, squeaky *pidik pik pidik peekado* song.
Similar Species: *Cassin's Kingbird* (p. 266): brighter yellow underparts; darker gray head and breast; contrasting white "mustache"; narrowly white-tipped, dark brown tail. *Tropical Kingbird* (p. 452) and *Couch's Kingbird* (p. 265): much longer bill; olive yellow upper breast; brownish tail. *Say's Phoebe* (p. 259): smaller; pale rufous belly and undertail; all-dark tail; dull gray upper-parts; wags tail.
Best Sites: urban areas in much of Texas; parks such as Lewisville Lake Park and Meridian SP.

EASTERN KINGBIRD

Tyrannus tyrannus

No one familiar with the pugnacity of the Eastern Kingbird is likely to refute its scientific name, *Tyrannus tyrannus*. This brawler fearlessly attacks crows, hawks and even humans that pass through its territory. Intruders are often vigorously pursued, pecked and plucked for some distance until the kingbird is satisfied that they pose no further threat. In contrast, its butterfly-like courtship flight, which is characterized by short, quivering wingbeats, reveals a gentler side of this bird. • During a summer drive through rural eastern Texas, you will likely spot at least one kingbird sitting on a fenceline or utility wire. Normally found in pairs, Eastern Kingbirds gather along the coast in late summer and fall in conspicuous flocks that may contain over a thousand birds. • Eastern Kingbirds rarely walk or hop on the ground—they prefer to fly, even for very short distances.

ID: dark gray to black upperparts; white underparts; black bill; small head crest; thin orange-red crown (rarely seen); no eye ring; white-tipped tail; black legs.

Size: *L* 8¾ in; *W* 15 in.

Status: common summer resident in eastern Texas, from the eastern Panhandle and eastern edge of the Edwards Plateau to the central Coastal Plain; rare to common migrant in all parts of the state.

Habitat: *Breeding:* open pinewoods or fields with scattered trees. *In migration:* any wooded habitat.

Nesting: on a horizontal tree or shrub limb or on a standing stump or upturned tree root; pair builds a cup nest of weeds, twigs and grass and lines it with root fibers, fine grass

and fur; female incubates 3–4 darkly blotched, white to pinkish white eggs for 14–18 days.

Feeding: sallies for insects in the air or on the ground; feeds on fruit during migration.

Voice: buzzy *dzee* call, often in a series.

Similar Species: *Eastern Phoebe* (p. 258): little seasonal overlap; smaller; head darker than back; tail lacks white band. *Eastern Wood-Pewee* (p. 247): smaller; bicolored bill; lacks white-tipped tail and all-white underparts. *Western Kingbird* (p. 267): gray head and breast; yellow belly and undertail coverts; black tail; white edge on outer tail feathers.

Best Sites: *Breeding:* Cedar Hill SP, Brazos Bend SP; Galveston Island SP; Sea Rim SP. *In migration:* migrant "traps" on the Coastal Plain.

SCISSOR-TAILED FLYCATCHER

Tyrannus forficatus

With the refined, long tail feathers of a tropical bird of paradise and salmon-pink underparts, the adult male Scissor-tailed Flycatcher tops many a birder's "must-see" list. This lovely bird often perches on roadside fences or utility wires, allowing observers to marvel at its beauty. • The name "Scissor-tailed" is derived from the male's habit of opening and closing the gap between his long tail feathers during courtship flights. The rollercoaster-like courtship ritual often includes dazzling backward somersaults that enhance the beauty of the male's tail. • These flycatchers aggressively defend their nests, giving shrill, piercing calls and attacking much larger birds. • After the breeding season, stray Scissor-tailed Flycatchers wander nationwide and may turn up in any of the lower 48 states, well away from their normal breeding range.

Status: common summer resident east of the Pecos R. and rare to uncommon in the Trans-Pecos; rare winter resident on the Coastal Plain and irregular elsewhere.
Habitat: perches on power lines over pastures, fields and other open habitats.
Nesting: usually in a fork high in a tree; female builds a bulky nest of twigs, rootlets and weed stems; female incubates 3–5 creamy white eggs, with dark blotches, for 12–13 days.
Feeding: sallies for insects (especially grass-hoppers) in the air or on the ground; also eats fruit.
Voice: call is a sharp, harsh *kek;* song consists of a low-pitched *pik pik pidEEK.*
Similar Species: *Fork-tailed Flycatcher:* casual visitor; darker gray upperparts; black head; white throat. *Northern Mockingbird* (p. 329): similar to female and juvenile, but tail shorter; 2 white wing bars; light gray underparts. *Western Kingbird* (p. 267): bright yellow underparts; square black tail.
Best Sites: open parklands throughout the eastern two-thirds of the state.

ID: long, black tail with white outer feathers; pale gray upperparts; mostly white head and underparts. *Male:* extremely long tail; bright pink under-wings and paler undertail coverts. *Female* and *juvenile:* shorter tail; pale pink or yellowish underparts.
Size: *L* 10 in (up to 15 in for male); *W* 15 in.

LOGGERHEAD SHRIKE

Lanius ludovicianus

Shrikes are small, predatory songbirds that impale their prey on barbed wire fences or thorny vegetation. Two species occur in Texas, but the Loggerhead Shrike is by far more common. A medium-sized songbird with a large head and hooked bill, the Loggerhead Shrike is largely resident in much of the western and southern U.S. and Mexico. • Shrikes have very acute vision and often perch atop trees and on wires to scan for small prey, which is caught in a fast, direct flight or a swooping dive. Without the talons and strong feet of hawks and owls, shrikes must impale their prey, hence the colloquial name "butcher bird." The hunting prowess of a male shrike helps him to attract a mate. • Loggerhead Shrikes are found in a variety of open habitats but seem unable to survive in developed areas, probably because many are struck by vehicles as they swoop down to capture prey. Populations continent-wide are declining about 7 percent per year, and some are now endangered.

ID: gray back and crown; wide, black mask; white throat; black wings with white primary patch; long, black tail with white corners; white underparts.
Juvenile: barred, brownish gray underparts.
In flight: fast wingbeats; white patches on wings and tail.
Size: *L* 9 in; *W* 12 in.
Status: rare to locally common resident statewide, though absent from parts of the South Texas Brush Country and the Lower Rio Grande Valley; rare to common migrant and winter resident statewide.
Habitat: open habitats, such as pastures, fields and prairies; also ball fields and cemeteries.

Nesting: in the crotch of a shrub or tree; bulky cup nest of twigs and grass is lined with animal hair, feathers and rootlets; female incubates 5–6 darkly spotted, pale buff to grayish white eggs for 15–17 days; 2 broods per year.
Feeding: swoops down on prey from a perch or attacks in pursuit; takes mostly large insects; regularly eats small birds and other vertebrates.
Voice: harsh *shack-shack* call; song is a series of warbles, trills and other notes.
Similar Species: *Northern Mockingbird* (p. 329): much thinner bill; no black mask; wings lighter; slower, buoyant wingbeats. *Northern Shrike* (p. 452): rare winter resident in Panhandle; larger; fine barring on sides and breast; more sinuous black mask does not extend above hooked bill.
Best Sites: any park with open, shrubby areas, including many suburban ones.

WHITE-EYED VIREO

Vireo griseus

Often a challenge to spot, the cryptic White-eyed Vireo can be readily identified by its variable songs, which start and end with an emphatic *chick* note. This bird is renowned for its complex vocalizations and may have a repertoire of a dozen or more songs. Also an excellent vocal mimic, it may incorporate the calls of other bird species into its own songs! • Like most vireos, the White-eyed Vireo remains out of sight as it sneaks through dense tangles of branches and foliage in search of insects. Although several vireo species share the same winter range, each forages in a specific niche to avoid competition. The White-eyed Vireo feeds at the middle heights of trees, whereas other vireos may stick to higher or lower sites. • Even more cryptic than the bird itself is the location of its nest.

ID: white eyes; yellow "spectacles"; gray face; white throat; greenish back and crown; 2 white wing bars; mostly yellow underparts. *Juvenile:* dark eyes.

Size: *L* 5 in; *W* 7¾ in.

Status: uncommon to common migrant and summer resident in the eastern two-thirds of the state and very rare in the western third; rare winter resident in the southern third of the state, becoming more common in the South Texas Plains and the Lower Rio Grande Valley.

Habitat: dense, shrubby undergrowth, scrub and woodland edges.

Nesting: in a deciduous shrub or small tree; intricately woven cup nest hanging from a horizontal fork consists of moss and the fibrous paper from a wasp nest; pair incubates 4 lightly speckled, white eggs for 13–15 days; pair feeds the young.

Feeding: gleans branches and foliage for insects; often hovers while gleaning.

Voice: loud, snappy, 4–7-note song, usually beginning and ending with *chick* notes; often mimics other birds.

Similar Species: bold white eyes and yellow "spectacles" distinguish the White-eyed Vireo from other vireos. *Bell's Vireo* (p. 272): with brown eyes and white "spectacles," may be taken for juvenile White-eyed Vireo.

Best Sites: any park with sufficient shrubbery habitat.

BELL'S VIREO

Vireo bellii

The subtle colors and markings of the Bell's Vireo can easily cause observers to mistakenly identify it as one of a number of similar birds, especially because some of the fine whitish markings around the eyes may be present in some individuals and not in others. Confusion is particularly likely during migration, when the midwestern olive-and-yellow morph can easily cross paths with southwestern gray forms. • Destruction of streamside habitat and nest parasitism from Brown-headed Cowbirds (facilitated by habitat fragmentation) have caused noticeable declines in Bell's Vireo populations throughout much of its range. • This small, active vireo is named after John Graham Bell (1812–1889), a famous New York taxidermist and bird collector who accompanied John James Audubon and John Cassin on various expeditions to the western frontier.

ID: *Eastern race:* pale gray head; thin, dark eyeline; broken eye ring; pale bill; olive back and rump; 2 wingbars, with lower bar usually much whiter and more obvious; white underparts with bright yellow sides, flanks and undertail; bluish gray legs. *Western race* and *hybrid:* brighter colors above replaced by gray; faint yellowish wash below; indistinct wingbars.
Size: *L* 4¼–5 in; *W* 7 in.
Status: rare to locally uncommon summer resident statewide except in the western half of the Panhandle and extreme Southeast; rare migrant statewide; very rare winter resident in the Lower Rio Grande Valley.
Habitat: dense riparian shrubs and thorny thickets in the southwest; brushy fields and second-growth scrub in the midwest; may also use chaparral, hedgerows between fields, scrub oaks or woodland edges.

Nesting: suspended in a fork of a horizontal shrub branch, usually within 5 ft of the ground; small hanging cup consists of woven vegetation; mostly the female incubates 3–5 white eggs, with dark dots, for about 14 days.
Feeding: gleans foliage, hawks or hovers for insects; also eats spiders and very few berries.
Voice: call may be a single *mire* or *chee* or a series of notes; song is a rapid, nonmusical series of harsh notes, *chu-che-chu-che-chu-che,* increasing in volume and often ending with an upward or downward inflection on the last note.
Similar Species: *Warbling Vireo* (p. 278): lankier; no wing bars; finer bill; sings an extended, slurred whistle series. *Gray Vireo* (p. 274): complete eye ring; 1 wing bar; *Blue-headed Vireo* (p. 276): more contrasting plumage; strong white "spectacles." *Philadelphia Vireo* (p. 452): longer proportions; dark lores, eye line and crown; no wingbars; more yellow on underparts. *Ruby-crowned Kinglet* (p. 315): bolder wing bars; elongated eye ring; sings 3-part, descending phrases.
Best Sites: riparian areas along the Rio Grande in the Trans-Pecos. *In migration:* any wooded area on the Coastal Plain.

BLACK-CAPPED VIREO

Vireo atricapilla

Federally endangered, the Back-capped Vireo is unique among the vireos in several ways. Its upside-down feeding habits mimic those of a chickadee, it is active and mobile like a wood warbler and, unlike others in the vireo family, the genders differ in their plumage. The Black-capped Vireo is the neighborhood chatterbox of the scrub-oak habitat; its raspy song is the first to greet the new day and the last to remain with the evening sky. • Each April, the Black-capped Vireo returns to its central Texas breeding zone to find its habitat dwindling as a result of urban sprawl and conifer succession caused by fire suppression. Birds lucky enough to establish a territory must endure heavy parasitism by the Brown-headed Cowbird. Because the incubation for the Back-capped Vireo is 15 days, the earlier-hatching Brown-headed Cowbird chicks have the advantage of being fed first and outcompete the vireo young.

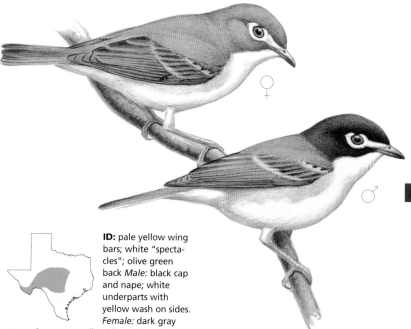

ID: pale yellow wing bars; white "spectacles"; olive green back *Male:* black cap and nape; white underparts with yellow wash on sides. *Female:* dark gray cap and nape; no yellowish wash on sides.
Size: *L* 4½ in; *W* 7 in.
Status: rare to locally uncommon summer resident on most of the Edwards Plateau and west to the Big Bend area.
Habitat: scrubby oak woodland and juniper.
Nesting: in a low, scrubby oak; in the fork of a horizontal branch; pair builds a hanging nest of leaves and coarse grasses bound with spider webs and long plant fibers; pair incubates 3–5 white eggs for 15 days; after the chicks have fledged, the female may start another brood with the same or a different male.

Feeding: usually gleans insects from leaves and stems; occasionally hangs upside down to glean leaves and bark for insects; also takes berries and other fruit.
Voice: call note resembles the scold note of the Bewick's Wren; song consists of husky, well-spaced and complex phrases.
Similar Species: *Blue-headed Vireo* (p. 276): little seasonal overlap; similar to female Black-capped Vireo but larger, with duller cap.
Best Sites: Balcones Canyonlands NWR; Dinosaur Valley SP; Kerr WMA; Lost Maples SP.

273

GRAY VIREO

Vireo vicinior

The Gray Vireo is a bird of the arid southwestern U.S. and northwestern Mexico. Although this energetic little bird is uncommon in the southern Trans-Pecos and western Edwards Plateau, its range in Texas appears to be expanding. • Watch for the Gray Vireo flitting between sparse patches of scrub and juniper, bobbing its tail and chirping briskly. Its species name of *vicinior* means "more neighborly" in Latin, highlighting its curious, welcoming nature. • The Gray Vireo's voice and habitat of thorn scrub and chaparral may be the determining factor in identifying the bird, because its plumage closely resembles that of bushtits, gnatcatchers and titmice. • During the nesting season, Gray Vireos are mostly insectivorous. In winter, their diets turn to the fruit of elephant trees in northwestern Mexico. • Some vireos, including the Gray Vireo, are parasitized by the Brown-headed Cowbird. If the intruder's eggs are discovered, a second bottom layer is added to the nest to cover the spoiled brood.

ID: gray plumage; paler underparts; faint white wingbar; white eye ring; sometimes raises and flips long tail.
Size: *L* 5¾ in; *W* 8 in.
Status: rare to uncommon local summer resident in the Trans-Pecos Mts. and the western Edwards Plateau.
Habitat: thorn scrub, chaparral or pinyon-juniper woodlands.
Nesting: attached to the fork of a horizontal branch in a thorny shrub or tree; deep, well-hidden hanging cup nest of plant fibers and stems is bound with cobwebs and decorated with leaves; pair incubates 3–5 white eggs with dark speckles for 13–14 days.
Feeding: forages on low bush branches or on the ground; eats mostly insects such as grasshoppers, beetles, cicadas and moths.
Voice: call is a low, harsh *churr;* song consists of 4–6 short, harsh-sounding repeated phrases; *cheeriup!... cheery!... cheerooo... cheeri-up!* .
Similar Species: *Plumbeus Vireo* (p. 452): holds tail still; larger body; bold white "spectacles"; 2 thicker wing bars; streaked flanks. *Bell's Vireo* (p. 272): western race is similar but smaller, with broken eye ring.
Best Sites: Balmorhea SP; Big Bend NP; Guadalupe Mountains NP.

YELLOW-THROATED VIREO

Vireo flavifrons

Mature, deciduous woodlands with little or no understory, particularly tall oak or maple groves, are favored by the Yellow-throated Vireo. This vireo forages high above the forest floor, making observation difficult. • An unmated male sings tirelessly as he searches for nest sites, often placing a few pieces of nest material in several locations. When a female appears, the male dazzles her with his displays and leads her on a tour of potential nest sites within his large territory. If the birds form a bond, they mate and build an intricately woven hanging nest in the forking branches of a deciduous tree. The male is a devoted helper, assisting the female to build the nest, incubate the eggs and rear the young. • The Yellow-throat is North America's most colorful vireo and the only vireo with a bright yellow throat and breast and a white lower belly. The scientific name *flavifrons* means "yellow front."

ID: bright yellow throat and "spectacles"; grayish green back and head; gray wings with 2 white bars; unstreaked, bright yellow breast and upper belly; white lower belly and undertail coverts.

Size: *L* 5¾ in; *W* 9¾ in.

Status: uncommon to common summer resident in the eastern two-thirds of the state and through most of the Edwards Plateau; uncommon to common migrant in the eastern half and rare in the western half of Texas.

Habitat: *Breeding:* mixed oak-pine stands, oak hammocks and maple groves. *In migration:* any wooded habitat.

Nesting: in a deciduous tree, usually more than 20 ft up; pair builds a hanging cup nest in the fork of a horizontal branch; pair incubates 4 darkly spotted, white to pinkish eggs for 14–15 days; parents take on guardianship of separate fledglings.

Feeding: mostly inspects the branches and foliage in the upper canopy for insects; also feeds on seasonally available berries.

Voice: call a harsh *shu-shu-shu;* song is a slowly repeated series of slurred phrases consisting of 2–3 notes each, often including *three-eight.*

Similar Species: *Pine Warbler* (p. 354): surprisingly similar; smaller bill; no yellow "spectacles"; indistinct streaking on sides of breast; rich *chip* call; song is 1-pitched trill. *White-eyed Vireo* (p. 271): white chin and throat; grayer head and back; white eyes.

Best Sites: Mother Neff SP; Daingerfield SP; Caddo Lake SP; Martin Dies, Jr., SP.

BLUE-HEADED VIREO

Vireo solitarius

From the canopies of shady woodlands, the purposeful, liquid notes of the Blue-headed Vireo penetrate the dense foliage. This vireo prefers different habitat than many of its relatives—it is the only vireo to commonly occupy coniferous forests. The Blue-headed Vireo breeds throughout Canada's boreal forests and the northeastern U.S. Unlike most vireos, the Blue-headed Vireo winters partially in the southern U.S., including the eastern two-thirds of Texas, rather than solely in the tropics. • In winter, the Blue-headed Vireo joins flocks of other small birds, such as the Downy Woodpecker, Tufted Titmouse, Ruby-crowned Kinglet and several species of warblers. • The distinctive "spectacles" that frame this bird's eyes are a good field mark. They are among the boldest of the eye rings seen on our songbirds. • Until 1997, the Blue-headed, Cassin's *(V. cassinii)* and Plumbeous *(V. plumbeus)* vireos were lumped together as one species, "Solitary Vireo."

ID: gray head; bold white "spectacles"; greenish gray back; white throat; white underparts with yellow flanks; 2 white wing bars.

Size: *L* 5–6 in; *W* 9¾ in.

Status: uncommon to common migrant east of the Pecos R. and rare in the Trans-Pecos; rare to locally uncommon winter resident in the eastern half of the state.

Habitat: found in most wooded habitats.

Nesting: does not nest in Texas.

Feeding: gleans foliage; feeds mostly on insects (especially caterpillars) and spiders.

Voice: harsh *shu-shu-shu* call.

Similar Species: *Yellow-throated Vireo* (p. 275): yellow "spectacles" and throat. *Cassin's Vireo* (p. 452): similar to female Blue-headed, but crown and back are same color.

Best Sites: *In migration:* wooded "traps" in the Coastal Plain. *Winter:* any wooded park.

HUTTON'S VIREO

Vireo huttoni

In early spring, male Hutton's Vireos sing continuously throughout the day, waging vocal battles in an attempt to defend their nesting territories. Their song is an oscillating, two-syllable *zuWEEM, zuWEEM, zuWEEM*. • Unlike most of their vireo relatives, Hutton's Vireos are locally common summer residents in the Davis and Chisos mountains but become less common in winter. • Birders can attract a Hutton's Vireo with persistent "pishing" or a convincing rendition of a Northern Pygmy-Owl call. The odds of seeing this vireo are in your favor—this sprite of deep live-oak shadows is far more numerous than inexperienced birders might imagine—although it does closely resemble kinglets, *Empidonax* flycatchers and even a few warblers. • John Cassin named this bird after William Hutton, a field collector who first obtained this bird for scientific study.

ID: grayish green upperparts; short, slim, hook-tipped bill; incomplete eye ring; smudgy loral dot; white wing bars. **Size:** *L* 4½–5 in; *W* 8 in.

Status: locally common summer resident and very rare to locally uncommon winter resident in the Davis, Guadalupe and Chisos mts. and very rare in extreme western Edwards Plateau.

Habitat: mixed conifer and oak forest; strongly partial to live oak, especially as a consistent understory.

Nesting: well above the ground, in the fork of an oak or on a conifer twig woven into the rim of the nest; pair builds a softball-sized open cup of grass, lichens, moss and bark fibers bound with spider webs, lined with fine grass and outwardly covered with whitish plant down and spider egg cases; pair incubates 4 white eggs, sparsely marked with small dark spots, for 14–16 days.

Feeding: hops from twig to twig in the inner canopy of trees and shrubs to glean or hover for insects; takes caterpillars, spiders, berries, small fruits and some plant galls.

Voice: routine call is a stuttered, *dzee? zeed-eed-eet!* Male: monotonous song is a nasal, buzzy series of tirelessly repeated, 2-syllable notes: *zuWhEEM, zuWhEEM, zuWhEEM.*

Similar Species: *Ruby-crowned Kinglet* (p. 315): smaller overall; smaller head and tail; thin, dainty black bill. *Orange-crowned Warbler* (p. 342): no wing bars. Empidonax *flycatchers:* longer tails and bodies; longer, flatter bills; erect posture.

Best Sites: Davis Mountains SP; Big Bend NP; Guadalupe Mountains NP.

WARBLING VIREO

Vireo gilvus

The charming Warbling Vireo is an uncommon, local summer resident in the mountains of the Trans-Pecos and northeastern Texas. By early May, its bubbly, unvireo-like voice may be heard in local parks and backyards—this vireo often settles close to urban areas. Without any splashy field marks, the Warbling Vireo is undetectable unless it moves from one leaf-hidden stage to another. • The Warbling Vireos that breed in the mountains of the Trans-Pecos belong to the western subspecies (*V.g. swainsonii*), which have a darker crown, smaller bill and paler underparts. Warbling Vireos found in northeastern Texas belong to the eastern subspecies (*V.g. gilvus*) and have brighter yellow flanks. • Population trends for this vireo are not well understood and vary geographically. In California, Warbling Vireo numbers have declined over the last two decades, whereas populations in eastern Canada have increased.

ID: partial, dark eye line borders white eyebrow; gray crown; olive gray upper-parts; no wing bars; yellowish flanks; white to pale gray underparts; bright birds have more yellow in plumage, especially in fall. *In flight:* broad winged; drab above, white below.

Size: *L* 5–5½ in. *W* 8–9 in.

Status: rare to uncommon summer resident in the Trans-Pecos Mts., the eastern Panhandle, north-central and wooded portions of northeastern parts of the state; uncommon migrant statewide.

Habitat: *Breeding:* deciduous rural and suburban woodlots in open situations; prefers riverside sycamores; less often in drier, upland areas. *In migration:* open deciduous woodlands; parks and gardens with deciduous trees.

Nesting: in a deciduous tree or shrub; in an outer horizontal fork; hanging, basket-like cup nest of grass, roots, plant down, spider silk and a few feathers; pair incubates 3–4 sparingly-marked, white eggs for 13–14 days.

Feeding: gleans upper-canopy foliage, occasionally hovering, for insects, especially caterpillars, moth pupae and ladybird beetles.

Voice: calls are rather catlike, often 2-syllabled, notes and a short, dry *gwit*. *Male:* song is a long, musical warble of slurred whistles.

Similar Species: *Philadelphia Vireo* (p. 452): yellow breast, sides and flanks; full, dark eye line bordering white eyebrow. *Bell's Vireo* (p. 272): smaller; brighter plumage; bright yellow flanks; usually 1 bright wing bar; bluish legs. *Red-eyed Vireo* (p. 279): black eye line extends to bill; bluish gray crown; red eyes. *Tennessee Warbler* (p. 341): bluish gray cap and nape; olive green back; slimmer bill.

Best Sites: *In summer:* Davis Mountains SP; Guadalupe Mountains NP; Big Bend NP. *In migration:* any wooded "trap" in the Coastal Plain.

RED-EYED VIREO

Vireo olivaceus

Undisputed as champions of vocal endurance, male Red-eyed Vireos carry on singing their robinlike songs for five or six hours after sunrise on spring and early summer mornings. One tenacious male set a record by singing 21,000 phrases in one day! • The Red-eyed Vireo is one of the most common songbirds in eastern North America. Texas marks the westernmost edge of this vireo's breeding range, and it can be a common summer resident throughout the swamps and the moist deciduous or mixed forests of the Edwards Plateau. This hard-to-see bird forages high in the canopy, where its dull colors offer camouflage. • The Red-eyed Vireo perches with a hunched stance and hops with its body turned diagonally to its direction of travel. • There is no firm agreement about the reason for this vireo's red eye color. Red eyes are very unusual among songbirds and tend to be more prevalent in nonpasserines such as hawks, grebes and some herons.

ID: olive green upperparts; gray crown; white eyebrow; black eye line; red eyes; white throat and underparts with yellow wash on flanks and undertail coverts, especially during fall.
Size: *L* 6 in; *W* 10 in.
Status: uncommon to common summer resident in eastern Texas; common migrant in eastern Texas and rare in the western half.
Habitat: *Breeding:* swamps, riparian areas and other wet deciduous woodlands. *In migration:* any wooded habitat.

Nesting: in a horizontal fork in a deciduous tree or shrub; hanging, basketlike cup is made of grass, roots, spider silk and cocoons; female incubates 4 darkly spotted, white eggs for 11–14 days.
Feeding: gleans foliage for prey; feeds mostly on insects and spiders but eats fruit during migration.
Voice: descending nasal *sherr* call; song is a variable series of short phrases with distinct pauses in between, uttered for long periods.
Similar Species: *Philadelphia Vireo* (p. 452) and *Warbling Vireo* (p. 278): smaller, thinner bill; duller eye line. *Tennessee Warbler* (p. 341): bluish gray cap and nape; olive green back; slimmer bill.
Best Sites: *In summer:* any wooded park. *In migration:* wooded "traps" in the Coastal Plain.

BLUE JAY

Cyanocitta cristata

Large suburban trees and bushy ornamental shrubs offer perfect habitat for the adaptable, mischievous Blue Jay. Common wherever there are fruit-bearing plants or backyard feeding stations stocked with sunflower seeds and peanuts, this jay is one of the most recognizable songbirds. Sometimes appearing greedy at the feeder, it is often only caching food for later use. • Beautiful, resourceful and vocally diverse, the Blue Jay embodies all the admirable traits and aggressive qualities of the corvid family, and it can easily mimic the call of a Red-tailed Hawk, American Crow or even a neighborhood cat. • Blue Jays are excellent sentinels for spotting predators, warning others with their loud *jay* calls. Fearless jays readily mob and attack hawks or owls. It seems that no predator, not even the Great Horned Owl, is too formidable for this bird to harass. • In some years, flocks containing thousands of Blue Jays are seen migrating through the eastern third of Texas.

ID: blue crest; black "necklace," eye line and bill; blue upperparts; white underparts; dark bars and white corners on blue tail; white bar and flecking on wings.

Size: *L* 11–12¾ in; *W* 16 in.

Status: common resident in the eastern half of the state and the eastern Panhandle, becoming rare on the South Plains; irregular migrant and winter visitor in the remainder of the state east of the Pecos R.

Habitat: mixed deciduous forests, agricultural areas, scrubby fields and townsites.

Nesting: in the crotch of a tree or tall shrub; pair builds a bulky stick nest; pair incubates 4–5 variably marked, greenish, buff or pale blue eggs for 16–18 days.

Feeding: forages on the ground and among vegetation for nuts, berries, eggs, nestlings and birdseed; also eats insects and carrion.

Voice: calls include *jay-jay-jay* and *queedle queedle queedle-queedle;* expert mimic of Red-shouldered Hawk and Osprey calls.

Similar Species: *Steller's Jay* (p. 453): local in Guadalupe Mts and Davis Mts.; dark head and back; dark blue wings and tail with no white markings. *Western Scrub-Jay* (p. 282) and *Pinyon Jay* (p. 453): no crest; no barring on tail or wings.

Best Sites: any park in the eastern half of Texas.

GREEN JAY

Cyanocorax yncas

Unmistakably a tropical bird, the Green Jay is known to many Texans as "Rio Grande Jay." Look for this agile bird as it searches every part of a tree for food, even hanging upside down when branches bend under its weight. • Green Jays in Texas live in family flocks but do not practice cooperative breeding (helpers at the nest) like other populations—instead, nonbreeders defend the family territory. In March, the entire family patrols the territorial boundaries together. The one-year-olds continue to chase intruders away during the nesting period but are quickly cast out of the family unit once the nestlings have fledged. • Green Jays have been observed inserting sticks under the bark of dead trees to draw out insects.

ID: green back; flashy yellow underparts; blue crown; black bib; sturdy bill; long, blue-green tail with yellow outer feathers. *Immature:* duller greens and yellows.

Size: *L:* 10½ in; *W* 13½ in.

Status: common resident in the Lower Rio Grande Valley and the southern half of the South Texas Brush Country and rare north to the Edwards Plateau and the central part of the Coastal Plain.

Habitat: open woodland; brushy thickets; dense second-growth forests; lowland, riparian areas.

Nesting: in a dense thicket; builds a bulky stick nest; eggs may be visible from below; female incubates 3–5 pale gray or greenish white eggs for 17–18 days.

Feeding: spirals through a tree for arthropods, seeds, nuts and fruit; also eats small rodents, lizards and other birds' eggs.

Voice: various noisy screams; rapid, rattling *jeek jeek jeek jeek;* mechanical *slik slik slik slik;* also a variety of quiet *green-reen* or *neek-neek* squeaks; mimics other birds.

Similar Species: none.

Best Sites: Anzalduas County Park; Bentson-Rio Grande SP; Santa Ana NWR; Laguna Atascosa NWR.

WESTERN SCRUB-JAY

Aphelocoma californica

This slender jay is often seen foraging among leaf litter or surveying its tree-dotted habitat from a perch atop a tall shrub. • Fallen acorns are a staple of the Western Scrub-Jay's winter diet. Each fall, this jay gathers and stores them individually in holes that it has dug in the ground with its strong bill. This intelligent bird often uses a rock or concrete slab as an "anvil" to assist in cracking open the shielding coat. • The Western Scrub-Jay has recently been granted full species status and is now distinguished from the Florida Scrub-Jay *(A. coerulescens)* and the Island Scrub-Jay *(A. insularis),* which is an endemic species of southern California's Santa Cruz Island.

ID: slim body; sky blue upperparts with gray back; long, unmarked tail; bluish "necklace" borders streaked, white throat; light gray underparts; dark, heavy bill; dark cheek patch; faint white eyebrow.

Size: *L* 11½ in; *W* 15½ in.

Status: common resident on the Edwards Plateau and much of the Trans-Pecos and rare in the Panhandle; rare to locally uncommon winter resident in the South Plains and Rolling Plains.

Habitat: chaparral and dry, brushy open areas of oak and pinyon-juniper woodlands, mixed oak-coniferous forests, broken mixed deciduous-coniferous woodlands and riparian woodlands; also found in suburban parks and gardens and urban shrubbery to 8000 ft (may wander to 11,000 ft).

Nesting: in a small conifer or small shrub; pair builds a bulky stick nest, usually lined with moss, grass and fur; female incubates 3–6 brown-flecked, white eggs, for 15–17 days.

Feeding: forages on the ground for insects and small vertebrates; also eats other birds' eggs and nestlings, acorns, pinyon nuts and many fruits.

Voice: harsh, repetitive *ike-ike-ike* perch call; rough, frequently repeated *quesh, quesh, quesh* in flight.

Similar Species: *Pinyon Jay* (p. 453): blue overall; shorter tail. *Steller's Jay* (p. 453): local; large, black crest; dark head, nape and back; blue underparts; barred wings and tail. *Mexican Jay* (p. 453): local; blue head; bluish back; whitish throat; gray underparts.

Best Sites: Hueco Tanks SP; Lost Maples SP; Pedernales Falls SP; Friedrich Wilderness Park; Guadalupe River SP.

AMERICAN CROW

Corvus brachyrhynchos

Texas is unique in supporting four of the five crow and raven species regularly found in North America. The American Crow is a common year-round inhabitant of eastern Texas. Along the Louisiana border, its range overlaps that of the Fish Crow. • American Crows are wary, intelligent birds that have flourished despite considerable human effort to reduce their numbers. As ecological generalists, they can survive in a wide variety of situations. In January, as crows in southern Canada are searching the snow-covered fields for mice or carrion, those in Texas are busy capturing lizards in the brushlands. • Able to cry like a child, laugh, whine like a dog or squawk like a hen, crows are impressive mimics. Some crows in captivity can repeat simple spoken words. • In some places, many thousands of crows may roost together—in aggregations known as "murders"—on any given fall night. • The cumbersome-sounding scientific name *Corvus brachyrhynchos* is Latin for "raven with the small nose."

ID: black body, bill and legs; slim, sleek head and throat; broad wings; square-shaped tail.
Size: *L* 17–21 in; *W* 3 ft.
Status: common to abundant resident from eastern Texas west to the eastern Panhandle, the eastern Edwards Plateau and the central part of the Coastal Plain; uncommon to locally abundant migrant and winter visitor on the High Plains, western parts of the Rolling Plains and the Edwards Plateau and the eastern half of the Lower Rio Grande Valley.
Habitat: pastures, agricultural fields, oak and mixed oak-pine woodlands; wooded urban areas.

Nesting: in a tree or on a utility pole; large stick-and-branch nest is lined with fur and soft plant materials; female incubates 4–6 grayish to bluish green eggs, blotched with brown and gray, for about 18 days.
Feeding: very opportunistic; eats carrion, small vertebrates, other birds' eggs and nestlings, berries, seeds, invertebrates and human food waste; visits bird feeders.
Voice: distinctive *caw-caw-caw*.
Similar Species: *Fish Crow* (p. 284): slightly smaller; smaller bill; longer tail and wings; usually readily distinguished by typical nasal *uh-uh* call, but nasal *car-car-car-car-car* is similar to American Crow's. *Common Raven* (p. 286) and *Chihuahuan Raven* (p. 285): larger; heavier bill; shaggy throat; Chihuahuan Raven has white-based neck feathers (usually hidden).
Best Sites: widespread.

FISH CROW

Corvus ossifragus

The Fish Crown is a coastal species found only in the eastern U.S., from Massachusetts to Texas. In Texas, it is an uncommon permanent resident along the Red River, Sabine River and Louisiana border, although it appears to be extending its range westward. It is often found near water, including coastal habitats. • Although Fish Crows and American Crows are virtually identical in plumage, their habitats and call notes readily distinguish the two species. The common call of a Fish Crow is a *uh* or *uh-uh*, whereas the common call of an American Crow is a raucous *caw!* • A large part of the Fish Crow's continuing success is a result of its ability to eat a diverse array of foods, including carrion, insects, crustaceans, fish, seeds and fruits. An effective combination of a nimble bill, strong, dexterous feet and the ability to learn allow the Fish Crow to solve most foraging problems.

ID: all black; smaller head and bill, with more pointed, swept-back wing tips, than American Crow; relatively long tail; best identified by voice.

Size: *L* 15¾ in; *W* 3 ft.

Status: uncommon resident in east Texas along the Sabine, Red and Sulphur river drainages and in the southeast along the Neches R.

Habitat: river valleys, flood plain forests and coastal habitats, including tidewater marshes and bayous.

Nesting: often in small, loose colonies; in the fork of a tree or large shrub; pair builds a bulky stick nest; female incubates 4–5 heavily marked, greenish eggs for 16–18 days.

Feeding: walks on the ground looking for prey or flies into wading bird rookeries; often scavenges; feeds on a wide variety of foods, including bird eggs, carrion, fish, marine crustaceans and insects.

Voice: nasal *uh* or *uh-uh* common call; less frequently utters nasal *car-car-car-car-car* reminiscent of American Crow.

Similar Species: *American Crow* (p. 283): slightly larger; well-known boisterous *caw!* is often doubled. *Common Raven* (p. 286) and *Chihuahuan Raven* (p. 285): larger; heavier bill; shaggy throat; Chihuahuan Raven has white-based neck feathers (usually hidden).

Best Sites: Caddo Lake SP; Sea Rim SP; Wright Patman L.

CHIHUAHUAN RAVEN

Corvus cryptoleucus

Unless it is a blustery day, you may not see the Chihuahuan Raven's hidden white neck feathers, the main distinguishing characteristic between it and the slightly larger Common Raven. The easiest way to tell the two apart is by habitat and call. The Chihuahuan Raven is usually found in areas that the Common Raven avoids—the flat, scrubby grasslands of the southern U.S. • Once thought to bother cattle and wild game, both of these species were historically persecuted. The Chihuahuan Raven was harder hit during these hunts, as their post-breeding social nature gathers them in groups of hundreds. Luckily for the birds, this myth has diminished, and flocks can still be seen scavenging at dumps or foraging through waste grain fields in fall. • With little cover for their broods in their arid breeding habitat, pairs become very territorial during breeding season.

ID: black plumage; hidden white neck feathers; tail only slightly wedge-shaped; thick bill with long nasal bristles.
Size: *L* 19–20 in; *W* 3½ ft.
Status: common resident from the Pecos R. through the High Plains and Rolling Plains south to the Lower Rio Grande Valley.
Habitat: brushy areas, arid grassland, yucca and garbage dumps.
Nesting: in a tree or on a utility pole or a yucca; platform of thorns and sticks is lined with grass, bark and hair; pair incubates

5–6 pale blue or blue-green eggs, marked with dark squiggles, for 18–21 days.
Feeding: eats carrion, eggs, insects, grain, berries, cactus fruit and garbage.
Voice: similar to Common Raven but without deep richness in its call: *craaaaag, craaaag*.
Similar Species: *Common Raven* (p. 286): larger body; thicker throat area; longer bill; distinct wedge shape to tail. *American Crow* (p. 283) and *Fish Crow* (p. 284): smaller; smaller head and bill; shorter, rounder wings; rounded tail; higher-pitched calls.
Best Sites: Abilene SP; Balmorhea L.; Big Spring SP; Falcon SP; Laguna Atascosa NWR.

COMMON RAVEN

Corvus corax

With a wingspan comparable to that of a hawk's, the Common Raven soars, traveling along coastlines, over deserts, along mountain ridges and even on the Arctic tundra. Few birds occupy such a large natural range. In Texas they are found from the Edwards Plateau west through the mountains of the Trans-Pecos. • Whether stealing food from a flock of gulls, harassing an eagle or scavenging from a carcass, the Common Raven is worthy of its reputation as a clever bird. Glorified in many cultures as a magical being, the raven does not act by instinct alone. From producing complex vocalizations to playfully sliding down snow banks, this raucous bird exhibits behaviors that many people once thought of as exclusively human. • Breeding ravens maintain lifelong pair bonds, enduring everything from harsh weather and food scarcity to the raising of young.

ID: all-black plumage; heavy, black bill; wedge-shaped tail; shaggy throat; broad, blunt-pointed wings.
Size: *L* 24 in; *W* 50 in.
Status: rare to uncommon resident in the Trans-Pecos Mts., east though much of the Edwards Plateau; rare winter resident in the northwestern Panhandle.
Habitat: most habitats from low elevations to over 14,000 ft, but tends to avoid habitats occupied by crows, such as urban parks, farmyards and orchards. *Foraging:* locally in towns and cities, especially along the north coast.
Nesting: on steep cliffs, ledges, bluffs, power poles and tall conifers; large stick and branch nest is lined with fur and soft plant materials; female incubates 4–6 light blue to pale green eggs, with dark blotches or streaks, for 18–21 days.
Feeding: carrion, small vertebrates, other birds' eggs and nestlings, berries, invertebrates and human food waste.
Voice: many vocalizations, from deep gargling croaks to high twanging notes; deep, far-carrying, croaking *craww-craww* or *quork quork;* juvenile contacts adults with a higher pitched croak.
Similar Species: *Chihuahuan Raven* (p. 285): higher pitched *craaaaag* call; smaller body; thinner throat area; shorter bill; less distinct wedge shape to tail. *American Crow* (p. 283) and *Fish Crow* (p. 284): smaller; smaller head and bill; shorter, rounder wings; fan-shaped tail; higher-pitched calls.
Best Sites: Guadalupe Mountains NP; Davis Mountains SP; Big Bend NP; Seminole Canyon SP.

HORNED LARK

Eremophila alpestris

An impressive, high-speed, plummeting courtship dive would blow anybody's hair back or, in the case of the male Horned Lark, his two unique black "horns." He begins his elaborate song-flight courtship display by flying and gliding in circles at heights of up to 800 feet, then issuing his sweet, tinkling song before closing his wings and plummeting downward in a dramatic, high-speed dive. • These open-country inhabitants are most common in migration and in winter as they congregate in flocks on farm fields, beaches and airfields, sometimes in the company of longspurs. Horned Larks are frequently found along the shoulders of gravel roads, searching for seeds. Easy to see but often tough to identify, they fly off into the adjacent fields at the approach of any vehicle. • One way to distinguish sparrows from Horned Larks is by their method of travel: Horned Larks walk, but sparrows hop.

ID: *Male:* small black "horns" (rarely raised); black line under eye extends from bill to cheek; light yellow to white face; dull brown upperparts; black breast band; dark tail with white outer feathers; pale throat. *Female:* less distinctively patterned; duller plumage.
Size: *L* 7 in; *W* 12 in.
Status: rare to common resident on the High Plains and along the coast; common migrant and winter resident in the northern half of the state and less common southward, becoming rare and local in the east.
Habitat: croplands. *Breeding:* open areas, including sparsely vegetated fields, weedy meadows and airfields. *In migration and winter:* fields and roadside ditches.

Nesting: on the ground; female chooses the nest site; in a shallow scrape lined with grass, plant fibers and roots; female incubates 3–4 brown-blotched, pale gray to greenish white eggs for 10–12 days.
Feeding: gleans the ground for seeds; feeds insects to the young.
Voice: tinkling *tsee-titi* or *zoot* call; flight song is a long series of tinkling, twittered whistles.
Similar Species: *Sparrows* (pp. 377–406, 457–58), *Lapland Longspur* (p. 409) and *American Pipit* (p. 335): all lack distinctive facial pattern, "horns" and solid black breast band.
Best Sites: *Summer:* Bolivar Flats Shorebird Sanctuary; Galveston Island SP; Big Spring SP; Rita Blanca National Grassland. *Winter:* open areas in such places as Benbrook L. and Cedar Hill SP.

287

PURPLE MARTIN

Progne subis

The Purple Martin is North America's largest swallow. It once nested in natural tree hollows and cliff crevices, but today it has all but abandoned natural nest sites. • To attract this large, vocal swallow to your backyard, make sure the cavity openings of your "martin condo complex" are the right size for Purple Martins and place it high on a pole in a large open area, preferably near water. The condo must be cleaned out and closed up each winter, and you should remove any House Sparrows and European Starlings that may lay claim to the site. If all goes well, a Purple Martin colony will return each spring. The result will be an endlessly entertaining summer spectacle as the adults spiral around the house in pursuit of flying insects and the young birds perch clumsily at the openings of their apartment cavities. • The scientific name *Progne* refers to Procne, the daughter of the king of Athens who, according to Greek mythology, was transformed into a swallow.

ID: shallowly forked tail. *Male:* wholly dark blue. *Female* and *juvenile:* gray forehead; "scaly," dark and whitish underparts.
Size: *L* 7–8 in; *W* 18 in.
Status: common summer resident in most of the state, less common in the South Plains and Rolling Plains and absent in the western Panhandle.
Habitat: semi-open areas, often near water; common in suburban areas.
Nesting: communal; usually in a human-made, apartment-style birdhouse or a hollowed-out gourd; rarely in a tree cavity or cliff crevice; nest materials include feathers, grass, mud and vegetation; female incubates 4–5 white eggs for 15–18 days.
Feeding: mostly while in flight; usually eats flies, ants, dragonflies and mosquitoes; may also walk on the ground, taking insects and rarely berries.
Voice: rich, fluty, robinlike *pew-pew*, often heard in flight.
Similar Species: *European Starling* (p. 334): longer bill (yellow in summer); unforked tail. *Barn Swallow* (p. 295): smaller; buff orange to reddish brown throat; deeply forked tail. *Northern Rough-winged Swallow* (p. 291): smaller; drab brown upperparts; square tail.
Best Sites: best seen at colonies in martin "houses" around human habitation. *Late summer:* large urban roosts.

TREE SWALLOW

Tachycineta bicolor

Tree Swallows are most common during migration, appearing like huge clouds of smoke over marshes or fields. In summer, they are uncommon breeders in northeast Texas, but, in winter, flocks can be locally abundant along the coast. • Tree Swallows are more cold-hardy than other swallows, which explains their presence in Texas during winter. They readily switch to a diet of berries when insects become scarce during cold weather—large flocks of Tree Swallows gleaning the abundant berries from Wax Myrtle bushes can be a common sight in southern areas. • In bright spring sunshine, the iridescent back of the Tree Swallow appears dark blue, but in fall it appears green. Unlike other North American swallows, the female Tree Swallow acquires its full adult plumage only in her second or third year. • The word *bicolor* is Latin for "two colors" and refers to the contrast between this bird's dark upperparts and white underparts.

ID: iridescent, dark blue or green head and upperparts; white underparts; no white on cheek; dark rump; small bill; long, pointed wings; shallowly forked tail. *Female:* slightly duller.
Size: *L* 5¾ in; *W* 14¾ in.
Status: common, often locally abundant migrant statewide; rare to uncommon winter resident in the southern half of the state, where it may be abundant along the coast and irregular in the Trans-Pecos; rare and local summer resident in the extreme northeast and in central Texas.
Habitat: forages over any habitat.

Nesting: in a tree cavity or nest box lined with weeds, grass and feathers; female incubates 4–6 white eggs for up to 19 days.
Feeding: plucks flying insects from the air or gleans berries (especially wax myrtle) from foliage.
Voice: metallic, buzzy *klweet* alarm call. *Male:* liquid, chattering twitter song.
Similar Species: *Violet-green Swallow* (p. 290): white on face extends above eye; emerald green back; white rump patches. *Barn Swallow* (p. 295): some birds appear wholly white below, but note deeply forked tail. *Eastern Kingbird* (p. 268): larger; white-tipped tail; longer bill; dark gray to blackish upperparts.
Best Sites: *In migration:* anywhere along the coast. *Summer:* L. Tawakoni; Granger L.

VIOLET-GREEN SWALLOW

Tachycineta thalassina

Considered the western equivalent of the Tree Swallow, the Violet-green Swallow demonstrates a greater aptitude for taking advantage of western montane habitats, being found around cliffs and treeless open areas far more often than its cousin. In summer and during migration, the Violet-green can routinely be seen darting above cliffs and rivers in the mountains of the Trans-Pecos. It is a rare winter visitor along the Rio Grande. • At first sight, Violet-greens look an awful lot like Tree Swallows, which is to be expected, given their close relationship. • Swallows occasionally eat mineral-rich soil, egg shells and exposed shellfish fragments, possibly to recoup the minerals lost during egg laying. • Swallows are swift and graceful flyers, routinely traveling at speeds of 30 miles per hour. • The scientific name *thalassina* is Latin for "sea green," a tribute to this bird's body color.

ID: white underparts, cheek and rump patches; small bill; long, pointed wings; shallowly forked tail; small feet. *Male:* iridescent, emerald green upperparts. *Female:* duller and more bronze than male.
Size: *L* 5 in; *W* 13½ in.
Status: uncommon summer resident in the Davis, Guadalupe and Chisos mts.; common migrant in the Trans-Pecos.
Habitat: open environments, including beaver ponds, marshes, townsites and mixed woodlands.

Nesting: in a tree cavity, rock crevice or nest box; nest is made of weeds, grass and feathers; female incubates 4–6 white eggs for up to 15 days.
Feeding: catches flying insects, such as leafhoppers, leafbugs, flies, ants and wasps; drinks on the wing.
Voice: buzzy, trilling *tweet tweet;* harsh *chip-chip.*
Similar Species: *Tree Swallow* (p. 289): no white cheek or white rump patches. *Bank Swallow* (p. 292): no white cheek; dark breast band contrasts with white throat and belly.
Best Sites: Davis Mountains SP; Guadalupe Mountains NP; Big Bend NP.

NORTHERN ROUGH-WINGED SWALLOW

Stelgidopteryx serripennis

Northern Rough-winged Swallows are more widespread in our state than most people realize. They typically nest in sandy banks along rivers and streams, excavating their own nesting burrow or reusing a burrow dug by another bird or rodent. Vertical cuts created by interstate highways have provided additional nesting crevices for these dusky little birds. Watch for Rough-wings zipping through busy intersections near banks, culverts and bridges. • Unlike other swallows, male Northern Rough-wings have curved barbs along the outer edge of their primary wing feathers. The purpose of this saw-toothed edge remains a mystery, but it may be used to produce sound during courtship displays. The Northern Rough-wing's English and scientific names relate to this structure; *Stelgidopteryx* means "scraper wing" and *serripennis* means "saw feather."

ID: dull brown upperparts, including head; indistinct brown wash on breast; whitish underparts. *Juvenile:* wide rufous wingbars. *In flight:* square tail.

Size: *L* 5½ in; *W* 14 in.

Status: rare to locally uncommon summer resident statewide except in the Rolling Plains and the southern half of the High Plains; common migrant throughout the state; rare winter resident on the Coastal Plain and along the Rio Grande to the Big Bend area.

Habitat: nests in riverbanks, drain pipes, exhaust pipes (!) or other artificial cavities; forages over most habitats, especially near water.

Nesting: sometimes in small colonies but usually solitary; pair excavates a burrow in an earthen bank and lines the nesting chamber with leaves and dry grass; mostly the female incubates 4–8 white eggs for 12–16 days.

Feeding: catches flying insects on the wing.

Voice: call is a short, squeaky note.

Similar Species: *Bank Swallow* (p. 292): brown breast band; white underparts. *Tree Swallow* (p. 289): drab birds appear brown above, but note pure white underparts.

Best Sites: *Breeding:* on most parts of the Rio Grande and other rivers with high banks. *In migration:* most bodies of water and on the Coastal Plain.

BANK SWALLOW

Riparia riparia

Highly social, the Bank Swallow is one of the most broadly distributed members of the swallow family; it is found throughout North America and northern Eurasia. In Texas, the Bank Swallow is seen mainly during migration, although small numbers also nest along the Rio Grande. • Small flocks of migrating Bank Swallows sometimes gather along our sandy shores to preen each other in a communal dust bath. They squat on the ground and spread out their wings while resting and sunbathing. • On their breeding grounds, Bank Swallows nest in burrows that are dug (initially with their bills, then later with their feet) into earthen river or stream banks; "*riparia*" is Latin for "riverbank." The Bank Swallow is known in the Old World as "Sand Martin." • In medieval Europe, it was believed that swallows spent winter in the mud at the bottom of swamps because they were not seen at that time of year. In those days, it was beyond imagination that these birds might fly south for winter.

ID: brown upperparts; light underparts; brown breast band; long, pointed wings; shallowly forked tail; white throat; grayish brown crown; dark cheek; small legs.

Size: *L* 5¾ in; *W* 13 in.
Status: locally common summer resident along the Rio Grande and rare on the southern Edwards Plateau; common migrant statewide; rare and irregular winter resident along the coast and up the Rio Grande.
Habitat: steep banks, lakeshore bluffs and gravel pits.

Nesting: singly or in small, loose colonies in burrows dug into stream banks; pair incubates 4–7 brown-spotted, white eggs for 13–17 days.
Feeding: catches flying insects on the wing.
Voice: call is a series of buzzy twitters.
Similar Species: *Tree Swallow* (p. 289) and *Violet-green Swallow* (p. 290): iridescent upperparts; no dark breast band. *Northern Rough-winged Swallow* (p. 291): stockier overall; no breast band; buffy throat and underparts; broader wings and square tail in flight.
Best Sites: *In migration:* anywhere along the coast or around inland bodies of water.

CLIFF SWALLOW

Petrochelidon pyrrhonota

If the Cliff Swallow were to be renamed in the 20th century, it would probably be called "Bridge Swallow," because so many bridges have a colony living under them. In recent decades, the Cliff Swallow has expanded its range across eastern North America, nesting on various human-made structures, including bridges and culverts. During breeding season, it may be the most common swallow in Texas. • Cliff Swallows roll mud into balls with their bills and press the pellets together to form their characteristic gourd-shaped nests. As brooding parents peer out of the circular neck of the nest, their white forehead patches warn intruders that somebody is home. • Agricultural fields and marshes are favorite foraging sites for the Cliff Swallow. To help in identification, watch for the square (not forked) tail, cinnamon-colored rump patch and distinctive flight pattern of ascending with rapid wing-strokes then gliding gracefully down.

ID: orangy rump; buff forehead; bluish gray head and wings; rusty nape, cheek and throat; buff breast; white belly; spotted undertail coverts; nearly square tail.
Size: *L* 5¾ in; *W* 13¾ in.
Status: common to abundant summer resident, uncommon to locally abundant migrant statewide.
Habitat: steep banks, cliffs, bridges and buildings, often near watercourses.
Nesting: colonial; under a bridge, overpass, the eaves of a barn, in a culvert or on a cliff or building; pair builds a gourd-shaped mud nest with a small opening near the bottom; pair incubates 4–5 brown-spotted, white to pinkish eggs for 14–16 days.

Feeding: forages over water, fields and marshes; catches flying insects and drinks on the wing; occasionally eats berries.
Voice: twittering chatter: *churrr-churrr; nyew* alarm call.
Similar Species: *Barn Swallow* (p. 295): deeply forked tail; dark rump; rust- to buff-colored underparts; rusty forehead. *Cave Swallow* (p. 294): darker forehead; pale throat. *Other swallows* (pp. 289–92): lack buff forehead and rump patch.
Best Sites: culverts, bridges and overpasses in any part of the state.

CAVE SWALLOW

Petrochelidon fulva

As their name suggests, Cave Swallows traditionally preferred the protection of limestone caves for nesting and roosting. Lately, Cave Swallows have also begun nesting in culverts and under bridges, allowing for a range expansion into southern and central Texas. • These swallows often share their traditional nest sites with bats but, aside from an occasional bat roosting in an old swallow nest, these two species are not known to interact. Swallows are active by day and bats by night, so they generally occupy the cave at different times, with the swallows settling in for the night just before the bats leave. However, because Cave Swallows tend to fly through the entrance at top speed, the two species occasionally collide. • Colonial birds such as swallows are believed to share information on food sources among the group. When a swallow cannot find food, it rejoins the group, then follows another swallow to find a more promising foraging area. • The Cave Swallow's genus name combines two Greek words: *petra* ("rock") and *chelidon* ("a swallow").

ID: dark back; cinnamon forehead; dark cap; pale tawny throat; light underparts. *In flight:* pointed wings, reddish orange rump.

Size: *L* 5¾ in; *W* 13¾ in.

Status: common to abundant summer resident in the southern half of Texas, north through the Edwards Plateau and north-central Texas; increasingly common winter resident from the coast into the Edwards Plateau and east-central Texas.

Habitat: open lands with culverts, bridges and overpasses, especially near water courses.

Nesting: colonial; in a cave or culvert or under a bridge; pair uses mud and plant material to attach a half-cup nest, which may be reused, to a vertical surface, often under an overhang and lines it with feathers and plant down; pair incubate 3–4 brown-speckled, white eggs for 15–18 days; pair feeds the young.

Feeding: gregarious; catches insects in flight.

Voice: soft, distinct *choo choo* call notes.

Similar Species: *Cliff Swallow* (p. 293): lighter forehead; dark, cinnamon-colored throat. *Barn Swallow* (p. 295): deeply forked tail. *Other swallows* (pp. 289–92) lack cinnamon forehead and rump patch.

Best Sites: any culvert, bridge or overpass within the breeding range.

BARN SWALLOW

Hirundo rustica

The Barn Swallow is the most widely distributed swallow in the world, as well as in North America and Texas. Although Barn Swallows do not occur in mass colonies, they are familiar birds because they usually build their nests on human-made structures. Barn Swallows once nested in entrances to caves and on cliffs, but their cup-shaped mud nests are now found under house eaves, in barns and boathouses, under bridges or on any other structure that provides shelter. • Unfortunately, not everyone appreciates nesting Barn Swallows—the young can be very messy—and people often scrape barn swallow nests off buildings just as the nesting season begins. Remember that these graceful birds are natural pest controllers, and their close association with urban areas and tolerance for human activity affords us the wondrous opportunity to observe and study the normally secretive reproductive cycle of birds. • *Hirundo* is Latin for "swallow," whereas *rustica* refers to this bird's preference for rural habitats.

ID: long, deeply forked tail; blue crown, nape and ear patch; orange forehead, cheek and throat; bluish black upperparts; rust- to buff-colored underparts; long, pointed wings.
Size: *L* 7 in; *W* 15 in.
Status: rare to common summer resident and common to abundant migrant statewide; rare and irregular winter resident on the Coastal Plain and inland to the southern part of the Edwards Plateau.
Habitat: open rural and urban areas where bridges, culverts and buildings are found near rivers, lakes, marshes or ponds.

Nesting: singly or in small, loose colonies; on a vertical or horizontal building structure under a suitable overhang, on a bridge or overpass or in a culvert; pair builds cup nest of mud and grass or straw; pair incubates 3–5 brown-spotted, white eggs for 13–17 days.
Feeding: catches flying insects on the wing.
Voice: continuous, twittering chatter; *wit* call, often doubled.
Similar Species: none; orange underparts and long, forked tail are diagnostic.
Best Sites: any building, culvert, bridge or overpass within its breeding range.

CAROLINA CHICKADEE

Poecile carolinensis

N
amed for their calls, chickadees are tiny songbirds with black bibs. Seven species are native to North America, but only two, the Carolina Chickadee and the Mountain Chickadee, occur regularly in Texas. • The Carolina Chickadee is a cavity nester, so it cannot survive in developed areas where snags are removed for aesthetics or safety. In rural areas, however, it will nest in birdhouses and does well in suburban areas. The species also is strongly attracted to bird feeders.• Outside the breeding season, chickadees join the company of foraging mixed-species flocks that also contain Downy Woodpeckers, Tufted Titmice, Blue-headed Vireos, White-eyed Vireos, Ruby-crowned Kinglets, Golden-crowned Kinglets and several warblers.

ID: black cap and bib separated by white cheeks; gray back; tiny bill; gray wings with pale edging on secondary feathers; whitish underparts with pale peach flanks.

Size: *L* 4¾ in; *W* 7½ in.

Status: common resident in the eastern two-thirds of the state and south along the riparian woodlands of the upper and central Coastal Plain and rare along rivers in the eastern Panhandle; very rare in winter west and south of the breeding range.

Habitat: most wooded habitats, including urban and suburban areas.

Nesting: in a snag or fence post (or a nest box); pair excavates a cavity and lines it with soft plant material and animal hair; female incubates 5–8 finely speckled, white eggs for 11–14 days.

Feeding: gleans vegetation for insects, spiders and some fruit, often while hanging upside down; also visits bird feeders.

Voice: rapid *chick-a-dee-dee* call; whistling 4-note *fee-bee fee-bay* song.

Similar Species: *Mountain Chickadee* (p. 454): ranges do not overlap; indistinct white eyebrow line; gray wings. *Black-crested Titmouse* (p. 298): larger and stockier; black crest. *Red-breasted Nuthatch* (p. 301) and *White-breasted Nuthatch* (p. 302): no black "bibs"; longer, thinner bills; climb headfirst down trees.

Best Sites: any wooded area within the breeding range.

TUFTED TITMOUSE

Baeolophus bicolor

This bird's amusing feeding antics and its insatiable appetite keep curious observers entertained at bird feeders. Grasping an acorn or sunflower seed with its tiny feet, the dexterous Tufted Titmouse strikes its dainty bill repeatedly against the hard outer coating, exposing the inner core. • The titmouse's call, a clear whistle usually written as *peter peter peter*, is a common avian sound of our pinewoods and oak hammocks. • When not breeding, Tufted Titmice join flocks composed of other small songbirds such as Carolina Chickadees, White-eyed Vireos, Blue-headed Vireos, Blue-gray Gnatcatchers and various warblers. They are often the first to detect danger, which they scold with loud harsh notes that attract other birds to help mob the predator. • A breeding pair of Tufted Titmice will maintain their bond throughout the year. Young from one breeding season will often stay with their parents long enough to help them with nesting and feeding duties the following year. In late winter, mating pairs break from their flock to search for nesting cavities and soft lining material. By setting out human or pet hair that has accumulated in a hairbrush, you may attract these curious birds, which will incorporate your offering into their nest.

ID: prominent crest; gray upperparts; white face with bold black eye; white underparts with orange flanks.
Size: *L* 6–6½ in; *W* 10 in.

Status: common resident in the eastern third of the state and west to the edge of the Rolling Plains and the Edwards Plateau.
Habitat: most wooded habitats.
Nesting: in a natural cavity lined with soft vegetation and animal hair; female may be fed by the male from courtship to time of

hatching; female incubates 5–6 finely dotted, white eggs for 12–14 days; both adults and occasionally a "helper" raise the young.
Feeding: forages on branches and occasionally on the ground for insects, spiders and seeds; also visits bird feeders.
Voice: harsh, scolding call; whistled *peter peter peter* song.
Similar Species: *Black-crested Titmouse* (p. 298): pale forehead; black crest; orange sides. *Juniper Titmouse* (p. 454): uniform gray overall; gray crest.
Best Sites: open woodlands within the breeding range.

BLACK-CRESTED TITMOUSE

Baeolophus atricristatus

Like the Tufted Titmouse (of which it was once believed to be a subspecies) the Black-crested comes to bird feeders and actively seeks sunflower seeds, which it pounds open. This species also associates with other small birds in flocks during the nonbreeding season and raises a fuss when disturbed, which quickly attracts other song birds. Although this bird's voice is not as distinctive as that of the Tufted Titmouse, it is easily recognizable. • These birds either seek out an existing cavity or excavate a new one in rotting wood to lay their eggs and raise their young. Black-crested Titmice feed in trees and shrubs, eating seeds, insects and other arthropods. • Black-crested Titmice narrowly overlap in their Texas distribution with Tufted Titmice. In the areas of overlap, the vocalizations are more distinct.

ID: gray upperparts; white forehead; black crest; white underparts with orange flanks.
Size: *L* 6–6½ in; *W* 10 in.
Status: common resident in north-central Texas and the eastern Panhandle, south through the Edwards Plateau to the Lower Rio Grande Valley and west to the eastern part of the Trans-Pecos.
Habitat: mostly open woodlands, especially "cedar breaks" on the Edwards Plateau.

Nesting: seeks out an existing cavity or constructs one in soft wood; lines the cavity with soft materials, including hair; pair incubates 5–6 white to creamy-white eggs, finely speckled with dark brown, for 12–14 days.
Feeding: forages in woody vegetation, occasionally on the ground.
Voice: similar to that of the Tufted Titmouse, but higher pitched and more rapid.
Similar Species: *Tufted Titmouse* (p. 297): black forehead; gray crest. *Juniper Titmouse* (p. 454): uniform gray overall, including crest.
Best Sites: open woodlands within the breeding range.

VERDIN

Auriparus flaviceps

Once classified as a member of the chickadee family, the Verdin is now considered to be North America's only member of the Remizidae family—the Old World tits. • During breeding season, males build several nests, only one of which will be used for brooding. The other nests provide shaded daytime roosts or nighttime protection. Nests built early in spring face away from the wind for added warmth, but nests constructed later face toward the wind and allow breezes to cool eggs hatched under the intense summer sun. Young Verdin leave the nest when they are about 21 days old. Both adults and immatures may return to the main nest or use alternate nest sites at any time of the year for roosting. • Native trees, shrubs, cactus and wildflowers in your yard can provide attractive habitat for the Verdin—thorny shrubs such as paloverde, mesquite, hawthorn and cholla cactus are particular favorites.

ID: gray overall, paler below; yellow head and throat; dark lores; short, black bill; dark eyes; red shoulder patch (sometimes hidden). *Immature:* gray head and shoulder; base of lower mandible is yellowish to pinkish.

Size: *L* 4–4½ in; *W* 6½ in.

Status: uncommon to common resident from the central Coastal Plain and Lower Rio Grande Valley north to the southern Panhandle and Rolling Plains and west through the Trans-Pecos.

Habitat: desert, thorny scrub thickets, riparian woods and low-elevation mesquite woodlands; common inhabitant of townsites and suburban parks and gardens.

Nesting: in a thorny shrub, low tree or cholla cactus; female chooses among many nests built by male; hollow, spherical to oval nest of thorny twigs is lined with grass, leaves, feathers and spider silk; female incubates

4–5 green to blue-green eggs with reddish brown spots for about 10 days.

Feeding: insects are caught during active foraging among foliage, stems and branches or on the wing; forages in flocks outside of breeding season; may eat berries, seeds and spiders; often takes nectar from flowers or hummingbird feeders.

Voice: call is a rapid *chip* series; song is 3–4 loud, whistled notes *tsee-tsee-tsee* (2nd note is higher).

Similar Species: *Bushtit* (p. 300): brown ear patch; all black bill; no yellow on head; no red shoulder patch; female has yellow eyes.

Best Sites: any park with appropriate habitat.

BUSHTIT

Psaltriparus minimus

There is a saying that the quality of the home reflects the character of its occupant. If it is true, then the tiny Bushtit is a noble resident. The intricate weave and elaborate shape of its hanging nest is an example of splendid architecture that is worthy of admiration and respect. • Intruders that violate the sanctity of a nest site can force the adults to switch mates, desert the nest or build a new one in a different location. • Best described as a hyperactive, tiny, gray cottonball with a long, narrow tail, the Bushtit seems to be constantly on the move. It bounces from one shrubby perch to another, looking for something to keep its hungry little engine running. • When they are not fully engrossed in the business of raising young, Bushtits travel in bands of up to 40 birds, filling the brushlands and woodlands with their charming bell-like tinkles. • *Psaltriparus* is derived from the Greek word *psaltris*, meaning "player of the lute" (or zither) and *parus*, the former Latin generic name for a titmouse.

ID: uniform, gray plumage; light brown cheek patch; long tail; no crest; coastal birds have brown cap. *Male:* dark eyes. *Female:* light eyes.

Size: *L* 4½ in; *W* 6 in.

Status: uncommon to common resident from the eastern and southern Panhandle south through Rolling and High Plains, the Edwards Plateau and the Trans-Pecos.

Habitat: various brushlands and woodlands, including pinyon-juniper-mahogany woodlands, riparian thickets, open oak woodlands, oak savannah and chaparral.

Nesting: pair builds a sock-like, hanging nest in a shrub or tree, woven with moss, lichens, cocoons, spider silk, fur and feathers, which can take up to 50 days to complete; pair incubates 5–7 white eggs for 12 days.

Feeding: gleans vegetation for insects; also eats small seeds; forages in constantly roving, cohesive flocks most of the year.

Voice: excited lisping notes; trilled alarm call.

Similar Species: *Juniper Titmouse* (p. 454): small crest; relatively shorter tail; lighter colored legs; no brown cheek patch. *Ruby-crowned Kinglet* (p. 315): distinct wing bars and eye ring; greener overall; persistently flicks wings. *Verdin* (p. 299): yellow head, red shoulder patch.

Best Sites: any park with appropriate habitat.

RED-BREASTED NUTHATCH

Sitta canadensis

The Red-breasted Nuthatch may look a little like a woodpecker, but it moves down tree trunks headfirst, cleaning up the seeds, insects and nuts that woodpeckers may have overlooked. • Red-breasted Nuthatches frequently join in on bird waves—groups of warblers, chickadees, kinglets, titmice and small woodpeckers that forage together through woodlands in winter or during migration. Nuthatches stand out from the other songbirds because of their unusual body form and habit of moving headfirst down tree trunks. When present, this irruptive species regularly visits backyard feeders in fall and winter. • The Red-breasted Nuthatch smears the entrance of its nest cavity with pitch from pine or spruce trees, perhaps to stop ants and other animals from entering.

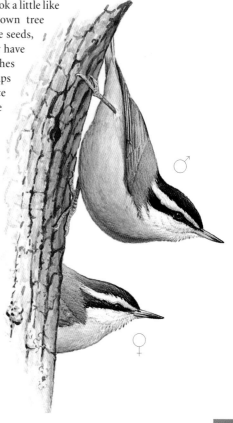

ID: rusty underparts; gray-blue upperparts; white eyebrow; black eye line; black cap; straight bill; short tail; white cheek. *Male:* deeper rust on breast; black crown. *Female:* light red wash on breast; dark gray crown. *In flight:* stubby look, with short, rounded wings and short tail with white flashes; fast, direct flight.

Size: *L* 4–4½ in; *W* 8 in.

Status: irregular and rare to uncommon migrant and winter visitor across the state; rarely in the South Texas Brushlands; irregular and rare summer resident in the Guadalupe Mts.

Habitat: mixed woodlands, especially those near birdfeeders.

Nesting: does not regularly nest in Texas.

Feeding: forages down trees while probing under loose bark for larval and adult invertebrates; eats pine and spruce seeds in winter; frequents feeders.

Voice: calls include slow, continually repeated, nasal *yank-yank-yank* or *rah-rah-rah-rah* and a short *tsip;* song consists of a series of slow, rising nasal notes *eeen, eeen.*

Similar Species: *White-breasted Nuthatch* (p. 302): larger; no black eye line or red underparts; undulating flight; white underwing patches. *Brown-headed Nuthatch* (p. 303): smaller; brown head; large white spot on nape; gray back; pale underparts; less white on wing and tail; heavier bill. *Pygmy Nuthatch* (p. 454): smaller; brownish gray head; paler back; light buff sides; gray flanks; heavier bill; limited to Guadalupe Mts. and Davis Mts.

Best Sites: *Winter:* mixed woodlands; feeders.

WHITE-BREASTED NUTHATCH

Sitta carolinensis

For a novice birder, seeing a White-breasted Nuthatch calling repeatedly while clinging to the underside of a branch is an odd sight. Moving headfirst down a tree trunk, the White-breasted Nuthatch forages for invertebrates, occasionally issuing a noisy call. • Unlike woodpeckers and creepers, nuthatches do not use their tails to brace themselves against tree trunks—they grasp the tree through foot power alone. • Nuthatches are presumably named for their habit of wedging seeds and nuts into crevices and hacking them open with their bills. • A regular visitor to most backyard feeders, the White-breasted Nuthatch sticks around just long enough to grab a seed and then dash off. Only an offering of peanut butter can persuade this tiny bird to remain in a single spot for any length of time.

ID: white underparts; white face; gray-blue back; rusty undertail coverts; short tail; short legs. *Male:* black cap. *Female:* dark gray cap.

Size: *L* 5½–6 in; *W* 11 in.

Status: rare to uncommon resident in the eastern third of the state north of the Coastal Plain, extending into the north-central region and in the Trans-Pecos Mts.; rare to uncommon migrant and winter visitor to most of Texas but absent from the South Plains, the upper and lower Coastal Plain and the Lower Rio Grande Valley.

Habitat: mixed forests, woodlots and wooded backyards.

Nesting: in a natural cavity or an abandoned woodpecker nest in a large deciduous tree; female lines the cavity with bark, grass, fur and feathers; female incubates 5–8 brown-spotted, white eggs for 12–14 days.

Feeding: forages headfirst down trees in search of larval and adult invertebrates; also eats nuts and seeds; regularly visits feeders.

Voice: calls include *ha-ha-ha ha-ha-ha, ank ank* and *ip;* song is a fast, nasal *yank-hank yank-hank*, lower than that of the Red-breasted Nuthatch.

Similar Species: *Brown-headed Nuthatch* (p. 303): brown cap; white spot on nape. *Red-breasted Nuthatch* (p. 301): black eye line; rusty underparts. *Carolina Chickadee* (p. 296): black "bib"; smaller bill.

Best Sites: Fairfield Lake SP; Huntsville SP; Tyler SP; Big Bend NP; Guadalupe Mountains NP.

BROWN-HEADED NUTHATCH

Sitta pusilla

One of the very few bird species found exclusively in the United States, the Brown-headed Nuthatch is endemic to the pine forests of the Deep South, including the Pineywoods of eastern Texas. It is also one of very few North American birds to use tools. Employing a flake of bark or a cone bract to pry off other bark flakes in search of prey hiding underneath, a bird may carry the tool from tree to tree or discard it once prey is found. • Like other nuthatches, the Brown-headed commonly forages in large, multi-species flocks that usually include Eastern Bluebirds, Carolina Chickadees, Tufted Titmice and Pine Warblers, along with other species during winter. • During the breeding season, when adult pairs break away from larger groups to establish small breeding territories, a nonbreeding male may join such a pair. This "helper" aids in excavating the nest cavity, gathering the soft nest lining or feed the nestlings.

ID: short, straight bill; dull blue-gray backs and wings; brownish gray nape and crown; white nape patch, cheek and throat; whitish underparts.

Size: L 4½ in; W 7½ in.

Status: rare to locally common resident in the Pineywoods of east Texas, south to the upper Coastal Plain.

Habitat: open and mixed pine woodlands.

Nesting: in a dead pine tree; pair excavates a nest cavity (often with many partial excavations) or may use an existing cavity; cavity is lined with softer materials; male feeds the female as she incubates 4–7 profusely speckled, white eggs for 13–15 days; pair

(and often a male "helper") raises young; may have 2 broods.

Feeding: forages along tree branches and trunks for pine seeds and insects; commonly seen walking headfirst down tree trunks; male may forage lower on tree; often stores seeds under pine bark for later retrieval.

Voice: repeated double call note has a squeaky quality; nasal, twittering *bit bit bit* call often given by foraging flocks.

Similar Species: *Red-breasted Nuthatch* (p. 301): black crown and eye line; white eyebrow and cheeks; rusty red to orange underparts. *White-breasted Nuthatch* (p. 302): larger; white face; male has dark stripe on crown. *Carolina Chickadee* (p. 296): black "bib"; smaller bill.

Best Sites: Daingerfield SP; Huntsville SP; Lake Livingston SP; Tyler SP; W.G. Jones State Forest.

BROWN CREEPER

Certhia americana

Never easy to find, the cryptic Brown Creeper inhabits old-growth forests for much of the year, and it often goes unnoticed until what looked like a flake of bark suddenly takes the shape of a bird. If a creeper is frightened, it freezes and flattens itself against a tree trunk, becoming even more difficult to see. • The Brown Creeper feeds by slowly spiraling up a tree trunk, searching for hidden invertebrates. When it reaches the upper branches, the creeper floats down to the base of a neighboring tree to begin another foraging ascent. Its long, stiff tail feathers prop it up against vertical tree trunks as it hitches its way skyward. • Like the call of the Golden-crowned Kinglet, the thin whistle of the Brown Creeper is so high pitched that many birders can't hear it. To increase the confusion, the creeper's song often takes on the boisterous, warbling quality of a wood-warbler song. • Many species of creepers inhabit Europe and Asia, but the Brown Creeper is the only member of its family found in North America.

Habitat: mature deciduous, coniferous and mixed forests, especially in wet areas with large dead trees; also found near bogs.

Nesting: a cavity in dead wood of a tree; nest of grass and conifer needles is woven together with spider silk; female incubates 5–6 whitish eggs, dotted with reddish brown, for 14–17 days.

Feeding: hops up tree trunks and large limbs, probing loose bark for adult and larval invertebrates.

Voice: high *tseee* call; faint, high-pitched song: *trees-trees-trees see the trees.*

Similar Species: plumage is unique. *Carolina Wren* (p. 308) and *Nuthatches* (p. 301–03, 454) forage on trunks but do not ascend trunks spiral fashion.

Best Sites: Guadalupe Mountains NP. *Winter:* almost any wooded area.

ID: mottled, brown and white upperparts; brown head; pale eyebrow; white throat; short, downcurved bull; white underparts; buffy undertail coverts; uses tail as prop.

Size: *L* 5–5½ in; *W* 7½ in.

Status: rare to uncommon migrant and winter visitor east of the Pecos R.; rare resident in the Guadalupe Mts.

CACTUS WREN

Campylorhynchus brunneicapillus

Throughout the hot Southern days, when most desert creatures are seeking shade, the Cactus Wren remains active. Perched upon a thorny bush, it utters loud, harsh calls throughout the day and year-round. Although its size distinguishes the Cactus Wren from other wrens, its heavily spotted breast may cause some birdwatchers to mistake it for a thrasher. • Bold and curious, the Cactus Wren is often approachable. It has even been known to forage for dead or dying insects stuck to the front grills of parked cars. Unlike other wrens, this one makes up to 20 percent of its diet with small fruits, berries, seeds and nectar. • This large wren weaves its football-shaped nest tightly within an impregnable fortress of cactus spines or thorny shrubs. The needle-sharp spines protect the nestlings from predators, including snakes, lizards, mammals and larger birds. As the female incubates her eggs, the male may build several other nests to use as roosting sites.

ID: relatively large; prominent white eyebrow; dark crown; long, curved bill; streaked back; black and white barring on wings and tail; densely spotted underparts.

Size: *L* 8½ in; *W* 11 in.

Status: locally common resident from the Lower Rio Grande Valley onto the central Coastal Plain, north through southern and western Edwards Plateau and west through the South Plains and the Trans-Pecos.

Habitat: desert habitats, chaparral and townsites with an abundance of cactus (especially cholla cactus), yucca, mesquite and other thorny shrubs.

Nesting: among the spines of a cholla cactus or thorny shrub; pair builds a bulky, domed, elongated nest of vegetation, animal hair and feathers; female incubates 4–5 pale,

purple-spotted eggs for 15–18 days; pair raises young; may mate for life.

Feeding: forages on the ground or at a tree base; probes for insects and spiders; may also eat small lizards and plant material including nectar, berries, seeds and small fruit.

Voice: year-round song is a low, harsh series of notes: *chur chur chur chur chur.*

Similar Species: *Thrashers* (p. 330–33, 454): no white eyebrows; unstreaked, gray-brown backs; unbarred wings and tails; *Canyon Wren* (p. 307): smaller; no white eye-brow; very long bill; rufous overall with white throat and upper breast.

Best Sites: Balmorhea SP; Garner SP; Goliad SP; Seminole Canyon SP.

ROCK WREN

Salpinctes obsoletus

Well-camouflaged plumage, secretive habits and echoing calls can make the Rock Wren difficult to spot. Singing males are experts at remaining concealed while bouncing their buzzy, trilling songs off canyon walls, maximizing the range and aural effect of the sound. • Rock Wren nests may be built in a sheltered, rocky crevice, in an animal burrow or even in an abandoned building. Nest entrances are typically "paved" with a few (occasionally up to 1600!) pebbles, bones or other debris items. This paving may protect the nest from moisture, make it easier to find in confusing rocky terrain or serve some other purpose. • Rock Wrens are typically identified at long range by their habit of bobbing atop prominent boulders. • *Salpinctes* is from the Greek word for "trumpeter," in reference to this bird's exclamatory call. The term *obsoletus* is Latin for "indistinct," describing the bird's dull, cryptic plumage.

Habitat: talus slopes, scree, outcrops, stony barrens and similar places with abundant crevices.

Nesting: in a crevice, hole or burrow; often places small stones at the opening; nest of grass and rootlets is lined with various items; female incubates 5–6 speckled, white eggs for up to 14 days.

ID: bluish gray to grayish brown upperparts with intricate light and dark flecking; cinnamon rump and tail; light underparts; finely streaked, white throat and breast; white eyebrow; slender bill; short, buff-tipped tail.

Size: *L* 6 in; *W* 9 in.

Status: common summer resident in western Texas and east through the Edwards Plateau and the Rolling Plains; common winter resident in the Trans-Pecos and uncommon in the Panhandle and along the Rio Grande.

Feeding: forages among rocks, boulders and logs and on the ground for insects and spiders.

Voice: repeated, accented 1–2-note phrases: *tra-lee tra-lee tra-lee; tick-EAR* alarm call.

Similar Species: *Canyon Wren* (p. 307): clean white throat; brown underparts; no eyebrow; very long bill. *House Wren* (p. 310): much smaller; unflecked, brown upperparts; shorter bill. *Bewick's Wren* (p. 309): grayish brown upperparts and rump; bold, white eyebrow borders dark eye line; clean white throat and breast.

Best Sites: Franklin Mountains SP; Guadalupe Mountains NP; Davis Mountains SP; Big Bend NP; Garner SP.

CANYON WREN

Catherpes mexicanus

Heard far more often than it is seen, the Canyon Wren has a beautiful, clear song that echoes across broad canyons, rippling and cascading downward in pitch as if recounting the action of tumbling pebbles. • With a somewhat flattened body shape, the Canyon Wren is able to pass easily through narrow crevices. This small bird forages tirelessly, even during the hottest parts of the day, searching nooks and crevices for hidden insects and spiders. Its quick, gliding movements suggest a small rodent. • While foraging and moving about its territory, a Canyon Wren quickly raises and lowers its hindquarters every few seconds, giving birders a clue to the bird's identity. • *Catherpes* is the latinized form of the Greek word *katherpein*, meaning "to creep."

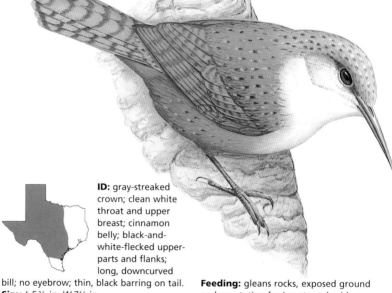

ID: gray-streaked crown; clean white throat and upper breast; cinnamon belly; black-and-white-flecked upperparts and flanks; long, downcurved bill; no eyebrow; thin, black barring on tail.

Size: *L* 5¾ in; *W* 7½ in.

Status: uncommon to locally common resident in the western half of the state, through the Rolling Plains and Edwards Plateau and south to the central Coastal Plain.

Habitat: precipitous cliffs, steep-walled streamside canyons, boulder piles and rocky slopes and outcroppings.

Nesting: in a crevice under rocks, on a ledge or on a shelf in a cave; cup nest of moss, twigs and spider silk is lined with fur and feathers; female incubates 5–6 lightly spotted, white eggs for up to 18 days; pair feeds the young.

Feeding: gleans rocks, exposed ground and vegetation for insects and spiders.

Voice: flat *jeet* call; song is a startling, descending, whistled *dee-ah dee-ah dee-ah dah-dah-dah.*

Similar Species: *Rock Wren* (p. 306): lightly streaked throat and upper breast; faint white eyebrow; bluish gray to grayish brown upperparts; light underparts; less partial to vertical cliffs. *Other wrens* (pp. 305–13): much shorter bills; prominent eyebrows.

Best Sites: Pedernales Falls SP; Guadalupe River SP; Palo Duro Canyon SP; Davis Mountains SP; Guadalupe Mountains NP; Seminole Canyon SP.

CAROLINA WREN

Thryothorus ludovicianus

Shy and retiring at times, the energetic Carolina Wren often hides deep inside dense shubbery, so wait until this large wren sits on a conspicuous perch and unleashes its impressive song. Pairs perform lively "duets" at any time of day and in any season, often beginning with introductory chatter by the female and followed by innumerable ringing variations of *tea-kettle tea-kettle tea-kettle tea* by her mate. • Watch for Carolina Wrens creeping up tree trunks or flitting low in search of food. They frequent most wooded habitats, but, because they forage and nest close to the ground, they cannot persist in heavily developed areas, where cats and other dangers lurk. Elsewhere, they readily nest in the brushy thickets of an overgrown backyard or in an obscure nook or crevice in a house or barn. Carolina Wrens seems to be able to make do with almost any nest cavity, including against radiators of cars and in forgotten boots and empty plant pots!

ID: rich brown upperparts, including nape and crown; longish, slightly downcurved bill; bold white eyebrow; rusty cheek; white throat; rich buffy underparts; relatively long tail.
Size: *L* 5½ in; *W* 7½ in.
Status: common resident in the eastern two-thirds of Texas, west through the Rolling Plains and Edwards Plateau and south to the Lower Rio Grande Valley, and rare to uncommon in the Panhandle.
Habitat: dense forest undergrowth, especially shrubby tangles and thickets.
Nesting: pair builds a dome nest in either an open cavity or unused garden nook;

female incubates 4–6 brown-flecked, creamy white eggs for 12–14 days; pair raises the young; 1–3 broods per season.
Feeding: usually in pairs on the ground and among vegetation; eats mostly insects and other invertebrates; also takes berries, fruits and seeds; takes peanuts and suet at feeders.
Voice: loud *tea-kettle-tea-kettle-tea-kettle* (or *video-vide- video* or *cheeseburger-cheeseburger-cheeseburger-cheese,* etc.); also a loud, ringing *churt* call.
Similar Species: *Bewick's Wren* (p. 309): lighter upperparts; white-tipped tail. *House Wren* (p. 310) and *Winter Wren* (p. 311): no prominent white eyebrow. *Red-breasted Nuthatch* (p. 301): blue-gray upperparts; black crown); calls not loud and ringing; descends trees headfirst; partial to pines.
Best Sites: parks with shrubby habitat.

BEWICK'S WREN

Thryomanes bewickii

This charming brown mite seems to investigate all the nooks and crevices of its territory with endless curiosity and exuberant animation. As a Bewick's Wren briefly perches to scan its surroundings for sources of food, its long, narrow tail flits and waves from side to side, occasionally flashing with added verve as the bird scolds an approaching intruder. • Bewick's Wren populations west of the Mississippi River are better off than those to the east, where numbers are declining because of habitat loss. • John James Audubon chose to honor Thomas Bewick in the name of this spirited bird. A respected friend of Audubon's, Bewick was an exceptionally talented wood engraver and the author and illustrator of *A History of British Birds*.

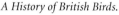

ID: long, bold white eyebrow; long tail trimmed with white spots; rich brown or grayish brown upperparts; clean, whitish underparts; slender, downcurved bill.
Size: *L* 5 ¼ in; *W* 7 in.

Status: uncommon to common resident in the western two-thirds of Texas, east into the Oak Woods & Prairies and the Edwards Plateau and south to the central Coastal Plain; uncommon to common migrant and winter resident across the state but rare on the upper Coastal Plain.

Habitat: chaparral, riparian thickets, dense vines and shrubby tangles bordering woodlands, parks and gardens, shrublands within pinyon-juniper or oak woodlands.
Nesting: often in a natural cavity or an abandoned woodpecker nest (sometimes in a bird box); nest of sticks and grass is lined with feathers; female incubates 5–7 white eggs, with dark speckles, for up to 14 days.
Feeding: gleans vegetation for insects, especially caterpillars, grasshoppers, beetles and spiders.
Voice: bold, clear *chick-click, for me-eh, for you*; peevish *dzeeeb* or *knee-deep* alarm call.
Similar Species: *Carolina Wren* (p. 308): richer, reddish brown back; buffy underparts. *House Wren* (p. 310) and *Winter Wren* (p. 311): shorter tail; faint buff eyebrow.
Best Sites: Lake Mineral Wells SP; Pedernales Falls SP; Lost Maples SP; Cedar Hills SP; Meridian SP.

HOUSE WREN

Troglodytes aedon

From nearby, the House Wren's loud, distinctive chatter will undoubtedly give away its presence. Hearing a House Wren is one thing, but getting a good look at this energetic little bird is quite another. It often hides among tangled bushes and brush piles, moving rapidly from one location to another, sending bird-watchers crashing through the brambles in pursuit. • This nervous bird spends winter in Texas and then announces the coming of spring with a bubbly song. It stays as a common summer resident in the northeastern Panhandle only, becoming rare farther west. • The scientific name of the House Wren reflects the similarity of the bird's wonderfully warbled song to that of a nightingale. In Greek mythology, Aedon was the jealous queen of Thebes, who accidentally killed her own son after plotting to murder her nephew. To ease her grief, Zeus transformed Aedon into a nightingale.

Nesting: in a natural or artificial cavity or abandoned woodpecker nest; cuplike depression in a pile of sticks is lined with feathers and fur; female incubates 6–8 heavily marked, white eggs for 12–15 days.
Feeding: gleans the ground and vegetation for insects, especially beetles, caterpillars, grasshoppers and spiders.
Voice: call consists of a variety of dry, short and often soft notes; smooth, running, bubbly, warbling song, *tsi-tsi-tsi-tsi oodle-oodle-oodle-oodle*, lasts about 2–3 seconds.
Similar Species: *Winter Wren* (p. 311): smaller; darker overall; much shorter, stubby tail; prominent dark barring on flanks. *Sedge Wren* (p. 312): faint white streaking on dark crown and back.
Best Sites: unpredictable; brushy thickets in parks, national refuges and wildlife management areas.

ID: brown upper-parts; fine, dark barring on upper wings and lower back; faint, pale eyebrow and eye ring; short, upraised tail finely barred with black; whitish throat; whitish to buff underparts; faintly barred flanks.
Size: *L* 4½–5 in; *W* 6 in.
Status: common to uncommon winter resident in most of the state, although rare in the north-central region.
Habitat: thickets and shrubby areas in or at the edges of deciduous or mixed woodlands or near buildings.

WINTER WREN

Troglodytes troglodytes

The upraised, mottled brown tail of the Winter Wren matches the gnarled, upturned roots and decomposing tree trunks it calls home. Although the Winter Wren blends well with its habitat, its distinctive, song gives away its presence and distinguishes it from other forest songbirds. The Winter Wren has one of the most vibrant songs of any species and certainly the loudest in terms of its relative size. Its song can be heard throughout the year, usually in the early morning during winter. • Winter Wrens occur in Texas from September to May. They are most common in northeastern and north-central Texas, where they lay claim to patches of moist coniferous forest. • This bird is known simply as "Wren" in other parts of the Northern Hemisphere.

ID: barred dark brown upperparts; short, upraised, barred tail; brown or rufous brown underparts, barred on flanks and undertail coverts; paler eyebrow; thin, dark bill; flesh-colored or dusky orange legs; northern migrants are paler in coloration.
Size: *L* 4 in; *W* 5½ in.
Status: uncommon migrant and winter resident in much of the state; rare from the South Plains to the Edwards Plateau.
Habitat: lowland forests, woodlands, thickets, brush piles and less often gardens.

Nesting: does not nest in Texas.
Feeding: forages on the ground, around tree trunks and in wood piles and tangles for invertebrates; also picks aquatic insects and larvae from the water surface or just below, especially in pools below tree roots.
Voice: the double-noted call has hard *tsip-tsip* or *chat-chat;* complex song includes trills and buzzes.
Similar Species: *House Wren* (p. 310): larger; longer tail; paler brown overall; longer, downcurved bill; shorter song; prefers drier and more open habitats. *Marsh Wren* (p. 313): more rufous; largely unstreaked; longer tail; rattling song; found only in aquatic vegetation.
Best Sites: unpredictable; Dinosaur Valley SP; Cedar Hill SP; Village Creek Wastewater Treatment Plant (Arlington); Bear Creek Pioneer Park (Houston).

SEDGE WREN

Cistothorus platensis

L ike most wrens, the Sedge Wren is secretive and difficult to observe. It is the least familiar of all our wrens, because it keeps itself well concealed in dense stands of sedges and tall, wet grass. This wren is also less loyal to specific sites than other wrens and may totally disappear from an area after a few years. Its transient nature may have to do with its unstable habitat, which changes annually with natural flooding and drying cycles. • Sedge Wrens breed in the northeastern United States and the Canadian Prairies. They are common to uncommon migrants through the eastern half of Texas and can be locally common winter residents along the Coastal Plain. • The scientific term *platensis* refers to the Rio de la Plata in Argentina, where another isolated population of this wren is found. • This bird used to be known as "Short-billed Marsh Wren" until the name was changed to emphasize habitat differences between it and the similar Marsh Wren.

Habitat: brackish or freshwater sedge meadows, marshes, bogs, beaver ponds and abandoned wet fields with dense weeds or grass; also pine savannas.
Nesting: does not nest in Texas.
Feeding: forages low in dense vegetation, for adult and larval insects and spiders; occasionally catches flying insects.
Voice: heard in northern Texas in spring; sharp *chat* or *chep* call; song is a few short, staccato notes followed by a rattling trill: *chap-chap-chap-chap, chap, churr-r-r-r-r-r*.
Similar Species: *Marsh Wren* (p. 313): conspicuous broad, white eyebrow; prominent white streaking on black back; unstreaked crown; prefers cattail marshes. *Winter Wren* (p. 311): darker overall; shorter, stubby tail; unstreaked crown. *House Wren* (p. 310): unstreaked, dark brown crown and back.
Best Sites: Sea Rim SP; Anahuac NWR; Brazoria NWR; Galveston Island SP; San Bernard NWR.

ID: short, narrow tail (often upraised); faint, pale eyebrow; dark crown and back faintly streaked with white; barring on wing coverts; whitish underparts with buff orange sides, flanks and undertail coverts.
Size: *L* 4–4½ in; *W* 5½ in.
Status: common to abundant migrant and winter resident on the Coastal Plain and uncommon and local in the rest of eastern Texas.

MARSH WREN

Cistothorus palustris

Fueled by newly emerged aquatic insects, the Marsh Wren zips about in short bursts through the tall grasses and cattails that surround wetlands. This expert hunter catches flying insects with lightning speed, but don't expect to see the Marsh Wren in action—this reclusive bird prefers to remain hidden deep within its dense marshland habitat. A patient observer might be rewarded with a brief glimpse of a Marsh Wren, but it is more likely that this bird's distinctive song will inform you of its presence. • This wren occasionally destroys the nests and eggs of other Marsh Wrens and other marsh-nesting songbirds such as the Red-winged Blackbird. Other birds are usually prevented from doing the same, because the Marsh Wren's globe nest keeps the eggs well hidden, and several decoy nests help to divert predators from the real nest. • This bird was formerly known as "Long-billed Marsh Wren."

ID: white chin and belly; white to light brown upperparts; white-streaked, black triangle on upper back; bold white eyebrow; unstreaked, brown crown; long, thin, downcurved bill.

Size: *L* 5 in; *W* 6 in.

Status: common resident in the marshes of the upper and central Coastal Plain and rare along the Rio Grande in Brewster Co.; rare to locally common migrant and winter resident statewide.

Habitat: freshwater, saltwater and brackish wetlands surrounded by tall grasses, bulrushes or cattails interspersed with open water; occasionally in tall grass-sedge marshes.

Nesting: in a brackish or salt marsh among cattails or tall emergent vegetation; weaves a globelike nest of cattails, bulrushes, weeds and grass and lines it with cattail down; female incubates 4–6 darkly marked, white to pale brown eggs for 12–16 days.

Feeding: gleans vegetation and flycatches for adult aquatic invertebrates, especially dragonflies and damselflies.

Voice: call is a harsh *chek. Male:* rapid, rattling, staccato warble sounds like an old-fashioned treadle sewing machine.

Similar Species: *Sedge Wren* (p. 312): smaller; streaked crown. *House Wren* (p. 310): faint eyebrow; unstreaked, black back. *Carolina Wren* (p. 308): larger; buff underparts; unstreaked, black back.

Best Sites: Sea Rim SP; McFaddin NWR; Galveston Island SP; Brazoria NWR.

GOLDEN-CROWNED KINGLET

Regulus satrapa

Not much larger than a hummingbird, the Golden-crowned Kinglet can be difficult to spot as it flits and hovers among coniferous treetops. Its high-pitched *tsee-tsee-tsee* call often goes unnoticed or gets lost in the woodland breeze. • Binoculars are a must to distinguish tiny Golden-crowned Kinglets from similar-sized Ruby-crowned Kinglets. If the yellow crown is hidden from view, look to the eyes—Golden-crowned Kinglets have a prominent white eye stripe whereas Ruby-crowned Kinglets sport a white eye ring. • In the northern part of their range, Golden-crowned Kinglets manage to survive low winter temperatures by roosting together in groups, often in empty squirrel nests. Like chickadees, these birds can lower their body temperatures at night to conserve energy.

ID: olive back; darker wings and tail; light underparts; dark cheek; 2 white wing bars; black eye line; white eyebrow; black border crown. *Male:* reddish orange crown. *Female:* yellow crown.
Size: *L* 4 in; *W* 7 in.
Status: uncommon to locally common migrant and winter resident statewide.
Habitat: coniferous, deciduous and mixed forests and woodlands.

Nesting: does not nest in Texas.
Feeding: gleans and hovers among the forest canopy for insects, berries and occasionally sap.
Voice: very high-pitched *tsee tsee tsee* call; song is a faint, high-pitched, accelerating *tsee-tsee-tsee-tsee, why do you shilly-shally?*
Similar Species: *Ruby-crowned Kinglet* (p. 315): broken, bold white eye ring; no black border to crown. *Carolina Chickadee* (p. 296): lacks bright, colorful crown.
Best Sites: any park, wildlife management area or national wildlife refuge with open woodlands.

RUBY-CROWNED KINGLET

Regulus calendula

Among the little brown perching birds that overwinter in Texas, the Ruby-crowned Kinglet is one of the most abundant. This energetic little bird visits birdfeeders or flits among branches along with warblers and vireos. It might be mistaken for an *Empidonax* flycatcher, but the kinglet's frequent hovering and energetic wing-flicking behavior set it apart from look-alikes. The wing flicking is thought to startle insects into movement, allowing the kinglet to spot them and pounce. • The Ruby-crowned Kinglet breeds largely in the western states, Alaska and Canada. The male erects his red crown only during courtship and when defending his territory.

ID: broken, bold white eye ring; 2 bold white wing bars; olive green upperparts; dark wings and tail; whitish to yellowish underparts; short tail; flicks its wings. *Male:* small, red crown (usually hidden). *Female:* no red crown.
Size: *L* 4 in; *W* 7½ in.
Status: common to abundant migrant and winter resident statewide.
Habitat: mixed woodlands and pure coniferous forests, especially those dominated by spruce; often found near wet forest openings and edges.
Nesting: does not nest in Texas.

Feeding: gleans and hovers for insects and spiders; also eats seeds and berries.
Voice: usually silent in Texas. *Male:* song is an accelerating and rising *tea-tea-tea-tew-tew-tew look-at-Me, look-at-Me, look-at-Me.*
Similar Species: *Golden-crowned Kinglet* (p. 314): dark cheek; black-bordered crown; male has yellow-bordered, orange crown; female has yellow crown. *Orange-crowned Warbler* (p. 342): no eye ring or wing bars. Empidonax *flycatchers* (pp. 248–56): complete eye ring, if any; larger bill; longer tail; no red crown.
Best Sites: any park, wildlife management area or national wildlife refuge with open woodlands.

BLUE-GRAY GNATCATCHER

Polioptila caerulea

Gnatcatchers are essentially a subtropical genus, yet the tiny Blue-gray Gnat-catcher is a true migrant that has expanded into temperate North America. The hyperactive, tiny Blue-gray Gnatcatcher is a restless inhabitant of wood-lands and brushy areas, flitting from shrub to shrub with its long tail raised in the air and moving from side to side. The scratchy, banjolike twanging calls announce progress and keep pairs close together. During courtship, as early as late April, a male gnatcatcher follows his prospective mate around his territory. Pair-bonded birds are inseparable, and the male takes a greater part in nesting and raising the young than in related species. • *Polioptila* is from the Greek for "gray-feathered," referring to the gray primary edges of the genus, and *caerulea* is Latin for "sky blue."

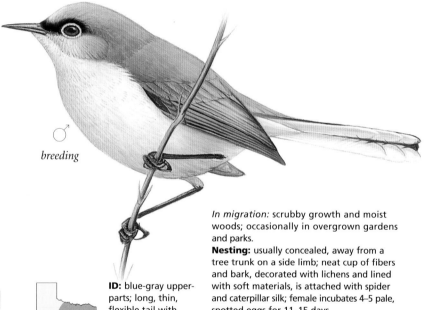

breeding

♂

ID: blue-gray upper-parts; long, thin, flexible tail with flashy white outer feathers; white eye ring; pale gray under-parts; dark legs; thin, dark bill (pale in winter). *Breeding male:* black forehead.
Size: *L* 4½ in; *W* 6½ in.
Status: rare to uncommon summer resident but absent from most of the Rolling Plains and High Plains; common migrant statewide; abundant winter resident in the Lower Rio Grande Valley and uncommon on the Coastal Plain.
Habitat: *Breeding:* abandoned pastures, urban parks, woodlands, floodplains; usu-ally near swamps, ponds, brooks or rivers.

In migration: scrubby growth and moist woods; occasionally in overgrown gardens and parks.
Nesting: usually concealed, away from a tree trunk on a side limb; neat cup of fibers and bark, decorated with lichens and lined with soft materials, is attached with spider and caterpillar silk; female incubates 4–5 pale, spotted eggs for 11–15 days.
Feeding: moves quickly through foliage, peering into cover and flicking its tail; also flycatches and gleans twigs for small insects and spiders.
Voice: calls are thin and high-pitched, single *see* notes or a short series of "mew-ing" or chattering notes; very accomplished songster mimics several species.
Similar Species: *Black-tailed Gnatcatcher* (p. 317) breeding male has black cap and tail. *Bushtit* (p. 300): grayer overall; wholly grayish brown tail; tiny bill; no eye ring; female has white eye; travels in flocks.
Best Sites: outer edges of woodland upper canopies; dry mesquite thickets; brushy grasslands.

BLACK-TAILED GNATCATCHER

Polioptila melanura

Two gnatcatchers occur in Texas, and the best way to tell them apart is by voice, range and the amount of white on their tails. As it's name implies, the Black-tailed Gnatcatcher has a mainly black tail, with white outer edges and two white spots on the end of the undertail. This permanent resident of the southwestern Trans-Pecos is usually seen in pairs, and its harsh calls resemble a crow calling at high speed. Similar-looking Blue-gray Gnatcatchers occur throughout Texas, have mainly white undertails and give thin, high-pitched *see* chips or slurs. • Black-tailed Gnatcatchers remain together for life, defending their permanent territories within the dry desert washes of the desert southwest. Breeding begins in February, with the pair building a small nest low within acacia or mesquite bushes. • The scientific name for this species means "black feather, gray tail" in Greek.

breeding

Status: rare to common resident in the Trans-Pecos and south along the Rio Grande to the western half of the South Texas Brush Country.
Habitat: semi-arid to arid deserts; low desert brush; acacia, mesquite and creosote bush.
Nesting: in the fork of a low bush; tightly knit cup of plant material is lined with plant down; pair incubates 3–4 eggs for about 14 days.
Feeding: hovers above foliage, gleaning for insects; sometimes eats seeds and berries.
Voice: raspy *kah-kah-kah;* also mews and gives a quick *chee* call note.
Similar Species: *Blue-gray Gnatcatcher* (p. 316): bluer upperparts; bolder white outer tail feathers; undertail appears mainly white; male has longer, well-defined eyebrow.
Best Sites: Hueco Tanks SP; Big Bend NP; Black Gap WMA; Seminole Canyon SP.

ID: small body; long tail; dark gray upperparts; light gray underparts; black eyebrow; black tail with white outer edges; undertail has 2 white spots per side toward tip. *Breeding male:* black crown.
Size: *L* 4–4½ in; *W* 5½ in.

EASTERN BLUEBIRD

Sialia sialis

Bluebirds are members of the thrush family, a diverse group of birds with slender, blunt bills, fairly long legs and musical, flutelike songs. All three North American bluebird species occur in Texas, but the lovely Eastern Bluebird is the most common and perhaps the most cherished. • This cavity nester's survival has been put to the test—populations have declined in the face of stiff competition from the introduced House Sparrow and European Starling. The removal of standing dead trees has diminished nest site availability, and agricultural pesticides have also negatively affected this insect-eating bird. Thankfully, bluebird enthusiasts have developed "bluebird trails," mounting nest boxes on fence posts along highways and rural roads, allowing Eastern Bluebird numbers to gradually recover. • Eastern Bluebirds are fond of fields, uncultivated farmlands and mature wood edges, but an elevated perch is necessary as a base from which to hunt insects.

ID: chestnut red chin, throat, breast and sides; dark bill and legs; white undertail coverts and belly. *Male:* deep blue upperparts. *Female:* thin, white eye ring; gray-brown head and back tinged with blue; blue wings and tail; paler chestnut on underparts.
Size: *L* 7 in; *W* 13 in.
Status: common summer resident west to the eastern High Plains and the eastern Edwards Plateau but rare on the rest of the High Plains and south to the central Coastal Plain; uncommon to common migrant and winter resident statewide.
Habitat: cropland fencelines, meadows, fallow and abandoned fields, pastures, forest clearings and edges; also golf courses, large lawns and cemeteries.

Nesting: in an abandoned woodpecker cavity, natural cavity or nest box; female builds a cup nest of grass, weed stems and small twigs and lines it with finer materials; mostly the female incubates 4–5 pale blue eggs for 13–16 days.
Feeding: swoops from a perch to pursue flying insects; also forages on the ground for invertebrates.
Voice: chittering *pew* call; rich, warbling *turr, turr-lee, turr-lee* song.
Similar Species: *Mountain Bluebird* (p. 320): blue overall, female may have some chestnut on breast. *Western Bluebird* (p. 319): little range overlap; darker upperparts; blue throat; usually has chestnut shoulder patches. *Indigo Bunting* (p. 417): blue throat, breast and sides; nonbreeding female is brown, with bluish wash on tail.
Best Sites: South Llano River SP; Fairfield Lake SP; Lake Livingston SP; Palmetto SP.

WESTERN BLUEBIRD

Sialia mexicana

Like the feathers of all blue birds, Western Bluebird feathers are not actually pigmented blue. The blue color is a result of the feather's microscopic structure: shiny blues that change hue and intensity with the angle of view are produced by iridescence; dull blues come from "Tyndall scatter," the same process that produces the blue of the sky. • The Guadalupe and Davis mountains mark the eastern limit of the Western Bluebird's breeding range. It is replaced in eastern Texas by the more common Eastern Bluebird. • In much of the breeding range, Western Bluebirds manage to raise two broods of young each year. A second clutch of eggs is often laid just as the first brood has left the nest, even though the first set of young still rely on their parents for food. • In fall and over winter, Western Bluebirds often flock together with Yellow-rumped Warblers around good crops of mistletoe berries or berry-producing shrubs.

ID: chestnut red breast; light gray belly and undertail coverts; dark bill and legs; chestnut shoulder-patch. *Male:* deep blue head, back, wings and throat; chestnut red sides and flanks. *Female:* light eye ring; grayish brown head and back; bluish wings and tail.

Size: *L* 7 in; *W* 13 in.

Status: uncommon resident in the Guadalupe Mts. and Davis Mts.; rare to common migrant and winter resident in the western third of the state and irregular through the Edwards Plateau.

Habitat: *Breeding:* broken oak and oak-conifer woodlands, oak savannahs, riparian woodlands and open pine forests. *In migration* and *winter:* lowland valleys, agricultural lands interspersed by woodlands and tree groves.

Nesting: in an abandoned woodpecker cavity, natural cavity or nest box; nest consists of stems, conifer needles and twigs; female incubates 4–6 blue eggs for up to 17 days.

Feeding: swoops from a perch to pursue flying insects; also forages on the ground for invertebrates; highly reliant on ground foraging or on mistletoe berries in winter.

Voice: soft *few* and harsh *chuck* calls; harsh *cheer cheerful charmer* song.

Similar Species: *Eastern Bluebird* (p. 318): little range overlap; chestnut throat; paler blue upperparts; no chestnut shoulder patch. *Mountain Bluebird* (p. 320): no chestnut on underparts; female is browner overall. *Townsend's Solitaire* (p. 321): grayish overall; white eye ring; peach-colored patches on wings and tail.

Best Sites: Davis Mountains SP; Guadalupe Mountains NP.

MOUNTAIN BLUEBIRD

Sialia currucoides

The vibrant male Mountain Bluebird is like a piece of spring sky come to life. Few birds rival him for good looks, cheerful disposition and boldness—it is not surprising that bluebirds are viewed as the "birds of happiness." Unfortunately for bluebirds, both good and bad have come from close association with humans. They have profited from the clearing of forests, raising of livestock and erection of nest boxes, but they have clearly suffered as a result of fire suppression and the manicuring of overgrown pastures. • The spring and fall migrations of the Mountain Bluebird routinely consist of small groups of birds, but occasional migrating flocks can number more than one hundred. Migrants and winter residents are most common in the Panhandle and the Trans-Pecos, rarely straying farther east.

ID: black eyes, bill and legs. *Male:* sky blue body; upperparts darker than underparts. *Female:* sky blue wings, tail and rump; bluish gray back and head; gray underparts.
Size: *L* 7 in; *W* 14 in.
Status: uncommon to common but irregular migrant and winter resident in the western two-thirds of the state and very rare east through the Edwards Plateau.
Habitat: open forests, forest edges, burned forests, agricultural areas and grasslands.
Nesting: does not usually nest in Texas; 1 breeding record from the Davis Mts.

Feeding: swoops from a perch for flying and terrestrial insects; also forages on the ground for various invertebrates, such as beetles, ants and bugs.
Voice: low *turr turr* call. *Male:* short, warbling song of *chur* notes.
Similar Species: *Eastern Bluebird* (p. 318) and *Western Bluebird* (p. 319): stockier overall; shorter tail; male has vibrant chestnut red breast. *Townsend's Solitaire* (p. 321): gray overall; white eye ring; peach-coloured patches on wings and tail; white outer tail feathers. *Pinyon Jay* (p. 453): larger overall; long, thick bill.
Best Sites: Franklin Mountains SP; Hueco Tanks SP; Balmorhea SP; Davis Mountains SP.

TOWNSEND'S SOLITAIRE

Myadestes townsendi

Few birds characterize the mountain forests of the West better than the Townsend's Solitaire. Slim and graceful, this bird makes up for its plain plumage with remarkable bursts of sustained song. An inconspicuous bird, it perches for minutes at a time at the top of a tall tree or snag or on the upturned roots of a fallen tree. From its perch, it flutters out to catch insects in midair or follows them to the ground and grasps them with a soft pounce. In flight, the warm, peachy wing linings of this beautiful bird shine like sunlight through a bedroom window. • Townsend's Solitaires have the unusual habit of picking fruit off trees while in flight. During winter, these birds defend feeding grounds with berry-laden junipers and other fruit-bearing trees. • Solitaires are true to their name in summer, when they are rarely seen in groups.

Habitat: woodland edges, especially in areas with fruit-bearing shrubs and trees.

Nesting: does not nest in Texas.

Feeding: flycatches and gleans vegetation and the ground for invertebrates and berries; plucks berries from branches while in flight.

Voice: harsh *piink* call. *Male:* long, bubbly, warbling song.

Similar Species: *Gray Catbird* (p. 328): black cap; red undertail coverts. *Western Bluebird* (p. 319) and *Eastern Bluebird* (p. 318): female may have pale orange breast but no peach-colored wing and tail patches or white outer tail feathers. *Mountain Bluebird* (p. 320): female has faint rusty breast and pale blue wings and tail.

Best Sites: Muleshoe NWR; Lake Meredith NRA; Davis Mountains SP; Guadalupe NP; Big Bend NP.

ID: gray body; darker wings and tail; peach-colored wing patches (very evident in flight); long tail; white eye ring; white outer tail feathers. *Immature:* brown body heavily spotted with buff; pale eye ring.

Size: *L* 8½ in; *W* 14½ in.

Status: uncommon to common but irregular migrant and winter resident in the western third of the state and rare through the Edwards Plateau and Rolling Plains.

VEERY

Catharus fuscescens

The Veery is the most reclusive and terrestrial of the *Catharus* thrushes. It nests and forages on the ground among tangled vegetation and gets around not by walking or running but in short, springy hops. • The Veery's reddish plumage distinguishes it from all other thrushes except the heavily spotted Wood Thrush. When startled by an intruder, it either flushes or faces the threat with its faintly streaked buff breast exposed, hoping for concealment. • First described by Alexander Wilson in 1831, the Veery was once best known as "Wilson's Thrush" or "Tawny Thrush." Its present name is an interpretation of its flutelike, cascading song. *Catharus* is derived from a Greek word that means "pure" and refers to the song of the thrush family, whereas *fuscescens* means "dusky."

ID: reddish brown upperparts; thin, pale buff eye ring; streaked cheeks; straight, pale bill; indistinct "mustache"; pale throat; spotted breast; white underparts; pale gray flanks; pale pink legs. *In flight:* clear, broad, buff inner stripe on underwings.
Size: *L* 7 in; *W* 12 in.
Status: uncommon migrant in the eastern half of the state and rare west of the Pecos R.
Habitat: almost any damp woodland habitat.
Nesting: does not nest in Texas.
Feeding: takes insects and fruit on the ground; also gleans foliage and performs short flycatching sallies; partial to beetles, ants and wasps.

Voice: generally silent in Texas; calls include a nasal, braying *jerrr*, a less harsh *veeyer* and a fast, harsh chuckle; song is a smooth, rolling, somewhat nasal series of descending phrases, usually uttered from a low perch.
Similar Species: *Swainson's Thrush* (p. 324): olive brown with russet tinge (especially younger birds); distinct "spectacles"; off-white belly tinged pale rusty; rufous-tinged olive flanks; rising, flutelike song. *Hermit Thrush* (p. 325): obvious rufous coloration restricted to tail (and sometimes back and wings); flutelike song with ascending and descending phrases. *Wood Thrush* (p. 326): slightly larger; bright orange-brown nape; boldly black-spotted underparts. *American Robin* (p. 327): larger; gray back; rustiness only on underparts and wing linings; young birds are spotted down to white undertail coverts.
Best Sites: migrant "traps" on the upper and central Coastal Plain, including Sabine Woods, High Island, Sea Rim SP, Brazos Bend SP and Blucher Park (Corpus Christi).

GRAY-CHEEKED THRUSH

Catharus minimus

The Gray-cheeked Thrush is the least colorful of the spotted thrushes in both plumage and song. What it lacks in appearance, the Gray-cheek more than makes up for in endurance. Some birds nest among willows and stunted black spruce of the Arctic muskeg and migrate, mostly at night, as far south as Peru. The migration route takes this species through eastern Texas, but, if you want to catch a migrant Gray-cheek out in the open, you'll need to arrive early in the morning—pit stops are brief and one glimpse is usually all you get. • A recent revision of North American bird species split the Bicknell's Thrush of the East off from the widespread Gray-cheeked Thrush, but Bicknell's Thrush has not yet been proven to occur in Texas.

ID: gray upperparts; brown-tinged wings and tail; streaked, gray cheeks; straight, relatively pale bill; fairly distinct "mustache"; pale throat; well spotted, buff breast; off-white underparts; olive-tinged gray flanks; pale pink legs. *Juvenile:* well spotted on back and belly until August; slowly loses finer breast streaks and light edge on tertials. *In flight:* clear, broad, buff inner stripe on underwings; brownish tail.

Size: *L* 7–7½ in; *W* 13 in.

Status: uncommon migrant in the eastern half of the state and rare elsewhere.

Habitat: almost any woodlands or thickets at lower elevations, including riparian woodlands, city parks and coastal thickets.

Nesting: does not nest in Texas.

Feeding: gleans vegetation and forages on the ground for invertebrates, including spiders; also eats berries and other small fruits, especially in migration.

Voice: down-slurred *wee-o* call; buzzy, descending *peeez* nocturnal migratory flight call; distinctive, high-pitched, nasal song (heard mostly at dusk or dawn) ends with a clear, descending whistle: *wee-a, wee-o, wee-a, titi, wheeeee.*

Similar Species: *Veery* (p. 322): rusty overall; indistinct eye ring; white belly; gray flanks; descending, flutelike song. *Hermit Thrush* (p. 325): rufous tail coloration (and sometimes on back and wings); flutelike song has ascending and descending phrases.

Best Sites: migrant "traps" on the upper and central Coastal Plain, including Sabine Woods, High Island, Sea Rim SP, Brazos Bend SP and Blucher Park (Corpus Christi).

SWAINSON'S THRUSH

Catharus ustulatus

During its migration through Texas, the Swainson's Thrush may be seen skulking low on the ground under shrubs and tangles, and it occasionally visits backyards and neighborhood parks. Although spring migrants occasionally add their inspiring song to the morning chorus, Texas birders are more likely to hear this thrush's distinctive nocturnal *eep!* call. • Most thrushes feed on the ground, but the Swainson's Thrush is also adept at gleaning the airy heights of trees for food, sometimes briefly hover-gleaning like a warbler or vireo. Search for this thrush in large, mixed species flocks that gather where berries are numerous, but be aware that this wary thrush does not allow many viewing opportunities and often gives a sharp warning call from some distance. • The English-born William Swainson was a zoologist and illustrator in the early 19th century. His name also graces the Swainson's Hawk.

ID: gray-brown upperparts; noticeable buff eye ring; buff wash on cheek and upper breast; spots arranged in streaks on throat and breast; white belly and undertail coverts; brownish gray flanks.

Size: *L* 7 in; *W* 12 in.

Status: uncommon to common migrant in the eastern half of the state and rare to uncommon in the western half.

Habitat: various forested areas, parks and backyards.

Nesting: does not nest in Texas.

Feeding: gleans vegetation and forages on the ground for invertebrates; also eats berries.

Voice: sharp *wick* call; distinctive *eep!* in migration; rarely heard in spring, song is a slow, rolling, rising spiral: *Oh, Aurelia will-ya, will-ya will-yeee.*

Similar Species: *Gray-cheeked Thrush* (p. 323): gray cheek; less buff wash (or none) on breast; no conspicuous eye ring. *Hermit Thrush* (p. 325): reddish tail and rump; grayish brown upperparts; darker breast spotting on whiter breast. *Veery* (p. 322): upperparts more reddish; faint breast streaking; no bold eye ring.

Best Sites: migrant "traps" on the upper and central Coastal Plain, including Sabine Woods, High Island, Sea Rim SP, Brazos Bend SP and Blucher Park (Corpus Christi).

HERMIT THRUSH

Catharus guttatus

This bird is considered to be one of the finest singers of all of North America's birds. Resembling the song of the Swainson's Thrush, the song of the Hermit Thrush is almost always preceded with a single questioning note. However, the Guadalupe Mountains mark the southernmost extension of this bird's breeding range, so the Hermit Thrush is primarily known as a winter resident in Texas, and its song is rarely heard here. This species migrates later in fall and earlier in spring than do the other spotted thrushes. • Although a rufous-colored tail is the trademark of Hermit Thrushes, these birds are otherwise extremely variable in color. The plumage of eastern populations is often tinged with reddish brown, whereas western birds are grayer. • True to its English name, the Hermit Thrush is never encountered in groups. The scientific term *guttatus* is Latin for "spotted" or "speckled," in reference to this bird's breast.

ID: reddish brown tail and rump; reddish brown upperparts; black-spotted throat and breast; pale underparts; gray flanks; thin, whitish eye ring; thin bill; pink legs.

Size: *L* 7 in; *W* 11½ in.

Status: common migrant and winter resident almost statewide, but uncommon in the Panhandle; common summer resident and breeder in the Guadalupe Mts. and Davis Mts.

Habitat: deciduous, mixed or coniferous woodlands; wet coniferous bogs bordered by trees; wooded urban parks.

Nesting: in a small tree or shrub (occasionally on the ground); female builds a bulky cup nest of vegetation; female incubates 4 light blue eggs for 11–13 days.

Feeding: forages on the ground and gleans vegetation for insects and other invertebrates; also eats berries.

Voice: calls include a faint *chuck* and a flutelike *treee;* occasionally heard in spring,

song is a series of beautiful flutelike notes, both rising and falling in pitch, usually preceded by a questioning note.

Similar Species: *Swainson's Thrush* (p. 324): buff cheek; buff wash on breast; grayish brown back and tail. *Veery* (p. 322): lightly streaked upper breast; reddish brown upperparts and tail. *Gray-cheeked Thrush* (p. 323): gray cheek; no conspicuous eye ring. *Fox Sparrow* (p. 400): stockier build; conical bill; brown breast spots.

Best Sites: *Breeding:* Guadalupe Mountains NP; Davis Mountains SP. *In migration:* migrant "traps" on the upper and central Coastal Plain, including Sabine Woods, High Island, Sea Rim SP, Brazos Bend SP and Blucher Park (Corpus Christi).

WOOD THRUSH

Hylocichla mustelina

Although the loud, warbled notes of the Wood Thrush still resound through many of our eastern woodlands and swamps in spring, forest fragmentation and urban sprawl have eliminated much of this bird's traditional nesting habitat. Openings into the forest have allowed for the invasion of open-area predators such as raccoons, skunks, crows, jays and cowbirds. Traditionally, these predators had little access to nests that were hidden deep within vast stands of hardwood forests. Many forests that have been urbanized or developed for agriculture now host families of American Robins rather than the once-prominent Wood Thrushes. Wood Thrushes that do nest in populated areas often fall victim to house cats. • Naturalist and author Henry David Thoreau considered the male Wood Thrush's song to be the most beautiful of avian sounds—and this bird can even sing two notes at once!

ID: plump body; large black spots on white breast, sides and flanks; bold white eye ring; streaked cheeks; rusty head and back; brown wings, rump and tail.

Size: *L* 8 in; *W* 13 in.

Status: uncommon summer resident in the eastern third of the state and west to the edge of the Rolling Plains and the Edwards Plateau; uncommon to common migrant in the eastern half and rare in the western half.

Habitat: moist, mature and preferably undisturbed deciduous woodlands and mixed forests.

Nesting: low in a fork of a deciduous tree; female builds a bulky cup nest of grass, twigs, moss, weeds, bark strips and mud and lines it with softer materials; female incubates 3–4 pale greenish blue eggs for 13–14 days.

Feeding: forages on the ground and gleans vegetation for insects and other invertebrates; also eats berries.

Voice: calls include a *pit pit* and *bweebeebeep. Male:* bell-like phrases of 3–5 notes, with each note at a different pitch and followed by a trill: *Will you live with me? Way up high in a tree, I'll come right down and...seeee!*

Similar Species: *Other thrushes* (pp. 321–27, 454): smaller spots on underparts; most have colored wash on sides and flanks; no bold white eye rings; caps and back not rusty.

Best Sites: *Breeding:* Daingerfield SP; Caddo Lake SP; Huntsville SP; W.G. Jones State Forest. *In migration:* migrant "traps" on the upper and central Coastal Plain, including Sabine Woods, High Island, Sea Rim SP, Brazos Bend SP and Blucher Park (Corpus Christi).

AMERICAN ROBIN

Turdus migratorius

Come spring, the familiar song of the American Robin may wake you early if you are a light sleeper. This abundant bird adapts easily to urban areas and often works from dawn until after dusk when there is a nest to be built or hungry young mouths to feed. An adult with its bill stuffed full of earthworms and grubs is a sign that offspring are close at hand. Young robins are easily recognized by their disheveled appearance and heavily spotted underparts. • A hunting robin apparently listening for prey is actually looking for movements in the soil— because its eyes are placed on the sides of its head, it needs to tilt its head to look downward. • English colonists named the American Robin after the European Robin *(Erithacus rubecula)*, a distantly related bird with similar looks and behavior. The Blackbird *(T. merula)*, which is identical in all aspects except plumage, is the American Robin's closest European relative.

ID: gray-brown back; dark head; white throat streaked with black; white undertail coverts; incomplete, white eye ring; black-tipped, yellow bill. *Male:* deep brick red breast; black head. *Female:* dark gray head; light red-orange breast.
Size: *L* 10 in; *W* 17 in.
Status: rare to common summer resident in the High Plains, western Trans-Pecos and eastern third of the state; common to locally abundant migrant and winter resident in the eastern two-thirds and less common in the western third of the state.
Habitat: residential lawns and gardens, pastures, urban parks, broken forests, bogs and river shorelines.

Nesting: in a tree or shrub; sturdy cup nest of grass, moss and loose bark is cemented with mud; female incubates 4 light blue eggs for 11–16 days; up to 3 broods per year.
Feeding: forages on the ground and among vegetation for larval and adult insects, earthworms, other invertebrates and berries.
Voice: rapid *tut-tut-tut* call; evenly spaced, warbling song: *cheerily cheer-up cheerio*.
Similar Species: *Clay-colored Robin* (p. 454): casual, in the Lower Rio Grande Valley only; light brown upperparts; warm buff underparts; light streaks on throat.
Best Sites: *Breeding:* suburban areas in the eastern third of the state. *In migration* and *winter:* large roosts form in woodlands, often near urban areas.

GRAY CATBIRD

Dumetella carolinensis

Calling with a catlike meow, the Gray Catbird—an accomplished mimic—may fool you as it shuffles through underbrush and dense riparian shrubs. Its mimicking talents are enhanced by its ability to sing two notes at once, using each side of its syrinx individually. • Catbirds are common migrants in the eastern third of Texas, and a few overwinter along the Gulf Coast. They can often be drawn out by a birder's "pishing." • Most Gray Catbirds breed farther north, but some build their loose cup nests deep within the impenetrable tangles of shrubs, brambles and thorny thickets of eastern Texas. By being very loyal to their nests, female catbirds leave little opportunity for parasitism by Brown-headed Cowbirds. They are also one of the few species able to recognize and remove foreign eggs. • Half of the catbird's diet is made up of insects, whereas fruit and berries make up the other half. Pokeberries and mulberries are favorites of this gray bird.

ID: dark gray overall; black cap; long, dark gray to black tail; chestnut undertail coverts; black eyes, bill and legs.
Size: *L* 8½–9 in; *W* 11 in.

Status: rare to locally common summer resident in the eastern half of the state; uncommon to common migrant throughout most of Texas; rare to uncommon winter resident on the Coastal Plain and in the Lower Rio Grande Valley, though it appears at many inland localities.

Habitat: dense thickets, brambles, shrubby or brushy areas and hedgerows, often near water.
Nesting: in a dense shrub or thicket; bulky cup nest is loosely built with twigs, leaves and grass and lined with finer materials; female incubates 4 greenish blue eggs for 12–15 days.
Feeding: forages on the ground and in vegetation for a wide variety of insects; also eats berries and visits feeders.
Voice: calls include a catlike meow and a harsh *check-check;* song is a variety of warbles, squeaks and mimicked phrases repeated only once and often interspersed with a *mew* call.
Similar Species: *Northern Mockingbird* (p. 329): no black cap or chestnut undertail coverts.
Best Sites: migrant "traps" on the Coastal Plain.

NORTHERN MOCKINGBIRD

Mimus polyglottos

Serenading into the night during a full moon, Northern Mockingbirds have an amazing vocal repertoire that includes over 400 different song types, which they belt out incessantly throughout the breeding season. Mockingbirds can imitate almost anything, from other birds and animals to musical instruments. They replicate notes so accurately that even computerized sound analysis may be unable to detect the difference between the original source and a mockingbird imitation. • Whether perched comfortably on a power pole or singing from a street lamp, Northern Mockingbirds have adapted remarkably well to urban environments. They thrive in a variety of habitats ranging from lush gardens to arid deserts and are currently expanding their range northward. Their common and widespread status inspired the Texas Federation of Women's Clubs to nominate the Northern Mockingbird as our state bird, a designation that became official on January 27, 1926. • The word *polyglottos*, Greek for "many tongues," refers to this bird's ability to mimic a wide variety of sounds.

ID: gray upperparts; dark wings; 2 thin, white wing bars; long, dark tail with white outer feathers; light gray underparts. *Immature:* paler overall; spotted breast. *In flight:* large white patch at base of black primaries.
Size: *L* 10 in; *W* 14 in.
Status: common resident statewide.
Habitat: hedges, suburban gardens and orchard margins with an abundance of available fruit; hedgerows of multiflora roses are especially important in winter.
Nesting: in a shrub or small tree; cup nest is made of twigs, grass, fur and leaves; female incubates 3–4 brown-blotched, bluish gray to greenish eggs for 12–13 days.

Feeding: gleans vegetation and forages on the ground for beetles, ants, wasps and grasshoppers; also eats berries and wild fruit; visits feeders for suet and raisins.
Voice: calls include a harsh *chair* and *chewk;* song is a medley of mimicked phrases, with the phrases often repeated 3 times or more.
Similar Species: *Loggerhead Shrike* (p. 270): thicker, hooked bill; black mask. *Gray Catbird* (p. 328): gray overall; black cap; chestnut undertail coverts; no white outer tail feathers. *Townsend's Solitaire* (p. 321): gray overall; white eye ring; small bill; buffy wing bars.
Best Sites: almost any terrestrial habitat except dense woodlands.

SAGE THRASHER

Oreoscoptes montanus

The smallest of our thrashers, the Sage Thrasher is intricately linked to the open flats of sagebrush of the western U.S. Belting out his long, warbling phrases, the male is regularly seen perched atop sage and other shrubs. • Although drab in color, the Sage Thrasher has a harmonious, flutelike song that may be heard throughout the day during breeding season and into the night during the full moon. This bird is also an accomplished mimic of other species, especially the Western Meadowlark and the Horned Lark, and was originally named "Mountain Mockingbird." Much like a mockingbird, the Sage Thrasher slowly raises and lowers its tail while perched, and it holds its tail high when running along the ground. • "Thrasher" is derived from "thrush"—thrashers belong to the family Mimidae, the mimic thrushes. Although the genus name *Oreoscoptes* is Greek for "mimic of the mountains," this bird's range lies largely in the intermountain Great Basin.

Habitat: sagebrush flats, open brushland and coastal sage scrub.

Nesting: does not nest in Texas.

Feeding: forages extensively among vegetation on the ground for invertebrates and larvae; also eats berries.

Voice: calls include a high *churr* and *chuck;* a notable night singer, the male's complex, warbled song lasts up to 2 minutes, with the phrases usually repeated without a pause.

ID: gray-brown upperparts; heavily streaked underparts; yellow eyes; short, slim, straight bill. *In flight:* white tail corners; 2 white wing bars (often faded).

Size: *L* 8 ½ in; *W* 12 in.

Status: rare to uncommon migrant and winter resident in the western two-thirds of the state.

Similar Species: *Curve-billed Thrasher* (p. 333): larger; longer, curved bill; light round spots on underparts. *Northern Mockingbird* (p. 329): juvenile has less heavily streaked underparts; large, white wing patches; white outer tail feathers. *Swainson's Thrush* (p. 324) and *Hermit Thrush* (p. 325): avoids sagebrush flats; stockier overall; no streaking on the belly; dark eyes; pinkish legs.

Best Sites: Hueco Tanks SP; Big Bend NP; Black Gap WMA; Seminole Canyon SP.

BROWN THRASHER

Toxostoma rufum

Amid the various chirps and warbles that rise from woodland and lakefront edges in spring and early summer, the song of the male Brown Thrasher stands alone—its lengthy, complex chorus of twice-repeated phrases is truly unique. This thrasher's vocal repertoire, which is estimated at up to 3000 distinctive combinations of various phrases, is the most extensive of any North American bird. • Despite its relatively large size, the Brown Thrasher generally goes unnoticed in its shrubby domain. A typical sighting of this thrasher consists of nothing more than a flash of rufous as it zips from one tangle to another. • Because Brown Thrashers nest on or close to the ground, their eggs and nestlings are particularly vulnerable to predation; the aggressive, vigilant, spirited defense of the parents is not always enough. • Unlike other notable singers, such as the Northern Mockingbird and the similarly shaped, shrub-dwelling Gray Catbird, the Brown Thrasher prefers to live well away from urban areas.

ID: reddish brown upperparts; pale underparts with heavy, brown spotting and streaking; long, slender, downcurved bill; yellow-orange eyes; long, rufous tail; yellow legs; 2 white wing bars.

Size: *L* 11½ in; *W* 13 in.

Status: uncommon to locally common resident in the eastern half of the state, west to the edge of the Rolling Plains and Edwards Plateau; uncommon to common migrant and winter resident in the western half and rare in the South Texas Brush Country.

Habitat: dense shrubs and thickets, overgrown pastures (especially those with hawthorns), woodland edges and brushy areas; rarely close to human habitation.

Nesting: usually in a low shrub; often on the ground; cup nest of grass, twigs and leaves is lined with fine vegetation; pair incubates 4 bluish white to pale blue eggs, dotted with reddish brown, for 11–14 days.

Feeding: gleans the ground and vegetation for larval and adult invertebrates; occasionally tosses leaves aside with its bill; also eats seeds and berries.

Voice: calls include a loud crackling note, a harsh *shuck*, a soft *churr* and a whistled, 3-note *pit-cher-ee;* sings a large variety of phrases, with each phrase usually repeated twice: *dig-it dig-it, hoe-it hoe-it, pull-it-up pull-it-up.*

Similar Species: *Long-billed Thrasher* (p. 332): range overlaps in winter only; browner, less rufous upperparts; gray cheeks; black-streaked, white underparts; streaked undertail coverts. *Thrushes* (pp. 321–27): shorter bill and tail; breast spotted, not streaked.

Best Sites: Daingerfield SP; Tyler SP; High I.; Bear Creek Pioneer Park (Houston).

LONG-BILLED THRASHER

Toxostoma longirostre

With a streaked belly and a rufous back, the Long-billed Thrasher looks nearly identical to the Brown Thrasher. These closely related species only share the same range when the Brown Thrasher moves to southern Texas for winter. The Long-billed Thrasher was once common throughout the Lower Rio Grande Valley, but 95 percent of its breeding habitat has now been destroyed. Ironically, the thrasher has extended its breeding range northward, where overgrazing and fire suppression have allowed brush to invade former grassland. • This shy, large, robin-sized bird sticks close to the ground, flying only short distances and retreating to dense thickets when approached. During breeding season, the male becomes bolder, singing melodiously from exposed perches. • Fossilized *Toxostoma* bones from the Quaternary period (10,000 to 1.6 million years ago) were found in a cave in southern New Mexico.

ID: rufous back; whitish underparts heavily streaked with black; gray face; long, slender, down-curved bill; long, rufous tail.
Size: *L* 9¾ in. *W* 13 in.

Status: uncommon to common resident from the Lower Rio Grande Valley north through the central Coastal Plain and southern Edwards Plateau, becoming rare along the Rio Grande in the southern Trans-Pecos and in the western Edwards Plateau.
Habitat: thorny shrubs, thick brush, dense thickets and riparian woodland.
Nesting: well hidden in dense understory 25 feet from the edge; cup nest of thorny twigs is lined with bark, straw or moss; pair

incubates 3–4 pale green eggs with brown spots for 13–14 days.
Feeding: forages on the ground, under dense cover; sweeps leaf litter aside with bill; eats arthropods, snails and slugs or berries in fall and winter.
Voice: melodious *kleek* (descending slightly) and loud *chak* calls; musical song with rich phrases, harsher and not as clearly paired as the Brown Thrasher's song.
Similar Species: *Brown Thrasher* (p. 331): ranges overlap in winter only; shorter, less curved bill; slighter lighter and brighter back, neck and sides; slightly buffier underparts. *Curve-billed Thrasher* (p. 333): paler and more gray-brown overall; dull gray-brown spots on breast.
Best Sites: Seminole Canyon SP; Lake Corpus Christi SP; Santa Ana NWR; Bentsen-Rio Grande Valley SP.

CURVE-BILLED THRASHER

Toxostoma curvirostre

Deserts filled with cholla, prickly-pear and saguaro cacti provide favored feeding, nesting and roosting habitat for the Curve-billed Thrasher. This sassy, familiar bird shares this harsh, sun-bleached habitat with the Cactus Wren, building its nest among the yucca or cholla (pronounced *choy-ah*) cactus. Within this fortress of sharp spines, eggs and nestlings are protected from predators, but fledglings must quickly master flying or risk being fatally pricked as they enter or exit the nest. • When foraging, the Curve-billed Thrasher digs in the soil for insects, propping its tail against the ground for reinforcement and then striking the soil with heavy, purposeful blows.

ID: long, dark, downcurved bill; bright yellow to orange eyes; pale, brownish gray upperparts; brownish to buffy gray underparts; large, blurry breast spots; birds in eastern part of range may show white wing bars; long tail may have whitish corners. *Juvenile:* shorter, all-dark bill.
Size: *L* 9½–11½ in; *W* 13½ in.
Status: uncommon to common resident in the western half of the state and east through the Rolling Plains, Edwards Plateau and central Coastal Plain.

Habitat: arid, brushy lowlands, desert and grasslands with cholla cactus.
Nesting: in a cholla cactus, yucca or thorny shrub; loose, bulky cup nest consists of grass, thorny twigs, feathers and animal hair; pair incubates 3 blue-green eggs, with brown spots, for 12–15 days.
Feeding: forages on the ground for insects, berries and seeds; often uses its long bill to dig in soil; readily takes cactus fruit and seeds.
Voice: sharp, liquidy *whit-wheat* call; song is a long, variable series of whistled phrases.
Similar Species: *Crissal Thrasher* (p. 454): unspotted, buffy brown breast and belly; rufous undertail coverts. *Sage Thrasher* (p. 330): smaller; shorter bill; thin streaks on underparts.
Best Sites: Davis Mountains SP; Big Bend NP; Seminole Canyon SP; Abilene SP; San Angelo SP.

EUROPEAN STARLING

Sturnus vulgaris

The European Starling was brought to North America in 1890 and 1891, when about 100 birds were released into New York's Central Park as part of the local Shakespeare society's plan to introduce all the birds mentioned in their favorite author's writings. The European Starling quickly established itself in the New York landscape and then spread rapidly across the continent, often at the expense of many native cavity-nesting birds, such as the Tree Swallow, Eastern Bluebird and Red-headed Woodpecker. Despite many concerted efforts to control or even eradicate this species, the European Starling will no doubt continue to assert its claim in the New World. The more than 200 million individuals in North America today are believed to have sprung from these first 100 birds. • Courting European Starlings are infamous for their ability to reproduce the sounds of other birds, such as Killdeers, Red-tailed Hawks, Soras and meadowlarks.

breeding

ID: short, squared tail; dark eyes. *Breeding:* iridescent, blackish plumage; yellow bill. *Nonbreeding:* blackish wings; feather tips heavily spotted with white and buff; dark bill. *In flight:* pointed, triangular wings. *Juvenile:* overall drab gray-brown plumage; dark bill.
Size: *L* 8½ in; *W* 16 in.
Status: uncommon to locally abundant resident statewide.
Habitat: agricultural areas, townsites, woodland edges, landfills and roadsides.
Nesting: in an abandoned woodpecker cavity, natural cavity or nest box; nest is made of grass, twigs and straw; mostly

the female incubates 4–6 bluish to greenish white eggs for 12–14 days.
Feeding: forages mostly on the ground; diverse diet includes many invertebrates, berries, seeds and human food waste.
Voice: various whistles, squeaks and gurgles; imitates other birds.
Similar Species: *Rusty Blackbird* (p. 425): longer tail; black bill; no spotting; yellow eyes; rusty tinge on upperparts in fall. *Brewer's Blackbird* (p. 426): longer tail; black bill; no spotting; male has yellow eyes; female is brown overall. *Brown-headed Cowbird* (p. 431): no spotting; male has longer tail, shorter, dark bill and brown head.
Best Sites: anywhere around human habitation.

AMERICAN PIPIT

Anthus rubescens

Each winter, roadsides, stubble fields and coastal shorelines become foraging grounds for American Pipits. Flocks of pipits fluctuate annually and may go unnoticed, because their dull brown and buff plumage blends into the landscape. But, to keen observers, the plain attire, slender bill, white outer tail feathers and habit of continuous tail wagging make these birds readily identifiable. The best indicator that pipits are near is their telltale, two-syllable call of *pip-it pip-it,* which is usually given in flight. • American Pipits may resemble sparrows, but the two move very differently. Pipits typically stride along the ground, whereas sparrows and most other passerines hop. The reason for these distinct movement styles may be simply that long-legged birds move a greater distance with one long stride, whereas a single hop takes short-legged birds farther. • This bird was formerly known as "Water Pipit" (*A. spinoletta*). • Pipits are found worldwide and occupy every continent except Antarctica.

ID: faintly streaked, gray-brown upperparts; lightly streaked "necklace" on upper breast; streaked sides and flanks; dark legs; dark tail with white outer feathers; buff-colored underparts; slim bill and body.
Size: *L* 6–7 in; *W* 10½ in.
Status: common migrant and winter resident in most of the state but rare in winter in the northern half of the Panhandle.
Habitat: agricultural fields, pastures and roadsides; coastal shorelines and shores of wetlands, lakes and rivers.

Nesting: does not nest in Texas.
Feeding: gleans the ground and vegetation for seeds and insects; eats agricultural pests, including grasshoppers and weevils; also takes aquatic invertebrates and mollusks.
Voice: familiar *pip-it pip-it* flight call. *Male:* song a harsh, sharp *tsip-tsip* or *chiwee.*
Similar Species: *Horned Lark* (p. 287): black "horns"; facial markings. *Sprague's Pipit* (p. 336): lighter back with strong streaking; paler buff breast.
Best Sites: agricultural lands, especially along the shores of lakes and ponds.

SPRAGUE'S PIPIT

Anthus spragueii

The Sprague's Pipit has the brown plumage pattern typical of prairie passerines but flashes white outer tail feathers in flight. Unlike most of the world's pipits, this species does not habitually wag its tail. • This solitary bird breeds in the northern Great Plains and Canadian prairies, where it delivers a musical courtship song while circling overhead. It migrates through most of Texas and overwinters in the eastern half of our state and southward into Mexico. • Unlike the American Pipit, this species occurs more on drier, often upland fields. • Isaac Sprague was a talented illustrator who accompanied John J. Audubon across the Great Plains in the 1840s. He later became one of America's foremost botanical artists.

ID: white outer tail feathers; thin bill; light-colored legs; grayish brown upperparts streaked with buff; lighter underparts; faint breast streaks.

Size: *L* 6½ in; *W* 10 in.

Status: uncommon migrant statewide; rare to uncommon winter resident south of the Panhandle, more prevalent on the Coastal Plain.

Habitat: native short-grass prairie.

Nesting: does not nest in Texas.

Feeding: searches the ground and grassy vegetation for seeds and small invertebrates.

Voice: generally silent in Texas; song is a swirling and descending, bell-like *choodly choodly choodly choodly chooodly*.

Similar Species: *American Pipit* (p. 335): darker plumage; darker legs; wags its tail. *Vesper Sparrow* (p. 390): heavier bill; chestnut shoulder patch. *Baird's Sparrow:* no white outer tail feathers.

Best Sites: Sea Rim SP; Anahuac NWR; Galveston Island SP; Brazos Bend SP; Padre Island National Seashore.

CEDAR WAXWING

Bombycilla cedrorum

With its black mask and slick hairdo, the Cedar Waxwing has a heroic look. This bird's splendid personality is reflected in its social feeding habits. If a bird's crop is full and it is unable to eat any more, it will continue to pluck fruit and pass it down the line like a bucket brigade, until the fruit is gulped down by a still-hungry bird. As flocks gorge on fermented berries in late winter and spring, birds will show definite signs of tipsiness. Planting mulberries, juniper or yaupon shrubs in your backyard can attract this bird and provide an opportunity to observe its striking plumage up close. • Practiced observers learn to recognize Cedar Waxwings by their high-pitched, trilling calls. Flocks are highly nomadic, and numbers vary each year. • Cedar Waxwings are named for their bright red wing tips, which look like they have been dipped in colored candle wax.

Status: common to abundant migrant and winter resident east of the Pecos R. and uncommon and irregular in most of the Trans-Pecos.
Habitat: wooded residential parks and gardens, overgrown fields, forest edges, second-growth, riparian and open woodlands.
Nesting: does not nest in Texas.
Feeding: eats large amounts of berries and wild fruit in winter and early spring; also catches flying insects on the wing or gleans vegetation, especially in summer.
Voice: faint, high-pitched, trilled whistle: *tseee-tseee-tseee.*
Similar Species: *Bohemian Waxwing:* casual winter visitor; more rufous on face; rufous undertail coverts.
Best Sites: any open woods and parks, rural or suburban, with a lot of berry-bearing shrubs.

ID: cinnamon crest; brown upperparts; black mask; yellow wash on belly; gray rump; yellow terminal tail band; white undertail coverts; small red "drops" on wings. *Immature:* no mask; streaked underparts; gray-brown body.
Size: *L* 7 in; *W* 12 in.

337

PHAINOPEPLA

Phainopepla nitens

The Phainopepla belongs to the Silky-flycatcher family, a small group of tropical, mainly fruit-eating birds. Despite its glossy plumage and saucy character, the Phainopepla leads a mysterious existence. Much of this bird's life revolves around mistletoe, which provides nesting habitat and a food source. Once eaten, the pulpy, sticky-coated seeds slip through the bird's digestive system to be deposited on a new host tree or shrub branch, helping the parasitic plant colonize new territory. The mistletoe's tangled growth, sprouting in bushy tangles from elevated tree and shrub branches, also provides a concealing foundation for the Phainopepla's nest. This close, mutually beneficial relationship between plant and bird is known as "mutualism." • The name *Phainopepla* is derived from Greek words meaning "shining robe," referring to the male's elegant plumage.

ID: raised crest; red eyes. *Male:* all-black plumage. *Female* and *immature:* dark wings and tail on otherwise gray body. *In flight:* long, square tail; white (male) or pale gray (female) wing patch.
Size: *L* 7 ¾ in; *W* 11 in.
Status: locally common resident throughout most of the Trans-Pecos and rare on the southernmost South Plains and the western third of the South Texas Brush Country.

Habitat: broken mixed-oak and oak woodlands and riparian woodlands containing mistletoe and other berry producing plants; occasionally attracted to exotic shrub plantings.
Nesting: in a mistletoe tangle or in the fork of a shrub or tree; male builds most of the shallow, cup-shaped nest of twigs, vegetation, animal hair and spider webs; pair incubates 2–3 dark-spotted, pale gray or pinkish eggs for 10–12 days; pair raises the young; may have 2 broods per year.
Feeding: eats mostly seasonally available berries and insects; takes insects by hawking or while flying or hovering.
Voice: low, liquid *wurp?* call note has an upslurred effect; seldom-heard song is a short warble.
Similar Species: *Cedar Waxwing* (p. 337): immature has streaked underparts, flattened, swept-back crest and yellow-tipped tail.
Best Sites: Davis Mountains SP; Big Bend Ranch SP; Big Bend NP; Black Gap WMA.

BLUE-WINGED WARBLER

Vermivora pinus

The Blue-winged Warbler introduces the large and diverse family of wood-warblers, an active group of small, brightly colored birds found only in the New World. Many of the approximately 50 wood-warblers that occur in North America pass through Texas at some point in the year, and an astounding number of them may be seen along our coastline during spring migration. Exhausted birds that have encountered sudden storms or extreme headwinds while crossing the Gulf of Mexico find shelter in the limited coastal woodlands, and, in some years, birders may see several dozen different species in a few hours. • During the mid-1800s, the Blue-winged Warbler began expanding its range eastward and northward from its home in the central midwestern U.S., finding new breeding territories among overgrown fields and pastures near abandoned human settlements.

ID: bright yellow head and underparts, except for white to yellowish undertail coverts; olive yellow upperparts; bluish gray wings and tail; black eye line; thin, dark bill; 2 white wing bars; bold white spots on underside of tail.
Size: L 4½–5 in; W 7½ in.
Status: rare to common migrant in the eastern half of the state.
Habitat: second-growth woodlands, willow swamps, shrubby, overgrown fields, pastures and woodland edges and openings.
Nesting: does not nest in Texas.

Feeding: gleans insects and spiders from the lower branches of trees and shrubs.
Voice: song is a buzzy, 2-note *beee-bzzz*.
Similar Species: *"Brewster's Warbler"* (hybrid): variable; may have pale or white underparts or yellow wing bars. *"Lawrence's Warbler"* (hybrid): usually shows black throat; often has yellow wing bars. *Cerulean Warbler* (p. 457): juvenile has bluish green upperparts, bold yellowish eyebrow and pale buff underparts, with some grayish streaking on flanks. *Pine Warbler* (p. 354): larger; much larger bill; no black eye line; "dirty" yellow underparts with olive streaking on breast and flanks. *Prothonotary Warbler* (p. 359): larger; no black eye line; no wing bars.
Best Sites: migrant "traps" on the Coastal Plain.

GOLDEN-WINGED WARBLER

Vermivora chrysoptera

A beautiful gray songbird with a black mask and a bright yellow cap and wing patches, the Golden-winged Warbler passes through eastern Texas during migration. It prefers abandoned farmlands, shrubby fields or new-growth habitats that follow fire and logging. • Because of habitat change, nest parasitism by the Brown-headed Cowbird and the range expansion of the Blue-winged Warbler, the Golden-winged Warbler is declining in numbers throughout its range. Where the ranges of these two warblers overlap, they may interbreed and produce hybrids known as "Brewster's Warblers," which have a black eye line and whitish underparts. These fertile hybrids can reproduce with either species or each other, producing a variety of forms, including the "Lawrence's Warbler."

ID: yellow fore-crown and wing patch; dark chin, throat and mask bordered by white; bluish gray upper-parts and flanks; white undersides; white spots on undertail. *Female* and *immature:* duller overall, with gray throat and mask.
Size: *L* 4¾ in; *W* 7½ in.
Status: rare to uncommon migrant in the eastern half of the state and very rare in the western half.
Habitat: moist shrubby fields, woodland edges and early-succession forest clearings.

Nesting: does not nest in Texas.
Feeding: gleans tree and shrub canopies for insects and spiders.
Voice: usually silent in Texas; call is a sweet *chip;* buzzy song begins with a higher note: *zee-bz-bz-bz.*
Similar Species: *"Brewster's Warbler"* (hybrid): yellow underparts; 2 yellow wing bars. *"Lawrence's Warbler"* (hybrid): usually shows yellow underparts and 2 white wing bars. *Carolina Chickadee* (p. 296): black crown and "bib"; no black ear patch; no yellow wing patch.
Best Sites: migrant "traps" on the Coastal Plain.

340

TENNESSEE WARBLER

Vermivora peregrina

Tennessee Warblers don't have the bold, bright features found on other warblers. Without their loud, twittering song, these birds would easily pass through Texas unnoticed. • Migrating Tennessee Warblers often sing their tunes and forage for insects high in the forest canopy. However, inclement weather and the need for food after a long flight can force these birds to lower levels in the forest. • Alexander Wilson discovered this bird along the Cumberland River in Tennessee and named it after that state. This warbler only migrates through Tennessee, though, and breeds in Canada, northern Michigan and northeastern Minnesota. • Tennessee Warblers thrive during spruce budworm outbreaks in the northern boreal forest. During times of plenty, these birds may produce more than seven young in a single brood.

♀

breeding

♂

ID: *Breeding male:* blue-gray cap; white eyebrow; black eye line; olive green back, wings and tail edgings; clean white underparts; thin bill. *Breeding female:* yellow wash on breast and eyebrow; olive gray cap. *Nonbreeding:* olive yellow upperparts; yellow eyebrow; yellow underparts except for white undertail coverts; male may have white belly.

Size: *L* 4½–5 in; *W* 8 in.

Status: common to abundant migrant in the eastern half of the state and rare in the western half; very rare winter resident on the Coastal Plain and in the Lower Rio Grande Valley.

Habitat: woodlands and areas with tall shrubs.

Nesting: does not nest in Texas.

Feeding: gleans foliage and buds for small insects, caterpillars and other invertebrates; also eats berries; occasionally visits suet feeders.

Voice: sweet *chip* call. *Male:* song is a loud, sharp, accelerating *ticka-ticka-ticka swit-swit-swit-swit chew-chew-chew-chew-chew.*

Similar Species: *Philadelphia Vireo* (p. 452): nonbreeding bird has very similar plumage but slower, more deliberate movements, thicker bill, blackish forehead and yellow throat. *Orange-crowned Warbler* (p. 342): tends to forage low to the ground; dull streaking on breast and flanks; yellow undertail coverts. *Warbling Vireo* (p. 278): stouter overall; thicker bill; much less green on upperparts.

Best Sites: migrant "traps" on the Coastal Plain.

341

ORANGE-CROWNED WARBLER

Vermivora celata

With its nondescript plumage, the Orange-crowned Warbler causes identification problems for many birders. Its drab, olive yellow appearance and lack of field marks make it frustratingly similar to females of other warbler species, and the male's orange crown patch is seldom visible. • Orange-crowned Warblers routinely feed on sap or insects attracted to the sap wells drilled by Yellow-bellied Sapsuckers. These small warblers have rather deliberate foraging movements and are usually seen gleaning insects from the leaves and buds of low shrubs, but they occasionally eat berries and fruit or visit suet feeders in winter. • *Vermivora* is Latin for "worm eating," and *celata* is derived from the Latin word for "hidden," a reference to this bird's inconspicuous crown.

ID: olive yellow to olive gray body; faintly streaked underparts; bright yellow undertail coverts; thin, faint, dark eye line; bright yellow eyebrow and broken eye ring; thin bill; faint orange crown patch in males (rarely seen).

Size: *L* 5 in; *W* 7 in.

Status: common migrant statewide; rare winter resident in the Panhandle and uncommon to locally common south of the Panhandle; uncommon summer resident in the Guadalupe Mts. and Davis Mts.

Habitat: woodlands and areas with tall shrubs.

Nesting: on the ground or in lower parts of shrubs; female builds a bulky nest of coarse grasses and bark; female incubates the 4–6 white eggs marked with reddish speckles or spots for 12–14 days; both parents raise the young.

Feeding: gleans foliage for invertebrates; also takes berries, nectar and sap; often hover-gleans.

Voice: clear, sharp *chip* call. *Male:* faint trill breaks downward halfway through.

Similar Species: *Tennessee Warbler* (p. 341): very similar juvenile has narrow, pale wing bars, paler undertail coverts than remainder of underparts, often more distinct eyebrow and no split eye ring. *Yellow Warbler* (p. 345): very drab juvenile has complete eye ring, with no eyebrow or eye line. *Common Yellowthroat* (p. 368): somewhat similar juvenile has complete eye ring but no eyebrow, eye line or breast streaking.

Best Sites: *Breeding:* Guadalupe Mountains NP; Davis Mountains SP. *In migration:* migrant "traps" on the Coastal Plain.

342

NASHVILLE WARBLER

Vermivora ruficapilla

Nashville Warblers have an unusual distribution, with two widely separated summer populations, one eastern and the other western. These populations are believed to have been created thousands of years ago when a single core population split apart during continental glaciation. • Nashville Warblers are uncommon to abundant migrants throughout Texas and rare winter residents in the Lower Rio Grande Valley and the Coastal Plain. They are best found in overgrown farmland and second-growth forest as they forage low in trees and thickets, often at the edge of a dry forest or burn area. • This warbler was first described near Nashville, Tennessee, but it does not breed in that state. This misnomer is not an isolated incident—the Tennessee, Cape May and Connecticut warblers all bear names that do not indicate their breeding distributions.

ID: yellow green upperparts; yellow underparts; white between legs; bold white eye ring. *Male:* bluish gray head; may show a small, chestnut red crown. *Female* and *immature:* duller overall; light eye ring; olive gray head; bluish gray nape.
Size: *L* 4½–5 in; *W* 7½ in.
Status: common to abundant migrant statewide except for the extreme western Trans-Pecos and the upper Coastal Plain, where it is rare to uncommon; uncommon winter resident in the Lower Rio Grande Valley and rare in the southern South Texas Brush country and on the Coastal Plain.
Habitat: prefers second-growth mixed woodlands; also uses wet coniferous forests, riparian woodlands, cedar-spruce swamps and moist, shrubby, abandoned fields.
Nesting: does not nest in Texas.
Feeding: gleans foliage for insects such as caterpillars, flies and aphids.
Voice: generally silent in migration; metallic *chink* call. *Male:* song begins with a thin, high-pitched *see-it see-it see-it see-it,* followed by a trilling.
Similar Species: *Common Yellowthroat* (p. 368) and *Wilson's Warbler* (p. 370): all-yellow underparts; females do not have grayish heads or bold white eye rings. *Connecticut Warbler* and *Mourning Warbler* (p. 366): yellow between legs; females have grayish to brownish hoods.
Best Sites: migrant "traps" on the central and lower Coastal Plain.

343

NORTHERN PARULA

Parula americana

Northern Parulas are common residents of habitats that contain an abundance of Spanish moss, in which the birds nest. The young spend the first few weeks of their lives enclosed in a fragile, socklike nest suspended from a tree branch. Once they have grown too large for the nest and developed their wing feathers, the young disperse among the surrounding trees and shrubs. With the arrival of fall, Northern Parulas migrate to the warmer climes of Central America or the Florida Keys. • Parulas are small birds, even by wood-warbler standards. Their name is a form of *Parus*—the genus of chickadees and titmice—and refers to the parula's size. • Parula has two correct pronunciations: *PAIR-yuh-luh* or *PAIR-uh-luh;* the pronunciation *puh-ROO-luh*, although popular, is incorrect.

Habitat: *Breeding:* oak hammocks, riparian woodlands, cypress swamps or other woodlands festooned in Spanish moss. *In migration* and *winter:* any wooded habitat, especially oak woodlands.

Nesting: suspended from a tree branch; pair builds a socklike cup nest within a clump of Spanish moss; pair incubates 4–5 brown-marked, whitish eggs for 12–14 days.

Feeding: forages for insects, spiders and other invertebrates by hovering, gleaning or hawking; occasionally eats fruit.

Voice: clear *chip* call; song is a rising, buzzy trill ending with a lower-pitched *zip*.

Similar Species: none; small size, bluish gray head, yellow-green back, white eye crescents and yellow breast are diagnostic.

Best Sites: *Summer:* Atlanta SP; Caddo Lake SP; Huntsville SP; Bear Creek Pioneer Park (Houston). *In migration:* migrant "traps" on Coastal Plain.

ID: yellowish green back; blue-gray head; conspicuous white eye crescents; yellow lower mandible; bold white wing bars on blue-gray wings; yellow throat and breast; white belly and undertail coverts. *Male:* narrow, blue and rufous breast band.

Size: *L* 4½ in; *W* 7 in.

Status: common summer resident in the eastern half of the state and the southern half of the Edwards Plateau; common migrant in the eastern half of the state and rare in the western half; rare winter resident in the Lower Rio Grande Valley.

YELLOW WARBLER

Dendroica petechia

Although Yellow Warblers occasionally overwinter in southern Texas, most Yellows arrive here in spring to refuel on insects before continuing their migration northward. Flitting from branch to branch among open woodland edges and riparian shrubs, these inquisitive birds seem to be in perpetual motion. • During fall migration, silent, plain-looking Yellow Warblers and other similar-looking warblers can cause confusion for birders who have been lulled into a false sense of familiarity with these birds. Watch for the unique yellow flashes on the sides of the tails to identify the Yellow Warblers. • Yellow Warblers are among the most frequent victims of nest parasitism by Brown-headed Cowbirds. Unlike many birds, they can recognize the foreign eggs and many pairs will either abandon their nest or build another nest overtop the old eggs, creating bizarre, multilayered, high-rise nests. • The Yellow Warbler is often mistakenly called "Wild Canary" because of its bright yellow plumage.

ID: bright yellow body; yellowish legs; black bill and eyes; bright yellow highlights on dark yellow olive tail and wings. *Male:* red breast streaks. *Female:* fainter breast streaks.

Size: *L* 5 in; *W* 8 in.

Status: common migrant statewide; former rare breeder but no longer nests in Texas.

Habitat: shrubby or wooded habitats, especially near water.

Nesting: does not nest in Texas.

Feeding: gleans vegetation for insects and spiders; occasionally takes fruit.

Voice: clear, loud *chip* call; song is a series of 6–8 high, *sweet-sweet* notes with a rapid ending.

Similar Species: *Orange-crowned Warbler* (p. 342): little seasonal overlap; darker olive plumage overall; pale eyebrow; dark eye line; dusky streaking on breast and flanks. *Common Yellowthroat* (p. 368): female stays close to ground and has olive upperparts, including nape and crown. *American Goldfinch* (p. 441): black wings and tail; male often has black forehead.

Best Sites: migrant "traps" on the Coastal Plain.

CHESTNUT-SIDED WARBLER

Dendroica pensylvanica

Most wood-warblers molt into a duller but still recognizable "winter" plumage after breeding, but the Chestnut-sided Warbler undergoes a dramatic transformation that causes its plumage in fall to bear little resemblance to its appearance in spring and summer. It breeds in southeastern Canada and the northeastern U.S. south through the Appalachian Mountains, and it winters from Mexico to Guatemala. • Chestnut-sided Warblers migrate through eastern Texas in spring, and the boldly patterned males never fail to dazzle onlookers. These birds are seldom seen during fall, though, because their southern migration route is east of our state. • A Chestnut-sided Warbler often feeds with its tail slightly upraised and its wings held slightly outward from its body, a posture not shown by Bay-breasted Warblers.

♀

♂

breeding

ID: 2 pale yellow wing bars. *Breeding:* yellow upperparts, including nape with black streaking; yellow crown; white cheek partially framed with black; white underparts with chestnut flanks. *Nonbreeding:* uncommon in Texas; yellow-green upperparts, usually with black streaking; yellow-green nape and crown; gray face with white eye ring; white throat; white underparts, plain (female and juvenile) or with some chestnut on flanks (male).

Size: *L* 5 in; *W* 8 in.
Status: uncommon to common migrant in the eastern half of the state and rare to casual westward; less common in fall.
Habitat: any wooded habitat, especially oak woodlands.
Nesting: does not nest in Texas.
Feeding: gleans foliage or flycatches; eats insects and spiders.
Voice: clear *chip* call; song (rarely heard in Texas) is usually written as *I'm so pleased to meetcha.*
Similar Species: yellow-green upperparts, gray face with white eye ring and yellow wing bars are generally diagnostic. *Bay-breasted Warbler* (p. 356): black face; dark chestnut hindcrown, upper breast and sides; buff belly and undertail coverts; white wing bars. *American Redstart* (p. 358): female has large yellow patches on wings and tail; more grayish overall.
Best Sites: migrant "traps" on the Coastal Plain.

MAGNOLIA WARBLER

Dendroica magnolia

This species was originally called "Black-and-yellow Warbler" by its discoverer, Alexander Wilson, but the name Magnolia Warbler was eventually chosen because the first specimen was collected from a magnolia. It is a striking warbler during spring but molts into a much duller nonbreeding plumage. • The Magnolia Warbler breeds across southern Canada and the extreme northern continental U.S., and it winters from Florida, Mexico and the West Indies to Panama. It migrates throughout eastern Texas but is encountered most frequently along the coast. • This active feeder often fans its tail to reveal the distinctive white band on the uppertail and the equally distinctive undertail pattern, with white at the base and black at the end.

breeding

ID: yellow rump; unique tail pattern: black uppertail with white spots; white undertail with black tip. *Breeding male:* black upperparts; gray crown; black mask; white eyebrow and lower eye arc; yellow throat; dark wings with white patch; yellow underparts with heavy black streaking. *Breeding female:* plumage duller. *Nonbreeding* and *juvenile:* gray upperparts may have black streaking; gray head; white eye ring; yellow throat; gray wings with 2 white wing bars; yellow underparts may have black streaking.
Size: *L* 4½–5 in; *W* 7½ in.

Status: uncommon to common migrant in the eastern half of the state and rare in the western half; rare winter vagrant on the Coastal Plain and in the Lower Rio Grande Valley.
Habitat: any wooded habitat, especially oak woodlands.
Nesting: does not nest in Texas.
Feeding: gleans vegetation and flycatches; eats insects and spiders; may also eat fruit.
Voice: hoarse *vink* call.
Similar Species: upper and lower tail patterns are unique. *Cape May Warbler* (p. 455): nonbreeding bird has pale eyebrow and no eye ring, often with pale underparts. *Prairie Warbler* (p. 355): bobs tail; yellow lower eye arc; no eye ring or yellow rump.
Best Sites: migrant "traps" on the Coastal Plain.

YELLOW-RUMPED WARBLER

Dendroica coronata

Yellow-rumped Warblers are the most abundant and widespread wood-warblers in North America. They may be seen statewide during migration and south of the Panhandle in winter, feeding at apple, juniper or sumac trees laden with fruit. • This species comes in two forms: the common, white-throated "Myrtle Warbler," which occurs in the eastern two-thirds of Texas, and the less common, yellow-throated "Audubon's Warbler," which is found in the west. • For night migrants such as the Yellow-rumped Warbler, collisions with human-made structures including buildings and towers cause hundreds of fatalities each year. • The scientific term *coronata*, Latin for "crowned," refers to this bird's yellow crown.

"Myrtle Warbler"

ID: yellow fore-shoulder patches and rump; white underparts; dark cheeks; faint white wing bars; thin eyebrow. *Male:* yellow crown; blue-gray upperparts with black streaking; black breast band and streaking along sides and flanks. *Female:* gray-brown upperparts with dark streaking; dark streaking on breast, sides and flanks.

Size: *L* 5–6 in; *W* 9 in.

Status: uncommon summer resident in the Davis Mts. and Guadalupe Mts., with nesting at high elevations; common to abundant migrant and winter resident statewide.

Habitat: *Breeding:* coniferous and mixed forests; rarely in pure deciduous woodlands. *In migration:* woodlands or shrubby areas.

Nesting: on a branch up to 25 ft up in a tree; female builds a nest of twigs, bark, grass and similar plant materials and lines it with hair and feathers; female incubates 4–5 smooth, buffy eggs with dark brown markings for 12–13 days.

Feeding: hawks and hovers for beetles, flies, wasps, caterpillars, moths and other insects; also gleans vegetation; sometimes eats berries.

Voice: sharp *chip* or *check* call. *Male:* song is a tinkling trill, often given in 2-note phrases that rise or fall at the end (there can be much variation among individuals).

Similar Species: combination of dull brown upperparts, yellow rump and yellow flank patch is diagnostic; little seasonal overlap with other yellow-rumped warblers.

Best Sites: *Breeding:* Davis Mountains SP; Guadalupe Mountains NP. *In migration* and *winter:* any park with wooded or shrubby areas.

348

GOLDEN-CHEEKED WARBLER

Dendroica chrysoparia

est seen sitting visibly upon the tops of junipers in central Texas, the Golden-cheeked Warbler is the only endemic breeding bird in the entire state. On the federal endangered list since 1990, this wood-warbler is a victim of both habitat loss and brood parasitism by the Brown-headed Cowbird. • Birders wishing to see this rare Texan treat will have to venture into the central Ashe juniper-oak woodlands. Beginning in mid-March, the males sing relentlessly, proclaiming the start of spring and declaring their territories. Anyone wanting to hear their song must do so before July, when this rare songbird migrates to Central America for winter. • The scientific name translates from Greek as "golden-cheeked tree inhabitant."

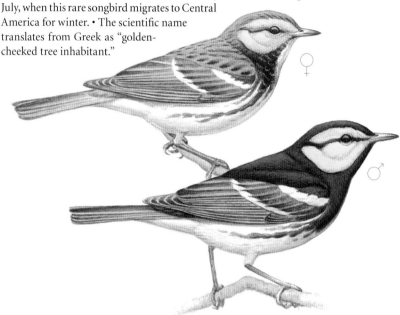

ID: black crown, bill, throat and "bib"; black eye line; golden cheeks; black upperparts; 2 white wing bars; clear white belly; black streaks on sides. *Juvenile:* olive green upperparts; eye line more faint; faint black "bib," throat and chin.
Size: *L* 5 in; *W* 7¾ in.
Status: federally endangered; rare to uncommon summer resident from the southeastern part of the Rolling Plains south through the eastern half of the Edwards Plateau; rare migrant south of the breeding range to the coast.
Habitat: endemic to the hillside "cedar breaks" of central Texas.

Nesting: in a fork of a horizontal branch; nest primarily of bark strips, moss, rootlets and leaves is camouflaged by bark strips held together by spider webs; female incubates 3–5 white to creamy-white eggs, marked with fine red or red-brown spots, for 12 days; both parents raise the young.
Feeding: gathers insects from branches and leaves in upper two-thirds of trees; also takes caterpillars and spiders.
Voice: distinctive *buzz*.
Similar Species: *Black-throated Green Warbler* (p. 350): little seasonal or range overlap; greenish cheek patch; olive green upperparts; yellowish below; faint eye line; black chin and throat.
Best Sites: Meridian SP; Balcones Canyonland NWR; Pedernales Falls SP; Lost Maples SP; Friedrich Wilderness Park (San Antonio); Emma Long Metropolitan Park (Austin).

BLACK-THROATED GREEN WARBLER

Dendroica virens

Accurately named, the male Black-throated Green Warbler has a green, black and white plumage unique among eastern wood-warblers. The female and juvenile are very similar, but with a mottled black or pale yellow throat. A diagnostic field mark of all plumages is a yellow wash to the undertail coverts. • The Black-throated Green Warbler breeds across southern Canada and the eastern U.S., and it winters from the southeastern states and Mexico through the West Indies and Central America to Panama. • This bird is generally an uncommon to common migrant in eastern Texas, but its migration period often lasts longer than those of other warblers. Small numbers also winter along the lower coast. The Black-throated Green Warbler is rarely observed in numbers, even during "fallouts" of migrants following strong winds. Rather, one or two birds are normally observed among flocks of other warblers or other small land birds.

ID: plain olive upperparts, including nape and crown; yellow face with faint olive eye line extending to cheek; blackish wings with 2 white bars; black breast and flanks; white underparts with pale yellow undertail coverts. *Male:* black throat. *Female:* yellow throat.
Size: *L* 4½–5 in; *W* 7½ in.
Status: common migrant in the eastern half of the state and rare in the western half; rare winter resident in the Lower Rio Grande Valley, on the Coastal Plain and inland to the southern half of the Edwards Plateau.
Habitat: any wooded habitat, especially oak woodlands.
Nesting: does not breed in Texas.
Feeding: gleans vegetation or flycatches for insects and spiders; also eats fruit.
Voice: clear *chip* call; song (rarely heard in Texas) is a series of 5 notes, the 4th lower-pitched.
Similar Species: *Blackburnian Warbler* (p. 352): female and juvenile have streaked back and orange or butterscotch on head and throat.
Best Sites: migrant "traps" on the Coastal Plain.

TOWNSEND'S WARBLER

Dendroica townsendi

A colorful black-and-yellow western species that seems to have found "greener pastures" in which to nest, the Townsend's Warbler still graces the Trans-Pecos during migration. A few may also be found in the Lower Rio Grande Valley during winter. • Conifer crowns are preferred foraging sites for many wood-warblers, making warbler watching a neck-straining experience. Because they feed largely in tall trees during winter, Townsend's Warblers are often "underlooked." Sharp eyes, good birding instincts and a bit of luck will go a long way in helping you meet the striking Townsend's Warbler. • This bird bears the name of one of the West's pioneer ornithologists, John Kirk Townsend (1809–51).

ID: yellow breast and sides streaked with black; white lower belly and undertail coverts; black ear patch encompasses eye; olive greenish upperparts; 2 white wing bars. *Male:* black chin, throat and crown. *Female:* yellow chin and throat; dusky crown and ear patch; white upper belly.
Size: *L* 5 in; *W* 8 in.
Status: uncommon to common migrant in the western third of the state and rare eastward in the Edwards Plateau and Lower Rio Grande Valley; very rare winter resident along the Rio Grande.

Habitat: lowland riparian and oak woodlands, mixed oak-coniferous forests, conifer and exotic tree groves and suburban parks and gardens. *Winter:* partial to semi-open, full-crowned lowland conifers.
Nesting: does not nest in Texas.
Feeding: gleans vegetation and flycatches for beetles, flies, wasps and caterpillars.
Voice: incisive *tzp* call sounds electronic; male's song (rarely heard in Texas) is wheezy, ascending and variable.
Similar Species: *Hermit Warbler* (p. 456): gray back; white breast, belly and undertail; all-yellow face with no dark ear patch.
Best Sites: Franklin Mountains SP; Guadalupe Mountains NP; Davis Mountains SP; Big Bend Ranch SP; Big Bend NP.

BLACKBURNIAN WARBLER

Dendroica fusca

A breeding-plumaged male Blackburnian Warbler is one of the most dazzling of North American birds. When this colorful bird forages high among the crowns of hardwoods, his fiery orange throat glows ablaze in spring. • Birders in eastern Texas may see this bird in breeding plumage for a brief time during April and May, following its migration across the Gulf of Mexico. It is generally more numerous here in spring relative to fall because the southbound migration route lies slightly east of Texas. The white or pale "braces" on the back, when present, are diagnostic of this species. • The Blackburnian Warbler was named after Anna Blackburne (1726–93), an English botanist and museum curator whose brother collected birds in the U.S. The Latin word *fusca*, meaning "dusky," is a strange name to be given to such a brightly colored species.

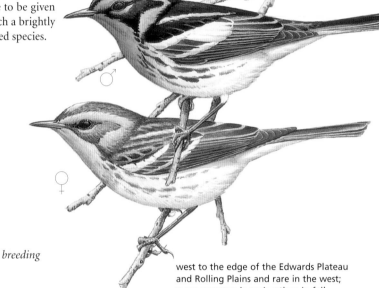

breeding

ID: distinctive face pattern of dark cheek patch and pale lower eye arc; white undertail coverts. *Breeding male:* black upperparts with pale "braces"; black nape and hindcrown; orange forecrown, face, lower eye-arc and throat; black cheek; black wings with white panel; orange breast; black streaking on flanks. *Breeding female:* duller upperparts; brown crown; duller orange areas; 2 white wing bars.

Size: *L* 4½–5½ in; *W* 8½ in.

Status: uncommon to locally common migrant from eastern parts of the state west to the edge of the Edwards Plateau and Rolling Plains and rare in the west; more common in spring than in fall.

Habitat: any wooded habitat, especially oak woodlands.

Nesting: does not nest in Texas.

Feeding: forages on uppermost branches, gleaning budworms, flies, beetles and other invertebrates; occasionally hover-gleans.

Voice: rich *chip* call; song (rarely heard in Texas) is a series of very high-pitched notes.

Similar Species: The orange on the adults is diagnostic. *Yellow-throated Warbler* (p. 353): tree-creeping behavior; blue-gray upperparts; white eyebrow and ear patch; bright yellow throat. *Prairie Warbler* (p. 355): faint yellowish wing bars; no distinct solid angular dark facial patch.

Best Sites: migrant "traps" on the Coastal Plain.

YELLOW-THROATED WARBLER

Dendroica dominica

When its bright, lemon-yellow throat and upper breast catch the sun, they give the Yellow-throated Warbler an unexpected flamboyance at odds with its generally quiet and unassuming demeanor. • Yellow-throats are fond of wet lowland forests, preferring the upper canopy. They forage more like creepers than warblers, inserting their unusually long bills into bark cracks and crevices. Yellow-throats often also forage on the undersides of horizontal branches and sometimes on the trunk, as does the Black-and-white Warbler. • This bird breeds in eastern Texas, and fall or early winter can produce the odd wayward Yellow-throat at backyard feeders, particularly along the coast. Three races exist, but Texan birds belong to the white-lored race *(D.d. albilora)*.

white-lored form

ID: triangular, black face mask; black forehead; bold white eyebrow and ear patch; yellow throat and upper breast; white underparts with black streaking on sides; 2 white wing bars; bluish gray upperparts.

Size: *L* 5–5½ in; *W* 8 in.

Status: rare to locally common summer resident from eastern Texas west through the Edwards Plateau; rare migrant in western Texas; rare winter resident in the Pineywoods of eastern Texas and on the Coastal Plain.

Habitat: primarily riparian woodlands; hardwood, pine and cypress forests; occasionally seen at backyard feeders in winter.

Nesting: high in an oak, cypress or pine tree, often near a branch tip; female builds a cup nest in Spanish moss and lines it with sycamore down and feathers; female incubates 4 variably marked, greenish or grayish white eggs for 12–13 days.

Feeding: gleans insects, spiders and other small prey from trunks or branches; also sallies for flying insects.

Voice: soft clear *chip* call; song is a beautiful series of down-slurred whistles ending with a 2-note flourish.

Similar Species: *Magnolia Warbler* (p. 347): black "necklace"; yellow breast, belly and rump; no white ear patch. *Blackburnian Warbler* (p. 352): yellow-orange to orange-red throat, eyebrow, ear patch and crown stripe; dark brown to blackish upperparts; often shows yellowish underparts. *Yellow-throated Vireo* (p. 275): no black and white on face; unstreaked sides.

Best Sites: Daingerfield SP; Huntsville SP; Jesse H. Jones Park (Houston); Garner SP.

PINE WARBLER

Dendroica pinus

Perfectly named for its habitat, the unassuming Pine Warbler is often difficult to find. It typically forages near the top of very tall, mature pine trees, preferring long-needled white pines and red pines. This preference limits its breeding to the Pineywoods of East Texas and the "Lost Pines" of the Edwards Plateau. Occasionally, a foraging Pine Warbler can be seen smeared with patches of pine resin. • The Pine Warbler's modest appearance, which resembles that of some immature and fall-plumaged vireos and warblers, forces birders to get a good, long look before making a positive identification. Female and immature Pine Warblers are most often confused with Bay-breasted Warblers or Blackpoll Warblers in fall plumage. • The Pine Warbler is one of the few wood-warblers with a range nearly limited to North America.

and rare from the South Plains to the Lower Rio Grande Valley.

Habitat: *Breeding:* open, mature pine woodlands and mature pine plantations. *In migration:* mixed and deciduous woodlands.

Nesting: toward a pine limb tip; female builds a deep, open cup nest of twigs, bark, weeds, grass, pine needles and spider silk lined with feathers; pair incubates 3–5 brown-speckled, whitish eggs for about 10 days.

Feeding: gleans from the ground or foliage (by climbing); may hang upside down on branch tips; eats mostly insects, berries and seeds.

Voice: sweet *chip* call note; song is a short, musical trill.

Similar Species: *Bay-breasted Warbler* (p. 356) and *Blackpoll Warbler* (p. 457): non-breeding and immature have dark streaking on head, back or both and long, thin, yellow eyebrow. *Prairie Warbler* (p. 355): dark facial stripes; darker side streaking; yellowish wing bars. *Yellow-throated Vireo* (p. 275): gray rump; unstreaked sides.

Best Sites: Daingerfield SP; Huntsville SP; W.G. Jones State Forest; Bastrop SP.

ID: *Male:* olive green head and back; dark grayish wings and tail; whitish to dusky wing bars; yellow throat and breast; faded streaking or dusky wash on sides; white undertail coverts and belly; faint dark eye line; broken, faint yellow eye ring. *Female:* duller, especially in fall.

Size: *L* 5–5½ in; *W* 8½ in.

Status: resident in the Pineywoods and the "Lost Pines"; rare migrant in the Panhandle, northern South Plains and the eastern Edwards Plateau; uncommon to common winter resident in the eastern third of Texas

PRAIRIE WARBLER

Dendroica discolor

Open scrublands host the summer activities of the inappropriately named Prairie Warbler. This conspicuous, tail-wagging, yellow warbler occupies early successional areas with such poor soil conditions that the vegetation remains short and scattered. • It is thought the Prairie Warbler was rare over much of its current breeding range in the early 1800s, before North America was widely colonized. As settlers cleared land, the Prairie Warbler gradually occupied what is now its current range. • A male Prairie Warbler may return each year to a favored nest site until the vegetation in that area grows too tall and dense, at which point he moves to a new area. • This bird's common name is derived from Alexander Wilson's discovery of the first bird on a Kentucky pine barren—a habitat referred to as a "prairie" in the Southeast.

ID: bright yellow face and underparts, with paler undertail coverts; wags tail. *Male:* dark cheek stripe and eye line; black-streaked sides; olive gray upperparts; inconspicuous chestnut back streaks; 2 faint yellowish wing bars. *Female:* less continuous, paler streaking; whitish "spectacles"; no black facial markings.
Size: L 4½–5 in; W 7 in.
Status: rare to locally uncommon summer resident in the Pineywoods; uncommon migrant in eastern Texas and rare west through the Edwards Plateau and Lower Rio Grande Valley to the eastern Trans-Pecos.
Habitat: shrubby areas; young pine stands. *Breeding:* dry, open, scrubby sand dunes.
Nesting: sometimes forms small, loose colonies; low in a shrub or small tree; female builds an open cup nest of soft vegetation lined with animal hair; female incubates 4 whitish

eggs with brown spots for 11–14 days; pair raises the young.
Feeding: gleans, hover-gleans and occasionally hawks for prey, mainly insects; also eats berries and tree sap exposed by sapsuckers; favors caterpillars for nestlings.
Voice: sweet *chip* call; buzzy song is an ascending series of *zee* notes.
Similar Species: *Pine Warbler* (p. 354): lighter side streaking; whitish wing bars; no distinctive dark streaking on face. *Yellow-throated Warbler* (p. 353): white belly; bold white wing bars, eyebrow and ear patch. *Bay-breasted Warbler* (p. 356) and *Blackpoll Warbler* (p. 457): nonbreeding and immature birds have white bellies and wing bars and lighter upperparts with dark streaking.
Best Sites: Caddo Lake SP; Martin Dies, Jr. SP; Big Thicket National Preserve.

BAY-BREASTED WARBLER

Dendroica castanea

L ike all migratory birds, Bay-breasted Warblers face many dangers on their travels. Their annual trip north to the spruce-fir forests of Canada, however, seems well worth it for the abundance of summer food found there. Although rare in some years, Bay-breasts may pass through the eastern Great Plains in large numbers in spring following a successful nesting season the previous year. • Bay-breasted Warblers are spruce budworm specialists, and their populations fluctuate from year to year along with the cyclical rise and fall of budworm numbers. In outbreak years, this species may eat over 5000 budworms per acre through the breeding season. Although Bay-breasts are insectivorous on their breeding grounds, they switch to an almost all-fruit diet while they winter in Panama and Colombia. • Most Bay-breasted Warblers spend winter close to the equator. Because the seasons and day length are similar year-round there, the birds rely heavily on their internal clocks, rather than external clues, to spark their spring migration northward.

breeding

ID: *Breeding male:* black face and chin; chestnut crown, throat, sides and flanks; creamy-colored belly, under-tail coverts and patch on side of neck; 2 white wing bars. *Breeding female:* paler colors overall; dusky face; whitish to creamy underparts and neck patch; faint chestnut cap; rusty wash on sides and flanks. *Nonbreeding:* yellow olive head and back; dark-streaked crown and back; whiter underparts.
Size: *L* 5–6 in; *W* 9 in.
Status: common to abundant spring migrant and uncommon fall migrant in the east and rare in the west.

Habitat: woodlands or areas with tall shrubs; coastal areas.
Nesting: does not nest in Texas.
Feeding: gleans vegetation for insects and spiders; may also eat fruit.
Voice: loud *chip* call; song (rarely heard in Texas) is a series of 3–10 high-pitched *see* or *see-see* notes.
Similar Species: Breeding adults are unmistakable. *Chestnut-sided Warbler* (p. 346): nonbreeding bird has greener upperparts, plain gray face with narrow, white eye ring, yellowish wing bars and white underparts. *Blackpoll Warbler* (p. 457): nonbreeding bird has white or pale yellow underparts, faint streaking on sides of neck and flanks, white undertail coverts and, usually, yellow legs and feet.
Best Sites: migrant "traps" on the Coastal Plain.

BLACK-AND-WHITE WARBLER

Mniotilta varia

The foraging behavior of the Black-and-white Warbler stands in sharp contrast to that of most of its kin. Rather than dancing or flitting quickly between twig perches, the Black-and-white Warbler behaves like a creeper or nuthatch—a distantly related group of birds. Birders with frayed nerves and tired eyes from watching flitty warblers will be refreshed by the sight of this bird as it methodically creeps up and down tree trunks, probing bark crevices. • Novice birders can easily identify this uniquely colored, two-tone warbler, which retains its standard plumage year-round. A keen ear also helps to distinguish this forest-dweller: its gentle, oscillating song—like a wheel in need of greasing—is easily recognized and remembered.

ID: black-and-white-striped crown; white-striped, dark upperparts; 2 white wing bars; white underparts with black streaking on sides, flanks and undertail coverts; black legs. *Male:* black cheeks and throat. *Female:* gray cheeks; white throat.

Size: *L* 4½–5½ in; *W* 8 in.

Status: uncommon to locally common summer resident in east Texas and west through the Edwards Plateau; uncommon to common migrant throughout most of the state, becoming less common in the western third; rare to uncommon winter resident on the Coastal Plain and in the Lower Rio Grande Valley.

Habitat: deciduous or mixed forests, often near water; also uses cedar swamps or thickets bordering wetlands.

Nesting: usually on the ground next to a tree, log or large rock; in a shallow scrape, often among a pile of dead leaves; female builds a cup nest of grass, leaves, bark strips, rootlets and pine needles and lines it with fur and fine grass; female incubates 5 brown-flecked, creamy white eggs for 10–12 days.

Feeding: gleans insect eggs, larval insects, beetles, spiders and other invertebrates while creeping along tree trunks and branches.

Voice: sharp *pit* and soft, high *seet* calls; series of high, thin, 2-syllable notes: *weetsee weetsee weetsee weetsee weetsee weetsee.*

Similar Species: *Yellow-throated Warbler* (p. 353): generally similar tree-climbing behavior and plumage, but with distinct yellow throat. *Blackpoll Warbler* (p. 457): spring male has solid black cap, clean white undertail coverts and yellow legs and feet.

Best Sites: *Breeding:* Daingerfield SP; Meridian SP; Bastrop SP; W.G. Jones State Forest. *In migration:* migratory "traps" on the Coastal Plain.

AMERICAN REDSTART

Setophaga ruticilla

Consistently listed as a favorite among birders, the supercharged American Redstart flits from branch to branch in dizzying pursuit of prey. Even when perched, its tail sways rhythmically back and forth. Few birds can rival a mature male redstart for his plumage of contrasting black and flaming orange, his approachability and his animated behavior. The American Redstart behaves much the same way on its wintering grounds in Latin America, where it is locally known as *candelita* ("little candle"). • Uniquely among warblers, Redstarts alternate between songs instead of sticking to one tune. Their high-pitched, lisping, trilly songs are so variable that even experienced birders faced with an unknown warbler song will exclaim, "It must be a Redstart!"

ID: white belly and undertail coverts. *Male:* black upperparts and breast; reddish orange foreshoulder, wing and tail patches. *Female:* olive brown upperparts; grayish green head; yellow foreshoulder, wing and tail patches. *In flight:* long tail with black tip and center; male has orange-tinged wing lining.

Size: *L* 5 in; *W* 8 in.

Status: very rare summer resident in the northeast; uncommon to common migrant in the eastern half of the state and rare to uncommon in the west.

Habitat: *Breeding:* open deciduous or mixed forests with a thick understory, often near water. *In migration* and *winter:* any wooded habitat.

Nesting: in the fork of a shrub or sapling, usually in a wet area; female builds a cup nest of twigs, plant down and lichen lined with feathers; female incubates 4 variably marked, whitish eggs for 11–12 days.

Feeding: actively gleans foliage and hawks for insects and spiders on leaves, buds and branches; often hover-gleans.

Voice: sharp, sweet *chip* call. *Male:* song is a highly variable series of *tseet* or *zee* notes, often at different pitches.

Similar Species: *Painted Redstart* (p. 457): found locally in Chisos Mts. only; black overall; bright red belly; white wing patches; white outer tail feathers. *Magnolia Warbler* (p. 347): can be confused in poor light; always yellow on throat and underparts; tail band white and closer to tip. *Tennessee Warbler* (p. 341): similar to 1st-year female; no yellow in tail and sides.

Best Sites: *Breeding:* check second-growth forest openings and power-line cuts for this colorful warbler. *In migration:* migrant "traps" on the Coastal Plain.

PROTHONOTARY WARBLER

Protonotaria citrea

The stunning Prothonotary Warbler is the only eastern wood-warbler that nests in cavities. It breeds throughout the eastern U.S. and winters from Mexico to northern South America. • Prothonotary Warblers breed in swamps and along rivers and creeks; snags in or near stagnant water provide ideal nesting habitat. They remain partial to forested wetlands even during migration. Prothonotary Warblers are usually found close to the ground, and they are often best located by their sharp *chink* calls. • This bird acquired its unusual name because its plumage was thought to resemble the yellow hoods worn by prothonotaries, who are high-ranking clerics in the Roman Catholic Church.

ID: relatively big, yellow head; conspicuous large, black eyes; yellow breast; shortish tail. *Male:* olive back; gray wings; yellow underparts with white undertail coverts; gray tail with white patches in outer feathers. *Female* and *juvenile:* duller head and underparts.

Size: *L* 5½ in; *W* 8½ in.

Status: uncommon to common summer resident from eastern Texas west to the edge of the Edwards Plateau and south through the eastern half of the South Texas Brush Country; uncommon to common migrant from eastern Texas south to the Lower Rio Grande Valley and rare in the rest of the state.

Habitat: deciduous or cypress swamps and riparian woodlands.

Nesting: in a natural cavity or birdhouse; mostly the male builds a cup nest of twigs and leaves, lined with finer materials; female incubates 4–6 brown-spotted, pale eggs for 12–14 days; 2 broods per year.

Feeding: gleans from vegetation; may also hop on floating debris or creep along tree trunks; eats various insects and small mollusks.

Voice: brisk *tink* call. *Male:* song is a loud, ringing series of *sweet* or *zweet* notes issued on a single pitch; flight song for both sexes is *chewee chewee chee chee.*

Similar Species: *Blue-winged Warbler* (p. 339): white wing bars; black eye line; yellowish white undertail coverts. *Yellow Warbler* (p. 345): dark wings and tail with yellow highlights; yellow undertail coverts; male has reddish streaking on breast. *Hooded Warbler* (p. 369): female has yellow undertail coverts and yellow olive upperparts.

Best Sites: *Breeding:* Caddo Lake SP; Daingerfield SP; Palmetto SP; Sea Rim SP; Brazos Bend SP. *In migration:* migrant "traps" on the Coastal Plain.

WORM-EATING WARBLER

Helmitheros vermivora

Eagerly sought during migration, the Worm-eating Warbler is a subtly attractive species. A largish warbler with a large head and bill and striped crown, it is typically seen along the coast, although it is likely to turn up elsewhere, especially in the eastern third of the state. Watch for this bird hopping from branch to branch or creeping along large branches, probing crevices for insects, spiders and caterpillars. While habitually searching clumps of dead leaves for prey, the Worm-eating Warbler often hangs upside-down. • The Worm-eating Warbler is the only Texas-breeding warbler that nests on the ground. Nests are typically built on slopes and near water, well hidden in the leaf litter. The female becomes completely still if she is approached while on the nest, relying on her striped crown for concealment. Parents will feign injury by dragging their tails or wings along the ground to lead predators away from their nests or fledglings.

ID: grayish buff tail, back and wings; grayish buff head; bold, black crown stripes; buffy underparts; pale legs and feet.
Size: *L* 5 in; *W* 8½ in.
Status: uncommon to common migrant in the eastern third of the state, rare in the central third and very rare in the western third; very rare and local summer resident in the middle third of the Pineywoods.
Habitat: steep, deciduous woodland slopes and ravines and swampy woodlands with shrubby understory cover.

Nesting: on the ground, usually on a hillside or ravine bank, often near water; hidden under leaf litter; female builds a cup nest of decaying leaves lined with fine grass, moss, plant stems and hair; female incubates 3–5 brown-speckled white eggs for about 13 days.
Feeding: gleans prey from the ground or foliage or probes clumps of dead leaves; feeds mostly on caterpillars and other insects and spiders.
Voice: loud *chip* call; song is a rapid dry trill.
Similar Species: *Swainson's Warbler* (p. 361): similar in plumage pattern and ground-dwelling habits but has rusty crown without black stripes. *Red-eyed Vireo* (p. 279): gray crown; white eyebrow; red eyes; yellow undertail coverts.
Best Sites: *Breeding:* Alabama Creek WMA (Davy Crockett National Forest); Huntsville SP; W.G. Jones State Forest. *In migration:* migrant "traps" on the Coastal Plain.

SWAINSON'S WARBLER

Limnothlypis swainsonii

A little-known inhabitant of dense thickets in the swamps of the Southeast, the Swainson's Warbler is distinguished from other wood-warblers by its plain looks and a large bill. It is an uncommon to locally common breeding resident in the eastern third of Texas. It breeds in canebrakes, saw palmetto and other thick underbrush in wet areas and along streams in our state. It remains on or near the ground, relying on its non-showy plumage and unassuming manner for concealment. • Excepting the presumably extinct Bachman's Warbler *(Vermivora bachmanii)*, the Swainson's Warbler is the only wood-warbler that lays unmarked, white eggs. • Like the Swainson's Hawk and the Swainson's Thrush, this species is named for William Swainson (1789–1855), a noted British writer and naturalist.

ID: fairly large bill; brown upperparts; rusty cap; pale face with whitish eyebrow and dark eye line; pale throat and underparts; pinkish legs.

Size: *L* 5½ in; *W* 9 in.

Status: uncommon to locally common summer resident in the eastern third of the state, rare west to the eastern edge of the Edwards Plateau and south to the central Coastal Plain; uncommon migrant in the eastern half of the state, becoming less common westward and very rare in the Trans-Pecos.

Habitat: *Breeding:* stands of saw palmetto and other dense thickets in wet areas and the edges of swamps. *In migration:* various habitats with dense vegetation.

Nesting: near the ground, often among palmetto fronds; female builds a bulky cup nest of leaves, pine needles and other vegetation; female incubates 3–5 sparsely spotted, white eggs for 13–15 days.

Feeding: gleans prey from the ground or foliage or flips over leaves; eats primarily insects, spiders and millipedes.

Voice: loud *chip* call; song is a short series of slurred, whistled notes, often ending with a rising *tea-o*.

Similar Species: *Worm-eating Warbler* (p. 360): shares plumage pattern and ground-dwelling habits but often found high in foliage; buffy crown boldly striped with black. *Red-eyed Vireo* (p. 279): red eyes; thicker bill; black line separates gray crown from white eyebrow.

Best Sites: *Breeding:* Alabama Creek WMA; Palmetto SP; Baytown Nature Center (Harris Co.); Brazos Bend SP. *In migration:* migrant "traps" on the Coastal Plain.

361

OVENBIRD

Seiurus aurocapilla

Plain olive upperparts and a spotted breast make the Ovenbird appear thrushlike, but its small size, striped crown and ground-nesting habits place it among the wood-warblers. • Although the Ovenbird nests in southeastern Oklahoma, there are no nesting records for our state; we encounter it primarily as a migrant in eastern Texas. • Ovenbirds are nearly exclusively terrestrial while in Texas, walking with deliberate steps around hammocks and other open woodlands like windup toys, often while bobbing their heads. They can be quite tame during migration, allowing the approach of a birder to within a few feet. At other times, Ovenbirds show agitation by slightly raising their crests and chipping loudly. • The plumages of Ovenbirds vary little between the genders and among age classes. • The name "Ovenbird" refers to this bird's unusual dome-shaped ground nest.

ID: olive brown upperparts; white eye ring; heavy, dark streaking on white breast, sides and flanks; rufous crown has black border; pink legs; white undertail coverts; no wing bars.
Size: *L* 6 in; *W* 9½ in.
Status: uncommon to common migrant in the eastern half of the state and rare in the western half; rare winter resident on the Coastal Plain and in the Lower Rio Grande Valley.

Habitat: open woodlands, especially those with streams and pools of water.
Nesting: does not nest in Texas.
Feeding: gleans the ground for worms, snails and insects; also gleans vegetation for fruit.
Voice: loud *chip* call; song (rarely heard in Texas) is a series of doubled notes increasing in volume.
Similar Species: *Thrushes* (pp. 321–27, 454): larger; no black-bordered, rufous crowns; most have buffy or dusky breasts with little or no streaking on lower belly. *Northern Waterthrush* (p. 363) and *Louisiana Waterthrush* (p. 364): wholly dark crown; bold white or yellowish eyebrow; no white eye ring; bob hind end constantly.
Best Sites: migrant "traps" on the Coastal Plain.

NORTHERN WATERTHRUSH

Seiurus noveboracensis

Although the Northern Waterthrush has a long body that looks "thrushlike," it is actually a large wood-warbler. • This bird skulks along the shores and fallen trees of deciduous swamps and coniferous bogs, often wagging or bobbing its tail. During spring and fall, migrating Northern Waterthrushes also appear among dry upland forests or along lofty park trails and boardwalks. Backyards featuring a small garden pond may also attract migrating waterthrushes. Typically, Northern Waterthrushes migrate later than similar looking Louisiana Waterthrushes. • The voice of the Northern Waterthrush is loud and raucous for such a small bird, and it was once known as "New York Warbler," in reference to the city so well known for its decibels. The word *noveboracensis* also means "of New York."

ID: pale yellowish to buff eyebrow; pale yellowish to buff underparts with dark streaking; finely spotted throat; olive brown upperparts; pinkish legs; frequently bobs tail.

Size: *L* 5–6 in; *W* 9½ in.

Status: uncommon to common migrant in the eastern half of the state and rare in the western half; rare winter resident in the Lower Rio Grande Valley.

Habitat: always around water; bayheads, swamps and riparian forests.

Nesting: does not nest in Texas.

Feeding: gleans the ground, leaf litter or low vegetation; eats insects, spiders, worms, snails and small crustaceans; often tosses aside leaf litter with bill; may even take small fish from shallow water.

Voice: loud, sharp *chink* call.

Similar Species: *Louisiana Waterthrush* (p. 364): broader, white eyebrow broadens behind eye; plain white throat; buff orange wash on flanks. *Ovenbird* (p. 362): does not bob tail; black-bordered, rufous crown; white eye ring; no eyebrow.

Best Sites: migrant "traps" on the Coastal Plain.

LOUISIANA WATERTHRUSH

Seiurus motacilla

The Louisiana Waterthrush is often seen sallying along the shorelines of babbling streams and gently swirling pools in search of its next meal. This bird inhabits swamps and sluggish streams throughout much of its North American range, but, where its range overlaps with that of the Northern Waterthrush, it inhabits shorelines near fast-flowing water. Louisiana Waterthrushes have never been recorded in great numbers in Texas, partly because little suitable habitat remains for them. • The Louisiana Waterthrush has a larger bill, pinker legs, whiter eye stripes and less streaking on its throat than the Northern Waterthrush. Both waterthrushes are easily identified by their habit of bobbing their heads and moving their tails up and down as they walk, but the Louisiana Waterthrush bobs its tail more slowly and also tends to sway from side to side. The scientific term *motacilla* is Latin for "wagtail."

ID: brownish upperparts; long bill; pink legs; white underparts; buff orange wash on flanks; long, dark streaks on breast and sides; buff and white eyebrow; clean, white throat.

Size: *L* 6 in; *W* 10 in.

Status: rare to uncommon summer resident from the eastern third of the state west to the eastern edge of the Edwards Plateau and south to the central Coastal Plain; uncommon migrant in the eastern half of the state and rare in the western half.

Habitat: wooded areas around water.

Nesting: concealed within a rocky hollow or tangle of tree roots; pair builds a cup nest of leaves, bark strips, twigs and moss lined with animal hair, ferns and rootlets; female incubates 3–6 speckled, creamy white eggs for about 14 days.

Feeding: gleans the ground, leaf litter or low vegetation; eats insects, spiders, worms, snails and small crustaceans; often tosses aside leaf litter with bill; may take small fish from shallow water.

Voice: loud, sharp *chink* call; song is a series of 3–4 distinctive slurred whistles followed by a descending twitter.

Similar Species: *Northern Waterthrush* (p. 363): yellowish to buff eyebrow narrows behind eye; streaked throat; underparts have no contrasting flanks. *Ovenbird* (p. 362): does not bob tail; black-bordered, rufous crown; white eye ring; no eyebrow.

Best Sites: *Breeding:* Daingerfield SP; W.G. Jones State Forest; Jesse H. Jones Park; Brazos Bend SP. *In migration:* migrant "traps" on the Coastal Plain.

KENTUCKY WARBLER

Oporornis formosus

Yet another eastern warbler found only in eastern Texas, the Kentucky Warbler is the only *Oporornis* warbler to nest south of Minnesota. Never an easy bird to see, the Kentucky Warbler rarely leaves the confines of its dense ground cover where it forages stealthily. • The shy and elusive males sing their loud springtime song from secluded perches. As a general rule, males of all warblers sing most actively and feed only intermittently in the morning, but they quiet down and feed more actively in the afternoon. Once the young hatch, singing becomes rare as both the male and the female spend much of their time feeding the young. Unmated males may continue to sing throughout summer. The Kentucky Warbler's song may be confused with that of the Carolina Wren, but the Kentucky Warbler will sing the same song pattern repeatedly, whereas the Carolina Wren varies its song constantly. • Like waterthrushes and Ovenbirds, Kentucky Warblers bob their tails up and down as they walk.

ID: olive upperparts, including nape; yellow "spectacles"; wholly yellow underparts; pink legs and feet; wags tail. *Male:* black crown; black patch below eye. *Female:* less black on crown; little or no black on face.

Size: *L* 5–5½ in; *W* 8½ in.

Status: uncommon to common summer resident and migrant in the eastern half of the state, west to the eastern edge of the Rolling Plains and Edwards Plateau; rare migrant in western Texas.

Habitat: dense understory of moist deciduous or mixed woodlands and riparian areas.

Nesting: on or near the ground; pair builds a cup nest of plant material lined with rootlets and hair; female incubates 4–5 cream-colored eggs, spotted or blotched with reddish brown, for 12–13 days; may produce 2 broods per year.

Feeding: flips over leaves or gleans the ground or low vegetation for insects and spiders; also takes fruit.

Voice: low *chuck* call; song is a rich and loud rolling series of 2- or 3-syllable notes, similar to the song of the Carolina Wren.

Similar Species: *Common Yellowthroat* (p. 368): no "spectacles"; dingier belly and undertail coverts; male's black mask includes forehead and eyes.

Best Sites: *Breeding:* Palmetto SP; Huntsville SP; W.G. Jones State Forest; Bear Creek Pioneer Park (Houston). *In migration:* migrant "traps" on the Coastal Plain.

MOURNING WARBLER

Oporornis philadelphia

Mourning Warblers seldom leave the protection of their dense, shrubby, often impenetrable habitat, and they tend to utter their *cheery* song only on their breeding territory. Riparian areas, regenerating cut-blocks and patches of recently burnt forest provide the low shrubs and saplings that these warblers rely on for nesting and foraging. They almost always choose areas with broadleaf shrubs. • Mourning Warblers are best seen during fall migration, when backyard shrubs and raspberry thickets may attract small, silent flocks. They are also seen in coastal locations where cover is more limited. • This bird's dark hood reminded pioneering ornithologist Alexander Wilson of someone dressed in mourning. Some birders like to remember this bird's name by thinking that it is mourning the loss of its eye ring.

ID: yellow underparts; olive green upperparts; short tail; pinkish legs. *Male:* usually no eye ring (possible broken eye ring); bluish gray hood; black upper breast patch. *Female:* possible thin eye ring; gray hood; whitish chin and throat. *Immature:* grayish brown hood; pale gray to yellow chin and throat; thin, incomplete eye ring.
Size: *L* 5–5½ in; *W* 7½ in.
Status: uncommon to common migrant from eastern Texas to the eastern portions of the Edwards Plateau and Rolling Plains and south to the Lower Rio Grande Valley and rare elsewhere.

Habitat: dense and shrubby thickets, tangles and brambles, often in moist areas of forest clearings and along the edges of ponds, lakes and streams.
Nesting: does not nest in Texas.
Feeding: forages in dense, low shrubs for caterpillars, beetles, spiders and other invertebrates.
Voice: loud, low *check* call; husky, 2-part song (rarely heard in Texas) is variable and lower-pitched at the end: *churry, churry, churry, churry, chorry, chorry.*
Similar Species: *Connecticut Warbler:* bold complete eye ring; no black breast patch; long undertail coverts make tail look very short; immature has light gray throat. *Nashville Warbler* (p. 343): bright yellow throat; dark legs. *MacGillivray's Warbler* (p. 367): incomplete white eye ring; darker gray hood; pale yellow underparts; longer tail with shorter undertail coverts; female has paler throat.
Best Sites: migrant "traps" on the Coastal Plain.

MACGILLIVRAY'S WARBLER

Oporornis tolmiei

A tendency to keep to dense, impenetrable thickets at high elevations makes it difficult to get a clear view of the MacGillvray's Warbler. Birders often have to make do with hearing its loud, rich *chip* call to ascertain its presence, but because it is not given to advertising itself, it is easily overlooked in our state. • Different species of wood warblers can coexist through a partitioning of foraging "niches" and feeding strategies, reducing competition for food sources and avoiding the exhaustion of particular resources. Some warblers inhabit high treetops, a few feed and nest along outer tree branches, some at high levels and some at lower levels, and others restrict themselves to inner branches and tree trunks. MacGillivray's Warblers have found their niche among dense understory shrubbery and brushy tangles. • Audubon named this warbler in honor of Scotsman William MacGillivray, who edited and reworked the manuscript of Audubon's classic work, *Ornithological Biographies,* in the 1830s.

ID: yellow underparts; olive green upperparts; broken bold white eye ring; pinkish legs. *Male:* slate gray hood; blackish "bib." *Female* and *immature:* light gray-brown hood and "bib"; white chin.

Size: *L* 5–5¾ in; *W* 5¼ in.

Status: uncommon migrant in the western half of the state and rare eastward along the central Coastal Plain and on the Blackland Prairies.

Habitat: moist, shady riparian thickets and other similar habitats.

Nesting: does not nest in Texas.

Feeding: gleans low vegetation and the ground for beetles, bees, leafhoppers, insect larvae and other invertebrates; does not ordinarily ascend high into tall trees.

Voice: low, rich *chip* call; song (rarely heard in Texas) is a clear, rolling *sweeter sweeter sweeter sugar sugar.*

Similar Species: *Nashville Warbler* (p. 343): yellow chin; complete eye ring; white between legs; bobs tail. *Common Yellowthroat* (p. 368): female has narrow pale eye ring and no grayish "bib."

Best Sites: almost any park in the western half of the state.

367

COMMON YELLOWTHROAT

Geothlypis trichas

The bumblebee colors of the male Common Yellowthroat's black mask and yellow throat identify this skulking wetland resident. He sings his *witchety* song from strategically chosen cattail perches that he visits in rotation, fiercely guarding his territory against intrusion by other males. The maskless female remains mostly hidden from view in thick vegetation while she tends to the nest. • Unlike most wood-warblers, the Common Yellowthroat prefers marshlands and wet, overgrown meadows to forests. • The Common Yellowthroat is one of the most numerous and widespread wood-warblers in North America, and it has more races than all but the Yellow Warbler. As many as ten races of the Common Yellowthroat have been recorded in our state. • Common Yellowthroats are very curious, and they readily respond to "pishing," often flying in to within a few feet of a birder.

ID: olive upperparts, including nape and hindcrown; pale to dusky belly and undertail coverts; pink legs and feet. *Breeding male:* black mask across forehead and forecrown, with pale rear border; yellow throat and breast. *Female:* no mask; olive face; narrow pale eye ring. *Juvenile:* similar to female; male shows hint of mask.

Size: *L* 5 in; *W* 6½ in.

Status: rare to locally uncommon summer resident in most of Texas; common migrant statewide; uncommon winter resident in eastern Texas, the Lower Rio Grande Valley and along the Rio Grande to Big Bend NP.

Habitat: marshes, palmetto thickets and other dense understory, often near water.

Nesting: on or near the ground, often in a small shrub or among emergent aquatic vegetation; female builds a bulky, open cup nest of weeds, grass, sedges and other materials lined with hair and soft plant fibers; female incubates 3–5 darkly spotted, creamy white eggs for about 12 days.

Feeding: gleans vegetation and hovers for adult and larval insects, including dragonflies, spiders and beetles; occasionally eats seeds.

Voice: sharp *tcheck* or *tchet* call; song is a clear, oscillating *witchety witchety witchety-witch.*

Similar Species: male's black mask is distinctive. *Kentucky Warbler* (p. 365): yellow "spectacles"; all-yellow underparts; half mask. *Yellow Warbler* (p. 345): brighter yellow overall; yellow wing highlights; all-yellow underparts. *Orange-crowned Warbler* (p. 342): dull yellow-olive overall; faint breast streaks.

Best Sites: *Breeding:* Coastal Plain marshlands. *In migration:* wetlands statewide.

HOODED WARBLER

Wilsonia citrina

Despite nesting low to the ground, Hooded Warblers require extensive mature forests, where fallen trees have opened gaps in the canopy, encouraging understory growth. • Just as different species of wood-warblers can coexist in a limited environment by selectively foraging exclusively in certain areas, Hooded Warblers also partition between the genders. Males tend to forage in treetops, and females forage near the ground. When Hooded Warblers arrive on their wintering grounds in Mexico and South America, the males and females segregate—a practice unknown in any other warbler species—with males using mature forests and females using shrubby and disturbed areas. • Unlike their female counterparts, male Hooded Warblers may return to the same nesting territory year after year. Once the young have left the nest, each parent takes on guardianship of half the fledged young.

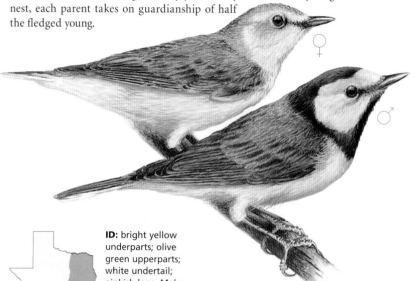

ID: bright yellow underparts; olive green upperparts; white undertail; pinkish legs. *Male:* black hood; bright yellow face. *Female:* olive crown; yellow face; may show faint traces of black hood.
Size: *L* 5½ in; *W* 7 in.
Status: uncommon to common summer resident from eastern Texas south onto the central Coastal Plain and west to the eastern Edwards Plateau; uncommon to common migrant in the eastern half of the state and the Lower Rio Grande Valley and rare in the west.
Habitat: *Breeding:* hardwood forests near water or in swamps. *In migration:* any wooded habitat with a dense understory.
Nesting: low in a deciduous shrub; mostly the female builds an open cup nest of fine grass, bark strips, dead leaves, animal hair, spider webs and plant down; female incubates

4 brown-spotted, creamy white eggs for about 12 days.
Feeding: gleans foliage or the ground for insects and spiders.
Voice: metallic *tink* call; song is a series of whistled phrases with the final note lower in pitch.
Similar Species: male's head pattern is diagnostic. *Common Yellowthroat* (p. 368): female has pale eye ring, yellow breast, pale or buffy belly and undertail coverts and wholly olive tail. *Kentucky Warbler* (p. 365): bold yellow "spectacles." *Wilson's Warbler* (p. 370): rare; wholly dark tail.
Best Sites: *Breeding:* Daingerfield SP; Huntsville SP; Baytown Nature Center (Harris Co.); Bear Creek Pioneer Park (Houston). *In migration:* migrant "traps" on the Coastal Plain.

WILSON'S WARBLER

Wilsonia pusilla

The petite Wilson's Warbler darts energetically through the undergrowth in its tireless search for insects. Fueled by its energy-rich prey, this indefatigable bird seems to behave as if a motionless moment would break some unwritten law of warblerdom. • Although this warbler may make brief stopovers in the shrubs of almost any backyard during spring or fall migration, it is most abundant in open woodlands. • The Wilson's Warbler is richly deserving of its name. Named after Scottish-born Alexander Wilson (1766–1813), this species epitomizes the energetic devotion that the pioneering ornithologist exhibited in his study of North American birds.

ID: yellow underparts; yellow-green upperparts; beady, black eyes; thin, pointed, black bill; orange legs. *Male:* black cap. *Female:* very faint or absent cap.

Size: *L* 4½–5 in; *W* 7 in.

Status: common migrant statewide; uncommon winter resident on the Coastal Plain to the Lower Rio Grande Valley and upriver through the South Texas Brush Country and rare inland.

Habitat: woodlands or areas with tall shrubs.

Nesting: does not nest in Texas.

Feeding: hovers, flycatches and gleans vegetation for insects.

Voice: flat, low *chet* or *chuck* call; song (rarely heard in Texas) is a rapid chatter that drops in pitch at the end: *chi chi chi chi chet chet.*

Similar Species: male's black cap is distinctive. *Yellow Warbler* (p. 345) male has red breast streaks and brighter yellow underparts. *Kentucky Warbler* (p. 365): yellow "spectacles"; angular dark half mask. *Orange-crowned Warbler* (p. 342): dull yellow olive overall; faint breast streaks. *Nashville Warbler* (p. 343): complete bold eye ring; bluish gray crown.

Best Sites: migrant "traps" on the Coastal Plain.

CANADA WARBLER

Wilsonia canadensis

Male Canada Warblers, with their bold white eye ring, have a wide-eyed, alert appearance. They are fairly inquisitive birds, and they occasionally pop up from dense shrubs in response to passing hikers. • Canada Warblers live in open defiance of winter: they never stay in one place long enough to experience one! After the summer's nesting, these warblers migrate to South America. • Although several wood-warblers breed exclusively in Canada, the Canada Warbler isn't one of them. Most Canada Warblers nest in eastern and northern Canada, but some can be found nesting in the Appalachians and northeastern states. Unlike most wood-warblers, the Canada has strong pair bonds, with pairs often migrating and wintering together.

ID: yellow forehead patch; complete white eye ring; yellow underparts, except for white undertail coverts; blue-gray upperparts; pale legs. *Male:* streaky black "necklace"; angular dark half mask. *Female:* blue-green back; faint "necklace." *1st-year:* yellow forehead; faint, gray "necklace."
Size: *L* 5–6 in; *W* 8 in.
Status: uncommon to common migrant from the eastern half of the state to the eastern parts of the Oaks and Prairies and the Edwards Plateau and rare elsewhere.
Habitat: varied habitats, especially damp situations.

Nesting: does not nest in Texas.
Feeding: gleans the ground and vegetation for beetles, flies, hairless caterpillars, mosquitoes and other insects; occasionally hovers.
Voice: loud, quick *chick* or *chip* call; song (rarely heard in Texas) begins with 1 or more sharp *chip* notes and continues with a rich, variable warble.
Similar Species: *Northern Parula* (p. 344): white wing bars; broken white eye ring; white belly. *Common Yellowthroat* (p. 368) and *Kentucky* (p. 365), *Mourning* (p. 366), *MacGillivray's* (p. 367) and *Wilson's* (p. 370) *warblers:* greenish on backs; contrasting head patterns; no "necklaces."
Best Sites: migrant "traps" on the Coastal Plain.

YELLOW-BREASTED CHAT

Icteria virens

The unique Yellow-breasted Chat, which measures over 7 inches in length, is almost a warbler and a half. Despite DNA evidence connecting the Chat with the wood-warbler family, its bill is thick and stocky, more like a tropical tanager, and its song and courtship displays are reminiscent of thrashers and mockingbirds. Chats typically thrash about in dense undergrowth, and they rarely hold back their strange vocalizations, often drawing attention to themselves. • During courtship, the male advertises for a mate by launching off his perch to hover in the air with head held high and legs dangling, chirping incessantly until he drops back down.

ID: white "spectacles"; white jaw line; heavy, black bill; yellow breast; white undertail coverts; olive green upperparts; long tail; grayish black legs. *Male:* black lores. *Female:* gray lores.
Size: L 7½ in; W 9½ in.
Status: common local summer resident in most of Texas, although rare in the Panhandle and very local in the South Plains, the Rolling Plains and the South Texas Brush Country; uncommon to common migrant statewide; rare winter resident in the lower Rio Grande and along the Rio Grande in the South Texas Brush Country.

Habitat: dense thickets and woodland edges.
Nesting: in shrubby vegetation, frequently along a stream; female builds a cup of coarse grass, dead leaves and similar vegetation and lines it with fine grass; female incubates 3–5 white or creamy eggs, splotched with reddish brown to gray blotches, for 11–12 days.
Feeding: gleans insects, spiders, small crustaceans and fruit from low vegetation.
Voice: calls include *whoit, chack* and *kook;* song is a series of whistles, squawks, grunts, squeals and various other sounds, uttered during an aerial display and sometimes at night.
Similar Species: none.
Best Sites: *Breeding:* shrubby vegetation along streams, in old pastures and at woodlot edges statewide. *In migration:* migrant "traps" on the Coastal Plain.

HEPATIC TANAGER

Piranga flava

The Tanagers are a large family of mostly tropical birds with highly variable, brightly colored plumage and fairly thick bills. In Central and South America, over 200 tanager species represent every color of the rainbow. All five North American species occur in Texas, although the Flame-colored Tanager *(P. bidentata)* is an extremely rare visitor only. • Our largest species, the Hepatic Tanager is a restless, jumpy bird that may fly long distances in search of food. Present in Texas only to breed, it can be found in the mid-elevation forests of the Chisos, Davis and Guadalupe Mountains. • The unflattering title of "hepatic" means "relating to the liver" and refers to the male's liver red plumage. The genus name of *Piranga* means "small bird" in an indigenous South American tongue, and the word *flava*, Latin for "yellow," indicates that the female was probably the first of this species to be described.

ID: dark bill and ear patch; long tail. *Male:* dull, dark red plumage with; brighter throat and crown. *Female* and *immature:* olive above; deep yellow below; bright orange throat; dark eye line.
Size: *L* 8 in; *W* 12½ in.
Status: uncommon summer resident in the Chisos, Davis and Guadalupe mts.; rare migrant throughout the Trans-Pecos, South Plains and South Texas Brush Country.
Habitat: mature oak and pine forests.
Nesting: in a forked branch high in a tree; saucer-shaped nest of grass is lined with flower petals; female incubates 3–5 bluish eggs for 12–14 days; pair feeds the young.
Feeding: gleans insects from foliage or sallies for flying insects.
Voice: *chuk* and *squeep* call notes; bold, short phrases; varied whistles at even intervals.
Similar Species: *Summer Tanager* (p. 374): brighter red plumage; pale bill; no dark cheek patch. *Scarlet Tanager* (p. 375): smaller bill; male is bolder red, with black tail and wings; female has darker wings, brighter underparts and uniformly olive upperparts.
Best Sites: Guadalupe Mountains NP; Davis Mountains SP; Big Bend NP.

SUMMER TANAGER

Piranga rubra

Summer Tanagers are a treat for southern birders—most of North America only gets a glimpse of these beauties if a rare individual flies off track. These striking birds breed throughout Texas's forested areas, favoring the edges of pine or pine-oak forests and riparian areas. • Summer Tanagers thrive on a wide variety of insects, but they are best known for their courageous attacks on wasps. These birds snatch flying bees and wasps from menacing swarms. They may even harass the occupants of a wasp nest until the nest is abandoned and the larvae inside are left free for the picking. • A courting male tanager entices a mate by offering her food and fanning his handsome crest and tail feathers. To ensure she notices him, the male hops persistently in front of the female and sometimes jumps right over her.

Nesting: on a high, horizontal tree limb; female builds a flimsy, shallow cup of grass, Spanish moss and twigs; female incubates 3–4 rust-spotted, pale blue-green eggs for 11–12 days.

Feeding: gleans insects from the tree canopy; may hover-glean or hawk insects in midair; raids wasp nests; also eats berries and small fruits.

Voice: *pit* or *pit-a-tuck* call; song is a series of 3–5 sweet, clear, whistled phrases, like a faster version of the American Robin's.

Similar Species: *Hepatic Tanager* (p. 373): dark bill; male is duller red and has dusky cheek patch. *Scarlet Tanager* (p. 375): smaller bill; male is bolder red, with black tail and wings; female has darker wings, brighter underparts and uniformly olive upperparts. *Northern Cardinal* (p. 411): red bill; prominent crest; male has black mask and "bib."

Best Sites: *Breeding:* most parks with woodlands. *In migration:* migrant "traps" on the Coastal Plain.

ID: pale bill. *Male:* rose red overall (patchy, red and greenish plumage on immature). *Female:* grayish yellow to greenish yellow upperparts; dusky yellow underparts; possible orange or reddish wash overall.

Size: *L* 7–8 in; *W* 12 in.

Status: rare to common summer resident except on the High Plains and the Rolling Plains and in the Lower Rio Grande Valley; uncommon to common migrant statewide; rare winter resident on the Coastal Plain and Lower Rio Grande Valley.

Habitat: mixed coniferous and deciduous woodlands, especially those with oak or hickory, or riparian woodlands with cotton-woods; occasionally in wooded backyards.

SCARLET TANAGER

Piranga olivacea

Each spring, as multitudes of spring migrants descend on our coastline, the lovely Scarlet Tanager outshines them all. The male's flaming red plumage contrasts with his slate black wings and tail to create one of our most beautiful birds. • When cold and rainy weather dampens spring birdwatching, you may find a Scarlet Tanager at eye level, foraging in the forest understory. At other times, this bird can be surprisingly difficult to spot as it darts through the forest canopy in pursuit of insect prey. • The Scarlet Tanager migrates farther than any other tanager, most of which are sedentary birds in Central and South American forests. • Unlike the male Summer Tanager, which remains red year-round, the male Scarlet Tanager molts into a female-like plumage after breeding.

breeding

ID: *Breeding male:* bright red body and head; pale bill; black wings and tail. *Fall male:* red areas become patchy with greenish yellow. *Nonbreeding male:* bright yellow underparts; olive upperparts. *Female:* uniformly olive upperparts; yellow underparts; grayish brown wings and tail.
Size: *L* 7 in; *W* 11½ in.
Status: uncommon to common spring migrant and rare fall migrant in the eastern half of the state and rare and irregular in the western half.
Habitat: fairly mature upland deciduous and mixed forests and large woodlands.
Nesting: does not nest in Texas.

Feeding: gleans insects from the tree canopy; hover-gleans or hawk or insects in midair; may forage at lower levels during cold weather; also takes some seasonally available berries.
Voice: *chip-burrr* or *chip-churrr* call; song is a series of 4–5 sweet, clear, whistled phrases, like a slurred version of the American Robin's.
Similar Species: *Summer Tanager* (p. 374): larger bill; male has red tail and wings; female has paler wings and is duskier overall, often with orange or reddish tinge. *Northern Cardinal* (p. 411): red bill, wings and tail; prominent head crest; male has black mask and "bib." *Orioles* (p. 432–36, 458–459): females have wing bars and sharper bills.
Best Sites: migrant "traps" on the Coastal Plain.

WESTERN TANAGER

Piranga ludoviciana

With a golden body accentuated by black wings and tail and an orange-red face, the male Western Tanager brings a splash of color to the foothills and low mountain slopes. Both the male and the female of this species are unique among Texas tanagers in having one yellow wing bar and one white one. • This bird of the West breeds locally in the Guadalupe and Davis Mountains. The male's courtship song can be confusing to the birder because it closely parallels the phrases of an American Robin's song. The tanager's notes are somewhat hoarser, as if the bird had a sore throat, and end with a distinctive, hiccup-like *pit-a-tik*.

breeding

ID: *Breeding male:* yellow underparts and rump; black back, wings and tail; 1 yellow and 1 white wing bar; red on forehead or entire head (variable); pale bill. *Female:* olive green overall; lighter underparts; darker upperparts; fainter wing bars. *Nonbreeding male:* duller plumage; less red on head.

Size: *L* 7 in; *W* 11½ in.

Status: uncommon summer resident in the Davis and Guadalupe mts.; uncommon migrant in the Trans-Pecos and High Plains and rare elsewhere.

Habitat: *Breeding:* a great variety of foothill and mountain forests and woodlands, generally tall conifers with or without a hardwood component, from sea level to 9000 ft.

In migration: almost any stand of trees, no matter how small or isolated.

Nesting: in a fork or on a horizontal branch of a conifer, placed well out from the trunk; builds a loose cup nest of twigs, grass and other plant materials, lined with fine vegetation; female incubates 3–5 pale blue, brown-speckled eggs for 13–14 days.

Feeding: gleans vegetation for wasps, beetles and other insects or catches them on the wing; also eats fruit; drinks from puddles on the ground or from the edge of a pond.

Voice: unique crisp *pritik* or *priterik* call; song is a hoarse, rapid series of dry 2- or 3-note phrases.

Similar Species: male is distinctive. *Bullock's Oriole* (p. 433): female has thinner, sharper bill and pale gray underparts with yellowish breast. *Summer Tanager* (p. 374): female has no wing bars.

Best Sites: Guadalupe Mountains NP; Davis Mountains SP.

OLIVE SPARROW

Arremonops rufivirigatus

Under the dense cover of thorn scrub habitat in southern Texas, the metallic song of the Olive Sparrow rings out. With a rhythm like a bouncing ball, the song is composed of accelerating *chip* or *tsip* notes, given in a musical burst. • Olive Sparrows forage close to the ground, using a peculiar double-scratch technique. While their bodies remain motionless, they claw both feet backward simultaneously, raking leaves aside and exposing seeds or insects on the ground. • Olive Sparrows require native thorn scrub vegetation. Although they avoid urban areas and disappear from overgrazed habitat, groups of Olive Sparrows have returned to abandoned agriculture fields that have been allowed to regrow. For instance, these birds have extended their range into areas across southern Texas and near Corpus Christi where light cattle grazing has changed former prairie into thorn scrub habitat.

ID: grayish overall; plain olive back; brownish rump; 2 brown head stripes, buff or pale gray underparts. *Immature:* pale wing bars; duller, buffy underparts with pale streaks.
Size: *L* 6¼ in; *W* 7¾ in.
Status: common resident in the South Texas Brush Country, rare north to the southern third of the Edwards Plateau and to the central Coastal Plain.
Habitat: near the ground in dense thorn scrub and brush.
Nesting: low to the ground in dense vegetation; constructs slightly dome-shaped nest of grasses, vines or weed stems; probably just the female incubates 4–5 white eggs for an unknown incubation period; may have 2 broods per year.
Feeding: scratches at the ground under dense cover; rarely feeds in open; food choice is poorly studied, probably eats insects, arthropods and seeds.
Voice: song consists of accelerating *chip* or *tsip* notes resembling a metal ball bouncing to a stop.
Similar Species: *Green-backed Sparrow:* brighter, more patterned olive back; lemon yellow undertail; no head stripes.
Best Sites: Bentsen-Rio Grande Valley SP; Santa Ana NWR; Laguna Atascosa NWR; Hazel Bazemore CP (Corpus Christi).

377

GREEN-TAILED TOWHEE

Pipilo chlorurus

Green-tailed Towhees favor arid scrub habitats in the western foothills and lower mountains. They can be common summer birds of hillsides and foothills while remaining entirely unknown in the nearby valleys. The best time to see Green-tailed Towhees is in spring, when the males give clear, whistled notes, raspy trills or catlike *mew* calls from exposed woody perches. Otherwise, they remain concealed in shrubby undergrowth, industriously scratching away debris with both feet in a double scratching motion in search of insects and hidden seeds. In advance of human intrusions, females on their nests will run from the area. • Green-tailed Towhees often join up with White-crowned Sparrows during their fall migration to Mexican wintering grounds. • *Pipilo* is derived from a Latin word meaning "to twitter"; *chlorurus* means "green tail."

ID: yellowish green upperparts, most intense on wings and tail; rufous orange crown; white throat with 2 dark stripes; sooty gray face and breast; conical, gray bill; gray legs. *Immature:* brownish overall; streaked upperparts and underparts; pale throat is bordered by a dark stripe and white stripe.

Size: *L* 6½–7¼ in; *W* 9¾ in.

Status: rare summer resident in the Trans-Pecos Mts.; uncommon to common migrant and winter resident in the western half of the state, rare east to the northcentral region south through the eastern Edwards Plateau to the central Coastal Plain.

Habitat: arid, shrubby hillsides featuring sagebrush, juniper or other well-spaced trees and shrubs; dense, low thickets.

Nesting: on the ground or very low in a bush; deep, bulky, thick-walled cup nest of twigs, grass and bark shreds is lined with fine materials; female incubates 3–4 darkly spotted, white eggs for 11 days.

Feeding: scratches the ground for insects, seeds and berries; drinks morning dew from leaves; occasionally visits feeders.

Voice: distinctive, nasal *mew* call; song consists of clear, whistled notes followed by squealing, raspy trills: *swee-too weet chur cheee-churr.*

Similar Species: *Chipping Sparrow* (p. 386): smaller; white eyebrow; black eye line; mottled, brown back. *Rufous-crowned Sparrow* (p. 384): reddish eye line; striped, gray and rufous back.

Best Sites: Guadalupe Mountains NP; Hueco Tanks SP; Davis Mountains SP; Big Bend NP.

SPOTTED TOWHEE

Pipilo maculatus

Spotted Towhees are often heard before they are seen. These noisy foragers rustle about in dense undergrowth, craftily scraping back layers of dry leaves to expose the seeds, berries or insects hidden beneath. Towhees prefer tangled thickets and overgrown gardens, especially if blackberries or other small fruits are available for the taking. Confined to the Trans-Pecos Mountains during the breeding season, the species ranges widely over the state as a migrant and winter resident. • Spotted Towhees rarely leave their subarboreal world, except to perform their simple courtship song or to furtively eye a threat to their territory; thus one will only have a brief glimpse of the bird before it darts out of sight.

ID: *Male:* black hood, back, wings and tail; rufous flanks; conical, dark bill; bold white spotting on wings; white-tipped outer tail feathers; white belly and undertail. *Female:* somewhat drabber and paler overall.
Size: *L* 7–8½ in; *W* 10½ in.
Status: resident in the Trans-Pecos Mts.; uncommon migrant and winter resident in the western two-thirds of the state and rare in the eastern third.
Habitat: riparian thickets, chaparral, brushy ravines; shady canyons and thick undergrowth in suburban parks and gardens.
Nesting: low in a bush, on the ground under cover or in a brushy pile; cup nest of leaves, grass and bark shreds is lined with fine materials; primarily the female incubates 3–4 brown-wreathed, white eggs for 12–13 days.
Feeding: scratches the ground vigorously for seeds and insects; periodically visits feeding stations; seldom feeds in trees; also eats berries and acorns, especially in winter.

Voice: raspy or whining *chee* or *chwaay* call; song is a simple, querulous trilling: *here here here PLEASE.*
Similar Species: *Eastern Towhee* (p. 380): inhabits eastern Texas; all-black head, back and wing coverts; single white wing patch. *Black-headed Grosbeak* (p. 414): stockier; much heavier bill; dark eyes; orange to whitish belly. *Dark-eyed Junco* (p. 407): smaller; "Oregon" race has pale rufous on back and sides. *American Redstart* (p. 358): much smaller, flittier; male has black breast, bright red sides, orange in wings and tail and no white wing spots.
Best Sites: Guadalupe Mountains NP; Davis Mountains SP; Big Bend NP.

EASTERN TOWHEE

Pipilo erythrophthalmus

Towhees are large members of the sparrow family, and, like several of our other towhees, the Eastern Towhee is a colorful bird. • The Eastern Towhee and its western relative the Spotted Towhee were once grouped together as a single species known as the "Rufous-sided Towhee," although they could equally be called the "Red-eyed Towhee." Both act in the same way, and both are eager to see what is going on around them. • Squeaking and pishing are irresistible for towhees, which quickly pop out from cover to investigate curious noises, but as quickly pop back into the vegetation. • The term *erythrophthalmus* is derived from Greek words that mean "red eye."

ID: rufous sides and flanks; white wing patches and outer tail corners; white lower breast and belly; buff undertail coverts; red eyes; dark bill. *Male:* black hood and upperparts. *Female:* brown hood and upperparts. *Juvenile:* very different; brownish, with distinct streaks on upper- and underparts; pale bill. *In flight:* short, rounded wings; long tail; dark above, with prominent white "wrist" patch and tail spots; rufous sides contrast with white below.

Size: *L* 7–8½ in; *W* 10–10½ in.

Status: common migrant and winter resident in the eastern half of the state and less common in the southern parts south to the eastern part of the Lower Rio Grande Valley.

Habitat: often along woodland edges and in shrubby, abandoned fields; takes readily to feeders near dense, low cover.

Nesting: does not nest in Texas.

Feeding: scratches at leaf litter for insects, seeds and berries; sometimes forages in low shrubs and saplings; scratching and mouse-like runs are distinctive.

Voice: scratchy, slurred *cheweee!* or *chewink!* call; song is 2 high, whistled notes followed by a trill, usually interpreted as *drink your teeeee*, but with many local variations.

Similar Species: *Spotted Towhee* (p. 379): bold white spotting on wings; 2 white wing bars. *Dark-eyed Junco* (p. 407): much smaller; pale bill; black eyes; white outer tail feathers; eastern male is slate colored; pink or pale rufous-sided western birds are sometimes found in migration and winter. *Sparrows* (pp. 377–406, 457–58): smaller; no wing patches.

Best Sites: any eastern park with open woods and shrubby understory.

CANYON TOWHEE

Pipilo fuscus

Few birds are as bold as the Canyon Towhee, well known for its scrappy, scolding disposition and habit of foraging among the gravel of parking lots, hopping underneath parked cars in search of shade and food. Like other towhees, it scratches the ground in a two-footed hopping motion in an attempt to uncover a variety of seeds and insects. • A pair of adult Canyon Towhees may mate for life, foraging together year-round and staying within the boundaries of their loosely protected territory. Depending on the availability of food and water, a breeding pair may raise up to three broods of young each year. • Until recently, the Canyon Towhee and its western relative the California Towhee were considered to be a single species, the "Brown Towhee."

ID: rusty cap and undertail coverts; buffy throat, breast and sides; central dark breast spot and "necklace" of dark spots; white belly; gray upperparts.

Size: *L* 8½ in; *W* 11½ in.

Status: rare to locally common resident from the Trans-Pecos east through the southern Panhandle, the South Plains and the Edwards Plateau; uncommon migrant and rare winter resident in the rest of the Panhandle and the Rolling Plains.

Habitat: canyons, chaparral, scrub desert and grassland, desert foothills and open pinyon-juniper woodlands.

Nesting: in a shrub, small tree or cactus; bulky, cup-shaped nest consists of twigs, bark, vegetation and animal hair; female incubates 3–4 sparsely marked, whitish or pale blue eggs for 11 days; pair raises the young.

Feeding: seasonally available seeds and insects are found while foraging on the ground, often under objects such as parked cars, benches, shrubs and logs; occasionally scratches dirt.

Voice: *chiup* call is typical; song is a chipping, musical trill.

Similar Species: *Green-tailed Towhee* (p. 378): brighter rufous cap; greenish wings and tail; white throat with 2 dark stripes.

Best Sites: Hueco Tanks SP; Guadalupe Mountains NP; Davis Mountains SP; Big Bend NP; Lost Maples SP.

CASSIN'S SPARROW

Aimophila cassinii

Dull and plain in appearance and extremely secretive most of the year, Cassin's Sparrows nest in scattered pairs in dense, tall grasslands with scattered bushes. A wet year often entices larger numbers of Cassin's Sparrows to visit Texas. Dry years force this bird to range more widely, as it follows the rains to find the more plentiful insects and seeds that result from the moisture. • In productive years, male Cassin's Sparrows have singing competitions from their grass tops, competing for breeding territory. Especially if another male enters his territory, a male will "skylark," launching from tall grasses to float down with the notes of his sweet, trilling song. • S.W. Woodhouse collected the first Cassin's specimen in San Antonio in 1851 and named it for John Cassin of the Academy of Natural Sciences in Philadelphia, Pennsylvania.

ID: round head; small, pale bill; finely streaked crown with pale stripe; pale eye ring; dark-bordered, white throat; gray breast with "necklace" of brownish rufous spots and streaks; brown-streaked flanks; white-edged tertials and coverts; gray to rufous face. *Juvenile:* no rufous; buff underparts with brown streaks; "scaly" back. *In flight:* broad, rounded wings; long, rounded tail with pale corners; male sings in flight.

Size: *L* 6 in; *W* 7½–8 in.

Status: rare to locally common summer resident in the western two-thirds of the state, east through the Rolling Plains and south through the Edwards Plateau to the Lower Rio Grande Valley.

Habitat: sand-sage prairies; arid grasslands with scattered shrubs; yuccas, rabbitbush or low trees, especially on open slopes. *In migration:* brushy draws and canyons.

Nesting: on the ground or in a grass clump or low shrub; female builds the nest of dry grasses, weed stems and fibers, lined with finer grasses, rootlets, grass tops and horsehair, and incubates 3–5 unspotted, white eggs for 10–11 days; pair feeds the young.

Feeding: *Summer:* picks insects off the ground. *In migration* and *winter:* eats mostly weed and grass seeds.

Voice: chipping and chittering calls. *Male:* variable, always sweet and memorable song in a dramatic larklike songflight.

Similar Species: *Grasshopper Sparrow* (p. 395): large, rufous spots on back and trailing edge of wing; unmarked, buffy underparts; shorter tail; white crown stripe; buffy, unbordered throat. *Other sparrows* (pp. 377–406, 457–58): lack rufous centers and white edges to tertials and coverts.

Best Sites: Hueco Tanks SP; Guadalupe Mountains NP; Davis Mountains SP; Big Bend NP; Seminole Canyon SP.

BACHMAN'S SPARROW

Aimophila aestivalis

Hiding in the grasses of mature pine forests and open fields, the reclusive Bachman's Sparrow is a shy, little bird that drops out of sight at the first sound of a birder's pishing. On early April evenings, though, this bird will quietly perch on a small branch and grace patient listeners with a varied and clear song. • Bachman's Sparrow is dependent on grass for nest material, cover and winter forage. Before the onset of heavy logging, mature southern pine forests provided an ideal meadowlike understory, but today this species is often found in cleared fields or utility rights-of-way. Local populations of this bird tend to flourish as fire or humans open grassy pastures and then crash as the understory grows in. • In 1837, William Swainson named this sparrow after John Bachman, an ornithologist and good friend of John James Audubon. The genus name *Aimophila* comes from the Greek for "thicket-loving."

ID: long, dark tail; white belly; buffy breast and sides; heavy gray and rust streaking above. *In flight:* buffy "wing pits."
Size: *L* 5–6 in; *W* 7 in.

Status: uncommon local resident in the Pineywoods of eastern Texas, south to the northern edge of the upper Coastal Plain.
Habitat: grassy understory of mature pine forest; open fields.
Nesting: on the ground, at the base of a grass clump or shrub; female builds a domed nest of grass, small roots and animal hair; female incubates 2–5 white eggs for 12–14 days; may have 2–3 broods.
Feeding: forages on the ground; sometimes jumps for seeds and insects.
Voice: varied; long clear note followed by a trill on a different pitch; mimics other birds.
Similar Species: *Chipping Sparrow* (p. 386): rufous cap; gray nape and cheek; solid gray chest.
Best Sites: Daingerfield SP; Alabama Creek WMA (Davy Crockett NF); Angelina NF; Roy E. Larsen Sandyland Sanctuary (Big Thicket NP).

RUFOUS-CROWNED SPARROW

Aimophila ruficeps

Many Texan sparrows favor prairie grasslands, dense chaparral and oak-dominated woodlands, but the Rufous-crowned Sparrow usually avoids these habitats. Instead, it remains devoted to the arid, grassy slopes and shrub-strewn, rocky outcroppings that carpet many bordering canyons and foothills. The Rufous-crowned Sparrow is a bird of brushy and grassy areas on rocky hillsides in the Panhandle, the Edwards Plateau and northcentral Texas. Thus, it fills the gap between the Bachman's Sparrow of east Texas and Cassin's Sparrow of the more arid west and south Texas regions. • In winter, the Rufous-crowned Sparrow can be seen hopping about in search of seeds from sun-dried grasses and herbaceous plants. • When alarmed or disturbed, this sparrow readily issues a nasal *deer-deer-deer.*

twigs, grass and plant fibers is often lined with animal hair; 3–4 pale bluish white eggs are incubated for 11–13 days; pair feeds the young.

Feeding: eats mostly grass and wildflower seeds, stems and shoots, with more insects in spring and summer.

Voice: sharp *deer* call, usually given in a series of 2–3; song is a series of rapid, bubbling warbles and *chip* notes.

Similar Species: *American Tree Sparrow* (p. 385): stubby, bicolored bill; buffish flanks; dark breast spot; 2 white bars; no throat stripe or pale crown stripe. *Chipping Sparrow* (p. 386) and *Clay-colored Sparrow* (p. 387): gray nape; darker back stripes; 2 white wing bars; no prominent throat stripe. *Swamp Sparrow* (p. 403): black and buff back stripes; rufous buff flanks; blurry brown breast streaks; rufous wings and rump.

Best Sites: Guadalupe Mountains NP; Big Bend NP; Palo Duro Canyon SP; Friedrich Wilderness Park (San Antonio); Pedernales Falls SP.

ID: rufous crown; gray eyebrow and cheek; rufous line behind eye; white eye ring; black and white whisker stripes; whitish throat; unstreaked, buffy gray breast. *Juvenile:* buffier overall; streaked breast and crown.

Size: *L* 6 in; *W* 7½–8 in.

Status: uncommon to locally common resident in the western third of the state and east through the Rolling Plains and Edwards Plateau.

Habitat: grassy shrublands and open woodlands on rocky hillsides and in canyons; rocky slopes of mesas.

Nesting: on the ground under a shrub or grass clump or in a low shrub; open cup of

AMERICAN TREE SPARROW

Spizella arborea

Most of us know the rufous-capped, spot-breasted American Tree Sparrow as a winter visitor to agricultural fields and backyard feeders, with numbers that fluctuate depending on the year and location. It is irregular in the northern third of Texas, often occurring in mixed flocks with Dark-eyed Juncos. • Although its name suggests a close relationship with trees or forests, the American Tree Sparrow actually prefers treeless fields and semi-open, shrubby habitats. It breeds at or above the treeline at northern latitudes, then returns to weedy fields in southern Canada and the northcentral states to overwinter. • This bird got its name because of a superficial resemblance to the Eurasian Tree Sparrow *(Passer montanus)* familiar to early settlers from Europe. Perhaps a more appropriate name for this bird would be "Subarctic Shrub Sparrow." With adequate food supplies, the American Tree Sparrow can survive temperatures as low as -28° F.

ID: gray, unstreaked underparts; central dark breast spot; pale rufous cap; rufous stripe behind eye; gray face; mottled, brown upperparts; notched tail; 2 white wing bars; dark legs; dark upper mandible; yellow lower mandible. *Nonbreeding:* central gray crown stripe. *Juvenile:* streaky breast and head.
Size: *L* 6–6½ in; *W* 9½ in.
Status: rare to locally common in the High Plains and Rolling Plains and irregular in the Trans-Pecos and northcentral region.
Habitat: brushy thickets, roadside shrubs, semi-open fields and croplands.
Nesting: does not nest in Texas.
Feeding: scratches exposed soil or snow for seeds in winter; eats mostly insects in summer; takes some berries; occasionally visits bird feeders.

Voice: 3-note *tsee-dle-ea* call; song consists of a high, whistled *tseet-tseet* followed by a short, sweet, musical series of slurred whistles; song may be given in late winter and during spring migration.
Similar Species: *Chipping Sparrow* (p. 386): clear black eye line; white eyebrow; no dark breast spot. *Swamp Sparrow* (p. 403): white throat; no dark breast spot or white wing bars. *Field Sparrow* (p. 389): white eye ring; orangy pink bill; no dark breast spot.
Best Sites: Palo Duro Canyon SP; Caprock Canyons SP; Buffalo Lake NWR; Gene Howe WMA.

CHIPPING SPARROW

Spizella passerina

The Chipping Sparrow and Dark-eyed Junco do not share the same tailor, but they must have attended the same voice lessons because their songs are very similar. Although the rapid trill of the Chipping Sparrow is slightly faster, drier and less musical than the junco's, even experienced birders can have difficulty identifying this singer. • Chipping Sparrows are found from the forest floor to the topmost spires of conifers. They commonly nest at eye level, so you can easily have the good fortune to watch their breeding and nest-building ritual close up. They are well known for their preference for conifers as a nest site and for hair as a lining material for the nest. • The Chipping Sparrow is the smallest and tamest of sparrows. "Chipping" refers to this bird's call, and *passerina* is Latin for "little sparrow."

breeding

ID: *Breeding:* prominent rufous cap; bold white eyebrow; black eye line; light gray, unstreaked underparts; mottled, brown upperparts; dark bill; 2 faint wing bars; pale legs. *Nonbreeding:* paler crown with dark streaks; brown eyebrow and cheek; pale lower mandible.
Size: *L* 5–6 in; *W* 8½ in.
Status: common to locally abundant resident in the Trans-Pecos, Edwards Plateau and eastern Texas woodlands.
Habitat: open conifers or mixed woodland edges; often in yards and gardens with tree and shrub borders.
Nesting: usually nests at midlevel in a coniferous tree; female builds a compact cup nest of woven grass and rootlets, often lined with hair; female incubates 4 pale blue eggs for 11–12 days.

Feeding: gleans seeds from the ground and from the outer branches of trees or shrubs; prefers seeds from grass, dandelions and clovers; also eats adult and larval invertebrates; occasionally visits feeders.
Voice: high-pitched *chip* call; song is a rapid, dry trill of *chip* notes.
Similar Species: *American Tree Sparrow* (p. 385): central dark breast spot; rufous stripe extends behind eye; no bold white eyebrow. *Swamp Sparrow* (p. 403): no white wing bars, white eyebrow or dark line behind eye. *Field Sparrow* (p. 389): rufous stripe extends behind eye; white eye ring; gray throat; orangy pink bill; no bold white eyebrow.
Best Sites: Hueco Tanks SP; Garner SP; Lost Maples SP; Tyler SP; Huntsville SP.

CLAY-COLORED SPARROW

Spizella pallida

For the most part, the Clay-colored Sparrow goes completely unnoticed because its plumage, habit and voice all contribute to a cryptic lifestyle. Even when a male is singing at the top of his vocal cords, he is usually mistaken for a buzzing insect. • Although it is subtle in plumage, the Clay-colored Sparrow still possesses an unassuming beauty. Birders looking closely at this sparrow to confirm its identity can easily appreciate its delicate shading, texture and form—features so often overlooked in birds with more colorful plumage. • Often found in shrubby, open bogs and willow scrub habitat, the Clay-colored Sparrow tags along with migrant and wintering Chipping Sparrows and Dark-eyed Juncos and shows up in a variety of open-ground habitats.

ID: unstreaked, white underparts; buff breast wash; gray nape; light brown cheek edged with darker brown; brown crown with dark streak and central pale stripe; white eyebrow; brown-bordered, white jaw stripe; white throat; mostly pale bill. *Juvenile:* dark streaks on buff breast, sides and flanks.
Size: *L* 5–6 in; *W* 7½ in.
Status: rare to common migrant statewide; rare to locally common winter resident from the eastern half of the Trans-Pecos and southern South Plains through the southern half of the Edwards Plateau and south to the Lower Rio Grande Valley and the central Coastal Plain.
Habitat: brushy open areas along forest and woodland edges; in forest openings, regenerating burn sites, abandoned fields and riparian thickets.
Nesting: does not breed in Texas.
Feeding: forages for seeds and insects on the ground and in low vegetation.
Voice: soft *chip* call; song is a series of 2–5 slow, low-pitched, insectlike buzzes.
Similar Species: *Chipping Sparrow* (p. 386): breeding bird has prominent rufous cap; gray cheek and underparts; 2 faint white wing bars; all-dark bill; juvenile has no gray nape or buff sides and flanks. *Brewer's Sparrow* (p. 388): light gray breast; brown jaw stripe.
Best Sites: Franklin Mountains SP; Big Bend NP; Hazel Bazemore CP (Corpus Christi); Big Spring SP.

BREWER'S SPARROW

Spizella breweri

Strip away all the breast streaks, contrasting caps, crown stripes and facial markings that adorn most other sparrows, and you're left with the Brewer's Sparrow. This sparrow does not oblige binocular-toting birders, because it infrequently perches in the open. Rather, its identity is often determined from its buzzy call and its characteristic quick getaway flights. • The Brewer's Sparrow is remarkably well adapted to its dry environments and can survive long periods of drought by getting sufficient water from its diet of seeds. This sparrow follows the seed crops and can be abundant in an area one year and absent the next. • It is most frequently encountered in sagebrush habitats, which, like this sparrow, have declined over time in our state. • This sparrow was named for Dr. Thomas Mayo Brewer (1814–80), who made significant contributions to the understanding of the breeding behavior of North American birds.

ID: light brown, unstreaked under-parts; brown cheek patch; faint eye ring; finely streaked, brown upperparts; light throat; pale eye-brow, bill and jaw stripes; light-colored legs.

Size: *L* 5 in; *W* 7–8 in.

Status: uncommon to common migrant and winter resident in the western third of the state and rare in the southern Panhandle and Lower Rio Grande Valley.

Habitat: sagebrush flats and grasslands.

Nesting: no longer breeds in Texas.

Feeding: forages on the ground and gleans low vegetation for adult and larval invertebrates and seeds.

Voice: buzzy call; extremely variable, canary-like song with buzzes and trills up to 10 seconds long, often including trills of different speeds and pitches in the same song.

Similar Species: *Clay-colored Sparrow* (p. 387): more pronounced facial markings and crown stripe; no eye ring.

Best Sites: Franklin Mountains SP; Hueco Tanks SP; Balmorhea SP; Big Bend NP.

FIELD SPARROW

Spizella pusilla

Deserted farmland may seem unproductive to some people, but to the Field Sparrow it is heaven. This species frequents overgrown fields, pastures and forest clearings, and, for nesting purposes, this pink-billed bird requires that these habitats must be scattered with shrubs, herbaceous plants and plenty of tall grass. • Unlike most songbirds, a nestling Field Sparrow leaves its nest prematurely if disturbed. • Over time the Field Sparrow has learned to recognize when its nest has been parasitized by the Brown-headed Cowbird. Because the unwelcome eggs are usually too large for this small sparrow to eject, the nest is simply abandoned. This sparrow may be so stubborn in refusing to raise young cowbirds that affected pairs of Field Sparrows may make numerous nesting attempts in a single season.

rufous morph

ID: orangy pink bill; gray face and throat; rusty crown with gray central stripe; rusty streak behind eye; white eye ring; 2 white wing bars; gray, unstreaked underparts with buffy red wash on breast, sides and flanks; pinkish legs.
Size: *L* 5–6 in; *W* 8 in.
Status: uncommon to common resident in the northern half of forested eastern Texas, the southern half of the Edwards Plateau and south to the central Coastal Plain; uncommon to common migrant and winter resident statewide.
Habitat: abandoned or weedy and over-grown fields and pastures, woodland edges and clearings, extensive shrubby riparian areas and young conifer plantations.
Nesting: on or near the ground, often sheltered by a grass clump, shrub or sapling; female weaves an open cup nest of grass and lines it with animal hair and soft plant material; female incubates 3–5 brown-spotted, whitish to pale bluish white eggs for 10–12 days.
Feeding: forages on the ground. *Summer:* mostly insects. *Spring* and *fall:* mostly seeds.
Voice: *chip* or *tsee* call; song is a series of woeful, musical, down-slurred whistles accelerating into a trill.
Similar Species: *American Tree Sparrow* (p. 385): central dark breast spot; dark upper mandible; no white eye ring. *Swamp Sparrow* (p. 403): white throat; dark upper mandible; does not have 2 white wing bars or white eye ring. *Chipping Sparrow* (p. 386): dark bill; white eyebrow; black eye line; light gray underparts.
Best Sites: Daingerfield SP; Cooper Lake SP; Meridian SP; Mitchell L. (San Antonio); Goose Island SP.

389

VESPER SPARROW

Pooecetes gramineus

For birders who frequent grassy fields or agricultural lands with multitudes of confusing little brown sparrows, the Vesper Sparrow offers welcome relief—white outer tail feathers and a chestnut shoulder patch announce its identity whether the bird is perched or in flight. The Vesper Sparrow is also known for its bold and easily distinguished song, which begins with two sets of unforgettable double notes: *here-here! there-there!* • These ground-dwelling birds expanded their range into the eastern U.S. from the Great Plains when European settlers began clearing forests for farmland. Today, Vesper Sparrows are declining in the Southeast as agricultural land reverts back to forest. • "Vesper" is Latin for "evening," a time when this bird often sings. *Pooecetes* is Greek for "grass dweller."

ID: chestnut shoulder patch; white outer tail feathers; pale yellow lores; weakly streaked flanks; white eye ring; dark upper mandible and lighter lower mandible; pale legs.

Size: *L* 6 in; *W* 10 in.

Status: uncommon to common migrant and winter resident statewide, rare winter resident in the Panhandle.

Habitat: open fields bordered or interspersed with shrubs, semi-open shrublands and grasslands; also uses agricultural areas, open, dry conifer plantations and scrubby gravel pits.

Nesting: does not nest in Texas.

Feeding: walks and runs along the ground, picking up grasshoppers, beetles, cutworms and other invertebrates as well as seeds.

Voice: sharp *chip* call.

Similar Species: *Song Sparrow* (p. 401) and *Savannah Sparrow* (p. 394): smaller; no eye ring. *Other sparrows* (pp. 377–406, 457–58): no white outer tail feathers or chestnut shoulder patch. *American Pipit* (p. 335): thinner bill; grayer upperparts without brown streaking; no chestnut shoulder patch.

Best Sites: any brushy roadside hedgerow.

LARK SPARROW

Chondestes grammacus

The Lark Sparrow's unique, quail-like facial pattern and unique tail pattern distinguishes it from all other sparrows. These large sparrows are typically seen in open, shrubby areas and "edge" habitats, but they occasionally venture into meadows and wooded areas and join flocks of Vesper Sparrows and Savannah Sparrows. • Courting males are conspicuous and active, singing clear, buzzy trills and spreading their wing and tail feathers in a manner that reminded early naturalists of the famed Sky Lark *(Alauda arvensis)* of Europe. The males challenge rivals near their nest but do not defend a large territory.

• During migration, small flocks of Lark Sparrows are regularly seen foraging alongside juncos, sparrows and towhees in suburban parks and gardens.

ID: chestnut red head with distinctive helmet consisting of white throat, eyebrow and crown stripe and several black lines; pale, unstreaked breast with central dark spot; black tail with white outer tail feathers; mottled, soft brown back and wings; light-colored legs.
Size: *L* 6 in; *W* 11 in.
Status: uncommon to common summer resident statewide; common migrant, though rare on the upper Coastal Plain; rare winter resident except in the Trans-Pecos Mts.

Habitat: semi-open shrublands, sandhills, sagebrush and occasionally pastures.
Nesting: on the ground or in a low bush; bulky cup nest consists of grass and twigs lined with finer material; occasionally reuses abandoned thrasher nests; female incubates 4–5 white eggs sparsely marked with dark specks or spots, for 11–12 days.
Feeding: walks or hops on the ground to glean seeds; also eats grasshoppers and other invertebrates.
Voice: call is a high *tsek;* variable, melodious song consists of short trills, buzzes, pauses and clear notes.
Similar Species: no other sparrow has this distinctive head pattern.
Best Sites: Garner SP; Pedernales Falls SP; Bear Creek Pioneer Park (Houston); Meridian SP.

BLACK-THROATED SPARROW

Amphispiza bilineata

Both the Black-throated Sparrow and the Sage Sparrow prefer the arid, sagebrush-dominated habitat of the Trans-Pecos, Edwards Plateau and South Texas. The close bond between these two species is further reflected in their similar preference for seeds and insects and in the similar appearance of the juvenile Black-throated Sparrow and the adult Sage Sparrow. • Because the Black-throated Sparrow shares the same hot, dry habitat used by the Sage Sparrow, it presumably copes with the lack of available drinking water in a similar way—with a super-efficient physiology that allows it to extract and recycle moisture from its food. • Nests built near the ground are especially subject to predation, making Black-throated Sparrow nestlings and eggs welcome food items for a number of lizards, snakes, ground squirrels and other animals.

ID: black tail with white-edged outer feathers; gray cheek and cap; prominent white eyebrow; black chin, throat and "bib"; broad, white jaw line; dark bill; unstreaked, light underparts. *Juvenile:* white chin and throat; dark-streaked upper breast; light lower mandible.
Size: *L* 4½–5½ in; *W* 9 in.
Status: common resident in the South Plains, the Rolling Plains, the western half of the Edwards Plateau, the South Texas Brush Country and the Trans-Pecos and rare in the Panhandle.
Habitat: rocky hills and flatlands covered with sagebrush, greasewood, saltbrush and rabbit brush; low mountain slopes with pinyon-juniper woodlands and an understory of open sagebrush.

Nesting: on the ground under the shelter of tall weeds, in a rocky cliff crevice, in a shrub or low in a tree; open cup nest of twigs, grass and weeds is lined with hair, fine grasses and rootlets; female incubates 4–5 darkly spotted, creamy to grayish white eggs over 11–12 days; pair feeds the young.
Feeding: forages on open ground by walking, often in small, loose flocks, or in low shrubs and trees. *Winter:* mostly seeds from the ground. *Summer:* mostly insects.
Voice: call is a series of faint, tinkling, chattery notes; simple, variable song often opens with a few clear notes followed by a light trill.
Similar Species: *Sage Sparrow* (p. 458): shorter, thinner white eyebrow; distinct dark streaking on sides; finely streaked head and back; runs with tail held high.
Best Sites: Hueco Tanks SP; Seminole Canyon SP; San Angelo SP; Pedernales Falls SP.

LARK BUNTING

Calamospiza melanocorys

Above the grasslands or hay fields of the Panhandle, birders might see the spectacular courtship flight of the male Lark Bunting. As he rises into the air, he flutters about in circles above the prairie, beating his wings slowly and deeply. His bell-like, tinkling song spreads over the landscape until he decides to fold his wings and float to the ground like a falling leaf. • Breeding-plumaged male Lark Buntings are so different from their mates that they might easily be taken for a completely different species. In this respect, they resemble the unrelated Bobolink. • The Lark Bunting is an unusual sparrow with a propensity for forming large winter flocks and nesting in loose colonies. Males molt in March and April and return to breeding territories where they display to later-arriving females. Loose colonies of males may encourage polygynous behavior because of the proximity between the pairs; most pairs, however, are stable.

♀ ♂

nonbreeding

ID: heavy, bluish, finchlike bill. *Breeding male:* black overall; white shoulder patch and wing feather edges. *Female:* brownish gray overall; heavy black streaking; white wing patch; white tail tip; prominent ear patch. *Nonbreeding male:* like female, but grayer with more white on shoulder patch.
Size: *L* 7 in; *W* 10½ in.
Status: uncommon and irregular summer resident in the Panhandle and western Edwards Plateau, occasionally breeding in both areas; uncommon to abundant migrant and winter resident in the western half of the state.
Habitat: *Breeding:* mixed- and short-grass prairies and grasslands, including old fields and agricultural areas. *In migration and*

winter: stubblefields, cattle feedlots, sand prairies and playas.
Nesting: on the ground; female scrapes a depression and builds a nest using grass, roots, leaves and hair provided by the male; pair incubates 2–5 pale, usually unmarked eggs for 10–12 days.
Feeding: *Summer:* gleans, hawks and stalks grasshoppers, weevils, ants, beetles, bugs, grains, seeds and leaves. *Winter:* eats weed seeds, wheat, leaves, insects and spiders.
Voice: calls include a soft, whistled *heew* or *howik*. *Male:* song is a series of low, liquid whistles overlaid with high, tinkling rattles at an extraordinarily (for a sparrow) slow tempo.
Similar Species: *Bobolink* (p. 420): male has straw-colored nape, white rump and back patch, pink legs and smaller bill. *Purple Finch* (p. 437): juvenile has very similar pattern to female and nonbreeding male but without white wing patch.
Best Sites: Muleshoe NWR; Franklin Mountains SP; Big Bend NP; Seminole Canyon SP.

393

SAVANNAH SPARROW

Passerculus sandwichensis

Our most common open-country bird in winter is the Savannah Sparrow. Its numbers peak from September to May. At one time or another, most people have probably seen or heard a Savannah, though they may not have been aware of it—this bird's streaky, dull brown, buff and white plumage resembles the plumages of so many of the other grassland sparrows that it is easily overlooked.
• You may see Savannahs darting across roads, foraging in open fields, marshes and sand dunes or perched on a fence, but, like most sparrows, they generally stay out of sight. When danger appears, they take flight only as a last resort, preferring to run swiftly and inconspicuously through the grass, almost like feathered voles.
• The common and scientific names of this bird reflect its broad North American distribution: "Savannah" refers to the city in Georgia, and *sandwichensis* is derived from Sandwich Bay in the Aleutian Islands off Alaska.

ID: pale, streaked underparts with finely streaked breast, sides and flanks and possible dark breast spot; mottled, brown upperparts; yellow lores; light jaw line; pale bill and legs.
Size: *L* 5–6 in; *W* 6½ in.
Status: uncommon to abundant migrant and winter resident statewide.
Habitat: agricultural fields, moist sedge and grass meadows, pastures, beaches, bogs and fens.

Nesting: does not nest in Texas.
Feeding: gleans insects and seeds while walking or running along the ground and occasionally scratches.
Voice: high, thin *tsit* call; song is a high-pitched, clear, buzzy *tea tea teeeeea today.*
Similar Species: *Vesper Sparrow* (p. 390): white outer tail feathers; chestnut shoulder patch. *Lincoln's Sparrow* (p. 402): buff jaw line; buff wash across breast; broad, gray eyebrow. *Grasshopper Sparrow* (p. 395): unstreaked breast. *Song Sparrow* (p. 401): triangular "mustache" stripes; central pale crown stripe; rounded tail; no yellow lores.
Best Sites: roadsides adjacent to open fields, pastures or lakeshores.

GRASSHOPPER SPARROW

Ammodramus savannarum

The Grasshopper Sparrow is not named for its diet but, rather, for its buzzy, insectlike song. Unique among sparrows, the male sings two completely different courtship songs: one ends in a short trill, and the other is a prolonged series of high trills that vary in pitch and speed. During courtship flights, he chases females through the air, buzzing at a frequency that is usually inaudible to human ears. • These open-country birds have the best chance of nesting successfully in pastureland, fallow fields or abandoned fields. Nests located in agricultural lands (or along roadsides) are often destroyed by mowing or early harvesting, because modern farming techniques involve earlier and more frequently cutting than half a century ago.

ID: unstreaked, white underparts with buff wash on breast, sides and flanks; flattened head profile; dark crown with central pale stripe; buff cheek; mottled, brown upperparts; black eyes; short tail; pale legs; possible small yellow patch on edge of forewing.

Size: *L* 5–5½ in; *W* 7½ in.

Status: rare to locally common summer resident statewide, becoming less common in the eastern forests and the Trans-Pecos; uncommon to common migrant but rare on the upper Coastal Plain; rare to uncommon winter resident statewide except for the High Plains and Rolling Plains.

Habitat: grasslands and grassy fields with little or no shrub or tree cover.

Nesting: in a shallow depression on the ground, usually concealed by grass; female builds a small cup nest of grass lined with rootlets, fine grass and hair; female incubates 4–5 creamy white eggs, spotted with gray and reddish brown, for 11–13 days.

Feeding: gleans various insects and seeds from the ground and grass.

Voice: call is a very high double *tsip;* song is a high, faint, buzzy trill preceded by 1–3 high, thin whistled notes: *tea-tea-tea zeeeeeeeeee.*

Similar Species: *Le Conte's Sparrow* (p. 397): buff-and-black-striped head with central white crown stripe; gray cheek; dark-streaked sides and flanks. *Nelson's Sharp-tailed Sparrow* (p. 398): buff orange face and breast; central gray crown stripe; gray cheek and shoulders.

Best Sites: *Breeding:* Goliad SP; Lake Corpus Christi SP. *In migration* and *winter:* any grassy field.

HENSLOW'S SPARROW

Ammodramus henslowii

It's difficult to predict when you'll see the next Henslow's Sparrow in our region—this bird makes irregular visits here, often appearing one year but not the next. Sometimes, a male has been known to occupy a field for a few weeks before suddenly disappearing, probably upon discovering the absence of potential mates. • This inconspicuous sparrow is almost impossible to observe, because it spends most of its time foraging alone along the ground. When disturbed, it may fly a short distance before dropping into cover, but it usually prefers to run through dense, concealing vegetation. Its habits and unpredictability have made the Henslow's difficult to study, so we have much more to learn about its habitat requirements and the reasons for its recent widespread decline. • John J. Audubon named this sparrow after his friend John Stevens Henslow (1796–1861), a naturalist and one-time teacher of Charles Darwin.

ID: flattened head profile; olive green face, central crown stripe and nape; dark crown and "whisker" stripes; rust-tinged back, wings and tail; white underparts with dark streaking on buff breast, sides and flanks; thick bill; deeply notched, sharp-edged tail. *Juvenile:* buff wash on most of underparts; faint streaking on sides only.
Size: *L* 5–5½ in; *W* 6½ in.
Status: rare migrant and winter resident in the eastern half of the state; formerly bred in Harris Co. but extirpated as a breeding bird since the mid-1980s.
Habitat: large, fallow or wild, grassy fields and meadows with matted ground layer of dead vegetation and scattered shrub or herb perches; often in moist, grassy areas.
Nesting: no longer nests in Texas.
Feeding: gleans insects and seeds from the ground.
Voice: call is a sharp *tick;* distinctive weak, liquidy, cricketlike *tse-lick* song is often given during periods of rain or at night.
Similar Species: *Other sparrows* (pp. 377–406, 457–58): no greenish face, central crown stripe or nape. *Grasshopper Sparrow* (p. 395): no dark "whisker" stripe or prominent streaking on breast and sides. *Savannah Sparrow* (p. 394): no buff wash on breast. *Le Conte's Sparrow* (p. 397): buff-and-black-striped head with central white crown stripe; gray cheek.
Best Sites: Fort Parker SP; Lake O' The Pines; Angelina NF.

LE CONTE'S SPARROW

Ammodramus leconteii

Their habitat preference, scattered distribution and secretive behavior make Le Conte's Sparrows difficult to find. They prefer to scurry along the ground in thick cover and resort to flight only for short distances before dropping out of sight again. • Even a singing male typically chooses a low, concealing perch from which to offer his gentle love ballads. Some skilled birders may follow the buzzy tune to its source and catch a fleeting glimpse of the singer before he dives into tall vegetation and disappears from view. • Although this bird's namesake, John Le Conte, was interested in all areas of natural history, he is best remembered as one of the preeminent American entomologists of the 19th century.

ID: buff orange face; gray cheek; black line behind eye; central pale crown stripe bordered by black stripes; buff orange upper breast, sides and flanks; dark streaking on sides and flanks; white throat, lower breast and belly; mottled, brown-black upperparts, with buff streaks on back; pale legs. *Juvenile:* duller overall; more streaking on breast.
Size: *L* 4½–5 in; *W* 6½ in.
Status: uncommon migrant and winter resident in the eastern half of the state and rare in the western half.
Habitat: grassy meadows with dense vegetation, riparian thickets and thorn forests.

Nesting: does not nest in Texas.
Feeding: gleans the ground and low vegetation for insects, spiders and seeds.
Voice: high-pitched, whistling alarm call; song is a weak, short, raspy, insectlike buzz: *t-t-t-zeeee zee* or *take-it ea-zeee*.
Similar Species: *Nelson's Sharp-tailed Sparrow* (p. 398): central gray crown stripe and nape; white streaks on dark back. *Grasshopper Sparrow* (p. 395): paler face; unstreaked underparts.
Best Sites: Sea Rim SP; Anahuac NWR; Brazoria NWR; Padre Island NS; Laguna Atascosa NWR.

397

NELSON'S SHARP-TAILED SPARROW

Ammodramus nelsoni

Nelson's Sharp-tailed Sparrows are hard to find without getting your feet wet. These relatively colorful sparrows conceal themselves in low coastal marsh grasses, then unexpectedly pop out of their soggy hiding places to perch completely exposed at a close distance. A few even venture into inland freshwater marshes and riparian margins. • The best way to identify a Nelson's Sharp-tail—and most other sparrows—is by sound. This sparrow produces a combination unique among our birds: a single sharp note followed by a buzzy trill. • Edward William Nelson was the president of the American Ornithologists' Union from 1908 to 1909 and chief of the U.S. Biological Survey Bureau from 1916 to 1927. His greatest contribution was the creation of the Migratory Bird Treaty in 1916, which is still in effect today. • In 1998, the Sharp-tailed Sparrow was split into two species—the Nelson's Sharp-tailed Sparrow and the coastal Saltmarsh Sharp-tailed Sparrow *(A. caudacutus)*, which favors the Atlantic Coast.

ID: buff orange face, breast, sides and flanks; gray cheek, central crown stripe and nape; dark line behind eye; light-streaked sides and flanks; white stripes on dark back; white to light buff throat; white belly.

Size: *L* 5 in; *W* 7 in.

Status: uncommon migrant in the eastern half of the state south to the Lower Rio Grande Valley and rare west to the eastern half of the Trans-Pecos; uncommon to locally common winter resident in the saltwater marshes of the Coastal Plain.

Habitat: marshlands with tall emergent vegetation and shoreline vegetation; coastal salt marshes and dunes.

Nesting: does not nest in Texas.

Feeding: gleans ants, beetles, grasshoppers and other invertebrates from the ground and low vegetation; also eats seeds.

Voice: call is a hard *tack;* song is a raspy *ts tse-sheeeee.*

Similar Species: *Le Conte's Sparrow* (p. 397): nape not gray; mottled, brown-black back with buff streaks. *Grasshopper Sparrow* (p. 395): unstreaked underparts. *Savannah Sparrow* (p. 394): notched tail; heavily streaked underparts. *Seaside Sparrow* (p. 399): no buff orange on face, breast or sides; strongly streaked breast and flanks.

Best Sites: Sea Rim SP; Anahuac NWR; Brazoria NWR; Padre Island NS; Laguna Atascosa NWR.

SEASIDE SPARROW

Ammodramus maritimus

Fortunate birders may delight in the view of a courting male Seaside Sparrow projecting his cheery, buzzing song from atop a nearby shrub or during a courtship flight. But, for most observers, meeting with this bird may be brief because a flushed bird usually flutters only a short distance before disappearing into thick vegetation. This secretive bird inhabits the tidal salt marshes of the Gulf Coast, where tall stands of marsh grasses, rushes and shrubs provide a perfect habitat. • Foraging primarily on the ground, this stocky little bird enjoys a diverse diet of insects, spiders, small aquatic invertebrates and seeds. Small, widely separated Seaside Sparrow populations living in slightly different salt marshes along the species' coastal range have evolved into a number of distinctive subspecies or races that, given time, may develop into fully separate and unique species.

ID: long bill; yellow lores; white chin; gray "whisker" stripes; olive gray upperparts; streaked, pale gray underparts. **Size:** *L* 6 in; *W* 7½ in. **Status:** uncommon to common resident in the saltwater marshes of the Coastal Plain.
Habitat: restricted to tidal salt marshes on the coast.
Nesting: in low marsh vegetation just above the high-tide mark; female builds a cup nest of grasses and rushes with a sheltering canopy; female incubates 4–5 brown-speckled, pale greenish white eggs for 11–12 days; pair feeds the young.

Feeding: forages on the ground among marsh vegetation or at the water's edge for insects, invertebrates and seeds; occasionally probes in mud.
Voice: call is a low, soft *tsup;* song is a series of soft notes followed by buzzes: *tup-tup zee-reeee.*
Similar Species: *Savannah Sparrow* (p. 394): paler undersides; streaked head and back. *Song Sparrow* (p. 401): darker streaking; breast spot; gray and brown lores. *Saltmarsh Sharp-tailed Sparrow:* orange facial triangle.
Best Sites: Sea Rim SP; Anahuac NWR; Brazoria NWR; Padre Island NS; Laguna Atascosa NWR.

FOX SPARROW

Passerella iliaca

Like the Eastern Towhee, the Fox Sparrow eagerly scratches out a living using both feet as it stirs up leaves and scrapes organic matter on the forest floor. This large sparrow's preference for impenetrable, brushy habitat makes it difficult to observe, even though its noisy foraging habits often reveal its whereabouts. • Unlike other songbirds, which may filter through the region in a series of lingering waves, Fox Sparrows generally appear in our region for only a few short weeks in a single wave before moving on to their nesting grounds farther north. • The overall reddish brown appearance of this bird inspired taxonomists to name it after the red fox.

ID: whitish underparts with heavy, reddish brown spotting and streaking that often converges into central breast spot; reddish brown wings, rump and tail; gray crown; brown-streaked back; gray eyebrow and nape; stubby, conical bill; pale legs.

Size: *L* 6½–7 in; *W* 10½ in.

Status: uncommon to common migrant in the eastern half of the state and rare from the southern parts of the Edwards Plateau south to the Lower Rio Grande Valley and west through the rest of the state.

Habitat: riparian thickets and brushy woodland clearings, edges and parklands.

Nesting: does not nest in Texas.

Feeding: scratches the ground to uncover seeds, berries and invertebrates. *In migration* and *winter:* visits backyard feeders.

Voice: calls include *chip* and *click* notes; does not sing in migration.

Similar Species: *Song Sparrow* (p. 401): central pale crown stripe; dark "mustache"; dark brownish rather than reddish streaking and upperparts. *Hermit Thrush* (p. 325): longer, thinner bill; pale eye ring; dark breast spots; unstreaked, olive brown and reddish brown upperparts; no heavy streaking on underparts.

Best Sites: White Rock Lake Park (Dallas); Village Creek Wastewater Treatment Plant (Arlington); Meridian SP; Bear Creek Pioneer Park (Houston).

SONG SPARROW

Melospiza melodia

Good numbers of Song Sparrows call the bushy fields, marshes and riparian thickets of Texas home each winter. They spend much of their time near the ground, flitting through the lower branches or hopping along the forest floor in hopes of scratching up some tasty insects or spiders. These curious little birds are easily identified by their streaky plumage, which converges into a prominent breast spot, and are readily drawn out for closer views by a birder's "pishing." • Young Song Sparrows and many other songbirds learn to sing by eavesdropping on their fathers or on rival males. By the time a young male is a few months old, he will have formed the basis for his own courtship tune. • There are about 31 different subspecies of Song Sparrow, from the pale desert birds to the larger and darker Alaskan forms; five subspecies have been reported from Texas but do not include these extremes.

ID: whitish underparts with heavy brown streaking that converges into central breast spot; grayish face; dark line behind eye; white jaw line bordered by two dark stripes; dark crown with pale central stripe; mottled, brown upperparts; rounded tail tip.

Size: L 5½–7 in; W 8½ in.

Status: uncommon to common migrant, though rare from the central Coastal Plain south to the Lower Rio Grande Valley.

Habitat: shrubby areas, often near water, including willow shrublands, riparian thickets, forest openings and pastures.

Nesting: does not nest in Texas.

Feeding: gleans the ground, shrubs and trees for invertebrates and seeds; also eats wild fruit and visits feeders.

Voice: calls include a short *tsip* and a nasal *tchep;* song, occasionally heard in Texas, is 1–4 distinctive introductory notes, such as *sweet, sweet, sweet,* followed by a buzzy *towee,* then a short, descending trill.

Similar Species: *Fox Sparrow* (p. 400): heavier breast spotting and streaking; reddish (not dark brownish) streaking and upperparts; no central pale crown stripe; no dark "mustache." *Lincoln's Sparrow* (p. 402): lightly streaked breast with buff wash; buff jaw line. *Savannah Sparrow* (p. 394): lightly streaked breast; yellow lores; notched tail; brownish face.

Best Sites: any park with brushy habitat in the eastern half of the state.

401

LINCOLN'S SPARROW

Melospiza lincolnii

There is a certain beauty in the plumage of a Lincoln's Sparrow that is greater than the sum of its feathers. Everything about this bird is refined and, dare we say, feminine, in comparison to the scruffier, chunkier and more masculine Song Sparrow. Sightings of this bird can bring joy to the hearts of perceptive birdwatchers, especially if they are lucky enough to hear its song. • Most Lincoln's Sparrows build their nests in the cool, moist muskeg of northern Canada, frequenting thickets, woodland edges, swamps and the margins of wetland areas in migration. • This sparrow bears the name of Thomas Lincoln, a young companion to John James Audubon on his voyage to Labrador in 1833.

ID: more delicate looking than other sparrows; buff breast band, sides and flanks with fine dark streaking; buff jaw stripe; gray eyebrow, face and collar; dark line behind eye; dark reddish cap with central gray stripe; white throat and belly; mottled, gray-brown to reddish brown upperparts; very faint white eye ring. *Juvenile:* brown on face, neck and back; heavy streaking on underparts, especially on breast.
Size: *L* 5½–6 in; *W* 7½ in.
Status: uncommon to common migrant and winter resident in the eastern two-thirds of the state and rare in the west.
Habitat: various open and scrubby habitats, particularly thickets, woodland edges, swamps, wet bottomlands and wetland margins.
Nesting: does not nest in Texas.

Feeding: scratches at the ground, exposing invertebrates and seeds; prefers insects, but also eats spiders and millipedes; occasionally visits feeding stations.
Voice: calls include a buzzy *zeee* and *tsup;* song (rarely heard in Texas) is a wrenlike musical mixture of buzzes, trills and warbled notes.
Similar Species: *Song Sparrow* (p. 401): heavier breast streaking; no buff wash on breast, sides or flanks. *Savannah Sparrow* (p. 394): yellow lores; white eyebrow and jaw line. *Swamp Sparrow* (p. 403): generally unstreaked breast; more contrast between red and gray crown stripes. *Nelson's Sharp-tailed Sparrow* (p. 398): orange-buff face and breast; central gray crown stripe; gray cheek and shoulders. Ammodramus *sparrows* (pp. 395–99): brighter head colors; stronger back patterns; large, flattened head; spiky tails; inhabits more open grasslands.
Best Sites: wet thickets, often in the company of larger sparrows.

SWAMP SPARROW

Melospiza georgiana

Swamp Sparrows are well adapted to life near water. These wetland inhabitants skulk among the emergent vegetation of cattail marshes, foraging for a variety of invertebrates, including beetles, caterpillars, spiders, leafhoppers and flies. Like other sparrows, they can't swim, but that is no deterrent to snatching many of their meals directly from the water's surface as they wade through the shallows.
• The Swamp Sparrow must keep a lookout for daytime predators such as Northern Harriers, Great Blue Herons and large snakes. At night, the key to survival is finding a secluded, concealed perch that provides safety from raccoons, skunks and weasels.
• The *chink* calls of Swamp Sparrows are heard throughout winter, and birders can "squeak" to draw these curious birds in for closer observation. The metallic trills of the males are occasionally heard in spring, just before they depart for their northern breeding grounds.

nonbreeding

ID: gray face; black stripes outline white throat and jaw; dark line behind eye; brownish upperparts; reddish brown wings; dark streaking on back; dull gray breast. *Breeding:* rusty cap; streaked, buff sides and flanks. *Nonbreeding:* streaked, brown cap with central gray stripe; more brownish sides.
Size: *L* 5–6 in; *W* 7½ in.
Status: common migrant in the eastern half of the state, uncommon in the western half and absent from the Rolling Plains; uncommon winter resident in much of the state, especially in eastern forests and on the upper Coastal Plain.
Habitat: cattail marshes, open wetlands, wet meadows and open deciduous riparian thickets.
Nesting: does not nest in Texas.
Feeding: gleans insects from the ground, vegetation and the water's surface; takes seeds in late summer and fall.

Voice: harsh *chink* call; song, occasionally heard in spring, is a slow, sharp, metallic trill: *weet-weet-weet-weet.*
Similar Species: *Chipping Sparrow* (p. 386): clean white eyebrow; full black eye line; uniformly gray underparts; white wing bars. *American Tree Sparrow* (p. 385): central dark breast spot; white wing bars; 2-tone bill. *Song Sparrow* (p. 401): heavily streaked underparts; no gray collar. *Lincoln's Sparrow* (p. 402): fine breast streaking; less contrast between brown and gray crown stripes.
Best Sites: any park with marshland in the eastern half of the state.

WHITE-THROATED SPARROW

Zonotrichia albicollis

The handsome White-throated Sparrow is easily identified by its bold white throat and striped crown. Two color morphs are common: one has black and white stripes on its head, and the other has brown and tan stripes. White-striped males are more aggressive than tan-striped males, and tan-striped females are more nurturing than white-striped females. These two color morphs are perpetuated because each morph almost always breeds with the opposite color morph. • In winter, White-throated Sparrows are common in the eastern two-thirds of Texas but may appear anywhere in the state. Urban backyards dressed with brushy fenceline tangles and a bird feeder brimming with seeds can attract good numbers of these delightful sparrows. • *Zonotrichia* means "hairlike," a reference to the striped heads of birds in this genus; *albicollis* is Latin for "white neck"—not quite accurate, because it is the bird's throat and not its neck that is white.

white-striped morph

ID: black and white (or brown and tan) head stripes; white throat; gray cheeks; yellow lores; black eye line; unstreaked, gray underparts; mottled, brown upperparts; grayish bill.
Size: *L* 6½–7½ in; *W* 9 in.
Status: common to abundant migrant and winter resident in the eastern two-thirds of the state, becoming less common from the central Coastal Plain southward and rare in the western third.
Habitat: backyards, woodlots and wooded parks with thick understory; riparian brush.

Nesting: does not nest in Texas.
Feeding: scratches the ground to expose invertebrates, seeds and berries; also takes insects from vegetation and while in flight. *Winter:* eats seeds from bird feeders.
Voice: sharp *chink* call; variable song, occasionally heard in spring, is a clear, distinct, whistled *Old Sam Peabody, Peabody, Peabody.*
Similar Species: *White-crowned Sparrow* (p. 406): pinkish bill; gray collar and throat; no yellow on lores. *Swamp Sparrow* (p. 403): smaller; gray and chestnut on crown; streaked underparts; lacks head pattern.
Best Sites: any park in the eastern third of the state with brushy habitat.

HARRIS'S SPARROW

Zonotrichia querula

Wintering Harris's Sparrows are very attractive, with warm brown or cinnamon-buff faces and variable amounts of black on the throat and upper breast. Flocks are typically midsized and cohesive, with call notes and songs maintaining contact and determining status within the flock. In winter, males establish dominance related to the size of the dark "bib" patch. This "bib" extends to the crown and lores in summer and further accentuates the bright pink bill. On the breeding grounds in the muskeg of the Canadian Arctic (Harris's Sparrows nest farther north than other *Zonotrichia* sparrows), the males use their high, whistled songs, practiced during winter, to affirm their status. • The scientific term *querula* means "plaintive" in Latin and refers to this bird's quavering, whistled song. • John J. Audubon named this sparrow after his friend and amateur naturalist, Edward Harris, with whom he traveled up the Missouri River in 1843.

nonbreeding

ID: mottled, brown-and-black upperparts; white underparts; pinkish orange bill. *Breeding:* black crown, ear patch, throat and "bib"; gray face; black streaks on sides and flanks; white wing bars. *Nonbreeding:* brown face; brownish sides and flanks; white flecks on black crown.
Size: *L* 7–7½ in; *W* 10½ in.
Status: common migrant and winter resident in the central third of the state from the eastern third of the Panhandle and eastern half of the Edwards Plateau through the north-central region and south to the Coastal Plain, and rare to uncommon elsewhere.
Habitat: brushy roadsides, shrubby vegetation, forest edges and riparian thickets.
Nesting: does not nest in Texas.
Feeding: gleans the ground and vegetation for seeds, fresh buds, insects and berries; occasionally takes seeds from bird feeders.

Voice: *jeenk* or *zheenk* call; flocks in flight may give a rolling *chug-up chug-up;* song (rarely heard in Texas) is a series of 2–4 long, quavering whistles.
Similar Species: *White-throated Sparrow* (p. 404): grayish bill; yellow lores; black-and-white-striped crown. *White-crowned Sparrow* (p. 406): black-and-white-striped crown; gray collar. *House Sparrow* (p. 442): male is brownish overall, with gray crown, broad brown band behind eye, broad whitish jaw band and dark bill.
Best Sites: Village Creek Wastewater Treatment Plant (Arlington); White Rock Lake Park (Dallas); Lake Tawakoni SP; Meridian SP.

WHITE-CROWNED SPARROW

Zonotrichia leucophrys

Brightening brushy hedgerows, overgrown fields and riparian areas, White-crowned Sparrows are bold and smartly patterned in winter. They typically appear singly, or in twos or threes, flitting through brushy fencerows and overgrown fields. • This bird has a widespread distribution in North America, and populations in different parts of its range vary significantly in behavior and in migratory and nesting habits. It breeds in the far north, in alpine environments and along the California coast. The White-crowned Sparrow is North America's most studied sparrow. Several races have been identified, though plumage differences are minor, and research has given science tremendous insight into bird physiology, homing behavior and the geographic variability of song dialects; only two subspecies occur in Texas.

ID: black and white head stripes; black eye line; pinkish orange bill; gray face; unstreaked, gray underparts; pale gray throat; mottled, grayish brown upperparts; 2 faint white wing bars. *Juvenile:* brown and tan head stripes.
Size: *L* 5½–7 in; *W* 9½ in.
Status: uncommon to common migrant and winter resident statewide, although less so in the eastern third.

Habitat: woodlots, brushy tangles and riparian thickets.
Nesting: does not nest in Texas.
Feeding: scratches the ground to expose insects and seeds; also eats berries, buds and moss caps; may take seeds from bird feeders.
Voice: high, thin *seet* or sharp *pink* call; song (rarely heard in Texas) is a frequently repeated variation of *I gotta go wee-wee now*.
Similar Species: *White-throated Sparrow* (p. 404): bold white throat; grayish bill; yellow lores; browner overall. *Swamp Sparrow* (p. 403): smaller; reddish tinge to wings.
Best Sites: any park with brushy habitat.

DARK-EYED JUNCO
Junco hyemalis

Juncos usually congregate in backyards with bird feeders and sheltering conifers—with such amenities at their disposal, more and more juncos are appearing in urban areas. • Juncos spend most of their time on the ground, and they are readily flushed from wooded trails and backyard feeders. Their distinctive white outer tail feathers flash in alarm as they seek cover in a nearby tree or shrub. • In 1973, the American Ornithologists' Union grouped five junco species into a single species called the Dark-eyed Junco. The five subspecies are closely related and have similar habits but differ in coloration and range, though they interbreed where their ranges meet. Three races commonly overwinter in Texas. The "Slate-colored Junco" *(J.h. hyemalis)* may be found statewide, though it is rare in the Trans-Pecos and the southern tip of Texas. The "Oregon Junco" *(J.h. oreganus)* is found in the western half of Texas, and the less common "Gray-headed Junco" *(J.h. caniceps)* is found mainly in the Panhandle and Trans-Pecos.

"Slate-colored Junco"

ID: white outer tail feathers; pale bill. *Male "Slate-colored Junco":* dark gray upperparts; pink bill; white belly. *Female "Slate-colored Junco":* duller plumage, with some brown in wings. *Male "Oregon Junco":* rusty upperparts and flanks strongly contrasted with black head. *Female "Oregon Junco":* muted colors; dark gray head. *"Gray-headed Junco":* pale gray hood; gray upperparts; bright rufous patch on back.
Size: *L* 5½–7 in; *W* 9½ in.
Status: common migrant and winter resident throughout most of the state, though uncommon to rare on the Coastal Plain.

Habitat: shrubby woodland borders; frequents backyard feeders.
Nesting: does not nest in Texas.
Feeding: scratches the ground for invertebrates; also eats berries and seeds.
Voice: generally silent in Texas; call is a smacking *chip* note, often given in a series; song is a long, dry trill, very similar to that of the Chipping Sparrow, but more musical.
Similar Species: plumage pattern, small size and ground-dwelling habits are distinctive. *Eastern Towhee* (p. 380) and *Spotted Towhee* (p. 379): larger; females have rufous sides, red eyes and grayish bills.
Best Sites: any park with open brushy habitat.

MCCOWN'S LONGSPUR

Calcarius mccownii

Longspurs are drab, sparrowlike birds that appear in Texas during winter. They may be distinguished by their distinctive white tail patterns and the long claw on the hind toe, for which these birds are named. Four species of longspurs occur in Texas, and all are usually found in grasslands and agricultural areas, congregating in large, mixed flocks with Horned Larks. • All longspurs breed in arctic tundra, the Canadian Prairies or the northern Great Plains. The breeding male McCown's distinctive plumage and bold black and white facial pattern are unmistakable, but they are usually seen only late in the season, just prior to spring migration. • John McCown (1815–79) was an American military officer posted in southern Texas, where he collected several birds, including the species that now carries his name.

nonbreeding

ID: rufous shoulder patch; tail has mainly white outer feathers with black tip and central stripe (inverted "T"). *Breeding male:* black cap, "bib" and whisker; light gray face and underparts; black bill. *Breeding female:* resembles male, but much drabber. *Nonbreeding male and female:* pinkish bill, pale gray-brown overall.
Size: *L* 6 in; *W* 11 in.
Status: rare to locally common migrant and winter resident west from the Pineywoods through the High Plains and Trans-Pecos and generally absent from the South Texas Brush Country and Lower Rio Grande Valley.
Habitat: short-grass prairie, native grasslands, pastures and agricultural areas.
Nesting: does not nest in Texas.

Feeding: walks on the ground gleaning seeds and invertebrates, especially grasshoppers, beetles and moths; occasionally drinks at shallow ponds.
Voice: *poik* call is a short, soft rattle; song is a fast, twittering warble (rarely heard in Texas) delivered on the wing.
Similar Species: longer bill and shorter tail than other longspurs. *Chestnut-collared Longspur* (p. 410): black triangle on white tail; breeding male has mostly black underparts. *Lapland Longspur* (p. 409): more central black tail feathers. *Smith's Longspur* (p. 458): rare (northeastern Texas only); white wing patch; buffy underparts; all-white outer tail feathers. *Vesper Sparrow* (p. 390): chestnut wing patch; more white on face. *Savannah Sparrow* (p. 394): wholly grayish brown tail.
Best Sites: open fields and grasslands in the Oakwoods & Prairies region.

LAPLAND LONGSPUR

Calcarius lapponicus

Throughout much of winter, Lapland Longspurs wheel about in large numbers over our fields. From day to day, their movements are largely unpredictable, but they typically appear wherever open fields offer an abundance of seeds or waste grain. Flocks of longspurs can be surprisingly inconspicuous until closely approached—anyone attempting a closer look at the flock will be awed by the sight of the birds suddenly erupting into the sky, flashing their white outer tail feathers. • In fall, these birds arrive from their breeding grounds looking like mottled, brownish sparrows, and they retain their drab plumage throughout winter. • The Lapland Longspur breeds in the northern polar region, including the area of northern Scandinavia known as Lapland.

nonbreeding

ID: *Breeding male:* black crown, face and "bib"; chestnut nape; broad, white stripe curving down to shoulder from eye (may be tinged with buff behind eye). *Breeding female:* mottled, brown and black upperparts with rufous wing coverts; lightly streaked flanks; narrow, lightly streaked, buff breast band; strong "ear" markings. *Nonbreeding:* black central tail feathers with few white outer tail feathers; pale bill; male has dark breast band.
Size: *L* 6½ in; *W* 11½ in.
Status: abundant migrant and winter resident in the Panhandle and rare to locally common through the Rolling Plains and Blackland Prairies and south through the Oakwoods & Prairies region.
Habitat: pastures, meadows and croplands.

Nesting: does not nest in Texas.
Feeding: gleans the ground and snow for seeds and waste grain.
Voice: musical calls; flight calls include a rattled *tri-di-dit* and a descending *teew;* flight song (rarely heard in Texas) is a rapid, slurred warble.
Similar Species: *Chestnut-collared Longspur* (p. 410): black triangle on white tail; breeding male has mostly black underparts. *McCown's Longspur* (p. 408): rufous shoulder patch; white tail with black inverted "T." *Smith's Longspur* (p. 458): rare (northeastern Texas only); completely buff to buff orange underparts; male has black-and-white face and buff orange nape.
Best Sites: open grasslands and fields in central parts of the state and the Panhandle.

409

CHESTNUT-COLLARED LONGSPUR

Calcarius ornatus

A native of the North American prairies, the Chestnut-collared Longspur breeds in the Great Plains and overwinters in the south-central states and northern Mexico. Before the plow arrived and altered the landscape, this colorful longspur was one of the most abundant grassland birds. Now it is found only in areas that have escaped cultivation or where the natural forces of the grasslands have restored once-plowed fields. Of the four longspurs, this species has the broadest distribution in Texas. On its wintering grounds here in our state, this species often occurs in flocks with the other longspurs and with Horned Larks, especially in plowed grainfields and on grasslands, where the flocks may number several hundred. • Longspurs are so named because they have an extremely long hind claw (the genus name *Calcarius* also refers to this feature). It is thought that this elongated appendage is beneficial to a bird that spends so much of its life on the ground.

♂

nonbreeding

ID: black triangle on white tail; white undertail coverts. *Breeding male:* mostly black underparts; chestnut nape; black cap; yellow throat; white eyebrow; mottled, brown upperparts. *Breeding female:* mottled, brown overall; light breast streaks; possible chestnut nape. *Nonbreeding male:* buff cap and underparts. *Nonbreeding female:* buffier overall.
Size: *L* 6 in; *W* 10 in.
Status: uncommon to locally common migrant and winter resident throughout much of the state, generally absent in the eastern woodlands and very rare south from the southern half of the Edwards Plateau.

Habitat: short-grass prairie; usually avoids tall grass.
Nesting: does not nest in Texas.
Feeding: gleans the ground for plant seeds and invertebrates.
Voice: call is a 2-note harsh *kettle;* song is a warble that begins high and loud and ends low and soft.
Similar Species: breeding male is distinctive. *McCown's Longspur* (p. 408): female has chestnut hints on wings. *Vesper Sparrow* (p. 390): chestnut wing patch; more white on face. *Savannah Sparrow* (p. 394): wholly grayish brown tail.
Best Sites: open grasslands and plowed fields throughout the High Plains, Rolling Plains and prairie regions.

NORTHERN CARDINAL

Cardinalis cardinalis

A bird as beautiful as the Northern Cardinal rarely fails to capture our attention and admiration: it is often the first choice for calendars and Christmas cards. Most people easily recognize this delightful year-round neighbor even without the help of a field guide. • This bird prefers the tangled shrubby edges of woodlands and is easily attracted to backyards with feeders and sheltering trees and shrubs. • Northern Cardinals form one of the bird world's most faithful pair bonds. The male and female remain in close contact year-round, singing to one another through the seasons with soft, bubbly whistles. The female sings while on the nest, possibly informing her partner whether or not food is needed. Highly territorial, the male will even challenge his own reflection in a window or shiny hubcap! • The Northern Cardinal owes its name to the vivid red plumage of the male, which resembles the red robes of Roman Catholic cardinals.

ID: *Male:* red overall; pointed crest; black mask and throat; conical, red bill. *Female:* brownish buff overall; red crest, wings and tail.

Size: *L* 7½–9 in; *W* 12 in.

Status: common to abundant resident in the eastern two-thirds of the state, less common in the west and rare in the western Trans-Pecos.

Habitat: brushy thickets and shrubby tangles along forest and woodland edges; backyards and suburban and urban parks.

Nesting: in a dense shrub, thicket, vine tangle or low in a conifer; female builds an open cup nest of twigs, weeds, grass, leaves and rootlets and lines it with hair and fine grass; female incubates 3–4 profusely marked, whitish to greenish eggs for 12–13 days.

Feeding: gleans seeds, insects and berries from low shrubs or while hopping along the ground; visits feeders.

Voice: metallic *chip* call; song is a variable series of clear, bubbly whistled notes: *what cheer! what cheer! birdie-birdie-birdie what cheer!*

Similar Species: *Pyrrhuloxia* (p. 412): gray overall; longer, red-tipped crest; yellow bill; male has red on face, underparts, wings and tail. *Summer Tanager* (p. 374) and *Scarlet Tanager* (p. 375): males have gray bill and no crest or black mask; Scarlet Tanager has black wings and tail.

Best Sites: parks in the eastern two-thirds of the state.

411

PYRRHULOXIA

Cardinalis sinuatus

Like its close relative the Northern Cardinal, the tropical-looking Pyrrhuloxia is a crested bird with a thick, stubby bill perfect for cracking seeds. The Pyrrhuloxia prefers drier, more open habitats than the cardinal but has similar behaviors and even songs. In Texas, it is a common to uncommon, year-round resident of the arid brush country and thorny desert scrub common to the southwest. Lush suburban gardens bursting with berries, seeds and fruit attract this parrot-billed bird. • In winter, Pyrrhuloxia forage with other birds in large flocks, readily visiting feeders and wandering northward, outside of their breeding range. In early spring, males become increasingly aggressive and break away from flocks to establish breeding territories which they defend until late summer.

ID: *Male:* grayish overall, with red on face, underparts, wings and tail; long, red-tipped crest; thick, stubby, orange-yellow bill. *Female:* less red than male. *Immature:* duller than female; dark bill; pale wing bars.
Size: *L* 8¾ in; *W* 12 in.
Status: uncommon to locally common resident from the Trans-Pecos and southern South Plains east through the southern half of the Edwards Plateau and south through the South Texas Brush Country and the Lower Rio Grande Valley.
Habitat: desert habitats, including arid canyons, mesquite and acacia thickets, brushy washes and scrubby riparian areas. *Winter:* may visit feeders and wander into hedgerows, open woodlands, farmlands.

Nesting: in a thorny shrub, tree or mistletoe tangle; female builds a cup-shaped nest of bark, thorny twigs and fine plant materials; female incubates 2–3 darkly spotted white or very pale green eggs for 14 days; pair raises the young.
Feeding: forages on or near the ground, in shrubs or low trees, for seeds, insects, berries and small fruits; may visit feeders.
Voice: common call is a sharp *chink;* song, shorter and thinner than that of the Northern Cardinal, is a varied series of liquid whistles: *what-cheer what-cheer.*
Similar Species: *Northern Cardinal* (p. 411): straighter, conical, red bill; thicker, shorter crest; black face; male is red overall; female and immature are warm brown with reddish wings; immature has dark bill.
Best Sites: open, brushy habitat in parks of the Trans-Pecos, southern South Plains, and Edwards Plateau or South Texas Brush Country.

ROSE-BREASTED GROSBEAK

Pheucticus ludovicianus

Spring in Texas is synonymous with migrating flocks of Rose-breasted Grosbeaks feasting on mulberries before continuing on to their northern breeding grounds. The male's striking red chest patch is offset by their bold black and white plumage, helping them to stand out among our rich assortment of migrant birds. The drab-colored female blends in with the foliage, though her distinct white "eyebrow," heavy bill and pink or yellowish breast help in identification. • The scientific term *ludovicianus*, Latin for "from Louisiana," is misleading, because this bird is only a migrant through Louisiana and other southern states.

♀

breeding

♂

ID: conical, pale bill; dark wings with small white patches; dark tail. *Breeding male:* black hood and back; red breast patch and inner underwings; white underparts and rump. *Female and non-breeding male:* bold whitish eyebrow; thin whitish crown stripe; brown upperparts; buff underparts with dark brown streaking; possible light pink or yellow tinge on breast in fall.

Size: *L* 7–8½ in; *W* 12½ in.

Status: uncommon to common migrant in the eastern half of the state and rare in the western half; rare winter resident on the upper Coastal Plain.

Habitat: deciduous and mixed forests.

Nesting: does not nest in Texas.

Feeding: gleans vegetation for insects, seeds, buds and fruit; occasionally hover-gleans, catches flying insects on the wing or visits feeders.

Voice: call is a distinctive squeak; song (rarely heard in Texas) is a long, melodious series of whistled notes, much like a fast version of an American Robin's song.

Similar Species: male is distinctive. *Black-headed Grosbeak* (p. 414): buff underparts; finer streaks on sides of breast; yellow underwing coverts. *Purple Finch* (p. 437) and *House Finch* (p. 438): females are much smaller and have heavier streaking on underparts. *Sparrows* (pp. 377–406, 457–58): smaller; much smaller bills.

Best Sites: migrant "traps" on the Coastal Plain.

413

BLACK-HEADED GROSBEAK

Pheucticus melanocephalus

Anyone birding in the Trans-Pecos Mountains in spring or summer quickly makes acquaintance with Black-headed Grosbeaks. These birds are marvelous singers, advertising breeding territories with extended bouts of complex, accented caroling. Males sing from slightly sheltered perches near the top of a tree, whereas females forage and conduct nesting chores within the cover of interior foliage, betraying their presence with frequent call notes. The female's lemon yellow wing linings and buffy breast, eye stripe and crown stripe distinguish it from the female Rose-breasted Grosbeak. • Black-headed Grosbeaks are most characteristic of riparian thickets, rich oak woodland and broken conifer forests with a strong hardwood component, but they also visit backyard feeders adjacent to dense woodlots. • The word *Pheucticus* is thought to be derived from the Greek *phyticos,* meaning "painted with cosmetics," referring to the male's coloration.

ID: large, conical, dark bill. *Male:* orangy brown underparts and rump; black head, back, wings and tail; white wing bars and undertail coverts. *Female:* dark brown upperparts; buff underparts; lightly streaked flanks; pale eyebrow and crown stripe.

Size: *L* 7–8 in; *W* 12 in.

Status: common summer resident in the Trans-Pecos Mts.; uncommon to common migrant in the High Plains and the Edwards Plateau and south to the Lower Rio Grande Valley, becoming very rare in the east; rare winter resident on the Coastal Plain and up the Rio Grande into the Trans-Pecos.

Habitat: *Breeding:* various forests and forest-edge situations, preferring deciduous riparian, oak, mixed oak-coniferous woodlands, farmyards, parks and suburban tree groves. *In migration:* almost any stand of trees or tall brush.

Nesting: in a tall shrub or deciduous tree, often near water; female loosely weaves a cup nest of twigs, stems and grasses; pair incubates 3–4 brown-spotted, pale blue eggs for 12–14 days.

Feeding: forages in the upper canopy for invertebrates and plant foods; occasionally visits feeders.

Voice: high-pitched, penetrating *eek* call; song is a loud, ecstatic caroling with exceptionally rich quality and many accented notes.

Similar Species: male is distinctive. *Rose-breasted Grosbeak* (p. 413): female has pale bill and streaked breast. *Purple Finch* (p. 437): female is much smaller and has heavily streaked underparts.

Best Sites: Guadalupe Mountains NP; Davis Mountains SP; Big Bend NP.

BLUE GROSBEAK

Passerina caerulea

Male Blue Grosbeaks owe their spectacular spring plumage not to a fresh molt but, oddly enough, to feather wear. While Blue Grosbeaks are wintering in Mexico and Central America, their brown feather tips slowly wear away, leaving the crystal blue plumage that is seen as they arrive on their breeding grounds. The lovely blue color of the plumage is not produced by pigmentation but by tiny particles in the feathers that reflect only short wavelengths in the light spectrum. • A pair of rusty wing bars, visible even on first-winter birds, distinguishes the Blue Grosbeak from the similar-looking, and much more common, Indigo Bunting. • In spring, watch for the tail-spreading, tail-flicking and crown-raising behaviors that suggest the birds might be breeding. • The term *caerulea* is from the Latin for "blue," a description that just doesn't grasp this bird's true beauty.

ID: large head; stubby, conical, pale grayish bill; 2 rusty wing bars. *Male:* blue overall; black around base of bill. *Female:* soft brown overall; whitish throat; faint blue wash on rump and shoulders. *1st-spring male:* resembles female, but with blue head.
Size: *L* 6–7½ in; *W* 11 in.
Status: rare to locally common migrant and summer resident statewide.
Habitat: thick brush, riparian thickets, shrubby areas and densely weedy fields near water.

Nesting: in a shrub or low tree; pair builds a cup nest of twigs, roots and grass lined with finer materials, including paper and occasionally a shed reptile skin; female incubates 2–5 pale blue eggs for 11–12 days.
Feeding: gleans insects from the ground while hopping; occasionally takes seeds; may visit feeding stations.
Voice: loud *chink* call; sweet, melodious, warbling song with phrases that rise and fall.
Similar Species: *Indigo Bunting* (p. 417): smaller body and bill; male has no wing bars; female has dark brown breast streaks.
Best Sites: Big Bend NP; Meridian SP; Mitchell L. (San Antonio); Bear Creek Pioneer Park (Houston).

LAZULI BUNTING

Passerina amoena

Small flocks of Lazuli Buntings migrate through western and central Texas, stopping off at feeders and desert oases along the route; they are more common during fall migration. Before migrating south, Lazuli Buntings undergo a partial molt, completing their change of plumage on their wintering grounds. • Lazuli Buntings breed in southern Canada and the western U.S., and they have occasionally nested in the Texan Panhandle. The males set up territorial districts in which neighboring males copy and learn their songs from one another, producing "song territories." Each male within a song territory sings with slight differences in the syllables, producing his own acoustic fingerprint. • Lazuli Buntings do not demand much of their environment—a selection of song perches, a bit of low, shrubby cover and somewhere to hunt for insects is all they require. They make use of dry brushlands and woodland edges, often sharing their quarters with Black-headed Grosbeaks working the upper canopy.

ID: stout, conical bill. *Male:* turquoise blue hood and rump; chestnut upper breast; white belly; dark wings and tail; 2 bold white wing bars. *Female:* soft brown overall; hints of blue on rump.
Size: *L* 5–6 in; *W* 8 in.
Status: rare migrant in the western two-thirds of the state, except for the Rolling Plains, and uncommon to locally common in the extreme western Trans-Pecos; rare summer resident in the Panhandle and has occasionally nested there.

Habitat: brushy fencerows and open brushy fields.
Nesting: low in a shrubby tangle, in an upright crotch; small cup nest is woven with grass and lined with finer grass and hair; female incubates 3–5 pale blue or light green eggs for 12 days.
Feeding: gleans the ground and low shrubs for grasshoppers, beetles, other insects and native seeds; visits bird feeders in some areas.
Voice: hard *pit* call. *Male:* song is a brief complex of whispering notes: *swip-swip-swip zu zu ee, see see sip see see.*
Similar Species: *Blue Grosbeak* (p. 415): larger; larger bill; rusty wing bars; male has all-blue underparts. *Western Bluebird* (p. 319): male is larger, with slimmer bill, more extensive chestnut on breast and no wing bars. *Indigo Bunting* (p. 417): no wing bars; male has all-blue underparts.
Best Sites: Franklin Mountains SP; Hueco Tanks SP.

INDIGO BUNTING

Passerina cyanea

A vivid electric blue, male Indigo Buntings are among the most spectacular birds in our region. Indigo Buntings arrive in eastern Texas in April or May, favoring raspberry thickets as nest sites. Dense, thorny stems keep most predators away, and the berries are a good food source. • A persistent singer, the male vocalizes even through the heat of a summer day. He learns his couplet song from neighboring males during his first year on his own. • The Indigo Bunting employs a clever foraging strategy to reach grass and weed seeds. It lands midway on a stem and then shuffles slowly toward the seed head, which eventually bends under the bird's weight, thus giving easier access. Planting coneflowers, cosmos or foxtail grasses may attract the Indigo Bunting.

♂

♀

breeding

ID: stout, conical, gray bill; black eyes; black legs; unbarred wings. *Breeding male:* blue overall; black lores; possible black on wings and tail. *Female:* soft brown overall; brown-streaked breast; whitish throat. *Nonbreeding male:* resembles female, but usually with some blue.
Size: *L* 5½ in; *W* 8 in.
Status: common to abundant summer resident as far west as the eastern High Plains and the South Texas Brush Country; common to abundant migrant in eastern Texas and rare in the west; rare winter resident on the Coastal Plain and in the Lower Rio Grande Valley.
Habitat: deciduous forest and woodland edges, regenerating forest clearings, shrubby fields, orchards, abandoned pastures and hedgerows; occasionally uses mixed woodland edges.
Nesting: usually in an upright fork of a small tree or shrub or in a vine tangle; female builds a cup nest of grass, leaves and bark strips lined with rootlets, hair and feathers; female incubates 3–4 white to bluish eggs for 12–13 days.
Feeding: gleans low vegetation and the ground for insects and larvae; also eats seeds of thistles, dandelions and other plants.
Voice: quick *spit* call; song consists of paired warbled whistles: *fire-fire, where-where, here-here, see-it see-it.*
Similar Species: *Varied Bunting* (p. 458): dark purplish plumage; red nape. *Blue Grosbeak* (p. 415): larger overall; larger bill; rusty wing bars; female has unstreaked breast. *Eastern Bluebird* (p. 318): larger; slimmer bill; orange or rufous below; male has pure blue wings and tail.
Best Sites: *Summer:* eastern parks with appropriate habitat. *In migration:* migrant "traps" on the Coastal Plain.

PAINTED BUNTING

Passerina ciris

Wearing almost every color of the rainbow, the stunning male Painted Bunting graces the thickets of the South with his sweet songs. Although not nearly as unmistakable as the adult male, the female bears a plumage that is still attractive: a rich greenish above and pale yellow below. Unlike some other finches, including the Indigo Bunting, the male Painted Bunting retains his bright colors during winter. • Painted Buntings have two separate breeding ranges: along the Atlantic Coast from North Carolina to Florida and mostly inland from Alabama to Mexico. These birds tend to be rather secretive on their breeding grounds, though, often hiding in dense foliage and making observation difficult despite the bright colors of the male.

ID: *Male:* blue head; red eye ring, underparts and rump; green back; dark wings and tail with reddish highlights. *Female:* green upperparts; yellow-green underparts.

Size: *L* 5½ in; *W* 8½ in.

Status: uncommon to common migrant and summer resident statewide; very rare winter resident on the Coastal Plain and in the Lower Rio Grande Valley.

Habitat: semi-open areas, including roadside thickets, hedgerows, woodland edges, clearings and undergrowth, parks, gardens and brushlands.

Nesting: in a low tree, dense shrubbery or a vine tangle; female weaves an open cup nest of grass, weed stems and leaves and lines it with fine plant material and animal hair;

female incubates 3–4 finely speckled, white eggs for 11–12 days; usually has 2 broods per year.

Feeding: forages on the ground or in low vegetation for seeds and insects; may also eat fruits and berries.

Voice: sharp *chip* call; song is a sweet, clear series of warbling notes.

Similar Species: male is distinctive. *Other female* and *immature buntings* (pp. 416–17, 458): brown overall.

Best Sites: *Summer:* any park with appropriate habitat. *In migration:* migrant "traps" on the Coastal Plain.

DICKCISSEL

Spiza americana

These "miniature meadowlarks" are a seminomadic, irruptive species that may be abundant one year and nearly absent the next. Whether Dickcissels remain in Texas to breed depends largely on environmental conditions—in drought years, migrants continue northward. Watch for them at bird feeders in the company of House Sparrows or on cattle farms, where they feed from the trough. • Although Dickcissels eat mostly insects on their breeding grounds, seeds and grain form the main part of their diet on their South American wintering grounds, making them unpopular with local farmers. Each year, large numbers of roosting birds are poisoned in efforts to reduce crop losses, which may partially explain the Dickcissel's pattern of absence and abundance. Because winter flocks can contain over one million birds, targeting a single roost can significantly affect the world population. • Dickcissels are polygynous—a male may mate with up to eight females in a single breeding season.

breeding

ID: yellow eyebrow; gray head and nape; white chin, conical, dark bill; pale grayish underparts; yellow breast with gray sides; brown upperparts; rufous shoulder patch. *Breeding male:* triangular, black "bib"; duller colors in nonbreeding plumage. *Female:* duller version of male; no dark "bib." *Nonbreeding male:* duller plumage.
Size: L 6–7 in; W 9½ in.
Status: uncommon to locally abundant migrant and summer resident east of the Pecos R. and rare and local in the Trans-Pecos; very rare winter resident on the Coastal Plain.
Habitat: abandoned fields, weedy meadows, croplands, grasslands and grassy roadsides.
Nesting: on or near the ground, well concealed among tall, dense vegetation; female builds a bulky, open cup nest of

grass and other vegetation; female incubates 4 pale blue eggs for 11–13 days.
Feeding: gleans the ground and low vegetation for insects and seeds.
Voice: buzzerlike *bzrrrrt* flight call; song consists of 2–3 single notes followed by a trill, often paraphrased as *dick dick dick-cissel*.
Similar Species: *House Sparrow* (p. 442): black bill, "bib" and lores; gray throat; no yellow on eyebrow or breast. *Meadowlarks* (pp. 422–23): much larger; long, pointed bill; yellow chin and throat with black "necklace." *American Goldfinch* (p. 441): white or buff yellow bars on dark wings; possible black forecrown; no black "bib."
Best Sites: weedy fields and pastures, especially in the eastern half of the state.

BOBOLINK

Dolichonyx oryzivorus

The Bobolink is the only North American icterid (the group that includes blackbirds, meadowlarks and orioles) that winters in the Southern Hemisphere, where it forms huge flocks. Some individuals migrate an amazing 12,000 miles annually between their breeding and wintering areas, making the Bobolink the premiere long-distance land bird in the Western Hemisphere. One banded female made the round-trip nine times during her lifetime, the equivalent to circling the Earth at the equator four times! • Bobolinks are generally uncommon to rare spring migrants and very rare fall migrants (when the bulk of their migration is well to the east) in the eastern half of Texas. • Bobolinks once benefited from increased agriculture, but modern practices, such as harvesting hay early in the season, continue to thwart the reproductive efforts of this bird. • Many people believe that the common name is a reference to the bird's song.

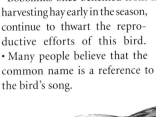

breeding

ID: *Breeding male:* black bill, head, wings, tail and underparts; buff nape; white rump and wing patch. *Breeding female:* yellowish bill; brown-buff overall; streaked back, sides, flank and rump; pale eyebrow; dark eye line; light central crown stripe bordered by dark stripes; whitish throat. *Nonbreeding male and female:* resembles breeding female, but darker above and rich golden-buff below.
Size: *L* 6–8 in; *W* 11–12 in (male is noticeably larger than female).
Status: rare to uncommon spring migrant from the eastern half of the state west to the eastern Panhandle and south to the Lower Rio Grande Valley; very rare in fall.
Habitat: grassy or brushy fields, dry prairie and agricultural fields.
Nesting: does not nest in Texas.

Feeding: forages on the ground and low vegetation for insects, spiders and seeds.
Voice: low *chuck* call; distinctive *ink* flight call; song (sometimes heard in spring) is a series of bubbly warbling notes.
Similar Species: *Smith's Longspur* (p. 458): more rounded wings; white outer tail feathers; gray underwings; little or no seasonal overlap. *Savannah Sparrow* (p. 394): dark breast streaking; yellow lores. *Vesper Sparrow* (p. 390): dark-streaked, white breast; white outer tail feathers.
Best Sites: grassy fields and pastures on the Coastal Plain, especially in spring.

RED-WINGED BLACKBIRD

Agelaius phoeniceus

Nearly every cattail marsh worthy of the name in Texas plays host to Red-winged Blackbirds during at least some of the year. • The male's bright red shoulders and short, raspy song are his most important tools in the often intricate strategy he employs to defend his territory from rivals. A flashy and richly voiced male that manages to establish a large and productive territory can attract several mates to his cattail kingdom. In field experiments, males that had their red shoulders painted black soon lost their territories to rivals they had previously defeated. • After the male has wooed the female, she starts weaving a nest amid the cattails. Cryptic coloration allows the female to sit inconspicuously upon her nest, blending in perfectly with the surroundings.

ID: *Male:* black overall, with large, red shoulder patch edged in yellow (occasionally concealed). *Female:* heavily streaked underparts; mottled, brown upperparts; faint red shoulder patch; pale eyebrow.
Size: *L* 7–9½ in; *W* 13 in.
Status: common to abundant resident statewide.
Habitat: cattail marshes, wet meadows and ditches, croplands and shoreline shrubs.
Nesting: colonial; in cattails or a shoreline bush, usually next to or over water; female weaves a deep cup nest of dried cattail leaves and grass and lines it with fine grass; female incubates 3–4 darkly marked, pale blue-green eggs for 10–12 days.
Feeding: gleans the ground for seeds, waste grain and invertebrates; also gleans vegetation for seeds, insects and berries; occasionally catches insects in flight; may visit feeders.
Voice: calls include a harsh *check* and a high *tseert;* song is a loud, raspy *konk-a-ree* or *ogle-reeeee;* female may give a loud *che-che-che chee chee chee.*
Similar Species: plumage of male is distinctive. Females resemble sparrows or finches but are much larger, are found in flocks in open habitats and have pointed bills. *Brown-headed Cowbird* (p. 431): female is dull gray-brown overall and has finely streaked underparts.
Best Sites: any marshland, especially if on the Coastal Plain.

EASTERN MEADOWLARK

Sturnella magna

The breeding ranges of the Eastern Meadowlark and the Western Meadowlark overlap in Texas, and both species wander widely in winter. They occasionally interbreed, but the offspring are infertile. • The two meadowlark species are very similar in appearance, so birders must distinguish them by their song. The Eastern Meadowlark's song is a series of distinct whistles, whereas the more varied song of the Western Meadowlark ends with a gurgle. • The drab plumage of most female songbirds protects them during the breeding season, but the female Eastern Meadowlark uses a different strategy. Her V-shaped "necklace" and bright yellow throat and belly create a colorful distraction that most predators cannot resist chasing. Once the female has led the predator away from the nest, she folds away her white tail flags, exposes her camouflaged back and disappears into the grass.

breeding

ID: *Breeding:* yellow underparts; broad, black breast band; mottled, brown upperparts; short, wide tail with white outer feathers; yellow lores; long, sharp bill; blackish eye line and crown stripes border pale eyebrow and median crown stripe; dark-streaked, white sides and flanks. *Nonbreediing:* duller plumage.
Size: *L* 9–9½ in; *W* 14 in.
Status: common resident, though absent from the Trans-Pecos Mts and the western half of the Panhandle.
Habitat: *Breeding:* grassy meadows and pastures; may use croplands, weedy fields, grassy roadsides and old orchards. *In migration* and *winter:* coastal barrens and fields, croplands and wasteland.

Nesting: in a depression on the ground, concealed by dense grass; female weaves a domed grass nest into surrounding vegetation; female incubates 3–7 brown-speckled, white eggs for 13–15 days.
Feeding: gleans grasshoppers, crickets, beetles and spiders from the ground and vegetation; probes the soil for grubs and worm; also eats seeds.
Voice: rattling flight call and a high, buzzy *dzeart;* song is a rich series of 2–8 distinct, melodic, slurred whistles: *see-you at school-today* or *this is the year.*
Similar Species: *Western Meadowlark* (p. 423): lighter upperparts, especially crown stripes and eye line; more yellow on throat and lower cheek; different call and song. *Dickcissel* (p. 419): smaller; dark crown; white chin; unstreaked sides.
Best Sites: most grassy fields and pastures.

WESTERN MEADOWLARK

Sturnella neglecta

The brightly colored Western Meadowlark is one of the most abundant and widely distributed birds in the western U.S. It is also one of the most popular—the Western Meadowlark is the state bird of six states. • Birders are encouraged to exercise extreme caution when walking through meadowlark nesting habitat. The grassy domed nests are extremely difficult to locate and are so well concealed that they are often accidentally crushed before they are seen. • The Western Meadowlark was overlooked by members of the Lewis and Clark expedition, who mistakenly thought it was the same species as the Eastern Meadowlark. This oversight is represented in the scientific name with *neglecta*. • Meadowlarks are not actually larks; they are members of the blackbird family. The similarities become very apparent when the birds are seen in silhouette.

breeding

ID: *Breeding:* dark-mottled, brown upperparts; yellow underparts and lower cheek; black breast band; yellow lores; sharp bill; brown crown stripes and eye line border; pale eyebrow and central crown stripe; dark-streaked, white sides and flanks. *Nonbreeding:* duller plumage.
Size: *L* 9–9½ in; *W* 14½ in.
Status: common resident from western Texas east through the Rolling Plains and the Edwards Plateau.
Habitat: grassy meadows and pastures; may use croplands, weedy fields and grassy roadsides.
Nesting: in a depression on the ground, concealed by dense grass or rarely low shrubs; female weaves a domed grass nest with a side entrance into surrounding vegetation; female incubates 3–7 white eggs, heavily spotted with brown and purple, for 13–15 days.
Feeding: gleans the ground and vegetation for insects and spiders; probes the soil for grubs and worms; also eats seeds.
Voice: calls include a low, loud *chuck* or *chup*, a rattling flight call and a few clear, whistled notes; song is a rich, melodic series of bubbly, flutelike notes that ends with a gurgle.
Similar Species: *Eastern Meadowlark* (p. 422): darker upperparts, especially crown stripes and eye line; yellow on throat does not extend onto lower cheek; different call and song. *Dickcissel* (p. 419): smaller; solid dark crown; conical bill; white chin; unstreaked sides.
Best Sites: grassy fields, pastures and agricultural fields in western Texas.

YELLOW-HEADED BLACKBIRD

Xanthocephalus xanthocephalus

The spectacular Yellow-headed Blackbird is most common in western Texas during migration, with a few birds lingering along the Rio Grande in winter. Summer residents can be locally common in the Panhandle, but Texas marks the southern limit of their breeding range and breeding records are rare. This bird often nests in small colonies and requires a marsh with a ratio of half emergent vegetation and half open water in which to breed. • Although you might expect this blackbird to have a song as splendid as its gold and black plumage, the courting male emits only pathetic grinding noise, possibly the worst song in North America. • The scientific term *xanthocephalus* means "yellow head."

ID: *Male:* yellow head and breast; black body; black lores; white wing patches; long tail; black bill. *Female:* dusky brown overall; yellow breast, throat and eyebrow; hints of yellow on face.

Size: *L* 8–11 in; *W* 15 in.

Status: rare summer resident and local breeder in the southern half of the Panhandle; common migrant in the western two-thirds of the state and rare to uncommon in the eastern third; rare winter resident in many parts of the state but locally abundant in the Trans-Pecos.

Habitat: *In migration* and *winter:* agricultural fields, dairy farms and cattle feedlots. *Summer:* deep marshes, sloughs, lakeshores and river impoundments with cattails.

Nesting: loosely colonial; female builds a deep basket of aquatic plants lined with dry grass and woven into surrounding vegetation over water; female incubates 4 pale green or gray eggs, marked with gray or brown, for 11–13 days.

Feeding: forages on the ground for grain, other seeds and insects; may visit bird feeders.

Voice: deep *croak* call; song is a strained, metallic grating note followed by a descending buzz.

Similar Species: adult male is distinctive. *Boat-tailed Grackle* (p. 428): female and juvenile resemble female or juvenile Yellow-headed Blackbird but are larger, with longer tails, buffy underparts and no white wing patches.

Best Sites: *Winter:* marshes of the Trans-Pecos. *In migration:* potentially any marsh in the state.

RUSTY BLACKBIRD

Euphagus carolinus

A rust-colored fall plumage is the reason for the Rusty Blackbird's name, but its moniker might as well reflect the grating, squeaky song, which sounds very much like a rusty hinge. • During migration and over winter, Rusty Blackbirds often intermingle with flocks of other blackbirds, sometimes blackening the rural skies. They spend their days foraging along the wooded edges of fields and wetlands, occasionally varying their routine to pick through the manure-laden ground of cattle feedlots. At day's end, foraging is curtailed, and most birds seek the shelter of trees and shrubs and the stalks of emergent marshland vegetation. • Rusty Blackbirds are generally less abundant and less aggressive than their blackbird relatives, and they tend to avoid most human-altered environments. In the 1950s, winter roosts in Texas sometimes contained thousands of birds, but numbers have declined substantially since then—roosts with several dozen birds are now more common.

nonbreeding

ID: yellow eyes; dark legs; long, sharp bill. *Breeding male:* dark gray, almost black plumage with subtle green gloss on body and subtle bluish or greenish gloss on head. *Female:* gray to brownish gray plumage with buffy underparts and rusty cheeks. *Nonbreeding male:* rusty wings, back and crown.

Size: *L* 9–9½ in; *W* 14 in.

Status: rare to uncommon migrant and winter resident from eastern Texas west to the Rolling Plains and southeastern Edwards Plateau and south to the central Coastal Plain, becoming very rare in the west and absent from the South Texas Brush Country and Lower Rio Grande Valley.

Habitat: swamps, marshes, beaver ponds, open fields, brushlands, feedlots and woodland edges near water; occasionally winters at feeders.

Nesting: does not nest in Texas.

Feeding: walks along shorelines taking waterbugs, beetles, dragonflies, snails, grasshoppers and occasionally small fish; also eats waste grain and seeds.

Voice: harsh *chack* call; song is a squeaky, creaking *kushleeeh ksh-lay*.

Similar Species: *Brewer's Blackbird* (p. 426): male is glossier overall, with no rust in winter plumage; female is drab gray-brown year-round and usually has dark eyes. *Common Grackle* (p. 427): longer, keeled tail; larger body and bill; more iridescent. *European Starling* (p. 334): speckled appearance; dark eyes.

Best Sites: Daingerfield SP; Huntsville SP; Armand Bayou Nature Center (Houston); Bear Creek Pioneer Park (Houston).

BREWER'S BLACKBIRD

Euphagus cyanocephalus

A relatively new addition to our avifauna, the Brewer's Blackbird has been expanding its nesting range eastward at an incredible rate of 11 miles per year for the last century by following roadways and taking advantage of cleared land. This bird of the West is most commonly found in western Texas during winter, when small flocks or single individuals show up along roadsides or in pastures, where they often probe cow patties in search of seeds. • The feathers of the Brewer's Blackbird show an iridescent quality as rainbows of reflected sunlight move along the feather shafts. As it walks, the Brewer's Blackbird distinguishes itself from other blackbirds by jerking its head back and forth like a chicken, enhancing the glossy effect. • John J. Audubon named this bird after Thomas Mayo Brewer (1814–80), a friend and prominent oologist (a person who studies eggs).

breeding

ID: *Breeding male:* iridescent, blue-green body and purplish head often look black; yellow eyes. *Female:* flat brown plumage; dark eyes. *Nonbreeding male:* may show some faint rusty feather edging.
Size: *L* 8–10 in; *W* 15½ in.
Status: common to locally abundant migrant and winter resident, becoming uncommon to rare in the forested areas of eastern Texas.
Habitat: moist, grassy meadows and roadsides with nearby wetlands and patches of trees and shrubs.
Nesting: loosely colonial; woven into vegetation over water; female builds a deep basket of aquatic plants lined with dry grass;

female incubates 4 gray- or brown-marked, pale green to gray eggs for 11–13 days.
Feeding: gleans the ground or manure piles for grain and other seeds; also eats some insects.
Voice: metallic *check* call; song is a creaking, 2-noted *k-shee*.
Similar Species: *Rusty Blackbird* (p. 425): longer, more slender bill; both genders have yellow eyes; male's plumage has subtler green gloss on body and subtle bluish or greenish gloss on head. *Common Grackle* (p. 427): much longer, keeled tail; larger body and bill. *Brown-headed Cowbird* (p. 431): shorter tail; stubbier, thicker bill; male has brown head; female has paler, streaked underparts and very pale throat. *European Starling* (p. 334): speckled appearance; dark eyes.
Best Sites: Village Creek Wastewater Treatment Plant (Arlington); Huntsville SP; Sea Rim SP; Goose Island SP.

COMMON GRACKLE
Quiscalus quiscula

Grackles are large, mostly terrestrial blackbirds with heavy bills and long, keel-shaped tails. All three North America species are found in Texas. • The Common Grackle is a poor but spirited singer. When courting, the male usually perches in a shrub. He slowly takes a deep breath to inflate his breast, causing his feathers to spike outward, then closes his eyes and gives out a loud, strained *tssh-schleek*. • Grackles are one of several species that practice "anting," a curious behavior that involves squishing ants into their feathers. The formic acid released from the ants' bodies helps eliminate parasites. When ants are not available, grackles may substitute lemons instead!

ID: long tail. *Male:* black overall, with purple iridescence on head, green on back and blue on tail; yellow eyes. *Female:* resembles male but duller, with less iridescence. *Juvenile:* resembles female, but with even less iridescence and dark eyes.
Size: *L* 11–13½ in; *W* 17 in.
Status: uncommon to common summer resident from eastern Texas west to the eastern Panhandle and south to the central Coastal Plain; uncommon to abundant migrant and winter resident in the east and rare in the west.
Habitat: most open or semiwooded upland habitats; also uses forested wetlands and suburban areas.
Nesting: singly or in a small colony; in dense tree or shrub branches or emergent vegetation, often near water; female builds a bulky, open cup nest of twigs, grass, plant fibers and mud lined with fine grass or feathers; female incubates 4–5 brown-blotched, pale blue eggs for 12–14 days.
Feeding: on or near the ground; feeds mostly on vegetable matter such as seeds, berries and acorns; also takes insects and other invertebrates and occasional small vertebrates.
Voice: loud *chack* call; song is a series of harsh, strained notes ending with a squeak.
Similar Species: *Boat-tailed Grackle* (p. 428): much larger, with larger tail; usually dark eyes; female has brown plumage and pale throat. *Rusty Blackbird* (p. 425) and *Brewer's Blackbird* (p. 426): in migration and winter only; much smaller; smaller bill; no keel on tail.
Best Sites: any park, refuge or wildlife management area with open woodlands in the eastern half of the state.

BOAT-TAILED GRACKLE

Quiscalus major

Well adapted to suburbia, the Boat-tailed Grackle can be found occupying most shopping-center parking lots, where it displays from planted trees and forages among cars and shoppers. It is also commonly seen nesting in stormwater retention ponds and is closely associated with coastal waters, where it wades through the shallows or walks on top of floating vegetation while searching for snails and mussels. • With fluffed feathers, spread tails, fluttering wings and bills held skyward, groups of male Boat-tailed Grackles display for females, uttering their loud *cheep* notes and other sounds in series. • Until the 1970s, the Boat-tailed Grackle and the Great-tailed Grackle were considered to be the same species. Their ranges partially overlap, and the birds have similarities in appearance and habit, but their failure to interbreed revealed their distinct identities.

ID: long, keel-shaped tail; long, dark bill; eye color varies from yellow to brown. *Male:* iridescent, green-blue plumage usually looks black. *Female:* orangy brown underparts; brown mask and crown; darker wings and tail.

Size: *Male: L* 16½ in; *W* 23 in. *Female: L* 14 in; *W* 17½ in.

Status: common to abundant resident in the marshlands of the upper and central Coastal Plain.

Habitat: usually near water, from salt to fresh, including stormwater retention ponds in suburban and urban areas.

Nesting: colonial; in vegetation at the edge of a marsh or other water body; female builds bulky cup nest from marsh vegetation and

mud; female incubates 2–3 darkly scrawled, pale blue eggs for 12–14 days and raises the young alone.

Feeding: forages on or near the ground or in shallow water; normally takes insects, crustaceans and other invertebrates, but may also eat small vertebrates and some seeds; sometimes gleans radiator grills for insects!

Voice: various calls, including rattles, chatters, squeaks and a soft *chuck*; song consists of harsh *jeeb* notes repeated in series.

Similar Species: *Great-tailed Grackle* (p. 429): slightly larger, with longer tail; male has iridescent, purplish blue plumage. *Common Grackle* (p. 427): much smaller, with shorter tail; yellow eyes; never has pale brown in plumage.

Best Sites: Sea Rim SP; Anahuac NWR; Galveston Island SP; Brazoria NWR; Brazos Bend SP.

GREAT-TAILED GRACKLE

Quiscalus mexicanus

One of our largest all-black birds—only ravens are larger—the Great-tailed Grackle is North America's largest grackle. With a tail so long that it acts as a sail on windy days, continually pointing the bird into the wind, the male Great-tailed Grackle has sacrificed function for beauty. • Great-tailed Grackles are farmland feeders, devouring waste grain before heading into suburban areas at night, announcing their presence with squeaks and hoots in a noisy gang. Particularly in winter, these gangs bully other birds from feeders. • In nesting colonies, females may steal nest material from each other, and both genders tend to stray from their mates, with females sometimes switching territories within a breeding season. • Since the 1960s, following increasing agriculture and urbanization, the Great-tailed Grackle population has expanded northward to northern Nebraska, southern Kansas and eastern Colorado.

ID: yellow eyes. *Male:* all-black body with bluish purple iridescence; very long, wide tail. *Female:* grayish brown body; lighter eyebrow and under- parts; shorter tail.

Size: *Male: L* 18 in; *W* 23 in. *Female: L* 15 in; *W* 19 in.

Status: common to abundant resident in the eastern two-thirds of the state and uncommon to locally common in the western third and in the woodlands of eastern Texas.

Habitat: open to semi-open habitat, includ- ing urban parks, farmland and wetlands.

Nesting: in a tree near water or in cattails; tree nest is made of mud, moss and varied

debris, and wetland nest is made of cattails and thick vegetation; female incubates 3–4 pale blue eggs, with purplish blotches and scrawling, for 13–14 days.

Feeding: forages on or near the ground or in shallow water; varied diet includes birds' eggs, grain, insects, crustaceans and other invertebrates.

Voice: very verbal; ascending whistles, hoots and squeaks; noisy chattering in large groups, especially in winter. *Male:* screeches to proclaim his territory.

Similar Species: *Boat-tailed Grackle* (p. 428): restricted to the upper Texas coast; slightly smaller; rounder head; iridescent, bluish green plumage. *Common Grackle* (p. 427): shorter tail and wings; smaller body; limited iridescence.

Best Sites: any area inhabited by humans that has some trees.

BRONZED COWBIRD

Molothrus aeneus

Opening the Southwest to cattle grazing and agriculture in the early 20th century created new habitat for the Bronzed Cowbird. Previously found only from Mexico to Panama, this brood parasite was first recorded in North America in Arizona in 1909, and it has been steadily spreading eastward ever since. • Like other cowbirds, Bronzed Cowbirds favor open areas such as parks and golf courses, and they gather at dairy farms and cattle feedlots. • The male Bronzed Cowbird courts the female with a display that includes fluffing out his ruff (the feathers on the nape), spreading his tail and walking toward her with his bright red eyes flared. As a parasitic nester, the female lays each egg in the nest of a "host" bird, sometimes poking holes in the rest of the eggs so hers will be the only one to receive parental attention.

ID: brownish black plumage; heavy, conical bill; red eyes. *Male:* thick neck ruff; iridescent, blue wings. *Female:* slightly duller overall; no blue on wings. *Juvenile:* resembles female but has dark eyes.
Size: *L* 8½–9 in; *W* 14 in (female is smaller than male).
Status: common resident from the Lower Rio Grande Valley to the western half of the Edwards Plateau and west through the Trans-Pecos and southern half of the High Plains; rare to locally common migrant and winter resident through the central third of the state.

Habitat: open or lightly wooded habitats, especially around cattle or farmland; also suburban areas.
Nesting: brood parasite; female lays 4–5 pale blue or blue-green eggs in nests of other birds, usually 1 egg per nest, and leaves adoptive parents to incubate eggs for 10–13 days and raise the young.
Feeding: forages on or near the ground; feeds mostly on grain and other seeds; also takes snails, insects and spiders.
Voice: varied high, bubbling whistles.
Similar Species: red eyes of adults are diagnostic. *Brown-headed Cowbird* (p. 431) and *Shiny Cowbird* : identification of juveniles may be difficult.
Best Sites: Davis Mountains SP; Choke Canyon SP; Santa Ana NWR; Bentsen-Rio Grande Valley SP; Goliad SP.

BROWN-HEADED COWBIRD

Molothrus ater

Historically, the nomadic Brown-headed Cowbird followed bison herds across the Great Plains (it now follows cattle), so it never stayed in one area long enough to build and tend a nest. Instead, the Brown-headed Cowbird lays its eggs in the nests of other birds, including 220 known species, making it the most successful brood parasite in North America. Although not all nest parasitism is successful—some birds eject the cowbird eggs or build new nests elsewhere, and others, such as doves, cannot properly feed the young cowbird—nearly 150 of the species parasitized by the Brown-headed Cowbird successfully raise the cowbird young. • As people have cleared forests and established cattle feedlots and dairy farms over the past century, this species has greatly expanded its range. It now breeds from southern Alaska to northern Mexico, and it winters in much of the continental U.S. and Mexico.

ID: thick, conical bill; shortish tail; raises tail when foraging. *Male:* black body with green iridescence; brown head. *Female:* dull grayish brown overall; pale throat; faint streaking on breast. *Juvenile:* resembles female, but with "scaly" back and wings and streaked underparts.
Size: *L* 6–8 in; *W* 12 in.
Status: common resident statewide, becoming locally abundant in winter.
Habitat: any habitat with at least scattered trees. *Winter:* large flocks frequent dairy farms and feedlots.

Nesting: brood parasite; female lays up to 30 variably marked, whitish eggs in nests of other birds, 1 egg per nest, and leaves adoptive parents to incubate eggs for 10–13 days and raise the young.
Feeding: forages on the ground for seeds; rarely takes insects.
Voice: squeaky, high-pitched *seep* call, often given in flight; also a fast, chipping *ch-ch-ch-ch-ch-ch;* song is a high, liquidy gurgle: *glug-ahl-whee.*
Similar Species: *Bronzed Cowbird* (p. 430): male has red eyes; female is uniformly dull black. *Rusty Blackbird* (p. 425) and *Brewer's Blackbird* (p. 426): slimmer, longer bills; longer tails; males have dark heads.
Best Sites: any park with open shrub habitat; often found in pastures with cattle.

ORCHARD ORIOLE

Icterus spurius

Orioles are members of the blackbird family that have brilliant orange or yellow plumages. Of North America's nine oriole species, seven have occurred in Texas. • Orchards may once have been the favored haunts of this oriole, but, with most orchards now heavily sprayed and manicured, you are unlikely to see this bird in such a locale. Instead, the Orchard Oriole is most commonly found in large shade trees that line roads, paths and streams. It is the smallest of all North American orioles. • Orioles are frequent victims of nest parasitism by Brown-headed Cowbirds. In some parts of its breeding range, over half of Orchard Oriole nests are parasitized by cowbirds.

ID: *Male:* mostly dark rufous, with black tail, back and head; black wing has rufous shoulder patch and 1 white bar. *Female:* yellow overall, darker on crown and nape, with greenish gray back; darkish wing with 2 white wing bars. *Juvenile male:* resembles female, but with black throat patch.

Size: *L* 6–7 in; *W* 9½ in.

Status: uncommon to locally common migrant and summer resident in the eastern two-thirds of the state and rare in the western third.

Habitat: open woodlands, suburban parklands, forest edges, hedgerows and groves of shade trees.

Nesting: in the fork of a deciduous tree or shrub; female weaves a hanging pouch nest from fine plant fibers; female incubates 4–5 pale bluish white eggs, blotched with gray, brown and purple, for about 12–15 days.

Feeding: gleans vegetation for insects, spiders and fruit.

Voice: quick *chuck* call; song is a loud, rapid, varied series of whistled notes.

Similar Species: *Baltimore Oriole* (p. 435): male has brighter orange plumage with orange in tail; female has orange overtones. *Scott's Oriole* (p. 436) and *Audubon's Oriole* (p. 434): larger; males have brighter yellow plumage. *Summer* (p. 374), *Scarlet* (p. 375) and *Hepatic* (p. 373) *tanagers:* females have thicker, pale bills and no wing bars.

Best Sites: *Summer:* Village Creek Wastewater Treatment Plant (Arlington); Meridian SP; Bear Creek Pioneer Park (Houston); Mitchell L. (San Antonio); Lost Maples SP. *In migration:* migrant "traps" on the upper and central Coastal Plain.

BULLOCK'S ORIOLE

Icterus bullockii

The Bullock's Oriole is common and widespread in the western half of Texas, yet most residents are unaware of it existence. The male's glowing orange, black and white plumage blends remarkably well with the sunlit and shadowed upper-canopy summer foliage where he spends much of his time. Finding the drab olive, gray and white female oriole is even more difficult, especially for predators. • Orioles build very elaborate hanging pouch nests that provide both shelter and protection, and a nest dangling in a bare tree in fall is sometimes the only evidence that the bird was there at all. • The name "oriole" comes from the Latin *aureolus*, meaning "golden"—most North American orioles are yellow or orange in color.

ID: *Male:* bright orange eyebrow, cheek, underparts, rump and outer tail feathers; black throat, eye line, cap, back and central tail feathers; large white wing patch. *Female:* dusky yellow face, throat and upper breast; gray underparts; olive gray upperparts and tail; small white wing patches.

Size: *L* 7–9 in; *W* 12 in.

Status: common migrant and summer resident in the western half of the state; rare migrant in the eastern half.

Habitat: deciduous riparian forests, willow shrublands and urban areas.

Nesting: high in a deciduous tree, suspended from a branch; mostly female weaves hanging pouch nest of fine plant fibers, hair, string and fishing line and lines it with horsehair, plant down, fur and moss;

female incubates 4–5 pale gray-white or bluish white eggs, marked with fine black or purplish black scribbling, for 12–14 days.

Feeding: gleans canopy vegetation and shrubs for caterpillars, beetles, wasps and other invertebrates; also eats fruit and nectar; occasionally visits hummingbird feeders or takes orange halves.

Voice: call is a series of slow chattering notes; song consists of an accented series of 6–8 whistled, rich and guttural notes.

Similar Species: *Baltimore Oriole* (p. 435): male has all-black head and less white on wings. *Hooded Oriole* (p. 458) and *Altamira Oriole* (p. 459): male has orange (or yellow) cap and smaller wing bars. *Western Tanager* (p. 376): yellow body plumage; no black on cap or throat. *Summer* (p. 374), *Scarlet* (p. 375) and *Hepatic* (p. 373) *tanagers*: females have thicker, pale bills and no wing bars.

Best Sites: Palo Duro Canyon SP; San Angelo SP; Lake Corpus Christi SP; Davis Mountains SP.

AUDUBON'S ORIOLE

Icterus graduacauda

Named after the great ornithologist John James Audubon, the Audubon's Oriole hides within the thick forests of the Rio Grande Valley. A native of Mexico, it reaches the northernmost extension of its range in the South Texas Brush Country. • Unlike the rest of the edge-loving oriole family, this modest bird prefers the deep parts of the forest. Unfortunately, the clearing of woodlands for agriculture or roadways and other forms of fragmentation has led to an increase of cowbird parasitism on Audubon's Oriole nests. Despite this increased cowbird parasitism, the species has expanded its range to the north onto the southern Edwards Plateau and up into the central Coastal Plain region.

ID: *Male:* black head; yellow-green back; black wings with white edges; black tail; yellow underparts, shoulders and rump. *Female:* same color pattern as male, but duller.

Size: *L* 8 in; *W* 12 in.

Status: uncommon resident in the Lower Rio Grande Valley, the South Texas Brush Country, the southern third of the Edwards Plateau and into the central Coastal Plain.

Habitat: varied, including open oak or pine-oak woodlands, mesquite forests and riparian areas; prefers dense areas of taller trees and scrubby vegetation.

Nesting: on a tree branch; female weaves a pendulant nest of grasses and lines it with finer grasses; female incubates 3–5 pale blue to gray-white eggs, marked with brown blotches and scribbling, for 12–14 days.

Feeding: eats invertebrates and wild berries; enters orchards for fruit.

Voice: repeated *yike yike yike!* call; song is a slow whistle that melds from one note to the next, the pitch constantly varying.

Similar Species: combination of yellow-green back and black head is diagnostic. *Scott's Oriole* (p. 436): ranges do not overlap; black breast and back. *Orchard Oriole* (p. 432) and *Hooded Oriole* (p. 458): juveniles are smaller and have black throats.

Best Sites: Chaparral WMA; Lake Corpus Christi SP; Santa Ana NWR; Bentsen-Rio Grande Valley SP; Falcon SP.

BALTIMORE ORIOLE

Icterus galbula

Striking, black and orange plumage marks the male Baltimore Oriole as he moves among our neighborhood treetops. He sings a rich, flutelike courtship song, vocalizing almost continuously until he finds a mate. • Because northeastern Texas marks the southernmost extension of the breeding range, breeding birds are uncommon and often difficult to locate. • For years, the Baltimore Oriole and the Bullock's Oriole were combined as the "Northern Oriole"; in 1995, the American Ornithologists' Union reinstated the birds as separate species. Where their ranges overlap, hybrids sometimes occur. • The Baltimore Oriole was named for the black and orange coat of arms of George Calvert, First Lord Baltimore, who was instrumental in the proclamation of Maryland as a British colony.

Nesting: high in a deciduous tree; female builds a hanging pouch nest of grass, bark shreds and grapevines; female incubates 4–5 darkly marked, pale gray to bluish white eggs for 12–14 days.

Feeding: gleans canopy vegetation and shrubs for caterpillars, wasps and other invertebrates; eats some fruit and nectar; visits hummingbird feeders and takes orange halves.

Voice: calls include a 2-note *tea-too* and a rapid chatter: *ch-ch-ch-ch-ch;* song consists of slow, loud, clear whistles: *peter peter peter here peter.*

ID: *Male:* black hood, back, wings and central tail feathers; bright orange underparts, shoulder, rump and outer tail feathers; white wing patch and feather edgings. *Female:* olive brown upperparts (darkest on head); dull yellow-orange underparts; white wing bar.

Size: *L* 7–8 in; *W* 11½ in.

Status: locally uncommon summer resident in the eastern Panhandle and the northern Rolling Plains, Oakwoods & Prairies and Blackland Prairies and rare in the northern Pineywoods; common migrant in eastern Texas.

Habitat: deciduous and mixed forests, particularly riparian woodlands, natural openings, shorelines, roadsides, orchards, gardens and parklands.

Similar Species: *Bullock's Oriole* (p. 433): male has bright orange eyebrow and cheek and large white wing patch; female has grayish wings and "jagged" edge to upperwing bar. *Orchard Oriole* (p. 432): male has darker chestnut plumage; female is olive yellow overall. *Summer* (p. 374), *Scarlet* (p. 375) and *Hepatic* (p. 373) *tanagers:* females have thicker, pale bills and no wing bars.

Best Sites: *Summer:* Fort Worth Nature Center; Cedar Hill SP (Dallas Co.). *In migration:* migrant "traps" on the Coastal Plain.

SCOTT'S ORIOLE

Icterus parisorum

Summer is when the Scott's Oriole can be found in the Southwest, nesting near a water supply within a stand of yuccas, oaks, sycamores or palm trees. Populations are slowly declining, but very little is known about this species, especially in relation to disturbances and habitat loss. • Scott's Oriole was named after Winfield Scott, a major general of the U.S. Army, presidential nominee and mediator of many disputes and controversies in the 19th century. Scott himself had no interest in ornithology, but his name was attached to the bird by an admiring soldier who thought he had found a new species and named it *I. scottii*. However, the ornithologist Charles-Lucien Bonaparte had previously assigned the species name *I. parisorum*, after the Paris brothers who collected the first specimens in Mexico, so only the common name was kept.

ID: yellow underparts and undertail coverts; yellow of rump extends onto tail; 2 white wing bars; black tail; blue legs. *Breeding male:* black head, back and breast. *Female* and *immature:* brown head and nape; female has dark throat.
Size: *L* 9 in; *W* 12½ in.
Status: uncommon to common summer resident in the Trans-Pecos and the southern half of the Edwards Plateau.
Habitat: open, arid grasslands; semi-arid areas with yucca or Joshua trees; riparian woodland.
Nesting: within a yucca, oak, Joshua tree or pinyon; female constructs a hanging nest of yucca leaves; female incubates 2–4 darkly blotched, pale blue eggs for approximately 14 days.
Feeding: feeds on insects, fruit and berries; may be attracted to feeders with sugar water.
Voice: call is a low, harsh *chuck;* song is a clear, fast whistle, with emphasis on the middle.
Similar Species: *Audubon's Oriole* (p. 434): yellow-green back; less black on breast; 1 white wing bar. *Hooded Oriole* (p. 458) and *Orchard Oriole* (p. 432): female has drabber upperparts, with yellow-green underparts; juvenile male has black throat and yellow head and nape.
Best Sites: Hueco Tanks SP; Guadalupe Mountains NP; Big Bend NP; Lost Maples SP.

PURPLE FINCH

Carpodacus purpureus

Despite the Purple Finch's name, this bird's stunning plumage is more of a raspberry red than a shade of purple. Roger Tory Peterson said it best when he described the Purple Finch as "a sparrow dipped in raspberry juice." Only the male is brightly colored, however—the female is a rather drab, unassuming bird by comparison. • The frequently given musical *pik* or *weet* call note is a good way to know if this finch is nearby. • A flat, raised, table-style feeding station and nearby tree cover will attract Purple Finches, and erecting a feeder may keep a small flock in your area over winter. These birds are erratic visitors, though, abundant throughout eastern Texas in some winters, then appearing only in the northeast in others.

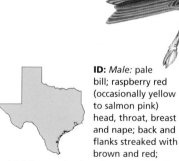

ID: *Male:* pale bill; raspberry red (occasionally yellow to salmon pink) head, throat, breast and nape; back and flanks streaked with brown and red; reddish brown cheek; red rump; notched tail; pale, unstreaked belly and undertail coverts. *Female:* dark brown cheek and jaw line; white eyebrow and lower cheek stripe; heavily streaked underparts; unstreaked undertail coverts.

Size: *L* 5–6 in; *W* 10 in.

Status: uncommon and irregular winter visitor in the eastern half of the state and rare elsewhere.

Habitat: forests and shrubby open areas; frequents feeders with nearby tree cover.

Nesting: does not nest in Texas.

Feeding: gleans the ground and vegetation for seeds, buds, berries and insects; readily visits table-style feeding stations.

Voice: call is a single metallic *pik* or *weet;* song (rarely heard in Texas) is a bubbly, continuous warble.

Similar Species: *House Finch* (p. 438): squared tail; male has brown-streaked flanks; female has plainer cheeks. *Cassin's Finch* (p. 459): rare winter visitor restricted to Trans-Pecos; brighter red forecrown; distinctly streaked, browner upperparts; female has narrow, crisp brown streaks on breast and weaker face pattern.

Best Sites: Daingerfield SP; Tyler SP; Cedar Hill SP (Dallas Co.); Hagerman NWR.

HOUSE FINCH

Carpodacus mexicanus

House Finches are familiar birds throughout the settled parts of Texas. Commonly seen in towns and cities, they are among the few species to nest within the urban core. Rural country dominated by agriculture or ranching is also to their liking. • A native of the western U.S. and Mexico, the House Finch was taken to eastern cities for the cage bird trade and sold as the "Hollywood Finch." When, in 1940, it became known that the House Finch was a protected species, some pet shop owners in New York City released their birds to avoid prosecution. From these few dozen birds, the population had by the late 1990s grown to exceed 10 million birds as the species colonized the entire eastern U.S. and extreme southern Canada! • The male often gives his pleasing spring song in extended bouts from a power line or rooftop antenna. The color of his head and breast can vary from red to yellow, but females prefer the reddest-plumaged males.

ID: streaked, brown upperparts; 2 pale wing bars; brown-streaked, whitish underparts. *Male:* brown crown; red (sometimes orange or yellow) forehead, throat and breast; reddish rump. *Female:* resembles male, but without red (or orange or yellow) areas.

Size: *L* 5–6 in; *W* 9½ in.

Status: uncommon to common resident statewide.

Habitat: urban, suburban and agricultural areas.

Nesting: in a natural or artificial cavity or in dense foliage of evergreen shrubs; female builds a cup nest of twigs and lines it with finer materials; female incubates 4–5 sparsely marked, pale blue eggs for 12–14 days.

Feeding: gleans vegetation and the ground for seeds; also takes berries, buds and some flower parts; often visits feeders.

Voice: sweet *cheer* flight call, given singly or in series; bright, disjointed, warbling song, about 3 seconds long, often ends with a harsh *jeeer* or *wheer*.

Similar Species: *Purple Finch* (p. 437): notched tail; male has more burgundy red cap, upper back and flanks; female has distinct cheek patch. *Cassin's Finch* (p. 459): rare winter visitor restricted to Trans-Pecos; brighter red forecrown; distinctly streaked, browner upperparts; female has narrow, crisp brown streaks on breast and weaker face pattern. *Red Crossbill* (p. 459): rare; crossed mandibles; male has more red overall and darker wings.

Best Sites: frequents suburban and urban areas.

PINE SISKIN

Carduelis pinus

Pine Siskins are unpredictable, social birds that may be abundant for a time and then suddenly disappear. Like other winter invasion species, siskins vary greatly in numbers and distribution in Texas from one year to the next. Because their favored habitats are widely scattered, flocks are constantly on the move, searching forests for the most abundant seed crops. These drab, sparrowlike birds are easy to overlook at first, but, once you learn to recognize their characteristic rising *zzzreeeee* calls and boisterous chatter, you will encounter them with surprising frequency. They often feed near the tops of trees, favoring coniferous and mixed woodlands and forest edges. Perhaps the best way to meet these birds is to set up a finch feeder filled with black niger seed in your backyard and wait for them to appear. • Unlike most finches, which have very different male and female plumages, the Pine Siskin shows little plumage difference between male and female.

Habitat: open coniferous or mixed forests; residential areas.
Nesting: does not nest in Texas.
Feeding: gleans the ground and vegetation for seeds; regularly visits bird feeders.
Voice: buzzy, rising *zzzreeeee* call; boisterous chattering.
Similar Species: *American Goldfinch* (p. 441): nonbreeding male has yellow head and shoulder patch, unstreaked, gray underparts and blacker tail. *Yellow-rumped Warbler* (p. 348): superficially similar, but with thin bill, unstreaked head, pale throat and yellow rump. *Purple Finch* (p. 437) and *House Finch* (p. 438): females have thicker bills and no yellow on wings or tail. *Sparrows* (pp. 377–406, 457–58): no yellow on wings or tail.
Best Sites: none; irruptive.

ID: faintly streaked, grayish brown upperparts; boldly streaked, dirty white underparts; 2 wing bars (yellow to white); yellow tail patches.
Size: *L* 4½–5½ in; *W* 9 in.
Status: common to abundant migrant and winter resident statewide, irregular everywhere except the Panhandle.

LESSER GOLDFINCH

Carduelis psaltria

A tiny, yellow and green bird, the Lesser Goldfinch is most often found in pairs or in small flocks. The eastern "black-backed" form or morph occurs in Texas, with adult males exhibiting glossy black upperparts, white wing and tail patches and bright yellow underparts. • Unlike the more common American Goldfinch, which is a winter visitor throughout Texas, the Lesser Goldfinch occurs year-round in arid parts of western Texas. It occupies a variety of habitats near fresh water, including dry, brushy expanses, open oak woodlands and agricultural lands. • Lesser Goldfinch pairs nest during spring or summer months with the most rainfall. In the interior states, including Texas, nesting takes place from June to September, whereas birds on the West Coast breed earlier in spring. • In fall and winter, family groups flock to a limited extent with other finches.

black-backed form

ID: lemon yellow underparts and undertail coverts; black wings and tail; small, stubby, black bill. *Male (black-backed form):* white wing and tail patches; black cap and back. *Female* and *immature male:* greenish upperparts; narrow, pale wing bars.
Size: *L* 4–4½ in; *W* 8 in.
Status: uncommon to common summer resident from the southern Panhandle through the central Edwards Plateau to the central Coastal Plain and south to the Rio Grande.
Habitat: various semi-open habitats near water; most numerous in oak woodland, chaparral and suburban and rural edge habitats.
Nesting: in a small tree or shrub, saddled on the outer portion of a limb; female weaves cup nest using grass, plant fibers, bark strips, moss and a few feathers; female incubates 4–5 pale bluish or bluish green eggs for 12–13 days.

Feeding: gleans the ground and vegetation for seeds and insects; attracted to salt and mineral licks; visits birdbaths, leaky garden hoses and feeders stocked with niger seed.
Voice: high, clear *teee* call, often with a final up-note; distinctive, breezy song of up-slurred and down-slurred *teeoo...tooee* notes; also chatters and snatches songs and calls from other species.
Similar Species: *American Goldfinch* (p. 441): white undertail coverts and rump; breeding male has black forehead and bright yellow body; nonbreeding male has olive brown back, yellow-tinged head and shoulder patches and gray underparts. *Pine Siskin* (p. 439): heavily streaked grayish brown upperparts and dirty white underparts; yellow flashes in wings and tail.
Best Sites: Hueco Tanks SP; Guadalupe Mountains NP; Davis Mountains SP; San Angelo SP; Garner SP.

AMERICAN GOLDFINCH

Carduelis tristis

Because of the male's bright plumage and musical song, the American Goldfinch is colloquially known as "Wild Canary." • American Goldfinches breed largely in southern Canada and the northern two-thirds of the continental U.S., but rare and local records of breeding exist for the northeastern corner of our state. The birds winter throughout the U.S. and northern Mexico. In Texas, American Goldfinches are best known as irruptive winter visitors and are found statewide during most years. They often remain in Texas until late May or early June, by which time they have molted into their breeding plumage, and the males have begun singing. • The scientific descriptor *tristis*, Latin for "sad," refers to the goldfinch's voice but seems a rather unfair choice for such a pleasing and playful bird.

nonbreeding

ID: stocky; bold wing bars; some yellow in plumage. *Breeding male:* bright yellow body; black wings with white bars; black forehead and tail. *Breeding female:* resembles male, but with duller body and no black on head. *Nonbreeding:* brownish or grayish upperparts; gray underparts; often some pale yellow on head and breast.
Size: L 4½–5½ in; W 9 in.
Status: uncommon to locally abundant migrant and winter resident statewide; rare summer resident in extreme northeastern Texas, where it is a local breeder, and along the eastern edge of the Panhandle.

Habitat: any weedy, shrubby or open woodland habitat, including suburbs.
Nesting: in the fork of a deciduous tree; female builds compact cup nest of plant fibers, grass and spider silk; female incubates 4–6 pale bluish eggs for 12–14 days.
Feeding: gleans the ground and vegetation, primarily for seeds, but also takes some fruit; commonly visits feeders for thistle seeds.
Voice: calls include *po-ta-to-chip* and *per-chic-or-ee* (often delivered in flight); song (heard during spring) is a long, varied series of trills, twitters, warbles and hissing notes.
Similar Species: *Lesser Goldfinch* (p. 440): male has black cap, black back and larger white wing and tail patches; female has olive green upperparts and narrow, pale wing bars. *Evening Grosbeak* (p. 459): rare and irruptive visitor; much larger; massive bill; gray or yellow forehead.
Best Sites: widespread; any area with weedy fields; best seen at bird feeders.

HOUSE SPARROW

Passer domesticus

A well-known, stocky resident of grocery-store signs, fast-food parking lots and gas stations, the House Sparrow is native to Europe and northern Africa. • Introduced to North America in the 1850s around Brooklyn, New York, House Sparrows were part of a plan to control insects that were damaging grain and cereal crops. Contrary to popular opinion at the time, this sparrow's diet is largely vegetarian, so its effect on crop pests proved to be minimal. • In Texas, House Sparrows were first released at Galveston in 1867, with additional releases over the following five years; by 1905, the birds were found pretty well statewide. Benefiting greatly from their close association with people, House Sparrows had soon colonized most human-altered environments on the continent. • Although House Sparrows have been blamed for the decline of native cavity-nesting species such as Eastern Bluebirds, populations of House Sparrows have also been declining for decades. • House Sparrows belong to the large Old World family of sparrows (Passeridae). They are only distantly related to native New World sparrows (Emberizidae).

breeding

ID: *Breeding male:* gray crown; black bill, chin, throat and breast form "bib"; chestnut nape; light gray cheek; 1 white wing bar; dark, mottled upperparts; gray underparts. *Female:* plain gray-brown overall, with paler underparts and streaked upperparts; buffy eyebrow. *Nonbreeding male:* smaller "bib"; pale bill.

Size: *L* 5½–6½ in; *W* 9½ in.

Status: common to abundant resident statewide.

Habitat: usually restricted to areas around human habitation.

Nesting: often communal; in a human-made structure, ornamental shrub or natural cavity; pair builds a large, dome-shaped nest of grass, twigs, plant fibers and litter and often lines it with feathers; pair incubates 4–6 whitish to greenish eggs, dotted with gray and brown, for 10–13 days.

Feeding: gleans the ground and vegetation for seeds, insects and fruit; frequently visits feeders for seeds.

Voice: short *chill-up* call; song is a plain, familiar *cheep-cheep-cheep-cheep.*

Similar Species: unlikely to be confused with any other species because no native species shares the same nesting habitat.

Best Sites: widespread.

OCCASIONAL BIRD SPECIES

BRANT
Branta bernicla

Very rare migrant and winter resident at scattered localities east of the Pecos River.

MUSCOVY DUCK
Cairina moschata

Rare resident in Hidalgo, Starr and Zapata counties of the Lower Rio Grande Valley. Difficult to distinguish feral individuals from domesticated stocks.

SURF SCOTER
Melanitta perspicillata

Rare migrant and winter visitor in many parts of the state, especially on the upper and central coasts.

WHITE-WINGED SCOTER
Melanitta fusca

Rare migrant and winter visitor in much of Texas, especially on the upper and central coasts; absent from the lower Rio Grande Valley and the Trans-Pecos.

BLACK SCOTER
Melanitta nigra

Rare migrant and winter visitor in the eastern half of Texas, especially on the upper and central coasts; very rare inland.

LONG-TAILED DUCK
Clangula hyemalis

Rare migrant and local winter visitor in many parts of the state.

LESSER PRAIRIE-CHICKEN
Tympanuchus pallidicinctus

Rare to locally uncommon resident in the Panhandle and western half of the South Plains; populations are declining.

MONTEZUMA QUAIL
Cyrtonyx montezumae

Rare to locally uncommon resident in the mountains of the Trans-Pecos and in Edwards and Val Verde counties of the western Edwards Plateau.

RED-THROATED LOON
Gavia stellata

Rare winter resident on reservoirs in the eastern half of Texas and along the coast; casual on reservoirs in the western half of the state.

PACIFIC LOON
Gavia pacifica

Rare winter resident on inland reservoirs and in coastal waters; vagrant in summer in coastal waters.

WESTERN GREBE
Aechmophorus occidentalis

Rare migrant and winter resident
on many reservoirs across the state;
uncommon local resident on reservoirs
in the western half of the Trans-Pecos.

CLARK'S GREBE
Aechmophorus clarkii

Uncommon local resident on reservoirs
in the western Trans-Pecos; rare winter
resident in the eastern Trans-Pecos,
southern High Plains and western
Edwards Plateau.

CORY'S SHEARWATER
Calonectris diomedea

Rare to uncommon visitor in offshore
waters in summer and fall; casual in
spring and winter.

AUDUBON'S SHEARWATER
Puffinus lherminieri

Rare to common visitor in offshore
waters in summer and fall, especially
over deep water.

BAND-RUMPED STORM-PETREL
Oceanodroma castro

Rare to uncommon visitor in offshore
waters in summer; casual in early fall.
(not illustrated)

HOOK-BILLED KITE
Chondrohierax uncinatus

Rare resident in Hidalgo, Starr and
Zapata counties of the Lower Rio
Grande Valley.

COMMON BLACK-HAWK
Buteogallus anthracinus

Rare summer resident in Jeff Davis,
Val Verde and Lubbock counties; rare
migrant in the Trans-Pecos along the
Rio Grande; very rare winter resident
in the western parts of the Lower Rio
Grande Valley.

GRAY HAWK
Buteo nitidus

Rare to locally uncommon resident in
the Lower Rio Grande Valley; rare and
irregular summer resident in Brewster
County of the Trans-Pecos.

YELLOW RAIL
Coturnicops noveboracensis

Rare migrant throughout most of the
eastern half of the state; rare to locally
uncommon winter resident in the
upper and central coastal marshes.

BLACK RAIL
Laterallus jamaicensis

Rare migrant in the eastern third of the
state, but absent from the forested areas;
rare to locally uncommon resident in
the upper and central coastal marshes.

WHIMBREL
Numenius phaeopus

Uncommon migrant in the eastern half of the state, rare in the western half; rare and irregular winter resident on the Coastal Plain.

HUDSONIAN GODWIT
Limosa haemastica

Uncommon to common spring migrant on the Coastal Plain; rare to locally common inland; very rare fall migrant on the Coastal Plain.

RED-NECKED PHALAROPE
Phalaropus lobatus

Uncommon migrant in the extreme western Trans-Pecos; rare and irregular elsewhere in the state, mostly in fall.

BLACK-LEGGED KITTIWAKE
Rissa tridactyla

Rare and irregular winter visitor along the coast and on inland reservoirs.

SOOTY TERN
Onychoprion fuscata

Rare and local summer resident on the central and lower coasts; often appears inland after hurricanes.

BRIDLED TERN
Onychoprion anaethetus

Rare to uncommon summer visitor in offshore waters; rare vagrant along the coast after hurricanes.

POMARINE JAEGER
Stercorarius pomarinus

Rare migrant and winter visitor along the coast and in offshore waters; very rare in summer; very rare and irregular on inland reservoirs.

PARASITIC JAEGER
Stercorarius parasiticus

Very rare fall migrant along the coast and in offshore waters; very rare and irregular on inland reservoirs.

RED-BILLED PIGEON
Patagioenas flavirostris

Rare to uncommon summer resident and very rare winter resident in the Lower Rio Grande Valley, upriver to Maverick County and along the coast to Kenedy County.

BAND-TAILED PIGEON
Patagioenas fasciata

Common summer and irregular winter resident at high elevatios in the Guadalupe, Davis and Chisos mountains and perhaps other Trans-Pecos Mountains; very rare visitor to the lowlands of the Trans-Pecos and High Plains.

GREEN PARAKEET
Aratinga holochlora

Uncommon to locally common resident in the Lower Rio Grande Valley and upriver to Webb county. The origin of these populations remains uncertain. (not illustrated)

RED-CROWNED PARROT
Amazona viridigenalis

Uncommon to locally common resident in the Lower Rio Grande Valley and upriver to Webb county. The origin of these populations remains uncertain.

FLAMMULATED OWL
Otus flammeolus

Rare to uncommon summer resident in the Guadalupe, Davis and Chisos mountains of the Trans-Pecos; very rare migrant in the rest of the Trans-Pecos and in the western half of the High Plains.

SPOTTED OWL
Strix occidentalis

Rare resident in the Guadalupe Mountains and Davis Mountains of the Trans-Pecos; very rare vagrant in fall and winter in El Paso county.

BROAD-BILLED HUMMINGBIRD
Cynanthus latirostris

Very rare to rare spring and fall visitor to the Trans-Pecos; very rare in winter in El Paso County; casual and irregular in the southern half of the state. (not illustrated)

BLUE-THROATED HUMMINGBIRD
Lampornis clemenciae

Uncommon summer resident in the
Chisos Mountains and rare in the Davis
Mountains and Guadalupe Mountains;
rare migrant in the western half of the
Trans-Pecos and along the Rio Grande
to the Lower Rio Grande Valley.

MAGNIFICENT HUMMINGBIRD
Eugenes fulgens

Rare to locally uncommon summer
resident in the Guadalupe, Davis and
Chisos mountains of the Trans-Pecos;
very rare migrant in the western half
of the Trans-Pecos.

LUCIFER HUMMINGBIRD
Calothorax lucifer

Common summer resident in the Chisos
Mountains and locally uncommon in
the Davis Mountains; vagrant in other
parts of the Trans-Pecos and Edwards
Plateau.

ANNA'S HUMMINGBIRD
Calypte anna

Rare and irregular migrant and winter
resident in the western two-thirds of the
state and on the upper Coastal Plain.

CALLIOPE HUMMINGBIRD
Stellula calliope

Rare to locally uncommon migrant in
the Trans-Pecos; very rare and irregular
elsewhere in the state; very rare and
irregular winter visitor on the Coastal
Plain, usually at feeders.

ALLEN'S HUMMINGBIRD
Selasphorus sasin

Rare to locally uncommon migrant and winter resident on the central and upper Coastal Plain, north into the southeastern portion of the Edwards Plateau; casual elsewhere.

LEWIS'S WOODPECKER
Melanerpes lewis

Very rare and irregular winter visitor in the western half of the state north of the South Texas Brush Country.

WILLIAMSON'S SAPSUCKER
Sphyrapicus thyroideus

Rare migrant and winter resident in the western third of the state, including the western half of the Edwards Plateau.

RED-NAPED SAPSUCKER
Sphyrapicus nuchalis

Rare migrant and winter resident in the Trans-Pecos and the western halves of the High Plains, Rolling Plains and Edwards Plateau; very rare summer resident in the Guadalupe Mountains.

NORTHERN BEARDLESS-TYRANNULET
Camptostoma imberbe

Rare to locally uncommon resident in the Lower Rio Grande Valley, up the Coastal Plain to Kenedy County.

TROPICAL KINGBIRD
Tyrannus melancholicus

Uncommon local resident in the Lower
Rio Grande Valley. Becoming increasingly
common in Cameron County and
Hidalgo County.

NORTHERN SHRIKE
Lanius excubitor

Rare winter resident in the northern
halves of the High Plains and Rolling
Plains; very rare and irregular in the rest
of the High Plains and the western half of
the Edwards Plateau.

PLUMBEOUS VIREO
Vireo plumbeus

Uncommon summer resident in the
Guadalupe, Davis and Chisos mountains;
common migrant throughout the Trans-
Pecos and rare to uncommon in the High
Plains and the western half of the
Edwards Plateau; rare winter resident in
the Trans-Pecos and on the Coastal Plain.

CASSIN'S VIREO
Vireo cassinii

Rare to uncommon migrant in the western
half of the Trans-Pecos and very rare in
the eastern half and on the High Plains;
very rare winter resident in the Trans-
Pecos and Lower Rio Grande Valley and
on the Coastal Plain.

PHILADELPHIA VIREO
Vireo philadelphicus

Uncommon spring and rare fall migrant
in the eastern half of the state; very rare in
the western half.

STELLER'S JAY
Cyanocitta stelleri

Locally common resident in the
Guadalupe Mountains and Davis
Mountains of the Trans-Pecos; very rare
and irregular winter visitor in the rest of
the Trans-Pecos, Panhandle and western
half of the Edwards Plateau.

BROWN JAY
Cyanocorax morio

Rare to uncommon local resident along
the Rio Grande in Starr county, in the
Lower Rio Grande Valley.

MEXICAN JAY
Aphelocoma ultramarina

Common resident in the Chisos
Mountains of the Trans-Pecos; rare
straggler north to Jeff Davis County.

PINYON JAY
Gymnorhinus cyanocephalus

Very rare winter visitor to the High
Plains, Trans-Pecos and western edge
of the Edwards Plateau. May occur in
large flocks.

TAMAULIPAS CROW
Corvus imparatus

Locally common winter resident
and very rare summer resident in
Cameron County, Lower Rio Grande
Valley, where it has bred. Numbers
seem to be decreasing.

MOUNTAIN CHICKADEE
Poecile gambeli

Common resident at high elevations in the Guadalupe Mountains and Davis Mountains; rare to uncommon migrant and winter visitor in the western Trans-Pecos and on the High Plains.

JUNIPER TITMOUSE
Baeolophus ridgwayi

Locally uncommon resident in the Guadalupe Mountains and Delaware Mountains; very rare winter visitor in El Paso County and Jeff Davis County.

PYGMY NUTHATCH
Sitta pygmaea

Rare to common resident in the Guadalupe Mountains and Davis Mountains; rare migrant and winter visitor elsewhere in the Trans-Pecos and southern Panhandle.

CLAY-COLORED ROBIN
Turdus grayi

Rare resident in the Lower Rio Grande Valley; casual and irregular along the Coastal Plain to Aransas County. Numbers seem to be increasing. (not illustrated)

CRISSAL THRASHER
Toxostoma crissale

Rare to locally common resident in the Trans-Pecos and western edge of the Edwards Plateau.

VIRGINIA'S WARBLER
Vermivora virginiae

Rare summer resident in the
Guadalupe Mountains and Davis
Mountains; uncommon migrant in the
Trans-Pecos; rare on the High Plains.

COLIMA WARBLER
Vermivora crissalis

Uncommon and local summer resident
in the Chisos Mountains.

LUCY'S WARBLER
Vermivora luciae

Rare to locally uncommon summer
resident in Brewster, Hudspeth and
Presidio counties of the Trans-Pecos.

TROPICAL PARULA
Parula pitiayumi

Rare resident in the Lower Rio Grande
Valley, on the Coastal Plain to
Calhoun County and Victoria County
and upriver to Val Verde County on the
Edwards Plateau.

CAPE MAY WARBLER
Dendroica tigrina

Rare in spring and very rare in fall in the
eastern quarter of Texas; very rare in
both seasons in the rest of the state.

BLACK-THROATED BLUE WARBLER
Dendroica caerulescens

Rare migrant in the eastern half of the state and very rare in the western half; very rare winter resident on the Coastal Plain.

BLACK-THROATED GRAY WARBLER
Dendroica nigrescens

Rare to uncommon migrant from the High Plains and Trans-Pecos east to the Brazos River and on the upper Coastal Plain; rare winter resident along the Rio Grande and low elevations in the Trans-Pecos.

HERMIT WARBLER
Dendroica occidentalis

Rare migrant in the Trans-Pecos; casual inland to the upper Coastal Plain.

GRACE'S WARBLER
Dendroica graciae

Rare summer resident at high elevations in the Guadalupe Mountains and Davis Mountains of the Trans-Pecos; uncommon migrant in the Trans-Pecos; rare in the southern half of the High Plains.

PALM WARBLER
Dendroica palmarum

Uncommon migrant east of the Pecos River; uncommon and local winter resident on the Coastal Plain; rare on the remainder of the Coastal Plain and inland to the Oaks & Prairies.

BLACKPOLL WARBLER
Dendroica striata

Uncommon spring migrant and rare fall migrant in the eastern half of the state; very rare in the western half.

CERULEAN WARBLER
Dendroica cerulea

Rare to uncommon spring migrant in the eastern half of the state south to the Lower Rio Grande Valley; very rare in the western half and very rare fall migrant in the eastern half.

PAINTED REDSTART
Myioborus pictus

Uncommon and irregular summer resident at high elevations in the Chisos Mountains; scattered records from many parts of the state.

WHITE-COLLARED SEEDEATER
Sporophila torqueola

Rare to uncommon local resident along the Rio Grande from Starr County in the Lower Rio Grande Valley to Webb county in the South Texas Brush Country.

BOTTERI'S SPARROW
Aimophila botterii

Uncommon to locally common summer resident on the lower Coastal Plain and southern third of the South Texas Brush Country.

BLACK-CHINNED SPARROW
Spizella atrogularis

Uncommon summer resident in the Trans-Pecos Mountains; casual vagrant from the southern High Plains and western Edwards Plateau.

SAGE SPARROW
Amphispiza belli

Uncommon migrant and winter resident in the Trans-Pecos; rare in the High Plains and western Edwards Plateau.

SMITH'S LONGSPUR
Calcarius pictus

Rare and irregular migrant and winter resident from the eastern edge of the Rolling Plains through the Blackland Prairies and the Oaks & Prairies regions.

VARIED BUNTING
Passerina versicolor

Rare to locally uncommon summer resident along the Rio Grande from the Lower Rio Grande Valley through the eastern half of the Trans-Pecos and western half of the Edwards Plateau.

HOODED ORIOLE
Icterus cucullatus

Rare to locally common summer resident from the Lower Rio Grande Valley through the southern half of the Edwards Plateau and the eastern half of the Trans-Pecos, north into the Davis Mountains and Guadalupe Mountains.

ALTAMIRA ORIOLE
Icterus gularis

Uncommon resident in the Lower Rio
Grande Valley; rare in the southern half
of the South Texas Brush Country and
lower Coastal Plain.

CASSIN'S FINCH
Carpodacus cassinii

Rare to uncommon and irregular winter
visitor in the Trans-Pecos, High Plains
and western edge of the Edwards
Plateau.

RED CROSSBILL
Loxia curvirostra

Rare and irregular summer resident
in the Guadalupe Mountains and Davis
Mountains; rare and irregular winter
visitor in many parts of the state. In
some years, the species may reach high
numbers.

EVENING GROSBEAK
Coccothraustes vespertinus

Irregular winter visitor in most of
the state; absent in most years, but
may appear in large numbers and
widespread.

GLOSSARY

accipiter: a forest hawk (genus *Accipiter*), characterized by a long tail and short, rounded wings; feeds mostly on birds.

altricial: birds that are hatched in a very helpless state, dependent on their parents, with eyes closed, no feathers and unable to walk.

anting: some birds let ants crawl on their feathers—the ants secrete acids that act as insecticide and discourage parasites.

avifauna: all the bird species of a given region or area.

brood parasite: a bird that lays its eggs in other birds' nests.

brood: *n.* a family of young from one hatching; *v.* to incubate the eggs.

buteo: a high-soaring hawk (genus *Buteo*), characterized by broad wings and a short, wide tail; feeds mostly on small mammals and other land animals.

cere: a fleshy area at the base of the bill that contains the nostrils.

clutch: the number of eggs laid by the female at one time.

corvid: a member of the family Corvidae; includes crows, jays, magpies and ravens.

covey: a small flock of birds, often grouse or quail, that stay together during fall and winter.

dabbling: a foraging technique used by some ducks, in which the head and neck are submerged but the body and tail remain on the water's surface; dabbling ducks can usually walk easily on land, can take off without running and have brightly colored speculums.

diagnostic: a distinctive or distinguishing characteristic that is used to specifically identify a species.

diurnal: most active during the day.

eclipse plumage: a cryptic plumage, similar to that of females, worn by some male ducks in fall when they molt their flight feathers and consequently are unable to fly.

endangered: a species that is facing extirpation or extinction in all or part of its range.

extirpated: a species that no longer exists in the wild in a particular region but occurs elsewhere.

exurban: prosperous communities that lie outside the suburbs of a major city; often bedroom communities.

fledged young: young birds that have developed flight feathers.

flushing: when frightened birds explode into flight in response to a disturbance.

flycatching: a feeding behavior in which the bird leaves a perch, snatches an insect in midair and returns to the same perch; also known as "sallying."

glean: a foraging style of a small bird that uses its bill to pick up food from leaf surfaces, the ground, etc.

gorget: a conspicuous area of the chin, throat and upper breast; is often iridescent.

hawking: attempting to capture insects through aerial pursuit.

intergrade: a bird that blends the characteristics of two subspecies, often found at the limits of their ranges.

irruption: a sporadic mass migration of birds into an unusual range.

kettle: a large concentration of hawks, usually seen during migration.

lek: a place where males (especially grouse and similar species) gather to display for females in spring.

lores: the small area found between the bill and the eyes.

mantle: the area that includes the back and uppersides of the wings.

migrant "trap": an area with conditions that encourage migrant birds to gather.

molt: the periodic shedding and regrowth of worn feathers (often twice a year).

nocturnal: most active at night.

oologist: a zoologist who specializes in the study of eggs.

peep: a sandpiper of the *Calidris* genus.

pelagic: inhabiting or occurring on the open ocean.

pishing: a repeated sibilant sound made especially to attract birds.

polyandry: a mating strategy in which one female breeds with many males.

polygyny: a mating strategy in which one male breeds with many females.

precocial: a bird that is relatively well developed at hatching; precocial birds usually have open eyes, extensive down and are fairly mobile.

primaries: the outermost flight feathers of a bird's wing.

raft: a gathering of birds resting on the water.

raptor: a carnivorous bird; includes eagles, hawks, falcons and owls.

riparian: habitat along rivers or streams.

sallying: a feeding behavior in which the bird leaves a perch, snatches an insect in midair and returns to the same perch; also known as flycatching.

sexual dimorphism: a difference in plumage, size or other characteristics between males and females of the same species.

special concern: a species that has characteristics that make it particularly sensitive to human activities or disturbance, requires a very specific or unique habitat or whose status is such that it requires careful monitoring.

speculum: a brightly colored patch on the wings of many dabbling ducks.

stage: to gather in one place during migration, usually when birds are flightless or partly flightless during molting.

stoop: a steep dive through the air, usually performed by birds of prey while foraging or during courtship displays.

syrinx: a bird's voice organ.

taxonomy: the system of classification of animals and plants.

threatened: a species likely to become endangered in the near future in all or part of its range.

understory: the shrub or thicket layer beneath a canopy of trees.

vagrant: a bird that has wandered outside of its normal migration range.

vent: the single opening for excretion of uric acid and other wastes and for sexual reproduction; also known as the "cloaca."

wattle: bare folded skin hanging from the lower bill or chin; seen on turkeys and domestic fowl.

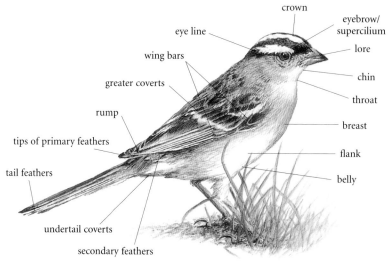

crown

eyebrow/ supercilium

eye line

lore

wing bars

chin

greater coverts

throat

rump

breast

tips of primary feathers

flank

tail feathers

belly

undertail coverts

secondary feathers

SELECT REFERENCES

American Ornithologists' Union. 1998. *Check-list of North American Birds.* 7th ed. (and its supplements). American Ornithologists' Union, Washington, D.C.

Brush, Timothy. 2005. *Nesting Birds of a Tropical Frontier.* Texas A&M University Press, College Station.

Eubanks, Ted. L., Jr., Robert A. Behrstock and Ron J. Weeks. 2006. *Birdlife of Houston, Galveston and the Upper Texas Coast.* Texas A&M University Press, College Station

Kyle, Paul D., and Georgean Z. Kyle. 2005. *Chimney Swifts: America's Mysterious Birds above the Fireplace.* Texas A&M University Press, College Station.

Lockwood, Mark W. 2001. *Birds of the Texas Hill Country.* University of Texas Press, Austin.

Lockwood, Mark W., and Brush Freeman. 2004. *The Texas Ornithological Society Handbook of Texas Birds.* Texas A&M University Press, College Station.

Peterson, James J., and Barry R. Zimmer. 1998. *Birds of the Trans-Pecos.* University of Texas Press, Austin.

Pulich, Warren M. 1988. *Birds of North Central Texas.* Texas A&M University Press, College Station.

Rappole, John A., and Gene W. Blacklock. 1985. *Birds of the Texas Coastal Bend: Abundance and Distribution.* Texas A&M University Press, College Station.

Seyffert, Kenneth D. 2001. *Birds of the Texas Panhandle.* Texas A&M University Press, College Station.

Shackelford, Clifford E., Madge M. Lindsay and C. Mark Klym. 2005. *Hummingbirds of Texas.* Texas A&M University Press, College Station.

Sibley, D.A. 2000. *National Audubon Society: The Sibley Guide to Birds.* Alfred A. Knopf, New York.

Sibley, D.A. 2001. *National Audubon Society: The Sibley Guide to Bird Life and Behavior.* Alfred A. Knopf, New York.

White, Matt. 2003. *Birds of Northeast Texas.* Texas A&M University Press, College Station.

CHECKLIST

The following is the official list of bird species accepted for Texas by the Texas Bird Records Committee (TBRC) of the Texas Ornithological Society. This list totals 629 species and includes taxonomic and nomenclatural changes outlined in the 47th supplement to the AOU Check-list of North American Birds. We wish to thank the Texas Ornithological Society for their kind permission to use their list as the basis for our list.

To be considered a fully accepted species on the Texas list, at least one of the following is required:
- An extant specimen identified by a recognized authority together with convincing evidence that the specimen was obtained within Texas.
- One or more photographs that clearly demonstrate definitive characters with convincing evidence that the photos were taken within Texas.
- An audio recording of a bird vocalization that clearly demonstrates definitive characters with convincing evidence that the recording was made within Texas.

In addition to the above, the record itself must be reviewed and accepted by the TBRC.

The following categories are noted:
I = Introduced   en=endangered
E = Extinct   th=threatened
e = extirpated

Waterfowl (Anatidae)
- ❏ Black-bellied Whistling-Duck
- ❏ Fulvous Whistling-Duck
- ❏ Greater White-fronted Goose
- ❏ Snow Goose
- ❏ Ross's Goose
- ❏ Brant
- ❏ Cackling Goose
- ❏ Canada Goose
- ❏ Trumpeter Swan
- ❏ Tundra Swan
- ❏ Muscovy Duck
- ❏ Wood Duck
- ❏ Gadwall
- ❏ Eurasian Wigeon
- ❏ American Wigeon
- ❏ American Black Duck
- ❏ Mallard
- ❏ Mottled Duck
- ❏ Blue-winged Teal
- ❏ Cinnamon Teal
- ❏ Northern Shoveler
- ❏ White-cheeked Pintail
- ❏ Northern Pintail
- ❏ Garganey
- ❏ Green-winged Teal
- ❏ Canvasback
- ❏ Redhead
- ❏ Ring-necked Duck
- ❏ Greater Scaup
- ❏ Lesser Scaup
- ❏ King Eider
- ❏ Harlequin Duck
- ❏ Surf Scoter
- ❏ White-winged Scoter
- ❏ Black Scoter
- ❏ Long-tailed Duck
- ❏ Bufflehead
- ❏ Common Goldeneye
- ❏ Barrow's Goldeneye
- ❏ Hooded Merganser
- ❏ Common Merganser
- ❏ Red-breasted Merganser
- ❏ Masked Duck
- ❏ Ruddy Duck

Chachalacas (Cracidae)
- ❏ Plain Chachalaca

Grouse & Allies (Phasianidae)
- ❏ Ring-necked Pheasant (I)
- ❏ Greater Prairie-Chicken
- ❏ Lesser Prairie-Chicken
- ❏ Wild Turkey

Quail (Odontophoridae)
- ❏ Scaled Quail
- ❏ Gambel's Quail
- ❏ Northern Bobwhite
- ❏ Montezuma Quail

Loons (Gaviidae)
- ❏ Red-throated Loon
- ❏ Pacific Loon
- ❏ Common Loon
- ❏ Yellow-billed Loon

Grebes (Podicipedidae)
- ❏ Least Grebe
- ❏ Pied-billed Grebe
- ❏ Horned Grebe
- ❏ Red-necked Grebe
- ❏ Eared Grebe
- ❏ Western Grebe
- ❏ Clark's Grebe

Albatrosses (Diomedeidae)
- ❏ Yellow-nosed Albatross

CHECKLIST

**Petrels & Shearwaters
(Procellariidae)**
❏ Black-capped Petrel
❏ Stejneger's Petrel
❏ White-chinned Petrel
❏ Cory's Shearwater
❏ Greater Shearwater
❏ Sooty Shearwater
❏ Manx Shearwater
❏ Audubon's Shearwater

**Storm-Petrels
(Hydrobatidae)**
❏ Wilson's Storm-Petrel
❏ Leach's Storm-Petrel
❏ Band-rumped Storm-
Petrel

**Tropicbirds
(Phaethontidae)**
❏ Red-billed Tropicbird

**Boobies & Gannets
(Sulidae)**
❏ Masked Booby
❏ Blue-footed Booby
❏ Brown Booby
❏ Red-footed Booby
❏ Northern Gannet

Pelicans (Pelecanidae)
❏ American White Pelican
❏ Brown Pelican

**Cormorants
(Phalacrocoracidae)**
❏ Neotropic Cormorant
❏ Double-crested
Cormorant

Darters (Anhingidae)
❏ Anhinga

**Frigatebirds
(Fregatidae)**
❏ Magnificent Frigatebird

Herons (Ardeidae)
❏ American Bittern
❏ Least Bittern
❏ Great Blue Heron
❏ Great Egret
❏ Snowy Egret

❏ Little Blue Heron
❏ Tricolored Heron
❏ Reddish Egret (th)
❏ Cattle Egret
❏ Green Heron
❏ Black-crowned Night-
Heron
❏ Yellow-crowned Night-
Heron

**Ibises
(Threskiornithidae)**
❏ White Ibis
❏ Glossy Ibis
❏ White-faced Ibis (th)
❏ Roseate Spoonbill

Storks (Ciconiidae)
❏ Jabiru
❏ Wood Stork (th)

Vultures (Cathartidae)
❏ Black Vulture
❏ Turkey Vulture

**Flamingos
(Phoenicopteridae)**
❏ Greater Flamingo

**Kites, Eagles & Hawks
(Accipitridae)**
❏ Osprey
❏ Hook-billed Kite
❏ Swallow-tailed Kite (th)
❏ White-tailed Kite
❏ Snail Kite
❏ Mississippi Kite
❏ Bald Eagle
❏ Northern Harrier
❏ Sharp-shinned Hawk
❏ Cooper's Hawk
❏ Northern Goshawk
❏ Crane Hawk
❏ Common Black-Hawk (th)
❏ Harris's Hawk
❏ Roadside Hawk
❏ Red-shouldered Hawk
❏ Broad-winged Hawk
❏ Gray Hawk (th)
❏ Short-tailed Hawk
❏ Swainson's Hawk
❏ White-tailed Hawk (th)
❏ Zone-tailed Hawk (th)

❏ Red-tailed Hawk
❏ Ferruginous Hawk
❏ Rough-legged Hawk
❏ Golden Eagle

Falcons (Falconidae)
❏ Collared Forest-Falcon
❏ Crested Caracara
❏ American Kestrel
❏ Merlin
❏ Aplomado Falcon
❏ Gyrfalcon
❏ Peregrine Falcon (th)
❏ Prairie Falcon

Rails (Rallidae)
❏ Yellow Rail
❏ Black Rail
❏ Clapper Rail
❏ King Rail
❏ Virginia Rail
❏ Sora
❏ Paint-billed Crake
❏ Spotted Rail
❏ Purple Gallinule
❏ Common Moorhen
❏ American Coot

Cranes (Gruidae)
❏ Sandhill Crane
❏ Whooping Crane (en)

**Thick-Knees
(Burhinidae)**
❏ Double-striped
Thick-knee

Plovers (Charadriidae)
❏ Black-bellied Plover
❏ American Golden-
Plover
❏ Pacific Golden-Plover
❏ Collared Plover
❏ Snowy Plover
❏ Wilson's Plover
❏ Semipalmated Plover
❏ Piping Plover (th)
❏ Killdeer
❏ Mountain Plover

**Oystercatchers
(Haematopodidae)**
❏ American Oystercatcher

Stilts & Avocets (Recurvirostridae)
❑ Black-necked Stilt
❑ American Avocet

Jacanas (Jacanidae)
❑ Northern Jacana

Sandpipers (Scolopacidae)
❑ Spotted Sandpiper
❑ Solitary Sandpiper
❑ Wandering Tattler
❑ Spotted Redshank
❑ Greater Yellowlegs
❑ Willet
❑ Lesser Yellowlegs
❑ Upland Sandpiper
❑ Eskimo Curlew (E)
❑ Whimbrel
❑ Long-billed Curlew
❑ Hudsonian Godwit
❑ Marbled Godwit
❑ Ruddy Turnstone
❑ Surfbird
❑ Red Knot
❑ Sanderling
❑ Semipalmated Sandpiper
❑ Western Sandpiper
❑ Red-necked Stint
❑ Least Sandpiper
❑ White-rumped Sandpiper
❑ Baird's Sandpiper
❑ Pectoral Sandpiper
❑ Sharp-tailed Sandpiper
❑ Purple Sandpiper
❑ Dunlin
❑ Curlew Sandpiper
❑ Stilt Sandpiper
❑ Buff-breasted Sandpiper
❑ Ruff
❑ Short-billed Dowitcher
❑ Long-billed Dowitcher
❑ Wilson's Snipe
❑ American Woodcock
❑ Wilson's Phalarope
❑ Red-necked Phalarope
❑ Red Phalarope

Gulls & Terns (Laridae)
❑ Laughing Gull
❑ Franklin's Gull
❑ Little Gull
❑ Black-headed Gull
❑ Bonaparte's Gull
❑ Heermann's Gull
❑ Black-tailed Gull
❑ Mew Gull
❑ Ring-billed Gull
❑ California Gull
❑ Herring Gull
❑ Thayer's Gull
❑ Iceland Gull
❑ Lesser Black-backed Gull
❑ Slaty-backed Gull
❑ Western Gull
❑ Glaucous-winged Gull
❑ Glaucous Gull
❑ Great Black-backed Gull
❑ Kelp Gull
❑ Sabine's Gull
❑ Black-legged Kittiwake
❑ Brown Noddy
❑ Black Noddy
❑ Sooty Tern (th)
❑ Bridled Tern
❑ Least Tern
❑ Gull-billed Tern
❑ Caspian Tern
❑ Black Tern
❑ Roseate Tern
❑ Common Tern
❑ Arctic Tern
❑ Forster's Tern
❑ Royal Tern
❑ Sandwich Tern
❑ Elegant Tern
❑ Black Skimmer

Skuas & Jaegers (Stercorariidae)
❑ South Polar Skua
❑ Pomarine Jaeger
❑ Parasitic Jaeger
❑ Long-tailed Jaeger

Pigeons & Doves (Columbidae)
❑ Rock Pigeon (I)
❑ Red-billed Pigeon
❑ Band-tailed Pigeon
❑ Eurasian Collared-Dove (I)
❑ White-winged Dove
❑ Mourning Dove
❑ Passenger Pigeon (E)
❑ Inca Dove
❑ Common Ground-Dove
❑ Ruddy Ground-Dove
❑ White-tipped Dove
❑ Ruddy Quail-Dove

Parakeets (Psittacidae)
❑ Monk Parakeet (I)
❑ Carolina Parakeet (E)
❑ Green Parakeet
❑ Red-crowned Parrot

Cuckoos & Anis (Cuculidae)
❑ Dark-billed Cuckoo
❑ Yellow-billed Cuckoo
❑ Mangrove Cuckoo
❑ Black-billed Cuckoo
❑ Greater Roadrunner
❑ Groove-billed Ani

Barn Owls (Tytonidae)
❑ Barn Owl

Owls (Strigidae)
❑ Flammulated Owl
❑ Western Screech-Owl
❑ Eastern Screech-Owl
❑ Great Horned Owl
❑ Snowy Owl
❑ Northern Pygmy-Owl
❑ Ferruginous Pygmy-Owl
❑ Elf Owl
❑ Burrowing Owl
❑ Mottled Owl
❑ Spotted Owl
❑ Barred Owl
❑ Long-eared Owl
❑ Stygian Owl
❑ Short-eared Owl
❑ Northern Saw-whet Owl

Nightjars (Caprimulgidae)
❑ Lesser Nighthawk
❑ Common Nighthawk
❑ Common Pauraque
❑ Common Poorwill
❑ Chuck-will's-widow
❑ Whip-poor-will

CHECKLIST

Swifts (Apodidae)
- ❏ White-collared Swift
- ❏ Chimney Swift
- ❏ White-throated Swift

Hummingbirds (Trochilidae)
- ❏ Green Violet-ear
- ❏ Green-breasted Mango
- ❏ Broad-billed Hummingbird
- ❏ White-eared Hummingbird
- ❏ Berylline Hummingbird
- ❏ Buff-bellied Hummingbird
- ❏ Violet-crowned Hummingbird
- ❏ Blue-throated Hummingbird
- ❏ Magnificent Hummingbird
- ❏ Lucifer Hummingbird
- ❏ Ruby-throated Hummingbird
- ❏ Black-chinned Hummingbird
- ❏ Anna's Hummingbird
- ❏ Costa's Hummingbird
- ❏ Calliope Hummingbird
- ❏ Broad-tailed Hummingbird
- ❏ Rufous Hummingbird
- ❏ Allen's Hummingbird

Trogons (Trogonidae)
- ❏ Elegant Trogon

Kingfishers (Alcedinidae)
- ❏ Ringed Kingfisher
- ❏ Belted Kingfisher
- ❏ Green Kingfisher

Woodpeckers (Picidae)
- ❏ Lewis's Woodpecker
- ❏ Red-headed Woodpecker
- ❏ Acorn Woodpecker
- ❏ Golden-fronted Woodpecker
- ❏ Red-bellied Woodpecker
- ❏ Williamson's Sapsucker
- ❏ Yellow-bellied Sapsucker
- ❏ Red-naped Sapsucker
- ❏ Red-breasted Sapsucker
- ❏ Ladder-backed Woodpecker
- ❏ Downy Woodpecker
- ❏ Hairy Woodpecker
- ❏ Red-cockaded Woodpecker (en)
- ❏ Northern Flicker
- ❏ Pileated Woodpecker
- ❏ Ivory-billed Woodpecker (e)

Flycatchers (Tyrannidae)
- ❏ Northern Beardless-Tyrannulet (th)
- ❏ Greenish Elaenia
- ❏ Tufted Flycatcher
- ❏ Olive-sided Flycatcher
- ❏ Greater Pewee
- ❏ Western Wood-Pewee
- ❏ Eastern Wood-Pewee
- ❏ Yellow-bellied Flycatcher
- ❏ Acadian Flycatcher
- ❏ Alder Flycatcher
- ❏ Willow Flycatcher
- ❏ Least Flycatcher
- ❏ Hammond's Flycatcher
- ❏ Gray Flycatcher
- ❏ Dusky Flycatcher
- ❏ Cordilleran Flycatcher
- ❏ Buff-breasted Flycatcher
- ❏ Black Phoebe
- ❏ Eastern Phoebe
- ❏ Say's Phoebe
- ❏ Vermilion Flycatcher
- ❏ Dusky-capped Flycatcher
- ❏ Ash-throated Flycatcher
- ❏ Great Crested Flycatcher
- ❏ Brown-crested Flycatcher
- ❏ Great Kiskadee
- ❏ Social Flycatcher
- ❏ Sulphur-bellied Flycatcher
- ❏ Piratic Flycatcher
- ❏ Tropical Kingbird
- ❏ Couch's Kingbird
- ❏ Cassin's Kingbird
- ❏ Thick-billed Kingbird
- ❏ Western Kingbird
- ❏ Eastern Kingbird
- ❏ Gray Kingbird
- ❏ Scissor-tailed Flycatcher
- ❏ Fork-tailed Flycatcher

Becards & Tityras (incertae sedis: family uncertain)
- ❏ Rose-throated Becard(th)
- ❏ Masked Tityra

Shrikes (Laniidae)
- ❏ Loggerhead Shrike
- ❏ Northern Shrike

Vireos (Vireonidae)
- ❏ White-eyed Vireo
- ❏ Bell's Vireo
- ❏ Black-capped Vireo (en)
- ❏ Gray Vireo
- ❏ Yellow-throated Vireo
- ❏ Plumbeous Vireo
- ❏ Cassin's Vireo
- ❏ Blue-headed Vireo
- ❏ Hutton's Vireo
- ❏ Warbling Vireo
- ❏ Philadelphia Vireo
- ❏ Red-eyed Vireo
- ❏ Yellow-green Vireo
- ❏ Black-whiskered Vireo
- ❏ Yucatan Vireo

Jays & Crows (Corvidae)
- ❏ Steller's Jay
- ❏ Blue Jay
- ❏ Green Jay
- ❏ Brown Jay
- ❏ Western Scrub-Jay
- ❏ Mexican Jay
- ❏ Pinyon Jay
- ❏ Clark's Nutcracker
- ❏ Black-billed Magpie
- ❏ American Crow
- ❏ Tamaulipas Crow
- ❏ Fish Crow
- ❏ Chihuahuan Raven
- ❏ Common Raven

Larks (Alaudidae)
❏ Horned Lark

Swallows (Hirundinidae)
❏ Purple Martin
❏ Gray-breasted Martin
❏ Tree Swallow
❏ Violet-green Swallow
❏ Northern Rough-winged Swallow
❏ Bank Swallow
❏ Cliff Swallow
❏ Cave Swallow
❏ Barn Swallow

Chickadees & Titmice (Paridae)
❏ Carolina Chickadee
❏ Black-capped Chickadee
❏ Mountain Chickadee
❏ Juniper Titmouse
❏ Tufted Titmouse
❏ Black-crested Titmouse

Verdins (Remizidae)
❏ Verdin

Bushtits (Aegithalidae)
❏ Bushtit

Nuthatches (Sittidae)
❏ Red-breasted Nuthatch
❏ White-breasted Nuthatch
❏ Pygmy Nuthatch
❏ Brown-headed Nuthatch

Creepers (Certhiidae)
❏ Brown Creeper

Wrens (Troglodytidae)
❏ Cactus Wren
❏ Rock Wren
❏ Canyon Wren
❏ Carolina Wren
❏ Bewick's Wren
❏ House Wren
❏ Winter Wren
❏ Sedge Wren
❏ Marsh Wren

Dippers (Cinclidae)
❏ American Dipper

Kinglets (Regulidae)
❏ Golden-crowned Kinglet
❏ Ruby-crowned Kinglet

Gnatcatchers (Sylviidae)
❏ Blue-gray Gnatcatcher
❏ Black-tailed Gnatcatcher

Thrushes (Turdidae)
❏ Northern Wheatear
❏ Eastern Bluebird
❏ Western Bluebird
❏ Mountain Bluebird
❏ Townsend's Solitaire
❏ Orange-billed Nightingale-Thrush
❏ Black-headed Nightingale-Thrush
❏ Veery
❏ Gray-cheeked Thrush
❏ Swainson's Thrush
❏ Hermit Thrush
❏ Wood Thrush
❏ Clay-colored Robin
❏ White-throated Robin
❏ Rufous-backed Robin
❏ American Robin
❏ Varied Thrush
❏ Aztec Thrush

Mockingbirds & Thrashers (Mimidae)
❏ Gray Catbird
❏ Black Catbird
❏ Northern Mockingbird
❏ Sage Thrasher
❏ Brown Thrasher
❏ Long-billed Thrasher
❏ Curve-billed Thrasher
❏ Crissal Thrasher
❏ Blue Mockingbird

Starlings (Sturnidae)
❏ European Starling (I)

Pipits (Motacillidae)
❏ American Pipit
❏ Sprague's Pipit

Waxwings (Bombycillidae)
❏ Bohemian Waxwing
❏ Cedar Waxwing

Silky-Flycatchers (Ptilogonatidae)
❏ Gray Silky-flycatcher
❏ Phainopepla

Olive Warbler (Peucedramidae)
❏ Olive Warbler

Wood-Warblers (Parulidae)
❏ Blue-winged Warbler
❏ Golden-winged Warbler
❏ Tennessee Warbler
❏ Orange-crowned Warbler
❏ Nashville Warbler
❏ Virginia's Warbler
❏ Colima Warbler
❏ Lucy's Warbler
❏ Northern Parula
❏ Tropical Parula (th)
❏ Yellow Warbler
❏ Chestnut-sided Warbler
❏ Magnolia Warbler
❏ Cape May Warbler
❏ Black-throated Blue Warbler
❏ Yellow-rumped Warbler
❏ Black-throated Gray Warbler
❏ Golden-cheeked Warbler (en)
❏ Black-throated Green Warbler
❏ Townsend's Warbler
❏ Hermit Warbler
❏ Blackburnian Warbler
❏ Yellow-throated Warbler
❏ Grace's Warbler
❏ Pine Warbler
❏ Prairie Warbler
❏ Palm Warbler
❏ Bay-breasted Warbler

CHECKLIST

❑ Blackpoll Warbler
❑ Cerulean Warbler
❑ Black-and-white Warbler
❑ American Redstart
❑ Prothonotary Warbler
❑ Worm-eating Warbler
❑ Swainson's Warbler
❑ Ovenbird
❑ Northern Waterthrush
❑ Louisiana Waterthrush
❑ Kentucky Warbler
❑ Connecticut Warbler
❑ Mourning Warbler
❑ MacGillivray's Warbler
❑ Common Yellowthroat
❑ Gray-crowned
  Yellowthroat
❑ Hooded Warbler
❑ Wilson's Warbler
❑ Canada Warbler
❑ Red-faced Warbler
❑ Painted Redstart
❑ Slate-throated Redstart
❑ Golden-crowned
  Warbler
❑ Rufous-capped Warbler
❑ Yellow-breasted Chat

Tanagers (Thraupidae)
❑ Hepatic Tanager
❑ Summer Tanager
❑ Scarlet Tanager
❑ Western Tanager
❑ Flame-colored Tanager

Sparrows & Allies (Emberizidae)
❑ White-collared
  Seedeater
❑ Yellow-faced Grassquit
❑ Olive Sparrow
❑ Green-tailed Towhee
❑ Spotted Towhee
❑ Eastern Towhee
❑ Canyon Towhee
❑ Cassin's Sparrow
❑ Bachman's Sparrow (th)
❑ Botteri's Sparrow
❑ Rufous-crowned
  Sparrow
❑ American Tree
  Sparrow
❑ Chipping Sparrow

❑ Clay-colored Sparrow
❑ Brewer's Sparrow
❑ Field Sparrow
❑ Black-chinned Sparrow
❑ Vesper Sparrow
❑ Lark Sparrow
❑ Black-throated Sparrow
❑ Sage Sparrow
❑ Lark Bunting
❑ Savannah Sparrow
❑ Grasshopper Sparrow
❑ Baird's Sparrow
❑ Henslow's Sparrow
❑ Le Conte's Sparrow
❑ Nelson's Sharp-tailed
  Sparrow
❑ Seaside Sparrow
❑ Fox Sparrow
❑ Song Sparrow
❑ Lincoln's Sparrow
❑ Swamp Sparrow
❑ White-throated
  Sparrow
❑ Harris's Sparrow
❑ White-crowned
  Sparrow
❑ Golden-crowned
  Sparrow
❑ Dark-eyed Junco
❑ Yellow-eyed Junco
❑ McCown's Longspur
❑ Lapland Longspur
❑ Smith's Longspur
❑ Chestnut-collared
  Longspur
❑ Snow Bunting

Grosbeaks & Buntings (Cardinalidae)
❑ Crimson-collared
  Grosbeak
❑ Northern Cardinal
❑ Pyrrhuloxia
❑ Rose-breasted
  Grosbeak
❑ Black-headed Grosbeak
❑ Blue Bunting
❑ Blue Grosbeak
❑ Lazuli Bunting
❑ Indigo Bunting
❑ Varied Bunting
❑ Painted Bunting
❑ Dickcissel

Blackbirds & Orioles (Icteridae)
❑ Bobolink
❑ Red-winged Blackbird
❑ Eastern Meadowlark
❑ Western Meadowlark
❑ Yellow-headed
  Blackbird
❑ Rusty Blackbird
❑ Brewer's Blackbird
❑ Common Grackle
❑ Boat-tailed Grackle
❑ Great-tailed Grackle
❑ Shiny Cowbird
❑ Bronzed Cowbird
❑ Brown-headed
  Cowbird
❑ Black-vented Oriole
❑ Orchard Oriole
❑ Hooded Oriole
❑ Streak-backed Oriole
❑ Bullock's Oriole
❑ Altamira Oriole
❑ Audubon's Oriole
❑ Baltimore Oriole
❑ Scott's Oriole

Finches (Fringillidae)
❑ Pine Grosbeak
❑ Purple Finch
❑ Cassin's Finch
❑ House Finch
❑ Red Crossbill
❑ White-winged Crossbill
❑ Common Redpoll
❑ Pine Siskin
❑ Lesser Goldfinch
❑ Lawrence's Goldfinch
❑ American Goldfinch
❑ Evening Grosbeak

Old World Sparrows (Passeridae)
❑ House Sparrow (I)

INDEX OF SCIENTIFIC NAMES

This index references only primary species and those found in the appendix and does not include subspecies.

INDEX OF COMMON NAMES

Page numbers in **boldface** type refer to the primary, illustrated species accounts.

ABOUT THE AUTHORS

Keith A. Arnold

Keith A. Arnold is a prominent expert on the birds of Texas. Having graduated with a PhD in Zoology and Physiology from Louisiana State University in 1966, Dr. Arnold taught ornithology for 40 years and is now Professor Emeritus at Texas A&M University. Among his professional honors, he is a Fellow of the American Ornithologists' Union, an Honorary Life Member of the Texas Ornithological Society and former President of both the Texas Ornithological Society and the Southwestern Association of Naturalists. His research on the impact of human communities on bird populations has taken him across the United States, as well as Mexico, Costa Rica, the Dominican Republic, Dominica and Tanzania. Today, Dr. Arnold continues to consult privately on endangered species of birds in Texas.

Gregory Kennedy

Gregory Kennedy has been an active naturalist since he was very young. He is the author of many books on natural history and has also produced film and television shows on environmental issues and indigenous concerns in Southeast Asia, New Guinea, South and Central America, the High Arctic and elsewhere. He has also been involved in numerous research projects around the world ranging from studies in the upper canopy of tropical and temperate rainforests to deepwater marine investigations.